PROCEEDINGS OF THE ROYAL IRISH ACADEMY • 120C

CLIMATE AND SOCIETY IN IRELAND

From prehistory to the present

Edited by James Kelly and Tomás Ó Carragáin

Climate and society in Ireland: from prehistory to the present

First published in 2021 by
ROYAL IRISH ACADEMY
19 Dawson Street,
Dublin 2,
Ireland
www.ria.ie

Copyright © Royal Irish Academy 2021

With the exception of 'Climate, disease and society in late-medieval Ireland' by Bruce M.S. Campbell and Francis Ludlow, © Authors. That work is an open access article licensed under a Creative Commons Attribution-Non Commercial-No Derivatives 4.0 International License.

All rights reserved. No part of this publication may be reprinted or reproduced or utilised in any electronic, mechanical or any other means, now known or hereafter invented, including photocopying and recording, or otherwise without either the prior written consent of the publishers or a licence permitting restricted copying in Ireland issued by the Irish Copyright Licensing Agency Ltd, The Writers' Centre, 19 Parnell Square, Dublin 1.

While every effort has been made to contact and obtain permission from holders of copyright, if any involuntary infringement of copyright has occurred, sincere apologies are offered, and the owner of such copyright is requested to contact the publisher.

ISBN 978-1-911479-73-4 (PB)
ISBN 978-1-911479-74-1 (pdf)
ISBN 978-1-911479-75-8 (epub)
ISBN 978-1-911479-76-5 (mobi)

Typesetting by Datapage International Ltd.
Printed in Ireland by Sprint-PRINT

A NOTE FROM THE PUBLISHER

We want to try to offset the environmental impacts of carbon produced during the production of our books and journals. For the production of our journals this year we will plant 20 trees with Easy Treesie.

The Easy Treesie – Crann Project organises children to plant trees. Crann – 'Trees for Ireland' is a membership-based, non-profit, registered charity (CHY13698) uniting people with a love of trees. It was formed in 1986 by Jan Alexander, with the aim of "Releafing Ireland". Its mission is to enhance the environment of Ireland through planting, promoting, protecting and increasing awareness about trees and woodlands.

www.easytreesie.com

EDITORS
Professor James Kelly, School of History and Geography, Dublin City University
Dr Tomás Ó Carragáin, Department of Archaeology, University College Cork

EDITORIAL BOARD
Dr Juliana Adelman, School of History and Geography, Dublin City University
Professor Lauren Arrington, Department of English, Maynooth University
Dr Sparky Booker, School of History, Anthropology, Philosophy and Politics, Queen's University Belfast
Dr Lindsey Earner-Byrne, School of History, University College Dublin
Dr Peter Harbison, Honorary Academic Editor, Royal Irish Academy
Professor Poul Holm, Trinity Centre for Environmental Humanities, Trinity College Dublin
Dr Tadhg O'Hannrachain, School of History, University College Dublin
Dr Michael Potterton, Department of History, Maynooth University
Dr Gill Plunkett, School of Natural and Built Environment, Queen's University Belfast
Professor Graeme Warren, School of Archaeology, University College Dublin

INTERNATIONAL ADVISORY BOARD
Dr Toby Barnard, Hertford College, University of Oxford
Professor Thomas Charles-Edwards, Jesus College, University of Oxford
Professor John Morton Coles, Fitzwilliam College, University of Cambridge
Dr Vicki Cummings, School of Forensic and Applied Sciences, University of Central Lancashire
Professor Sir Barry W. Cunliffe, Institute of Archaeology, University of Oxford
Professor Thomas M. Devine, School of History, Classics & Archaeology, University of Edinburgh
Professor Robin Frame, Department of History, University of Durham
Dr Melanie Giles, Department of Archaeology, University of Manchester
Professor Michael W. Herren, Department of Humanities, York University, Toronto; and Centre for Medieval Studies, University of Toronto
Professor J. Th. Leerssen, Department of European Studies, University of Amsterdam
Professor Bernard Lightman, Humanities Department, McLaughlin College, York University, Toronto, Ontario
Professor Elisabeth Lorans, School of Archaeology, Université François-Rabelais de Tours
Professor Máire Ní Mhaonaigh, St John's College, University of Cambridge
Professor Quentin R.D. Skinner, Faculty of History, University of Cambridge
Professor Sir David Mackenzie Wilson, University College London
Professor Alexandra Walsham, Faculty of History, Trinity College Cambridge

CONTENTS

JAMES KELLY AND
TOMÁS Ó CARRAGÁIN

Introduction: constructing the history
of climate and society in Ireland   i

GRAEME WARREN

Climate change and hunter gatherers in
Ireland: problems, potentials and
pressing research questions   1

MERIEL MCCLATCHIE AND
AARON POTITO

Tracing environmental, climatic and
social change in Neolithic Ireland   23

PHIL STASTNEY

A question of scale? A review of
interpretations of Irish peatland
archaeology in relation to Holocene
environmental and climate change   51

GILL PLUNKETT,
DAVID M. BROWN AND
GRAEME T. SWINDLES

Siccitas magna ultra modum: examining
the occurrence and societal impact
of droughts in prehistoric Ireland   83

BENJAMIN GEAREY,
KATHARINA BECKER,
ROSIE EVERETT AND
SEREN GRIFFITHS

On the brink of Armageddon? Climate
change, the archaeological record and
human activity across the Bronze Age–
Iron Age transition in Ireland   105

LISA COYLE MCCLUNG AND
GILL PLUNKETT

Cultural change and the climate record
in final prehistoric and early
medieval Ireland   129

BRUCE M.S. CAMPBELL AND
FRANCIS LUDLOW

Climate, disease and society in
late-medieval Ireland   159

RAYMOND GILLESPIE

Climate, weather and social change in
seventeenth-century Ireland   253

JAMES KELLY

Climate, weather and society in Ireland
in the long eighteenth century: the
experience of the later phases of the
Little Ice Age   273

LUCY COLLINS

'Nature herself seems in the vapours
now': poetry and climate change
in Ireland 1600–1820   325

MÁIRE NÍ ANNRACHÁIN

Seeing the natural world:
Comhbhá an Dúlra   349

SIMON NOONE AND
CONOR MURPHY

Reconstruction of hydrological drought
in Irish catchments (1850–2015)   365

JOHN SWEENEY

Climate and society in modern Ireland:
past and future vulnerabilities   391

Introduction

Constructing the history of climate and society in Ireland

James Kelly and Tomás Ó Carragáin

In Ireland, as elsewhere on the planet, the proliferation in recent years of extreme weather events has amplified interest in the reconstruction of an accurate history of climate and weather. Yet, as John Sweeney explains in his contribution to this collection (chapter 13) in which he traces the appreciation in 'societal awareness' of climate change, appreciation of its implications emerged slowly. Indeed, though the nineteenth-century Irish born scientist John Tyndall was one of the first to identify the warming effects of greenhouses gases, 'climate change was not deemed a serious issue in Ireland…at either the academic or public level for a number of years' after the establishment (at the instigation of the World Meteorological Organisation (WMO) and the United Nations Environment Programme (UNEP)) in 1988 of the Intergovernmental Panel on Climate Change (IPCC). This was not a tenable position, given the weight of scientific evidence pointing to the acceleration in 'global warming', but the Irish scholarly community was poorly positioned to identify the likely implications as climate modelling was still in its infancy and the research infrastructure required to investigate the phenomenon was basic at best. Moreover, the meteorologists, climate geographers and others who were in the vanguard of inquiry in this respect could not appeal to the history of climate in Ireland either for context or direction since the discipline of History seemed disinterested, while Geography did not prioritise historical climate inquiry. By comparison, archaeologists and scholars in cognate disciplines afforded it more prominence in their narratives, though their hypotheses were rarely demonstrable evidentially.

The modern study of Ireland's climate can be said to have been inaugurated in the mid-seventeenth century with Gerard Boate (1604–50) who engaged with the subject in a number of sections of his pioneering 'Natural history', which was published posthumously in 1652.[1] Boate's account was necessarily brief and impressionistic, but it established weather and climate as key environmental issues requiring investigation, and they feature among the wide array of matters that elicited the attention of the Dublin Philosophical Society, which constitutes the

---

doi: https://doi.org/10.3318/PRIAC.2020.120.14

[1] Gerard Boate, *A natural history of Ireland* (London, 1652). A later edition of the work was published in 1755.

most striking manifestation of the engagement with the 'new learning' that is identifiable in Ireland in the later decades of the seventeenth century.[2] Notable though this was, it was both less systematic and less successful in the generation of useful data than that pursued in the eighteenth century by the Dublin-based physician John Rutty (1697–1775), who, mirroring the appreciating interest in the subject that can be identified in England and elsewhere in Europe, had recourse to 'a raingauge and a crude sponge-hygrometer' as well as his own observation as he pursued his lifelong inquiry into the influence and impact of the weather on health and wellbeing.[3] Rutty was, as this implies, primarily interested in the weather for therapeutic reasons, but his published work spawned few imitators, with the notable exception of the scientist, Richard Kirwan (1733–1812). This might reasonably be characterised as a lost opportunity, since Kirwan's meteorological investigation overlapped with the establishment, in Armagh in 1790, of an astronomical observatory and, in Dublin in 1795, of the Royal Dublin Society's Botanic Garden, both of which engaged in the systematic collection of weather data.[4] The beginnings of the professionalising of such information aggregation, which accelerated in the nineteenth century, did not interrupt the parallel collection by individuals of their own data or the maintenance of weather diaries, though it is only now that these documents are being identified and scrutinised for what they reveal of the history of climate and weather and how the latter phenomena shaped and influenced the lives of people.[5] The increased amount of space devoted to reporting the weather in newspapers, which also emerged as an identifiable trend in the final decades of the eighteenth century, attests to the fact that this was a subject in which there was mounting public interest in the nineteenth century, though the involvement of newspapers in its publication and dissemination was intermittent and largely determined by weather conditions. Matters were not destined to remain in this inherently inchoate state however, and a turning point was reached in 1860 when 'real time' weather observations were made at Valentia Island on behalf of the

---

[2] K. Theodore Hoppen (ed.), *Papers of the Dublin Philosophical Society* (2 vols, Dublin, 2008), passim; K. Theodore Hoppen, *The common scientist in the seventeenth century: a study of the Dublin Philosophical Society, 1683–1708* (London, 1970).

[3] John Rutty, *A chronological history of the weather and seasons, and of the prevailing diseases in Dublin, with their various periods, successions, and revolutions during the space of forty years, with a comparative view of the differences of the Irish climate and diseases and those of England and other countries* (Dublin, 1770); John Rutty, *An essay towards a natural history of the county of Dublin* (2 vols, Dublin, 1772), ii, 271–9.

[4] Brendan McWilliams, 'The kingdom of the air: the progress of meteorology' in John Wilson Croker (ed.), *Nature in Ireland: scientific and cultural history* (Dublin, 1997),124–5; F.E. Dixon, 'Meteorology in Ireland', *Weather*, 5:2 (1950), 63–5; C.J. Butler et al., 'Air temperatures from Armagh Observatory, Northern Ireland, from 1796 to 2002', *International Journal of Climatology* 25 (2005),1055–79.

[5] Mairead Treanor, 'Meteorological collections at the Royal Irish Academy and Met Eireann Libraries', in Siobhán Fitzpatrick (ed.), *Science at the Royal Irish Academy: an exhibition* (Dublin, 2012), 28–36; Stephen O'Connor et al., 'A weather diary from Donegal, Ireland, 1846–1875', *Weather*, 10.1002/wea.3818.

Introduction — Constructing the history of climate and society in Ireland

recently established (1854) Meteorological Committee of the British Board of Trade. It was an early intimation of the reliance of the increasingly industrial and globalising world upon secure meteorological knowledge, and it established a precedent that was augmented and reinforced, in the teeth of considerable scepticism as to its utility, in succeeding decades.

Be that as it may, the fact that there was no Irish equivalent to the British Meteorological Service until 1936, when the Irish Meteorological Service was constituted to provide the aviators of the recently established national airline (Aer Lingus, 1936) with the information they needed to operate safely, represents a telling pointer as to its position in the hierarchy of public services and the population's prior dependence on a variety of quarters for even basic information. One of the unanticipated consequences of the establishment of the Irish Meteorological Service was an engagement with the history of the weather and climate, though in keeping with the fact that this was subordinated to the provision of accurate weather information in the present, it was fitful as well as unsystematic. It seems reasonable to conclude, moreover, that the enquiries that were then pursued into aspects of the history of the weather and climate in Ireland attracted few readers outside of the limited circle of professional meteorologists at which it was targeted. Economic historians, who might have been expected to seek to factor climatic and weather conditions into their efforts to plot the economic trajectory of the island, were few in number and disinclined to access or to integrate the information that might have been located in the handful of weather diaries then in the safekeeping of libraries and archives into their narrative, while the still smaller number of statistical series that had been constructed by interested meteorologists remained largely unheralded.

Of its nature, the situation was somewhat different in Archaeology. Even before the development of palaeoclimatology, archaeologists seeking to provide an overview of their discipline were obliged to confront the question of climate change when dealing with the colonisation of Ireland after the Last Glacial Period. Before the 1930s this was usually done in a very cursory manner.[6] For example, climate is mentioned only briefly in the first edition of R.A.S Macalister's *The archaeology of Ireland*, published in 1928.[7] In the second edition published in 1949, the issue receives more attention. Climate is cited as a possible factor, not only in the initial colonisation of Ireland, but also in later changes in the archaeological record.[8] There are also general comments on the importance of climate, and he posits a positive correlation over the millennia between 'fluctuations' in climate and culture. On this basis he concluded that 'what might be called the "Historical Climatology" of any country is a necessary preliminary to the study of its History, or Historical Geography'.

---

[6] For example, P. Power, *Prehistoric Ireland: a manual of Irish pre-Christian Archaeology* (Dublin, 1923), 11.
[7] R.A.S. Macalister, *The archaeology of Ireland* (London, 1928), 9.
[8] R.A.S. Macalister, *The archaeology of Ireland* (2nd ed., London, 1949), 170.

Individuals, including 'great men' are 'mere puppets', while manuscripts and other historical sources are of secondary importance, for 'the essential history is enshrined in minute grains of pollen, embedded in the mud of peat-bogs'.[9] This contrast between the two editions reflects the emergence of palaeoclimatology and environmental archaeology in the intervening years. The first pollen analysis undertaken in Ireland was published by Gunnar Erdtman in 1928.[10] Five years later the Royal Irish Academy's Committee for Quaternary Research was established. With three archaeologists (Macalister, Adolf Mahr and Claude Blake Whelan) among its membership, this was a milestone in the integration of evidence from archaeology and the natural sciences.[11] Knud Jessen undertook the extensive pollen analysis that was prioritised by the Committee and, as Gill Plunkett has observed, its publication in *Proceedings of the Royal Irish Academy Section B* in 1949 placed Ireland at the forefront of pollen analytical studies in Europe.[12]

The framework this research provided for 'all sub periods of the Great Ice Age and the ensuing climatic oscillations which gradually led up to our present climate' increasingly informed subsequent archaeological narratives.[13] For example, Joseph Raftery's *Prehistoric Ireland*, published in 1951, considered the possible effects of climate change on population groups, including the deterioration posited by Jessen in the Late Bronze Age.[14] The interdisciplinary ethos

---

[9] Macalister, *The archaeology of Ireland* (1949), 12–13. This expands on ideas first put forward by Macalister in 1935, drawing upon C.E.P Brooks's *Climate through the ages* (London, 1926). R.A.S. Macalister, *Ancient Ireland* (London, 1935), 277–80. Both his 1935 and 1949 books also include observations on the relationship between climate and society that now appear eccentric. In the latter, citing S.F. Markham's *Climate and the energy of nations* (Oxford, 1942), he argued that, along with 'insular remoteness', the 'time-lag' evident in Ireland 'whereby archaeological phenomena survived long after they had been discarded elsewhere' was due to climate: 'in the race of Civilization Ireland was heavily handicapped: the hot winds and ocean-streams of the Atlantic having had an enervating effect upon human energy and initiative', ix; see also Macalister, *Ancient Ireland*, 280–81.

[10] G. Erdtman, 'Studies in the post-Arctic history of the forests of northwestern Europe', *Geologiska Föreningens i Stockholm Förhandlingar* 50 (1928), 123–92.

[11] A. Mahr, 'Quaternary research in Ireland, 1934, from the archaeological viewpoint', *Irish Naturalists Journal* 5 (1934), 137–44.

[12] Knud Jessen, 'Studies in Late Quaternary deposits and flora-history of Ireland', *Proceedings of the Royal Irish Academy* 52B (1949), 85–290; G. Plunkett, 'Pollen analysis and archaeology in Ireland,' in E.M. Murphy and N.J. Whitehouse (eds) *Environmental archaeology in Ireland* (Oxford, 2007), 221–40: 224.

[13] Mahr, 'Quaternary research', 138; K. Jessen and A. Farrington, 'The bogs at Ballybetagh, near Dublin with remarks on late-glacial conditions in Ireland', *Proceedings of the Royal Irish Academy* 44B (1938), 205–60: 216; Jessen, 'Studies', 89.

[14] Joseph Raftery, *Prehistoric Ireland* (London, 1951), 1–8; for a contemporary discussion of Jessen's results, and the challenges of integrating palynology and archaeology, see H. Hencken, 'Palaeobotany and the Bronze Age', *Journal of the Royal Society of Antiquaries of Ireland* 81 (1951), 53–64.

Introduction — Constructing the history of climate and society in Ireland

of the Committee for Quaternary Research was carried forward into the latter half of the twentieth century by Frank Mitchell (1912–97), a towering figure in Irish Quaternary Studies who was trained by Jessen among others. Though a natural scientist first and foremost, Mitchell made extensive use of archaeological evidence, and conducted several excavations.[15] The relationship, over the long term, between people and the Irish environment, not least its climate, was central to his research and, in addition to his prodigious academic output, he illuminated the subject for a wide audience in *The Irish Landscape,* published in 1976, and in successor publications.[16] The utility of palynology for palaeoclimatology was greatly enhanced by the application of radiocarbon dating from the 1960s and of tephrochronology from the 1990s.[17] The construction, between 1970 and 1984, of a master chronology for Irish oak by Michael Baillie, David Brown and others at Queen's University Belfast, provided researchers with another vital tool for understanding past environments and climates.[18] Though now more cautious about assuming a causal link, it was not uncommon for scholars to cite climate change as the principal explanation for changes in the archaeological record and by extension in social organisation. An example is Barry Raftery's characterisation, in 1997, of Late Bronze Age society as 'on the brink of Armageddon' due in large part to a deteriorating climate, an interpretation that fitted the evidence available at the time, but which has been since been brought into question.[19]

In parallel with these developments, there was a modest increase in research by historians and geographers on climatology of the recent past. Initially, this was heavily reliant on British publications, *Weather* and the *Journal of Royal Meteorological Society* in particular, and upon the formative inquiries pursued by English geographers such as Hubert Lamb (1913–97) (who worked in the Irish Meteorological Service for a time shortly after its foundation) and Gordon Manley (1902–80). Following in the footsteps of Manley, who published the first

---

[15] For example, G.F. Mitchell, 'The relative ages of archaeological objects recently found in bogs in Ireland', *Proceedings of the Royal Irish Academy* 50C (1944–5), 1–19; G.F. Mitchell, 'Studies in Irish Quaternary deposits: No. 7', *Proceedings of the Royal Irish Academy* 53B (1951), 111–206; G.F. Mitchell, 'A pollen diagram from Lough Gur, County Limerick (Studies in Irish Quaternary Deposits: No. 9), *Proceedings of the Royal Irish Academy* 56C (1953–4), 481–8; G.F. Mitchell, 'The Mesolithic site at Toome Bay, Co. Londonderry', *Ulster Journal of Archaeology* 18 (1955), 1–16.

[16] G.F. Mitchell, *The Irish landscape* (London, 1976); G.F. Mitchell, *The Shell guide to reading the Irish landscape* (Dublin, 1986); G.F. Mitchell and M. Ryan, *Reading the Irish landscape* (Dublin, 1997).

[17] Plunkett, 'Pollen analysis', 225–6.

[18] J.R. Pilcher *et al.*, 'A 7,272-year tree-ring chronology for Western Europe', *Nature*, 312 (1984), 150–2.

[19] Barry Raftery, *Pagan Celtic Ireland* (London, 1997), 37; cf. Ian Armit *et al.*, 'Rapid climate change did not cause population collapse at the end of the European Bronze Age', *Proceedings of the National Academy of Sciences* 111, 48 (2014), 17045–49; see further, Geary *et al.*, chapter 5 below.

iteration of his seminal Central English Temperature series in 1953,[20] F.E. Dixon, who spent his working life in the Irish Meteorological Service, published the results of his interrogation of an early weather diary in the *Quarterly Journal of the Royal Meteorological Society* in 1959, which, after years of oversight, is now a standard, and increasingly frequently cited source of information on Irish weather in the eighteenth century.[21] The discipline of Geography, where the pedagogy of climate and weather were nested, did not prioritise inquiry into climatology in either the present or the past, however. Indicatively, in a review published in 1970 of the content of the first twenty-seven years of *Irish Geography*, the journal of the Geography Society of Ireland (1934), G.L. Davies reported that the journal had 'never published a paper on climatology' still less on the history of weather and climate in Ireland.[22] The situation did not change much during the following two decades, or until 'studies of the implications of climate change' began to acquire traction in the public realm in the 1990s.[23] Thereafter there were a number of significant studies of climate in particular locations, among which J.G. Tyrell's investigations in the 1990s of Munster stand out.[24] It may be that the inquiry he pursued that registers most visibly in this volume is that into climate patterns in Cork in the mid-eighteenth century and that political historians will also have encountered his exploration of the part the weather played in scuppering the *Expédition d'Irlande* commanded by Lazare Hoche which sought to make land at Bantry in December 1796.[25] But a good case can be made that the work he published with Kieran Hickey on establishing 'a flood chronology for Cork City' provides a more precise pointer to the direction in which the study of the history of Irish climate was to take, both because it set the precedent for a range of allied studies (notably by Dr Hickey) that were published in the course of the next two decades and because it was temporally focused on the nineteenth and twentieth centuries.[26] Moreover, it demonstrated the necessity for, and the

---

[20] Gordon Manley, 'The mean temperature of central England, 1698–1952', *Quarterly Journal of the Royal Meteorological Society* 79 (1953), 242–61.

[21] F.E. Dixon, 'An Irish weather diary of 1711–1725', *Quarterly Journal of the Royal Meteorological Society*, 85 (1959), 371–85.

[22] G.L. Davies, 'Twenty-seven years of Irish Geography', *Irish Geography*, 6:2 (1970), 190.

[23] Brendan McWilliams, *Climatic change: studies on the implications for Ireland* (Department of the Environment, Dublin, 1992); See McWilliams, 'The kingdom of the air', 115–32, for a review of the engagement with the issue as it stood in the 1990s.

[24] J.G. Tyrrell, 'Paraclimatic statistics and the study of climate change: the case of the Cork region in the 1750s', *Climatic Change* 29:2 (1995), 231–45.

[25] J.G. Tyrell, 'The weather and political destiny' in J.A. Murphy (ed.), *The French are in the Bay: the expedition to Bantry Bay 1796* (Cork, 1997), 25–47.

[26] J.G. Tyrell and Kieran Hickey, 'A flood chronology for Cork city and its climatological background', *Irish Geography* 24:2 (1991), 81–90; K.R. Hickey, 'The Storminess Record from Armagh Observatory 1796–1999', *Weather* 58:1 (2003), 28–35; E. Hanna, K.R. Hickey *et al.*, 'New insights into North European and North Atlantic surface pressure variability, storminess and related climate change since 1830', *Journal of Climate* 21:12 (2008), 6739–66; K.R. Hickey, 'The historic record of cold spells in Ireland',

value of, such investigation, and the potential of archivally informed historic climate inquiries such as have resulted in important contributions by J.K. Mitchell and is now being pursued on many fronts by Conor Murphy, Simon Noone and others in the ICARUS centre at Maynooth University, which may reasonably be identified as the most active unit of historic climate inquiry in Ireland.[27]

Internationally, the burgeoning interest in climate history is manifested in the number of journals devoted to publishing the fruits of this endeavour and, in the discipline of History, by the number of interpretative works published in recent years that have either explored the significance and impact of climate and weather on the societies that are their focus, or that have integrated the question of climate into an environmental approach. One may instance Bruce Campbell's warmly applauded exploration of climate, disease and society in the late medieval world; Geoffrey Parker's timely updating of the thesis of a 'seventeenth-century crisis', once scaffolded by war, rebellion and political events to embrace the Little Ice Age; and Dagomar DeGroot's arresting rewriting of the history of the Dutch Golden Age, while the foregrounding of climate in recent studies of the European settlement of North America and migration from Scotland further highlights its range and potential.[28] Archaeologists, too, are increasingly preoccupied with how the long-term perspective on human adaptations to climate change provided by their discipline might inform our responses to the unfolding challenge.[29] The accelerated rate of destruction of the archaeological record

---

Irish Geography 44:2–3 (2011), 303–21; K.R. Hickey, 'Identifying volcanic signals in Irish temperature observations since AD 1800', *Irish Geography* 44:1 (2011), 97–110; K.R. Hickey, 'The hourly gale record from Valentia Observatory, SW Ireland 1874–2008 and some observations on extreme wave heights in the NE Atlantic', *Climatic Change* 106:3 (2011), 483–506; Michelle McKeown, A.P. Potito and K.R. Hickey, 'The long term instrumental temperature record from Markree Observatory, Co. Sligo 1842–2011', *Irish Geography* 45:3 (2012), 257–82.

[27] J.K. Mitchell, 'Looking backward to see forward: historical changes of public knowledge about climatic hazards in Ireland', *Irish Geography* 44:1 (2011), 7–26; Conor Murphy *et al.*, 'A 305-year continuous monthly rainfall series for the island of Ireland (1711–2016)', *Climate of the Past* 14 (2018), 413–40; Conor Murphy *et al.*, 'The forgotten drought of 1765–68: reconstructing and re-evaluating historic droughts in the British and Irish Isles', *International Journal of Climatology* 40 (2020), 1–23; Simon Noone *et al.*, 'A 250 year drought catalogue for the island of Ireland', *International Journal of Climatology* 37 (2017), 239–54; chapter 12 below.

[28] B.M.S. Campbell, *The great transition: climate, disease and society in the late-medieval world* (Cambridge, 2016); Geoffrey Parker, *Global crisis: war, climate change and catastrophe in the seventeenth century* (Yale, 2013); Dagomar Degroot, *The frigid golden age: climate change, the Little Ice Age and the Dutch Republic 1560–1720* (Cambridge, 2018); Sam White, *The Little Ice Age and Europe's encounters with North America* (Cambridge, MA, 2017); Graeme Morton, *Weather, migration and the Scottish diaspora* (London, 2020).

[29] For example, Keith Kintigh *et al.*, 'Grand challenges for archaeology', *Proceedings of the National Academy of Sciences* 111 (2014), 879–80; T.J. Braje, 'Earth systems, human agency, and the Anthropocene: Planet Earth in the human age', *Journal of Archaeological*

(a precious, non-renewable resource) due to coastal erosion among other processes, has made archaeologists acutely aware of the threat posed by anthropogenic climate change, not just for inanimate archaeological strata, but also for living communities.[30] One might question the extent to which knowledge of past strategies of climate resilience can feed into real world decisions about the future of heavily industrialised societies, especially if the changes wrought in the Anthropocene are more rapid and dramatic than the climatic shifts encountered by complex societies in the past.[31] However, to paraphrase Graeme Warren in his contribution to this collection (chapter 1), it is vitally important to understand the full spectrum of human responses to past climate change at a time when some find it difficult to respond meaningfully to the current crisis due to the seemingly overwhelming scale of the challenge, while others continue to deny it altogether.

In Ireland, the inclusion of a chapter on climate and the environment in the *Cambridge History of Ireland* published in 2018 and the devotion in 2019 by the *Irish University Review* of an issue to the theme of 'food, energy and climate' is testament to the expanding disciplinary appeal of climate history to which this collection also attests.[32] The growing interest in ecocriticism, including representations and perceptions of weather and climate in literature, is represented here by the papers of Collins (chapter 10) and Ní Annracháin (chapter 11). When it comes to History, specifically, it is important not to understate how much remains to be undertaken. There are profound evidential, methodological and organisational issues that may be said to stand in the way. For example, it is necessary to take cognisance of the enduring scepticism that exists as to how the historical narrative, which prioritises human agency, can accommodate the more depersonalised methods of scientifically grounded inquiry. This scepticism is evident, for example, in R. Gillespie's contribution in this collection (chapter 8) where he justifiably queries if it is necessary to invoke hemispheric climatic forces by looking closely at one such episode. Others (Campbell and Ludlow (chapter 7), Kelly

---

Research 23 (2015), 369–96; J. Brewer and F. Riede, 'Cultural heritage and climate adaptation: a cultural evolutionary perspective for the Anthropocene', *World Archaeology* 50 (2018), 554–69; T.C. Rick and D.H. Sandweiss, 'Archaeology, climate, and global change in the Age of Humans', *Proceedings of the National Academy of Sciences of the United States of America* 117 (2020), 8250–53.

[30] For example, T. Dawson, *et al.*, 'Coastal heritage, global climate change, public engagement, and citizen science', *Proceedings of the National Academy of Sciences of the United States of America* 117 (2020), 8280–87; CHERISH—Climate, Heritage and Environments of Reefs, Islands and Headlands (www.cherishproject.eu/en/).

[31] For discussion see, for example, Braje, 'Earth systems', 386–85; E. Costello, 'Hill farmers, habitats and time: the potential of historical ecology in upland management and conservation', *Landscape Research* 45 (2020), 951–965: 951.

[32] Francis Ludlow and Arlene Crampsie, 'Environmental history of Ireland, 1550–1830' in Jane Ohlmeyer (ed.), *The Cambridge history of Ireland, volume 2* (Cambridge, 2018), 608–37.

(chapter 9)) argue, either implicitly or explicitly, for the integration of weather and climate into the explanatory narrative in a manner that suggests that they conceive of it as a logical feature of the greater inclusivity of modern social and economic history. Another challenge is posed by the longstanding tendency of historians to work alone. If, as seems inevitable, this disposition will weaken as the multi-dimensional, multi-spectrum approach of the sciences achieves a more commanding hold in the discipline, it would be a matter of regret if the diversity of disciplinary approaches that informs this collection was lost for each has something unique to offer.

The methods and demands of scientific and laboratory-based inquiry are more visible in Archaeology and in Geography. Interdisciplinary collaboration brings its own challenges, however. It is not easy to integrate evidence from archaeology and palaeoecology to create coherent narratives, not least because their respective chronologies have been established at different scales, the former to record short-term events, the latter to track continuous sequences of activity, as discussed in this volume by McClatchie and Potito (chapter 2) as well as by Stastney (chapter 3). In areas of the globe subject to climatic extremes it is sometimes relatively straightforward to demonstrate a causal link between climatic shifts and marked changes in human demography, settlement patterns and trade.[33] Not so in Ireland where changes in the predominantly temperate oceanic climate rarely had such thoroughgoing, long-term effects on human populations. As the contributions to this volume attest, most scholars now reject what Geary and colleagues (chapter 5) describe as, 'compelling but rather uncomplicated, totalising narratives in which climate is the sole, or at least the primary, driver of cultural change'. However, in no way has this diminished their interest in, and commitment to, more nuanced investigations of the complex relationship between climate and society. Notwithstanding the challenges just highlighted, Ireland also has distinct advantages in this regard, in addition to the wealth of palaeoenvironmental evidence cited above. To name the most obvious, Ireland's unusually extensive compilations of medieval annals provide a rich seam of evidence, both for one-off extreme weather events and longer-term climatic trends, that can fairly be claimed to be of international significance (chapters 6 and 7). In recent years it has been mined to great effect, and expertly combined with other strands of evidence, by Francis Ludlow.[34] Looking forward, in addition to refined chronological precision and better integration of disparate datasets, the application of new palaeoenvironmental techniques, such as sedaDNA and biomarker analysis, will undoubtedly enhance our ability to investigate the

---

[33] For example, M.D. Petraglia *et al.*, 'Human responses to climate and ecosystem change in ancient Arabia', *Proceedings of the National Academy of Sciences of the United States of America* 117 (2020), 8263–70.

[34] Francis Ludlow, 'Medieval Irish chronicles reveal persistent volcanic forcing of severe cold events, 431–1649 CE', *Environmental Research Letters* 8 (2013), 024035; the works by Ludlow cited in this collection.

relationship between demography and climate change over the long term, as discussed by Plunkett and colleagues below (chapter 4).

This volume is the third in the sequence of special, or themed, issues of *Proceedings of the Royal Irish Academy*. Like its predecessors, which engaged with 'domestic life' and 'food and drink' in Ireland,[35] it aspires to provide an multi-period, interdisciplinary perspective on an important theme, combining synthesis of existing knowledge with new insights and approaches. The editors wish to express their gratitude to the contributors without whom this project could never have been realised, for their commitment, professionalism and co-operation. They are grateful also for the support they have received in the conception and development of this volume to the Editorial Board of the journal and to the Academy's Publication Office and Publication Committee. Particular thanks are extended to Jonathan Dykes, Liz Evers and Trevor Mullins for their assistance in the production of the volume. The papers collected herein highlight the vibrancy of research on the history and archaeology of climate and society in Ireland. The more information that is gathered the more complex the relationship between the two appears, and scholarship has long moved beyond the initial temptation, evident in some of the earlier works cited above, to offer reductive explanations of it. As the challenge of climate change compels us to alter our behaviour in the present, it is essential that we equip ourselves with a full and detailed appreciation of how our forebears did so in the past. This will not provide us with all the answers we may need in the years ahead, but it should assist us in understanding the order and range of the problems that will be posed, while also underscoring the unprecedented nature of the current crisis.

---

[35] 'Domestic life in Ireland', *Proceedings of the Royal Irish Academy*, 111C (2011); 'Food and drink in Ireland', *Proceedings of the Royal Irish Academy*, 115C (2015).

Climate change and hunter gatherers in Ireland: problems, potentials and pressing research questions

GRAEME WARREN*

[Accepted 10 September 2019. Published 03 March 2020.]

Abstract

This paper reviews evidence for the potential impact of climate change on the earliest human settlement of Ireland, primarily within the Mesolithic period. Three key areas are examined: the broad correlation between climate change and the timing of the settlement of Ireland; the impact of climatically driven sea level change; and finally, the influence of key Holocene climate 'events' such as the 8.2 cal BP Event. Ireland should be well-placed to contribute to debates about the impact of climate change on prehistoric hunter-gatherers, but much of our data is insufficiently precise to understand this in detail.

Introduction

This paper explores the relationship between climate change and the timing, character and extent of the settlement of Ireland by hunter-gatherers. This includes material from two geological epochs: recently identified evidence for Upper Palaeolithic activity in the Late Glacial period of the Pleistocene, and the more substantial evidence for Mesolithic activity in the Holocene. At one level, the influence of climate change on this topic is profound: the archaeological period names are themselves products of our understanding of climate change, with the shift from the Pleistocene to Holocene at 11,700 cal BP[1] often seen as the transition from the Upper Palaeolithic to Mesolithic. However, whilst a very broad relationship between climate change and the timing of human colonisation of Ireland by hunter-gatherers can be identified, understanding how this influenced hunter-gatherers once the island was settled is not clear. The lack of data with appropriate resolution to examine this relationship is a key problem.

Understanding the relationship between climate change and human social transformations is one of archaeology's 'grand challenges',[2] potentially allowing the discipline to make a contribution to our understanding of one of the major existential crises facing humanity in the twenty-first century. Claiming

---

*Author's email: graeme.warren@ucd.ie
ORCID Id: https://orcid.org/0000-0001-6280-2576
doi: https://doi.org/10.3318/PRIAC.2020.120.01
[1] All dates in calibrated years Before Present (cal BP) unless stated otherwise.
[2] Keith Kintigh et al., 'Grand challenges for archaeology', *Proceedings of the National Academy of Sciences* 111 (2014), 879–80.

that an understanding of how climate change affected small-scale societies 10,000 years ago may help us identify strategies and possibilities for responding to the impacts of anthropogenically driven climate change on an industrialised world in the present may seem far-fetched, but understanding the varied human responses to climate change is of great significance in a world where many still deny anthropogenic climate change, or find difficulty in responding to it meaningfully due to the apparently overwhelming scale of the challenge.

It is also important to recognise that contemporary hunting and gathering communities are amongst the most vulnerable to the effects of anthropogenically driven climate change.[3] This is not because hunting and gathering groups are less resilient in the face of change, or less able to adapt their routines. An enormous body of work has demonstrated that hunter-gatherer societies are not solely products of their environment, but are the outcome of dynamic histories of change in forms of belief and tradition as well as expressions of agency within particular environments, which in turn shape those environments.[4] Rather, today's hunter-gatherers are especially vulnerable because they often live in environments where the effects of climate change are more marked, such as the Arctic. For such groups, changing climates and environments are having profound effects not just on the distribution of resources, but also on the ability to sustain traditions, customs and world views.[5] It is for this reason that climate change presents an existential challenge. Their identities are bound to the places they inhabit and formed through routines of movement and practice. Simply moving or changing their ways of life is not an easy response, as it may mean the end of their traditional cultures. On this basis, over a decade ago the Inuit Circumpolar Conference argued that because climate change was leading to a loss of identity it was an infringement of their human rights.[6]

Understanding the impact of climate change on past hunter-gatherers therefore provides an important contribution to a key problem. Ireland should be well placed to contribute to such debates, not least because it is an island in an ecologically marginal position at the north-western extremity of Europe.[7]

---

[3] Victoria Reyes-Garciá and Aili Pyhälä, 'Introduction: hunter-gatherers in a *fast* changing world', in Victoria Reyes-Garciá and Aili Pyhälä (eds), *Hunter-Gatherers in a changing world*, i-xxxviii. (Cham, 2017), i–xxxviii.

[4] Kenneth Sassaman and Donald Holly (eds), *Hunter-Gatherer archaeology as historical process* (Tucson, 2011).

[5] Susan Crate, 'Gone the bull of winter? grappling with the cultural implications of and anthropology's role(s) in global climate change'. *Current Anthropology* 49 (2008), 569–97.

[6] Anisimov O.A. *et al.*, 'Polar regions (Arctic and Antarctic)', in Martin Parry *et al.* (eds), *Climate change 2007: impacts, adaptation and vulnerability. Contribution of working group ii to the fourth assessment report of the Intergovernmental Panel on Climate Change* (Cambridge, 2007), 653–85.

[7] Graeme Warren, 'The adoption of agriculture in Ireland: perceptions of key research challenges', *Journal of Archaeological Method and Theory* 20 (2013), 525–51.

Ireland's north Atlantic position also means that it should be sensitive to changes in oceanic thermohaline circulation, often considered a key contributor to Holocene climate change. Ireland has been an island since *c.* 16,000 cal BP[8] and this island status is associated with a limited diversity of plants and animals. This may have augmented the effects of climate change in Ireland because of the greater vulnerability of an ecosystem with fewer components. Interdisciplinary work to examine the question of the comparative ecological complexity and resilience of early Holocene Ireland is a compelling need. Thus Ireland should provide an important case study of the relationship between climate change and hunter-gatherers. Unfortunately, as will be demonstrated in this paper, notwithstanding this potential, problems of data resolution mean this cannot be realised at present.

Climate and the archaeology of hunter-gatherers: key problems

The hunting and gathering communities who settled in Ireland in the early Holocene lived through very significant climate change. This included multiple processes, operating at very different temporal and geographical scales. These changes to the climate were manifest and experienced as changes to the environment, which are often seen as having a determining impact on hunter-gatherer lifeways. Indeed, the environment has always influenced accounts of Ireland's earliest settlers. Macalister, for example, characterised them as fearful inhabitants scared of dense forests.[9]

Understanding how Mesolithic groups experienced and reacted to climate change is profoundly challenging: put simply, the available data are either not of sufficient resolution to examine these questions in detail, or where the data are available it has not been analysed appropriately. In terms of understanding climate change, we can document key climate events and processes at a regional level through the use of a number of proxies, although our ability to identify how these manifested themselves in specific changes to eco-systems in specific places and at specific times, is variable. This modelling is not a straightforward process and integrating different proxies and the reconstructions arising from them is a significant challenge, even before we attempt to align these with the human record. Archaeologically, we can also identify the presence of human groups in specific parts of the Irish landscape through the presence of a different set of proxies (material culture) and use this to consider changes in their behaviours.

Unfortunately, it is often very difficult to provide robust analytical mechanisms to associate changes in the climate with changes in human behaviour.

---

[8] Robin Edwards and Kieran Craven, 'Relative sea-level change around the Irish coast', in Peter Coxon *et al.* (eds), *Advances in Irish Quaternary Studies* (Paris, 2017), 181–216; Robin Edwards and Anthony Brooks, 'The island of Ireland: drowning the myth of an Irish land-bridge', In J.L. Davenport *et al.* (eds), *Mind the Gap: postglacial colonisation of Ireland* (Special Supplement to the *Irish Naturalists' Journal* 2008), 19–34.

[9] Robert Macalister, *Ancient Ireland: a study in the lessons of archaeology and history,* (London,1935).

Even setting aside the epistemological issues about aligning interdisciplinary data of very varied character, there are two specific data problems. First, our archaeological and palaeoenvironmental data are often not from the same locations, and in some instances, the spatial and temporal variability in the impact of a climate event is not well understood. Second, it is difficult to chronologically associate climate change, its environmental implications and human behaviour. In 1991 Mike Baillie used the phrase 'suck-in and smear' to characterise the temptation to assume a link between poorly dated phenomena at a time when the number of available radiocarbon dates was limited and most were imprecise.[10] Since then advances in statistical modelling of large data sets, such as the increasingly common use of Bayesian and summed probability distribution (SPD) analysis of radiocarbon data sets, offer important advances in this regard, but they also introduce new interpretative challenges.[11] Where precision is a problem 'facts' become self-perpetuating as more and more explanatory power is assigned to a climate event. This is especially problematic when people with detailed knowledge of *either* the archaeology or climate records, but not both, look for correlations to justify grant awards. Ongoing developments in how universities are audited also encourage publications with big stories and high impact results.

The problem of precision is exacerbated when the dating of key environmental changes is still subject to debate. Demonstrating synchronicity between environmental and archaeological events can involve comparing proxies from ice cores (measured in ice core years) to sedimentary records (often dated by radiocarbon), with samples sometimes collected from geographically diverse regions. It has recently been argued that changes in the behaviour of pines in the north of Ireland, indicating the dry conditions associated with the sharp climate deterioration of 8,200 cal BP—henceforth the 8.2 Event (see page 14 for discussion)—demonstrate that the key ice core chronologies are 'too old by 65–75 years for the early Holocene'.[12] Whilst 70 years may not seem a substantial difference when we are dealing with events 8,200 years ago, in terms of cause and effect and correlation of different data it is very significant, representing two to three human generations. Tipping and colleagues have recently emphasised that the generational or decadal time resolution required to address these relationships is now available to us through the application of chronological modelling and they emphasise the need to develop clear, testable hypotheses that allow us to separate correlation and cause.[13]

---

[10] Mike Baillie, 'Suck-in and smear: two related chronological problems for the 90s', *Journal of Theoretical Archaeology* 2 (1991), 12–16.

[11] Alan Williams, 'The use of summed radiocarbon probability distributions in archaeology: a review of methods', *Journal of Archaeological Science* 39 (2012), 578–89.

[12] Max Torbenson *et al.,* 'Asynchrony in key Holocene chronologies: evidence from Irish bog pines', *Geology* 43 (2015), 799–802: 801.

[13] Richard Tipping *et al.,* 'Moments of crisis: climate change in Scottish prehistory', *Proceedings of the Society Antiquaries of Scotland* 142 (2012), 9–25.

Unfortunately, the archaeological evidence available from the Mesolithic of Ireland is not of a sufficient resolution to allow generational or decadal chronological precision. This paper therefore reviews the impact of climate change on human lives in this period at a general level. Rather than establish causal relationships, I will highlight the ways in which climate change shaped the archaeological record and describe some of the key events which *may have* influenced human activity. In some instances, such as the 8.2 Event, claims have been made for a direct causal relationship; these will be reviewed and found to be insufficiently grounded in the data. This review first provides a broad chronological framework before considering two main facets of climate change that have been claimed to influence Mesolithic lives: sea level change and particular episodes of climatic deterioration during the Holocene.

First settlement and its climatic context

At the broadest level, the (re)colonisation of Britain and Ireland by human groups after the Late Glacial Maximum is demonstrably related to climate change (see Fig. 1 for overview). The movement north and west of groups of hunter-gatherers as climate change led to transformations in the availability of key resources is evidenced across northern Europe.[14] The human pioneer settlement of new landscapes is sometimes cast either as a heroic, exploratory endeavour, or as a manifestation of an inherent human urge to explore, both characterisations often embodying a heavily gendered set of associations. In contrast, McCannon highlights that these climate changes led to considerable challenges: 'Some were crowded out of more desirable ecozones by accelerating population growth. Others had their skills and folkways rendered obsolete by changes to their habitat. Many were refugees, fleeing environmental shocks and stresses'.[15] For some, the movement north was not a heroic exploration but a process of following their world as the ecologies that had sustained it moved north.

In Britain, which at this time of lower sea level was linked to Europe, the first evidence of hunting and gathering groups is clearly associated with the warming of the Bølling-Allerød interstadial, c. 14,600 cal BP.[16] These hunter-gatherers are best considered part of the Magdalenian complex of northern Europe, linked by technology, religious practice and art forms, and their presence in Britain may have been limited in extent.[17] The ongoing climatic and environmental changes of

---

[14] Brian Wygal and Stephan Heidenreich, 'Deglaciation and human colonization of northern Europe', *Journal of World Prehistory* 27 (2014), 111–44.

[15] John McCannon, *A history of the Arctic: nature, exploration and exploitation*, (London, 2012), 40.

[16] Roger Jacobi and Tom Higham, 'The Later Upper Palaeolithic recolonisation of Britain: new results from AMS radiocarbon dating', in Nick Ashton *et al.* (eds), *The ancient human occupation of Britain,* Developments in Quaternary Science Volume 14 (London, 2011), 223–47.

[17] Paul Pettitt and Mark White, *The British Palaeolithic: human societies at the edge of the Pleistocene world* (London, 2012).

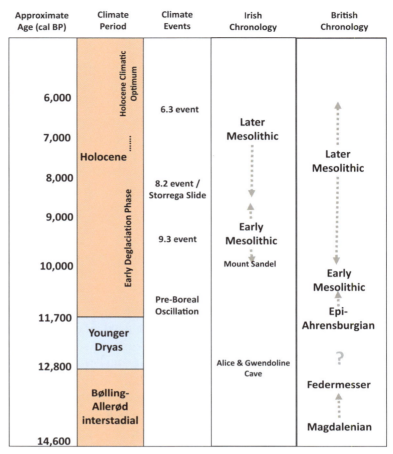

Fig. 1—A simplified and approximate timeline for the periods discussed.

the interstadial saw the reorganisation of hunter-gatherer technologies and adaptations across northern Europe. Characteristic Hamburgian and Federmesser assemblages have been recovered from Britain and show that hunter-gatherers in this area formed part of the broader European response to climate change. The onset of cold conditions with the Younger Dryas stadial (12,800 cal BP) seems to have led to the abandonment of Britain.[18]

There is no evidence of human activity in Ireland until c. 12,800–12,500 cal BP, some 2,000 years later than Britain.[19] The delay is likely to be linked to Ireland's island status: partly because of the challenges of colonising islands, but more likely because of the limited mammalian fauna present. The Quaternary Fauna Project suggested that only reindeer, hare and possibly giant deer were present in Ireland during the interstadial, whereas in Britain mammalian fauna

---

[18] Pettitt and White, *The British Palaeolithic*.
[19] Graeme Warren, 'The human colonisation of Ireland in northwest European context', in Peter Coxon *et al.* (eds), *Advances in Irish Quaternary studies* (Paris, 2017), 293–316.

included red deer, reindeer, elk, mammoth and horse.[20] The absence of wild horse may have been particularly significant given its critical importance to Magdalenian groups.[21] A recently discovered anthropogenically cut-marked bear patella from the Alice and Gwendoline cave in Co. Clare dates to 12,800–12,500 cal BP[22] placing it right at the end of the interstadial period, indeed within a period when activity in Britain was declining significantly because of cold conditions at the onset of the Younger Dryas. Quite what hunter-gatherer groups were doing in the west of Ireland during the early stages of a period of major climate deterioration is not yet clear.

After about 12,000 years cal BP, hunting and gathering groups were moving back into Britain and parts of Scandinavia. Stone-tool assemblages associated with these groups are described variously in different research traditions as long blade, Ahrensburgian or Epi-Ahrensburgian. In the south of England 'long blade' assemblages were present from the very end of the Younger Dryas.[23] Ahrensburgian (or Epi-Ahrensburgian) assemblages have recently been found in Scotland: Mithen and colleagues argue that settlement at Rubha Port an t-Seilich, Islay, at the end of the Younger Dryas was associated with very seasonal climate, with warm summers, reduced sea ice and storms.[24] Britain may have been very briefly abandoned again around 11,300 cal BP when changes in north Atlantic thermohaline circulation caused by a flood from the ice-dammed North American Lake Agassiz caused the 'Preboreal oscillation' climatic deterioration.[25] Mesolithic settlement follows, with the classic Early Mesolithic site of Star Carr in eastern England occupied from *c*. 11,300–10,500 years ago.[26]

---

[20] Peter Woodman *et al.*, 'The Irish Quaternary fauna project', *Quaternary Science Reviews* 16 (1997), 129–59.

[21] Jacobi and Higham 'The Later Upper Palaeolithic recolonisation of Britain', 243.

[22] Marion Dowd and Ruth Carden, 'First evidence of a Late Upper Palaeolithic human presence in Ireland', *Quaternary Science Reviews* 139 (2016), 158–63.

[23] Chantal Conneller and Tom Higham, 'Dating the Early Mesolithic: new results from Thatcham and Seamer Carr', in Nick Ashton and C. Harris (eds), *No stone unturned: papers in honour of Roger Jacobi*, Lithic Studies Society Occasional Paper 9 (London, 2015), 157–66.

[24] Steve Mithen *et al.*, 'A Lateglacial archaeological site in the far north-west of Europe at Rubha Port an t-Seilich, Isle of Islay, western Scotland: Ahrensburgian-style artefacts, absolute dating and geoarchaeology', *Journal of Quaternary Science* 30 (2015), 396–416.

[25] Chantal Conneller *et al.*, The resettlement of the British landscape: towards a chronology of Early Mesolithic lithic assemblage types. *Internet Archaeology* 42 (2016), https://doi.org/10.11141/ia.42.12; Conneller and Higham, 'Dating the Early Mesolithic'.; Timothy Fisher *et al.*, 'Preboreal oscillation caused by a glacial Lake Agassiz flood', *Quaternary Science Reviews* 21 (2002), 873–78.

[26] Alex Bayliss *et al.*, 'Dating the archaeology and environment of the Star Carr embayment', in Nicky Milner *et al.* (eds), *Star Carr volume 2: studies in technology, subsistence and environment* (York, 2018), 33–112; Nicky Milner *et al.* 'Interpretative narrative of the history of occupation', in Nicky Milner *et al.* (eds), *Star Carr volume 1: a persistent place in a changing world* (York, 2018), 225–44.

Again, evidence for comparable activity in Ireland is lacking.[27] A cut-marked bear vertebra from the Catacombs, Co. Clare, shows some presence of humans c. 11,100–10,500 cal BP, broadly contemporary with Star Carr.[28] Clear evidence of settlement, though later, is present at Mount Sandel c. 9,700 cal BP, when large circular huts paralleled in northern Britain were constructed on a bluff above the Bann.[29] The reasons for this second delay in the settlement of Ireland are not well understood, but again we may suspect that the limited range of mammalian fauna was a factor. Following the appearance of the Earlier Mesolithic at Mount Sandel, it is widely assumed that the Mesolithic presence in Ireland was continuous.

Sea level change

Changes in relative sea level caused by deglaciation represent one of the most significant impacts of Holocene climate change on the archaeology of Irish hunter-gatherers. In simple terms, this relates to the differential pace of absolute sea level rise caused by ice melt (glacio-eustasy) and rebound as the earth's crust is released from the weight of ice (glacio-isostasy), but modelling this process is highly complex.[30] In Ireland sea levels have risen since the start of the Mesolithic and relative sea level (RSL) for most of the Mesolithic is now below present sea level with the exception of the north-east of Ireland where very late Mesolithic RSL was at or above the current shoreline.[31] Changing sea level impacts the Mesolithic of Ireland in two ways: firstly, changing RSL would have been noticeable in the past, and human decisions and actions most likely attempted to cope with this. Secondly, changing RSL means that many Mesolithic sites that were once on dry land are now submerged, creating a very significant taphonomic bias in our attempt to understand hunter-gatherer lives. For example, in the south-west of Ireland, any coastal sites contemporary with Mount Sandel are now below 30–45m of water.

Our data rarely allows us to consider the response of groups of hunter-gatherers to sea level change driven by long-term climate change. One of

---

[27] Warren, 'The human colonisation of Ireland in Northwest European context'.

[28] Dowd and Carden, 'First evidence of a Late Upper Palaeolithic human presence in Ireland'.

[29] Alex Bayliss and Peter Woodman, 'A new Bayesian chronology for Mesolithic occupation at Mount Sandel, Northern Ireland', *Proceedings of the Prehistoric Society* 75 (2009), 101–23.

[30] Robin Edwards *et al.*, 'Resolving discrepancies between field and modelled relative sea-level data: lessons from western Ireland', *Journal of Quaternary Science* 32 (2017), 957–75.

[31] Graeme Warren and Kieran Westley, '" …they made no effort to explore the interior of the country…": coastal landscapes, hunter-gatherers and the islands of Ireland', in Almüt Schülke (ed.), *The coastal landscapes of the Mesolithic* (London, forthcoming).

Climate change and hunter gatherers in Ireland

Fig. 2—Diver with an Earlier Mesolithic flint blade recovered from the seabed, *c*. 2m water depth. Eleven Ballyboes, Co. Donegal © W Forsythe.

the most detailed studies is Westley's reconstruction of changing settlement patterns in Inishowen, Co. Donegal.[32] Here changing sea levels throughout the Mesolithic are associated with changing settlement patterns. Sea level change was initially relatively rapid and saw the inundation of dry land areas. This would have flooded Earlier Mesolithic sites located in estuarine environments, as seen for example at Eleven Ballyboes (Fig. 2).[33] As RSL change

---

[32] Warren and Westley, '"…they made no effort to explore the interior of the country…"'.
[33] Kieran Westley, 'Submerged Mesolithic landscape investigation, Eleven Ballyboes, Republic of Ireland', *International Journal of Nautical Archaeology* 44 (2015), 243–57.

slowed, new and comparatively stable shallow water and intertidal environments were created in embayments. These in-shore environments, as well as estuaries, appear to have been the focus of long-term activity based on exploitation of these in-shore environments: evidenced by lithic scatters and shell middens, the latter, such as Baylet, showing the types of resources used. In this case, the landscape distribution of hunter-gatherer activity appears to show human responsiveness to the changing environments provided by sea-level change. Even here, however, Westley stresses the difficulties caused by the coarse and differing chronological resolution of the archaeological materials (many of which are only dated on typological grounds) and the palaeo-geographic models. The causal relationships are not very clear and further work on dating and refining the archaeological chronologies would be a first step to providing a better understanding of the relationship of sea level change and human responses.

In some instances, locations appear to persist through long and radical changes in RSL, such as at Cushendun, Co. Antrim (Fig. 3). Here Mesolithic activity persisted in a landscape where falling and rising sea levels transformed a location from two different periods of lagoons through to a series of beach

Fig. 3—The classic Cushendun section, with Mesolithic artefacts recovered from layers B, D and E.

deposits.³⁴ It would be tempting to consider this as evidence of the persistent significance of this specific place despite fundamental landscape changes, but given that many of the artefacts that were recovered have been redeposited by incursions of the sea and are in secondary contexts it is not possible to demonstrate this.

Elsewhere, little detail is available. Although Nunn argues that a folk memory of north European sea level change is preserved in myth and legend³⁵ there is little compelling evidence to demonstrate how Mesolithic communities experienced this change.³⁶ As I have argued elsewhere,³⁷ sea level change was a transformation that was visible to Mesolithic communities in north-west Europe, a process of change that was recognised and perhaps experienced as a loss of familiar landscapes. At present, however, we cannot assess how it was understood in an Irish context because of a lack of data.

The Storegga Tsunami

As well as long-term processes of sea level change, it is argued that the Holocene has been characterised by rapid sea level events. The most widely discussed of these is the tsunami caused by the submarine Storrega Slide at 8,175–8,120 BP, which had a profound impact on many areas of the North Atlantic, with run ups greater than 20m proposed in the Shetland islands.³⁸ This major event coincided with the ongoing inundation of the low-lying coastal landscapes of Doggerland and with the 8,200 BP climate event (see Weninger, 2008). Wicks and Waddington highlight the potentially catastrophic consequences of the tsunami to Mesolithic communities in north-east Britain, as well as the potential taphonomic consequence of removing evidence of earlier coastal settlement.³⁹

---

[34] Hallam Movius *et al.*, 'An early Post-Glacial archaeological site at Cushendun, County Antrim', *Proceedings of the Royal Irish Academy Section C: Archaeology, Celtic Studies, History, Linguistics, Literature* 46 (1940), 1–84; Warren and Westley, '" …they made no effort to explore the interior of the country…"'.

[35] Patrick Nunn, *The edge of memory: ancient stories, oral tradition and the post-glacial World* (London, 2018).

[36] Jim Leary, 'Perceptions of and responses to the Holocene flooding of the North Sea lowlands', *Oxford Journal of Archaeology* 28 (2009), 227–37; Jim Leary, *The remembered land: surviving sea-level rise after the last Ice Age.* (London, 2015).

[37] Graeme Warren, 'Transformations? The Mesolithic of north-west Europe', in Vicki Cummings *et al.* (eds), *The Oxford handbook of the archaeology and anthropology of hunter-gatherers* (Oxford, 2014), 537–55.

[38] Stein Bondevik *et al.*, 'The Storegga Slide tsunami—comparing field observations with numerical simulations', in A. Solheim *et al.* (eds), *Ormen Lange–an integrated study for safe field development in the Storegga submarine area* (Oxford, 2005), 195–208; Stein Bondevik *et al.*, 'Green mosses date the Storegga tsunami to the chilliest decades of the 8.2 ka cold event', *Quaternary Science Reviews* 45 (2012), 1–6; Bernhard Weninger *et al.*, 'The catastrophic final flooding of Doggerland by the Storegga Slide tsunami', *Documenta Praehistorica* XXXV (2008), 1–24.

[39] Clive Waddington and Karen Wicks, 'Resilience or wipe out? Evaluating the convergent impacts of the 8.2 ka event and Storegga tsunami on the Mesolithic of northeast Britain', *Journal of Archaeological Science: Reports* 14 (2017), 692–714.'

As Blankholm has recently argued, despite the attention the tsunami has received, caution is required in relation to its putative effects, particularly on areas away from the epicentre of its impact.[40] There is also increasing evidence for other rapid sea level change through this period, which needs to be distinguished from the field evidence for the tsunami. For example, based on field observations in south-west Scotland, Lawrence and colleagues argue that sudden meltwater discharges associated with the down-wasting of the North American ice sheets led to pulses of sea level rise at 8,760–8,640 (RSL increase of 0.35m), 8,595–8,465 (0.7m), and 8,330–8,220 (0.4m) cal BP.[41] Differentiating between Storegga deposits, storm deposits and other marine transgressions is not straightforward.

Little attention has been paid to the potential impact of the Storegga tsunami on Ireland. Recent models suggest that it would have affected Ireland, with waves of *c.* 5m on the west coast,[42] but field observations of deposits that may relate to the event are rare, not surprising given that with the possible exception of parts of the north-east, most of the Mesolithic shorelines contemporary with this event are submerged, possibly by as much as 20m.[43] In the Shannon estuary, Edwards and colleagues have highlighted a truncation of peat and infilling of sediments following 8,700 cal BP, but the cause of this is not clear.[44]

In the absence of any meaningful data it is therefore not possible to speculate on the potential impact of the tsunami on hunting and gathering groups in Ireland, not least because separating the impact of the tsunami from the 8.2 Event is not straightforward. Whilst the potential destructive capacity of a wave modelled at 5m high is not to be underestimated, it is important to note that Ireland has long been characterised by high waves of different kinds and causes.[45] Although the atmospheric circulation conditions of the early Holocene are not directly comparable to those of today, contemporary Atlantic hurricanes can generate waves 7.5–16m high. Hunting and gathering communities living on the west of Ireland would have been very familiar with extreme events associated with the

---

[40] Hans Peter Blankholm, 'In the wake of the wake. An investigation of the impact of the Storegga tsunami on the human settlement of inner Varangerfjord, northern Norway', *Quaternary International* (2018).

[41] Thomas Lawrence *et al.*, 'Relative sea-level data from southwest Scotland constrain meltwater-driven sea-level jumps prior to the 8.2 kyr BP event', *Quaternary Science Reviews* 151 (2016), 292–308.

[42] Jon Hill *et al.*, 'How does multiscale modelling and inclusion of realistic palaeobathymetry affect numerical simulation of the Storegga Slide tsunami?', *Ocean Modelling* 83 (2014), 11–25.

[43] Edwards and Craven, 'Relative sea-level change around the Irish coast'.

[44] Edwards *et al.*, 'Resolving discrepancies between field and modelled relative sea-level data'.

[45] O'Brien L *et al.*, 'Extreme wave events in Ireland: 14680 BP-2012', *Natural Hazards and Earth System Sciences* 13 (2013), 625–48.

sea. This far from its epicentre, the tsunami may not have been of unprecedented magnitude although aspects of a tsunami wave's behaviour, including the retreat of the sea before the wave arrives, may have been less familiar.

Holocene climate change and the Mesolithic of Ireland

The Mesolithic falls broadly within two periods of Holocene climate, interrupted by events of differing magnitude. First, during the 'early deglaciation phase', from the onset of the Holocene at 11,700 cal BP through to 7,000 cal BP, northern latitudes were characterised by a cool or temperate climate, strongly influenced by ongoing deglaciation.[46] Much of the Irish Mesolithic falls within this period. Following this, and running through to c. 4,200 cal BP, the 'Holocene climate optimum' saw summer temperatures higher than preindustrial levels. These broad trends were interrupted by climate (and other) events of differing kinds. Events at 9,200, 8,200 and 6,300 cal BP are potentially significant, but it is important to note that these are not the only periods of deterioration. The variable oxygen isotope ($\delta^{18}O$) proportions in a spelothem (stalagtite) from Crag Cave, Co. Kerry, shows a clear series of warming and cooling events throughout the Holocene including other cooling events centred on c. 7,730 and 7,010 cal BP.[47]

Of the three major events, that at 9,200 cal BP is the most recently identified, possibly because it was short and therefore may not appear in some climate reconstructions.[48] It was a sharp cold anomaly, suggested by Fleitmann to be similar in magnitude to the 8.2 Event. Wicks and Waddington suggest it lasted about 50 years and caused reductions in average July temperatures of c. 1.6 degrees in north-west England. Attempts to identify a relationship between this event and the hunter-gatherer settlement of north-east Britain were inconclusive[49] and there is also little evidence of its impact on western Scotland.[50] Although this event has been correlated with environmental changes in Ireland,[51] there is insufficient archaeological data from this period to assess its possible impact on human settlement.

---

[46] Heinz Wanner et al., 'Structure and origin of Holocene cold events', *Quaternary Science Reviews* 30 (2011), 3109–123: 3117.

[47] Frank McDermott et al., 'Centennial-scale Holocene climate variability revealed by a high-resolution speleothem δ18O record from SW Ireland', *Science* 294 (2001), 1328–331.

[48] Dominik Fleitmann et al., 'Evidence for a widespread climatic anomaly at around 9.2 ka before present', *Paleoceanography* 23 (2008), PA1102.

[49] Waddington and Wicks, 'Resilience or wipe out?'.

[50] Karen Wicks and Steve Mithen, 'The impact of the abrupt 8.2 ka cold event on the Mesolithic population of western Scotland: A Bayesian chronological analysis using 'activity events' as a population proxy', *Journal of Archaeological Science* 45 (2014), 240–69.

[51] Beatriz Ghilardi and Michael O'Connell, 'Early Holocene vegetation and climate dynamics with particular reference to the 8.2 ka event: pollen and macrofossil evidence from a small lake in western Ireland', *Vegetation History and Archaeobotany* 22 (2013), 99–114.

The 8.2 Event

Of the Holocene cooling events that may have impacted hunter-gatherer groups, the one that has received most attention from archaeologists is that at *c.* 8,200 cal BP, the so-called 8.2 Event. This was caused by a significant meltwater pulse into the north Atlantic associated with the draining of glacial Lake Agassiz in North America. The pulse led to changes in north Atlantic thermohaline circulation.[52] Tipping and colleagues review evidence that it was only following the 8.2 Event that recognisable Holocene climatic patterns stabilised, with the persistent presence of large amounts of ice in the northern hemisphere prior to this date influencing atmospheric circulation.[53] The impacts of the 8.2 Event are spatially variable in north-west Europe, but in general the event was cold and dry, the most significant cooling event of the entire Holocene.[54]

Its potential impact on vegetation in Ireland and Atlantic Britain has been summarised by Wicks and Mithen.[55] In Ireland this includes the expansion of cool-tolerant birch and pine at the expense of hazel and oak in Sligo, variations in the presence of juniper in Inis Oírr and erosion in Connemara. Torbenson and colleagues highlight a large-scale expansion of bog pine at three sites in the north of Ireland at this time,[56] demonstrating drier conditions. Speleothem data from south-west Ireland shows that both the beginning and end of the event were abrupt, and that the event was characterised by increased seasonality in quantities of rainfall.[57] A range of evidence therefore supports the idea that the 8.2 Event brought about cold, dry conditions in Ireland. However, we must be careful given the limitations in chronological precision discussed above. For example, evidence from Lough Maumeen of an expansion of Pinus and decline in Corylus associated with erosion is cited by Wicks and Mithen as an expression of the 8.2 Event, but this evidence is not closely dated and several other major episodes of erosion take place before and after the claimed 8.2 impact. The 8.2 Event itself takes place within a longer-term colder period, and Head and colleagues found it very difficult to differentiate the potential effect of the 8.2 Event from that of longer-term cooling on a shift to a grass-dominated landscape on Achill.[58]

---

[52] Timothy Daley *et al.*, 'The 8200yr BP cold event in stable isotope records from the North Atlantic region', *Global and Planetary Change* 79 (2011), 288–302.

[53] Tipping *et al.*, 'Moments of crisis: climate change in Scottish prehistory', 11.

[54] Wanner *et al.*, 'Structure and origin of Holocene cold events'.

[55] Wicks and Mithen, 'The impact of the abrupt 8.2 ka cold event on the Mesolithic population of western Scotland'.

[56] Although see above for their concern about the dating of this; Torbenson *et al.*, 'Asynchrony in key Holocene chronologies'.

[57] James Baldini *et al.*, 'Structure of the 8200-Year cold event revealed by a speleothem trace element record', *Science* 296 (2002), 2203–206.

[58] Katie Head *et al.*, 'Problems with identifying the ?8200-year cold event? in terrestrial records of the Atlantic seaboard: a case study from Dooagh, Achill Island, Ireland', *Journal of Quaternary Science* 22 (2007), 65–75.

Elsewhere in Europe, the possible relationship between this cold and dry period and Mesolithic activity has seen extensive discussion in recent years. For example, Bicho has argued that on the Portuguese coast the cold marine conditions of the 8.2 Event led to a decline in marine productivity and increased up-swellings which led to a shift in settlement to the sheltered and stable Tagus estuary.[59] There are also cautious voices: Robinson and colleagues have highlighted that a lack of chronological precision means that assuming a causal relationship between the 8.2 Event and the broadly contemporary end of the Middle Mesolithic of the Rhine-Meuse-Scheldt region is problematic.[60] In northern Britain, Wicks and Mithen[61] have used SPDs[62] of radiocarbon dates from archaeological contexts from Mesolithic sites as a proxy for population to examine this relationship. Their focus on northern Britain also allowed them to consider the relationship between the 8.2 Event and the Storegga tsunami. Their interpretation is dramatic: in western Scotland 'a c. 90% reduction in the population density occurred post 8.2 ka, hence it follows that estimates for the number of people in western Scotland dropped to between c. 25 and 240 people during its aftermath'.[63] In the north-east of Britain, radiocarbon frequencies drop to c. 5% following the event and this depressed population levels for 1,000 years.[64] Wicks and Mithen highlight the implications of the combination of the cold and windy conditions of the 8.2 Event in the north-west of Britain for maritime mobility and the maintenance of fishing economies. They argue that the collapse of population was too rapid to allow innovative solutions to be maintained. A loose model is provided suggesting a movement to higher ground in the following period, with parallels to interpretations developed for Portugal.[65]

In Ireland two research teams have made claims about the relationship between the 8.2 Event and human activity. Both use radiocarbon dates as proxies for human activity. Riede and colleagues used SPDs to argue for population

---

[59] Nuno Bicho *et al.*, 'The emergence of Muge Mesolithic shell middens in central Portugal and the 8200 cal yr BP cold event', *The Journal of Island and Coastal Archaeology* 5 (2010), 86–104.

[60] Erik Robinson *et al.*, 'Radiocarbon chronology and the correlation of hunter-gatherer sociocultural change with abrupt palaeoclimate change: the Middle Mesolithic in the Rhine-Meuse-Scheldt area of northwest Europe', *Journal of Archaeological Science* 40 (2013), 755–63.

[61] Wicks and Mithen, 'The impact of the abrupt 8.2 ka cold event on the Mesolithic population of western Scotland'; Waddington and Wicks, 'Resilience or wipe out?'.

[62] Alan Williams 'The use of summed radiocarbon probability distributions in archaeology'.

[63] Wicks and Mithen, 'The impact of the abrupt 8.2 ka cold event on the Mesolithic population of western Scotland', 232.

[64] Waddington and Wicks, 'Resilience or wipe out?'.

[65] Penelope González-Sampériz *et al.*, 'Patterns of human occupation during the early Holocene in the central Ebro Basin (NE Spain) in response to the 8.2 ka climatic event', *Quaternary Research* 71 (2009), 121–32.

decline associated with the event,[66] while Griffiths and Robinson used Bayesian modelling to argue that there is no associated impact.[67] Even setting aside the question of whether radiocarbon dates are an effective proxy for population, both claims are problematic.

Riede and colleagues argue for a connection between climate change, lower population levels and technological change in the Irish Mesolithic. Specifically, they focus on the changing stone-tool technologies of the Mesolithic in Ireland. In the Earlier Mesolithic, blade-based technologies produced microliths which were used in compound tools, in keeping with technological traditions across much of Europe. Microlith production stopped in the Later Mesolithic, being replaced by a focus on larger flakes and blades – a development distinctive to Ireland (and related forms from the Isle of Man). Drawing upon a model developed for Tasmania, Riede argues that the proposed low level of population in Ireland led to an inability to maintain complex technologies. The Irish data therefore 'conform(s) well to the specific predictions laid out by the model: a targeted loss of more complex technologies (composite tools, organic technology, etc.) but a maintenance of or even improvement in simple technologies'.[68] It is debateable, however, whether the shift from Earlier to Later Mesolithic stone-tool technologies really represents a loss of complexity. It could simply represent a shift of that complexity into materials that do not preserve so well in the archaeological record, for example the fish traps known from the Later Mesolithic.[69] However this may be, Riede and colleagues essentially argue that climate change caused population collapse which in turn caused a technological change which we observe in the archaeological record. In contrast to the detailed model of impacts on maritime conditions and economies developed by Wicks and Mithen, no clear explanatory framework is provided for how climate change drives population collapse. There is simply an implicit assumption that the harder conditions of the 8.2 Event lead to population decline. Riede's articles have been influential. For example, Wicks and Mithen's detailed account of

---

[66] Felix Riede *et al.*, 'Tracking Mesolithic demography in time and space and its implications for explanations of culture change', in Phillipe Crombé *et al.* (eds), *Chronology and evolution within the Mesolithic of North-West Europe: proceedings of an international meeting, Brussels, May 30th-June 1st 2007* (Newcastle, 2009), 177–94; Felix Riede, 'Climate and demography in early prehistory: using calibrated 14c dates as population proxies', *Human Biology* 81 (2009), 309–37.

[67] Seren Griffiths and Erik Robinson, 'The 8.2 ka BP Holocene climate change event and human population resilience in northwest Atlantic Europe', *Quaternary International* 465 (2018), 251–57.

[68] Riede, 'Climate and Demography in Early Prehistory', 318.

[69] Melanie McQuade and Lorna O'Donnell, 'Late Mesolithic fish traps from the Liffey estuary, Dublin, Ireland', *Antiquity* 81 (2007), 569–84; Matt Mossop, 'Lakeside Developments in County Meath, Ireland: a Late Mesolithic fishing platform and possible mooring at Clowanstown 1', in Sinead McCartan *et al.* (eds), *Mesolithic horizons: papers presented at the seventh international conference on the Mesolithic in Europe, Belfast 2005* (Oxford, 2009), vol 2, 895–99.

the impact of the 8.2 Event in Scotland cites them as evidence for the claim that Ireland sees 'climate-driven population collapse during the ninth millennium BP' and that 'Irish demographic collapse may have been more severe than that occurring in western Scotland'.[70]

Given the significance of these claims it is important to examine the evidential basis carefully. Woodman was categorical that the technological changes that Riede seeks to explain through population change start earlier that 8,200 cal BP, and are therefore not caused by this event.[71] His most recent statements place the shift from Earlier to Later Mesolithic at *c.* 8,800/8,600 cal BP: therefore the 8.2 Event 'only happened at the end, if not after, this period of change'.[72] The two publications by Riede presenting the results of their analysis of the radiocarbon dates are slightly inconsistent in their chronological claims. In one a clear link is made with key climate events; periods with few dates 'coincide with major early Holocene climatic upheavals, such as the preboreal oscillation [and] the 8,200 event'.[73] (Note that there is no evidence of human settlement in Ireland prior to or during the Preboreal oscillation). In the other, following Woodman, the stone-tool transition is dated to 9,000–8,500 cal BP and it is argued that 'during the transition period the number of dates remains depressed and marked troughs are contemporary with the 8.2k BP event'.[74] The climate-driven explanation for population driven technological collapse is only demonstrated if Riede's radiocarbon data is reliable for the period 9,000–8,500 cal BP. Riede's database is, unfortunately, very weak. It comprises only dates obtained before 2002,[75] that is before the major expansion of archaeological work as part of the 'Celtic Tiger' boom. The total number of dates is also very small. Once multiple dates from phases are combined the data set comprises only 22 events which is a long way away from the 500 dates suggested by Williams for statistically reliable analysis.[76] Setting this issue aside, inspection of Riede's plot shows a decline in the number of dates following *c.* 9,500 cal BP, followed by an *increase* from *c.* 9,000 cal BP and a *peak* in dates *c.* 8,500 cal BP, rather than the claimed continuing decline.

---

[70] Wicks and Mithen, 'The impact of the abrupt 8.2 ka cold event on the Mesolithic population of western Scotland', 255.
[71] Peter Woodman, 'Challenging times: reviewing Irish Mesolithic chronologies', in Phillipe Crombé *et al.* (eds), *Chronology and evolution within the Mesolithic of North-West Europe: proceedings of an international meeting, Brussels, May 30th-June 1st 2007* (Newcastle, 2009) 195–216: 211.
[72] Peter Woodman, *Ireland's first settlers: time and the Mesolithic*, (Oxford, 2015): 227.
[73] Riede, 'Climate and Demography in Early Prehistory', 317
[74] Riede *et al.*, Tracking Mesolithic demography in time and space, 187.
[75] Riede *et al.*, Tracking Mesolithic demography in time and space, 182.
[76] Williams, The use of summed radiocarbon probability distributions in archaeology; a full audit and analysis of all Mesolithic C14 dates from Ireland is forthcoming (Chapple, McLaughlin and Warren, *An audit of Mesolithic radiocarbon dates from Ireland* (in prep)). At a preliminary stage this includes *c.* 50 definitely Mesolithic and over 80 possible Mesolithic sites with C14 dates.

There is a rapid fall following 8,200 cal BP. Whilst this may indicate a relationship between the 8.2 Event and radiocarbon date frequency, it is not plausible to relate this to technological change which happened in the period 9,000–8,500 cal BP. Thus, Riede's argument cannot be accepted.

Griffith and Robinson also review radiocarbon data from regions of north-west Europe including Ireland. They criticise SPD analysis for not providing data relevant to understanding the appropriate time scales for human response to climate change and instead use Bayesian approaches to modelling the chronological data from a *c.* 1,000 year period focused on 8,200 cal BP.[77] Their review includes sixteen sites from Ireland, some with multiple dates, and all claimed to be on 'anthropogenic' materials. Based on their review, they conclude that 'there does not seem to be a significant difference for activity at sites either side of the 8.2 ka BP event in northwest Atlantic Europe as a whole'.[78] Setting aside the question of whether SPD or Bayesian analysis provides the most appropriate mechanism to assess whether radiocarbon dates are a proxy for population levels, unfortunately Griffith and Robinson's Irish data set is also weak. Many of their radiocarbon dates are not demonstrably anthropogenic, including a date from an unmodified stoat bone from Keshcorran caves; two charcoal samples of Mesolithic date from much later sites (Rathgall and Lismore); sites whose archaeological status is questioned (Lullymore bog); and dates such as the pig ulna from Sutton, which are considered unreliable because it has been treated with preservative.[79] When these are removed there remains only eleven sites, many of which have very large standard deviations or significant questions about the associations between dated material and the archaeology (e.g. Newferry). Given these problems it is difficult to have confidence in the models generated by Griffith and Robinson for the Irish material. The impact of the 8.2 Event on human populations in Ireland is therefore unclear. The two most systematic attempts to analyse it have reached different conclusions, and each are based on poor data.

There has been little or no consideration of whether the 8.2 Event had a taphonomic impact on the archaeological record. Following the end of the dry period of the event, an extensive phase of river flooding is noted,[80] which might create conditions where riverine sites are more likely to be disturbed or buried. This is interesting, because such flood regimes may limit the creation of large palimpsest assemblages in riverine locations, separating episodes of activity with flood deposits. In turn, this could help generate a perception of smaller sites, characterised by fewer artefacts, a widely held understanding of the Irish Later Mesolithic. It is interesting to note, for example, that the accumulation of deposits

---

[77] Griffiths and Robinson, The 8.2 ka BP Holocene climate change event and human population resilience in northwest Atlantic Europe, 252.
[78] Griffiths and Robinson, The 8.2 ka BP Holocene climate change event and human population resilience in northwest Atlantic Europe, 255.
[79] Woodman *et al.*, The Irish quaternary fauna project, 144.
[80] Jonathan Turner *et al.*, 'New perspectives on Holocene flooding in Ireland using meta-analysis of fluvial radiocarbon dates', *Catena* 82 (2010), 183–90.

at Newferry may begin following 8,200 cal BP.[81] Possible human activity on basal sands in Zone 9 is poorly dated, with wood from this layer (not clearly associated with human activity) dating to *c.* 9,480–8,780 cal BP (UB-487, 8190±120 BP uncal). This is followed by the classic archaeological sequence, with the initiation of a sequence of variable artefact-bearing diatomites, silt and sands. Dating the initiation of this sequence is difficult. The date of 8,980–8,045 cal BP (UB-641, 7630±195 BP uncal) associated with Later Mesolithic activity in Zone 8 'is from the peat underlying the occupation layer',[82] whilst a *terminus ante quem* is provided by a range of dates from Zone 7, clustering at *c.* 8,000 cal BP. Although many of these dates have very large calibrated ranges, this hints that the accumulations of material at Newferry may be related to the changed flood environment following the cessation of the 8.2 Event. Further work to explore these issues is urgently needed given the potential taphonomic significance of changing flood regimes caused by climate change.

The 6.3 Event and the end of the Mesolithic

The period from *c.* 6,500 and 5,900 BP (sometimes referred to as the 6.3 Event) was also cold[83] although the combination of changes at this time is highly complex.[84] Tipping offers a summary of impacts on Britain and Ireland through this period.[85] Climate changes include a significant decline in sea temperatures west of Ireland, possibly associated with increased iceberg transport after *c.* 6,500 cal BP. Changing oceanic circulation led to increased sedimentation in the Irish Sea, which may have become much more seasonally variable in temperature, with winter sea-surface temperatures less than 5°C. Atlantic storms increased from *c.* 6,400 cal BP, possibly causing increased dune mobilisation in the north of Ireland. At a regional level temperature was colder from *c.* 6,750–6,550 cal BP, with a warmer period following. The period after 6,500 cal BP was significantly drier. Whitehouse *et al.* review evidence from Irish bog pines for drier conditions following *c.* 6,100 cal BP,[86] highlighting complex regional variation in the impact of these changes.

At a regional level, some claims have been made that the adoption of agriculture in Britain and Ireland was caused by climate change and that this

---

[81] Peter Woodman, 'Recent excavations at Newferry, Co. Antrim', *Proceedings of the Prehistoric Society* 43 (1977), 155–99.
[82] Woodman, 'Recent excavations at Newferry, Co. Antrim', 161.
[83] Wanner *et al.*, 'Structure and origin of Holocene cold events'.
[84] Tipping *et al.*, 'Moments of crisis: climate change in Scottish prehistory'.
[85] Richard Tipping, 'The case for climatic stress forcing choice in the adoption of agriculture in the British Isles', in Bill Finlayson and Graeme Warren (eds), *Landscapes in transition,* Levant Supplementary Series 8 (Oxford, 2010), 66–76.
[86] Nicki Whitehouse *et al.*, 'Neolithic agriculture on the European western frontier: the boom and bust of early farming in Ireland', *Journal of Archaeological Science* 51 (2014), 181–205.

was associated with changing hunter-gatherer behaviour. Tipping highlights the potential impact of the 6.3 Event on marine ecologies and the challenges this represented in terms of how the sea was used. He also argues that the sequence of profound ecological changes may have caused a loss of confidence amongst hunter-gatherers in their way of life and world-view, and encouraged them to consider new economic strategies. In a review of the evidence from north-west Europe (albeit with a Scottish focus), Bonsall and colleagues argued that the adoption of agriculture at *c.* 5,750 cal BP was associated with a change to drier climatic conditions combined with warmer summers and colder winters *c.* 6,050–5,150 cal BP, with the driest at *c.* 5,750 cal BP.[87] They argue that this reduced waterlogging and increased the potential for cereal cultivation, making agriculture more attractive to the indigenous hunter-gatherer population of Britain and Ireland. It has also been argued that this change in climate facilitated the geographical expansion of farming communities.[88] Regardless of who is doing the farming, the consensus view is that early agriculture in Ireland was initiated at a time of environmentally favourable conditions, especially between 5,950 and 5,550 cal BP.[89]

Unfortunately, there are few data available on how the varied processes that were part of the 6.3 Event played out in an Irish environmental context: Whitehouse and colleagues highlight that 'with some exceptions … there have been few attempts to examine in detail the nature of the Late Mesolithic Irish pollen record using high resolution pollen and charcoal counts, supported by a rigorous radiometric dating programme'.[90] This is unfortunate: Schulting has argued that assuming a large-scale unidirectional climate change at this time does not do justice to evidence for variation within and between areas of Europe and that more local detail is required.[91] Obtaining high resolution records of the environmental impact of this complex event is a pressing research priority, not least because it happened at a time of fundamental social change.

Turning to the archaeological evidence, precision about the processes through which agriculture replaced hunting and gathering in Ireland remains elusive. After many years of debate, multiple lines of evidence now suggest that the adoption of agriculture in Ireland involved the movement of farmers to the island, although questions surrounding their interaction with indigenous hunting and gathering groups remain. A clearly identifiable Neolithic is present in

---

[87] Clive Bonsall *et al.*, 'Climate change and the adoption of agriculture in North-West Europe', *European Journal of Archaeology* 5 (2001), 7–21.
[88] Glynis Jones *et al.*, 'Phylogeographic analysis of barley DNA as evidence for the spread of Neolithic agriculture through Europe', *Journal of Archaeological Science* 39 (2012), 3230–238.
[89] Whitehouse *et al.*, 'Neolithic agriculture on the European western frontier'.
[90] Whitehouse *et al.*, 'Neolithic agriculture on the European western frontier:', 183.
[91] Rick Schulting, 'Holocene environmental change and the Mesolithic-Neolithic transition in north-west Europe: revisiting two models', *Environmental Archaeology* 15 (2010), 160–72.

Ireland from c. 5,800–5,700 cal BP, but the period from 5,950–5,800 cal BP is still difficult to understand.[92] Some aspects of Neolithic activity appear to be present, but there is also continuity from the Mesolithic at some sites. Mesolithic groups in Ireland appear to have been in contact with farmers from the Continent from c. 6,300 cal BP, as evidenced by the appearance of a domesticated cattle bone at Ferriter's Cove.[93]

The presence of cattle at this date is in keeping with models of early migration of Breton farming communities through the western seaways, although this interpretation remains contentious.[94] The period following c. 6,300 cal BP therefore sees significant climate change, with poorly understood impacts on the Irish environment. This takes place alongside key social changes, including significant changes to the nature of human impact on the environment. With the data currently available, however, it is not possible to identify causal relationships, or even clear correlations.

Conclusion

As noted in the introduction, Ireland should provide a good case study for understanding the impact of climate change on hunter-gatherer behaviour in the early Holocene. Ireland had a limited range of fauna and flora, potentially magnifying the impact of environmental changes, and its marginal position in the Atlantic means that it should have been very sensitive to climate change, key aspects of which were driven by north Atlantic thermohaline circulation. It therefore has the potential to contribute more broadly to our understanding of the impact of climate change on hunter-gatherer groups.

At the broadest levels, the timing of the arrival of hunter-gatherers in Ireland appears to relate to climate change: the periods of warming and cooling at the end of the last ice age. In comparison to Britain, there appear to be delays in the timing of human arrivals in Ireland. This may be a product of the more restricted range of flora and fauna of this island environment, perhaps illustrating how ecological factors structure the impacts of climate change. However, following the colonising of the island, with the exception of the influence of sea-level change, and in contrast to later periods of Irish prehistory, there is little meaningful data available to understand the relationship between climate change and the changing character of hunter-gatherer activity in Ireland.

Sea-level change has long been associated with the study of the Mesolithic in Ireland and greatly influences our understanding of the period. As noted

---

[92] Nicki Whitehouse et al., 'Neolithic agriculture on the European western frontier:'.
[93] Peter Woodman and Margaret McCarthy, 'Contemplating some awful(ly interesting) vistas: importing cattle and red deer into prehistoric Ireland', in Ian Armit et al. (eds), *Neolithic settlement in Ireland and Western Britain* (Oxford, 2003), 31–9.
[94] Alison Sheridan 'The Neolithization of Britain and Ireland: the 'big picture'', in Bill Finlayson and Graeme Warren (eds), *Landscapes in transition,* Levant Supplementary Series 8 (Oxford, 2010), 89–105; Alasdair Whittle et al. *Gathering time: dating the early Neolithic enclosures of southern Britain and Ireland* (Oxford, 2011).

above, in part this is because of the significant taphonomic filter it represents: in many areas Mesolithic landscapes are now submerged and our sample of sites, especially for early periods, is constrained. But sea-level change would also have impacted on hunter-gatherer lifestyles, most likely forcing changes in routines of movement and resource exploitation. The details of these changes are harder to access, although in some areas such as Westley's work in Inishowen, relationships can be drawn out. The impact of sudden events of potentially serious magnitude, such as the Storegga tsunami, is wholly unclear. Turning to broader climate and environmental change, the relationship between human activity in Ireland and significant climate 'events' such as the substantial climate deterioration associated with the 8.2 Event and the more complex series of changes with the 6.3 Event is not well established. Statistical analyses of Mesolithic radiocarbon dates have been used to provide two sets of contradictory claims have been made for the impact of the 8.2 Event. These two claims use different statistical modelling techniques which helps explain their differing conclusions, but both are flawed because of the quality of the radiocarbon data they use. Insufficient data is available to assess the role of the 6.3 Event, which broadly coincides with considerable socio-cultural change in Ireland. In none of the areas reviewed is it yet possible to marry the climate and archaeological records with a suitable degree of resolution nor to speak meaningfully of relationships between the two. This is a pressing research deficit. Bridging the gap will require sustained collaboration between archaeologists and palaeoenvironmental researchers. Such collaborations will also require a detailed understanding of the interaction of the different processes discussed: from climate, through a series of environmental proxies, through to human behaviour. This is not just a challenge of data and resolution – although these are significant, and opportunities and deficits were highlighted above – but also of integrating contrasting views of the world that exist within different academic disciplines.

Acknowledgements

I am grateful to Tomás Ó Carragáin for the invitation to contribute to this volume and for precise editing. Robin Edwards, Fraser Mitchell, Gill Plunkett, Richard Tipping and Kieran Westley provided information, responded generously to queries and provided Fig. 2. Rosie Bishop, Ben Elliott and Richard Tipping gave valuable feedback on a draft. An anonymous referee provided generous and helpful comments which extended my argument in different directions: restrictions on space made it hard to deal with these issues in the depth they required. I am responsible for any errors of fact or misunderstanding which remain.

Tracing environmental, climatic and social change in Neolithic Ireland

Meriel McClatchie*
School of Archaeology, University College Dublin, Ireland

Aaron Potito
Palaeoenvironmental Research Unit, School of Geography, Archaeology and Irish Studies, National University of Ireland Galway, Ireland

[Accepted 8 April 2020. Published 18 June 2020.]

Abstract

This paper reviews archaeological and palaeoecological evidence for environments and climate in Neolithic Ireland (4000–2500 BC) and considers their complex relationships with contemporary social change. The introduction of farming into Ireland fundamentally changed how society was organised and the environments in which people lived. It is not yet clear if climatic change played a role in the initial uptake of farming during the Early Neolithic or in its decreased signal during the Middle–Later Neolithic. This issue is explored using evidence from archaeology, archaeobotany, zooarchaeology, palynology, palaeolimnology, organic residues, stable isotopes and sediment geochemistry. Climate reconstructions from northern Europe and the North Atlantic region further contextualise evidence for environmental change in Ireland. Integrated analysis of these diverse datasets does not reveal straightforward links between changing climatic conditions and human activities. Instead, this study highlights the complexities and challenges of an interdisciplinary approach and the need for additional high-resolution data.

Introduction

The Neolithic period in Ireland (4000–2500 BC) was a time of profound social change. When compared with the preceding Mesolithic period, Neolithic communities developed new ways of constructing their houses, burying their dead, and procuring and preparing their food. Recognising and understanding these changes have long been a focus of scholarship in Irish archaeology. Until relatively recently, the environmental and climatic contexts of these changes have been less well understood, in part because tracing environmental and climatic change is challenging. This issue can be addressed, however, through an interdisciplinary approach. This paper will review our understanding of environments and climate in Neolithic Ireland, drawing

---

*Author's email: meriel.mcclatchie@ucd.ie
ORCID iD: https://orcid.org/0000-0001-6371-333X
doi: https://doi.org/10.3318/PRIAC.2020.120.05

upon evidence from archaeology, archaeobotany, zooarchaeology, palynology, palaeolimnology, organic residues, stable isotopes and sediment geochemistry (Fig. 1). These sources have been selected because they provide diverse datasets and theoretical perspectives; integration of these sources has the potential to facilitate more nuanced understandings of how people interacted with their environments in Neolithic Ireland, and the potential impacts of changing environments and climate. The paper will start by exploring how different data sources can be drawn upon, followed by a diachronic perspective towards examining environmental interactions and climatic change at different times during the Neolithic. The paper will discuss the implications of these data for understanding past societies, environments and climate, and concludes with an assessment of whether, and if so to what extent, social and environmental changes in Neolithic Ireland were linked.

Archaeobotany, palynology and zooarchaeology

For many decades, archaeobotany, palynology and zooarchaeology have enabled insights into local environments, and human interactions with plants and animals. During archaeological excavations, soil samples are often taken from deposits to recover plant macro-remains (including seeds, nutshell, wood and charcoal; Pl. 1) and smaller or fragmented animal and fish bone. Larger animal bone may also be gathered during excavations. Such material is directly linked to past human activity because it is derived from stratified archaeological deposits, and it provides a datable source of information on several aspects of human behaviour. For the Neolithic period, analyses of these remains have often focused on determining past foodways.[1] Plant macro-remains can also provide information on local environments, because their presence can infer specific ecological conditions.[2] Plant macro-remains often provide insights into short-term events—such as plant foods being prepared over a hearth—but palynology tends to explore longer-term vegetation change at different spatial and temporal scales. Pollen samples from enclosed areas at an archaeological excavation can provide information on the immediate background environment, whilst samples

---

[1] Rick Schulting, 'On the northwestern fringes: earlier Neolithic subsistence in Britain and Ireland as seen through faunal remains and stable isotopes', in Sue Colledge, James Conolly, Keith Dobney, Katie Manning and Stephan Shennan (eds), *The origins and spread of domestic animals in southwest Asia and Europe* (Walnut Creek, 2013), 313–38; McClatchie *et al.*, 'Food production, processing and foodways in Neolithic Ireland', *Environmental Archaeology* (2019), https://doi.org/10.1080/14614103.2019.1615215.

[2] McClatchie *et al.*, 'Neolithic farming in north-western Europe: archaeobotanical evidence from Ireland', *Journal of Archaeological Science* 51 (2014), 206–15; Lorna O'Donnell, 'Appendix 7: Wood report', in Matt Mossop and Emma Mossop, *Report on the archaeological excavation of Clowanstown 1, Co. Meath* (Drogheda, 2008).

Tracing environmental, climatic and social change in Neolithic Ireland

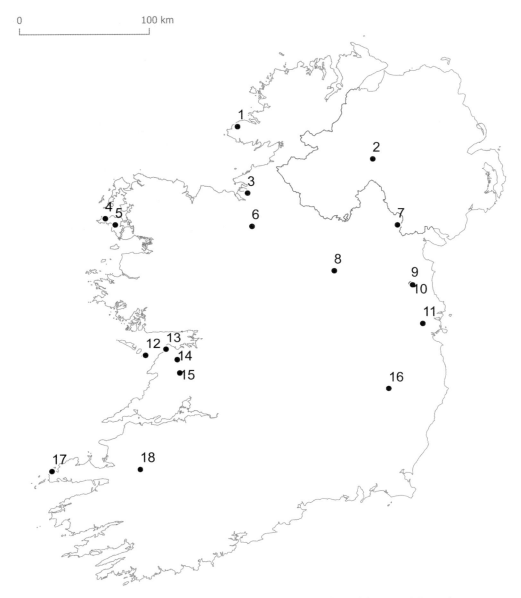

Fig. 1—Map of Ireland showing locations of sites mentioned in text: 1 Lough Meenachrinna, Co. Donegal; 2 Altanagh, Co. Tyrone; 3 Magheraboy, Co. Sligo; 4 Lough Nakeeroge, Co. Mayo; 5 Achill Island, Co. Mayo; 6 Lough Templevanny, Co. Sligo; 7 Lough Muckno, Co. Monaghan; 8 Derragh Bog, Co. Longford; 9 Knowth, Co. Meath; 10 Newgrange, Co. Meath; 11 Kilshane, Co. Meath; 12 An Loch Mór, Inis Oírr, Co. Galway; 13 Fanore More, Co. Clare; 14 Poulnabrone, Co. Clare; 15 Lough Inchiquin, Co. Clare; 16 Baltinglass, Co. Wicklow; 17 Ferriter's Cove, Co. Kerry; 18 Crag Cave, Co. Kerry.

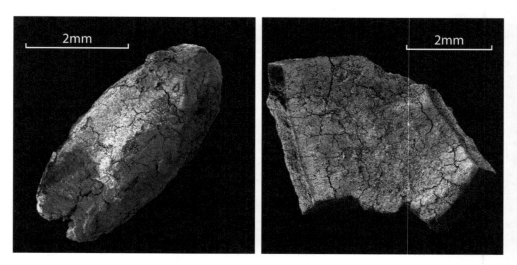

Pl. 1—Left: charred wheat grain (possible emmer wheat); Right: charred hazelnut shell.

from larger lakes and peatland deposits can reveal more regional vegetation histories.[3] Several major reviews of material from Neolithic Ireland have been undertaken in recent years, including plant macro-remains, animal bone and pollen.[4] While plant macro-remains and animal bone can provide insights into human-environment interactions and environmental change, they have more limited value in exploring climatic change. By contrast, palynology, particularly when explored along with palaeolimnological data, has been more successful in inferring climatic change.

Organic residues and stable isotopes in archaeology

Archaeobotany, palynology and zooarchaeology can provide clear insights into the categories of plant and animal species being targeted by humans in Neolithic Ireland, but details on food preparation and consumption practices are not

---

[3] G.W. Dimbleby, *The palynology of archaeological sites* (London, 1985).
[4] McClatchie *et al.*, 'Neolithic farming in north-western Europe'; McClatchie *et al.*, 'Farming and foraging in Neolithic Ireland: an archaeobotanical perspective', *Antiquity* 90:350 (2016), 302–18; McClatchie *et al.*, 'Food production, processing and foodways in Neolithic Ireland'; Schulting, 'On the northwestern Fringes'; Michael O'Connell and Karen Molloy, 'Farming and woodland dynamics in Ireland during the Neolithic', *Biology and Environment: Proceedings of the Royal Irish Academy* 101B:1–2 (2001), 99–128; Beatrice Ghilardi and Michael O'Connell, 'Fine-resolution pollen-analytical study of Holocene woodland dynamics and land use in north Sligo, Ireland', *Boreas* 42:3 (2013), 623–49; Whitehouse *et al.*, 'Neolithic agriculture on the European western frontier: the boom and bust of early farming in Ireland', *Journal of Archaeological Science* 51 (2014), 181–205.

as easily determined. Ceramic vessels are new introductions to Ireland during the early centuries of the Neolithic, and they provided new ways of preparing foods, and perhaps the creation and learning of novel food traditions.[5] Organic residue analysis is a relatively new technique that explores how these pots were used by undertaking biomolecular analyses of preserved residues. In the case of Neolithic Ireland, organic residue studies usually focus on lipids absorbed into the vessels, for example during cooking, and these have provided clear evidence for the use of pots in preparing both dairy and meat dishes.[6] Animal-derived lipids provide a signal that is more easily identifiable than plant-derived lipids—the plants seem to be 'drowned out' by the animals[7]—and so the organic residue data for Neolithic Ireland reveals relatively little about plant foods.[8] There has also been an increase in Ireland in stable isotope analysis, which is most often conducted on human bone to determine the relative contribution of terrestrial and marine sources of protein to human diets ($\delta^{13}C$) and the trophic level of protein components in human diets ($\delta^{15}N$) to distinguish between primarily vegetarian, omnivore, carnivore and marine diets.[9]

Palaeolimnology

Palaeolimnology, the study of past conditions in lake and river basins, uses physical, chemical and biological indicators (i.e. proxy data) preserved in sediment profiles to reconstruct past environments. These aquatic systems respond to both climatological change and anthropogenic influences. As human impacts within lake catchments can override climate effects in palaeolimnological records, climate and anthropogenic reconstructions are often derived from separate lake sediment records.[10] In an Irish context, palaeolimnological records have been used to explore Holocene climate change, and reconstruct prehistoric and historic anthropogenic influences on aquatic systems.[11] Although palaeolimnological

---

[5] McClatchie *et al.*, 'Food production, processing and foodways in Neolithic Ireland'.
[6] Jessica Smyth and R.P. Evershed, 'The molecules of meals: new insight into Neolithic foodways', *Proceedings of the Royal Irish Academy* 115C (2015), 27–46; Jessica Smyth and R.P Evershed, 'Milking the megafauna: using organic residue analysis to understand early farming practice', *Environmental Archaeology* 21:3 (2016), 214–29.
[7] Simon Hammann and L.J.E. Cramp, 'Towards the detection of dietary cereal processing through absorbed lipid biomarkers in archaeological pottery', *Journal of Archaeological Science* 93 (2018), 74–81.
[8] Smyth and Evershed, 'The molecules of meals'; Smyth and Evershed, 'Milking the megafauna'.
[9] Schulting, 'On the northwestern Fringes'; McClatchie *et al.*, 'Food production, processing and foodways in Neolithic Ireland'.
[10] Michelle McKeown and A.P. Potito, 'Assessing recent climatic and human influences on chironomid communities from two moderately impacted lakes in western Ireland', *Hydrobiologia* 765:1 (2016), 245–63.
[11] Holmes *et al.*, 'Multi-proxy evidence for Holocene lake-level and salinity changes at An Loch Mór, a coastal lake on the Aran Islands, western Ireland', *Quaternary Science*

and other sedimentary records (including pollen) can be important indicators of prehistoric human-environment interactions, care must be taken in interpreting these reconstructions. Pollen records can show local- to regional-level landscape change, and limnological records can show local- to catchment-level influence on lake systems. Whilst these are extremely useful indicators of human-landscape interactions, over-interpretation must be avoided, and spatial resolution must always be borne in mind.

Chironomids

Chironomid (Diptera: Chironomidae) subfossils in lake sediment cores are an excellent biological method for reconstructing past limnological conditions, as chironomid larvae are extremely sensitive to changes within freshwater lake systems.[12] Chironomid communities are affected directly and indirectly by a wide variety of environmental variables, including ambient air temperature, lake water pH, dissolved oxygen content, lake depth, benthic substrate and lake nutrient status.[13] Recent studies in Ireland highlight the potential for species-specific chironomid autecology in archaeological contexts, including timing and ecological impacts of crannóg development, lake-basin modifications, increased soil erosion and alterations to aquatic plant communities, and nutrient loading and subsequent lake productivity changes associated with pastoral farming (Pl. 2).[14]

Reviews 26 (2007), 2438–62; McKeown *et al.*, 'Complexities in interpreting chironomid-based temperature reconstructions over the Holocene from a lake in Western Ireland', *Quaternary Science Reviews* 222 (2019), https://doi.org/10.1016/j.quascirev.2019.105908; Taylor *et al.*, 'Impact of early prehistoric farming on chironomid communities in northwest Ireland', *Journal of Paleolimnology* 57:3 (2017), 227–44; Chique *et al.*, 'Tracking recent human impacts on a nutrient sensitive Irish lake: integrating landscape to water linkages', *Hydrobiologia* 807:1 (2018), 207–31.

[12] I.R. Walker, 'Midges: Chironomidae and related Diptera', in J.P. Smol, H.J.B. Birks and W.M. Last (eds), *Tracking environmental change using lake sediments* (Dordrecht, 2001), vol. 4, 43–66.

[13] Hilde Eggermont and Oliver Heiri, 'The chironomid-temperature relationship: expression in nature and palaeoenvironmental implications', *Biological Reviews* 87:2 (2012), 430–56.

[14] O'Brien *et al.*, 'A sediment-based multiproxy palaeoecological approach to the environmental archaeology of lake dwellings (crannogs), central Ireland', *The Holocene* 15:5 (2005), 707–19; Zoe Ruiz, A.G. Brown and P.G. Langdon, 'The potential of chironomid (Insecta: Diptera) larvae in archaeological investigations of floodplain and lake settlements', *Journal of Archaeological Science* 33:1 (2006), 14–33; McGinley *et al.*, 'Lough Lugh, Uisneach: from natural lake to archaeological monument?', *Journal of Irish Archaeology* 24 (2015), 115–30; Taylor *et al.*, 'Response of chironomids to Neolithic land-use change in northwest Ireland', *The Holocene* 27:6 (2017), 879–89; Taylor *et al.*, 'Palaeolimnological impacts of early prehistoric farming at Lough Dargan, County Sligo, Ireland', *Journal of Archaeological Science* 40:8 (2013), 3212–21; Taylor *et al.*, 'Impact of early prehistoric farming on chironomid communities in northwest Ireland'; Taylor *et al.*, 'Response of chironomids to Neolithic land-use change in northwest Ireland'.

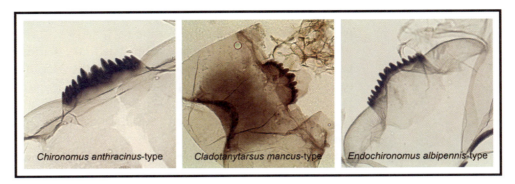

Pl. 2—Chironomid subfossils that are commonly abundant in 'impacted' prehistoric lakes. Images by Dr Karen Taylor.

Chironomids have also been used to reconstruct summer temperatures in Ireland using an expanded modern calibration set of lakes in western Ireland (r^2_{jack} = 0.63; root mean square error of prediction (RMSEP) = 0.56 °C).[15]

Stable Isotopes and Sediment Geochemistry

Lake sediments are comprised of both autochthonous (within lake) and allochthonous (catchment-derived) material, and geochemical analysis of the organic portion of the sediments can offer invaluable insights into past lake conditions by providing information on nutrient loading, lake productivity, sources of lake-sediment organic matter and changing land-use practices.[16] Agricultural inputs are a major influence on $\delta^{15}N$ values in the organic portion of surface sediments of modern Irish lakes,[17] and elevated $\delta^{15}N$ values have been shown to coincide with prehistoric pastoral farming at several lake sites in western Ireland.[18] $\delta^{13}C$ values are often used in conjunction with $\delta^{15}N$ to help determine sediment organic matter terrestrial and aquatic sources. $C_{organic}$:N ratios have been explored in an archaeological context in Ireland to determine

---

[15] Potito *et al.*, 'Modern influences on chironomid distribution in western Ireland: potential for palaeoenvironmental reconstruction', *Journal of Paleolimnology* 52 (2014), 385–404; Taylor *et al.*, 'A mid to late Holocene chironomid-inferred temperature record from northwest Ireland', *Palaeogeography, Palaeoclimatology, Palaeoecology* 505 (2018), 274–86; McKeown *et al.*, 'Complexities in interpreting chironomid-based temperature reconstructions over the Holocene from a lake in Western Ireland'.
[16] A.S. Cohen, *Paleolimnology: the history and evolution of lake systems* (Oxford, 2003).
[17] C.A. Woodward, A.P. Potito, and D.W. Beilman, 'Carbon and nitrogen stable isotope ratios in surface sediments from lakes of western Ireland: implications for inferring past lake productivity and nitrogen loading', *Journal of Paleolimnology* 47 (2012), 167–84.
[18] Taylor *et al.*, 'Impact of early prehistoric farming on chironomid communities in northwest Ireland'.

relative abundances of aquatic and terrestrial sources of lake sediment organic matter in relation to land-use change.[19]

Stable isotopes from within Irish lake sediments have been applied in palaeoclimate reconstructions that span the Neolithic. Stable strontium isotope ratios in ostracod shells have been used as part of a multi-proxy reconstruction of lake levels and lake salinity from An Loch Mór, Inis Oírr, Co. Galway.[20] Analyses of pollen and lake sediment geochemistry have been applied to investigate Neolithic landscape and climate change at Lough Templevanny, Co. Sligo.[21] A $\delta^{13}C$ record from Lough Inchiquin, Co. Clare, has been shown to reflect landscape change from the late Glacial to the early Neolithic.[22] The $\delta^{18}O$ record from a speleothem in Crag Cave, Co. Kerry, is also notable in that it is a high-resolution proxy for air temperature and precipitation that spans the Holocene.[23]

Palaeoclimate Modelling

All palaeoecological climate proxies will respond to environmental variables other than the reconstructed variable of interest. Comparison of proxy records to regional palaeoclimate simulations has been recommended, therefore, as an effective strategy in interpreting proxy-based reconstructions.[24] The Hadley Centre Coupled Model has been run at 500-year intervals through the Holocene and simulations applied in several recent palaeoclimate studies.[25] The climate model has been downscaled and localised in northern Achill Island, Co.

---

[19] McGinley *et al.*, 'Lough Lugh, Uisneach'.
[20] Holmes *et al.*, 'Multi-proxy evidence for Holocene lake-level and salinity changes at An Loch Mór'.
[21] Stolze *et al.*, 'Evidence for climatic variability and its impact on human development during the Neolithic from Loughmeenaghan, County Sligo, Ireland', *Journal of Quaternary Science* 27:4 (2012), 393–403; Stolze *et al.*, 'Solar influence on climate variability and human development during the Neolithic: evidence from a high-resolution multi-proxy record from Templevanny Lough, County Sligo, Ireland', *Quaternary Science Reviews* 67 (2013), 138–59.
[22] Diefendorf *et al.*, 'Evidence for high-frequency late Glacial to mid-Holocene (16,800 to 5500 cal yr B.P.) climate variability from oxygen isotope values of Lough Inchiquin, Ireland', *Quaternary Research* 65:1 (2008), 78–86.
[23] Frank McDermott, D.P Mattey and Chris Hawkesworth, 'Centennial-scale Holocene climate variability revealed by a high-resolution speleothem δ18O record from SW Ireland', *Science* 294:5545 (2001), 1328–31.
[24] Marsicek *et al.*, 'Reconciling divergent trends and millennial variations in Holocene temperatures', *Nature* 554 (2018), 92–6.
[25] HadCM3; Valdes *et al.*, 'The BRIDGE HadCM3 family of climate models: HadCM3@Bristol v1.0', *Geosciences Model Development* 10 (2017), 3715–43. See, for example, Swindles *et al.*, 'Ecosystem state shifts during long-term development of an Amazonian peatland', *Global Change Biology* 24:2 (2018), 738–57.

Mayo for a study of Holocene climate change.[26] Simulations for temperature and precipitation from this recent study offer a broad context for regional climate signals from the proxy records reviewed below. Further insights are gained from a compiled peatland water table reconstruction from eight sites across Ireland that was developed to interpret evidence of climate change through the Neolithic.[27]

Comparisons of proxy records from different sites with palaeoclimate simulations can be challenging due to differences in sampling resolution and the inexact nature of dating models. Palaeoclimate models simulate conditions within specified slices of time and are often at broader time intervals than proxy records, as was the case in applications of the Hadley Centre Coupled Model cited above.[28] While statistical techniques can be used to accurately compare detailed proxy records with broader palaeoclimate simulations,[29] data resolution is compromised. Dating uncertainties in proxy records can further compromise this comparison. Sediment records are often dated using a series of non-overlapping radiocarbon dates, with ages of intermediate depths interpolated using the existing dates. Dating uncertainties in the original dates and sedimentation variations in the interpolated depths add further uncertainty to dating of sediment proxy records. Bayesian calibration models and an increase in dating resolution have helped to reduce this error[30] but dating uncertainties should be recognised in any cross-record comparison.

Thus, a wide variety of analyses can be undertaken to explore environmental and climatic change in Neolithic Ireland at a range of scales and with variable success. Whilst studies comparing climate and social change have been undertaken, including studies focused on the Mesolithic/Neolithic transition,[31] this paper represents the first time that such a diverse variety of analyses have been collated and integrated to investigate the Irish Neolithic. The paper is focused on detecting change, and whilst there are clear social and environmental

---

[26] McKeown *et al.*, 'Complexities in interpreting chironomid-based temperature reconstructions over the Holocene from a lake in Western Ireland'.
[27] Swindles *et al.*, 'Centennial-scale climate change in Ireland during the Holocene', *Earth Science Reviews* 126 (2013), 300–20.
[28] Swindles *et al.*, 'Ecosystem state shifts during long-term development of an Amazonian peatland'; McKeown *et al.*, 'Complexities in interpreting chironomid-based temperature reconstructions over the Holocene from a lake in Western Ireland'.
[29] McKeown *et al.*, 'Complexities in interpreting chironomid-based temperature reconstructions over the Holocene from a lake in Western Ireland'.
[30] Christopher Bronk Ramsey, 'Bayesian analysis of radiocarbon dates', *Radiocarbon* 51 (2009), 337–60
[31] Bonsall *et al.*, 'Climate change and the adoption of agriculture in north-west Europe', *European Journal of Archaeology* 5:1 (2002), 9–23; Turney *et al.*, 'Holocene climatic change and past Irish societal response', *Journal of Archaeological Science* 33 (2006), 34–8; Rick Schulting, 'Holocene environmental change and the Mesolithic-Neolithic transition in north-west Europe: revisiting two models', *Environmental Archaeology* 15:2 (2010), 160–72.

changes around the beginning of the Irish Neolithic (the Early Neolithic), these changes are not island-wide and some of these changes do not persist, while new trends are evident later in the Neolithic. The following sections will therefore explore environment and climate through a diachronic perspective, investigating evidence from three sub-periods—the Early, Middle and Late Neolithic—and assessing the scientific evidence within the context of wider social changes.

Early Neolithic (4000–3600 BC)

The Early Neolithic is suggested to have begun around 4000 BC in Ireland, but recent studies have questioned how we determine the exact timing of the start of the Neolithic.[32] Early Neolithic societies and economies are often characterised by the introduction of rectangular houses, ceramics, mortuary monuments for the dead (portal tombs, court tombs and 'simple' passage tombs) and domesticated plants and animals.[33] These are all regarded as innovations: they involved new ways of engaging with landscapes, with associated environmental impacts. In the first two centuries of the fourth millennium BC, however, there is relatively little well-dated evidence for what might be considered diagnostic Neolithic material and sites in Ireland. Careful analysis in recent years of radiocarbon dates has revealed that most Early Neolithic sites post-date 3750 BC, and earlier evidence for Neolithic activity is scarce.[34] To complicate the issue further, 'Neolithic' remains are sometimes found at Late Mesolithic sites (such as the domesticated cattle bone at Ferriter's Cove, Co. Kerry), while some sites with Early Neolithic radiocarbon dates contain assemblages that would fit better into a Late Mesolithic context (such as the lithics at Fanore More 1, Co. Clare).[35]

A substantial proportion of sites dating to the period between 4000-3750 BC are burial deposits and structures (such as Poulnabrone portal

---

[32] Gabriel Cooney, *Landscapes of Neolithic Ireland* (London, 2000), 14; Cooney *et al.*, 'Ireland', in Alasdair Whittle, Frances Healy and Alex Bayliss (eds), *Gathering time: dating the early Neolithic enclosures of southern Britain and Ireland* (Oxford, 2011), 562–669. Seren Griffiths, 'A cereal problem? What the current chronology of early cereal domesticates might tell us about changes in late fifth and early fourth millennium cal BC Ireland and Britain', *Environmental Archaeology* (2018) https://doi.org/10.1080/14614103.2018.1529945.

[33] Jessica Smyth, *Settlement in the Irish Neolithic* (Oxford, 2014); McLaughlin *et al.*, 'The changing face of Neolithic and Bronze Age Ireland: a big data approach to the settlement and burial records', *Journal of World Prehistory* 29:2 (2016), 117–53.

[34] Cooney *et al.*, 'Ireland'; Whitehouse *et al.*, 'Neolithic agriculture on the European western frontier'.

[35] P.C. Woodman, Elizabeth Anderson and Nyree Finlay, *Excavations at Ferriter's Cove, 1983–1995: last foragers, first farmers in the Dingle Peninsula* (Bray, 1999); Michael Lynch, 'The Later Mesolithic on the north-west coast of Clare', *Archaeology Ireland*

tomb, Co. Clare, Altanagh court tomb, Co. Tyrone and Baltinglass passage tomb, Co. Wicklow), and a substantial causewayed enclosure was uncovered at Magheraboy, Co. Sligo.[36] Neolithic-style artefacts are also recorded, for example, ceramics and axeheads at Magheraboy. While some sites are suggested to have been constructed in already 'open' landscapes,[37] it is not clear if others were constructed in existing gaps within the mosaic of woodland or if they required woodland clearance.[38] Pollen evidence can be an excellent indicator of land use, but unfortunately high-precision dating is often lacking in palynological evidence for these centuries, which means it is difficult to determine land-use patterns at the Mesolithic/Neolithic transition. A major palynological 'event' previously thought to characterise the start of the Neolithic period in Ireland was the Elm Decline, reflecting a decline in the presence of elm across north-western Europe.[39] Re-analysis of chronologies associated with the Elm Decline in Ireland suggests, however, that it was not a synchronous event, and while in some locations it is associated with the earliest evidence for farming, overall the 'start' of the Elm Decline spans almost a millennium.[40] Changing landscape engagements are suggested, however, by a rise in ribwort plantain pollen (*Plantago lanceolata*),

---

31:4 (2017), 24–8; Jessica Smyth, Meriel McClatchie and Graeme Warren, 'Exploring the 'somewhere' and 'someone' else: an integrated approach to Ireland's earliest farming practice, in K.J. Gron, Lasse Sørensen and Peter Rowley-Conwy (eds), *Farmers at the frontier: a pan-European perspective on Neolithisation* (Oxford, 2020), 425–41.

[36] Ann Lynch, *Poulnabrone: an Early Neolithic portal tomb in Ireland* (Dublin, 2014); Murphy *et al.*, 'INSTAR: The people of prehistoric Ireland: Phase 1', *Archaeology Ireland* 24:1 (2010), 23–5; McLaughlin *et al.*, 'The changing face of Neolithic and Bronze Age Ireland'; Schulting *et al.*, 'Radiocarbon dating of a multi-phase passage tomb on Baltinglass Hill, Co. Wicklow, Ireland', *Proceedings of the Prehistoric Society* 83 (2017), 305–23; Ed Danaher, *Monumental Beginnings: the archaeology of the N4 Sligo Inner Relief Road* (Dublin, 2007).

[37] Kevin Kearney, 'Vegetation impacts and early Neolithic monumentality: a palaeoenvironmental case study from south-west Ireland', *Journal of Archaeological Science: Reports* 27 (2019), https://doi.org/10.1016/j.jasrep.2019.101940.

[38] O'Connell and Molloy, 'Farming and woodland dynamics in Ireland during the Neolithic'; Chris Caseldine and Ralph Fyfe, 'A modelling approach to locating and characterising elm decline/landnam landscapes', *Quaternary Science Reviews* 25 (2006), 632–44.

[39] J.R. Pilcher and A.G. Smith, 'Palaeoecological investigations at Ballynagilly, a Neolithic and Bronze Age settlement in County Tyrone, Northern Ireland', *Philosophical Transactions of the Royal Society* 286B (1979), 345–69; Caseldine and Fyfe, 'A modelling approach to locating and characterising elm decline/landnam landscapes'.

[40] Whitehouse *et al.*, 'Neolithic agriculture on the European western frontier'; Kevin Kearney and B.R. Gearey, 'The elm decline is dead! Long live declines in elm: revisiting the chronology of the elm decline in Ireland and its association with the Mesolithic/Neolithic transition', *Environmental Archaeology* (2020) https://doi.org/10.1080/14614103.2020.1721694.

which can be seen from around 4000/3900 BC in several locations.[41] Ribwort plantain is often interpreted as reflecting open landscapes and agricultural activity,[42] and its rise in the pollen record may reflect episodes of woodland clearance. Evidence for arable activity is absent from the plant macro-remains record before 3750 BC,[43] and pollen arable indicators pre-3750 BC seem unreliable.[44] There is, however, evidence for pastoral activity in the form of lipid residues on ceramics and domesticated animal bone. Biomolecular analysis of ceramics from primary fills of the enclosure at Magheraboy signals the presence of ruminant dairy fats, presumed to be cattle or sheep/goat.[45] There is also occasional zooarchaeological evidence for domesticated animals, such as the sheep/goat bone in primary fills of the enclosure ditch at Magheraboy.[46]

It is not until the thirty-eighth century BC that we see regular evidence for characteristically Neolithic activity, including both domesticated plants and animals, substantial rectangular houses, and significantly increased records of tombs and ceramics.[47] The landscape impacts of these new activities become more apparent in the archaeological and palaeoecological records as people created new environments and arenas for social engagement. There is widespread archaeological evidence for arable and pastoral activity immediately following 3750 BC; this evidence most often derives from the rectangular houses. Plant macro-remains analyses show that cereals—predominantly emmer wheat, with a little barley—were incorporated into many different contexts (Fig. 2), suggesting widespread uptake, although in many cases cereals are recorded in small quantities.[48] There is occasional evidence for other crops, such as flax.[49] While analyses of the cereal grains and chaff shows what people were farming, analyses of arable weeds (growing alongside the cereals and inadvertently harvested) provide insights into how people were farming. The predominance of annual weeds that thrive in disturbed habitats suggest that these early farmers were not undertaking shifting agriculture, but were instead engaged in garden-style intensive agriculture, thereby creating a sense of place, not only in the building of houses and tombs, but also in their manner of food production.[50]

---

[41] Whitehouse *et al.*, 'Neolithic agriculture on the European western frontier'.
[42] Willy Groenman-van Waateringe, 'Grazing possibilities in the Neolithic of the Netherlands based on palynological data', in K.-E. Behre (ed.), *Anthropogenic indicators in pollen diagrams* (Rotterdam, 1986), 187–202.
[43] McClatchie *et al.*, 'Neolithic farming in north-western Europe'; McClatchie *et al.* 'Farming and foraging in Neolithic Ireland'.
[44] Whitehouse *et al.*, 'Neolithic agriculture on the European western frontier'.
[45] Smyth and Evershed, 'Milking the megafauna'.
[46] Danaher, *Monumental Beginnings: the archaeology of the N4 Sligo Inner Relief Road.*
[47] McLaughlin *et al.*, 'The changing face of Neolithic and Bronze Age Ireland'.
[48] McClatchie *et al.*, 'Neolithic farming in north-western Europe'.
[49] McClatchie *et al.*, 'Neolithic farming in north-western Europe'.
[50] McClatchie *et al.*, 'Neolithic farming in north-western Europe'.

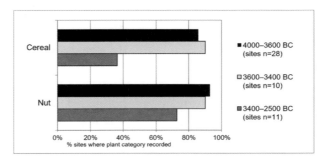

Fig. 2—Relative occurrence of categories from Neolithic plant macro-remains record.[51]

The rise in ribwort plantain pollen that began in some areas soon after 4000 BC becomes more pronounced between 3750 and 3600 BC, suggesting increased woodland clearance to accompany new living and farming practices.[52] Modelling of pollen data suggests a gradual opening of the landscape, rather than a short-lived clearance 'event'.[53] Pollen analyses also show increased diversity, suggesting organisation of the landscape varied regionally and temporally. In the midlands, there appears to have been relatively little woodland clearance, while in the west, landscapes appear considerably more open, perhaps reflecting communities taking advantage of already open habitats, as well as new clearance episodes.[54] A large-scale recent review of woodland engagement, based on wood and charcoal macro-remains, has not been completed for Neolithic Ireland, but regional and site-based studies indicate gathering of a wide variety of species, often dominated by wood available locally from primary woodland and understoreys and scrubland.[55]

Animal bone has been recorded at fewer locations than the remains of plants, but to some extent this reflects recovery strategies (including a lack of soil sieving for smaller bones) and acidic soil conditions at many sites, which does not support bone preservation. Where recovered, animal bone is often found in small quantities, but the standard 'triumvirate' of animals recorded elsewhere in

---

[51] Whitehouse *et al.*, 'Neolithic agriculture on the European western frontier'.

[52] Whitehouse *et al.*, 'Neolithic agriculture on the European western frontier'.

[53] Whitehouse *et al.*, 'Neolithic agriculture on the European western frontier'; Whitehouse *et al.*, 'Prehistoric land-cover and land-use history in Ireland at 6000 BP', *Past Global Changes* 26:1 (2018), 24–5; Kearney, 'Vegetation impacts and early Neolithic monumentality'.

[54] O'Donnell, 'Appendix 7: Wood report'; Ellen O'Carroll, '6.2: Wood remains', in R.M. Cleary and Hilary Kelleher, *Archaeological excavations at Tullahedy, County Tipperary: Neolithic settlement in North Munster* (Cork, 2011), 186–208.

[55] After McClatchie, 'Farming and foraging in Neolithic Ireland'.

northern Europe—cattle, pig and sheep/goat—is present in Ireland.[56] Further evidence for animal management is found in biomolecular analysis of ceramic sherds, which regularly reveals evidence for ruminant dairy fats, as well as some evidence for ruminant adipose fats.[57] While the management of domesticated plants and animals is clearly a feature of life in Early Neolithic Ireland, wild resources were not abandoned. There is extensive evidence for the gathering of wild plants, including nuts, fruits and greens (Fig. 2).[58] The zooarchaeological record suggests wild animals played a significantly less important role in food systems, however, and evidence from stable isotope analysis of human bone (particularly ^{13}C) indicates a shift away from marine resources towards terrestrial resources.[59]

Palaeolimnological analyses provide further indicators of pastoral activity. Evidence from three small lakes in Co. Sligo suggests that the onset of farming in the Early Neolithic was a significant enough change to immediately impact on freshwater ecology.[60] Nutrient loading, associated with a rise in δ^{15}N values and a turnover to eutrophic chironomid taxa, was concomitant with the onset of pastoral farming practices at all three sites. Although arable farming was also evident in these records, statistical association of lake changes with pastoral farming indicators reflect the greater impact of pastoral farming (versus arable farming) on lake productivity. This could be due to scale of activity (e.g. more widespread pastoral farming), location of pastoral farming near the lakeside, or taphonomic considerations such as differing pollen production rates and depositional pathways. At two larger Irish lakes—Lough Muckno, Co. Monaghan and Lough Inchiquin, Co. Clare—pastoral and arable farming was evident but not on a large enough scale to impact the ecology of the lakes, which did not exhibit cultural eutrophication until the Early Bronze Age.[61] Variability in Early Neolithic agricultural impacts on Irish lakes is therefore apparent.

The environmental context for these new ways of living suggests local conditions were drier post-4100 BC when compared with previous centuries, based upon an increase in bog-oak populations.[62] Several other analyses also

---

[56] Schulting, 'On the northwestern Fringes'; McClatchie et al., 'Food production, processing and foodways in Neolithic Ireland'.

[57] Smyth and Evershed, 'The molecules of meals'.

[58] McClatchie et al., 'Neolithic farming in north-western Europe'; McClatchie et al., 'Farming and foraging in Neolithic Ireland'.

[59] Schulting, 'On the northwestern Fringes'; McClatchie et al., 'Food production, processing and foodways in Neolithic Ireland'.

[60] Taylor et al., 'Impact of early prehistoric farming on chironomid communities in northwest Ireland'.

[61] Carlos Chique, 'Paleolimnological investigations on a nutrient polluted freshwater lake – reconstructing anthropogenic impacts across timescales', unpublished PhD thesis, National University of Ireland Galway, 2018; Daisy Spencer, 'People, land use and time: Linking multi-proxy palaeoenvironmental evidence to the Neolithic and Bronze Age archaeological record of the Burren and central Clare, western Ireland', unpublished PhD thesis, National University of Ireland Galway, 2019.

[62] Whitehouse et al., 'Neolithic agriculture on the European western frontier'.

suggest warmer conditions. During the Early Neolithic, there was an increase of 1.6 °C in chironomid-inferred July temperatures from Lough Meenachrinna in Co. Donegal from 3940 to 3620 BC.[63] This warming phase of ~300 years corresponds with several peatland studies in Scotland and Ireland, showing a period of drier climatic conditions and/or decreased peat accumulation rates.[64] A high-resolution pollen and geochemical record from Templevanny Lough in Co. Sligo also infers a period of elevated spring/summer temperatures and decreased precipitation from 3910 to 3670 BC.[65] This evidence is supported by a new marine sediment core record from the Irish Continental Shelf, which shows a general warming in bottom-water-temperature at the onset of the Neolithic.[66]

There are, however, other datasets that provide a contrasting picture in relation to palaeoclimate. Some proxies infer warm/dry climates in Ireland in the centuries preceding the Neolithic, with cool/wet conditions emerging during the Early Neolithic. The chironomid collector-filter guild from Lough Nakeeroge in Achill Island, Co. Mayo, the standardised Irish bog water table compilation and the Crag Cave, Co. Kerry $\delta^{18}O$ record all suggest warmer/drier conditions before 3850 BC, followed by the onset of cooler/wetter conditions during the Early Neolithic.[67] The HadCM3 climate model for northern Achill Island also suggests warmer summers at 4000 BC and cooler summers by 3500 BC.[68] Differences in proxy evidence show the complexities in palaeoclimatic interpretations but may also be due to sampling resolution and dating uncertainties.

Middle Neolithic (3600–3000 BC)

The Middle Neolithic is generally considered to have begun around 3600 BC and continued until 3000 BC, but recent studies have identified two sub-periods:

---

[63] Taylor *et al.*, 'A mid to late Holocene chironomid-inferred temperature record from northwest Ireland'.

[64] D.E. Anderson, 'A reconstruction of Holocene climatic changes from peat bogs in north-west Scotland', *Boreas* 27:3 (1998), 208–24; Caseldine *et al.*, 'Evidence for an extreme climatic event on Achill Island, Co. Mayo, Ireland around 5200-5100 cal. yr BP', *Journal of Quaternary Science* 20 (2005), 169–78.

[65] Stolze *et al.*, 'Solar influence on climate variability and human development during the Neolithic'.

[66] Curran *et al.*, 'Atmospheric response to mid-Holocene warming in the northeastern Atlantic: implications for future storminess in the Ireland/UK region', *Quaternary Science Reviews* 225 (2019), https://doi.org/10.1016/j.quascirev.2019.106004.

[67] McKeown *et al.*, 'Complexities in interpreting chironomid-based temperature reconstructions over the Holocene from a lake in Western Ireland'; Swindles *et al.*, 'Centennial-scale climate change in Ireland during the Holocene'; McDermott *et al.*, 'Centennial-scale Holocene climate variability revealed by a high-resolution speleothem $\delta 18O$ record from SW Ireland'.

[68] McKeown *et al.*, 'Complexities in interpreting chironomid-based temperature reconstructions over the Holocene from a lake in Western Ireland'.

3600–3400 BC and 3400–3000 BC.[69] During the first two centuries of the Middle Neolithic, there are changes in the archaeological record when compared with the Early Neolithic. Rectangular houses become rare, and 'domestic' activity is represented by pits (both single pits and complexes) and midden material, with relatively few formal and easily identifiable structures.[70] It has been argued that this may reflect a change in construction of houses and how they are detected in the archaeological record, rather than abandonment of house building.[71] Some tombs constructed during the Early Neolithic continue to be used and modified, but it is not clear to what extent new tombs were constructed.[72] During these first two centuries, archaeobotanical and zooarchaeological remains confirm the continuation of agricultural activity in many locations.[73] There is evidence for emmer wheat and some barley, and well as domesticated animals, although there are fewer records when compared with the Early Neolithic (Fig. 2). Analysis of the ecological habitats of arable weeds indicates decreasing soil fertility from 3550 BC, which may have resulted in a decline in agricultural production.[74] By contrast, lipid analyses of ceramics suggest that pastoral farming continued to play an important role during the first two centuries of the Middle Neolithic, with evidence for ruminant dairy fats common.[75] While most zooarchaeological assemblages are small around this time, there are exceptions that suggest domesticated animals played a key role in foodways. At Kilshane, Co. Meath, bones from at least 58 cattle were placed into the ditch of an enclosure, reflecting their deposition on separate occasions, rather than a gradual accumulation.[76] Field systems in Co. Mayo, assumed to reflect pastoral activity, are also suggested to date to around this time or even a little earlier.[77] Analysis of stable isotopes from

---

[69] Cooney, *Landscapes of Neolithic Ireland*; Whitehouse *et al.*, 'Neolithic agriculture on the European western frontier'; McLaughlin *et al.*, 'The changing face of Neolithic and Bronze Age Ireland'.

[70] McLaughlin *et al.*, 'The changing face of Neolithic and Bronze Age Ireland'.

[71] Jessica Smyth, 'Tides of changes? The house through the Irish Neolithic', in Daniela Hoffman and Jessica Smyth (eds), *Tracking the house in Neolithic Europe* (New York, 2013), 301–27.

[72] McLaughlin *et al.*, 'The changing face of Neolithic and Bronze Age Ireland: a big data approach to the settlement and burial records'; Schulting *et al.*, 'Radiocarbon dating of a multi-phase passage tomb on Baltinglass Hill, Co. Wicklow, Ireland'.

[73] McClatchie *et al.*, 'Farming and foraging in Neolithic Ireland: an archaeobotanical perspective'.

[74] Colledge *et al.*, 'Neolithic population crash in northwest Europe associated with agricultural crisis', *Quaternary Research (2019)*, https://doi.org/10.1017/qua.2019.42.

[75] Smyth and Evershed, 'The molecules of meals: new insight into Neolithic foodways'.

[76] Dermot Moore, *Report on archaeological excavation of Site 5, Kilshane, County Dublin* (Drogheda, 2009).

[77] Seamus Caulfield, R.G. O'Donnell and P.I. Mitchell, '14C dating of a Neolithic field system at Céide Fields, County Mayo, Ireland', *Radiocarbon* 40 (1998), 629–40; Cooney *et al.*, 'Ireland'; Michael O'Connell, Karen Molloy and Eneda Jennings, 'Long-term human impact and environmental change in mid-western Ireland, with particular

human bone continue to show a preference for terrestrial rather than marine sources of proteins, right through the Middle Neolithic into the Late Neolithic.[78]

Ribwort plantain features in pollen records at the beginning of Middle Neolithic, suggesting the maintenance or opening of newly cleared landscapes for farming and other activities.[79] By around 3500 BC, however, ribwort plantain begins to reduce significantly or even disappear (this has been labelled the '*Plantago* gap'), which may reflect less intensive use of the landscape and/or regeneration of woodland.[80] While agricultural indicators continue to be recorded in some locations,[81] increased woodland indicators, particularly hazel, are recorded in many pollen records from this time or in the following centuries.[82] Charcoal and wood studies indicate that a wide variety of wood species were gathered from both primary woodland and understoreys/scrubland.[83]

A decline in bog oaks can be seen around 3500 BC, which has been interpreted as reflecting an increase in climate-derived wetness in Ireland,[84] but in some locations, humification records indicate continued dry conditions, with a shift to wetter conditions not occurring until the Late Neolithic.[85] A decrease of 1.3 °C in chironomid-inferred temperatures at Lough Meenachrinna, Co. Donegal is evident at 3540 BC,[86] coinciding with cooler summers in the HadCM3 climate model for northern Achill Island, Co. Mayo at 3500 BC.[87] Outside Ireland higher

---

reference to Céide Fields – an overview', *E&G Quaternary Science Journal* 69 (2020), 1–32. It has been argued that the field systems are significantly later in date (Bronze Age), however; Andrew Whitefield, 'Neolithic 'Celtic' fields? A reinterpretation of the chronological evidence from Céide Fields in northwestern Ireland', *European Journal of Archaeology* 20 (2017), 257–79.

[78] Schulting, 'On the northwestern Fringes'; McClatchie *et al.*, 'Food production, processing and foodways in Neolithic Ireland'.

[79] Whitehouse *et al.*, 'Neolithic agriculture on the European western frontier'.

[80] Whitehouse *et al.*, 'Neolithic agriculture on the European western frontier'.

[81] For example, see Plunkett *et al.*, 'Vegetation history at the multi-period prehistoric complex at Ballynahatty, Co. Down, Northern Ireland', *Journal of Archaeological Science* 35:1 (2008), 181–90.

[82] O'Connell and Molloy, 'Farming and woodland dynamics in Ireland during the Neolithic'; Michael O'Connell, Beatrice Ghilardi and Liam Morrison, 'A 7000-year record of environmental change, including early farming impact, based on lake-sediment geochemistry and pollen data from County Sligo, western Ireland', *Quaternary Research* 81:1 (2014), 35–49; Whitehouse *et al.*, 'Neolithic agriculture on the European western frontier'; Whitehouse *et al.*, 'Prehistoric land-cover and land-use history in Ireland at 6000 BP'.

[83] O'Carroll, '6.2: Wood remains'.

[84] Whitehouse *et al.*, 'Neolithic agriculture on the European western frontier'.

[85] Caseldine *et al.*, 'Evidence for an extreme climatic event on Achill Island, Co. Mayo, Ireland around 5200-5100 cal. yr BP'.

[86] Taylor *et al.*, 'A mid to late Holocene chironomid-inferred temperature record from northwest Ireland'.

[87] McKeown *et al.*, 'Complexities in interpreting chironomid-based temperature reconstructions over the Holocene from a lake in Western Ireland'

lake levels have been reported in the Swiss Alps between 3600 and 3350 BC with a strong cooling episode at 3600 BC, which coincides with glacier advancement and tree-limit decline.[88] Sea surface temperatures from the North Atlantic also indicate a rapid cooling event at 3550 BC.[89]

Significant changes in burial, settlement, agricultural and other activities can be identified between 3400 and 3000 BC. This is the period when 'developed' passage tombs are widespread—including some of the best-known from Ireland, such as Newgrange and Knowth, Co. Meath—and other burial traditions are recorded, such as Linkardstown-type burials and other megaliths.[90] Whilst monumental burial architecture flourishes, settlement evidence becomes harder to detect; where recorded, it usually consists of pit complexes or occasional structures.[91] Some studies suggest that this reduced settlement evidence, further inferred by a reduction in ^{14}C dates post-3400 BC, indicates declining population levels and perhaps increasing mobility,[92] but the impact of potentially diverse social, construction and deposition practices—as indicated by diversity in the burial record—should also be considered.

It is clear, however, that arable indicators become rarer in archaeological and palaeoecological records. There are some pollen records for arable activity, including the well-dated deposits from the passage tomb at Newgrange,[93] but cereal macro-remains are rare at sites dating between 3400 and 3000 BC (Fig. 2).[94] None of these cereal macro-remains have been directly dated and it is possible that at least some are intrusive. Both emmer wheat and barley are present, but wheat is not clearly predominant, in contrast with earlier centuries. Given the small numbers, it would be unwise to interpret this as a shift to barley; it may be better viewed as persistence in barley, which tends to be a more resilient crop.[95] Domesticated animal bone continues to be recorded, but at relatively few sites,[96]

---

[88] Michel Magny and J.N. Haas, 'A major widespread climatic change around 5300 cal. yr BP at the time of the Alpine Iceman', *Journal of Quaternary Science* 19:5 (2004), 423–30.

[89] E.J. Farmer, M.R. Chapman and J.E. Andrews, 'Centennial-scale Holocene North Atlantic surface temperatures from Mg/Ca ratios in *Globigerina bulloides*'. *Geochemistry, Geophysics, Geosystems* 9:12 (2008), https://doi.org/10.1029/2008GC002199.

[90] McLaughlin *et al.*, 'The changing face of Neolithic and Bronze Age Ireland'.

[91] McLaughlin *et al.*, 'The changing face of Neolithic and Bronze Age Ireland'.

[92] C.J. Stevens and D.Q. Fuller, 'Did Neolithic farming fail? The case for a Bronze Age agricultural revolution in the British Isles'. *Antiquity* 86:333 (2012), 707–22; Bevan *et al.*, 'Holocene fluctuations in human population demonstrate repeated links to food production and climate', *PNAS* 114:9 (2017), E10524–31.

[93] Ann Lynch, 'Newgrange revisited: new insights from excavations at the back of the mound, 1984–8', *Journal of Irish Archaeology* 23 (2014), 13–82.

[94] McClatchie *et al.*, 'Farming and foraging in Neolithic Ireland'.

[95] C.J. Stevens and D.Q. Fuller, 'Alternative strategies to agriculture: the evidence for climatic shocks and cereal declines during the British Neolithic and Bronze Age (a reply to Bishop)', *World Archaeology* 47:5 (2015), 856–75.

[96] McClatchie *et al.*, 'Food production, processing and foodways in Neolithic Ireland'.

and it is possible that some animal remains may be intrusive, particularly at tombs revisited for centuries. Pastoral evidence is evident from lipid analyses of ceramics, often reflecting ruminant dairy fats,[97] but there are fewer records when compared with the Early Neolithic. Palaeolimnological records show lake system recovery from Early Neolithic farming impacts, with several lakes in northwest Ireland returning to their 'pre-impacted' state during this time,[98] suggesting a reduction in pastoral activity.

Changing landscape use is evident from many strands of archaeological evidence, therefore. Climatic variability during the final centuries of the Middle Neolithic has been demonstrated by several palaeoclimate proxies. A shift to wetter conditions has been noted at 3670 BC in the pollen and geochemical record in Templevanny Lough, Co. Sligo,[99] coinciding with an increase in bog-surface wetness at Derragh Bog, Co. Longford in the Irish midlands.[100] It has been suggested that in some cases, abandonment of landscapes followed extreme climatic events, such as the 3100 BC storm(s) that deposited an extensive layer of silt across blanket peat in the north-west of Ireland.[101] Other records emphasise the impact of wetter conditions, for example in bog-oak records that suggest a peak in wetness around 3300 BC and with a narrow-ring event at 3190 BC, but bog oaks do start to recover around 3100 BC, and sub-fossil pine records similarly suggest environmental conditions became less wet around this time.[102] The chironomid collector-filter guild from Lough Nakeeroge in Achill Island, Co. Mayo, the standardised Irish bog water table compilation and the Crag Cave $\delta 18O$ record all suggest that wet/cool conditions persisted through the Middle Neolithic.[103] These conditions coincide with a peak in ice-rafted debris in the North Atlantic and a decrease in solar irradiance.[104] There is also evidence for

---

[97] Smyth and Evershed, 'The molecules of meals'.
[98] Taylor et al., 'Impact of early prehistoric farming on chironomid communities in northwest Ireland'.
[99] Stolze et al., 'Solar influence on climate variability and human development during the Neolithic'.
[100] Langdon et al., 'Regional climate change from peat stratigraphy for the mid- to late Holocene in central Ireland', *Quaternary International* 268 (2012), 145–55.
[101] Caseldine et al., 'Evidence for an extreme climatic event on Achill Island, Co. Mayo, Ireland around 5200-5100 cal. yr BP'.
[102] M.G.L. Baillie, 'A view from outside: recognising the big picture', *Journal of Quaternary Science* 14:6 (1999), 625–35; Whitehouse et al., 'Neolithic agriculture on the European western frontier'.
[103] McKeown et al., 'Complexities in interpreting chironomid-based temperature reconstructions over the Holocene from a lake in Western Ireland'; Swindles et al., 'Centennial-scale climate change in Ireland during the Holocene'; McDermott et al., 'Centennial-scale Holocene climate variability revealed by a high-resolution speleothem $\delta 18O$ record from SW Ireland'.
[104] Bond et al., 'Persistent solar influence on North Atlantic climate during the Holocene', *Science* 294:5549 (2001), 2130–36; Friedhelm Steinhilber, Juerg Beer and Claus

cooler conditions from Greenland in the NGRIP and GISP2 $\delta^{18}O$ records.[105] Palaeoclimate models have suggested that the expansion of sea-ice led to cooler conditions across the North Atlantic region at this time.[106]

Late Neolithic (3000–2500 BC)

Change can be seen again from the Late Neolithic, when there is an increased settlement signal in the archaeological record, particularly in the north and east of the island. These sites consist of complexes of pits, postholes and spreads in many cases.[107] The construction of passage tombs largely ceases around this time, and overall there are fewer burials recorded; where they are found, burials are deposited into pits, cairns and existing tombs.[108] Timber circles, subcircular structures and embanked enclosures (henges) appear, with a concentration around the area of the Boyne Valley, Co. Meath passage tombs (including Newgrange and Knowth), emphasising the continued importance of this region, although it is not clear if these newer sites are always focused on ceremonial activities.[109] Grooved Ware is a new ceramic style often associated with this period, reflecting a tradition introduced from northern Britain.[110]

As well as an increased settlement signal, the '*Plantago* gap' that was clear in the final centuries of the fourth millennium BC is not so apparent during the Late Neolithic in Ireland, suggesting changing landscape management practices,[111] but this may not reflect a widespread return to farming practices.[112] Indeed, some pollen data suggest an absence of farming activity during

---

Fröhlich, 'Total solar irradiance during the Holocene', *Geophysical Research Letters* 36:19 (2009), https://doi.org/10.1029/2009GL040142.

[105] Minze Stuiver, P.M. Grootes and T.F. Braziunas, 'The GISP2 δ18O climate record of the past 16,500 years and the role of the sun, ocean, and volcanoes', *Quaternary Research* 44:3 (1995), 341–54; R.B. Alley, 'Ice-core evidence of abrupt climate changes', *Proceedings of the National Academy of Sciences* 97:4 (2000), 1331–34.

[106] Hans Renssen, Hugues Goosse and Raimund Muscheler, 'Coupled climate model simulation of Holocene cooling events: oceanic feedback amplifies solar forcing', *Climate of the Past* 2:2 (2006), 79–90.

[107] Whitehouse *et al.*, 'Neolithic agriculture on the European western frontier'; McLaughlin *et al.*, 'The changing face of Neolithic and Bronze Age Ireland.

[108] Schulting *et al.*, 'Dating the Neolithic human remains at Knowth', in George Eogan and Kerri Cleary (eds), *Excavations at Knowth 6: The passage tomb archaeology of the great mound at Knowth* (Dublin, 2017), 331–85.

[109] McLaughlin *et al.*, 'The changing face of Neolithic and Bronze Age Ireland'.

[110] Neil Carlin, 'Getting into the groove: exploring the relationship between Grooved Ware and developed passage tombs in Ireland *c.* 3000–2700 cal bc', *Proceedings of the Prehistoric Society* 83 (2017), 155–88.

[111] Whitehouse *et al.*, 'Neolithic agriculture on the European western frontier'.

[112] O'Connell and Molloy, 'Farming and woodland dynamics in Ireland during the Neolithic'.

Tracing environmental, climatic and social change in Neolithic Ireland

the initial centuries of the Late Neolithic where there was farming evidence earlier in the Neolithic, for example in areas of Co. Sligo[113]. When farming activity here becomes evident towards the end of the Late Neolithic, the scale of activity and nutrient influx is large enough to affect the ecology of small lakes, returning lakes to more eutrophic conditions.[114] While there are clear changes in some aspects of the archaeological record, cereal macro-remains continue to be rare at Late Neolithic sites, and where recorded, none have been directly dated (Fig. 2).[115] Both wheat and barley are present, with barley recorded at slightly more sites, but barley cannot be regarded as dominant. Domesticated animals (most often cattle and pig) continue to be recorded,[116] but much like the cereal remains, direct dating is often absent. Evidence from lipid analyses of ceramics is stronger, however, indicating that pastoral farming continued, particularly dairying,[117] but again there are fewer records when compared with the Early Neolithic.

Changing landscape interactions during the Late Neolithic coincide with warmer and/or drier conditions in several Irish palaeoclimate records. Chironomid-inferred July air temperatures are high during the Late Neolithic in both the Lough Meenachrinna, Co. Donegal and Lough Nakeeroge, Co. Mayo records in northwest Ireland.[118] The standardised Irish bog water table compilation shows dry conditions during this time.[119] This corresponds with a dry phase at 3250–2810 BC in the Irish midlands.[120] Annual precipitation begins to decrease in the HadCM3 climate model for northern Achill Island, Co. Mayo from 3000 BC.[121] A marine sediment core record from the Irish

---

[113] Ghilardi and O'Connell, 'Fine-resolution pollen-analytical study of Holocene woodland dynamics and land use in north Sligo, Ireland'; O'Connell *et al.*, 'A 7000-year record of environmental change, including early farming impact, based on lake-sediment geochemistry and pollen data from County Sligo, western Ireland'.

[114] Taylor *et al.*, 'Impact of early prehistoric farming on chironomid communities in northwest Ireland'; Taylor *et al.*, 'Response of chironomids to Neolithic land-use change in northwest Ireland'.

[115] McClatchie *et al.*, 'Farming and foraging in Neolithic Ireland: an archaeobotanical perspective'.

[116] McClatchie *et al.*, 'Food production, processing and foodways in Neolithic Ireland'.

[117] Smyth and Evershed, 'The molecules of meals: new insight into Neolithic foodways'.

[118] Taylor *et al.*, 'A mid to late Holocene chironomid-inferred temperature record from northwest Ireland'; McKeown *et al.*, 'Complexities in interpreting chironomid-based temperature reconstructions over the Holocene from a lake in Western Ireland'.

[119] Swindles *et al.*, 'Centennial-scale climate change in Ireland during the Holocene'.

[120] Langdon *et al.*, 'Regional climate change from peat stratigraphy for the mid- to late Holocene in central Ireland'.

[121] McKeown *et al.*, 'Complexities in interpreting chironomid-based temperature reconstructions over the Holocene from a lake in Western Ireland'.

Continental Shelf also shows a general warming trend in bottom water temperatures from 3000 BC.[122]

Discussion

This study was ambitious insofar as it attempted to compare diverse datasets in order to refine our understanding of how people interacted with their environments in Neolithic Ireland, and of the potential impacts of changing environments and climate. It focused on evidence from archaeology, archaeobotany, zooarchaeology, palynology, palaeolimnology, organic residues, stable isotopes and sediment geochemistry. Whilst some broad trends are apparent, these diverse datasets provide different and sometimes contrasting insights. It is not possible at this stage to develop a robust climate reconstruction for Neolithic Ireland against which archaeological and other palaeoecological evidence can be considered. In some cases, the data do not agree, and in others they derive from different timescales and sampling intervals, which means that direct comparison would be unwise. This study has, however, highlighted several important aspects of changing human activities and environmental interactions during the Irish Neolithic that merit further reflection.

A clear picture of the extent and nature of land-use practices around the time of the Mesolithic/Neolithic transition has yet to emerge. During the first two centuries of the fourth millennium BC, there is some evidence for burial sites and structures, including activity at portal, court and passage tombs, as well as a substantial causewayed enclosure.[123] Activities continue at several of these locations into the period after 3750 BC, suggesting people were beginning to create a sense of place that persisted into later centuries. There is little evidence for settlements, however, no evidence for cereal cultivation, and only occasional suggestions that animal husbandry was taking place. Whilst it would be unwise to assume that a full 'package' of Neolithic materials is required to assign Neolithic status to activities during the first two centuries of the fourth millennium BC, it is not clear what these early activities reflect, socially or economically, and what impact they had on surrounding landscapes. Evidence for animal husbandry was recorded at the causewayed enclosure of Magheraboy, Co. Sligo, where sheep/goat bone was found in primary fills of the enclosure ditch, and biomolecular analysis of ceramics from these fills signals the presence of ruminant dairy fats.[124] Cattle and sheep/goat were new introductions to Ireland during the Neolithic, having no wild predecessors here.[125] These animals are likely to have had a significant im-

---

[122] Curran *et al.*, 'Atmospheric response to mid-Holocene warming in the northeastern Atlantic'.

[123] Lynch, *Poulnabrone*; Murphy *et al.*, 'INSTAR: The people of prehistoric Ireland'; McLaughlin *et al.*, 'The changing face of Neolithic and Bronze Age Ireland'; Schulting *et al.*, 'Radiocarbon dating of a multi-phase passage tomb on Baltinglass Hill, Co. Wicklow, Ireland'; Danaher, *Monumental Beginnings*.

[124] Danaher, *Monumental Beginnings*; Smyth and Evershed, 'Milking the megafauna'.

[125] G.M. Warren, Steve Davis, Meriel McClatchie and Rob Sands, 'The potential role of humans in structuring the wooded landscapes of Mesolithic Ireland: a review of data

pact on the landscape, perhaps including the clearing of woodland for grazing. Further woodland clearance may have been associated with the construction of large monuments like Magheraboy. Indeed, in several locations across Ireland, pollen studies show a rise in ribwort plantain pollen from around 4000/3900 BC, which may reflect woodland clearance and the start of agricultural activity.[126] But there are also sites where pollen evidence suggests some level of 'openness' in Late Mesolithic landscapes and that subsequent activity during the early fourth millennium BC took place in pre-existing woodland clearings, rather than undertaking new woodland clearance.[127] Diversity can also be traced in the timing of the decline of elm woodland, which is not a marker of the Mesolithic/Neolithic transition, but instead took place during both the Mesolithic and Neolithic periods, at different times in different places.[128] While many Irish records show a warming during this transition,[129] others show a general cooling from 4000 BC (Fig. 3).[130] Although it is possible that these differences are due to sampling resolution and dating model inaccuracies, or mixed responses of important palaeoclimatological proxies, it means that a robust reconstruction of climate is not currently achievable for these important centuries, when hugely significant social innovations began to be enacted in Ireland.

From around 3750BC, there is extensive evidence for changing landscapes. The period 3750 to 3600 BC is sometimes referred to as 'the house horizon' in Ireland, such is the proclivity for constructing rectangular houses for around one century only, as confirmed by careful analysis and modelling of radiocarbon dates.[131] Settlement evidence is widespread and agricultural activity also takes place in many different locations and social contexts. Dairying appears to be an important component of food production,[132] and it is likely this activity had landscape impacts, such as the clearing of woodland and construction of fields. There is also regular evidence for cereal cultivation, which it is argued was intensive, perhaps occurring in garden-style spaces close to settlements. Having said this, it is likely that farming was undertaken on a spectrum of

---

and discussion of approaches', *Journal of Vegetation History and Archaeobotany* 23 (2014), 629–46.

[126] Whitehouse *et al.*, 'Neolithic agriculture on the European western frontier'.

[127] Kearney, 'Vegetation impacts and early Neolithic monumentality'.

[128] Whitehouse *et al.*, 'Neolithic agriculture on the European western frontier'; Kearney and Gearey, 'The elm decline is dead!'.

[129] Taylor *et al.*, 'A mid to late Holocene chironomid-inferred temperature record from northwest Ireland'.

[130] McKeown *et al.*, 'Complexities in interpreting chironomid-based temperature reconstructions over the Holocene from a lake in Western Ireland'. This issue of contrasting signals was previously highlighted by Schulting, 'Holocene environmental change and the Mesolithic-Neolithic transition in north-west Europe'.

[131] Cormac McSparron, 'Have you no homes to go to?', *Archaeology Ireland* 22:3 (2008), 18–21; Cooney *et al.*, 'Ireland'; Whitehouse *et al.*, 'Neolithic agriculture on the European western frontier'.

[132] Smyth and Evershed, 'The molecules of meals'.

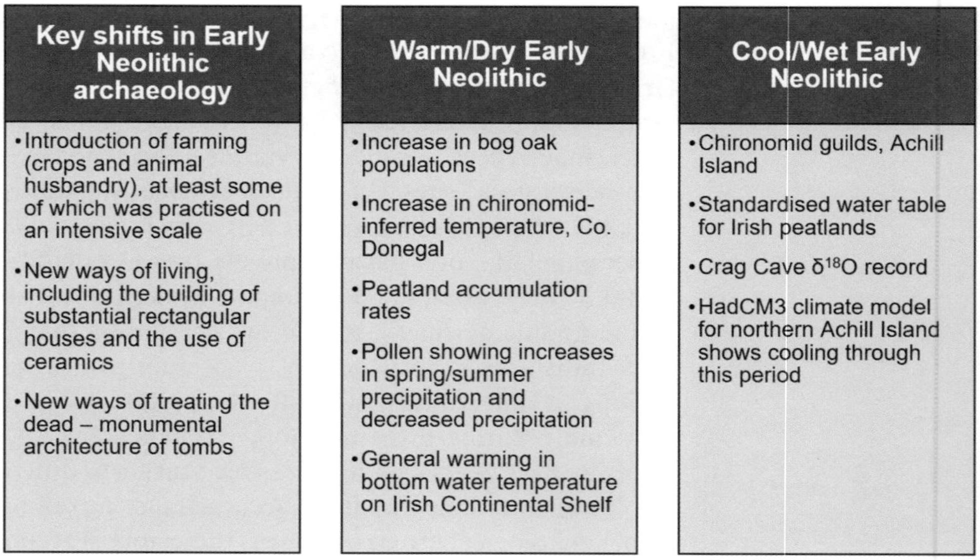

Key shifts in Early Neolithic archaeology	Warm/Dry Early Neolithic	Cool/Wet Early Neolithic
• Introduction of farming (crops and animal husbandry), at least some of which was practised on an intensive scale • New ways of living, including the building of substantial rectangular houses and the use of ceramics • New ways of treating the dead – monumental architecture of tombs	• Increase in bog oak populations • Increase in chironomid-inferred temperature, Co. Donegal • Peatland accumulation rates • Pollen showing increases in spring/summer precipitation and decreased precipitation • General warming in bottom water temperature on Irish Continental Shelf	• Chironomid guilds, Achill Island • Standardised water table for Irish peatlands • Crag Cave $\delta^{18}O$ record • HadCM3 climate model for northern Achill Island shows cooling through this period

Fig. 3—Comparison of archaeological evidence and climate reconstructions from Early Neolithic Ireland; contrasting results are evident in broadly contemporary climatic records, with some suggesting warm/dry conditions, and others indicating cool/wet conditions.

intensity depending on local circumstances; variability can be seen, for example, in the types of crops being grown and consumed at individual sites.[133] Gathered foods were not abandoned, but instead formed an integral element of foodways, with regular evidence for nuts, fruits and greens.[134] It appears, therefore, that open and wooded landscapes were the primary locations for food production, with management of crops and animals perhaps close to settlements (given the evidence for intensive agriculture and dairying), as well as foraging in the wider wooded landscapes. Not all areas of the island engaged in these practices; the midlands, for example, are rather quiet in terms of an agricultural and woodland clearance signal.[135] But overall, these new (or at least more widespread) practices of constructing houses, raising animals and cultivating crops created new arenas for social and landscape interactions, and may also have been significant in expressing and reinforcing social identities.[136] Whilst it may be tempting to link these changing human activities to the generally warm/dry conditions evidenced in several Irish records during the early Neolithic, there are also records that

---

[133] McClatchie *et al.*, 'Farming and foraging in Neolithic Ireland'.

[134] McClatchie *et al.*, 'Neolithic farming in north-western Europe'; McClatchie *et al.*, 'Farming and foraging in Neolithic Ireland'.

[135] Whitehouse *et al.*, 'Neolithic agriculture on the European western frontier'; Whitehouse *et al.*, 'Prehistoric land-cover and land-use history in Ireland at 6000 BP'.

[136] McClatchie *et al.*, 'Food production, processing and foodways in Neolithic Ireland'.

suggest more challenging environmental conditions (Fig. 3). Furthermore, dating uncertainties do not allow for causal interpretation of a climate change/land-use change dynamic.

The picture from the first two centuries of the Middle Neolithic (from 3600 BC) is more mixed. Cereals are still recorded in excavated deposits, but not to the same extent. This may be because cereals were most often associated with rectangular houses during the Early Neolithic, so when the houses disappeared, deposition practices changed also. It is not clear, therefore, if this reduced cereal record reflects changing deposition practices or a reduction in agricultural activity. But decreasing soil fertility has been identified from 3550 BC,[137] which may reflect a shift from intensive to more extensive agricultural practices. Furthermore, several (but not all) pollen studies suggest an increase in hazel and a reduction in ribwort plantain and cereals. This does not necessarily mean abandonment of land or population decline; instead it may reflect changes in the location of activities, or perhaps increased hazel pollen production due to woodland 'management' practices associated with nut and wood gathering.[138] Whilst interpretation of these changes (decreased cereals and ribwort plantain, and increased woodland indicators) is not straightforward, it does seem clear that human engagement with landscapes was changing. Lipid analyses suggest that animal husbandry, particularly dairying, continued to be important, however,[139] and the significant role that animals played in foodways and social occasions is suggested by the recovery of an enormous cattle bone assemblage from an enclosure ditch at Kilshane, Co. Dublin.[140]

By around 3400 BC, significant changes are apparent across a spectrum of activities. Diversity in burial traditions is notable and settlements become more elusive in the archaeological record. Indicators of agricultural activity (including pastoral) are reduced in many pollen and other records, and while lipid studies suggest animal husbandry continues, it may not be to the same level as previously, and there is very little plant macro-remains evidence for cereals. In southern Britain around the same time, cereals also seem to almost disappear from the archaeological record,[141] although it has been suggested that cereals persist in areas of northern Britain.[142] In the case of Ireland, there is not a shift towards wild plants,[143] and it is not clear if the evidence reflects an abandonment

---

[137] Colledge *et al.*, 'Neolithic population crash in northwest Europe associated with agricultural crisis'.
[138] Whitehouse *et al.*, 'Prehistoric land-cover and land-use history in Ireland at 6000 BP'.
[139] Smyth and Evershed, 'The molecules of meals'.
[140] Moore, *Report on archaeological excavation of Site 5, Kilshane, County Dublin*.
[141] Stevens and Fuller, 'Did Neolithic farming fail?'.
[142] R.R. Bishop, 'Did Late Neolithic farming fail or flourish? A Scottish perspective on the evidence for Late Neolithic arable cultivation in the British Isles', *World Archaeology* 47:5 (2015), 834–55.
[143] McClatchie *et al.*, 'Farming and foraging in Neolithic Ireland: an archaeobotanical perspective'; McClatchie *et al.*, 'Food production, processing and foodways in Neolithic Ireland'.

of arable agriculture because crops struggled due to changing climatic conditions, which could have included unstable conditions, colder winters and wetter summers,[144] or if crops failed to thrive in less fertile soils.[145] Perhaps pests and diseases affected crop yields and reliability, following an early 'honeymoon' period when crops were introduced to Ireland.[146] It is also possible that the decrease in cereal recovery reflects changing culinary, commensality and deposition practices, including the relative lack of 'domestic' deposits.[147] Given the wide-ranging evidence for reduced agricultural activity from many different datasets, however,[148] it is becoming increasingly difficult to interpret this as anything other than a significant agricultural decline. It has been suggested that reduced agricultural productivity in Ireland and Britain could be related to a climatic downturn at this time.[149] Whilst this is a possibility, climatic and agricultural records are often derived through independent chronosequences, and a cause/effect relationship is difficult to discern. Precisely how a change in climate could so drastically impact farming practices, and especially pastoral farming practices, in an Irish context remains unclear.

For the Late Neolithic (from 3000 BC), there is generally less palaeoenvironmental evidence available and where it exists, diverse activities seem apparent. While animal husbandry, particularly dairying, is evidenced by lipid studies, again very few cereal macro-remains are recovered. It is important to consider that this may not reflect continuation of arable practices established during the Middle Neolithic—the record is far too sparse to make such assumptions. The rare recovery of cereals is interesting, however, given the increased visibility of domestic sites in the archaeological record. Pollen evidence suggests an increase in agricultural activity, but only in some locations. The Late Neolithic in Ireland is generally warm and dry, as evidenced in terrestrial and marine palaeoclimate proxy records as well as regional model simulations.[150] However, due to

---

[144] Stevens and Fuller, 'Did Neolithic farming fail?'; Stolze *et al.*, 'Solar influence on climate variability and human development during the Neolithic'; Bevan *et al.*, 'Holocene fluctuations in human population demonstrate repeated links to food production and climate'.

[145] Colledge *et al.*, 'Neolithic population crash in northwest Europe associated with agricultural crisis'.

[146] Petra Dark and Henry Gent, 'Pests and diseases of prehistoric crops: a yield 'honeymoon' for early grain crops in Europe?' *Oxford Journal of Archaeology* 20:1 (2001), 59–78.

[147] McClatchie *et al.*, 'Food production, processing and foodways in Neolithic Ireland'.

[148] Stephen Shennan, *The first farmers of Europe: an evolutionary perspective* (Cambridge, 2018).

[149] Bevan *et al.*, 'Holocene fluctuations in human population demonstrate repeated links to food production and climate'.

[150] Swindles *et al.*, 'Centennial-scale climate change in Ireland during the Holocene'; Curran *et al.*, 'Atmospheric response to mid-Holocene warming in the northeastern Atlantic'; McKeown *et al.*, 'Complexities in interpreting chironomid-based temperature reconstructions over the Holocene from a lake in Western Ireland'.

inherent dating uncertainties, it cannot be said that improved climate conditions influenced any increase in farming activity.

Conclusions

This paper has shown how integration of a wide variety of analyses can provide a more nuanced understanding of societies, environments and climate in Neolithic Ireland. The emerging picture is not straightforward, and in some cases—particularly around the first and last centuries of the Neolithic—further analyses are clearly required. Further studies in palaeoentomology, for example, have the potential to provide new insights into changing landscapes and climates through detecting thermophilous species that may point towards fluctuating climates.[151] Further chironomid-based temperature reconstructions from 'isolated' lake catchments away from significant prehistoric human impacts would also be useful. Integration of further datasets may be beneficial, including emerging data from approaches that may make significant contributions in the future, such as aDNA and sedaDNA.[152]

We should not assume that when farming arrived in Ireland it was practised at a similar intensity throughout the island and for the entire Neolithic period. Rather, people made individual choices at different times and in varying circumstances. Drawing upon existing evidence, there are significant changes in land use when we compare the Early, Middle and Late Neolithic periods. The Early Neolithic and the early centuries of the Middle Neolithic are characterised in some locations (but not all) by regular evidence for settlement and farming from 3750 BC onwards (resulting in nutrient-loading in lakes) and increased woodland clearance. Some studies suggest climatic conditions were drier, which could be inferred as facilitating these new land-use practices, while other studies indicate the onset of cooler/wetter conditions. During the later centuries of the Middle Neolithic, there is reduced evidence for farming and settlement perhaps accompanied by woodland regeneration. Climatic records also suggest wetter/cooler conditions during this period. During the Late Neolithic, there is an increased signal for settlement and some farming activities, broadly coinciding with warmer/drier conditions.

Although several records for shifts in climate roughly align with changes in land use, a cause-effect relationship is not discernible and should not be assumed. In the Irish context, it is difficult to envisage a mechanism whereby climate change could have altered farming practices so drastically, especially pastoral farming. It is important to remember that chronologies may be established at different scales in archaeology and palaeoecology, perhaps because archaeology usually undertakes radiocarbon dating to determine the timing of short-term

---

[151] Eileen Reilly, 'The insect fauna (Coleoptera) from the Neolithic trackways Corlea 9 and 10: the environmental implications', in Barry Raftery (ed.), *Trackway excavations in the Mountdillon Bogs, Co. Longford 1985–91* (Dublin, 1996), 403–9.

[152] Clarke *et al.*, 'Holocene floristic diversity and richness in northeast Norway revealed by sedimentary ancient DNA (sedaDNA) and pollen', *Boreas* 48:2 (2019), 299–316.

events, while palaeoecology is more interested in tracking longer or continuous sequences of activity. Although we may detect changing land use and climate during the Middle Neolithic, for example, this is a period of several hundred years, and it is not clear to what extent changes really coincided. Indeed, based upon current chronological models, climate change may have followed land-use change in many instances. Further work, including refinement of chronologies, is essential. This paper has highlighted the real value of applying an integrated, interdisciplinary approach to tackle a complex issue. It is hoped that this approach will encourage more collaboration in addressing the big questions about Ireland's distant past.

Acknowledgements   We thank the editor and two anonymous reviewers for useful comments and suggestions on an earlier draft of this paper. We are grateful to Dr Karen Taylor for provision of images in Pl. 2.

A question of scale? A review of interpretations of Irish peatland archaeology in relation to Holocene environmental and climate change

PHIL STASTNEY*

Museum of London Archaeology, Mortimer Wheeler House, London

[Accepted 24 October 2019. Published 28 February 2020.]

Abstract

Irish peatlands contain rich archaeological and palaeoenvironmental archives allowing exploration of the relationship between past human activity and Holocene climatic variability. The existing literature on this topic is reviewed, and methodological and theoretical approaches are critically examined. Several underlying challenges associated with archaeo-environmental datasets emerge: chronological uncertainties, spatial scale, and non-linear relationships between data. Defining appropriate scales of analysis is a challenge: broad scales of analysis risk conflating small-scale trends, whilst at smaller scales the incompleteness and uncertainties associated with data are foregrounded. Understanding these challenges is essential to overcoming them. A case-study from bogs in Co. Tipperary is utilised to illustrate these challenges and evaluate various interpretive approaches. One novel technique, borrowed from literary criticism, is an 'unframed' reading in which both archaeological and palaeoenvironmental datasets are considered across large spatial and chronological scales. This approach circumvents methodological challenges and allows for the creation of meaningful narratives relevant to concerns about present and future climate change.

Introduction

Peatlands cover approximately one fifth of the surface of the island of Ireland,[1] and are well-established archives of palaeoenvironmental data, preserving sensitive records of past climatic change.[2] Irish bogs are also well-known for their

---

*Author's email: pstastney@mola.org.uk
ORCID iD: https://orcid.org/0000-0003-4556-9148
doi: https://doi.org/10.3318/PRIAC.2020.120.02

[1] John Connolly and N.M. Holden, 'Mapping peat soils in Ireland: updating the derived Irish peat map', *Irish Geography* 42:3 (2009), 343–52.

[2] K.E. Barber, 'Peatlands as scientific archives of past biodiversity', *Biodiversity and Conservation* 2 (1993), 474–89; K.E. Barber and D.J. Charman, 'Holocene palaeoclimate records from peatlands', in Anson Mackay *et al.* (eds), *Global change in the Holocene* (London, 2003), 210–26; D.J. Charman, *Peatlands and environmental change* (Chichester, 2002); Rixt de Jong *et al.*, 'Peatlands and climate', in John Dodson (ed.), *Changing climates, earth systems and society* (Dordrecht, 2010), 85–121; K.E. Barber, *Peat stratigraphy and climatic change: a paleoecological test of the theory of cyclic peat bog regeneration* (Rotterdam, 1981).

Fig. 1—Photographs of excavated peatland structures at Littleton bog, Co. Tipperary North. Clockwise from top left: Iron Age platform TN-LTN30; Middle Bronze Age plank path TN-LTN006; Late Bronze Age corduroy trackway TN-LTN001. Scale sub-divisions 0.5m.

internationally-important archaeology, with over 3,500 peatland structures, mostly timber trackways of various kinds (see Fig. 1), recorded in the Irish Sites and Monuments Record.[3] Ironically, this vast archaeological record has largely been revealed by the exploitation of bogs for peat extraction, a process which threatens this resource and adds urgency to the need to adequately record and understand it.[4] Meanwhile, increasing recognition of anthropogenic climate

---

[3] National Monuments Service, 'Map viewer', 2012, http://webgis.archaeology.ie/NationalMonuments/FlexViewer/.

[4] 'There is some argument for saying that the Irish bogs still hold more information about the past than any wetland in Europe; but time is running out.' Bryony Coles and John Coles, *People of the wetlands* (London, 1989), 159.

change since the 1990s[5] has renewed interest in human–environment interactions.[6] Given the direct association of archaeological and palaeoenvironmental data in Irish bogs, peatland trackways present an opportunity to study in microcosm the relationship between past human activity and environmental change. As concerns about the impacts of future climate change and the loss of the Irish peatland archive grow, so too does the importance of investigating past human–environmental interactions in these unique, and ultimately irreplaceable, settings.

The purpose of this paper is to provide a review of research on past human–environmental interactions in Irish peatlands, and in particular to critically examine the ways in which peatland archaeological and palaeoenvironmental ('archaeo-environmental') datasets have been interpreted and understood. Following a brief overview of the literature, it becomes clear that there is no consensus on the influence of past environmental change on human activity in Irish bogs. In order to explore the reasons for this, the specific methodological challenges and theoretical considerations associated with the study of peatland archaeo-environmental datasets are then explored. A case-study from a small group of bogs in Co. Tipperary is then introduced to illustrate these methodological issues and to evaluate a number of contrasting interpretive approaches, including a novel technique borrowed from the emerging field of ecocriticism. Finally, the various approaches are discussed and evaluated in relation to methodological and theoretical considerations, and the following overarching research questions are addressed:

1. What are the methodological challenges inherent in comparing the archaeological and palaeoenvironmental datasets obtained from Irish bogs?
2. What underlying theoretical assumptions underpin existing interpretations of past human–environment interactions in Irish bogs? Could theoretical developments in other disciplines offer any new insights?
3. How, armed with an understanding of the methodological challenges and recognition of underlying theoretical assumptions, could such novel insights be applied in practice?

A review of Irish peatland archaeology and Holocene environmental change

Changing intellectual fashions through the twentieth century onwards have seen the rise of classical environmental determinism,[7] its critique and fall from

---

[5] F.M. Chambers and S.A. Brain, 'Paradigm shifts in Late-Holocene climatology?', *The Holocene* 12:2 (2002), 239–49.

[6] Paul Coombes and K.E. Barber, 'Environmental determinism in Holocene research: causality or coincidence?', *Area* 37:3 (2005), 304; K.W. Kintigh *et al.*, 'Grand challenges for archaeology', *Proceedings of the National Academy of Sciences* 111:3 (2014), 879–80.

[7] This is exemplified by works such as Ellsworth Huntington, *Civilization and climate* (New Haven, 1924).

favour,[8] and, more recently, a resurgence in popular nonfiction[9] and academic research in regions such as South America[10] and the Near East.[11] In parallel, within environmental archaeology and Quaternary science, where past human–environment interactions have long been a focus of research, debates have encompassed a variety of methodological and theoretical issues. Following initial attempts at global syntheses that noted broad correspondence between periods of social change and climatic change,[12] some researchers have argued that ever-improving chronological precision in archaeological and palaeoenvironmental records would eventually be sufficient to prove causal links between climatic and social change,[13] whilst others have expressed scepticism about the existence of any linkages at all.[14] A growing number of researchers, however, have recently attempted more nuanced explorations of human–environment interactions that critically assess deterministic models, and allow for more sophisticated interpretations taking into account past demographics and varying social structures.[15]

A certain lack of engagement with wider theoretical debates has been noted amongst both environmental and wetland archaeologists.[16] Phenomenology provides an interesting case in point: first proposed and discussed in relation to

---

[8] Stephen Frenkel, 'Old theories in new places? Environmental determinism and bioregionalism', *Professional Geographer* 46:3 (1994), 289–295; Richard Peet, 'The social origins of environmental determinism', *Annals of the Association of American Geographers* 75:3 (1985), 309–33.

[9] Jared Diamond, *Collapse: how societies choose to fail or survive* (London, 2011); Jared Diamond, *Guns, germs and steel: a short history of everybody for the last 13,000 years*, New ed. (London, 2005).

[10] C.L. Erickson, 'Neo-environmental determinism and agrarian "collapse" in Andean prehistory', *Antiquity* 73 (1999), 634–42.

[11] H.E. Wright, 'Environmental determinism in near eastern prehistory', *Current Anthropology* 34:4 (1993), 458–69.

[12] W.M. Wendland and R.A. Bryson, 'Dating climatic episodes of the Holocene', *Quaternary Research* 4:1 (1974), 9–24.

[13] B.E. Berglund, 'Human impact and climate changes — synchronous events and a causal link?', *Quaternary International* 105:1 (2003), 7–12.

[14] Coombes and Barber, 'Environmental determinism in Holocene research'.

[15] Gill Plunkett et al., 'Environmental indifference? A critique of environmentally deterministic theories of peatland archaeological site construction in Ireland', *Quaternary Science Reviews* 61 (2013), 17–31; J.G. Evans, *Environmental archaeology and the social order* (London, 2003); Arlene Miller Rosen, *Civilizing climate: social responses to climate change in the ancient near east* (Lanham, MD, 2007); James Morris and Mark Maltby (eds) *Integrating social and environmental archaeologies: reconsidering deposition*, BAR International Series 2077 (Oxford, 2010); A.G. Brown, 'The Bronze Age climate and environment of Britain', *Bronze Age Review* 1 (2008), 7–22.

[16] Julian Thomas, 'Silent running: the ills of environmental archaeology', *Scottish Archaeological Review* 7 (1990), 2–7; Robert Van de Noort and Aidan O'Sullivan, *Rethinking wetland archaeology*, Duckworth Debates in Archaeology (London, 2007).

archaeology by Christopher Tilley,[17] it has since been widely incorporated into the study of British[18] and Irish[19] landscape archaeology. Tilley frequently discusses paths and formal routeways as ways in which experiences and identities are created, so it is perhaps ironic, given the abundance of paths and physical routeways (i.e. trackways) in the Irish peatland archaeological record, that such theoretical approaches have rarely been applied to Irish bogs.[20]

Aidan O'Sullivan highlighted the range of activities that is represented by the archaeological record of raised bogs in a comprehensive review of wetland archaeology in Ireland: hunting, fowling, the gathering of plants for medicine and crafts, grazing, preserving butter, seasoning wood, as well as religious and ritual practices.[21] Platform structures, for example, clearly imply some form of activity within raised bogs requiring a stable surface – hunting or fowling, or perhaps ritual activity of some kind, and whilst notable concentrations of these are known, for example at Edercloon, Co. Longford,[22] their exact functions remain elusive.[23]

Evidence for ritual activity in Irish raised bogs consists principally of votive deposits, including Bronze Age hoards[24] and bog bodies.[25] This pattern appears to be broadly in line with evidence in Britain and the European mainland for the importance of wetlands in late prehistoric ritual practice.[26] It has been argued, for example, that Iron Age bog bodies are related to rituals connected

---

[17] Christopher Tilley, *A phenomenology of landscape: places, paths, and monuments* (Oxford, 1994).
[18] Joanna Brück, 'Experiencing the past? The development of a phenomenological archaeology in British prehistory', *Archaeological Dialogues* 12 (2005), 45–72.
[19] Gabriel Cooney, *Landscapes of Neolithic Ireland* (London, 2000).
[20] Van de Noort and O'Sullivan, *Rethinking wetland archaeology*.
[21] Aidan O'Sullivan, 'Exploring past people's interactions with wetland environments in Ireland', *Proceedings of the Royal Irish Academy. Section C: Archaeology, Celtic Studies, History, Linguistics, Literature* 107C (2007), 175–6.
[22] Conor McDermott *et al.*, 'A colossus of roads: the Iron Age archaeology of Ireland's peatlands', in Gabriel Cooney *et al.* (eds), *Relics of old decency: archaeological studies in later prehistory. Festchrift for Barry Raftery* (Dublin, 2009), 49–66.
[23] Richard Brunning and Conor McDermott, 'Trackways and roads across the wetlands', in Francesco Menotti and Aidan O'Sullivan (eds), *The Oxford handbook of wetland archaeology* (Oxford, 2013), 367.
[24] George Eogan, *Hoards of the Irish later Bronze Age* (Dublin, 1983).
[25] A.L. Brindley and J.N. Lanting, 'Irish bog bodies: the radiocarbon dates', in R.C. Turner and R.G. Scaife (eds), *Bog bodies: new discoveries and new perspectives* (London, 1995), 133–6; Eamonn Kelly, 'Secrets of the bog bodies', *Archaeology Ireland* 20:1 (2006), 26–30; Sarah Forde, 'Dying for their king: a critical analysis of the relationship between Iron Age bog bodies and boundaries', *Trowel* 12 (2010), 20–30; M.J. Aldhouse-Green, *Bog bodies uncovered: solving Europe's ancient mystery* (London, 2015).
[26] Richard Bradley, *The passage of arms: an archaeological analysis of prehistoric hoards and votive deposits*, 2nd ed. (Oxford, 1998); Richard Bradley, *An archaeology of natural places* (London, 2000); David Yates and Richard Bradley, 'Still water, hidden depths: the deposition of Bronze Age metalwork in the English fenland', *Antiquity* 84:324 (2010), 405–15.

to kingship and boundaries, physical, political and spiritual.[27] Although evidence directly linking trackways to ritual deposits is rare, recent excavations of Iron Age trackways in Counties Longford (Fig. 2, 2)[28] and Tipperary (Fig. 2, 5)[29] have uncovered assemblages of unused objects apparently deposited in these bogs.

The larger types of wooden trackway (e.g. Class 1 toghers[30] such as TN-LTN006 and TN-LTN001 in Fig. 1) are often the focus of interpretations of human activity in Irish bogs, and therefore, as Michael Stanley points out, many archaeologists have tended to over-emphasise the notion that bogs represented obstacles, and so functional interpretations of trackways predominate.[31] In this vein, Barry Raftery interpreted the trackways of the Mountdillon bogs (Fig. 2, A) largely in utilitarian terms, albeit alongside a recognition that trackways could project ideas of prestige, power and belief (especially in the case of the massive Corlea 1 trackway (Fig. 2, 1)).[32] In Tipperary, the suite of wetland and dryland archaeological sites uncovered during the Lisheen mine archaeological project[33] (Fig. 2, 4) was interpreted as a 'vernacular landscape. Neither an obstacle to be overcome nor a place of ceremony'.[34]

Since peatland trackways occur in such distinctive environmental settings, it is unsurprising that implicit in many accounts of trackways and other structures is the notion that construction is contingent on the environmental conditions of the bog in some way: that structures were either constructed to compensate for wet and treacherous conditions, or conversely, that construction could only take place if the bog surface was relatively dry and stable. Raftery's study of the Mountdillon bogs was the first major project to integrate palaeoenvironmental analysis with archaeological investigation of Irish trackways; conclusions relating to the environmental or climatic context of trackway construction were tentative although a 'national pattern' of episodes of trackway construction was discerned.[35]

---

[27] Kelly, 'Secrets of the bog bodies'.
[28] Caitríona Moore, 'Old routes to new research: the Edercloon wetland excavations in County Longford', in Jerry O'Sullivan and Michael Stanley (eds), *Roads, rediscovery and research: proceedings of a public seminar on archaeological discoveries on national road schemes, August 2007* (Dublin, 2008), 1–12.
[29] Kate Taylor, 'At home and on the road: two Iron Age sites in County Tipperary', *Seanda* 3 (2008), 54–5.
[30] National Monuments Service, 'Monument class', undated, http://webgis.archaeology.ie/NationalMonuments/WebServiceQuery/Lookup.aspx#TOGP.
[31] Michael Stanley, 'Archaeological survey of Irish bogs: information without understanding?', *Journal of Wetland Archaeology* 3 (2003), 65.
[32] Barry Raftery, *Trackway excavations in the Mountdillon bogs, Co. Longford, 1985–1991*, Irish Archaeological Wetland Unit Transactions 3 (Dublin, 1996).
[33] Margaret Gowen, John O'Neill and Michael Phillips (eds), *The Lisheen mine archaeological project 1996–8* (Bray, 2005).
[34] Sarah Cross May *et al.*, 'Archaeological conclusions', in Gowen, O'Neill and Phillips (eds), *The Lisheen mine archaeological project 1996–8*, 363.
[35] Raftery, *Trackway excavations in the Mountdillon bogs*, 411–13.

Irish peatland archaeology in relation to Holocene environmental and climate change

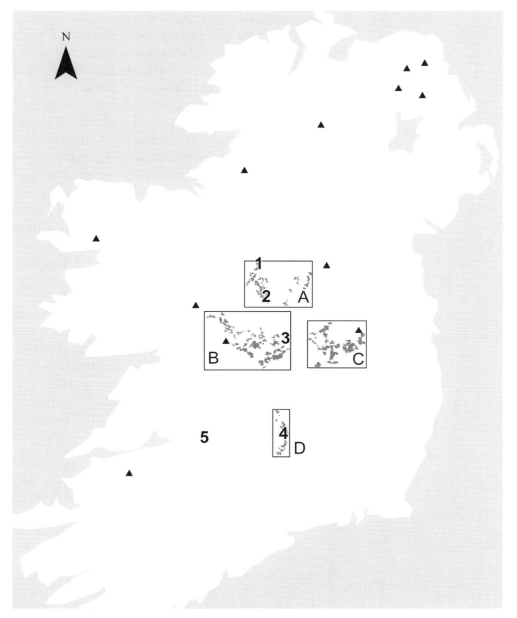

Fig. 2—Location of sites referred to in the text: 1) Edercloon, Co. Longford; 2) Corlea, Co. Longford; 3) Kilnagarnah, Co. Offaly; 4) Derryville, Co. Tipperary; 5) Annaholty, Co. Tipperary. Boxes indicate main groups of milled bogs subject to previous archaeological survey: A) Mountdillon group; B) Boora-Blackwater group; C) Derrygreenagh; D) Littleton group. The extent of milled production bogs in these groups is shown by the dark grey shading. Black triangles show the location of peatland palaeohydrological records utilised by Plunkett *et al.*, 'Environmental indifference?'.

The chronological clustering of trackways has in itself been interpreted, notably by Michael Baillie and colleagues, as evidence for social responses to environmental change. Since clusters appear to be related to growth-ring anomalies in Irish oaks, it has been suggested that trackway construction could be a response either to wetter[36] or drier conditions.[37] These studies have stimulated growing discourse about the role of climate in driving social change in Ireland.[38] Tensions between the intuitive notion that environmental conditions (especially 'bog surface wetness') are likely to have affected human behaviour (e.g. trackway construction), and the methodological (principally chronological) and conceptual difficulties (a general aversion to environmental determinism) associated with testing positivist hypotheses of human–environment interactions can be observed in the literature on Irish trackways. Brindley and Lanting, for example, suggested correlations between increased trackway construction and drier bog conditions,[39] although the palaeoenvironmental inference was based on the circular argument that archaeological sites were preserved by a later rise in water tables, and thus are likely to have been built during a preceding dry interval, in addition to potentially spurious links with dendroclimatological data.[40] Later work by Benjamin Gearey and Christopher Caseldine, based on combined archaeological and palaeoenvironmental investigations of a single site in Co. Tipperary (Fig. 2, 4), related trackway construction to bog surface wetness (BSW)[41] which they argued in this case may *not* have been a climatically sensitive record.[42] Thus implying that trackway construction was related to local bog conditions rather than climate *per se*. Similarly, Nóra Bermingham examined archaeological and palaeoenvironmental records from a bog in Co. Offaly (Fig. 2, 3), and argued that trackway con-

---

[36] M.G.L. Baillie, 'Dark ages and dendrochronology', *Emania* 11 (1993), 3–12.

[37] M.G.L. Baillie and D.M. Brown, 'Oak dendrochronology: some recent archaeological developments from an Irish perspective', *Antiquity* 76 (2002), 497–505.

[38] C.S.M. Turney *et al.*, 'Holocene climatic change and past Irish societal response', *Journal of Archaeological Science* 33:1 (2006), 34–8; G.T. Swindles and Gill Plunkett, 'Testing the palaeoclimatic significance of the Northern Irish bog oak record', *The Holocene* 20:2 (2010), 155–9; Plunkett *et al.*, 'Environmental indifference?'; N.C. Bermingham, 'Palaeohydrology and archaeology in raised mires: a case study from Kilnagarnagh', unpublished PhD thesis, University of Hull, 2005; Phil Stastney, 'The late prehistoric "dark age" in Ireland and climate fluctuation: buffering strategies and the agency of the environment', in E.M. van der Wilt and Javier Martínez Jiménez (eds), *Tough times: the archaeology of crisis and recovery*, BAR International Series 2478 (Oxford, 2013), 115–24.

[39] A.L. Brindley and J.N. Lanting, 'Radiocarbon dates for Irish trackways', *Journal of Irish Archaeology* 9 (1998), 45–67; Benjamin Gearey and Christopher Caseldine, 'Archaeological applications of testate amoebae analyses: a case study from Derryville, Co. Tipperary, Ireland', *Journal of Archaeological Science* 33:1 (2006), 49–55.

[40] Brindley and Lanting, 'Radiocarbon dates for Irish trackways'.

[41] Gearey and Caseldine, 'Archaeological applications of testate amoebae analyses'.

[42] Christopher Caseldine and Benjamin Gearey, 'A multiproxy approach to reconstructing surface wetness changes and prehistoric bog bursts in a raised mire system at Derryville bog, Co. Tipperary, Ireland', *The Holocene* 15:4 (2005), 585–601.

struction was not related to climate, but rather appeared to be related to periods of local, mostly autogenic hydrological change. It was therefore concluded that trackway construction was an 'opportunistic venture' based on a combination of environmental conditions and cultural factors.[43]

Revisiting the apparent national chronological pattern of trackway construction,[44] Gill Plunkett and colleagues critically examined the links between climate and trackway construction. A database of all published trackway dates in Ireland was compared with a composite palaeoclimate record based on six testate amoebae and six peat humification records from Ireland (see Fig. 2), explicitly excluding records showing evidence for autogenic processes or 'considerable human impact'.[45] No consistent relationship between BSW and trackway construction was found, leading to the conclusion that trackway construction was governed by 'wider cultural trends'.[46] Meanwhile, the local trends posited by Bermingham and Gearey and Caseldine were dismissed as being unable to explain the strong chronological clustering visible in the archaeological record as a whole. Although Plunkett *et al.*'s study is a robust critical examination of a deterministic link between climate and trackway construction, the study does not directly address the question of relationships between local or short-term (not necessarily climate-driven) conditions and human activity, a point raised in a recent study of German bogs by Inke Achterberg and colleagues.[47]

Trackway construction might have been related to a wide range of human behaviours: not only traversing bogs, but also other everyday economic and ritual practices.[48] Many of these are arguably 'culturally-determined'[49] whilst simultaneously being fundamentally linked to, and contingent upon, the bog environment, with its distinctive flora, fauna and physical characteristics.[50] So, whilst it is important to 'draw attention to the potential pitfalls of interpreting cause-and-effect on the basis of close temporal proximity of cultural and climate changes',[51] it seems that alternative means of thinking about human–environment interactions are required.

---

[43] Bermingham, 'Palaeohydrology and archaeology in raised mires', 266.
[44] Raftery, *Trackway excavations in the Mountdillon bogs, Co. Longford, 1985–1991*; Brindley and Lanting, 'Radiocarbon dates for Irish trackways'.
[45] Plunkett *et al.*, 'Environmental indifference?', 21.
[46] Plunkett *et al.*, 'Environmental indifference?', 29.
[47] Inke Achterberg *et al.*, 'Contemporaneousness of trackway construction and environmental change: a dendrochronological study in northwest-German mires', *Interdisciplinaria Archaeologica* 6:1 (2015), 26.
[48] O'Sullivan, 'Exploring past people's interactions with wetland environments in Ireland', 170–71.
[49] Plunkett *et al.*, 'Environmental indifference?', 28.
[50] G.F. Mitchell and Michael Ryan, *Reading the Irish landscape*, 3rd revised ed. (Dublin, 1997).
[51] Plunkett *et al.*, 'Environmental indifference?', 18, 29.

Methodological challenges

Dating the past is fundamental to all archaeological and palaeoenvironmental research and both chronologies are associated with their own methodological concerns and sources of uncertainty. In addition to improvement in radiocarbon techniques, now in the throes of a third 'revolution',[52] peatland archaeology in Ireland has benefitted from the development of dendrochronology, allowing oak timbers to be dated to annual, or even sub-annual, precision.[53] Thanks to these techniques, the archaeology of Irish peatlands is generally well-dated: of the estimated 3,500 peatland structures that have been recorded in Ireland, more than 350, approximately 10%, have been dated.[54] Palaeoenvironmental records from Irish peatlands are typically based on analysis of core samples which can be readily dated using radiocarbon, and used to construct robust Bayesian chronologies using various freely-available software packages.[55] In some cases, peat chronologies have been further refined through the use of volcanic tephra horizons as precise chronological markers.[56]

Although robust chronologies for individual archaeological and palaeoenvironmental sequences from Irish peatlands can be developed without much difficulty, comparing these chronologies remains a challenge. Baillie coined the phrase 'suck-in and smear' to characterise the dangers that can confound comparisons between chronologies: both the temptation to conflate two unrelated but near-synchronous events, and the tendency of statistical scatter to lead to the 'smearing' of events that were in fact either synchronous or very brief in duration.[57] At larger scales of analysis, where multiple datasets with independent chronologies are to be compared, these problems become amplified.[58]

---

[52] Alex Bayliss, 'Rolling out the revolution: using radiocarbon dating in archaeology', *Radiocarbon* 51:1 (2009), 123–47; Alex Bayliss, 'Quality in Bayesian chronological models in archaeology', *World Archaeology* 47:4 (2015), 677–700.

[53] M.G.L. Baillie, *A slice through time: dendrochronology and precision dating*, 1st ed. (London, 1997); Baillie and Brown, 'Oak dendrochronology'; M.G.L. Baillie, *Tree-ring dating and archaeology* (London, 2014).

[54] Brunning and McDermott, 'Trackways and roads across the wetlands', 361; R.M. Chapple, *Catalogue of radiocarbon determinations & dendrochronology dates (March 2018 release)* (Belfast, 2018).

[55] C. Bronk Ramsey, 'Radiocarbon calibration and analysis of stratigraphy: the OxCal program', *Radiocarbon* 37:2 (1995), 425–30; Christopher Bronk Ramsey, 'Deposition models for chronological records', *Quaternary Science Reviews* 27:1–2 (2008), 42–60; Maarten Blaauw and J.A. Christen, 'Flexible paleoclimate age-depth models using an autoregressive gamma process', *Bayesian Analysis* 6:3 (2011), 457–74.

[56] Gill Plunkett *et al.*, 'New dates for first millennium BC tephra isochrones in Ireland', *The Holocene* 14:5 (2004), 780–86; H.A. Rea, G.T. Swindles and H.M. Roe, 'The Hekla 1947 tephra in the north of Ireland: regional distribution, concentration and geochemistry', *Journal of Quaternary Science* 27:4 (2012), 425–31.

[57] M.G.L. Baillie, 'Suck-in and smear – two related chronological problems for the 90s', *Journal of Theoretical Archaeology* 2 (1991), 12–16.

[58] Maarten Blaauw, 'Out of tune: the dangers of aligning proxy archives', *Quaternary Science Reviews* 36 (2012), 38–49; Niels Bleicher, 'Summed radiocarbon probability

Palaeoenvironmental proxy records rely on the principle of uniformitarianism to allow inferences made on data from the micro-scale (e.g. pollen grains measuring less than a tenth of a millimetre) to be applied at spatial scales several orders of magnitude larger (e.g. a site that may be tens or hundreds of metres across). In the context of peatland palaeoenvironmental studies, which are based on the climatic sensitivity of ombrotrophic bogs,[59] this 'up-scaling' occurs at multiple levels: individual proxy indicators such as testate amoebae (typically 10–300μm across) are counted on a microscope slide prepared from a single 1cm thick slice of peat;[60] these data are then used, via a statistical model based on modern data from across Europe, to infer changes in conditions at the location the peat core was collected from (typically a 5–10cm diameter area);[61] this in turn is used to infer changes in the hydrology of the bog system as a whole;[62] and this, perhaps incorporated into a regional record compiled from several bogs,[63] is used to infer changes in precipitation balance[64] which, at last, is used as a proxy for large-scale, climatically-driven changes in atmospheric circulation.[65] At each stage the validity of these inferences relies on sound under-

---

density functions cannot prove solar forcing of central European lake-level changes', *The Holocene* 23:5 (2013), 755–65; Alex Bayliss *et al.*, 'Bradshaw and Bayes: towards a timetable for the Neolithic', *Cambridge Archaeological Journal* 17 (2007), 1.

[59] Bent Aaby, 'Cyclic climatic variations in climate over the past 5,500 yr reflected in raised bogs', *Nature* 263:5575 (September 23, 1976), 281–4; Barber, *Peat stratigraphy and climatic change*.

[60] D.J. Charman, Dawn Hendon and W.A. Woodland, *The identification of testate amoebae (Protozoa:Rhizopoda) in peats*, Technical Guide 9 (London, 2000).

[61] M.J. Amesbury *et al.*, 'Development of a new pan-European testate amoeba transfer function for reconstructing peatland palaeohydrology', *Quaternary Science Reviews* 152 (November 2016), 132–51.

[62] P.J. Morris, L.R. Belyea and A.J. Baird, 'Ecohydrological feedbacks in peatland development: a theoretical modelling study', *Journal of Ecology* 99 (2011), 1190–201; R.S. Clymo, 'The limits to peat bog growth', *Philosophical Transactions of the Royal Society of London. B, Biological Sciences* 303:1117 (1984), 605–54; L.R. Belyea and R.S. Clymo, 'Feedback control of the rate of peat formation', *Proceedings of the Royal Society B Biological Sciences* 268:1473 (June 22, 2001), 1315–21.

[63] D.J. Charman *et al.*, 'Compilation of non-annually resolved Holocene proxy climate records: stacked Holocene peatland palaeo-water table reconstructions from northern Britain', *Quaternary Science Reviews* 25:3–4 (February 2006), 336–50; G.T. Swindles *et al.*, 'Centennial-scale climate change in Ireland during the Holocene', *Earth-Science Reviews* 126 (2013), 300–20.

[64] K.E. Barber and P.G. Langdon, 'What drives the peat-based palaeoclimate record? A critical test using multi-proxy climate records from northern Britain', *Quaternary Science Reviews* 26:25–28 (2007), 3318–27; D.J. Charman *et al.*, 'Climate drivers for peatland palaeoclimate records', *Quaternary Science Reviews* 28:19–20 (2009), 1811–19; D.J. Charman *et al.*, 'A 1000-year reconstruction of summer precipitation from Ireland: calibration of a peat-based palaeoclimate record', *Quaternary International* 268 (2012), 87–97.

[65] H.H. Lamb, R.P.W. Lewis and A. Woodroffe, 'Atmospheric circulation and the main climatic variables between 8000 and 0 BC: meteorological evidence', in J.S.

standing of the underlying processes, and unsurprisingly several aspects of the method, such as the validity of transfer functions[66] and the difficulty in compiling composite records[67] have been, and will continue to be, subject to criticism.

Spatial scale in archaeological data is less challenging, but the effect of differing size of study area on the interpretation of archaeo-environmental data is nevertheless worth considering. Previous studies of the relationships between environmental conditions and trackway construction have broadly fallen into two groups: those that take a broad view, collating data from the whole region,[68] and those that have focused on single sites.[69] Whilst there is no clear consensus amongst these studies as to the exact nature of the relationship between trackway construction and environmental conditions, it is perhaps revealing that the regional syntheses have tended to focus on the existence (or lack thereof) of climatically-determined forcing factors, whilst studies based on single sites have tended to emphasise the importance of more localised factors. Since these studies address different questions, one approach cannot be argued to be in any way 'better' than the other, however, neither approach seems to adequately explain both broad cultural trends and regional peculiarities evident in the archaeological record, nor do they address the similarly nested effects of scale inherent in palaeoenvironmental data.

The complexity of the peatland palaeoenvironmental record is further illustrated by rare examples in the literature of autogenic environmental change that, nonetheless appear to be climatically-driven: during well-attested periods of rapid climatic change such as the so-called '2.8 Event' in the Late Bronze Age.[70] This is typically represented by a widespread shift to wetter conditions,[71] a few sites in both the Netherlands and Ireland show the opposite

---

Sawyer (ed.), *World climate from 8000 to 0 BC*, (London, 1966); K.E. Barber *et al.*, 'A sensitive high-resolution record of Late Holocene climatic change from a raised bog in northern England', *The Holocene* 4:2 (1994), 198–205; Swindles *et al.*, 'Centennial-scale climate change in Ireland during the Holocene'.

[66] L.R. Belyea, 'Revealing the emperor's new clothes: niche-based palaeoenvironmental reconstruction in the light of recent ecological theory', *The Holocene* 17:5 (2007), 683–8.

[67] Blaauw, 'The Integration of ice core, marine and terrestrial records'.

[68] Turney *et al.*, 'Holocene climatic change and past Irish societal response'; Plunkett *et al.*, 'Environmental indifference?'

[69] Bermingham, 'Palaeohydrology and archaeology in raised mires'; Gearey and Caseldine, 'Archaeological applications of testate amoebae analyses'.

[70] Paul Mayewski *et al.*, 'Holocene climate variability', *Quaternary Research* 62:3 (2004), 243–55.

[71] F.M. Chambers *et al.*, 'Globally synchronous climate change 2800 years ago: proxy data from peat in South America', *Earth and Planetary Science Letters* 253 (3–4) (2007), 439–44; Gill Plunkett and G.T. Swindles, 'Determining the sun's influence on lateglacial and Holocene climates: a focus on climate response to centennial-scale solar forcing at 2800cal.BP', *Quaternary Science Reviews* 27:1–2 (2008), 175–84.

response: a phenomenon that has been interpreted as evidence for 'bog bursts'[72] – catastrophic failures of the mire surface resulting in drastic falls in water levels[73] – potentially caused by a non-linear response to the same climatic forcing that caused wetter conditions at other bogs.[74]

How does non-linearity in palaeoenvironmental records impact our understanding of past human–environment interactions? Understandably, some syntheses have excluded records from sites that show non-linear climatic response signals from their analysis.[75] However, this approach relies to a certain extent on the circular argument that records which are alike are climatically-sensitive, and those that differ are in some way insensitive or otherwise unsuitable for further analysis. Nevertheless, if the object is to assess regional-scale climatic forcing, then it is reasonable, and necessary, to exclude any sources of noise – that is records dominated by localised phenomena – that may obscure the climatic signal. Here the importance of scale in understanding human–environment interactions should again be highlighted: it is vital not to conflate the more abstract concept of a regional climatic signal with local, site-specific environmental conditions, just as it is important to acknowledge the distinction between broad regional trends in the archaeological record and the interpretation of individual sites and features. At larger scales of investigation, where climatic signals are compared with similarly broad patterns in archaeological data, non-linear relationships between proxy records (e.g. BSW) and the actual environmental variables they are used to infer (e.g. past precipitation balance) should be identified and ideally excluded from further analysis; an example of this type of non-linearity would be a bog burst event, which may cause a temporary decoupling or inversion of the normal relationship between BSW and precipitation balance. However, at smaller scales of enquiry, it is local environmental conditions and not synthesised regional climatic signals that should be compared with local archaeological data and in these cases non-linear behaviour in palaeoenvironmental records may be

---

[72] Wil Casparie, 'Prehistoric building disasters in Derryville bog, Ireland: trackways, floodings and erosion', in Barry Raftery and Joyce Hickey (eds), *Recent developments in wetland research* (Dublin, 2001), 115–28; Caseldine and Gearey, 'A multiproxy approach to reconstructing surface wetness changes and prehistoric bog bursts'; Bas Van Geel et al., 'Bog burst in the eastern Netherlands triggered by the 2.8 Kyr BP climate event', *The Holocene* 24:11 (November 1, 2014), 1465–77; Phil Stastney, D.S. Young and N.P. Branch, 'The identification of Late-Holocene bog bursts at Littleton bog, Ireland: ecohydrological changes display complex climatic and non-climatic drivers', *The Holocene* 28:4 (2018), 570–82.
[73] J.H. Tallis, 'Bog bursts', *Biologist* 48:5 (2001), 218–23; A.P. Dykes and Jeff Warburton, 'Mass movements in peat: a formal classification scheme', *Geomorphology* 86:1–2 (2007), 73–93.
[74] Van Geel et al., 'Bog burst in the eastern Netherlands triggered by the 2.8 Kyr BP climate event'.
[75] Swindles et al., 'Centennial-scale climate change in Ireland during the Holocene'; Plunkett et al., 'Environmental indifference?'

one of several contingent factors influencing human–environment interactions at small spatial and temporal scales.

The challenges posed by the variable and imperfect chronological and spatial resolutions of archaeological and palaeoecological datasets are often acknowledged, but the question of how realistic it is to expect a consistent (spatially or temporally) or *linear* relationship between palaeoecological and archaeological variables is less frequently articulated. As such, *non-linear* human behaviour poses a further challenge to the study of past human–environment interactions. A general consideration of the agency of humans to behave in a manner that is not determined by their social and environmental milieu is well beyond the scope of this paper, but the complexity of these issues notwithstanding, the possibility that people in the past did not *always* behave in predictable or linear ways must be acknowledged. Relationships that may hold good in certain places at certain times may not be the same everywhere and at every time. A hypothetical example may be useful: it is possible that the construction of peatland trackways might be encouraged by dry climatic conditions during a certain period, but conversely, in a later period, it may be that increasingly wet conditions necessitate the construction of trackways in order to maintain pre-existing routes of communication. At some times it may be a sudden change in conditions that could drive a near-immediate response, but at other times it may be that a response to environmental conditions is prompted by longer-term trends, perhaps where social and economic networks were resilient to shorter-term environmental change. In this hypothetical example the relationship between trackway construction and environmental conditions changes across time and space and so these data would not show a linear relationship. But can the absence of a *linear* relationship truly prove the absence of a meaningful association given that climate change, albeit in opposite directions, drove trackway construction during both periods? If it is not realistic to always expect linear relationships between human behaviour and environmental conditions, then other ways of measuring, evaluating and discussing past human–environment interactions are needed.

Theoretical underpinnings: challenges and novel approaches

There have been challenges to the dominance of functionalist and economically deterministic approaches in environmental archaeology.[76] Lesley Head has discussed the 'trouble' that physical geographers (and palaeoecologists) are having with 'culture' and goes on to discuss ways in which approaches based on contingency, borrowed from the humanities, may offer better interpretive frameworks. Head argues that human society and the natural environment are mutually constituted,[77] and has subsequently gone on to challenge the very concept of 'human impacts' on the environment.[78] Environmentally deterministic models

---

[76] Evans, *Environmental archaeology and the social order*.
[77] Lesley Head, *Cultural landscapes and environmental change* (London, 2000), 3, 8.
[78] Lesley Head, 'Is the concept of human impacts past its use-by date?', *The Holocene* 18:3 (2008), 373.

of human–environment relationships have, rightly, been largely rejected as over-simplistic,[79] and, in the case of the Irish peatland archaeological record, are not supported by the data.[80] Nevertheless, natural places were clearly significant to past societies,[81] and palaeoenvironmental work provides objective representations of past environments through which social relationships were explored.[82] Thus, adopting conceptual models that emphasise contingent relationships might provide a more useful understanding of the archaeology of wetlands.[83]

Whilst many scientists and physical geographers are having 'trouble' with culture,[84] researchers within the humanities have begun to engage with the science of climate change.[85] One product of this engagement is the concept of resilience and the development of resilience theory, which has recently become prominent in archaeological and palaeoenvironmental studies, which are developing their own increasingly sophisticated terminology.[86] In essence, resilience theory is concerned with studying how past societies adapted and responded to challenges posed by changing environments, whilst at the same time recognising that past societies are embedded in a complex of contingent social and ecological processes and relationships.

A further point of contact between the humanities and human–environment studies is to be found within literary criticism. Ecocriticism, defined as 'the study of the relationship between literature and the physical environment',[87] is a branch of criticism that has developed in recent decades in response to growing awareness of environmental change. Greg Garrard highlights a number of recurrent themes, common in ecocritical readings of literary texts such as 'pollution', 'wilderness', 'apocalypse' and 'dwelling', which may have relevance to interpretations of past human–environment interactions.[88] Garrard's discussion of tragic and comic time – the former 'predetermined and epochal', the latter 'open-ended and episodic'[89] – resonates with debates around past human–environment

---

[79] Thomas, 'Silent running'; Coombes and Barber, 'Environmental determinism in Holocene research'.
[80] Plunkett *et al.*, 'Environmental indifference?'.
[81] Bradley, *An archaeology of natural places*; O'Sullivan, 'Exploring past people's interactions with wetland environments in Ireland'.
[82] Evans, *Environmental archaeology and the social order*.
[83] Head, *Cultural landscapes and environmental change*.
[84] Head, *Cultural landscapes and environmental change*, 3.
[85] Timothy Clark, *Ecocriticism on the edge: the Anthropocene as a threshold concept* (London, 2015).
[86] C.L. Redman, 'Resilience theory in archaeology', *American Anthropologist* 107:1 (2005), 70–77; Marcel Bradtmöller, Sonja Grimm and Julien Riel-Salvatore, 'Resilience theory in archaeological practice – an annotated review', *Quaternary International* 446 (2017), 3–16.
[87] Cheryll Glotflety and Frederick Morgan (eds), *The ecocriticsm reader: landmarks in literary ecology* (London, 1996), xix.
[88] Greg Garrard, *Ecocriticism*, 2nd ed., New Critical Idiom (London and New York, 2012).
[89] Garrard, *Ecocriticism*, 95.

interactions, deterministic models equating to the 'tragic' readings of time, and contingency to 'comic'. Resonances like these might force archaeologists to be more critically aware of assumptions that underpin interpretive models, for example: might ecocritical discussion of the concept of 'ecophobia' (an aversion or fear of the natural world) and its identification in literary texts[90] be revealing about the way in which we expect people to have responded to past environmental change?

Beyond providing 'food for thought' for environmental archaeologists, ecocriticism might also lead towards novel interpretive methodologies; might archaeo-environmental datasets be 'read' in the same way that ecocritics read literary texts? Simon Estok, in calling for the 'narrativizing [of] science', argues that literature and science are intrinsically similar in that they are both ways of telling stories to explain why we are here.[91] Timothy Clark describes a way of reading a text at a variety of increasingly broad spatial and chronological scales, using the example of 'Elephant', a 1981 short story. Readings encompassed an initial, personal, scale, a second national-cultural scale, and a third, 'unframed' long-term global-scale reading that emphasises the now dominant effect that modern western material infrastructure is having on global ecosystems.[92] Perhaps a similar 'unframed' approach applied to archaeology might resolve the challenges of chronological and spatial scaling that bedevil studies of human–environment interactions. Crucially, Clark makes the point that 'reading at several scales at once cannot be just concerned with the abolition of one scale in the greater claim of another' but should instead enrich and creatively inform reading.[93]

A case study: Littleton bogs, Co. Tipperary North

The themes discussed above are illustrated using records from the Littleton group of bogs (Fig. 1, D). These are intended to illustrate the limitations and challenges of a typical small archaeo-environmental dataset, and the potential pitfalls, challenges and opportunities provided by multiple interpretive approaches. The sites – Inchirourke bog, Longfordpass bog, Littleton bog and Killeen bog – are all milled peat production bogs forming part of a chain of bogs stretching approximately 40km between the Slieve Bloom mountains to the north and Cashel to the south (Fig. 3).

Archaeological investigations in these bogs began in the mid-twentieth century when Etienne Rynne carried out the first investigations on the large Late Bronze Age trackway (TN-LTN001, Fig. 1, bottom) at Littleton.[94] Following more recent survey in 2006, features from the four bogs were

---

[90] S.C. Estok, 'Narrativizing science: the ecocritical imagination and ecophobia,' *Configurations* 18:1–2 (2010), 141–59; Clark, *Ecocriticism on the edge*, 109–12.
[91] Estok, 'Narrativizing science'.
[92] Clark, 'Scale framing: a reading', *Ecocriticism on the edge*, 97–114.
[93] Clark, *Ecocriticism,* 108.
[94] Etienne Rynne, 'Toghers in Littleton bog, Co. Tipperary', *North Munster Antiquarian Journal* 9 (1965), 138–44.

Irish peatland archaeology in relation to Holocene environmental and climate change

Fig. 3—Location of sites in the Littleton chain of bogs, Co. Tipperary North. Quartered circles show the location of the core samples and the general locations of the archaeological excavations are indicated by the dashed rectangles.

excavated between 2008 and 2010.[95] These investigations revealed timber structures of various kinds, of which a broadly representative sample were dated. Dendrochronological and radiocarbon dates for these structures are

---

[95] N. Rohan and Jane Whitaker, 'Preliminary report on archaeological excavations in Lurgoe townland, Killeen bog, Co. Tipperary', Unpublished report (Kells, 2011); Jane Whitaker, 'Preliminary report on archaeological excavations in Inchirourke townland: Inchirourke bog, Co. Tipperary', Unpublished report (Kells, 2011); S. Turrell, 'Excavations in Littleton bog, Co. Tipperary for Bord Na Móna Ltd', Unpublished report (Kells, 2008).

Table 1—Dendrochronological dates from trackways in the Littleton bogs.

Feature	Site	Type	Felling date
TN-IRK001	Inchirourke	Plank path	After 1607 BC
TN-LTN006	Littleton	Plank path	1571±9 BC
			1502±9 BC
			1522±9 BC
TN-LFP005	Longfordpass	Plank path	1559±9 BC
TN-LFP003	Longfordpass	Roundwood path	After 1035 BC
TN-LFP002	Longfordpass	Plank path	After 1004 BC
TN-LFP001	Longfordpass	Corduroy trackway	After 986 BC

given in Table 1 and Table 2, respectively.[96] Trackway construction in these bogs is broadly clustered in four main phases. The Middle Bronze Age, when plank paths at Inchirourke (TN-IRK001), Longfordpass (TN-LFP005) and Littleton (TN-LTN006 (Fig. 1, top right) and TN-LTN002) are all potentially contemporary and have direct parallels with similar plank paths Cooleeny 22 and Derryfadda 23, excavated only a few kilometres to the north.[97] The Late Bronze Age, with TN-LFP003, TN-LFP002, and corduroy trackways TN-LFP001 and TN-LTN001 all potentially contemporary, and all possibly part of the same communication network, the latter also associated with the, apparently votive, deposition of a Class IV bronze sword (NMI1990.25) within the timbers of a repair phase.[98] During the Iron Age, activity appears to be confined to Littleton bog, and comprises a number of brushwood trackways and platforms. And finally, activity during the very late Iron Age or early medieval periods was concentrated in Killeen bog and appears to be focused on the nearby dryland island of Derrynaflan, the site of a monastic foundation and a ninth-century metalwork hoard.[99]

After drilling a series of boreholes to characterise the underlying basins, one location at each bog was sampled to provide sequences of peat cores for palaeoenvironmental analysis. The cores were logged and subsampled for peat humification, plant macrofossil and testate amoebae analyses, and radiocarbon dating.[100]

---

[96] Terminology for trackway types follows Raftery, *Trackway excavations in the Mountdillon bogs*, 211–18.

[97] Sarah Cross May et al., 'Catalogue of wetland sites', in Gowen, O'Neill and Phillips (eds), *The Lisheen mine archaeological project 1996–8*, 223, 233.

[98] A.L. Brindley, 'Tomorrow is another day: some radiocarbon dates for Irish bronze artefacts', in W.H. Metz, B.L. Van Beek and H. Steegstra (eds), *PATINA, essays presented to Jay Jordan Butler on the occasion of his 80th Birthday*, (Gronigen, 2001), 155.

[99] M. Ryan, 'An early Christian hoard from Derrynaflan, Co. Tipperary', *North Munster Antiquarian Journal* 22 (1980), 9–26; Michael Ryan, 'The Derrynaflan hoard and early Irish art', *Speculum* 72:4 (1997), 995–1017.

[100] Stastney, Young and Branch, 'The identification of Late-Holocene bog bursts at Littleton bog, Ireland'; Stastney, 'The late prehistoric "Dark Age" in Ireland and climate

TABLE 2—Radiocarbon dates from peatland structures in the Littleton bogs.

Feature	Site	Type	Lab code	14C date (BP)	Calibrated date (95% confidence)
TN-LTN002	Littleton	Plank path	BETA-222650	3300±70	1750–1710 cal BC (4.6%)1700–1430 cal BC (90.4%)
TN-LTN001	Littleton	Corduroy trackway	BETA-222649	2860±50	1200–900 cal BC (95%)
TN-KLN004	Killeen	Platform	BETA-222646	2550±70	830–430 cal BC (95%)
TN-LFP004	Longfordpass	Archaeological wood (animal trap?)	BETA-222648	2360±50	750–680 cal BC (8.7%)670–640 cal BC (2.7%)590–575 cal BC (0.5%)565–350 cal BC (82.2%)280–250 cal BC (0.9%)
TN-LTN009	Littleton	Brushwood trackway	BETA-222652	2220±50	400–170 cal BC (95%)
TN-LTN028	Littleton	Brushwood trackway	BETA-222655	2170±70	390–50 cal BC (95%)
TN-LTN029	Littleton	Brushwood trackway	BETA-222656	2180±70	390–50 cal BC (95%)
TN-LTN010	Littleton	Brushwood trackway	BETA-222653	2100±70	360–270 cal BC (13.2%)260 cal BC–cal AD 30 (81.2%)cal AD 40–50 (0.6%)
TN-LTN004	Littleton	Brushwood trackway	BETA-222651	2040±60	200 cal BC–cal AD 80 (95%)
TN-LTN031	Littleton	Platform	BETA-222657	2010±60	180 cal BC–cal AD 90 (93%)cal AD 100–130 (2%)
TN-LTN030	Littleton	Platform	UBA-11366	2001±32	90–75 cal BC (1.9%)60 cal BC–cal AD 75 (93.1%)
TN-LTN017	Littleton	Platform	UBA-11363	1880±21	cal AD 70–180 (86.4%)cal AD 190–215 (8.5%)
TN-LTN025	Littleton	Platform	UBA-11365	1865±19	cal AD 85–220 (95%)
TN-LTN024	Littleton	Platform	UBA-11364	1814±18	cal AD 130–245 (95%)
			BETA-222654	1740±60	cal AD 140–400 (95%)
TN-KLN002	Killeen	Corduroy trackway	BETA-222645	1720±60	cal AD 130–430 (95%)
TN-KLN007	Killeen	Roundwood path	BETA-222647	1290±60	cal AD 640–890 (95%)

69

As the sites are former ombrotrophic raised bogs, water table levels in these mires would have previously been at least partly controlled by changes in precipitation balance[101] and records of past BSW should therefore contain a climatic signal as well as recording local changes, although, as discussed above, disentangling local and climatic influences is complex. Fig. 4 shows the reconstructed water table records from each site, generated using the European testate amoebae transfer function and expressed as standard deviations from the mean,[102] plotted against the weighted mean age depth model for each core generated using the Bacon software package.[103] Positive values indicate drier conditions, negative values indicate wetter. Potentially synchronous wet-shifts at around 1100 BC, 800 BC and 200 BC at Inchirourke and Longfordpass, the latter also evident at Littleton, and sharp shifts to drier conditions – possible bog bursts – coinciding at Littleton and Killeen at around AD 600, indicate at least some climatic influence on the water table data from these bogs. A tuned and stacked composite record, generated using the same procedures as a previously published composite record from Northern Britain,[104] is also shown. Although the 'tuning and stacking' methodology has been extensively criticised,[105] and is not advocated here, the stacked record is shown as an example of a 'regional' record for comparison with the individual site records.

Summed probability density functions (PDFs) of the radiocarbon dated archaeological structures are also shown in Fig. 4 as shaded curves along the bottom of each panel. To facilitate comparison with the other datasets and to allow their inclusion in the PDFs, dendrochronological dates were converted to equivalent radiocarbon date ranges using the 'Simulate' function in OxCal v4.3.[106]

---

fluctuation'; Phil Stastney, 'Examining the relationships between Holocene climate change, hydrology and human society in Ireland', unpublished PhD Thesis, University of Reading, 2015.

[101] D.J. Charman, 'Summer water deficit variability controls on peatland water-table changes: implications for Holocene palaeoclimate reconstructions', *The Holocene* 17:2 (2007), 217–27; Barber and Langdon, 'What drives the peat-based palaeoclimate record?'; Barber and Charman, 'Holocene palaeoclimate records from peatlands'.

[102] Amesbury *et al.*, 'Development of a new pan-European testate amoeba transfer function'.

[103] Blaauw and Christen, 'Flexible paleoclimate age-depth models using an autoregressive gamma process'.

[104] Charman *et al.*, 'Compilation of non-annually resolved Holocene proxy climate records'.

[105] Blaauw, 'The integration of ice core, marine and terrestrial records of the last termination (INTIMATE) 60,000 to 8000 BP'; G.T. Swindles *et al.*, 'Examining the uncertainties in a "tuned and stacked" peatland water table reconstruction', *Quaternary International* 268 (2012), 58–64.

[106] Bronk Ramsey, 'Radiocarbon calibration and analysis of stratigraphy'; Christopher Bronk Ramsey, 'Development of the radiocarbon calibration program', *Radiocarbon* 43:2A (2001), 355–63; Christopher Bronk Ramsey *et al.*, 'Developments in the calibration and modelling of radiocarbon dates', *Radiocarbon* 53:2 (2010), 953–61; Christopher

Irish peatland archaeology in relation to Holocene environmental and climate change

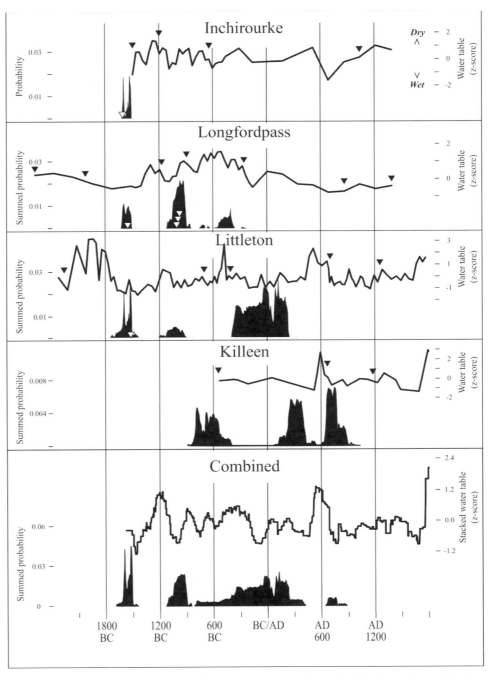

Fig. 4—Archaeological and bog surface wetness data from the Littleton bogs. Black filled curves are summed probability density functions of the dated peatland structures, and the black lines represent testate amoebae-derived reconstructed water tables from the individual bogs (top four panels), and a composite tuned-and-stacked water table record (bottom panel). Filled triangles indicate the position of dated horizons in the water table records, and unfilled triangles indicate dendrochronological dates from archaeological features.

The use of summed PDFs as a proxy for human activity,[107] although widespread within archaeology and Quaternary science,[108] has been criticised both for inherent potential for taphonomic bias[109] and the tendency to aggregate statistical scatter, thus over-estimating the duration of activity.[110] Furthermore, the conversion of dendrochronological dates to inherently less precise radiocarbon dates is naturally counter-intuitive, and is not advocated as a methodology here, but is instead intended to illustrate the complexities inherent in comparing datasets of varying chronological resolutions. Nevertheless, PDFs are used here to illustrate comparison of archaeological and palaeoenvironmental data 'by eye', and allow the calculation of correlations between the two datasets to illustrate the application, and shortcomings, of such an approach.

Visual comparison and correlations

Visual comparisons show no obvious trends. Peaks in the combined PDF from the sites seem to somewhat coincide with dips in the stacked water table record – especially the apparent peak in trackway construction and wet shift at around 1000 BC, although this is not so apparent in the records from the individual sites, since this same peak in the Longfordpass PDF seems to coincide with a period of drier local conditions. The earliest peak in activity, during the Middle Bronze Age, reflecting the potentially contemporary plank paths at three of the bogs, appears to occur at a time of major environmental change at Inchirourke and Littleton, as indicated by the transition from fen to bog.[111] At other periods there is little correspondence between the datasets, except that sharp peaks in the water tables at Littleton and Killeen – probable bog bursts – seem to coincide with lulls in trackway construction.

Unsurprisingly, there were no significant correlations between datasets from individual sites (Longfordpass $r = -0.27$; Littleton $r = -0.27$; Killeen $r = -0.13$), and the correlation obtained between the stacked water table and combined PDF is similarly weak, albeit statistically significant ($r = -0.24$, $p < 0.001$). Although all these relationships are negative – that is when drier

---

Bronk Ramsey, 'Methods for summarizing radiocarbon datasets', *Radiocarbon* 59:2 (2017), 1809–33.

[107] J.W. Rick, 'Dates as data: an examination of the Peruvian pre-ceramic radiocarbon record', *American Antiquity* 52:1 (1987), 55–73; Tom Aitchison, Barbara Ottaway and A.S. Al Ruzaiza, 'Summarizing a group of 14C dates on the historical time scale: with a worked example from the late Neolithic of Bavaria', *Antiquity* 65 (1991), 108–16.

[108] A.N. Williams, 'The use of summed radiocarbon probability distributions in archaeology: a review of methods', *Journal of Archaeological Science* 39:3 (2012), 578–89.

[109] T.A. Surovell *et al.*, 'Correcting temporal frequency distributions for taphonomic bias', *Journal of Archaeological Science* 36:8 (2009), 1715–24.

[110] Bayliss *et al.*, 'Bradshaw and Bayes', 9–11.

[111] Stastney, Young and Branch, 'The identification of Late-Holocene bog bursts at Littleton bog, Ireland'.

BSW conditions are indicated the level of activity indicated by the PDF tends to be lower – this relationship is too weak to be convincing and seems to be largely an artefact of the correspondence between the possible bog bursts and gaps in the archaeological records at Littleton and Killeen.

Interpretation 1: environmental determinism

An environmentally deterministic interpretation would require a strong relationship between the palaeoenvironmental and archaeological records that should hold true at both the local and regional scale, and this does not exist. A statistically significant correlation was obtained between the combined PDF and stacked BSW curve, but this relationship is too weak to adequately explain the variation observed in the archaeological record.

Interpretation 2: environmental indifference

The opposite of a deterministic interpretation might be that people were entirely indifferent to the bog surface conditions they encountered. Such an interpretation would be consistent with the lack of correlation between the records, but would not explain the local associations like the apparent coincidence between the establishment of the system of Middle Bronze Age plank paths and the transition from fen to raised bog at Inchirourke and Littleton, and the lulls in trackway construction at Littleton and Killeen coinciding with the possible bog bursts. Instead, these patterns suggest an active engagement with local environmental conditions, although those conditions do not absolutely determine patterns of human activity.

Interpretation 3: resilience

Resilience might, arguably, be inferred in the data from these bogs. The archaeological records from the site show a long-lived pattern of trackway construction spanning more than two and a half millennia, maintained through numerous periods of both environmental and cultural change (from the Bronze Age to the early medieval period). A certain level of continuity, as expressed by long-term repetition or re-occurrence of patterns of activity and connectivity, is evident in the apparent renewal of significant routeways, sometimes separated by considerable gaps in time – as at Killeen where TN-KLN002 and TN-KLN007, are built on similar alignments perhaps more than 500 years apart – a reflection, perhaps of the notion of trackways as physical manifestations of long-lived routeways, potentially much earlier in origin.[112] Resilience appears to offer a model that fits the data from the Littleton bogs reasonably well, accommodating long-term

---

[112] Henry Chapman, *Iconoclasm in later prehistory* (London, 2018), 174.

continuity and episodic renewal of activity as well as local engagement with, and adaption to, environmental changes.

Interpretation 4: scale framing

Finally, how could a series of interpretations, at multiple spatial and chronological scales, inspired by Timothy Clark's 'unframed' approach to reading the short story 'Elephant',[113] inform interpretations of the data from these bogs? The smallest scale at which the evidence can be read is that of the individual features, each viewed in isolation and compared with the contemporary environmental data from the same bog. At this scale, no meaningful patterns can be discerned: some trackways seem to be built during relatively dry periods, others during wet periods. At this scale, the difficulty in comparing chronologies is highlighted, given the dating uncertainties of both the archaeology and of the palaeoenvironmental data. This first scale is clearly naïve in that it can only reveal anything useful if there is a simple, linear relationship, which in any case, could hardly be discerned given the inherent chronological uncertainties of the data.

A second level of reading might expand the chronological perspective to consider the whole span of time recorded by the archaeo-environmental data from a single bog. At this scale, depending on which bog is being examined, there do appear to be some weak associations, but these are not consistent across sites. At the second scale, the dominant story seems to be one of episodic trackway construction, accompanied by a similarly episodic and variable pattern of environmental change. At this scale any vague patterns linking trackway construction to BSW appear to be localised, contingent phenomena.

Reading at the third scale entails attempting a consideration of the data as a whole, across all four bogs, and spanning a large portion of the Late Holocene. At this scale, the short-term episodic chronological tempo observed at the second scale disappears, and is instead replaced by a spread of near-continuous human activity on these bogs. At this scale, of course, the uncertainties inherent in radiocarbon dates are blurred, further reducing chronological resolution; but it is not the duration of individual events or even their frequency that is evident at the third scale, but rather the overall distribution and general chronological spread that is highlighted. At this scale, regional and local trends are conflated, and so, at first glance, this tells us little about past human–environment interactions. However, what is emphasised is a wider impression of millennia of human dwelling in these once dynamic environments. To the builders of the latest trackway at Killeen in the early medieval period, the people who built the first plank paths during the Middle Bronze Age were far more distant in time than we are to them; and yet, consider how much has changed in so short a period of time: a dynamic landscape of peatlands that people had lived in and around for twenty centuries or more has now largely disappeared. This is a salutary

---

[113] Clark, *Ecocriticism on the edge*.

lesson about the extent of the ecological destruction caused by humans in recent centuries, and how this destruction has not only altered the landscape but also distanced modern societies from those of the past.

Discussion

The data from this case study, in common with other Ireland-wide syntheses,[114] show that linear correlations between BSW and the archaeological data are weak at best, and so deterministic models of interpretation seem inadequate. By producing multiple interpretations, however, the importance of spatial and chronological scale are highlighted, and at some scales contingent relationships between environmental conditions and trackway construction become apparent. Variability in palaeoenvironmental and archaeological data examined on a site-by-site basis exhibit 'temporality … consonant with human dwelling'.[115] In other words, hydrological change at each bog appears at times to occur over timescales that are likely to have been perceived within the span of a single human lifetime, or at least a few generations. In some cases, for example at Littleton, a series of rapid shifts to dry conditions may be the result of bog bursts occurring over much shorter timescales, within a single day. Although no consistent linear relationship is evident between BSW and the construction of archaeological structures in the case study, patterns of environmental and archaeological change show a variety of contingent relationships reflecting the 'temporality of the landscape'[116] and the phenomenological experience[117] of living in and around these environments.

At the regional scale, comparisons between archaeological and palaeoenvironmental records[118] are confounded not only by the scale of chronological uncertainties but also by the degree of local variability of both records. It is also clear that there is no simple, predictable, relationship between human activity and environmental conditions in raised bogs. Instead, trackways are constructed as a result of the interaction between social and/or economic imperatives (the maintenance of routes of exchange or communication, the religious or ritual significance of dryland 'islands', or the importance of activities, ritual or otherwise, on the bogs themselves) and a response to the specific environmental characteristics of the bogs (wet, soft, marshy ground, uneven surface, pools, hummocks etc.). As such trackways cannot be understood without considering their specific environmental context. Indeed, many 'socio-economic' and 'environmental' factors may be inextricably linked: for example, dryland islands were considered appropriate locations for monastic sites, such as Derrynaflan, precisely because they were surrounded by wetlands, thus necessitating the construction

---

[114] Plunkett *et al.*, 'Environmental indifference?'
[115] Timothy Ingold, 'The temporality of the landscape', *World Archaeology* 25:2 (1993), 168.
[116] *Sensu* Ingold, 'The temporality of the landscape'.
[117] *Sensu* Tilley, *A phenomenology of landscape*.
[118] Such as Plunkett *et al.*, 'Environmental indifference?'

of communication routes to them. Although relationships may not be linear or predictable, understanding the environmental context of individual archaeological sites is important. Such relationships are contingent and variable, and therefore may be best explored on a site-by-site basis.

The challenges posed by comparing different chronologies notwithstanding, the actual meaning of gaps or lulls in trackway construction may also be problematic. The length of time that any one trackway might have been in use is rarely clear, but where this has been directly investigated, estimates range from less than a year, in the case of Cooleeny 31 which was partially destroyed by a bog burst,[119] to less than a decade at Corlea 1 in Co. Longford,[120] up to 20–40 years or more in the case of Killoran 18, in Derryville bog.[121] The variability in lifespan of trackways will undoubtedly affect the ultimate resolution at which, even with perfect annually-resolved chronologies, causal relationships between trackway construction and environmental conditions can be examined. The approach adopted by Gearey and Caseldine, where the average *rate* of site construction was calculated and compared with environmental data,[122] may offer a partial solution, but this is only really practicable at sites subject to full excavation and where almost every trackway or platform is dated such as Derryville, an exercise unlikely to be repeated regularly.

It has been suggested that trackways represent a formalisation of pre-existing routeways through the landscape.[123] If so, the frequency of use of such routes will similarly affect how quickly trackway construction could respond to any external determining factor. This will undoubtedly vary according to the type of route formalised by a trackway and the sorts of activities facilitated by its use. Derryville bog again provides one of the few studies where a distinction could be clearly drawn between trackways traversing the entire bog, which may have been part of long-distance communication networks, and those that appeared to facilitate access *into* the bog; it is notable that trackways in the first category were rare, and therefore their construction was highly sporadic, whilst those in the second category were far more numerous, and their use and construction was so frequent as to give the impression of near-continuous activity.[124] This example also illustrates the mixing of scales inherent in the peatland archaeological record, in this case activity relating to a large spatial scale being chronologically

---

[119] Gowen, O'Neill and Phillips (eds), *The Lisheen mine archaeological project 1996–8*, 364.

[120] Wil Casparie and A. Moloney, 'Corlea 1. Palaeo-environmental aspects of the trackway', in Barry Raftery (ed.), *Trackway excavations in the Mountdillon bogs, Co. Longford, 1985–1991*, Irish Archaeological Wetland Unit Transactions 3 (Dublin, 1996), 367–77.

[121] Gowen, O'Neill, and Phillips, *The Lisheen mine archaeological project 1996–8*, 63.

[122] Gearey and Caseldine, 'Archaeological applications of testate amoebae analyses'.

[123] Henry Chapman, *Iconoclasm and later prehistory* (London, 2018), 174; Christopher Tilley, 'Round barrows and dykes as landscape metaphors', *Cambridge Archaeological Journal* 14:2 (2004), 185–203.

[124] Gowen, O'Neill and Phillips, *The Lisheen mine archaeological project 1996–8*, 364–65.

restricted to discrete episodes, whilst much more localised activity seems to be more intense and so apparently quasi-continuous.

A further contrast produced by the mixing of scales is found in the distinction between *climatic* and *environmental* change in relation to the peatland archaeological record: all climatic change is environmental change, but not all environmental change is necessarily 'climate-driven'; some scale effects are evident here. Consider the related distinction between weather and climate as we experience it in the present day: a widely accepted definition being that 'weather refers to short-term changes in the atmosphere, climate describes what the weather is like over a long period of time in a specific area'.[125] This distinction is both an issue of chronological *and* spatial scale. In the archaeological and palaeoenvironmental archives, almost everything is viewed from a longer-term perspective. As far as these abstract notions can be unpicked, the distinction is, however, almost always expressed at the *spatial* scale: regional coherence of palaeoenvironmental records is read (quite sensibly, of course) as climatic forcing, whilst discordance is typically thought to indicate more localised, shorter term or autogenic environmental change. When considering the relationship between peatland palaeoenvironmental archives and trackways, a number of complicating factors emerge: studies that have focused on individual large trackways have shown that these usually cross diverse bog micro-habitats spanning a wide range of wetness conditions.[126] And whilst the climatic sensitivity of ombrotrophic peatlands is well established,[127] not all parts of a raised mire system are always thought to be equally responsive to climatic influence.[128] By extension this may suggest that not all bogs are equally sensitive to climate due to site-specific internal feedback mechanisms.[129]

Furthermore, comparison of records from across Ireland has shown that coherence of the BSW record is often poor except at periods of heightened climatic variability.[130] *Climate* 'happens' all the time, but could this mean that some or all peatland records are only *climate-driven* at key periods of rapid change? It is clear therefore that in the peatland archaeo-environmental record, climate and environment are intricately, perhaps even hopelessly, entwined. If separating

---

[125] NOAA, 'What's the difference between weather and climate?', National Centers for Environmental Information (NCEI), 2018, www.ncei.noaa.gov/news/weather-vs-climate.

[126] e.g. Casparie and Moloney, 'Corlea 1. Palaeo-environmental aspects of the trackway'.

[127] Aaby, 'Cyclic climatic variations in climate over the past 5,500 yr reflected in raised bogs'; Barber, *Peat stratigraphy and climatic change*.

[128] Barber, 'Peatlands as scientific archives of past biodiversity', 483; K.E. Barber *et al.*, 'Replicability and variability of the recent macrofossil and proxy-climate record from raised bogs: field stratigraphy and macrofossil data from Bolton Fell Moss and Walton Moss, Cumbria, England', *Journal of Quaternary Science* 13:6 (1998), 527.

[129] G.T. Swindles *et al.*, 'Ecohydrological feedbacks confound peat-based climate reconstructions', *Geophysical Research Letters* 39;11 (2012).

[130] Swindles *et al.*, 'Centennial-scale climate change in Ireland during the Holocene'.

climate from other *environmental* change in our palaeoenvironmental proxy records is so difficult, what should this mean for the questions that we ask of the data and the way we interpret the results? A recent study from Germany explicitly avoided any attempt to distinguish climate from non-climatic environmental change, instead comparing dates of individual trackways to 'short-term environmental changes' and found a consistent association between wetter conditions and trackway construction.[131] Certainly it would seem sensible at least to acknowledge the difficulty in achieving a clear separation between climatic and non-climatic environmental change in peatland palaeoecological records, and to be wary of attempting to treat 'climate' as an independent variable that can be correlated with the archaeological record. Some previous studies have implied a clear and unproblematic separation between 'natural' environments, landscapes and processes, and 'human' factors, such as societies, sites and artefacts, cultural landscapes and cultural processes.[132] This duality is expressed as one between 'natural' climate change and processes of bog ecosystems on the one hand, and the social act of constructing trackways, and the cultural choices, technological and economic imperatives that this entails on the other. In this line of reasoning, it follows that since the 'natural' and the 'human' factors are independent variables, the lack of a clear correlation between the two lines of evidence imply that natural processes do not play an important role in cultural processes. There would be little room for contingency in these relationships. It is argued here that the absence of contingency in these theoretical models restricts their usefulness. If the 'natural' and the 'human' are so easily separable and environmentally deterministic models of human activity so obviously fail to account for the evidence at hand, what is the point of studying human–environment interactions at all? Contingency provides a more useful model. This is based on the belief that human and natural influences are mutually constituted and thus inseparable, that the boundaries between the human and the natural are in fact socially constructed.[133] Contingency 'highlights the historical and local specificity that has to be accounted for in complete understanding and effective manipulation of ecological systems'.[134]

There is abundant evidence for contingent relationships in Irish prehistory: the ritual importance of wet places in the prehistory of Ireland as evidenced by the votive deposition of metalwork in bogs, lakes and streams, especially during the Bronze Age;[135] and the siting of *fulachtaí fiadh* beside streams and at

---

[131] Achterberg *et al.*, 'Contemporaneousness of trackway construction and environmental change: a dendrochronological study in northwest-German mires', 26.

[132] These studies draw upon C. Sauer, 'The morphology of landscape', *University of California Publications in Geography* 2:2 (1925), 19–54.

[133] Head, *Cultural landscapes and environmental change*, 7–8.

[134] V.T. Parker *et al.*, *Restoration ecology and sustainable development* (Cambridge, 1997), 18.

[135] Bradley, *The passage of arms*.

the edges of bogs during similar periods;[136] bog bodies, deposited mostly during the Iron Age;[137] the location of monastic and other ecclesiastical foundations in the early medieval period;[138] and the construction, use and changing meanings of *crannóga* into the medieval period.[139] These examples are rooted in what might be thought of as primarily 'cultural' processes reflecting economic practices, religious beliefs and social mores, but no satisfactory interpretation of any of them can fail to take account of their embeddedness within the 'natural' environment. There is clearly a dialectical relationship between changing environments, changing perceptions and connotations of these environments, and social change. Understanding these historically contingent dialectical relationships is a central part of understanding and interpreting past human activities and should be a focus for future research. Models that emphasise contingency, such as resilience theory,[140] as well as other developments in the humanities, including the emerging field of ecocriticism,[141] may provide valuable new ways of thinking, discussing, reading and 'narrativising'[142] these relationships, that may be fruitfully explored by researchers seeking to make sense of the relationships between past societies and environmental change.

Conclusions and future directions

To conclude we return to the questions outlined in the introduction in order to make recommendations on the direction of future research into past human–environment interactions in Irish peatlands.

What are the methodological challenges inherent in comparing the archaeological and palaeoenvironmental datasets obtained from Irish bogs?

Broadly, the comparison of archaeological and palaeoenvironmental datasets from Irish peatlands is complicated by challenges in three areas: chronological uncertainty, which affects both datasets, and which is multiplied when comparing datasets; issues of spatial scale, which are complicated by the fact that both palaeoenvironmental and archaeological datasets use observations made at small spatial scales to make inferences at much larger scales; and the complexity of

---

[136] John Waddell, *The prehistoric archaeology of Ireland* (Galway, 1998), 174; O'Sullivan, 'Exploring past people's interactions with wetland environments in Ireland', 162.
[137] Brindley and Lanting, 'Irish bog bodies'; Aldhouse-Green, *Bog bodies uncovered*.
[138] L.M. Bitel, *Isle of the saints: monastic settlement and Christian community in early Ireland* (Cork, 1990).
[139] Christina Frendengren, *Crannogs: a study of people's interaction with lakes, with special reference to Loch Gara in the north west of Ireland* (Bray, 2002).
[140] Redman, 'Resilience theory in archaeology'.
[141] Garrard, *Ecocriticism*; Serpil Oppermann et al. (eds), *The future of ecocriticism: new horizons* (Newcastle upon Tyne, 2011).
[142] Estok, 'Narrativizing science'.

response between the phenomena we wish to study (e.g. climate change or social organisation) and the evidence used as a proxy for them (e.g. BSW or trackway construction), a phenomenon referred to here as 'non-linearity'.

What underlying theoretical assumptions underpin existing interpretations of past human–environment interactions in Irish bogs? Could theoretical developments in other disciplines offer any new insights?

Existing interpretative models of human–environment interactions in Irish bogs have tended to rely on a clear separation between 'natural' and 'cultural' factors in order to evaluate their relative influence on past human activity. Challenges to this have emerged from several sources, most prominently from the humanities, and in response, new models that see human society and nature as being mutually constituted have emerged.[143] Meanwhile, in recent decades other disciplines such as literary criticism have begun to engage with the issue of environmental change, and the field of 'ecocriticism' has emerged to explore perceptions of and interactions with the natural world.[144]

How, armed with an understanding of the methodological challenges and recognition of the underlying theoretical assumptions, could such novel insights be applied in practice?

It is important to be realistic, both about how problematic the separations between 'social' and 'natural' influences, 'climatic' and 'non-climatic' environmental change are, and about the inherent uncertainties in the peatland archaeo-environmental archive. Whilst at first glance these challenges appear to be insurmountable, there are also opportunities: for example, awareness of the challenges and uncertainties may facilitate the exploration and evaluation of multiple interpretations of the same data. The 'scale framing' approach to reading literary texts may also prove useful. 'Reading' archaeo-environmental data at a variety of scales exposes the various effects of chronological and spatial scale in operation, and reveals differing perspectives on the same data depending on which scale they are being viewed from. At the broadest, 'unframed', perspective, the chronological uncertainties and variable spatial patterning of the data become blurred, and wider narratives about the long-term interactions between past societies and peatlands in Ireland become more prominent. At the unframed scale, the principal story to emerge is one of repeated, near-continuous, engagement between people and the peatland environment over several millennia which contrasts markedly with the disengagement and widespread degradation of the natural world in the present day.

---

[143] Head, *Cultural landscapes and environmental change*.
[144] Garrard, *Ecocriticism*; Clark, *Ecocriticism on the edge*.

Such narratives of the past may prove to be increasingly relevant as society struggles to come to terms with present and future climate change.[145]

Acknowledgements   This paper is based in large part on research carried out as part of a PhD project based at, and funded by, the School of Archaeology, Geography and Environmental Sciences, University of Reading, UK, and supervised by Professor Nick Branch and Dr Stuart Black. Access to the case study sites was provided by Bord na Móna plc. Support for dating the palaeoenvironmental sequences was provided by NERC and IQUA. Thanks also go to the two anonymous reviewers whose helpful comments greatly improved this manuscript. Finally, I would also like to thank Dr Suzi Richer and Dr Benjamin Gearey for their inspiring conversations that also contributed valuably to this paper.

---

[145] Estok, 'Narrativizing science'; Kintigh *et al.*, 'Grand challenges for archaeology'; P.J. Lane, 'Archaeology in the age of the Anthropocene: a critical assessment of its scope and societal contributions', *Journal of Field Archaeology* 40:5 (2015), 485–98.

Siccitas magna ultra modum[1]: examining the occurrence and societal impact of droughts in prehistoric Ireland

Gill Plunkett*
Archaeology and Palaeoecology, School of Natural and Built Environment, Queen's University Belfast, Northern Ireland

David M. Brown
Archaeology and Palaeoecology, School of Natural and Built Environment, Queen's University Belfast, Northern Ireland

Graeme T. Swindles
Geography, School of Natural and Built Environment, Queen's University Belfast, Northern Ireland
Ottawa-Carleton Geoscience Centre and Department of Earth Sciences, Carleton University, Ottawa, Ontario, Canada

[Accepted 19 July 2019. Published 25 March 2020]

Abstract — When considering past human–environment relationships in Ireland, we rarely contemplate the potentially detrimental effects of drought on populations. The summer of 2018 drew attention, however, to some of the ways in which reduced precipitation can impact on societies, even in an oceanic setting such as Ireland. Here, we examine ways in which we can identify the past occurrence of droughts through palaeoenvironmental records. We focus on three time intervals (*c.* 6200 BC, 3200 BC and 900 BC) for which there is evidence for centennial-scale droughts—drought phases—and consider the available archaeological and palynological records to evaluate whether the droughts may have triggered economic responses or population collapses. We find little evidence to confirm that any of these events undermined the subsistence base to the extent of triggering population collapse. We briefly explore alternative mechanisms by which the drought phases might have impacted upon human perception of their environment.

Introduction — Ireland is not a location known for its droughts. Rather, its frequent rainfall is internationally infamous, and a common source of conversation and

---

*Author's email: G.Plunkett@qub.ac.uk
ORCID iD: https://orcid.org/0000-0003-1014-3454
doi: https://doi.org/10.3318/PRIAC.2020.120.03
[1]This reference (translated 'An abnormally great drought') is from the *Annals of Ulster*, AD 764.7, celt.ucc.ie//published/T100001A/index.html.

consternation across the island. Yet the atypical hot, dry summer of 2018 (lasting from June to August), while lauded by many inhabitants, brought unexpected hardship to farmers, as grass growth declined and led to a shortage of fodder, and crops risked failing due to a lack of irrigation.[2] There were health consequences too, as larger than usual numbers of individuals presented to hospitals with severe cases of sunburn,[3] and in at least one instance, a child was admitted with a rare skin disease that may have been aggravated by the unusual heat.[4] All this transpired just months after the 'Beast from the East' saw an anticyclonic arctic airmass bring exceptional cold and heavy snow that caused considerable societal and economic disruption.[5]

While the extreme summer of 2018 may be symptomatic of the climate crisis that currently confronts us, droughts have featured in the Irish climate in the past. Instrumental climate records are of course a relatively recent innovation; for Ireland, the longest-running continuous sequence of weather data—from Armagh Observatory—was established a little over two centuries ago,[6] within which time the climate has emerged from the Little Ice Age and post-Industrial warming began. For an understanding of longer-term natural climate behaviour, one must turn to historical and palaeoenvironmental proxy records. An entry in the *Annals of Ulster* for the year AD 749 tells of 'Snow of unusual depth so that nearly all the cattle of the whole of Ireland perished, and the world afterwards was parched by unusual drought',[7] extremes that are rather reminiscent of the spring and summer of 2018. The consequences of droughts for farmers can also be gleaned from earlier chronicles: for example, the *Annals of Ulster* records for the year AD 773 an 'Unaccustomed drought and heat of the sun so that nearly all bread [grain] failed. Abundance of oak-mast afterwards'.[8] These references serve as salutary reminders of the detrimental societal impacts even one dry

---

[2] Rebekah Logan, 'NI Heatwave is posing challenges for some farmers', BBC News NI (3 July 2018), www.bbc.co.uk/news/uk-northern-ireland-44685611; Joe Leogue, 'Warm weather to continue but at cost to farmers', *Irish Examiner* (2 August 2018), www.irishexaminer.com/breakingnews/ireland/warm-weather-to-return-but-at-cost-to-farmers-859400.html.

[3] Ali Gordon, 'Heatwave sunburn: 220 people treated in NI hospitals', BBC News NI (20 July 2018), www.bbc.co.uk/news/uk-northern-ireland-44808082.

[4] Aisha Ijaz *et al.*, 'The hazards of an Irish heatwave; ecthyma', *Archives of Disease in Childhood* 104 (Supplement 3) (2019), A:246.

[5] Met Éireann, 'Storm Emma: An analysis of Storm Emma and the cold spell which struck Ireland between the 28th of February and the 4th of March 2018', www.met.ie/cms/assets/uploads/2019/02/EmmaReport2019.pdf.

[6] C.J. Butler *et al.*, 'Air temperatures at Armagh Observatory, Northern Ireland, from 1796 to 2002', *International Journal of Climatology* 25 (2005), 1055–79: 1056.

[7] *Annals of Ulster* 748.3, celt.ucc.ie//published/T100001A/index.html. This date has been corrected to AD 749 following synchronisation of sources by D.P. McCarthy, *Chronological synchronisation of the Irish Annals* (4th edition), www.scss.tcd.ie/misc/kronos/chronology/synchronisms/Edition_4/K_trad/K_synch.htm.

[8] *Annals of Ulster* 773.4, celt.ucc.ie//published/T100001A/index.html.

season can trigger. What then if such conditions persisted over many years as 'drought phases'? Palaeoenvironmental data suggest that they did.

One of the upsides of Ireland's pervasive wet climate is that it has resulted in ample bogs whose distinctive qualities have allowed them to capture records of past environmental change as they formed and accumulated peat through the millennia. Specifically, the inhibition of biological decay has ensured the partial preservation of plant and animal remains that once lived on the bogs, communities of which were strongly influenced by the degree of bog surface wetness. In peatlands that are independent of the water table (raised and blanket bogs), bog surface wetness is at least in part governed by climate: the drier and/or warmer the conditions, the drier the bog surface, while the colder and/or wetter the condition, the higher the water level at the bog surface. While the degree of wetness is therefore a product of both temperature and precipitation, it is thought that summer effective precipitation is the leading variable reflected in palaeohydrology records.[9] Examining changes in biotic communities preserved within the peat, linked as they are to bog surface wetness, can therefore yield indirect (proxy) records of past climate variability (Fig. 1). During drier phases, the peat itself will undergo a greater degree of decomposition (humification), so humification levels too are an index of past conditions. Subfossilised remains of bog oaks and pines also give insights into changing hydrological conditions through the dates of their establishment and die-off. Successful germination and establishment of such trees on bog surfaces will only occur during periods of lower water tables.[10]

Using a multi-proxy approach on peat sequences extending back to the Early Bronze Age (2500 BC), Swindles, Blundell and Roe identified three periods of potentially extended drought dating respectively to 1150–800 BC, 320 BC–AD 150 and AD 250–470, in addition to an extended period of drought in the post-Industrial era.[11] The climate signal in the upper levels of the bogs is, however, confounded by direct human impacts on bog hydrology, such as peatland drainage. A subsequent study entailing a wider selection of sites upheld the

---

[9] D.J. Charman *et al.*, 'Testing the relationship between Holocene peatland palaeoclimate reconstructions and instrumental data at two European sites', *Quaternary Science Reviews* 23 (2004), 137–43.

[10] D.N. McVean, 'Ecology of Scots pine in the Scottish Highlands', *Journal of Ecology* 51 (1963), 671–86: 672; J.R. Pilcher *et al.*, 'Hydrological data from the long Irish subfossil oak records', in J.S. Dean, D.M. Meko and T.W. Swetnam (eds), *Tree rings, environment, and humanity*. Proceedings of the International Conference, Tucson, Arizona, 17–21 May 1994. *Radiocarbon* (special issue) (1996), 259–64; A.K. Moir *et al.*, 'Dendrochronological evidence for a lower water-table on peatland around 3200–3000 BC from subfossil pine in northern Scotland', *The Holocene* 20 (2010), 931–42: 937.

[11] G.T. Swindles *et al.*, 'A 4500-year proxy climate record from peatlands in the north of Ireland: the identification of widespread summer "drought phases"?', *Quaternary Science Reviews* 29 (2010), 1577–89.

Plunkett et al.

Fig. 1—Examples of palaeohydrological indicators in bogs. a) A stockpile of bog timbers extracted from Ballymacombs More, Co. Londonderry; b) A peat section in Sluggan Bog, Co. Antrim, showing large-scale change in peat humification (decomposition) from dark, well-humified peat to light, less decomposed peat (highlighted by arrow). More discreet changes in humification can be quantified using laboratory techniques; c) An example of a testate amoeba (*Archerella flavum*, previously called *Amphitrema flavum*), a microscopic single-celled organism found in abundance in peat bogs. Different species have specific hydrological preferences and sensitivities, rendering them an important indicator of past water levels on the bog. For instance, *Archerella flavum* usually indicates wet conditions (near-surface water tables) in peatlands.

identification of these intervals as drier phases,[12] although Plunkett saw the first of these events as two distinct dry events, separated by a wet shift.[13] These findings imply that extended drought phases did indeed transpire in the past.

Here we examine three time-intervals for which there has been posited evidence for droughts phases during Irish prehistory, and for which we can avail of precisely-dated data from bog oaks and pines[14] to evaluate the evidence for and

---

[12] G.T. Swindles *et al.*, 'Centennial-scale climate change in Ireland during the Holocene', *Earth-Science Reviews* 126 (2013), 300–20: 316.

[13] Gill Plunkett, 'Tephra-linked peat humification records from Irish ombrotrophic bogs question nature of solar forcing at 850 cal. yr BC', *Journal of Quaternary Science* 21 (2006), 9–16.

[14] Dendrochronological data are drawn from the Belfast Master Chronology, a database comprising over 2,500 archaeological and natural timbers collected and dated by various

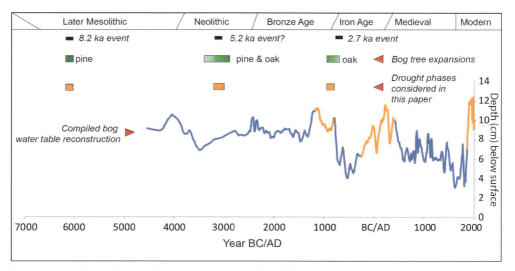

Fig. 2—Outline of drought phases discussed in this paper, showing timing in relation to subfossil tree records (selected intervals only) and a compiled testate amoeba-derived water table reconstruction from Irish bogs illustrating average reconstructed depth of the water table below surface and highlighting (orange line) notable dry shifts in the record (based on Swindles *et al.*, 'Centennial-scale climate change').

timing of these events (Fig. 2).[15] We consider the impacts these changes might have had on human populations, specifically from an economic perspective, and examine whether environmentally-driven interpretations stand up to critical analysis. The locations of key sites producing subfossilised oaks and pines referred to in the text are shown in Fig. 3.

The 8.2 ka Event

The '8.2 ka Event' is thought to be a potentially global phenomenon characterised by a rapid cooling lasting *c.* 150 years, possibly the most extreme climate perturbation since the end of the last glacial period.[16] It is dated in Greenland

---

workers from the 1970s. These timbers were measured and cross-correlated using standard methodologies: M.G.L. Baillie, *Tree-ring dating and archaeology* (London, 1982); M.A.R. Munro, 'An improved algorithm for crossdating tree-ring series', *Tree Ring Bulletin* 44 (1984), 17–27; J.R. Pilcher *et al.*, 'A 7272-year tree-ring chronology from western Europe', *Nature* 312 (1984), 150–2; D.M. Brown *et al.*, 'Dendrochronology – the absolute Irish standard', *Radiocarbon* 28 (1986), 279–83.

[15] See Lisa Coyle-McClung and Gill Plunkett, 'Cultural change and the climate record in Final Prehistoric and early medieval Ireland', *Proceedings of the Royal Irish Academy* 120C, for consideration of the Iron Age droughts identified by Swindles *et al.*, 'Centennial-scale climate change'.

[16] R.B. Alley *et al.*, 'Holocene climatic instability: A prominent, widespread event 8200 yr ago', *Geology* 25 (1997), 483–6.

Plunkett et al.

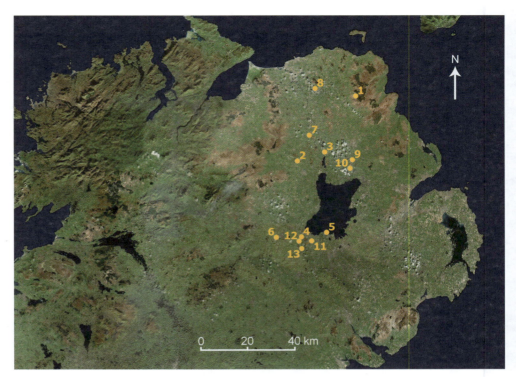

Fig. 3—Location of sites from which subfossil trees remains discussed in this paper have been derived. 1) Altnahinch, Co. Antrim; 2) Ballinderry, Co. Londonderry; 3) Ballymacombs More, Co. Londonderry; 4) Blackwater, Co. Tyrone; 5) Derrycrow, Co. Armagh; 6) Eskragh, Co. Fermanagh; 7) Fallahogy, Co. Londonderry; 8) Garry Bog, Co. Antrim; 9) Sharvogues, Co. Antrim; 10) Sluggan Moss, Co. Antrim; 11) St Patrick's Road, Co. Armagh; 12) Tamlaghtmore, Co. Tyrone; 13) Tullyroan, Co. Armagh.

ice cores to 8247±47 years before present (BP),[17] or approximately 6300 BC, although this date is subject to revision.[18] The climate anomaly has had little recognition in Irish palaeoecological records: difficulties in dating sedimentary records with such high precision, coupled with the relatively short duration of the event, renders it challenging to discern any expression of a climate perturbation at this time. A speleothem-derived temperature anomaly at 8300±120 years BP reported from Crag Cave, Co. Kerry,[19] has since been shown to be the result

---

[17] E.R. Thomas *et al.*, 'The 8.2 ka event from Greenland ice cores', *Quaternary Science Reviews* 26 (2007), 70–81.

[18] In this paper, primacy is given to the AD–BC timescale, with 'cal. BC' differentiating ^{14}C-derived dates from absolute dates derived from precisely-dated tree-ring chronologies; the term BP (before present) is used only with reference to events that are so-named.

[19] Frank McDermott, D.P. Mattey and Chris Hawkesworth, 'Centennial-scale Holocene climate variability revealed by a high-resolution speleothem δ18O record from SW Ireland', *Science* 294 (2001), 1328–31.

of a data calibration issue.[20] However, the germination of pines—precisely dated using dendrochronology—on bogs in the north of Ireland strongly points to a change towards drier conditions shortly after 6250 BC;[21] trees continued to establish on the bogs over the next 150 years, after which it appears rising water levels prevented their successful establishment. A 15- to 20-year-long growth downturn can been seen in the pine growth-rings at 6070 BC and signals a further climate impact, likely a shift to cooler summer temperatures. All in all, it would appear that Ireland experienced a *c.* 150-year phase of colder, drier conditions around 6250 BC, with perhaps a more severe episode of cold conditions around 6120 BC. The findings accord with multi-proxy records from Lake Holzmaar, Germany, where the 8.2 ka Event manifested as reduced winter and summer precipitation, as well as cooler summers.[22]

From an Irish archaeological perspective, the climate anomaly occurs within the Mesolithic period. For a long time dominated by consideration of lithic technology and site functions—lithic scatters representing the bulk of the archaeological assemblage, with a notable dearth of known structural remains—our understanding of the Irish Mesolithic has increased considerably in the last two decades, with the discovery of sophisticated fish traps in wetland locations, evidence for woodland management, ritualised behaviour and burial,[23] as a result of which more nuanced perspectives on the Irish Mesolithic are emerging.[24] Drawing upon published ^{14}C dates from Irish Mesolithic sites, Riede and colleagues have interpreted fluctuations in the number of dated archaeological sites as indications of changing population densities,[25] an approach based on

---

[20] I.J. Fairchild *et al.*, 'Modification and preservation of environmental signals in speleothems', *Earth-Science Reviews* 75 (2006), 105–53.

[21] M.C.A. Torbenson *et al.*, 'Asynchrony in key Holocene chronologies: Evidence from Irish bog pines', *Geology* 43 (2015), 799–802.

[22] Sushma Prasad *et al.*, 'The 8.2 ka event: Evidence for seasonal differences and the rate of climate change in western Europe', *Global and Planetary Change* 67 (2009), 218–26.

[23] M. Mossop, 'Lakeside developments in Co. Meath, Ireland: a Late Mesolithic fishing platform and possible mooring at Clowanstown 1', in S.B. McCartan *et al.* (eds), *Mesolithic Horizons II, papers presented at the 7th International conference on the Mesolithic in Europe, Belfast, 2005* (Oxford, 2009), 895–9; Melanie McQuade and Lorna O'Donnell, 'Late Mesolithic fish traps from the Liffey estuary, Dublin, Ireland', *Antiquity* 81 (2007), 569–84; Tracy Collins, 'Hermitage, Ireland: life and death on the western edge of Europe', in S.B. McCartan *et al.* (eds), *Mesolithic Horizons II*, 876–9; Aimée Little *et al.*, 'Stone dead: uncovering early Mesolithic mortuary rites, Hermitage, Ireland', *Cambridge Archaeological Journal* 27 (2017), 223–43.

[24] Aimée Little, 'Fishy settlement patterns and their social significance: a case study from the northern midlands of Ireland, in S.B. McCartan *et al.* (eds), *Mesolithic Horizons II*, 698–705; Nyree Finlay, 'Futile fragments? – some thoughts on microlith breakage patterns', in Nyree Finlay *et al.* (eds), *From Bann flakes to Bushmills: papers in honour of Professor Peter Woodman*, Prehistoric Society Research Paper 1 (Oxford, 2009), 22–30.

[25] Felix Riede, 'Climate and demography in early prehistory: using calibrated ^{14}C dates as population proxies', *Human Biology* 81 (2009), 309–38; Felix Riede, Kevan Edinborough

the premise that the more people there are in an area, the more sites they will leave behind for archaeologists to discover and date. They argue that dips in population coincide with climatic perturbations, including the 8.2 ka Event. Wicks and Mithen have similarly argued for a demographic impact in the Mesolithic of western Scotland.[26] Conversely, using a Bayesian approach to examine the probability that site number declined following the 8.2 ka Event, Griffiths and Robinson found that across northwest Europe, including Ireland, there was no evidence for a catastrophic decline in the number of Mesolithic sites at this time.[27] Indeed, securely-dated Mesolithic sites in Ireland are few and sporadic through time which limits the ability to identify significant demographic oscillations. Riede's dataset includes 94 dates from 22 sites spanning a >4,000-year period; this sample size falls well below the threshold generally considered sufficient to produce a statistically reliable summed probability curve.[28] The technological developments—specifically the transition from a microlithic composite tool tradition to that of a larger, broad blade industry—that differentiate the Later Mesolithic from the Earlier Mesolithic certainly point to some sort of transformation, be it in procurement strategies or population,[29] but Woodman places this shift prior to 8,500 years ago, perhaps between 7000 and 6500 BC.[30] All in all, given the low numbers and ephemeral nature of Mesolithic sites over this interval, interpretations of demographic fluctuations seem imprudent for the time being. Nevertheless, in view of the palaeoenvironmental evidence for a prolonged period of relative drought coupled with colder conditions, it is worthwhile considering the potential impact of the 8.2 ka Event on successive generations, specifically through the availability of food resources.

What we know of Mesolithic subsistence is restricted to the ecofactual evidence from a very small number of sites. Still, and despite Ireland's limited post-glacial fauna and flora, early settlers evidently availed themselves of a wide

---

and Mark Thomas, 'Tracking Mesolithic demography in time and space and its implications for explanations of culture change', in Marijn van Gils, Bart Vanmontfort and Marc De Bie, *Chronology and evolution in the Mesolithic of N(W) Europe* (Cambridge, 2009), 177–94.

[26] Karen Wicks and Steven Mithen, 'The impact of the abrupt 8.2 ka cold event on the Mesolithic population of western Scotland: a Bayesian chronological analysis using "activity events" as a population proxy', *Journal of Archaeological Science* 45 (2014), 240–69.

[27] Seren Griffiths and Erick Robinson, 'The 8.2 ka BP Holocene climate change event and human population resilience in northwest Atlantic Europe', *Quaternary International* 465 (2018), 251–7.

[28] A.N. Williams, 'The use of summed radiocarbon probability distributions in archaeology: a review of methods', *Journal of Archaeological Science* 39 (2012), 578–89.

[29] L.J. Costa, F. Sternke and P.C. Woodman, 'Microlith to macrolith: the reasons behind the transformation of production in the Irish Mesolithic', *Antiquity* 79 (2005), 19–33.

[30] Peter Woodman, *Ireland's first settlers: time and the Mesolithic* (Oxford, 2015): 226.

range of fish, shellfish, birds, small game and plants.[31] Warren notes the diversity of diet, not just in terms of the choice of foods available but also in terms of what foods were consumed at which sites.[32] Given the lack of large game in Ireland, it is perhaps not surprising that fish and shellfish remains dominate ecofactual assemblages.

Attempts to quantify the climate impact of the 8.2 ka Event have tended to focus on temperature changes, with a decline of about 1°C suggested for northwest Europe in general.[33] It is important to consider, however, that conditions prior to the 8.2 ka Event were unlike those of today. At this stage of the Holocene, Ireland's climate may have been more continental,[34] with greater seasonal differences. How the 8.2 ka Event cooling impacted on temperatures in Ireland has yet to be determined empirically, but the absence of varved lake sequences at this time may imply that winters were not so harsh as to feature frozen lakes for extended periods. Changes in water temperatures—marine and freshwater—may have impinged upon fish stocks or diversity, as might lower lake and river levels and any resultant changes in water chemistry following an extended drought phase. As yet, we have no data with which to evaluate such changes, but recent advances in biomolecular and sedaDNA analysis may in future place us in a position to tackle such questions. Migratory bird patterns may also have been altered, given the spatial scale of the 8.2 ka Event.

From a vegetation perspective, hazelnuts appear to have been a consistent element of the diet through the Irish Mesolithic. Hazel is sensitive to drought, particularly in relation to the successful germination of hazelnuts, although it is capable of vegetative reproduction.[35] Ghilardi and O'Connell recognise a *c.* 100 year decrease in *Corylus* pollen concomitant with increases in *Pinus* and *Betula* that they attribute to the 8.2 ka Event, and they note similar phenomena in several other pollen records from the west of Ireland. It is possible, therefore, that hazelnut production declined in response to the drought phase. However, *Corylus* remains the leading contributor to Irish pollen records during this time, and it is unlikely that the hazelnut supply dwindled to critical levels.

All things considered, despite lacking sufficient data with which to examine changes in diet during or subsequent to the 8.2 ka Event, we can reasonably assume that the climate perturbations were significant enough to be perceived by the population in Ireland at the time. Furthermore, it is highly likely that

---

[31] Graeme Warren, '"Mere food gatherers they, parasites upon nature…": Food and drink in the Mesolithic of Ireland', *Proceedings of the Royal Irish Academy* 115C (2015), 1–26; Woodman, *Ireland's first settlers*.
[32] Warren, '"Mere food gatherers they, parasites upon nature…"', 23.
[33] Hans Renssen, *et al.*, 'The 8.2 kyr BP event simulated by a global atmosphere—sea-ice—ocean model', *Geophysical Research Letters* 28 (2001), 1567–70.
[34] F.J.G. Mitchell, 'The Holocene', in C.H. Holland and I.S. Sanders (eds), *The Geology of Ireland* (Edinburgh, 2009), 397–404.
[35] P.A. Tallantire, 'The early-Holocene spread of hazel (*Corylus avellana* L.) in Europe north and west of the Alps: an ecological hypothesis', *The Holocene* 12 (2002), 81–96.

food resources were impacted to some degree, although thus far our evidence is limited to some dips in hazel pollen representation. At this point in time, we can only speculate about how such changes might have impacted at a psychological level, as evidence for ritualised behaviour is severely lacking. There presently exists, however, little evidence to substantiate an argument for a critical reduction in environmental productivity that might have threatened human demographics in any substantial way.

The Middle Neolithic

The Early Neolithic in Ireland is both clearly defined and relatively restricted in its chronology to *c*. 4000–3600 cal BC. The period sees a 'veritable explosion' of activity entailing a distinctive settlement type (rectangular houses), landscape clearances for mixed farming and the initiation of court tomb construction at approximately 3750–3600 cal BC. [36] A new material culture also appears, including pottery and a range of novel lithic forms. Some studies have suggested that this main pulse of Neolithic expansion began amidst a dry period identified through peatland proxies and subfossil tree population data,[37] but as yet, the palaeoclimate of this interval has not been adequately investigated. By the Middle Neolithic (*c*. 3600–3100 BC), a decline in activity is observed in both the archaeological and palynological records, amidst what may have been a shift to wetter conditions, inferred by Whitehouse and colleagues from declining bog oak populations.[38] Using multi-proxy data from two Irish bogs (Sluggan, Co. Antrim, and Fallahogy, Co. Londonderry), Roland and colleagues also identified a multi-centennial wet shift commencing sometime between 3550–3000 cal BC which they dub the '5.2 ka event'.[39]

In Whitehouse and colleagues' seminal analysis of Irish Neolithic sites, the archaeological decline occurs after 3400 cal BC and is inferred from the cessation of rectangular house construction and a decline in the construction of court tombs, a shift to more ephemeral occupation sites characterised by pits and postholes, and generally a major reduction in the number of known archaeological sites.[40] McLaughlin and colleagues place the bottom of this trough in human activity at 3300 cal BC, with an upturn in settlement evidence only after

---

[36] N.J. Whitehouse *et al.*, 'Neolithic agriculture on the European western frontier: the boom and bust of early farming in Ireland', *Journal of Archaeological Science* 51 (2014), 181–205: 188; Cormac McSparron, 'Have you no homes to go to?', *Archaeology Ireland* 22:3 (2018), 18–21. R.J. Schulting *et al.*, 'New dates from the north and a proposed chronology for Irish court tombs', *Proceedings of the Royal Irish Academy* 112C (2012), 1–60.

[37] Chris Caseldine *et al.*, 'Evidence for an extreme climatic event on Achill Island, Co. Mayo, Ireland around 5200–5100 cal. yr BP', *Journal of Quaternary Science* 20 (2005), 169–78.; Whitehouse *et al.*, 'Neolithic agriculture', 194.

[38] Whitehouse *et al.*, 'Neolithic agriculture', 199.

[39] T.P. Roland *et al.*, 'The 5.2 ka climate event: Evidence from stable isotope and multi-proxy palaeoecological peatland records in Ireland', *Quaternary Science Reviews* 124 (2015), 209–23.

[40] Whitehouse *et al.*, 'Neolithic agriculture', 190, 199.

3000 cal BC.[41] This is complemented by palynological evidence indicating widespread forest regeneration signalling reduced levels of land-use in the final centuries.[42] Smyth notes, however, that a shift to sod-built structures could explain the apparent decline in settlement evidence.[43] And while court tomb construction may have waned, persistence of tomb use is apparently evident at some megalithic tombs, such as Parknabinnia, Poulnabrone and Poulawack, Co. Clare, where human bones remains have been dated to the closing centuries of the millennium.[44] Exceptions to the pattern of decline in the pollen record include sequences from Glenulra and Garrynagran, Co. Mayo, where farming continues to be evident until around 3200 cal BC, with the former sequence showing indications of drier conditions from around 3350 cal BC,[45] and Ballynahatty, Co. Down, where signs of continued land-use through to the later fourth millennium BC can be seen.[46]

It is against the backdrop of this lull in activity that characterises the Middle Neolithic that the acme of the passage tomb tradition was reached, as exemplified by the Boyne Valley monuments, Knowth, Dowth and Newgrange.[47] Indeed, the most complex tombs appear to have been built and used in the final centuries of the fourth millennium BC,[48] corresponding to the nadir

---

[41] T.R. McLaughlin *et al.*, 'The changing face of Neolithic and Bronze Age Ireland: A big data approach to the settlement and burial records', *Journal of World Prehistory* 29 (2016), 117–53: 143.

[42] Michael O'Connell and Karen Molloy, 'Farming and woodland dynamics in Ireland during the Neolithic', *Biology and Environment: Proceedings of the Royal Irish Academy* 101B (2001), 99–128; Whitehouse *et al.*, 'Neolithic agriculture', 199.

[43] Jessica Smyth, 'The house and group identity in the Irish Neolithic', *Proceedings of the Royal Irish Academy* 111C (2011), 1–31.

[44] R.J. Schulting *et al.*, 'New dates from the north', 33 (Fig. 10).

[45] Karen Molloy and Michael O'Connell, 'Palaeoecological investigations towards the reconstruction of environment and land-use changes during prehistory at Céide Fields, western Ireland', *Probleme der Küstenforschung im Südlichen Nordseegebiet* 23 (1995), 187–225; O'Connell and Molloy, 'Farming and woodland dynamics'.

[46] Gill Plunkett *et al.*, 'Vegetation history at the multi-period prehistoric complex at Ballynahatty, Co. Down, Northern Ireland', *Journal of Archaeological Science* 35 (2008), 181–90.

[47] Gabriel Cooney *et al.*, 'Ireland', in Alasdair Whittle, Frances Healy and Alex Bayliss, *Gathering time: dating the early Neolithic enclosures of southern Britain and Ireland* (Oxford, 2011), 562–669: 657.

[48] R.J. Schulting, 'Dating the construction of Newgrange', in A. Lynch, 'Newgrange revisited: new insights from excavations at the back of the mound 1984–5', *Journal of Irish Archaeology* 23 (2014), 46–50; Alex Bayliss and Muiris O'Sullivan, 'Interpreting chronologies for the Mound of the Hostages, Tara and its contemporary contexts in Neolithic and Bronze Age Ireland', in Muiris O'Sullivan, Chris Scarre and Maureen Doyle (eds), *Tara—from the past to the future: towards a new research agenda* (Dublin, 2013), 26–104; R.J. Schulting *et al.*, 'Dating the human remains from Knowth', in George Eogan and Kerri Cleary (eds), *Excavations at Knowth 6: the archaeology of the large passage tomb at Knowth, Co. Meath* (Dublin, 2017). 331–79.

in many other aspects of the archaeological record. These major architectural attainments, showing strong connectivity with passage tomb builders along the Atlantic façade, seem to have been built during a widespread drought phase towards the end of the millennium. On Achill Island, Co. Mayo, Caseldine and colleagues report, on the basis of peat humification values, dry conditions from 3750 cal BC—at odds with the mid-millennium BC wet-shift proposed by Whitehouse and colleagues—that became drier still around 3150 cal BC, followed by an abrupt event (possibly a storm or series of storms) that triggered extensive soil erosion; the bog surface was subsequently colonised by pines.[49] A significant growth anomaly characterised by reduced annual ring widths in the 3190s BC in Irish bog oaks and pines, mirrored in North American bristlecone pines, also points to an extreme event at a supra-regional scale,[50] but the causes of such phenomena are elusive. In fact, this downturn is now known to be characterised by two phases in Ireland: an initial downturn at 3199 BC is followed by a second at 3193 BC.[51]

To get a better handle on hydrological changes at the end of the fourth millennium BC, we consider evidence for bog tree germination events. One of the most extensive collections of bog wood comes from Garry Bog, Co. Antrim, on which both oaks and pines were growing at this time. Oak start dates re-commence, after a hiatus, at 3451 BC, but recruitment is fairly evenly staggered until a *c.* 150-year hiatus beginning at 3081 BC. Oak assemblages from a small number of other bogs start to grow during the same timeframe (Fig. 4a). Pine start dates are recorded from 3418 BC, but the 3250s stand out as having a slightly higher frequency of recruitment. At Ballymacombs More, Co. Londonderry, pine expansion seems to have commenced later at 3138 BC, and there is a steady recruitment thereafter until the early third millennium BC. Pine assemblages from elsewhere in the north of Ireland show a range of start dates in the final centuries of the fourth millennium BC, all but one dating to after 3200 BC, continuing to 2925 BC (Fig. 4b). The bog trees appear, therefore, to reflect a gradual transition to dry conditions suitable for oak to grow on the bogs from *c.* 3400 BC and pine expansion following *c.* 3200 BC. These data are hard to reconcile with Roland and colleagues' peatland evidence for wetter conditions unless the latter corresponds with a reduction in oak and pine recruitment before *c.* 3400 BC or after 2900 BC. A shift to drier conditions around 3200 BC is also evident

---

[49] Caseldine *et al.*, 'Evidence for an extreme environmental event'.
[50] M.G.L. Baillie, and M.A.R. Munro, 'Irish tree rings, Santorini and volcanic dust veils', *Nature* 332 (1988), 344–6: 345; M.G.L. Baillie, 'A view from outside: recognising the big picture', *Journal of Quaternary Science* 14 (1999), 625–35: 627.
[51] Mike Baillie, personal communication.

Examining the occurrence and societal impact of droughts in prehistoric Ireland

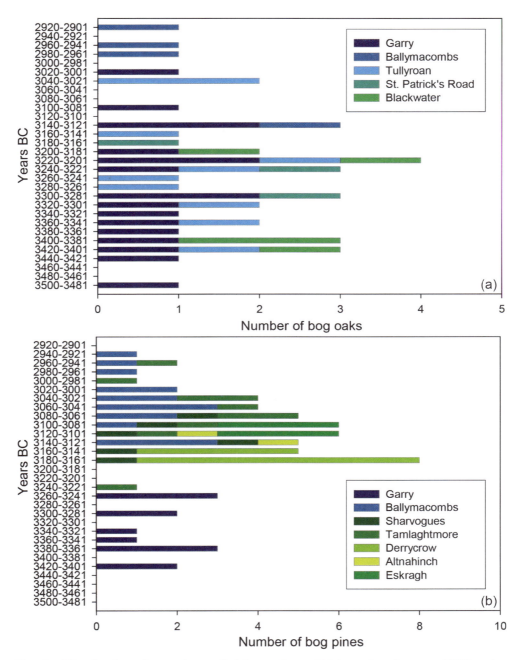

Fig. 4—Distribution of start dates of a) bog oaks and b) bog pines between 3500 and 2901 BC, drawn from the Belfast Master Chronology database. All wood samples had centres present, and were sampled shortly above the buttress. Start dates are therefore likely to lag germination dates by not more than 10 years.

in English[52] and Scottish[53] tree-ring chronologies. The bog tree records mirror the peatland record from Achill Island: dry conditions, getting drier still before an extreme event (the nature of which is uncertain but which may have entailed increased storminess, as evidenced at Achill), followed by more pronounced dry conditions favourable to the expansion of pine. We believe that the more precisely dated evidence presented here does indeed point to a 5.2 ka Event, but one characterised by dry rather than wet conditions.

What does this mean in terms of potential societal impacts? The archaeological record gives us little insight into the nature of settlement or economy at 3200 BC, and pollen records are generally rather mute in terms of human impacts at this time. As outlined above, the impetus for this 'bust' was in place several centuries before. The burial record provides hints that social changes accompanied the decline of the settlement evidence, with increasing complexity demonstrated by the passage tomb tradition. Importantly, as Carlin points out, the large passage tomb cemeteries, especially the sophisticated Boyne Valley monuments, and the mass burials in the Mound of the Hostages, Tara, Co. Meath, are not consistent with a reduced population.[54] Given how little we know of the economic basis of the Middle Neolithic—apart from the fact that it was sufficiently non-intensive to escape notice in most pollen records—it is difficult to envisage how a drought phase might have impacted upon the subsistence base, but a hydrological drought need not equate to an agricultural one, particularly in non-intensive farming subsistence regimes. Quite possibly, however, a shift in climate regime could have stimulated an ideological transformation, including a greater preoccupation with seasonal cycles, encapsulated in monument orientations on key solar events and megalithic art, the most spectacular examples of which emerge after 3200 BC. Such conjecture may not be testable, of course, but serves to draw attention to an alternative mode by which environmental changes could play a role in social transformations.

The end of the Bronze Age

Moving forward two millennia or so, the Dowris Phase, the *belle époque* of Irish Later Prehistory, comprises the final interval of the Irish Late Bronze Age, characterised by widespread settlement evidence,[55] a thriving and creative metalwork

---

[52] M.G.L. Baillie, *A slice through time* (London, 1995).

[53] A.K. Moir *et al.*, 'Dendrochronological evidence for a lower water-table on peatland around 3200–3000 BC from subfossil pine in northern Scotland', *The Holocene* 20 (2010), 931–42.

[54] Neil Carlin and Gabriel Cooney, 'Transforming our understanding of Neolithic and Chalcolithic society (4000–2200 BC) in Ireland', in Michael Stanley, Rónán Swan and Aidan O'Sullivan (eds), *Stories of Ireland's past: knowledge gained from NRA roads archaeology* (Dublin, 2017), 23–56.

[55] V.R. Ginn, *Mapping society: settlement structure in Later Bronze Age Ireland* (Oxford, 2016).

industry[56] and widespread forest clearance,[57] dating to approximately 1000–800 BC. The reasons behind the collapse of the Bronze Age have long been debated, some proposing an environmental trigger, others pointing to the potential impacts of increasing social complexity or the emergence of iron-working.[58] An environmental downturn at 850 BC manifesting as cooler/wetter conditions in north-west Europe was reported by van Geel and his colleagues.[59] In Ireland, tephrochronologically dated hydrological reconstructions from ombrotrophic (rain-fed) bogs suggest that the timing of this wet/cool shift was later by approximately a century.[60] The event occurs close in time to the end of the Irish Late Bronze Age, but a detailed analysis of the dating evidence for the archaeological sites indicates that the seeming decline of the Bronze Age began closer to 900 BC, before the onset of the climatic 'deterioration'.[61] At this time, the Irish peatland records indicate that instead conditions were relatively warm and dry.[62] The inherent uncertainty in ^{14}C-dated proxy records, despite the use of wiggle-match constrained tephrochronology in the Irish peatland sites, has led to a blurring

---

[56] George Eogan, 'The Later Bronze Age in Ireland in the light of recent research', *Proceedings of the Prehistoric Society* 14 (1964), 268–351.

[57] Gill Plunkett, 'Land-use patterns and cultural change in the Middle to Late Bronze Age in Ireland: inferences from the pollen record', *Vegetation History and Archaeobotany* 18 (2009), 273–95.

[58] B.G. Scott, 'Some notes on the transition from bronze to iron in Ireland' *Irish Archaeological Research Forum* I (1974), 9–24; Barry Raftery, 'Dowris, Hallstatt and La Tène in Ireland: problems of the transition from bronze to iron', in S.J. de Laet (ed.), *Acculturation and continuation in Atlantic Europe* (Brugge, 1976), 189–97; B.G. Scott, 'The introduction of non-ferrous and ferrous metal technologies to Ireland: motives and mechanisms', in Michael Ryan (ed.), *The origins of metallurgy in Atlantic Europe, Proceedings of the 5th Atlantic Colloquium* (Dublin 1979), 189–204; Timothy Champion, 'From Bronze Age to Iron Age in Ireland', in M.L. Stig-Sørensen and R. Thomas (eds), *The Bronze Age-Iron Age transition in Europe*, British Archaeological Reports International Series 483 (Oxford, 1989), 287–303; Barry Raftery, *Pagan Celtic Ireland* (London, 1994), 36–7.

[59] Bas van Geel, J. Buurman and H.T. Waterbolk, 'Archaeological and palaeoecological indications of an abrupt climate change in The Netherlands, and evidence for climatological teleconnections around 2650 BP', *Journal of Quaternary Science* 11, 451–60; Bas van Geel *et al.*, 'The sharp rise of Δ^{14}C ca. 800 cal BC: possible causes, related climatic teleconnections and the impact on human environments', *Radiocarbon* 40 (1997), 535–50.

[60] Plunkett, 'Tephra-linked peat humification records'; Graeme T. Swindles, Gill Plunkett and Helen Roe, 'A delayed climatic response to solar forcing at 2800 cal. BP: multi-proxy evidence from three Irish peatlands', *The Holocene* 17 (2007), 177–82; Gill Plunkett and Graeme T. Swindles, 'Determining the sun's influence on Late Glacial and Holocene climates: a focus on climate response to centennial-scale solar forcing at 2800 cal. BP', *Quaternary Science Reviews* 27 (2008), 175–84.

[61] Ian Armit *et al.*, 'Rapid climate change did not cause population collapse at the end of the European Bronze Age', *Proceedings of the National Academy of Sciences* 111 (2014), 17045–9.

[62] Plunkett, 'Tephra-linked peat humification records'; Armit *et al.*, 'Rapid climate change'.

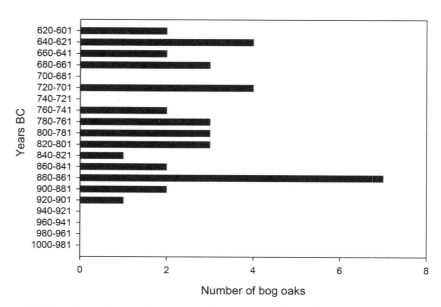

Fig. 5—Distribution of start dates from Garry Bog oaks dating to the period 1000–601 BC (data from the Belfast Master Chronology database). All wood samples had centres present, and were sampled shortly above the buttress. Start dates are therefore likely to lag germination dates by not more than 10 years.

of the precise timing of the '2.8 ka Event' (alternatively, '2.7 ka Event', which seems more accurate for Ireland at least), and the socio-economic significance of the warm/dry phase that apparently preceded this in Ireland during the ninth century BC has not yet been examined.

We turn again to the tree-ring data from Garry Bog, the site with the largest single dataset of bog oaks for this interval, and from which a peat humification record clearly shows a dry shift in bog surface wetness in the ninth century followed by a wet shift in the eighth century. The trees span a wide age range in both their start and death dates, beginning at 907 BC but with a large concentration of trees commencing growth in the period 880–861 BC (Fig. 5) that is symptomatic of a change to more favourable germination conditions following a reduction in bog surface wetness. We dub this the 'Terminal Dowris Drought'. Thereafter, start dates are more or less evenly staggered until 750 BC, when a c. 40-year gap in germination can be observed between 751 and 713 BC, and another between 709 and 668 BC. It is notable that the timing of this first hiatus in germination is coeval with the 2.7 ka wet-shift identified in the Irish peatland records and lends further support for the dating of this event to c. 750 BC.[63]

All in all, the precisely-dated tree-ring records from Garry Bog provide supporting evidence for the nature and timing of the hydrological swings observed at this and other sites in Ireland towards the end of the Late Bronze Age. There remains the difficulty of reconciling the timing of these environmental changes

---

[63] Plunkett, 'Tephra-linked peat humification records'.

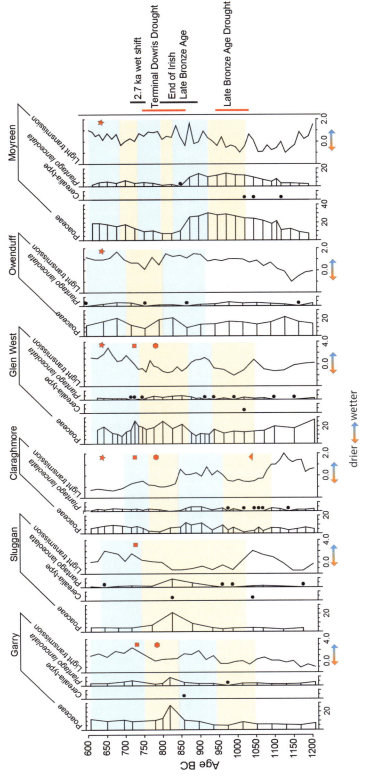

Fig. 6—Relationship between humification levels (shown as standardised light transmission values) (Plunkett, 'Tephra-linked peat humification records') and key anthropogenic indicators from six Irish bogs (dots indicate values of <1% of total dryland pollen) (Plunkett, 'Land-use patterns'). All records are shown on a common age scale but the chronological precision of each site is variable to c. 30–50 years. Inferred shifts to wetter bog surface conditions are highlighted in blue, and to drier conditions in orange. The positions of key tephras in each record are shown (triangle—Hekla 3; hexagon—GB4-150; square—Microlite; star—BMR-190): these tephras not only aid the dating of each sequence but also provide unequivocal tie-points between the records.

with the archaeological record. Dendro-dated trackways peak in the tenth century BC, but decline during the ninth century BC, although trackway construction may have continued using less substantial or non-oak materials for a time.[64] Indeed, no dendro-dated archaeological sites of any kind are recorded between 856 and 685 BC.[65] By and large, then, dendro-dated sites substantiate the seeming reduction in building activities during the ninth century BC inferred from the ^{14}C-dated archaeological record.[66] The timing of this decline raises the question of whether a subsistence crisis triggered by a prolonged water deficit might have played a role in the collapse of the Irish Bronze Age.

Fortunately, this theory is testable, as some palaeohydrological records are directly associated with pollen records that can shed light on land-use and farming activities. Fig. 6 presents key anthropogenic indicators from six sites alongside their humification-derived index of relative bog surface wetness.[67] Although peat humification is no longer a leading proxy for hydrological reconstructions, the dry to wet trends observed in these records have been replicated by semi-quantitative testate-amoebae reconstructions at Glen West (discussed here) and other Irish sites.[68] The humification records suggest an earlier dry phase commencing around the eleventh century BC that brackets the start of the Dowris Phase but is distinct from the Terminal Dowris Drought. Strong intersite correlations are afforded by the presence of the well-dated tephras GB4-150 (800–758 cal BC), Microlite (755–680 cal BC) and BMR-190 (705–585 cal BC).[69] Moreover, irrespective of chronological precision, uncertainty regarding the relative timing of the hydrological and land-use proxies is eliminated entirely by virtue of the two proxies being from the same peatland cores.

Expansions in land-use during the Late Bronze Age are evident to varying degrees in the pollen records, with the two western sites (Owenduff and Moyreen) showing strong increases in anthropogenic indicators as early as *c.* 1100 BC. In the more northerly sites, the main expansions occur later, in the tenth (Claraghmore, Garry, Sluggan) or early ninth (Glen West) centuries BC. By and large, these expansions coincide with the Dowris Phase. Declines in activity are similarly time-transgressive, occurring during the ninth century BC at Claraghmore, Owenduff and

---

[64] Gill Plunkett *et al.*, 'Environmental indifference? A critique of environmentally deterministic theories of peatland archaeological site construction in Ireland', *Quaternary Science Reviews* 61 (2013), 17–31.

[65] Based on Queen's University Belfast dendrochronological database.

[66] Armit *et al.*, 'Rapid climate change'.

[67] G.M. Plunkett, 'Environmental change in the Late Bronze Age in Ireland (1200–600 cal. BC)', unpublished PhD, Queen's University Belfast, 1999; Plunkett, 'Tephra-linked peat humification records'; Plunkett, 'Land-use patterns'.

[68] Swindles *et al.*, 'Centennial-scale climate change', *Earth-Science Reviews* 126 (2013), 300–20.

[69] G.M. Plunkett *et al.*, 'New dates for first millennium BC tephra isochrones in Ireland', *The Holocene* 14 (2004), 780–6; Plunkett, 'Tephra-linked peat humification records'; Plunkett, 'Land-use patterns'.

Moyreen, and during the early eighth century BC at Garry, Sluggan and Glen West. Irrespective of any chronological imprecision, the timings of these declines have variable relationships to hydrological changes. At Moyreen and Owenduff, reduced human activity occurs within a wet phase; at Claraghmore, the start of the decline begins immediately prior to a shift towards drier conditions; and at Garry, Sluggan and Glen West, activity declines during the spell of drier bog surface wetness. From an economic perspective, therefore, it would seem that changing levels of land-use were not driven by any specific climate event of the early first millennium BC.

Notwithstanding variations in the timing of changes in the pollen records, there were evidently widespread declines in farming levels (whether in expanse or intensity) in the period between 900 and 800 BC, coinciding with the fall-off in both ^{14}C- and dendro-dated archaeological sites and the inferred end of the Late Bronze Age.[70] Clearly, we are witnessing at this time a social transformation that impacted settlement patterns, material culture and economy, and very possibly overarching social organisation. Thanks to the complementary pollen and hydrological records, we can disentangle the impact of environmental change and state that neither the Terminal Dowris Drought nor the 2.7 ka Event triggered a complete collapse of the subsistence base. A mixed subsistence economy and a largely self-sufficient mode of production[71] may have ensured some degree of resilience against weather extremes. Moreover, we see evidence of recovery in the pollen records, with levels of land-use during the eighth and seventh centuries BC—the Early Iron Age—that are on par with pre-Dowris Phase activity. Similar recurrence of clearances and farming are evident in many Irish pollen records.[72] The island was evidently not depopulated by any means, but those responsible for the clearings and farming left comparatively little trace in the material and settlement records. Their environmental footprint betrays their presence and underlines the inadequacy of inferring population collapses from periods of low visibility in the archaeological record.

Might then the Terminal Dowris Drought have influenced an ideological shift that undermined the social structure of the Dowris Phase? As for the Middle Neolithic, such a hypothesis can only be speculative, but it is worth noting

---

[70] Plunkett *et al.*, 'Environmental indifference?'; Armit *et al.*, 'Rapid climate change'.

[71] Ginn, *Mapping society*, 188.

[72] Karen Molloy and Michael O'Connell, 'Holocene vegetation and land-use dynamics in the karstic environment of Inis Oírr, Aran Islands, western Ireland: pollen analytical evidence evaluated in light of the archaeological record', *Quaternary International* 113 (2004), 41–64; Karen Molloy, 'Holocene vegetation and land-use history at Mooghaun, south-east Clare, with particular reference to the Bronze Age', in Eoin Grogan, *The North Munster Project, Vol. 1: The Later Prehistoric landscape of South-East Clare*, Discovery Programme Reports No. 6 (Dublin, 2005), 255–87; D.A. Weir, 'A palynological study of landscape and agricultural development in County Louth from the second millennium BC to the first millennium AD. Final report', *Discovery Programme Reports* 2 (1995), 77–126; Karen Molloy and Michael O'Connell, 'Boom or bust or sustained development? Fossil pollen records and new insights into Bronze Age farming in County Clare', *Past Times, Changing Fortunes* (2011), 57–71.

the significance of wet places in the Late Bronze Age, and in particular their association with bronze and gold deposition. A drought manifesting in conjunction with the appearance of a new metal (iron) might have been perceived as portentous, enough perhaps to destabilise the existing social order.

The impact of droughts in Irish prehistory: a summary

We have examined three periods of Irish prehistory for which there is evidence of extended drought phases. While not denying that even short periods of drought can have severe detrimental effects on human populations, we find limited evidence that these drought phases were drivers of economic change. For the Mesolithic, the palaeoenvironmental evidence for changes associated with the 8.2 ka Event strongly points to a centennial-scale drought phase, likely coupled with cooler conditions. The archaeological record for this interval, however, is simply too sparse to enable a critical evaluation of impacts these changes might have had either on subsistence or demographics. Nevertheless, there remains considerable scope to investigate the possible impact on aquatic and forest ecosystems through sedimentary records as a first step towards understanding potential repercussions for contemporary populations.

The Middle Neolithic decline appears to have commenced during a period of wetter conditions; there is conflicting evidence for hydrological changes in the centuries around 3400 BC, but a clearer picture emerges of a period of prolonged dryness from 3200 BC following an extreme event of some sort. The environmental evidence supports the recognition of a 5.2 ka Event in Ireland, but we propose that this event comprised an abrupt event in the 3190s BC that was followed by a multi-centennial drought phase. Again, a paucity of evidence for the prevailing economy limits our ability to infer the economic impacts of this series of changes. We consider instead the timing of the dry phase with respect to the emergence of greater complexity and solar symbolism within the passage tomb tradition, and hypothesise an ideological response to the challenges or opportunities that the dry conditions may have brought.

Finally, we examined for the first time the potential role of a drought phase on the demise of the Irish Late Bronze Age. While it appears that the Dowris Phase decline broadly coincided with the onset of drier conditions in the ninth century BC (the 'Terminal Dowris Drought'), we demonstrate variability in the relationship between the dry phase and changing levels of land-use, and we conclude that drought did not drive a collapse in the subsistence economy. We raise the possibility that the changing conditions could have had an impact on the social system or power relations at this time, an idea which, though speculative, is worth considering given the importance of wet places for metal deposition in the final stages of the Late Bronze Age.

To conclude, the palaeoenvironmental evidence points to recurrent and prolonged drought phases during the course of Irish prehistory. The examples we have examined lie close to periods of social transformation. We find little convincing evidence of population declines at these times, nor signs that the droughts exerted any specific influence on the subsistence economy, although for the Mesolithic in particular, we lack data to evaluate the impact on food resources. It may well be that the nature of the drought phases—the way in which precipitation was distributed throughout the year—did not noticeably disrupt the prevalent subsistence regimes. That said, the changes were almost certainly of sufficient magnitude to be perceptible to the generations who lived through these transitions, and we cannot exclude the possibility that the drought phases impacted on the worldviews of individuals, groups of individuals or entire societies to the extent that existing ideologies were transformed. It remains to be seen if and how present and future generations will alter their behaviour and belief systems in response to the unprecedented climate scenarios that await us.

Reimagining environmental impacts on past societies

Our analysis highlights the wealth of palaeoenvironmental archives available in Ireland with which to examine the occurrence and impact of past climate change, mainly those occurring over longer, multi-generational timescales—decades to centuries—but in some instances, over the course of a few years. Dendrochronological records are currently dominated by those from the north of Ireland, reflecting decades of research in this region, but there is considerable scope to extend this work to the Irish Midlands. In terms of marrying past climate change with the archaeological record, sedimentary records afford important opportunities to overcome the first critical hurdle, that of establishing the relative timing of any observed changes. That climate change happened in the past is indisputable, but much less certain is how such changes might have affected populations living in a world vastly different to that of today, or even of the recent past. As yet, we know little of the vulnerability, or resilience, of past populations living in lower densities, operating different modes of production under different group dynamics and socio-political regimes; of whether mobility was a solution, or indeed a problem, in the face of an environmental crisis; or of mortality and recovery rates following abrupt and severe events.

How to begin to address these complex issues? To the extensive vegetation histories offered by pollen records and the increasing number of peatland palaeohydrological reconstructions, a diverse range of emerging methodologies promises to provide greater and deeper insights into past environmental change and human activity. From a palaeoenvironmental perspective, it is through methods such as sedaDNA (ancient DNA reconstructions from sediment) and biomarker (organic molecule) analysis, combined with more traditional approaches, that we may be able to glean changes in the nature and scale of human activity through time, independently of dated archaeological sites, akin to the Late Bronze Age case study considered in this paper. Then, we may be able to 'see' elusive Mesolithic inhabitants, and track the 'disappearing' Neolithic and Bronze Age populations, pinpoint when and where pivotal changes occurred, and most importantly, directly evaluate changes in human activity—at least in terms of population levels and environmental impacts—with respect to manifestations of climate change. In the meantime, we need to adopt a more critical approach to our investigations of past climate impacts on societies, and consider too the impacts that the *perception* of those changes might have had on the populations who experienced them.

Acknowledgments   We wish to thank Siobhán McDermott and Libby Mulqueeny for their assistance in the production of the location map. We are grateful to the Editor, Tomás Ó Carragáin, and to two anonymous referees for their comments and suggestions that have helped improve this paper.

On the brink of Armageddon? Climate change, the archaeological record and human activity across the Bronze Age–Iron Age transition in Ireland

BENJAMIN GEAREY*
Department of Archaeology, UCC, Connolly Building, Dyke Parade, Cork City

KATHARINA BECKER
Department of Archaeology, UCC, Connolly Building, Dyke Parade, Cork City

ROSIE EVERETT
Department of Archaeology, UCC, Connolly Building, Dyke Parade, Cork City

SEREN GRIFFITHS
School of Forensic and Investigative Sciences, University of Central Lancashire

[Accepted 22 June 2020. Published 18 August 2020.]

Abstract

Palaeoclimatic proxies from records in northwest Europe evidence a climatic deterioration, known as the '2.8 ka Event', which broadly coincided with the transition from Later Bronze Age to Iron Age in Ireland. This Bronze Age–Iron Age transition in Ireland has been invoked in various hypotheses concerning the relationship between environmental and cultural change. This paper offers a brief review of contrasting archaeological interpretations of the transition, outlines the gaps and uncertainties in current knowledge and highlights the role of climate change in some of these uncertainties. This is followed by a discussion of palaeoclimate records from peatlands, and in particular the utility of bog surface wetness records (BSW) to identify geographically and chronologically coherent periods of Holocene climate change, including the period around 750 BC (2.8 ka), which is apparent in both UK and Irish records. Whilst BSW records provide evidence of relative shifts from wet/cold to warm/dry conditions, quantitative indices of temperature and precipitation cannot be derived from these data. Recent work discounting a link between a demographic 'collapse' and climate change is considered, as is the importance of local-scale records for understanding the archaeology of peatlands. The role of 'bog burst' events (catastrophic hydrological failures of the physical integrity of peatland) in driving palaeohydrological changes in certain Irish peatlands is outlined. Whilst 'bog bursts' might confound the extraction of regional climatic meaning, they provide important contextual

*Author's email: b.gearey@ucc.ie
ORCID iD: https://orcid.org/0000-0003-0323-4921
doi: https://doi.org/10.3318/PRIAC.2020.120.06

evidence for human activity and the associated archaeological record. Although there are some coherent patterns in palynological records, others demonstrate spatial and chronological differences in vegetation change and human impact across the Late Bronze Age to Iron Age, but the implications for changes in the distribution of human populations are unclear. The paper concludes with a consideration of the importance of robust chronologies for integrating archaeological, palaeoenvironmental and palaeoclimatological data to investigate potential links between climate and cultural change. The importance of different analytical, spatial and chronological scales to investigate the complex and recursive nature of the relationship between human activity and climatic change is discussed.

Introduction

The 'upheaval' of Late Bronze Age societies around the eighth century BC has been linked to climate change across northwest Europe, which has in turn been associated with the impact of a decline in solar output dated to 850–550 BC.[1] Evidence for climatic deterioration in later prehistory was first advanced during the late nineteenth and early twentieth century and peat deposits in particular have long provided an important 'archive' of climate change.[2] In Ireland, this period has been much discussed, as the archaeological record of the Late Bronze Age to Iron Age transition has also presented an interpretive challenge. The apparent 'absence' of an early Iron Age in the archaeological record raised the possibility of a long, drawn out Bronze Age or a gap in human activity in the form of an Iron Age 'Dark Age'.[3] Climate change has featured prominently in these debates.[4] The evidence for climatic deterioration and archaeological indications of cultural 'decline' have often been causally linked,[5] but the 'climatic impact' narrative has also been the subject of considerable debate, for various reasons, in particular as many scholars are wary of linking cultural to environmental changes in a manner regarded as 'environmentally deterministic'.[6]

In this paper we consider these cultural and climatic changes in Ireland in the period long known as 'the sub-Boreal to sub-Atlantic' transition, or more recently

---

[1] For example, see Martin-Puertas *et al.*, 'Regional atmospheric circulation shifts induced by a grand solar minimum', *Nature Geoscience* 5 (2017), 397–401.

[2] For example, see Bent Aaby, 'Cyclic climatic variations in climate over the past 5,500 yr reflected in raised bogs', *Nature* 263 5575, (1976), 281–84; Keith E. Barber, *Peat stratigraphy and climatic change: a paleoecological test of the theory of cyclic peat bog regeneration* (Paris, 1981).

[3] For example, see Gabriel Cooney and Eoin Grogan, *Irish prehistory: a social perspective* (Bray, 1999); J.C. Henderson, *The Atlantic Iron Age. Settlement and identity in the first millennium BC* (London, 2007).

[4] For example, see Barry Raftery, *Pagan Celtic Ireland. The enigma of the Irish Iron Age* (London, 1994), 37.

[5] For example, see Turney *et al.* 'Holocene climatic change and past Irish societal response', *Journal of Archaeological Science* 33:1 (2006), 34–38.

[6] Plunkett *et al.* 'Environmental difference? A critique of environmentally deterministic theories of peatland archaeological site construction in Ireland', *Quaternary Science* 61

the '2.8 ka Event'.[7] We begin with a brief overview of archaeological evidence for the transition between the Late Bronze Age and Iron Age. We examine palaeohydrological data from bog surface wetness (BSW), the source of the most recent research on climatic changes across this period in Ireland. We then consider the evidence for the claim that climate change should be essentially 'decoupled' from the Bronze Age to Iron Age transition in Ireland.[8] We discuss processes that confound and complicate the extraction of palaeoclimatic data from peatland records and the implications of this for archaeological understanding. This is followed by a short review of palynological evidence for vegetation change and human activity from the Late Bronze Age into the Iron Age, an important strand of evidence. We conclude with a discussion of issues and problems raised and present a short case study to illustrate one potential methodological framework for future work.

The Bronze Age to Iron Age transition: archaeological evidence

The Irish Late Bronze Age (c. 1150 to 800–600 BC) is regarded as one of economic prosperity, based on the bronze and gold artefacts of the Dowris metalworking industry (Figure 1), named after the large hoard from Co. Offaly (see Figure 2).[9] It is often conceptualised as a complex and highly stratified society, with the wealth and power of the elite manifesting itself in rich bronze and gold artefacts as well as the construction of hillforts, which stand in stark contrast to the small farmsteads of the period.[10] The range and quality of metalwork implies the Dowris phase was a period of international connections, technological innovation, great wealth and industrial output, in which 'metal was

---

(2013), 17–31; B.E. Berglund, 'Human impact and climate changes—synchronous events and a causal link?', *Quaternary International* 105:1 (2003), 7–12.

[7] Van Geel *et al.*, 'A bog burst in the Netherlands triggered by the 2.8 kyr BP event', *The Holocene* 24, 11 (2014), 1465–77; B. Van Geel, J. Buurman and H.T. Waterbolk, 'Archaeological and palaeoecological indications of an abrupt climate change in The Netherlands and evidence for climatological teleconnections around 2650 BP', *Journal of Quaternary Science* 11 (1996), 451–60.

[8] Armit *et al.*, 'Rapid climate change did not cause population collapse at the end of the European Bronze Age', *Proceedings of the National Academy of Sciences* 111:48 (2014), 17045–49.

[9] George Eogan, *The hoards of the Irish Later Bronze Age* (Dublin, 1983); George Eogan, 'The Later Bronze Age in Ireland in the light of recent research' *Proceedings of the Prehistoric Society* 30 (1964), 268–351.

[10] For example, see Eogan, *The hoards of the Irish Later Bronze Age*; John Waddell, *The prehistoric archaeology of Ireland* (Bray, 2010); Raftery, *Pagan Celtic Ireland*, 36; Eogan 'The Later Bronze Age in Ireland in the light of recent research'; Cooney and Grogan, *Irish prehistory: a social perspective*, 149–67: 235; Henderson, *The Atlantic Iron Age. Settlement and identity in the first millennium BC*, 91–93; William O'Brien and James O'Driscoll, *Hillforts, warfare and society in Bronze Age Ireland*, (Oxford, 2017), 321–42; E. Grogan, *The North Munster Project. The later prehistoric landscape of south-east Clare* (Discovery Programme Monograph 6, Bray, 2005).

Gearey et al.

Fig. 1—Objects from the Dowris Hoard, Co. Offaly, dating to *c.* 1000–800 BC. Whilst referred to as a 'hoard', this group of objects may in fact have been deposited over a period of time. Image reproduced by kind permission of the National Museum of Ireland.

plentiful and craftsmen prolific'.[11] The fact that so many hoard deposits of Late Bronze Age date are found across Ireland is, as in other parts of Europe, often seen as evidence for this prosperity, though it has also been discussed as evidence for an offloading of material at the start of an impending crisis for ritual reasons or due to its redundancy when iron became the main working material.[12]

Hillforts such as that at Mooghaun, Co. Clare, promontory forts such as Dún Aonghasa (Fig. 2), as well as *crannogs* show the characteristic form of post and wattle and daub built houses—mostly round—of which the recent decades of infrastructural development have produced great numbers in small enclosed and unenclosed clusters in the lowlands.[13] *Fulachtaí fia*, the most common later

---

[11] Eogan, 'The Later Bronze Age in Ireland in the light of recent research'.
[12] Eogan, *The hoards of the Irish Later Bronze Age*; Katharina Becker, 'Transforming identities – New approaches to Bronze Age deposition in Ireland' *Proceedings of the Prehistoric Society* 79 (2013), 1–39; John Coles and Dennis Harding, *The Bronze Age in Europe* (London, 1979); Stuart Needham, '800 BC: The great divide', in C. Haselgrove and R. Pope (eds), *The earlier Iron Age in Britain and the near Continent* (Oxford, 2006), 39–43.
[13] Claire Cotter, *The Western Stone Forts Project. Excavations at Dún Aonghasa and Dún Eoghanachta* (Dublin, 2012); Rose Cleary, *The Archaeology of Lough Gur* (Bray, 2018), 150–214; Martin Doody, *Excavations at Curraghatoor, Co. Tipperary* (Cork, 2007);

On the brink of Armageddon?

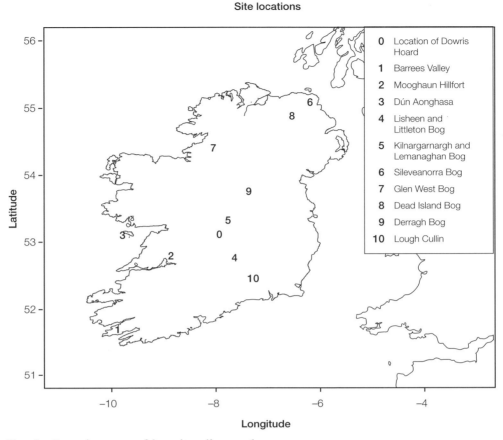

Fig. 2—Location map of key sites discussed.

prehistoric field monuments, and cremation cemeteries comprise further elements of the Bronze Age landscape.

To explain the apparent gap between the Late Bronze Age and the La Tène Iron Age of Ireland (*c.* fourth century BC onwards), some scholars have suggested the Irish Bronze Age continued until the second half of the first millennium BC, albeit with little archaeological visibility. Encapsulating the problems in defining this material absence, and the implied absence of human activity, Eogan referred to the 'darkness' of his Dowris B phase after the 'light' of the

---

John Ó Néill, *Inventory of Bronze Age structures,* Report to the Heritage Council 2009; Victoria Ginn, *Mapping society. Settlement structure in Later Bronze Age Ireland* (Oxford, 2016); Joanna Brück, *Personifying prehistory. Relational ontologies in Bronze Age Britain and Ireland* (Oxford, 2019), 125–62; Alan Hawkes, *The archaeology of prehistoric burnt mounds in Ireland* (Oxford, 2018).

Late Bronze Age.[14] If the Late Bronze Age is regarded as ending *c.* 600 BC, as suggested by the metalwork corpus, this implies the onset of a 'Dark Age' in the form of low levels of human activity, representing a societal crisis.[15] The absence of artefacts to fill the gap until the onset of La Tène metalworking traditions would mean a sudden 'crash' in metalworking and hoard deposition from *c.* 600 BC. This in turn could be interpreted as evidence for economic and social collapse, possibly as a response to the introduction of iron or environmental changes, as proposed for similar patterns across parts of Europe at the transition between the Bronze Age and the Iron Age (see below).[16] Some scholars argued for continuity rather than collapse between these periods, discounting a dramatic hiatus with associated loss of traditions of deposition and site use, and rejecting any significant cultural impact related to the introduction of iron or to the end of bronze trade networks.[17]

In contrast, Raftery painted a vivid picture of the possible impact of climatic deterioration: 'With waterlogged and ruined crops, with rivers bursting their banks and weeks of leaden skies and unceasing rain, Ireland's Late Bronze Age farmers – soaked, cold and hungry – could have felt themselves on the brink of Armageddon'.[18] Although recognising that the palaeoclimatic evidence was somewhat equivocal, this 'environmental impact' narrative drew a direct connection between climatic deterioration and the perceived processes of economic stagnation and decline in the archaeological record. The initial Iron Age 'withered as the country slipped into uncharacteristic 'insular isolation''.[19] Most recently, this scenario has been questioned, stressing the importance of integrating archaeological and palaeoenvironmental records, and arguing for a decrease in human activity prior to climatic deterioration.[20] In the next section

---

[14] Eogan, 'The Later Bronze Age in Ireland in the light of recent research'.

[15] Brian G. Scott, *Early Irish Iron working* (Belfast, 1990); Timothy Champion, 'The end of the Irish Bronze Age', *North Munster Antiquarian Journal* 14 (1971), 17–24.; Timothy Champion, 'From bronze to iron in Ireland', in Marie Luise Stig Sørensen and Richard Thomas (eds), *The Bronze Age–Iron Age transition in Europe*. British Archaeological Reports, International Series 483.2 (Oxford, 1989), 287–303.

[16] For example, see B.G. Scott, 'Some notes on the transition from Bronze to Iron in Ireland', *Irish Archaeological Research Forum* 1 (1974), 9–24; James Mallory and T.E. McNeill, *The archaeology of Ulster: from colonization to plantation,* (Queen's University Belfast, 1991), 140; Raftery, *Pagan Celtic Ireland,* 35–37; Barry Raftery, 'Dowris, Hallstatt and La Tène in Ireland: problems of the transition from bronze to iron', in S.J. De Laet (ed.), *Acculturation and continuity in Atlantic Europe, mainly during the Neolithic period and the Bronze Age,* (Ghent, 1976), 189–97.

[17] Cooney and Grogan, *Irish prehistory: a social perspective*, 179–184; Henderson, *The Atlantic Iron Age*, 96–97; John Waddell, 'The Irish Sea in Prehistory', *Journal of Irish Archaeology* 6 (1991/1992), 29–40.

[18] Raftery, *Pagan Celtic Ireland.*

[19] Raftery, *Pagan Celtic Ireland.*

[20] Armit *et al.*, 'Rapid climate change did not cause population collapse at the end of the European Bronze Age'.

we outline the role that palaeohydrological data obtained from peatlands have played in understanding of the timing and nature of climatic change during later prehistory.

Examining climate change in Ireland: the peatland record

Peatlands are important palaeoclimatic archives for terrestrial areas, as fluctuations in temperature and/or precipitation from wet/cold to warm/dry climatic conditions may be preserved within ombrotrophic (i.e. rain-fed) peat deposits.[21] Variations in bog surface wetness (BSW) can be derived from analyses of subfossil proxies (below) and since peat may accumulate in continuous or near continuous stratigraphic order, records of several millennia are possible.[22] Three main palaeohydrological proxies are utilised to track changes in BSW: peat humification, that is, the extent to which the peat has decayed (drier/warmer conditions result in greater decay than wetter/colder conditions); plant macrofossils, the subfossil remains of peat forming plants, such as *Sphagnum*, which can have different hydrological tolerances; and testate amoebae, unicellular shelled animals (Protozoa: Rhizopoda) that live on the peatland surface (see Fig. 3) and can have very specific hydrological preferences.[23] Palaeohydrological data derived from these proxies are generally expressed as the parameter referred to as 'Bog Surface Wetness', the relative depth of the watertable of a peatland at a given point in time.[24] A watertable close to or above (in the case of standing water) the surface of a peatland indicates a wet bog surface, whilst deeper watertables imply drier bog surfaces. Generally, the identification of climatic shifts thus turns on identifying and dating shifts from shallow to deeper watertables and vice versa. The primary controlling variable is regarded as changes in the past evapotranspiration ratio, which is in turn controlled by fluctuations in rainfall and temperature. In general, the BSW record is regarded as driven by summer moisture deficits, rather than precipitation and temperature *per se*.[25] Brown has suggested

---

[21] Keith E. Barber, *Peat stratigraphy and climatic change: a paleoecological test of the theory of cyclic peat bog regeneration* (Rotterdam, 1981).

[22] For example, see Frank M. Chambers, 'The development and refinement of proxy climate indicators from peat', *Quaternary International* 203 (2012), 21–33.

[23] Dan J. Charman, Dawn Hendon and Wendy A. Woodland, *The identification of testate amoebae (Protozoa:Rhizopoda) in Peats*, QRA Technical Guide 9 (London, 2000).

[24] For example, see Mike G. Baillie, 1992, 'Dendrochronology and past environmental change', *Proceedings of the British Academy* 77 (2012), 5–23; Frank McDermott, David Mattey and C.J. Hawksworth, 'Centennial scale climate variability revealed by a high resolution speleothem delta O-18 record from SW Ireland', *Science* 294 (2001), 1328–31; Dan J. Charman, 'Climate drivers for peatland palaeoclimate records', *Quaternary Science Reviews* 28 (2009), 1811–19.

[25] Charman *et al.*, 'A 1000-Year reconstruction of summer precipitation from Ireland: calibration of a peat-based palaeoclimate record', *Quaternary International* 268 (2012), 87–97; Dan J. Charman, 'Summer water deficit variability controls on peatland watertable changes: implications for Holocene palaeoclimate reconstructions', *The Holocene* 17:2 (2007), 217–27.

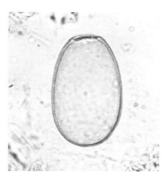

Fig. 3—Photomicrograph of testate amoeba *Hyalosphenia subflava*, an indicator of relatively dry BSW conditions (length: *c.* 70 μm).

this should be interpreted as 'principally a response to north Atlantic sea surface temperatures mediated through prevailing synoptic regimes and the resultant summer water deficit'.[26]

As greater confidence may be attributed to patterns of change in BSW recorded in more than one proxy, 'multi-proxy' studies incorporate testate amoebae, humification and plant macrofossil analyses.[27] However, humification and plant macrofossil analyses tend to yield at best semi-quantitative data indicating *relative* changes in BSW; that is, from wetter/colder to warmer/drier or vice versa.[28] The development of statistical transfer functions in the early 1990s has permitted quantitative estimates of BSW changes using testate amoebae records.[29] This has been one of the most significant developments in peatland palaeoclimate research across Europe and indeed further afield over the last two decades.[30] However, caution has been urged in the interpretation of BSW data derived from testate amoebae, with a focus on directional shifts (i.e. wet to dry) rather than absolute fluctuations in reconstructed water-table depths.[31]

It has been suggested that BSW records from peatlands across northwest Europe show a 'strong' degree of synchronicity between periods of wetter

---

[26] Tony Brown, 'The Bronze Age climate and environment of Britain', *Bronze Age Review* 1 (2008), 7–22.

[27] For example, see Dan J. Charman, Dawn Hendon and Susan Packman, 'Multiproxy surface wetness records from replicate cores on an ombrotrophic mire: implications for Holocene palaeoclimate records', *Journal of Quaternary Science* 14 (1999), 451–63.

[28] For example, see Gill Plunkett, 'Tephra linked peat humification records from Irish ombrotrophic bogs question nature of solar forcing at 850 cal. Yr BC', *Journal of Quaternary Science* 21:1 (2006), 9–16.

[29] Charman *et al.*, *The identification of testate amoebae (Protozoa: Rhizopoda) in Peats*.

[30] Chambers *et al.*, 'Globally synchronous climate change 2800 years ago: proxy data from peat in South America', *Earth and Planetary Science Letters* 253 (2007), 439–44.

[31] Turner *et al.*, 'Comparing regional and supra-regional transfer function from Holocene peatlands', *Palaeogeography, Palaeoclimatology, Palaeoecology* 369 (2013), 395–408; Amesbury *et al.*, 'Development of a new pan European testate amoeba transfer function for reconstructing peatland palaeohydrology.' *Quaternary Science Reviews* 152 (2016), 132–51.

conditions over the mid- to late Holocene in particular.[32] Charman highlighted four periods of high precipitation-evaporation ratios (i.e. wetter/colder conditions) in multiple palaeoclimate proxy records from the UK relevant to the Late Bronze Age to Iron Age transition: *c.* 1110–920 BC, 820–790 BC, 620–510 BC and 310–190 BC.[33] These phases do not all correlate with other proxy climate records, such as the Greenland ice cores, speleothem, tree line and tree ring, lake level and ice drift records.[34] The postulated correlations also vary in terms of the magnitude of implied climatic changes and associated chronology (provided by radiocarbon dating supplemented with tephrochronology). Charman also identified the period between *c.* 1150 to 950 BC as potentially one of rising temperatures, with a general cooling trend from *c.* 50 BC, but stressed that unequivocal evidence for temperature changes are based on very few reliable records, another interpretative problem when it comes to reconstructing climatic variables.[35]

A meta-analysis of ten Irish BSW records—including both testate amoebae derived watertable reconstructions and peat humification data from sites including Derragh Bog, Glen West and Slieveanorra (see Fig. 1)—by Swindles and colleagues identified shifts to wetter/colder conditions *c.* 750 BC, 550 AD and 1450–1850 AD, and they linked the deterioration of the eighth to ninth centuries BC to changes in the North Atlantic thermohaline circulation.[36] The same paper also urges caution in interpretation of Irish BSW records due to 'marked variability of… palaeoclimatic proxy data…associated with proxy complexities and chronological uncertainties'.[37]

Very few reconstructions of palaeotemperature are available, but recent data (expressed as mean July air temperature, referred to as

---

[32] For example, see Dawn Hendon, Dan J. Charman and Martin J. Kent, 'Comparison of the palaeohydrological records derived from testate amoebae from peatlands in northern England within site variability, between site comparability and palaeoclimatic implications', *The Holocene* 11 (2001), 127–48; Charman *et al.*, 'Compilation of non-annually resolved Holocene proxy climate records: stacked Holocene peatland palaeo-watertable reconstructions from northern Britain', *Quaternary Science Reviews* 35 (2006), 336–50; Hughes *et al.*, Mire development pathways and palaeoclimatic records from a full Holocene peat archive at Walton Moss, Cumbria, England', *The Holocene* 10 (2000), 465–79.

[33] Dan J. Charman, 'Centennial scale climate variability in the British Isles during the mid to late Holocene' *Quaternary Science Reviews* 29 (2010), 1539–54.

[34] O'Brien *et al.*, 'Complexity of Holocene climate as reconstructed from a Greenland ice core', *Science* 270 (1995), 1962–1964; Bond *et al.*, 'Persistent solar influence on North Atlantic climate during the Holocene', *Science* 294 (2001), 2130–36; M.G.L. Baillie and M.A.R. Munroe, 'Irish tree rings, Santorini and volcanic dust veils', *Nature* 332 (1998), 344–34; A.J. Gear and B. Huntley, 'Rapid changes in the range limits of Scots' Pine 4000 years ago', *Science* 241 (1991), 544–47.

[35] Charman, 'Centennial scale climate variability in the British Isles during the mid to late Holocene'.

[36] Swindles *et al.*, 'Centennial scale climate change in Ireland during the Holocene', *Earth Science Reviews* 126 (2013), 300–20.

[37] Swindles *et al.*, 'Centennial scale climate change in Ireland during the Holocene'.

Chironomid-inferred temperatures (C-ITs)) have been derived from a record from Lough Meenachrinna, Co. Donegal. Table 1 presents a comparative summary of selected data discussed in this paper, namely the estimated timing of the transition from the Late Bronze Age to the Iron Age; reconstructions of demographic change; and reconstructions of the palaeoclimate using mean June temperature reconstructions derived from chironomid analyses, with possible drought phases (DP) indicated by falls in bog surface wetness. In addition, palynological data from the five sites discussed in this paper are summarised, distinguishing between episodes of woodland clearance for settlement and agriculture as indicated by reductions in arboreal pollen and increases in herbs, etc., and episodes of reduced human activity leading to woodland regeneration as indicated by increasing arboreal pollen, reductions in herbs, etc. The phases of falling bog surface wetness attributed to 'bog bursts' are indicated for Lisheen. Cultural divisions follow Becker *et al.*;[38] estimates of demography and bog surface wetness (BSW) are from Armit *et al.*;[39] drought phase (DP) data is from Swindles *et al.*;[40] Chironomid inferred temperatures (C-ITs) are from Taylor *et al.*[41] The C-ITs are estimated as 11.5 °C during the Early Bronze Age (*c.* 1390 BC), rising into the Middle Bronze Age (*c.* 1310–1100 BC) to peak at 13.5 °C (*c.* 1260 BC), falling to *c.* 12 °C at the beginning of the Late Bronze Age (*c.* 1150–960 BC). Slight increases in C-ITs to 12.8 °C are recorded from the end of the Bronze Age into the Iron Age (*c.* 920–620 BC), later dropping to 11.4 °C (*c.* 660–480 BC). Taken at face value, these data imply that the climatic deterioration of *c.* 750 BC (above) took place during a period of rising summer temperatures. However, the significance of these temperature estimations in terms of the BSW record and island-wide climatic conditions is unclear.

Although interpretation of BSW records tend to focus on wet/cold shifts, Swindles and colleagues presented data from Northern Ireland, suggesting summer moisture deficits may have affected some peatlands leading to 'summer drought phases' during the Bronze Age (*c.* 1150–800 BC), Iron Age (*c.* 320 BC to 150 AD) and Late Iron Age to early medieval period (*c.* AD 250–470).[42] On the basis of these data, the climatic deterioration of the mid-eighth century BC was potentially preceded by a drier and warmer period during the Late Bronze Age,

---

[38] Becker *et al.*, *New perspectives on the Iron Age*.
[39] Armit *et al.* 'Rapid climate change did not cause population collapse at the end of the Irish Bronze Age'.
[40] Swindles *et al.*, 'A 4500 year proxy climate record from peatlands in the North of Ireland the identification of widespread summer drought phases', *Quaternary Science Reviews* 29 (2010), 1577–89.
[41] Taylor *et al.*, 'A mid to late Holocene chironomid-inferred temperature record from northwest Ireland', *Palaeogeography, Palaeoclimatology, Palaeoecology* 505:15 (2018), 274–86.
[42] Swindles *et al.*, 'A 4500 year proxy climate record from peatlands in the North of Ireland'.

TABLE 1—Summary of selected data discussed from c. 1500 BC to c. 300 BC. DP = drought phase; BB = bog burst; C-ITs = Chironomid-inferred temperatures; 🗿: palynological evidence for woodland regeneration/reduced human impact; dashed line: palynological evidence for human impact/agriculture. The relative intensity of such activity is not represented.

Date (cal. BC)	Period	Demography	Palaeo climate	Meenachrinna	Inchiquin	Lisheen	Muckno	Barrees
300	Developed Iron Age		**DP begins**			🗿		🗿
400			*11.4°C*		— 🗿	BB		🗿
500	....		*12.5°C*		🗿	🗿		—
600	Transition		*WET/COLD SHIFT*		🗿	BB		—
700								—
800	....	RAPID DECLINE	**DP ends**		—		—	—
900		DECLINE	*12.8°C*		🗿	BB	🗿	—
1000	Late Bronze Age	PEAK	**DP begins**		🗿	—	🗿	—
1100			*12°C*		🗿		🗿	—
1200			*13.5°C*			BB		—
1300			*11.5°C*			🗿		🗿
1400						🗿		
1500								

although how this correlates with the Lough Meenachrinna palaeotemperature reconstruction is unclear (see above).[43]

Bog bursts and palaeohydrological changes in Irish peatlands

Although some records indicate wetter/colder conditions during the Late Bronze Age to Iron Age transition, other BSW data appear to show the opposite. Multi-proxy BSW analyses from Lisheen Bog, part of the Littleton Bog complex, Co. Tipperary (Fig. 2) demonstrate abrupt *dry/warm* shifts at dates of *c.* 1250 BC, 750 BC, 600 BC/400 BC, with recoveries to wetter BSW between these dates.[44] The second dry shift (*c.* 750 BC) is notable as it falls at the same time that the BSW meta-analyses described above indicate wetter/colder conditions potentially across both Ireland and the UK. Recent palaeohydrological investigations of the Littleton Bog complex some five kilometres south of Lisheen have also identified dry shifts in BSW records at dates of *c.* 1190 BC, 660 BC and 440 BC.[45] Integrated archaeological and palaeoenvironmental research associated with the excavation of a medieval 'bog body' in the Kilnagarnagh Bog complex, Co. Offaly (Fig. 2), identified a very wet fen environment until *c.* 1000–950 BC, when a sudden shift to drier conditions was indicated.[46] Palaeohydrological investigations by Bermingham in an adjacent part of the Kilnagarnagh Complex at Lemanaghan also identified pronounced shifts from wet to dry conditions *c.* 980–820 BC in multiple BSW records.[47]

However, these BSW data from these sites do not reflect climate in an unambiguous manner, for the dry shifts have been interpreted as signals of events known as 'bog bursts': catastrophic structural failure of an area of peatland, driven by excessive hydrological recharge.[48] Studies of contemporary bog bursts suggest they often occur following episodes of extreme weather, in particular following sustained rainfall.[49] Although possibly caused by processes that might be

---

[43] Taylor *et al.*, 'A mid to late Holocene chironomid-inferred temperature record'.
[44] Margaret Gowen, John O'Neill and Michael Phillips (eds), *The Lisheen Mine archaeological project* 1996–1998, (Bray, 2003); Christopher J. Caseldine and Benjamin R. Gearey, 'Evaluation of a multi-proxy approach to reconstructing surface wetness changes on a complex raised mire system at Derryville Bog, Co. Tipperary, Ireland: identification of responses to a series of prehistoric bog bursts', *The Holocene* 15 (2005), 585–601.
[45] Phil Stastney, Daniel S. Young and Nick Branch, 'The identification of late-Holocene bog bursts at Littleton Bog, Ireland: ecohydrological changes display complex climatic and non-climatic drivers', *The Holocene* 28:4 (2017), 1–13.
[46] Nora Bermingham and Máire Delaney, *The bog body of Tumbeagh* (Bray, 2006).
[47] Nora Bermingham, '*Palaeohydrology and archaeology in raised mires: a case study of Kilnagarnagh Bog*', unpublished Ph.D. Thesis, University of Hull, UK, 2005.
[48] J. Couwenberg and H. Joosten, 'Self organisation in raised bog patterning: the origin of microtope zonation and mesotope diversity', *Journal of Ecology* 93:6 (2005), 1238–48.
[49] Elizabeth Feldmeyer-Christe, Meinrad Küchler and Otto Wildi, 'Patterns of early succession on bare peat in a Swiss mire after a bog burst. *Journal of Vegetation Science* 22:5 (2011), 943–54.

associated with climatic deterioration (i.e. increased rainfall), these events result in dry/warm rather than wet/cold signals in BSW records. There is persuasive evidence that peatlands in the Irish midlands were particularly susceptible to bog bursts.[50] Casparie speculated that 'large scale erosion, as a result of bog bursts, was quite normal in Irish raised bog growth, discharging the excess water on the bog surface in a very short time'.[51]

The BSW records from Lisheen, Littleton and Kilnagarnagh might therefore be rejected as unsuitable for palaeoclimatic interpretation, because the data are 'confounded' by these 'bog burst' signals.[52] However, 'bog bursts' were identified at these two sites due to detailed stratigraphic investigations informed by multiproxy palaeoenvironmental and archaeological data. In the absence of such integrated analyses, the causes of these abrupt falls in BSW would have remained unclear. These datasets provide insights into peatlands as dynamic systems and are critical for the interpretation of the associated peatland archaeological record. As explored further in the next section, past human activity in wetland environments took place both *in* climates and *on* bog surfaces; there is not necessarily an unambiguous correlation between the two.

Anthropogenic activity on changing bogs and in changing climates?

The peatland archaeological record from Lisheen shows a close correspondence between the construction of archaeological sites such as timber trackways and platforms and the fluctuations in BSW during the Bronze Age and Iron Age (Fig. 4; data from Gearey and Caseldine).[53] Human activity and construction of sites, on and across the peatland, during the Later Bronze Age was associated with drier BSW, following falls in the watertable driven by bog burst at *c.* 1055 BC, 750 BC and 600 BC. The 'high bog' (the central areas of the peatland), became more accessible during these periods, allowing access at least on a seasonal basis.

The pattern changes during the Iron Age *c.* 400 BC when BSW records indicate a shift back to extremely wet conditions (see Fig. 4;); the construction of sites such as wooden trackways and platforms also increased at this time, but the spatial focus of activity shifted to the very edge of the bog. A close relationship between local bog hydrology and archaeological site construction is also apparent at Kilnagarnagh during the Late Bronze Age; the construction of a number of wooden trackways in the Lemanaghan complex between *c.* 960–940 BC followed closely after drier conditions on the bog surface, resulting from the drainage of

---

[50] J. Feehan and G. O'Donovan, *The bogs of Ireland* (Dublin, 1996).
[51] Wil Casparie, 'Prehistoric building disasters in Derryville bog, Ireland: trackways, floodings and erosion', in Barry Raftery and Joyce Hickey (eds), *Recent developments in wetland research,* (Dublin, 2001), 115–28.
[52] Swindles *et al.*, 'Centennial-scale climate change in Ireland during the Holocene'.
[53] Benjamin R. Gearey and Chris J. Caseldine. 'Archaeological applications of testate amoebae analyses: a case study from Derryville, Co. Tipperary, Ireland', *Journal of Archaeological Science* 33 (2006), 49–55.

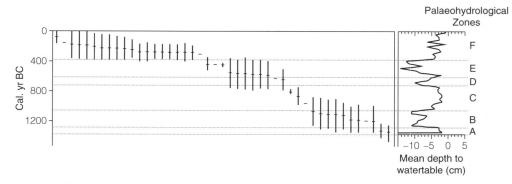

Fig. 4—Plot showing the radiocarbon (two standard deviation) and dendrochronological dates for the peatland archaeological structures at Lisheen Bog. Plotted against BSW (right) and palaeohydrological zones.

a 'bog lake' due to a bog burst around 1000 BC. Although the reasons for the construction of these trackways must be sought in social factors associated with the requirement to cross or access the peatland, human activity can be enabled, as well as constrained, by changes in specific local environmental conditions.

Hence, not all palaeohydrological 'events' in Irish BSW records unambiguously reflect a palaeoclimatic signal, but as observed at Lisheen and Kilnagarnagh, dry shifts related to bog bursts did have local, site specific significance for human activity and the archaeological record. McDermott (2001) attributed the increase in the construction of trackway structures in the Lemanaghan complex to more accessible bog surfaces related to a drier climate, indicated by a 'narrowest ring event' in the dendrochronological record at 1159 BC.[54] However, as the stratigraphic and palaeoenvironmental analyses at Tumbeagh demonstrate, these proxy records diverge from the dendroecological data: the bog system was highly saturated at this time, and only became relatively dry after c. 1000 BC. It is also possible that human activity at Lisheen during the Iron Age might have impacted directly on local peatland hydrology: the construction of a large timber trackway across a discharge channel at the western edge of the peatland damned the drainage system, resulting in a bog burst evident in both the stratigraphic and BSW records c. 600 BC.[55] As outlined earlier, possible drivers of hydrological change have focussed on climate or often ill-defined 'bog system dynamics'.[56] The direct role of human activity is a potential variable rarely considered.

---

[54] Bermingham and Delaney, *The bog body of Tumbeagh*.
[55] Gearey and Caseldine. 'Archaeological applications of testate amoebae analyses'
[56] Dan J. Charman, 'A 1000-year reconstruction of summer precipitation from Ireland: calibration of a peat-based palaeoclimate record, *Quaternary International* 268 (2012), 87–97.

Human activity during the Late Bronze Age and Iron Age: evidence for climatic and environmental change

A methodological problem of investigating the potential impact of climate change on terrestrial areas during the Later Bronze Age concerns collating, summarising and correlating patterns of cultural and environmental change on an island-wide scale. To address this, Armit and colleagues analysed over 2000 aggregate archaeological radiocarbon dates (summed probability functions: SPFs) from between 1200 BC to AD 400 across Ireland, concluding that 'there appears to be a distinct peak in human activity in Ireland *c.* 1050–900 BC, followed by a steady decline to around 800 BC and a rapid fall to 750 BC'.[57] The statistical aggregation (LOWESS curve) of eight BSW datasets indicates a trend to wetter conditions between 750 BC and 550 BC, with the former described as a 'major, rapid climate deterioration to much wetter conditions.' However, the relative timing of climatic deterioration, post-dating the demographic fall interpreted from the archaeological data, is interpreted as implying the 'crisis' at the end of the Irish Bronze Age might have been caused by socio-economic rather than environmental factors related to this climatic deterioration.

The palynological record is the third important component of discussions and debates concerning the pattern and process of environmental change and human activity from the Late Bronze Age into the Iron Age. Many Irish pollen records indicate woodland clearance and associated increases in pastoral and arable agriculture across the Bronze Age, generally complementing the archaeological evidence for the expansion of human activity, but with fluctuations in the intensity of this activity at different times in different locations.[58] Plunkett presented palynological data from four lowland raised bogs (Garry and Sluggan, Co. Antrim; Claraghmore, Co. Tyrone; Glen West, Co. Fermanagh) and two blanket bogs (Owenduff, Co. Mayo and Moyreen, Co. Limerick) with chronological control provided by tephrochronology.[59] These records suggest variations in the extent of agriculture corresponding to the Roscommon Phase of the Bronze Age (*c.* 1200 to 1000 BC) with good representation of arable farming in records such as those from Loughnashade and Mooghaun Lough. The Later Bronze Age (Dowris Phase; *c.* 1000 to 600 BC) apparently witnessed a general expansion of settlement, but with palynological evidence regarded as indicating 'instability in settlement patterns' possibly related to the consolidation of human activity to specific parts of the Irish landscape.[60]

Apparent spatial and chronological fluctuations in the relative intensity of land use in pollen diagrams indicate a reduction in human activity from

---

[57] Armit *et al.*, 'Rapid climate change did not cause population collapse at the end of the Irish Bronze Age'.

[58] The chronological data reported in this section are drawn directly from the relevant publications. Most estimates are generally based on 'centre points' of age depth models which do not present the full probabilistic calibrated ranges.

[59] Gill Plunkett, 'Land-use patterns and cultural change in the Middle to Late Bronze Age in Ireland: Inferences from pollen records', *Vegetation history and Archaeobotany* 18:4 (2008), 273–95.

[60] Plunkett, 'Land-use patterns and cultural change in the Middle to Late Bronze Age in Ireland'.

c. 1000 BC, suggesting a contraction in settlement, agriculture and associated woodland regeneration that may reflect the postulated 'demographic fall' (above). However, this pattern is not pervasive, and other records demonstrate continued human activity after *c.* 900 BC, hence during and after the demographic fall (Table 1).[61] The pollen record from Lough Mennachrinna indicates that agriculture continued, apparently uninterrupted from *c.* 1780 BC to 100 BC, with steady reductions in arboreal pollen across this period.[62] Recent palynological data from Lough Muckno, Co. Monaghan, demonstrates strong evidence for human activity between *c.* 1490–1300 BC, followed by a decrease in intensity from *c.* 1300 to 650 BC prior to a resurgence from *c.* 650 to 220 BC, described as 'comparable to land use dynamics in the Middle Bronze Age'.[63] The pollen record from Lough Inchiquin in the south of the Burren, suggests the Middle Bronze Age was distinguished by a period of woodland regeneration, *c.* 1540 to 1320 BC, with intense land-use between *c.* 1200 and 1000 BC, then an expansion of woodland from *c.* 1000 to 900 BC, implying a reduction in human activity, followed by renewed clearance and farming activity *c.* 900 to 750 BC.[64] Multiple pollen records from Lisheen Bog, Co. Tipperary (see above; Fig. 1) shows woodland regeneration from *c.* 1310 to 1050 BC, with clearance beginning from the latter date until *c.* 600 BC, at which time woodland recovered again, until further human impacts on the landscape after *c.* 200 BC.

Given that most records are from the lowlands, palynological data from the Barrees valley in the uplands of the Beara Peninsula, southwest Ireland are important.[65] Human activity, including pastoral and arable farming, intensified from the mid-Late Bronze Age and into the Iron Age, from *c.* 1400 BC through to *c.* 400 BC, with 'major reductions' in arboreal pollen from *c.* 1400–900 BC and again from *c.* 850–400 BC. This study is also significant as the analysis of multiple records from the study area of the Barrees valley, demonstrates spatial variation in land use during the mid to late Iron Age, with human activity taking place both in the lower areas of the landscape and also the uplands

---

[61] Armit *et al.*, 'Rapid climate change did not cause population collapse at the end of the Irish Bronze Age'.

[62] Taylor *et al.*, 'A mid to late Holocene chironomid-inferred temperature record from northwest Ireland', *Palaeogeography, Palaeoclimatology, Palaeoecology* 505:15 (2018), 274–86.

[63] Carlos Chique, Karen Molloy and Aaron P. Potito, 'Mid-Late Holocene vegetational history and land-use dynamics in County Monaghan, Northeastern Ireland: the palynological record of Lough Muckno', *Journal of the North Atlantic* 32, (2017), 1–24.

[64] Spencer *et al.*, 'New insights into Late Bronze Age settlement and farming in the southern Burren, Western Ireland', *Vegetation History and Archaeobotany* 29, (2019), 339–56.

[65] Annette Overland and Michael O'Connell, 'Fine spatial palaeoecological investigations towards the reconstruction of late Holocene environmental change, landscape evolution and farming activity in Barrees, Beara Peninsula', *Journal of the North Atlantic* 1:1 (2008), 27–73.

(over 200m asl).[66] In general, there are few other 'three dimensional' studies available that permit investigation of variations in patterns of change across relatively discrete spatial extents of the landscape.

The chronological precision of radiocarbon determinations varies, and in particular is constrained by the impact of the 'Homeric minimum' on radiocarbon calibration, the so-called Hallstatt Plateau, which effectively means that radiocarbon dates falling from *c.* 750 to 400 BC have calibrated (calendrical) ranges of several centuries.[67] However, recent palaeoenvironmental research in southeast Ireland has significantly refined the precision of determinations for a pollen record from Lough Cullin, Co. Waterford using Bayesian modelling (Fig. 1).[68] This sequence indicates that following a well-defined phase of intensive human activity (including pastoral and arable agriculture) during the Middle Bronze Age, from 1500–1470 BC to 1230–990 BC, there was a reduction in activity from the latter date leading to some woodland recovery.[69] After 805–710 BC, human activity appears to have ceased completely, but this was a relatively short-lived hiatus as woodland clearance and agriculture commenced again after 680–535 BC, continuing until 430–235 BC.

There are of course variations in the number of individual radiocarbon determinations obtained for the pollen sequences discussed above, and for all other records that cover the later prehistoric period in Ireland. The number and relative density of radiocarbon determinations has implications for the chronological precision that can be obtained, especially for the estimation of palynological 'events' that have not been directly dated.[70] While the chronology for the Lough Cullin sequence is based on an unusually high density of dates across the later prehistoric period, the range of modelled date estimates is variable and still cannot be resolved to decadal precision.

There are potentially coherent patterns of implied vegetation change; for example, human activity seems to have been variable during the Later Bronze Age, with reduced evidence possibly a feature of records from the north and west

---

[66] Overland and O'Connell, 'Fine spatial palaeoecological investigations towards the reconstruction of late Holocene environmental change'.

[67] Jacobsson *et al.*, 'Refining the Hallstatt plateau: short-term 14C variability and small scale offsets in 50 consecutive single tree-rings from southwest Scotland dendro-dated to 510–460 BC', *Radiocarbon* 60:1 (2017), 219–37.

[68] Becker *et al.*, '"Seeing beyond the site" Settlement and landscapes in later prehistoric Ireland: INSTAR-funded project AR04557, Phase 1 report to the Heritage Council', University College Cork, 2016; Christopher Bronk Ramsey, 'Deposition models for chronological records', *Quaternary Science Reviews* 27:1–2 (2008), 42–60.

[69] These are date ranges (at two standard deviations) or *posterior density estimates*, derived from Bayesian modelling of the radiocarbon chronology.

[70] For example, see Benjamin Gearey, Peter Marshall and Derek Hamilton, 'Correlating archaeological and palaeoenvironmental records using a Bayesian approach: a case study from Sutton Common, south Yorkshire, England', *Journal of Archaeological Science* 7 (2009), 1477–87.

of Ireland.[71] Given the hypothesised demographic collapse, an important question is how contrasting palynological evidence for anthropogenic activity in different geographical areas relates to possible changes in the distribution of human populations, as reflected by local archaeological datasets.[72] In practical terms, a review and statistical analysis of the chronological robustness of relevant Irish pollen records would be required to determine the precision of these datasets and hence better establish the relationship between records of environmental change and available archaeological data and chronologies.[73]

Building upwards? A case study of southeast Ireland

What approaches might we adopt and adapt to deal with some of the problems and uncertainties of the Late Bronze Age to Iron Age transition? How can we build upon previous research and identify and define local, regional and ultimately island-wide patterns of change across this period? What are the gaps in knowledge, which of these may remain beyond the reach of current methods, and which might be tackled by future research?

The Lough Cullin pollen diagram discussed above was part of an integrated programme of archaeological and palaeoenvironmental research on the Bronze Age to Iron Age transition in southeast Ireland (Cos Kilkenny and Waterford).[74] It provides closely dated evidence for reductions in human activity, one of the most pronounced of which dates to 760–535 BC, coinciding with the postulated climatic deterioration (c. 750 BC). These 'events' can therefore be described as imbricated, with chronology used 'purely [as] a means to establish... overlap (or not)', without loading this correlation with causational significance.[75] This example demonstrates the role of a robust chronological framework especially for estimating the degree of 'imbrication' between environmental and archaeological 'events', in explicitly defined spatial and geographical areas.[76] Whilst we might regard chronological correspondence between evidence for climatic and cultural change as a 'smoking gun' in terms of causality, this depends

---

[71] Spencer *et al.*, 'New insights into Late Bronze Age settlement and farming'.

[72] Carleton Jones, 'Climate change and farming response in a temperate oceanic zone: the exploitation of a karstic region in Western Ireland in the third and second millennia BC', *The Journal of Island and Coastal Archaeology* (2019), 1–22.

[73] P. Dark, 'Climate deterioration and land-use change in the first millennium BC: perspectives from the British palynological record', *Journal of Archaeological Science* 33, (2006), 1381–95; Chapman and Gearey, *Modelling archaeology and palaeoenvironments in wetlands*; Kevin Kearney and Benjamin R. Gearey, 'The elm decline is dead! Long live declines in elm: revisiting the chronology of the elm decline in Ireland and its association with the Mesolithic/Neolithic Transition', *Environmental Archaeology* 25, (2020), 1–14.

[74] Becker *et al.*, '"Seeing beyond the site" Settlement and landscapes in later prehistoric Ireland'.

[75] Gavin Lucas, 'Archaeology and contemporaneity', *Archaeological Dialogues* 22:1 (2015), 1–15, DOI: 10.1017/S1380203815000021

[76] Gearey *et al.*, 'Correlating archaeological and palaeoenvironmental records using a Bayesian approach'.

on the rate, scale and character of change in both records and, as observed above, our ability to reliably reconstruct these varies in practice. This is especially problematic for the Late Bronze Age to Iron Age because, as we have seen, the chronology and character of cultural processes as interpreted from the archaeological record are uncertain and contested.

The aforementioned project, focused on the southeast, aimed to tackle some of the methodological and theoretical problems and complexities considered in this paper.[77] A review of archaeological information, including Bayesian modelling of radiocarbon dates from excavated archaeological sites was undertaken, alongside a review of associated plant macrofossil and archaeozoological remains. Analysis of the spatial distribution of archaeological sites was performed within a Geographical Information System. Relatively few paleoenvironmental studies have been carried out in the southeast and modelling of the available records indicated some chronological problems. There are no BSW records or palaeotemperature data available from southeast Ireland. Hence palaeoclimatic data could only be obtained from either the closest available records or utilising the aggregate reconstructions described earlier, with due recognition of the generalised nature of these datasets.[78]

A range of archaeological sites was identified, but the Bronze Age archaeology was dominated by *fulachtai fia* and burnt mounds, thus establishing chronologies for these features was critical to an understanding of their longevity in the landscape. Poor preservation of plant macrofossil and faunal remains impacted on the detailed reconstruction of later prehistoric changes in farming and subsistence. In terms of vegetation and environmental change, the palynological analyses of a core from Lough Cullin were outlined in brief above. Significant improvements in precision were obtained across the 'Hallstatt Plateau' permitting finer-grained temporal resolution for the pollen record. Palynological analyses from blanket peat in the Comeragh Mountains implies variation in the intensity of pastoral farming in the uplands during later prehistory, but this record is compromised by problems with the radiocarbon chronology. The limited availability of other palaeoecological records in the study area curtailed reconstruction of wider regional spatial and chronological patterns of environmental change, but comparison with patterns of human activity inferred from archaeological sites within the pollen catchment of Lough Cullin allowed the formulation of hypotheses that can be tested by further study.

Discussion

At the heart of the challenge of correlating past climatic change (and for that matter environmental change in general) to human activity are issues of scale: both the analytical (geographical) scale adopted by researchers, and the inherent

---

[77] Becker *et al.*, '"Seeing beyond the site" Settlement and landscapes in later prehistoric Ireland'.
[78] Armit *et al.*, 'Rapid climate change did not cause population collapse at the end of the Irish Bronze Age'.

spatial and chronological limitations and constraints of available analytical methods. For example, BSW records from testate amoebae analyses are intrinsically hyperlocal; the spatial scale that testate amoebae communities occupied is the film of water on a *Sphagnum* leaf, which can be measured in millimetres cubed. The derivation of 'climatic meaning' from these records—at the level of site, region, island and beyond—therefore rests on the demonstration of teleconnections: coherent directional patterns of hydrological change across space and time. The closer the correspondence between the direction, degree and chronology of change in different records from different geographical areas, the more confident we can be that climate was the common driver of change.[79] However, the recursive relationship between environmental change and human activity—as reflected, for example, by the records from Lisheen and Lemanaghan—can only be understood on a site-specific, local scale.[80] If we want to drill down into the complexities of the mechanisms linking past climatic and ecosystem change to human activity, we need studies that work with, as opposed to against, these complexities and uncertainties of scale.

To move forward, we require a nuanced multiscalar perspective and multiple datasets that can be explicitly integrated from the bottom up: local narratives of specific sites and places are ultimately what compose the big picture.[81] Robust and precise chronological control is obviously important for both archaeological and palaeoclimatic records, and variable degrees of precision for either will constrain integrated interpretation. In order to fully represent the degree of chronological certainty attached to specific palaeoenvironmental and archaeological records, it is also essential that chronological age model uncertainties are always specified and discussed.[82] This is important for quantifying the degree of 'imbrication' between 'events' (see above), especially relevant for periods of abrupt, rapid change (decadal and below) which arguably were more likely to have impacted on human communities than gradual (centurial or millennial) processes. Meta-analyses of aggregated datasets are important tools to summarise broad scale patterns of change, but we should be wary of utilising these approaches shorn of the foundation and context provided by smaller scale studies, which are essential to unpick past processes that were undoubtedly complex, variable and nuanced across both time and space. Further proxy analyses and archaeological studies are necessary, and may lead towards improved, or at least less ambiguous conclusions, but we should be

---

[79] Langdon *et al.*, 'Regional climate change from peat stratigraphy from the mid-to late Holocene in central Ireland', *Quaternary International* 268 (2012), 145–55.
[80] See also Stastney, this volume.
[81] Chapman and Gearey, *Modelling archaeology and palaeoenvironments in wetlands*.
[82] Seren Griffiths and Benjamin Gearey, 'The Mesolithic-Neolithic transition and the chronology of the 'Elm Decline': a case study of east Yorkshire and Humberside U.K.', *Radiocarbon* 59 (2017), 1321–45; Terri Lacourse and Konrad Gajewski, 'Current practices in building and reporting age-depth models', *Quaternary Research* (2020), 1–11 https://doi.org/10.1017/qua.2020.47

aware there is no *a priori* reason to assume that bigger datasets always bring greater clarity or better answers.

We have examined, unevenly and incompletely, the three distinct but interconnected strands of research that together constitute narratives of the Late Bronze Age to Iron Age transition, namely archaeology, palaeohydrology/palaeoclimatology and palaeoecology. There has clearly been significant progress in archaeological and palaeoenvironmental research, shedding considerable light on patterns and processes of environmental and cultural change across this period. However, as Brown observed, 'the chances of finding correlations between climatic fluctuations and cultural changes by chance is almost certainly very high and rises with the increasing number and precision of palaeoclimatic records'.[83] As more data are generated, robustly correlating and integrating records therefore represents a theoretical as well as a methodological challenge.

In terms of the archaeological record, the character and chronology of the Late Bronze Age to Iron Age transition continues to present interpretative problems, not least the question of how and what we define as the 'end' of the Bronze Age. While the 'Hallstatt plateau' affects chronological precision for both archaeological and palaeoenvironmental records, attention has been drawn to evidence of pronounced changes in the archaeological record that have emerged through recent programmes of radiocarbon dating. These are suggestive of a broader cultural change in the eighth century BC that can be regarded as an Early Iron Age horizon.[84] This interpretation also rules out a 'longer' Bronze Age as previously envisaged, further stressing the complex nature of this transition.

The BSW data indicate a wet/cold shift occurred during the mid-eighth century BC but based on aggregated archaeological radiocarbon dates as a proxy for human activity, this does not seem to have contributed to the 'crisis' of the Later Bronze Age, because the postulated demographic drop seems to have commenced about a century and a half earlier (*c.* 900 BC).[85] However, the chronology and character of both 'events' are still not fully resolved. Using the best-dated site, Glen West (Co. Fermanagh), the climatic shift was 'constrained to 748 cal. BC (maximum probability) or 786–703 cal. BC (modelled range)',

---

[83] Brown, 'The Bronze Age climate and environment of Britain'.
[84] Katharina Becker, 'The introduction of iron working to Ireland', in A. Kern, and J. Koch (eds), *Technologieentwicklung und – transfer in der Eisenzeit.* Tagungsbericht der AG Eisenzeit, Hallstatt 2009. Beiträge zur Ur-und Frühgeschichte Mitteleuropas, (Langenweissenbach, 2012), 173–80; Katharina Becker, 'The dating of Late Bronze Age Dowris metalwork – a pilot study', *Journal of Irish Archaeology* 21 (2013), 7–15; Katharina Becker, Ian Armit and Graeme Swindles, 'New perspectives on the Irish Iron Age: the impact of NRA development on our understanding of later prehistory', in M. Stanley (ed.), *Stories of our past* (Bray, 2017), 85–100.
[85] Armit *et al.*, 'Rapid climate change did not cause population collapse at the end of the Irish Bronze Age'.

but another site, Derragh Bog (Co. Longford), gave a significantly wider range of 791–429 cal. BC (see Fig. 1).[86] We have not considered in detail how BSW records correlate and articulate with other proxy climate records: for example, it has been argued on the basis of the Irish 'bog oak' records that a shift to 'extreme wet' conditions in Ireland and the United Kingdom began *c.* 1000 BC.[87] Nor have we discussed the potential impact of warmer/drier climatic conditions that have been identified for the Later Bronze Age (see above).[88]

Assuming climate deterioration can be reliably anchored to *c.* 750 BC and is robustly represented by a single curve, we still cannot derive estimates of the absolute severity or nature of this change. We do not know how this might have affected environmental variables important for subsistence and agriculture, such as seasonality, the length of growing season, or if increased levels of precipitation could have led to reduced agricultural yields.[89] These are important in terms of human populations which, following the demographic data, had apparently been under some form of stress for perhaps a century and a half. In practice, as mentioned above in relation to the southeast case study, poor preservation of macrobotanical and faunal remains from excavated archaeological sites means our ability to identify and reconstruct changes in subsistence may be rather limited. The dearth of quantitative palaeotemperature reconstructions further constrains interpretation and inferences but offers potential for future enhanced understanding.[90]

Pollen records are a key component of reconstructing changes in human activity, and available data suggest some potentially coherent regional patterns in the form of reductions in human activity during the Later Bronze Age into the Iron Age. However, their exact significance for regional fluctuations in the distribution and character of human populations and settlement are unclear. As outlined above, some pollen records indicate reductions in human activity which appear to be coeval with the climatic deterioration of *c.* 750 BC, but further study is required. We must also be cautious of assuming that a lack of palynological evidence for human activity always reflects complete abandonment of a landscape: for example, the pollen record from Lisheen implies woodland regeneration between *c.* 1310–1000 BC, but the archaeological record demonstrates continuing construction of sites such as trackways in the

---

[86] Armit *et al.*, 'Rapid climate change did not cause population collapse at the end of the Irish Bronze Age'.

[87] Turney *et al.*, 'Extreme wet conditions coincident with upland abandonment in southwest Britain', *Anthropocene* 13 (2016), 69–79.

[88] Swindles *et al.*, 'A 4500-year proxy climate record from peatlands in the North of Ireland'.

[89] Richard Tipping, '"I have not been able to discover anything of interest in the peat": landscapes and environments in the Later Bronze and Iron Ages in Scotland', in F. Hunter and I. Ralston, (eds) *Scotland in later prehistoric Europe* (Edinburgh, 2015), 103–19.

[90] Taylor *et al.*, 'A mid to late Holocene chironomid-inferred temperature record'.

peatland throughout this period (see Fig. 4).⁹¹ These variations, uncertainties and gaps in the different datasets allow for a profusion of reasonable hypotheses which are often effectively impossible to prove or disprove. This arguably has resulted in the polarisation of interpretative positions, with some scholars looking to socio-cultural factors (often ill-defined) to explain patterns in the archaeological record, while others envisage climatic drivers wiping out Bronze Age communities ill-prepared for 'catastrophe', even though such drivers are also poorly defined and understood.

To tackle some of these problems, the case study focused on southeast Ireland described above attempted to refine the chronology and character of cultural and environmental changes across the Late Bronze Age to Iron Age transition. All available archaeological and palaeoecological data were considered and a rigorous approach was taken to the 'chronological hygiene' of associated radiocarbon determinations.⁹² The production of a new, high resolution palynological record from Lough Cullin meant the archaeological sites and inferred human activity within its defined pollen catchment could be contextualised. Wider patterns of regional environmental change cannot be extrapolated from this record, but hypotheses could be formulated. The adoption of a formal Bayesian approach to modelling and correlating the archaeological and palaeoecological chronologies permitted statistical assessment of the chronological relationships between inferred patterns of change. Further regional scale studies offer one way to build a wider island-wide picture, incorporating and allowing for varying strengths, shortcomings and imprecisions of relevant datasets and ensuring that these uncertainties always remain in the foreground of our interpretations.

Linking palaeoclimatic records with archaeological evidence always runs the risks of raising the 'spectre' of environmental determinism, a continuing issue for some researchers.⁹³ Determining the chronological relationship between changes identified in the archaeological, palaeoclimatological and palaeoecological datasets might be regarded as a first order requirement.⁹⁴ This would possibly help define *potential* scenarios and formulate hypotheses concerning climate and cultural changes, that can be tested through further research. Further theoretical reflection on how we can produce balanced accounts of climatic and cultural change is also needed.

---

[91] Gowen *et al.*, *The Lisheen Mine archaeological project*.
[92] Kearney and Gearey, 'The elm decline is dead'.
[93] Paul Coombes and Keith Barber, 'Environmental determinism in Holocene research. Causality or coincidence?', *Area* 37:3 (2005), 303–11; Arponen *et al.*, 'Environmental determinism and archaeology. Understanding and evaluating determinism in research design', *Archaeological Dialogues* 26 (2019), 1–9.
[94] For example, see Seren Griffiths and Erick Robinson, 'The 8.2 ka BP climate change event and human resilience in northwest Europe', *Quaternary International* 465 (2018), 251–57.

Conclusion

We have deliberately drawn attention to some of the issues that confound or complicate the production of straightforward narratives of human–environment relationships in later prehistory. Whilst rooted in different and sometimes conflicting paradigms and derived using discrete methods and techniques, the climatic, environmental and archaeological records have, through time, been woven in a complex and recursive manner into narratives with distinct and variable emphases. The gaps and omissions in these narratives are just as significant as the more complete sections; incomplete or inconclusive evidence will allow for different interpretations and hypotheses. The recognition of such gaps can also help define and shape future research, but understanding of cultural and environmental changes is often focused at variable, and sometimes coarse, chronological and spatial scales.[95] This is partly due to the inherent shortcomings of the available methodologies as well as the analytical precision and detail of individual records, rather than a lack of research interest. Current scholarship has largely turned away from compelling but rather uncomplicated, totalising narratives in which climate was the sole, or at least the primary, driver of cultural change in late prehistory. While this is to be welcomed, the challenge is now to embark on a more nuanced exploration of the relationship between climatic change and cultural change in the Late Bronze Age and Iron Age, and for this we need better understandings of both processes.

Acknowledgements

The authors would like to acknowledge funding from the Heritage Council and Transport Infrastructure Ireland for the project 'Seeing beyond the site' Settlement and landscapes in Later Prehistoric Ireland' (AR04557/AR06241) under the INSTAR (Irish National Strategic Archaeological Research Programme). We are very grateful for the advice, assistance and patience of the Editors and for the helpful comments of two anonymous referees. This paper is based in part on a presentation given by BRG at the Palaeoecology Laboratory, University of Southampton.

---

[95] Langdon *et al.*, 'Regional climate change from peat stratigraphy'.

Cultural change and the climate record in final prehistoric and early medieval Ireland

Lisa Coyle McClung and Gill Plunkett*

Archaeology and Palaeoecology, School of Natural and Built Environment, Queen's University Belfast, Northern Ireland.

[Accepted 01 July 2019. Published 25 March 2020.]

Abstract

To what extent did climate change steer the trajectories of early societies? The final prehistoric (Developed to Late Iron Age) and early medieval periods in Ireland witnessed several major transformations in settlement, economy, material culture and ideology. Here, we review the palaeoenvironmental records to contextualise these transformations in terms of both climate oscillations and land-use history to evaluate whether climate change may have played a role in altering the socio-economic or political framework. We find little evidence that climate change coincided with major cultural alterations in the archaeological record, with pollen records providing important insights into ongoing human activity during times of reduced archaeological visibility. Although palaeoenvironmental records rarely provide sufficient chronological resolution with which to test the effects of abrupt environmental changes on populations, we note no lasting impacts following the proposed downturns that would implicate climate as a determinant of enduring cultural change during these periods.

Introduction

There is a frequent, if often implicit, tendency to assume that cultural transitions of past societies were environmentally-driven and that climatic deteriorations, through their detrimental effects on the environment and subsistence economy, were the main agents of cultural decline.[1] This environmentally-deterministic theory is often considered over and above other more intrinsic factors such as socio-political or economic turmoil. Climate does assert an important influence on the success and productivity levels of farming economies, but the relationship between climate and culture is not straightforward. Various complex influences—including social structure, technology and resources—will determine whether a community is sufficiently resilient to adapt and flourish at times

---

* Author's email: G.Plunkett@qub.ac.uk
ORCID iD: https://orcid.org/0000-0003-1014-3454
doi: https://doi.org/10.3318/PRIAC.2020.120.04

[1] M.G.L. Baillie and M.A.R. Munro, 'Irish tree rings, Santorini and volcanic dust veils', *Nature* 332 (1988), 344–6; M.G.L. Baillie, 'Great oaks from little acorns...: precision and accuracy in Irish dendrochronology', in F.M. Chambers (ed.), *Climate change and human impact on the landscape* (London 1993), 33–41; Ulf Büntgen *et al.*, '2500 years of European climate variability and human susceptibility', *Science* 331 (2011), 578–82.

of climate change or if it will collapse into crisis.[2] Even when the occurrence of past climate changes can be substantiated, establishing a temporal correlation—much less a causal link—between climate and cultural change is fraught with difficulties, given the chronological uncertainties that frequently beset both the archaeological and palaeoclimate records.

Typically, environmentally deterministic models of past cultural change have focused on the impact climate change exerted on the subsistence base.[3] Such a premise lends itself to testing through an examination of the palynological record. Landscape manipulation has long been associated with the subsistence economies of past populations and the pollen record can highlight key transitions in agricultural management. Simply put, the pollen record provides insight into the nature and intensity of farming in the past, though interpretation of the data can be complex. Ideally, pollen and palaeoclimate reconstructions from the same sedimentary sequence enable the relative timing of past climate and land-use changes to be identified unequivocally.[4] Few such studies have yet been undertaken, however, perhaps partly due to a lack of interdisciplinary engagement.

The end of the prehistoric era (the Developed to Late Iron Age) and the dawn of the historic (early medieval) period in Ireland feature several culturally distinct developments within the archaeological record, including 'periods of much building',[5] changes in settlement types and patterns, and changes in economic practices. Perhaps not surprisingly, these changes have been attributed by some to climate fluctuations that at times benefitted, and at times undermined, social development (Table 1).[6] This paper explores the likelihood of environmentally-driven cultural change in Ireland during the Developed to Late Iron Age

---

[2] P.B. deMenocal, 'Cultural responses to climate change during the late Holocene', *Science* 292 (2001), 667–3; K.W. Butzer, 'Collapse, environment, and society', *Proceedings of the National Academy of Sciences* 109 (2012), 3632–9; Jago Cooper, 'Weathering climate change. The value of social memory and ecological knowledge', *Archaeological Dialogues* 19 (2012), 46–51; T.J. Wilkinson, 'Weather and climate proxy records', *Archaeological Dialogues* 19 (2012), 57–62.

[3] Robert van de Noort, 'Conceptualising climate change archaeology', *Antiquity* 85 (2011), 1039–48; Toby Pillatt, 'From climate and society to weather and landscape', *Archaeological Dialogues* 19 (2012), 29–42.

[4] Gill Plunkett, 'Tephra-linked peat humification records from Irish ombrotrophic bogs question nature of solar forcing at 850 cal. yr BC', *Journal of Quaternary Science* 21 (2006), 9–16; Gill Plunkett, 'Socio-political dynamics in later prehistoric Ireland: Insights from the pollen record', in T.L. Thurston and R.B. Salisbury (eds), *Reimagining regional analyses: The archaeology of spatial and social dynamics* (Cambridge, 2009), 42–66.

[5] Richard Warner, 'Tree-rings, catastrophes and culture in Early Ireland: Some comments', *Emania* 11 (1993), 13–9: 13.

[6] Iron Age population collapse: D.A. Weir, 'An environmental history of the Navan area, Co. Armagh', unpublished PhD thesis, Queen's University Belfast, 1993; Impacts of dust veil events at 207 BC, 44–42 BC and AD 536–540: M.G.L. Baillie, 'Dark ages and dendrochronology', *Emania* 11 (1993), 5–12; M.G.L. Baillie, 'Patrick, comets and Christianity', *Emania* 13 (1995), 69–78; Tenth century decline: D.M. Brown and M.G.L.

TABLE 1—Outline of the main cultural events in the Developed to Late Iron Age and early medieval period that have been attributed to climate change.

Cultural event	Timing	Symptoms	Suggested environmental cause*
Flurry of large-scale constructions during the Developed Iron Age	150–95 BC	Social/ideological upheaval leading to construction of ritual and defensive sites such as Navan and the Dorsey	Volcanic event at 207 BC, aggravated by further dust-veil event at 44–42 BC
Late Iron Age Lull	200/100 BC–early centuries AD	Widespread forest regeneration; absence of conspicuous archaeological record	Depopulation following extreme and rapid climate change
Start of early medieval period proper	Mid-sixth century AD	Spread of Christianity, surge in building activity	Dust-veil events at AD 536 and 540, contributing to spread of plague
Tenth century decline	Tenth century AD	Building gap in oak chronology	Volcanic eruption

*See text for references.

and early medieval period by (i) reviewing archaeological evidence for cultural developments during these times that have been attributed to climate variability; (ii) evaluating palaeoclimate records from Ireland to identify potential climate events and transitions; and (iii) examining pollen records to identify if cultural or palaeoclimate changes coincided with variations in subsistence economy.

Cultural developments in final prehistoric and early medieval Ireland

The to-ing and fro-ing of the Irish Iron Age

The Irish Iron Age (c. 700 BC–AD 400) has long been known for the emergence of large-scale construction projects and the manufacture of elaborate metalwork and apparent ritualised offerings,[7] all of which materialised during the last three centuries BC in the period now known as the Developed Iron Age. The scale of collaboration needed for the monumental constructions of this period has been taken to signify the emergence of a new ruling-class keen to establish their territorial boundaries.[8] Navan Fort (Emain Macha), Co. Armagh, Knockaulin

---

Baillie, 'Confirming the existence of gaps and depletions in the Irish oak tree-ring chronology', *Dendrochronologia* 30 (2012), 85–91.

[7] Barry Raftery, *Pagan Celtic Ireland: The enigma of the Irish Iron Age* (London, 1994), 64–97, 147–199.

[8] Raftery, *Pagan Celtic Ireland*, 65; Ian Armit, 'Social landscapes and hidden identities in the Irish Iron Age', in Colin Hasselgrove and Tom Moore (eds), *The later Iron Age in*

(Dún Ailinne), Co. Kildare, Rathcroghan (Cruachain), Co. Roscommon, and Tara (Teamhair), Co. Meath, have frequently been referred to in the literature as 'royal' sites. These localities are embedded in Irish mythology describing warrior champions such as Cú Chulainn;[9] and are believed to have been ceremonial centres and places of assembly.[10] Dendrochronological dating of an oak timber post from the '40m structure' at Navan Fort placed its construction at 95 BC,[11] and excavations at Knockaulin suggest it, too, is broadly contemporary, though perhaps a little later.[12] Additional building developments included extensive manmade linear earthworks, such as the impressive Black Pig's Dyke, thought to be an ancient boundary in southern Ulster. Oak timbers from a section of the Dyke, known as the Dorsey, Co. Armagh, were dendrochronologically dated to 140 BC and 95 BC,[13] the younger date concurrent with that derived from the Navan Fort central post. A date of 148 BC was recorded from Corlea, Co. Longford,[14] arguably the most impressive of Irish wetland trackway (togher) constructions in the prehistoric period. Warner has proposed that such large-scale endeavours are symptomatic of a society under stress and Baillie has pointed to a growth downturn in Irish oaks at 207 BC that may bear testimony to an environmental trigger for such stress.[15] In contrast, Becker has surmised that the Developed Iron Age arose amid a period of climatic improvement.[16]

The emergence of a new material culture in this period, comprising La Tène-style metalwork, has been associated with a warrior elite and horsemanship.[17] Most of the Irish La Tène artefacts have been recovered from wetland environments suggesting they may have been ritualistic, votive offerings.[18] There is also evidence for more gruesome ritual offerings. While bog bodies are not

---

Britain and beyond (Oxford, 2007), 130–9.

[9] Ann Hamlin, 'Emain Macha: Navan Fort', *Seanchas Ardmhacha: Journal of the Armagh Diocesan Historical Society* 11 (1985), 295–300.

[10] S.A Johnston, 'Revisiting the Irish royal sites', *Emania* 20 (2006), 53–9; S.A. Johnston, P.J. Crabtree and D.V. Campana, 'Performance, place and power at Dún Ailinne, a ceremonial site of the Irish Iron Age', *World Archaeology* 46 (2014), 206–23; Patrick Gleeson, 'Assembly and élite culture in Iron Age and late Antique Europe: a case-study of Óenach Clochair, Co. Limerick', *Journal of Irish Archaeology* 23 (2014), 171–87: 171–2.

[11] M.G.L. Baillie, 'The dating of the timbers from Navan Fort and the Dorsey, Co. Armagh', *Emania* 4 (1988), 37–40.

[12] S.A. Johnston, 'Chronology', in S.A. Johnston and Bernard Wailes, '*Dún Ailinne: Excavations at an Irish royal site 1968–1975*' (Dublin, 2007), 182.

[13] Baillie, 'The dating of the timbers from Navan Fort and the Dorsey'.

[14] Raftery, *Pagan Celtic Ireland*, 99.

[15] Warner, 'Tree-rings, catastrophes and culture in early Ireland', 13–9; Baillie, 'Great oaks from little acorns'.

[16] Katharina Becker, 'Relics of old decency', in Gabriel Cooney et al. (eds), *Archaeological studies in later prehistory: Festschrift for Barry Raftery* (Dublin 2009), 353–61: 358.

[17] Raftery, *Pagan Celtic Ireland*, 141.

[18] Raftery, *Pagan Celtic Ireland*, 183; E.P. Kelly, 'Secrets of the bog bodies: The enigma of the Iron Age explained', *Archaeology Ireland* 20:1 (2006), 26–30.

unique to Ireland and cover many cultural periods, those dated to the Iron Age display evidence for deliberate mutilation prior to death, intimating ceremonial killings or even sacrifices. It has been speculated that votive offerings in wetland sites, such as La Tène metalwork and bog bodies, were deliberately positioned to demarcate ancient political territories.[19] In the 2015 BBC production *4,000-year-old cold case: The body in the bog*, it was posited that such ritualised killings were prompted by climate deterioration.

The general scarcity of evidence for non-elite settlement throughout the period led Raftery to coin the phrase 'the invisible people' for the Iron Age population of Ireland.[20] During the Late Iron Age (*c.* AD 1–400), the paucity of information is particularly acute. The available evidence suggests that large-scale structures ceased to be built although there are some indications that smaller-scale elite complexes were in use at the 'royal' sites of Navan Fort, Rathcroghan and Tara, and elsewhere at sites such as Raffin Fort.[21] A recent study revealed an unambiguous hiatus in trackway building across Irish wetland sites dated between *c.* AD 25 and 400.[22] A similar gap in construction was noted during the creation of the Belfast Oak Chronology with, until recently, no Irish archaeological oak timbers found that dated between 40 BC–AD 550.[23] This seeming decline of the Iron Age culture in Ireland has long puzzled archaeologists, and the apparent paucity of the archaeological record over the early centuries AD led to speculation that there was a major demographic crisis,[24] potentially triggered by a global volcanic dust-veil at 44–42 BC.[25] Although about 400 sites of varying type attributable to the Late Iron Age can now be identified thanks to recent development-led rescue archaeology,[26] the current archaeological record remains poorly-defined, characterised by little more than about a dozen houses, an assortment of burial and ritual sites, and an increasing body

---

[19] Kelly, 'Secrets of the bog bodies'.

[20] Raftery, *Pagan Celtic Ireland*, 112.

[21] S.A. Johnston, 'Revisiting the Irish royal sites', *Emania* 20 (2006), 53–9; Eoin Grogan, '*The rath of the Synods, Tara, Co. Meath: Excavations by Seán P. Ó Riordáin*' (Dublin, 2008), 97; Conor Newman, 'Reflections on the making of a "royal site" in early Ireland', *World Archaeology* 30 (1998), 127–41.

[22] Gill Plunkett *et al.*, 'Environmental indifference? A critique of environmentally deterministic theories of peatland archaeological site construction in Ireland', *Quaternary Science Reviews* 61 (2013), 17–31.

[23] M.G.L. Baillie, 'Marking in marker dates: Towards an archaeology with historical precision', *World Archaeology* 23 (1991), 233–43.

[24] D.A. Weir, 'Dark ages and the pollen record', *Emania* 11 (1993), 21–30.

[25] Baillie, 'Great oaks from little acorns'; Brown and Baillie, 'Confirming the existence of gaps and depletions'.

[26] Ger Dowling, 'Landscape and settlement in late Iron Age Ireland: Some emerging trends. Late Iron Age and "Roman" Ireland', *Discovery Programme Reports* 8 (2014), 151–74: 151.

of artefactual remains indicating interactions with the Romano-British world.[27] The vast majority of sites comprise hearths, pits and post-holes dating to the early centuries AD, whose distribution reveals that Late Iron Age activity was in fact widespread across the island.[28] Recognition of this activity has been hindered, in the absence of absolute dates, by its often ephemeral and nondescript nature. Research on Romano-British artefacts and seemingly intrusive burials (inhumations that stand in contrast to the long-held tradition of cremation) in Ireland highlights two periods for which links between Ireland and the Roman and post-Roman world are particularly evident, namely the first–second centuries AD and fourth–sixth centuries AD.[29] Strontium analysis of tooth enamel from seven crouched burials dating to between the second century BC and second century AD confirms that three of the individuals were unlikely of local origin, but included possibly migrants from Britain; of three crouched burials dating to between the fourth and seventh centuries, two were non-local, one perhaps hailing from as far south as the Mediterranean, while eleven out of twenty extended inhumations were of non-local origin.[30]

Others have suggested increased population mobility, perhaps associated with a more fragmented, kin-based system of social structure and a pastoral-based economy, as an alternative explanation for the perceived 'invisibility' of Late Iron Age folk.[31] Dowling argues that there is a greater incidence of enclosed sites from the third century AD, perhaps a sign of more permanent ties with place, and highlights the growing recognition of Iron Age activity beneath early medieval raths and crannogs, that may betray the origins of this later settlement tradition.[32] Recently, there has also been appreciation that corn-drying kilns were in use during the Late Iron Age, notably

---

[27] Katharina Becker, 'Redefining the Irish Iron Age', in Michael Potterton and Christiaan Corlett (eds), *Life and death in Iron Age Ireland* (Dublin, 2012), 1–14; Cóilín Ó Drisceoil and E. Devine, 'Invisible people or invisible archaeology? Carrickmines Great, Co. Dublin, and the problem of Irish Iron Age settlement', in Christiaan Corlett and Michael Potterton (eds), *Life and death in Iron Age Ireland in the light of recent archaeological excavations* (Dublin, 2012), 249–65.

[28] Dowling, 'Landscape and settlement in late Iron Age Ireland'.

[29] Philip Freeman, 'The archaeology of Roman material in Ireland', *Proceedings of the Harvard Celtic Colloquium* 15 (1995), 69–74; Jacqueline Cahill Wilson, 'Romans and Roman material in Ireland: A wider social perspective', *Discovery Programme Reports* 8 (2014), 11–58; Jacqueline Cahill Wilson, Christopher Standish and Elizabeth O'Brien, 'Investigating mobility and migration in the later Irish Iron Age', *Discovery Programme Reports* 8 (2014), 127–49.

[30] Jacqueline Cahill Wilson and C.D. Standish, 'Mobility and migration in Late Iron Age and early medieval Ireland', *Journal of Archaeological Science: Reports* 6 (2016), 230–41.

[31] C.J. Lynn, 'Ireland in the Iron Age: A basket case?', *Archaeology Ireland* 17:2 (2003), 20–23; Armit, 'Social landscapes and hidden identities'; Brian Dolan, 'Beyond elites: Reassessing Irish Iron Age society', *Oxford Journal of Archaeology* 33 (2014), 361–77.

[32] Dowling, 'Landscape and settlement'.

between AD 200–400.[33] These sites have been considered as an indication of an expansion of cereal production despite 'an increasingly damp climate'[34] and were possibly inspired by Romano-British parching ovens.[35] Monk and Power note that that the earliest and greatest concentration of kilns centres around counties Dublin and Meath,[36] where a considerable number of Roman finds and intrusive burials have been discovered.[37] At Baysrath, Co. Kilkenny, the recovery of a possible Romano-British iron spearhead from a first–second century AD enclosed settlement associated with a corn-drying kiln suggests that an external stimulus for this new technology was not restricted to north Leinster.[38] There are, therefore, signs of changes within the economic structure of the Late Iron Age that may have been fuelled, if not driven, by connections with the Roman world. It is possible that the same connections inspired the formation of new social identities and fostered increasing social stratification.[39]

Boom and bust in the early medieval period

Immense cultural and economic changes occur within the early medieval period (*c.* AD 400–1100), with the emergence of new settlement types, shifts in agricultural practices, trackway and watermill construction phases, and the spread of the Church and literacy. While the first missionaries arrived in the fifth century AD, few textual sources pre-dating the seventh century survive. Along with annals, an extensive corpus of law tracts dating to the seventh and eighth centuries provide detailed insights into socio-economic and political structures, although only later copies of these texts have survived.[40] Notably, the texts paint a picture of a fragmented political structure characterised by around 150–200 *túatha*

---

[33] Scott Timpany, Mick Monk and Orla Power, 'Agricultural boom and bust in medieval Ireland: Plant macrofossil evidence from kiln sites along the N9/N10 road scheme', in Sheelagh Conran, Ed Danaher and Michael Stanley (eds), *Past times, changing fortunes*, National Roads Authority Monograph Series No. 8 (Dublin, 2011), 73–84; Mick Monk and Orla Power, 'More than a grain of truth emerges from a rash of corn-drying kilns', *Archaeology Ireland* 26:2 (2012), 38–41; Mick Monk and Orla Power, 'Casting light from the fires of corn-drying kilns on the Later Irish Iron Age', *Archaeology Ireland* 28, 28:3 (2014), 39–42.
[34] Monk and Power, 'Casting light from the fires of corn-drying kilns on the Later Irish Iron Age', 42.
[35] Monk and Power, 'More than a grain of truth emerges from a rash of corn-drying kilns', 39.
[36] Monk and Power, 'More than a grain of truth emerges from a rash of corn-drying kilns', 39.
[37] Cahill Wilson and Standish, 'Mobility and migration'.
[38] Dowling, 'Landscape and settlement'.
[39] Armit, 'Social landscapes and hidden identities', 137.
[40] Fergus Kelly, *Early Irish farming, a study based on the law-texts of the seventh and eighth centuries AD: with minor revisions and corrections* (Dundalk, 2000), 6–7.

(singular: *túath*) or petty kingdoms,[41] while cows underpinned the Irish economy and were status markers of the wealthy elites during the early centuries of the early medieval period.[42]

In tandem with the spread of the Church, and in stark contrast to the Late Iron Age, we observe relatively abundant evidence for secular settlement near the start of the early medieval period. During the sixth century, the rath, or ringfort, emerged as the predominant settlement type.[43] Generally interpreted as farmsteads surrounded by an earthen bank and ditch (*vallum*), these settlements have been closely associated with pastoral farming and their construction appears to have peaked during the seventh century.[44] Crannogs—artificial islands typically, though not exclusively, associated with elites—were constructed in shallow lakes. While some date to the later prehistoric period,[45] the early medieval crannogs appear to cluster in the late sixth to early seventh centuries and after the mid-eighth century (according to the temporal distribution of dendrochronologically-dated sites).[46] This expansion in activity is matched by a large increase in the number of trackways built across Irish wetlands in the period *c.* AD 550–750.[47] The dendrochronological record highlights that, more generally, oak-based constructions were at their height between AD 540 and 650.[48] Although Timpany and colleagues identify evidence for a slight decrease in corn-drying kiln numbers during the sixth century, on a national level, these features peak between the fifth and seventh centuries, evidently expanding beyond Leinster from this time.[49] Baillie has postulated that the major cultural change seen from the sixth century was facilitated by a rapid spread of Christianity following a series of closely-spaced environmental downturns that began in AD 536 (discussed later).[50]

Technological advances occurred with the introduction of the watermill from at least the early seventh century.[51] A concentrated building phase of

---

[41] Newman, 'Reflections on the making of a "royal site" in Ireland', 127–41.
[42] Kelly, *Early Irish farming*, 27.
[43] Thomas Kerr and Finbar McCormick, 'Statistics, sunspots and settlement: Influences on sum of probability curves', *Journal of Archaeological Science* 41 (2014), 493–501.
[44] Thomas Kerr, G.T. Swindles and Gill Plunkett, 'Making hay while the sun shines? Socio-economic change, cereal production and climatic deterioration in early medieval Ireland', *Journal of Archaeological Science* 36 (2009), 2868–74.
[45] Christina Fredengren, *Crannogs: A study of people's interaction with lakes, with particular reference to Lough Gara in the north-west of Ireland* (Dublin, 2002), 96.
[46] David Brown, personal communication.
[47] Plunkett *et al.*, 'Environmental indifference?'.
[48] Brown and Baillie, 'Confirming the existence of gaps and depletions'.
[49] Timpany, Monk and Power, 'Agricultural boom and bust in medieval Ireland'; Monk and Power, 'More than a grain of truth emerges from a rash of corn-drying kilns', 39.
[50] Baillie, 'Patrick, comets and Christianity'.
[51] Colin Rynne, 'Some observations on the production of flour and meal in the early historical period', *Journal of the Cork Historical and Archaeological Society* 95 (1990), 20–9.

Fig. 1—Key-hole type corn-drying kiln at Tullahoge, Co. Tyrone, dated to the eight to tenth centuries (Photograph: B. Sloan).

horizontal mills (AD 750–850)—inferred from a rise in the number of dendrochronologically-dated sites from this time interval—is contemporary with an overall decline in corn-drying kiln numbers but possibly, according to Monk and Power, with an increase in potentially more efficient and larger keyhole type kilns (Fig. 1).[52] Recently, Rynne has dismissed the significance of this seeming mill-building phase, arguing that the early texts indicate the existence of widespread mills in the seventh century, and pointing to the relative lack of Anglo-Norman mills in the archaeological record that conflicts with documentary evidence for their ubiquity.[53]

The changes in cereal-related structures support the notion of a shift in agricultural practices, with the AD 750–850 peak in horizontal mills argued by some to reflect increased grain production for an expanding population.[54] Conversely, drawing on an extensive database of dated early medieval sites, Hannah and McLaughlin have proposed that populations peaked in

---

[52] Monk and Power, 'More than a grain of truth emerges from a rash of corn-drying kilns', 40.

[53] Colin Rynne, 'Technological change in the agrarian economy of early medieval Ireland: New archaeological evidence for the introduction of the coulter plough', *Proceedings of the Royal Irish Academy* 118C (2018), 37–66: 57; Colin Rynne, 'Technological continuity, technological "survival": The use of horizontal mills in western Ireland, *c.* 1632–1940', *Industrial Archaeology Review* 33 (2011), 96–105.

[54] Rynne, 'Some observations on the production of flour and meal in the early historical period'.

the late seventh century, and declined steadily thereafter.[55] However, the disparity between the seemingly industrial level of grain processing and a decrease in archaeological visibility may perhaps be explained at least in part by changing settlement patterns. It has been suggested that greater control of cereal production by the elite may have been a factor in the contraction of kiln numbers.[56] Raised or platform raths—in which the enclosed area was artificially raised—emerged around the same time. These sites have been linked to an arable economy on the basis of their frequent occurrence close to high quality soils, and soon after their emergence, there is a decline in the construction of other rath types.[57] Variations in the agricultural economy are observed from the ninth century onwards, as pigs and sheep became more prominent in some areas while cattle appear to have declined in relative terms.[58] These changes are evident across Ulster and the west of Ireland, suggesting a possible shift in the socio-political and economic regime at least at a regional level.[59] The number of archaeological sites yielding archaeobotanical evidence for cereal cultivation increases between the seventh and tenth centuries, and greater diversity of crops is also observed from this time.[60] McCormick proposes that these changes may be symptomatic of a shift away from a cattle-based economy towards one fuelled by surplus agricultural production.[61]

Notwithstanding Rynne's objections, the available data imply that the erection of horizontal mills declined after AD 850, and dendrochronological evidence suggests that oak woodland began to regenerate from the mid-ninth century.[62] The following century sees a decline in many facets of the archaeological record. A further gap in dendro-datable, oak-built structures occurred during the period AD 930–1010,[63] and this is mirrored by a general lull in bog trackway constructions across Ireland.[64] Despite some continuity of use into the

---

[55] Emma Hannah and Rowan McLaughlin, 'Long-term archaeological perspectives on new genomic and environmental evidence from early medieval Ireland', *Journal of Archaeological Science* 106 (2019), 23–8.

[56] Monk and Power, 'More than a grain of truth emerges from a rash of corn-drying kilns', 40.

[57] T.R. Kerr, *Early Christian settlement in north-west Ulster*, British Archaeological Reports Series 430, (Oxford, 2007).

[58] Aidan O'Sullivan *et al.*, *Early medieval Ireland, AD 400–1100, the evidence from archaeological excavations,* Royal Irish Academy Monographs (Dublin, 2013), 210.

[59] O'Sullivan *et al.*, *Early medieval Ireland, AD 400–1100*, 210.

[60] Muriel McClatchie *et al.*, 'Early medieval farming and food production: A review of the archaeobotanical evidence from archaeological excavations in Ireland', *Vegetation History and Archaeobotany* 24 (2015), 179–86.

[61] Finbar McCormick, 'Agriculture, settlement and society in early medieval Ireland', *Quaternary International* 346 (2014), 119–30: 128.

[62] Brown and Baillie, 'Confirming the existence of gaps and depletions'.

[63] Brown and Baillie, 'Confirming the existence of gaps and depletions'.

[64] Plunkett *et al.*, 'Environmental indifference?'.

high medieval period and beyond,[65] in many areas the 'terminal decay' of raths as a settlement type appears to have begun around this time,[66] and corn-drying kilns also decline.[67] In view of the apparent fall-off in human activity during the tenth century inferred from some aspects of the archaeological record, a population crash has been proposed, attributed to the possible impact of a large-scale volcanic eruption, perhaps that of Eldgjá in Iceland, in the late AD 930s.[68]

Reconstructing the climate of final prehistoric and early medieval Ireland

The climate of the final centuries BC and first millennium AD has been characterised as part of the broader Subatlantic period (from c. 800 BC), which has traditionally been defined by cool summers, increased storminess and milder winters across north-west Europe. Centennial-scale climatic reconstructions over the past few decades have, however, demonstrated that this definition is an oversimplification of the meteorological conditions for the period[69] and have identified three main climatic shifts: the Roman Warm Period,[70] the Dark Age Climatic Deterioration[71] and the Medieval Warm Period.[72] However, to assess the relationship between environmental and social change, regionally relevant climate records are crucial. We consider to what extent these phases are represented within Ireland by examining the available palaeoclimate records from across the island.

Irish palaeoclimate records include but one temperature reconstruction from south-west Ireland, in the form of oxygen isotope analyses from a speleothem record from Crag Cave, Co. Kerry.[73] Furthermore, with chronological

---

[65] Elizabeth Fitzpatrick, 'Native enclosed settlement and the problem of the Irish "ringfort"', *Medieval Archaeology* 53 (2009), 271–307.
[66] Kerr and McCormick, 'Statistics, sunspots and settlement', 499.
[67] Timpany, Monk and Power, 'Agricultural boom and bust in medieval Ireland'.
[68] Brown and Baillie, 'Confirming the existence of gaps and depletions'.
[69] P.G. Langdon, 'Reconstructing Holocene climate change in Scotland utilising peat stratigraphy and tephrochronology', unpublished PhD thesis, University of Southampton, 1999; Anthony Blundell, 'Late-Holocene multi-proxy climate records from Northern Britain and Ireland derived from raised peat stratigraphy', unpublished PhD thesis, University of Southampton, 2002; G.T. Swindles, Gill Plunkett and H.M. Roe, 'A multi-proxy climate record from a raised bog in County Fermanagh, Northern Ireland: A critical examination of the link between bog surface wetness and solar variability', *Journal of Quaternary Science* 22 (2007), 667–79; G.T. Swindles et al., 'Centennial-scale climate change in Ireland during the Holocene', *Earth-Science Reviews* 126 (2013), 300–20; M.J. Amesbury, 'Fine-resolution peat-based palaeoclimate records of the late-Holocene', unpublished PhD thesis, University of Southampton, 2008.
[70] H.H. Lamb, *Climate: past present and future,* 157.
[71] J.J. Blackford and F.M. Chambers, 'Proxy record of climate from blanket mires: Evidence for a Dark Age (1400BP) climatic deterioration in the British Isles', *The Holocene* 1 (1991), 63–7.
[72] H.H. Lamb, 'The early medieval warm epoch and its sequel', *Palaeogeography, Palaeoclimatology, Palaeoecology* 1 (1965), 13–37.
[73] Frank McDermott et al., 'Holocene climate variability in Europe: Evidence from δ^{18}O, textural and extension-rate variations in three speleothems', *Quaternary Science Review*

error margins of ±200 years for the end of the first millennium AD,[74] the dating precision of this record is inadequate for identifying centennial and sub-centennial climate impacts on society. In contrast, the Belfast Oak Chronology is a precisely-dated dendrochronological archive that displays growth anomalies that reflect environmental stress during the trees' growing season (Fig. 2),[75] as well as longer-run phases of woodland regeneration and dying-off.[76] This chronology contributes to the recent Old World Drought Atlas (OWDA), a tree-ring derived model of annual and spatial hydroclimate variability (specifically, in summer season precipitation) across Europe during the last two millennia.[77] The Atlas data can be tailored to provide a precisely-dated reconstruction of precipitation in Ireland.

Peat-based palaeohydrological records based on humification, plant macrofossils and/or testate amoebae analyses from ombrotrophic bogs have for some time formed the backbone of Irish palaeoclimate reconstructions for the last several millennia. These proxies can be employed to demonstrate shifts in bog surface wetness (BSW), the level of which reflects the complex interplay between temperatures and rainfall and their impact on bog hydrology.[78] Essentially, wetter bog surfaces can result from increased rainfall and/or a reduction in surface water evaporation due to lower atmospheric temperatures; conversely drier bog surfaces arise due to decreased precipitation and/or higher atmospheric temperatures. Studies examining recent bog hydrology suggest that BSW in Atlantic Europe is more closely linked to changes in the summer precipitation deficit, that is, the moisture balance achieved specifically during the growing season by the combined effects of rainfall and surface water evaporation, the latter determined by temperature.[79] Recently, Swindles and colleagues compiled palaeoclimate

---

18 (1999), 1021–38; Frank McDermott, D.P. Mattey and Chris Hawkesworth, 'Centennial-scale Holocene climate variability revealed by a high-resolution speleothem $\delta^{18}O$ record from SW Ireland', *Science* 294 (2001), 1328–31.

[74] McDermott *et al.*, 'Holocene climate variability in Europe'; McDermott, Mattey and Hawkesworth, 'Centennial-scale Holocene climate variability'.

[75] M.G.L. Baillie, *A slice through time: Dendrochronology and precision dating* (London, 1995).

[76] H.H. Leuschner *et al.*, 'Subfossil European bog oaks: Population dynamics and long-term growth depressions as indicators of changes in the Holocene hydro-regime and climate', *The Holocene* 12 (2002), 695–706.

[77] E.R. Cook *et al.*, 'Old World megadroughts and pluvials during the Common Era', *Science Advances* 1 (2015), e1500561.

[78] Blackford and Chambers, 'Proxy record of climate from blanket mires'; D.J. Charman, 'Summer water deficit variability controls on peatland water-table changes: Implications for Holocene palaeoclimate reconstructions', *The Holocene* 17 (2007), 217–27; Swindles *et al.*, 'Centennial-scale climate change'.

[79] Charman, 'Summer water deficit variability controls on peatland water-table changes'; G.T. Swindles *et al.*, 'A 4500-year proxy climate record from peatlands in the north of Ireland: the identification of widespread summer "drought phases"?', *Quaternary Science Reviews* 29 (2010), 1577–89.

Fig. 2—Detail of oak timber, showing annual growth rings defined by spring vessels and summer growth. A growth anomaly (here dating to AD 540) is characterised by closely spaced series of spring vessels with relatively little summer wood, indicating poor growing conditions in successive years.

proxy records from across Ireland and performed a meta-analysis to examine centennial-scale climate variability during the last 5,000 years.[80]

The Roman Warm Period

The Roman Warm Period (c. 300 BC–AD 350) is generally described as a period of climatic amelioration across Europe coinciding with the pinnacle of the Roman Empire's expansion.[81] Climate-proxy evidence from Europe suggests that favourable meteorological conditions enabled alpine pines to extend to higher altitudes, which coincided with a contraction of the Gepatschferner glacier.[82]

---

[80] Swindles et al. 'Centennial-scale climate change'.
[81] Ting Wang, Donna Surge and Steven Mithen, 'Seasonal temperature variability of the Neoglacial (3300–2500 BP) and Roman Warm Period (2500–1600 BP) reconstructed from oxygen isotope ratios of limpet shells (*Patella vulgata*), northwest Scotland', *Palaeogeography, Palaeoclimatology, Palaeoecology* 317–8 (2012), 104–13.
[82] Kurt Nicolussi et al., 'Holocene tree-line variability in the Kauner Valley, Central Eastern Alps, indicated by dendrochronological analysis of living trees and subfossil

A variety of ocean sediment cores are also indicative of warmer sea temperatures between *c.* 400 BC and AD 450,[83] and further evidence of a climatic improvement is displayed in the isotope record of the Greenland Ice Core Project (GRIP) ice core.[84] Chronologically, these conditions appear to have prevailed during the Irish cultural phases of the Developed Iron Age and the Late Iron Age.

In Ireland, speleothem-based temperature reconstructions from Crag Cave, Co. Kerry, indicate a shift towards warmer climatic conditions from *c.* 250 BC.[85] BSW records from Slieveanorra, Co. Londonderry, and Dead Island, Co. Antrim, show two phases of reduced water tables indicative of a drier/warmer climate *c.* 320 BC–AD 470,[86] while the palaeoenvironmental reconstruction from Glen West Bog, Co. Fermanagh,[87] and Ardkill Moss, Co. Kildare,[88] display comparable results. On the basis of their meta-analysis of Irish palaeoclimate data, Swindles and colleagues suggest that the period *c.* 300 BC–AD 400 was mainly characterised by dry/warm conditions.[89] This conclusion is supported by the OWDA reconstructions that demonstrate generally drier conditions in Ireland in the first centuries AD, particularly pronounced during the fourth century, but interrupted by a short, wet interval in the third century AD.[90]

Within these broader trends that may or may not have been perceptible at a generational timescale, certain individual years, or sets of years, have been singled out in the literature as representing particularly anomalous conditions that are more likely to have been notable within a human lifetime. The dendrochronological record indicates a period of short-lived environmental stress for Irish oaks at 207 BC that is matched in German oaks and North American bristlecone pines.[91] Historical accounts from China and Egypt record this as

---

logs', *Vegetation History Archaeobotany* 14 (2005), 221–34: 228.

[83] H.C. Hass, 'Northern Europe climate variations during late Holocene: Evidence from marine Skagerrak', *Palaeogeography, Palaeoclimatology, Palaeoecology* 123 (1996), 121–45; Jón Eiríksson *et al.*, 'Variability of the North Atlantic Current during the last 2000 years based on shelf bottom water and sea surface temperatures along an open ocean/shallow marine transect in western Europe', *The Holocene* 16 (2006), 1017–29; C.S. Andresen *et al.*, 'Interactions between subsurface waters and calving of the Jakodshavn Isbræ during the late Holocene', *The Holocene* 21 (2010), 211–24.

[84] Willy Tinner *et al.*, 'Climatic change and contemporaneous land-use phases north and south of the Alps 2300 BC to 800 AD', *Quaternary Science Reviews* 22 (2003), 1447–60.

[85] McDermott *et al.*, 'Holocene climate variability in Europe'.

[86] Swindles *et al.*, 'A 4500-year proxy climate record'.

[87] Swindles, Plunkett and Roe, 'A multiproxy climate record'.

[88] Blundell, 'Late-Holocene multi-proxy climate records'; Anthony Blundell, D.J. Charman and K.E. Barber, 'Multi-proxy late Holocene peat records from Ireland: Towards a regional palaeoclimate curve', *Journal of Quaternary Science* 23 (2008), 59–71.

[89] Swindles *et al.*, 'Centennial-scale climate change'.

[90] Cook *et al.*, 'Old World megadroughts'.

[91] M.G.L. Baillie, 'Irish oaks record volcanic dust veils drama!', *Archaeology Ireland* 2:2 (1988), 71–4; Baillie, 'Marking in marker dates'; Baillie, 'Great oaks from little acorns'.

a time of devastating famine and social upheaval,[92] suggesting that whatever caused the trees stress—possibly a volcanic eruption, given the occurrence of large acid spikes in Greenland ice cores at this time—may also have had wider environmental and social repercussions. A similar series of tree growth anomalies, ice core acid layers and historical accounts of extreme weather signifying a global dust veil can be observed at 44–42 BC,[93] but the event is not evident in the few Irish oaks that span this period, or indeed in British timbers,[94] perhaps implying that the British Isles were buffered from this downturn. Arguably, such events are too short-lived to be detectable in other, less well-resolved palaeoclimate records.

The Dark Age Climatic Deterioration

The majority of European climate proxies demonstrate a shift to wetter/cooler conditions in the mid-sixth century in a phase that has been named the Dark Age Climatic Deterioration.[95] Temperature reconstructions from pine trees across Europe indicate cooler summer temperatures during the mid-sixth century,[96] while a variety of tree species record a growth anomaly indicating stress on the trees during their growing season c. AD 540.[97] European peatlands experienced a significant increase in BSW,[98] while a rise in lake-levels across

---

[92] Baillie, 'Marking in marker dates'; Baillie, 'Great oaks from little acorns'; M.G.L. Baillie and Jonny McAneney, 'Tree ring effects and ice core acidities clarify the volcanic record of the first millennium', *Climate of the Past Discussions* 11 (2015), 105–14; Francis Ludlow and J.G. Manning, 'Revolts under the Ptolemies: A paleoclimatic perspective', in J.J. Collins and J.G. Manning (eds), *Revolt and resistance in the ancient classical world and the Near East: The crucible of empire*, Culture and History of the Ancient Near East Series (Leiden, 2016), 154–71.

[93] Baillie, 'Marking in marker dates'; Baillie, 'Great oaks from little acorns'; Michael Sigl *et al.*, 'Timing and climate forcing of volcanic eruptions for the past 2,500 years', *Nature* 523 (2015), 543–9.

[94] David Brown, personal communication.

[95] Blackford and Chambers, 'Proxy record of climate from blanket mires'.

[96] K.R. Briffa *et al.*, 'Fennoscandian summers from AD 500: Temperature changes on short and long timescales', *Climate Dynamics* 7 (1992), 111–9; Samuli Helama *et al.*, 'The supra-long Scots pine tree-ring record for Finnish Lapland: Part 2, interannual to centennial variability in summer temperatures for 7500 years', *The Holocene* 12 (2002), 681–7.

[97] Baillie and Munro, 'Irish tree rings, Santorini and volcanic dust veils'; Briffa *et al.*, 'Fennoscandian summers from AD 500: Temperature changes on short and long timescales', 111–9; Leuschner *et al.*, 'Subfossil European bog oaks'; M.M. Naurzbaev *et al.*, 'Summer temperatures in eastern Taimyr inferred from a 2427-year late-Holocene tree-ring chronology and earlier floating series', *The Holocene* 12 (2002), 727–36.

[98] Bent Aaby, 'Cyclic climatic variations in climate over the past 5,500 years reflected in raised bogs', *Nature* 263 (1976), 281–4; K.E. Barber, F.M. Chambers and Darrel Maddy, 'Late Holocene climatic history of northern Germany and Denmark: Peat macrofossil investigations at Dosenmoor, Schleswig-Holstein and Svanemose, Jutland', *Boreas* 33 (2004), 132–44; Uulle Sillasoo *et al.*, 'Peat multi-proxy data from Männikjärve bog as

Europe also suggest the onset of wetter conditions.[99] Until recently, the duration of the climate downturn was not well defined, with many peatland-based palaeohydrological records suggesting various timeframes for its end, ranging from *c.* AD 600–800. Using tree-ring derived temperature reconstructions from the Alps and the Altai Mountains, Büntgen and colleagues have now identified a period of cooling that lasted from AD 536 to approximately AD 660, and have called this phase the 'Late Antique Little Ice Age'.[100] They suggest that rapid climate deterioration may have triggered a series of political upheavals and migrations and may have been a factor in the spread of the Justinian Plague in the early 540s. The start of the cooling coincides with growth downturns first noted in the Belfast Oak dendrochronological series at AD 536 and AD 541.[101] Baillie and McAneney's suggestion that these environmental downturns were the direct result of large-scale volcanic eruptions has been substantiated by the revised dating of the Greenland and Antarctic ice core records that attest volcanic events at these times.[102] A downturn in solar output during the seventh century may also have impacted on climate,[103] although the mechanisms and manifestation of such an impact are poorly understood.

In Ireland, peatland records demonstrate a gradual shift to elevated water tables from the mid-sixth century,[104] but due to a lack of chronological precision the exact timing of this event has been elusive. Mongan Bog, Co. Offaly, was the subject of three separate palaeohydrological investigations, all of which recorded increased BSW within this timeframe.[105] Elevated

---

indicators of late Holocene climate changes in Estonia', *Boreas* 36 (2007), 20–37; Amesbury, 'Fine-resolution peat-based palaeoclimate records of the late-Holocene'.

[99] Michel Magny, 'Holocene climate variability as reflected by mid-European lake-level fluctuations and its probable impact on prehistoric human settlements', *Quaternary International* 113 (2004), 65–79.

[100] Ulf Büntgen *et al.*, 'Cooling and societal change during the Late Antique Little Ice Age from 536 to around 660 AD', *Nature Geoscience* 9 (2016), 231–6.

[101] Baillie and Munro, 'Irish tree rings, Santorini and volcanic dust veils'.

[102] Baillie and McAneney, 'Tree ring effects'; Sigl *et al.*, 'Timing and climate forcing of volcanic eruptions'.

[103] C.A. Perry and K.J. Hsu, 'Geophysical, archaeological, and historical evidence support a solar-output model for climate change', *Proceedings of National Academic Science* 97 (2000), 12433–8.

[104] Swindles *et al.*, 'Centennial-scale climate change'.

[105] C.J. Haslam, 'Late Holocene peat stratigraphy and climatic change – a macrofossil investigation from the raised mires of north western Europe', unpublished PhD thesis, University of Southampton, 1987; K.E. Barber, F.M. Chambers and Darrel Maddy, 'Holocene palaeoclimates from peat stratigraphy: Macrofossil proxy climate records from three oceanic raised bogs in England and Ireland', *Quaternary Science Reviews* 22 (2003), 521–39; V.A. Hall and Dmitri Mauquoy, 'Tephra-dated climate- and human-impact studies during the last 1500 years from a raised bog in central Ireland', *The Holocene* 15 (2005), 1086–93.

water tables for the same period were observed at Letterfrack, Co. Galway,[106] Cloonoolish Moss, Co. Galway[107] and Fallahogy Bog, Co. Londonderry.[108] Swindles and colleagues reported a trend towards wetter conditions in the north-east of Ireland from the seventh century, with a more distinct wet shift occurring at *c.* AD 770.[109] More recently, Swindles and colleagues place the start of a widespread wet phase at *c.* AD 550, with wet conditions persisting until *c.* AD 800, although these conditions are not recorded at all sites for the same duration.[110]

The OWDA largely corroborates these changes, with extended wet phases evident between the mid-sixth and late seventh centuries and between the mid-eighth and mid-ninth centuries.[111] The tree-ring data also highlight short phases of wetter (early fifth century) and drier (early eighth century) conditions not easily determined by the peatland records. These fluctuations are further supported by annalistic records that reveal a series of severe droughts from the mid-seventh to mid-eighth centuries, followed by a period of more frequent heavy snows and storms from the mid-eighth to early ninth centuries.[112]

The Medieval Warm Period

Towards the end of the first millennium AD, a climatic amelioration, widely known as the Medieval Warm Period[113] or the Medieval Climatic Anomaly,[114] appears to have occurred across Europe. Temperature reconstruction from Fennoscandian Scots pines suggest a warming trend from the mid-tenth century,[115] while the evidence from European oak cohorts indicate mild and humid summers across central Europe between AD 700–1000.[116] Various climate reconstructions from numerous ocean core sediments point to warming sea surface temperatures in the period between AD 950–1150.[117] There is, however, a conflicting body of evidence that suggests not all areas experienced this climatic amelioration, with cooler conditions observed in Siberia during the tenth

---

[106] Blackford and Chambers, 'Proxy record of climate from blanket mires'.
[107] Blundell, Charman and Barber, 'Multi-proxy late Holocene peat records from Ireland'.
[108] Amesbury, 'Fine-resolution peat-based palaeoclimate records of the late-Holocene'.
[109] Swindles *et al.*, 'A 4500-year proxy climate record'; Kerr, Swindles and Plunkett, 'Making hay while the sun shines?'.
[110] Swindles *et al.*, 'Centennial-scale climate change'.
[111] Cook *et al.*, 'Old World megadroughts'.
[112] Kerr, Swindles and Plunkett, 'Making hay while the sun shines?'.
[113] Lamb, 'The early medieval warm epoch and its sequel'.
[114] Scott Stine, 'Extreme and persistent drought in California and Patagonia during mediaeval time', *Nature* 369 (1994), 546–9.
[115] Briffa *et al.*, 'Fennoscandian summers from AD500'.
[116] Büntgen *et al.*, '2500 years of European climate variability'.
[117] Dierk Hebbeln *et al.*, 'Late Holocene coastal hydrographic and climate changes in the eastern North Sea', *The Holocene* 16 (2006), 987–1001; Andresen *et al.*, 'Interactions between subsurface waters'.

century[118] and glacier advances in Switzerland and Norway.[119] Further research has led to the suggestion that the North Atlantic area may have experienced increased storminess during this time.[120]

Temperature reconstructions from Crag Cave in south-west Ireland are suggestive of warmer temperatures in the closing centuries of the first millennium AD; however, the chronological precision of the record is poor for this period.[121] Results from the Irish peatland records are variable. Some sites, such as Cloonoolish Moss, Co. Galway, and Ardkill Moss, Co. Kildare, register low water tables until the beginning of the tenth century prior to a rise in BSW.[122] Two independent investigations from Mongan Bog, Co. Offaly, gave conflicting results: Barber and colleagues record increased BSW from the Dark Age Climatic Deterioration until after AD 1000,[123] while Hall and Mauquoy find drier/warmer conditions from the end of the ninth century.[124] The compiled peatland records show a shift to warmer/drier conditions during the ninth century, though this is mainly evident in sites in the north and east.[125] None of the Irish annals gives any entries for favourable meteorological conditions from AD 800–1000, though their emphasis is characteristically upon extreme weather, and there are numerous references to severe winters and storms during this interval.[126] The OWDA provides the most compelling evidence for drier conditions that persist from the mid-ninth century until the twelfth century.

Climate impacts on subsistence? An assessment of the pollen record

Pollen records spanning the Late Bronze and Iron Ages in Ireland have recently been reviewed in order to discern patterns in landscape use as a backdrop to

---

[118] Christophe Corona *et al.*, 'Long-term summer (AD751–2008) temperature fluctuation in the French Alps based on tree-ring data', *Boreas* 40 (2011), 351–66.

[119] Johann Stötter *et al.*, 'Holocene palaeoclimatic reconstruction in northern Iceland: Approaches and results', *Quaternary Science Reviews* 18 (1999), 457–74; J.A. Matthews *et al.*, 'Holocene glacier variations in central Jotunheimen, southern Norway based on distal glaciolacustrine sediment cores', *Quaternary Science Reviews* 19 (2000), 1625–47; Hanspeter Holzhauser, Michel Magny and H.J. Zumbuühl, 'Glacier and lake-level variations in west-central Europe over the last 3500 years', *The Holocene* 15 (2005), 789–801.

[120] Hass, 'Northern Europe climate variations'; Malgorzata Witak *et al.*, 'Holocene North Atlantic surface circulation and climatic variability: evidence from diatom records', *The Holocene* 15 (2005), 85–96; A.K. Dugmore *et al.*, 'The role of climate in settlement and landscape change in the north Atlantic Islands: An assessment of cumulative deviations in high-resolution proxy climate records', *Human Ecology* 35 (2007), 169–78.

[121] McDermott, Mattey and Hawkesworth, 'Centennial-scale Holocene climate variability'.

[122] Blundell, Charman and Barber, 'Multi-proxy late Holocene peat records from Ireland'.

[123] Barber, Chambers and Maddy, 'Holocene palaeoclimates from peat stratigraphy'.

[124] Hall and Mauquoy, 'Tephra-dated climate- and human-impact studies'.

[125] Swindles *et al.*, 'Centennial-scale climate change', Fig. 5.

[126] Kerr, Swindles and Plunkett, 'Making hay while the sun shines?'.

changes in the cultural record.[127] Many pollen records reveal woodland clearance at c. 300 BC that can be associated with the start of the Developed Iron Age.[128] While this pattern was generally ubiquitous across the Irish landscape, the timing of the initial clearance was not synchronous, nor are there any signs of coherent spatial patterning where renewed farming first began.[129] For example, an agricultural expansion occurred at Caheraphuca, Co. Clare, at c. 450 BC[130] but clearances were not observed at Derryville Bog, Co. Tipperary, until the third century BC.[131] Although the level of woodland clearance is generally quite modest, implying that farming was not particularly intensive, the pollen record is testament to a predominantly pastoral-based subsistence (inferred from the comparatively low representation of cereals in pollen records of this period) during the Developed Iron Age that is otherwise difficult to discern in the archaeological record.[132] The pollen record associated with the bog body dubbed Oldcroghan Man shows that the deposition of this individual in the bog occurred as agriculture began to expand in the area surrounding Clonearl Bog, Co. Offaly, in the early third century BC,[133] a finding that does not seem symptomatic of a subsistence economy threatened by environmental stress *contra* some explanations for apparent sacrifices such as this. Notwithstanding the comparatively poor chronological precision and the temporal resolution of pollen records, there are currently no

---

[127] Plunkett, 'Tephra-linked peat humification records'; Lisa Coyle McClung, 'The Late Iron Age Lull—not so Late Iron Age after all!', *Emania* 21 (2013), 73–83.

[128] C.J. Caseldine and Jackie Hatton, 'Early land clearance and wooden trackway construction in the third and fourth millennia BC at Corlea, Co. Longford', *Proceedings of the Royal Irish Academy* 96B (1996), 11–9; C.J. Caseldine and Ben Gearey, 'A multiproxy approach to reconstructing surface wetness changes and prehistoric bog bursts in a raised mire system at Derryville Bog, Co. Tipperary, Ireland', *The Holocene* 15 (2005), 585–601; Gill Plunkett *et al.*, 'A multi-proxy palaeoenvironmental investigation of the findspot of an Iron Age bog body from Oldcroghan, Co. Offaly, Ireland', *Journal of Archaeological Science* 36 (2009), 265–77; Karen Molloy, Ingo Feeser and Michael O'Connell, 'A pollen profile from Ballinphuill Bog: Vegetation and land-use history', in Jim McKeon and Jerry O'Sullivan (eds), *The quiet landscape: Archaeological and palaeoecological investigations on the M6 Galway to Ballinasloe national road scheme*, National Roads Authority Scheme Monograph 15 (Dublin, 2014), 116–8.

[129] Plunkett, 'Socio-political dynamics in later prehistoric Ireland'.

[130] Karen Molloy and Michael O'Connell, 'Prehistoric farming in western Ireland: Pollen analysis at Caheraphuca, Co. Clare', in Shane Delaney *et al.*, (eds), *Borderlands. Archaeological investigations along the route of the M18 Gort to Crusheen road scheme*, National Roads Authority Scheme Monograph 9 (Dublin, 2012), 109–22.

[131] Caseldine and Gearey, 'A multiproxy approach to reconstructing surface wetness changes'.

[132] Note, however, that cereal pollen is generally poorly dispersed and is underrepresented in many pollen records.

[133] Plunkett *et al.*, 'A multi-proxy palaeoenvironmental investigation of the findspot'.

indications that this subsistence base changed in any appreciable way in the period following the 207 BC oak growth anomaly.

Evidence for farming in the pollen record generally declines around the turn of the millennium, a phenomenon widely referred to the as the Late Iron Age Lull.[134] The extent of woodland regeneration has been interpreted by some to signify a collapse of the subsistence economy and has led Weir to posit a severe population crash,[135] potentially as a result of the 44–42 BC global volcanic dust veil.[136] But while the majority of pollen records demonstrate this lull, there are notable exceptions, such as low levels of arable agriculture identified at Emlagh Bog, Co. Meath,[137] and in the area surrounding Cornaher Lough, Co. Westmeath.[138] Furthermore, recent research has demonstrated that the lull observed within the pollen records can be better characterised as a protracted shift, the onset of which varied considerably between approximately 200 BC and AD 200;[139] its diachronic nature, spanning many generations of Iron Age society, renders it highly unlikely to have been triggered by any single rapid or extreme event. Indeed, the lull seems to have endured across a relatively dry period but it cannot presently be established if such conditions were in any way a deterrent to cultivation or a facilitator of alternative subsistence practices. Regardless, the growing body of pollen evidence suggests that the lull represents a gradual shift in land-use that began within the Developed Iron Age.

For the most part, evidence for human activity in the pollen record remains limited, but not entirely invisible, through much of the Late Iron Age. Many pollen records show signs of renewed farming activity from c. AD 200–300,[140] coinciding, it would seem, with an increase in the numbers of recorded corn-drying kilns,[141] though the scale of arable production suggested

---

[134] G.F. Mitchell, 'Littleton bog, Tipperary: An Irish agricultural record', *Journal of the Royal Society of Antiquaries Ireland* 95 (1965), 121–32.

[135] Weir, 'Dark ages and the pollen record'; D.A. Weir, 'A palynological study of landscape and agricultural development in County Louth from the second millennium BC to the first millennium AD', *Discovery Programme Reports* 2 (1995), 77–126.

[136] Baillie, 'Great oaks from little acorns'.

[137] Conor Newman et al., 'Interpretation of charcoal and pollen data relating to a late Iron Age ritual site in eastern Ireland: A holistic approach', *Vegetation History and Archaeobotany* 16 (2007), 349–65.

[138] Alyson Heery, 'The vegetation history of the Irish midlands: Palaeoecological reconstructions of two lake sites adjacent to eskers', unpublished PhD thesis, Trinity College Dublin, 1998.

[139] Coyle McClung, 'The Late Iron Age Lull'.

[140] Gill Plunkett, 'Pollen analysis and archaeology in Ireland', in Eileen Murphy and N.J. Whitehouse (eds), *Environmental Archaeology in Ireland* (Oxford, 2007), 221–40; Carlos Chique, Karen Molloy and A.P. Potito, 'Mid-late Holocene vegetational history and land-use dynamics in County Monaghan, northeastern Ireland—the palynological record of Lough Muckno', *Journal of the North Atlantic* 32 (2017), 1–24.

[141] Timpany, Monk and Power, 'Agricultural boom and bust in medieval Ireland'; Monk and Power, 'More than a grain of truth emerges from a rash of corn-drying kilns'; Monk

by the pollen evidence is by no means intensive at this time. The third century wet-shift indicated by the OWDA illustrates a possible climatic incentive for the wider uptake of corn-drying facilities, but the archaeological evidence lacks the chronological resolution needed to scrutinise this relationship. Cereals can of course be dried by other means such as sheaf-burning,[142] as they must have been before kilns began to be constructed, even when wetter conditions prevailed. The development of kilns need not therefore have been a direct response to climate change, but may simply reflect exposure to a novel technology, possibly through contacts with Roman Britain. Rye too may have been introduced around this time, with *Secale cereale* pollen (Fig. 3) recorded from the first century AD, and more widely from the fourth century (Fig. 4), coinciding with what seems to be a second wave of Romano-British influences. The combined archaeological and palaeoenvironmental evidence highlights a gradual economic and social change within the Late Iron Age that was possibly stimulated by contacts with, and perhaps migrants from, the Roman world as early as the first century AD during a period of relatively dry conditions, and again but with wider impact in the fourth and fifth centuries.

The post-Late Iron Age resurgence of farming clearly begins prior to the early medieval period and the introduction of Christianity. Only in the west of Ireland do clearances certainly post-date the mid-fifth century.[143] The pollen record shows that agriculture was well-established in some areas before the founding of local monasteries,[144] suggesting that the Church was not the main, or at least not the initial, driver of the wider economy. Vegetation reconstructions at a number of sites in Ulster and Leinster demonstrate a short downturn in farming, particularly in arable representation, following initial signs of land clearance, although this is by no means a universal phenomenon.[145] For example, a decline in the mixed subsistence economy at Lake View, Co. Down, lasted around a century,[146] and a similar interruption occurred at Cornaher Lough, Co. Westmeath.[147] At Garry Bog, Co. Antrim, and Lake View, Co. Down, the decline commences between the mid-fifth to mid-sixth centuries AD, but the dating at other sites is less precise and age estimates span the

---

and Power, 'Casting light from the fires of corn-drying kilns on the Later Irish Iron Age'.
[142] Rynne, 'Some observations on the production of flour and meal in the early historical period'.
[143] Lisa Coyle McClung, 'A palynological investigation of land-use patterns in first millennium AD Ireland', unpublished PhD thesis, Queen's University Belfast, 2012, 201.
[144] V.A. Hall, 'The vegetation history of monastic and secular sites in the midlands of Ireland over the last two millennia', *Vegetation History and Archaeobotany* 15 (2005), 1–12.
[145] Coyle McClung, 'A palynological investigation of land-use patterns in first millennium AD Ireland', 203.
[146] Coyle McClung, 'A palynological investigation of land-use patterns in first millennium AD Ireland', 182.
[147] Heery, 'The vegetation history of the Irish midlands'.

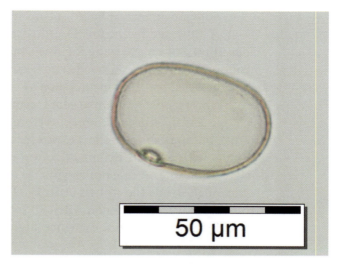

Fig. 3—A pollen grain from *Secale cereale* (rye). This cereal pollen is easily distinguished from wild and other domesticated grasses by its large size and the positioning of its pore (bottom left) towards the side of the grain.

period AD 350–1100.[148] This phase of reduced farming would seem to straddle the period in which raths emerge. In view of the dating uncertainty, it is conceivable that a disruption to or shift within the subsistence economy around this time was triggered by the two extreme events recorded by Irish oaks at AD 536 and AD 540, or by the shift towards wetter conditions indicated by the OWDA data for Ireland, but the chronological resolution of the pollen records is simply insufficient to determine the precise timing of the land-use change and establish such a correlation. At Mongan Bog, Co. Offaly, however, from which there exists a combined palynological and climate proxy record, a decline in farming indicators at this time coincides with a shift to drier bog surfaces.[149] More such integrated records are required to elucidate the relationship between climate and land-use changes.

The main rath building phase, AD 550–750, therefore transpired against a background of potentially inclement climate and spatially variable degrees of land clearance and farming. By the mid-eighth to early ninth centuries, some sites display a distinct expansion in mixed agriculture with increased emphasis on arable cultivation, while others go into decline. Sites such as Monteith's Lough, Co. Down,[150] Killymaddy Lough, Co. Tyrone,[151] Abbeyknockmoy,

---

[148] Coyle McClung, 'A palynological investigation of land-use patterns in first millennium AD Ireland', 182.

[149] Hall and Mauquoy, 'Tephra-dated climate- and human-impact studies'.

[150] Coyle McClung, 'A palynological investigation of land-use patterns in first millennium AD Ireland'.

[151] K.R. Hirons, 'Palaeoenvironmental investigations in east Co. Tyrone, Northern Ireland', unpublished PhD thesis, Queen's University Belfast, 1984.

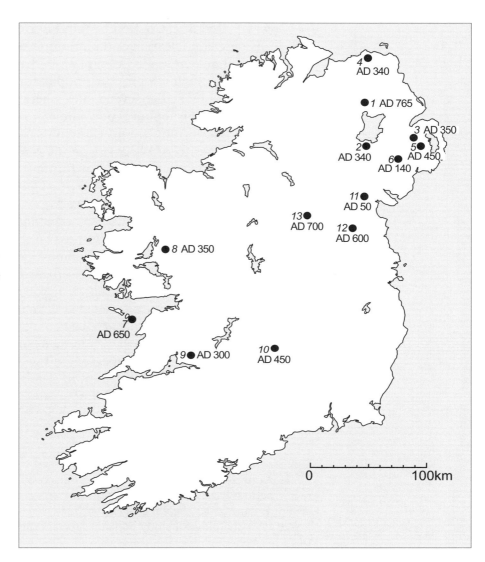

Fig. 4—Distribution of pollen sites showing evidence for *Secale* pollen in the first millennium AD (based on published data). 1. Ballyscullion East Bog (V.A. Hall, J.R. Pilcher and F.G. McCormac, 'Tephra-dated lowland landscape history of the north of Ireland, AD 750–1150', *New Phytologist* 125 (1993), 193–202); 2. Loughnashade (D.A. Weir, 'Dark ages and the pollen record', *Emania* 11 (1993), 21–30); 3. Long Lough (Valerie Hall, 'Recent landscape history from a Co. Down lake deposit', *New Phytologist* 115 (1990), 377–83); 4. Garry Bog (Lisa Coyle McClung, 'A palynological investigation of land-use patterns in first millennium AD Ireland', unpublished PhD thesis, Queen's University Belfast, 2012); 5. Lake View (Coyle McClung, 'A palynological investigation of land-use patterns in first millennium AD Ireland'); 6. Monteith's Lough (Coyle McClung, 'A palynological investigation of land-use patterns in first millennium AD Ireland'); 7. An Loch Mór (Karen Molloy and Michael O'Connell, 'Holocene vegetation and land-use dynamics in the karstic environment of Inis Oírr, Aran Islands, western Ireland: Pollen analytical evidence evaluated in light of the archaeological record', *Quaternary International* 113 (2004), 41–64); 8. Lough Fark (J.L. Fuller, 'Past vegetation and land-use dynamics in Mayo Abbey, central Mayo', *Archaeology Ireland* 16:3 (2002), 20–23); 9. Mooghaun (Karen Molloy, 'Holocene vegetation and land-use history at Mooghaun, south-east Clare, with particular reference to the Bronze Age', in E. Grogan (ed.), The north Munster project Volume 1: The later prehistoric landscape of south-east Clare, Discovery Programme Reports (Bray, 2002), 255–301); 10. Derryville Bog (V.A. Hall, 'The vegetation history of monastic and secular sites in the midlands of Ireland over the last two millennia', *Vegetation History and Archaeobotany* 15 (2005), 1–12); 11. Red Bog (D.A. Weir, 'A palynological study of landscape and agricultural development in County Louth from the second millennium BC to the first millennium AD', Discovery Programme Reports 2 (1995), 77–126); 12. Emlagh Bog (Conor Newman et al., 'Interpretation of charcoal and pollen data relating to a late Iron Age ritual site in eastern Ireland: A holistic approach', *Vegetation History and Archaeobotany* 16 (2007), 349–65); 13. Derragh Bog (A.G. Brown et al., 'Vegetation, landscape and human activity in midland Ireland: Mire and lake records from Lough Kinale-Derragh Lough area, central Ireland', *Vegetational History and Archaeobotany* 14 (2005), 81–98).

Co. Galway,[152] Red Bog, Co. Louth,[153] and Barrees on the Beara Peninsula, Co. Cork,[154] display land clearances on an unprecedented scale, which continued into the second millennium AD, and this evidence is difficult to reconcile with Hannah and McLaughlin's proposed population decline.[155] The timing of this expansion can be refined at several sites where the 'AD860B' tephra has been recorded (Fig. 5). This tephra is now known to correspond to the White River Ash (Eastern Lobe) from Mount Churchill, Alaska,[156] and has been dated in Greenland ice cores to AD 852/3±1 on the NS1–2011 ice core timescale.[157] In the pollen record, an intensification of farming, including a peak in cereal production can be seen to occur in the century before this tephra was deposited on the bogs. The timing of this shift overlaps with the increasing frequency of severe weather conditions reported by the annalists from the mid-eighth and ninth centuries.[158] The coincidence of the two changes does not certainly prove cause-and-effect, but it can now be demonstrated that the peak in horizontal mill construction (inferred from the dendrochronologically dated sites) and the putative shift to larger, more efficient, if fewer, corn-drying kilns (as proposed by Monk and Power)[159] was associated with an intensification of cereal cultivation, and that these changes occurred against the backdrop of an increasingly harsh climate, as discussed earlier. Intensive land-use continued until the mid-ninth century and may have impacted on the availability of mature oaks for construction purposes, as reflected in the dendrochronological record.

Following the AD860B tephra, at sites such as at Fallahogy, Co. Londonderry, Ballyscullion, Co. Antrim, and Cloonoolish Moss, Co. Galway, farming declines, but does not cease.[160] Elsewhere, such as at Clonfert, Co. Galway

---

[152] S.H. Lomas-Clarke and K.E. Barber, 'Palaeoecology of human impact during the historic period: Palynology and geochemistry of a peat deposit at Abbeyknockmoy, Co. Galway, Ireland', *The Holocene* 14 (2004), 721–31.

[153] Weir, 'A palynological study of landscape and agricultural development in County Louth'.

[154] Anette Overland and Michael O'Connell, 'Fine-spatial palaeoecological investigations towards reconstructing late Holocene environmental change, landscape evolution and farming activity in Barrees, Beara Peninsula, southwestern Ireland', *Journal of the North Atlantic* 1 (2008), 37–73.

[155] Hannah and McLaughlin, 'Long-term archaeological perspectives'.

[156] B.J.L. Jensen *et al.*, 'Transatlantic distribution of the Alaskan White River Ash', *Geology* 42 (2014), 875–8.

[157] S.E. Coulter *et al.*, 'Holocene tephras highlight complexity of volcanic signals in Greenland ice cores', *Journal of Geophysical Research – Atmospheres* 117 (2012), D21303; Sigl *et al.*, 'Timing and climate forcing of volcanic eruptions'.

[158] Kerr, Swindles and Plunkett, 'Making hay while the sun shines?'.

[159] Monk and Power, 'More than a grain of truth emerges from a rash of corn-drying kilns', 40.

[160] V.A. Hall, J.R. Pilcher and F.G. McCormac, 'Tephra-dated lowland landscape history of the north of Ireland, AD 750–1150', *New Phytologist* 125 (1993), 193–202; Plunkett, unpublished data.

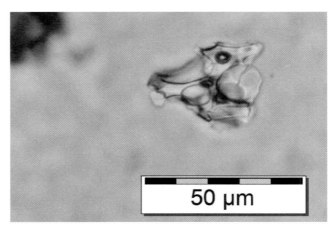

Fig. 5—Tephra (volcanic ash) shard from the 'AD860B' tephra from Churchill, Alaska. This tephra, erupted during the winter of AD 852/3±1, is widely found in Irish peat and lake sediments.

(Fig. 6), Garry Bog, Co. Antrim, and Emlagh Bog, Co. Meath, farming appears to have continued at the same level as before.[161] Like the palaeoclimate record, then, the pollen data reveal spatial variability towards the end of the millennium, and there currently appears to be little evidence to support the suggestion of an environmentally-triggered downturn in human activity in the tenth century. The building gap identified by Brown and Baillie in the dendro-dated archaeological record cannot therefore be accounted for simply by a widespread population decline.

Discussion

This paper aimed to consider the relationship between cultural and environmental change in final prehistoric and early medieval Ireland, specifically with respect to some of the main examples offered in the literature that associate climatic and societal change. Despite the difficulties of evaluating short-term, but potentially severe, environmental events in all but the most highly resolved palaeoenvironmental records, we find little convincing evidence of cultural collapse during this time that might have been prompted by environmentally-driven perturbation of the subsistence base (Fig. 7). Recent archaeological research has clearly shown that in the Late Iron Age the island was certainly not depopulated, debunking hypotheses of an environmentally-triggered demographic crisis.[162] Rather, we can see that there was widespread activity represented by mainly ephemeral archaeological remains and an increasing body of evidence for interactions with

---

[161] Coyle McClung, 'A palynological investigation of land-use patterns in first millennium AD Ireland', Fig. 7.1; Anette Overland and Michael O'Connell, 'New insights into late Holocene farming and woodland dynamics in western Ireland with particular reference to the early medieval horizontal watermill at Kilbegly, Co. Roscommon', *Review of Palaeobotany and Palynology* 163 (2011), 205–26.

[162] Weir, 'Dark ages and the pollen record'.

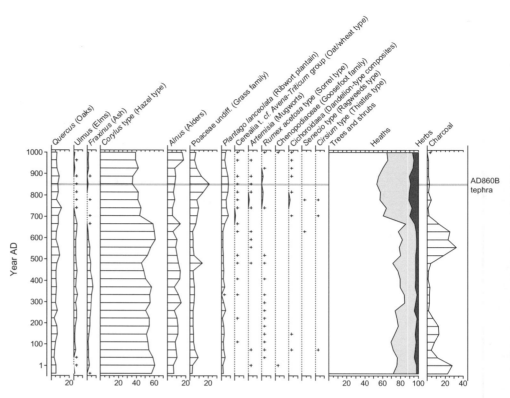

Fig. 6—Illustrative percentage pollen diagram from Clonfert, Co. Galway, based on data in Valerie Hall, 'The vegetation history of monastic and secular sites in the midlands of Ireland over the last two millennia', *Vegetation History and Archaeobotany* 15 (2006), 1–12. + indicates percentages <1%.

Roman Britain. It may, therefore, have been the absence of long-term settlement and fixed agriculture that prompted the decline in the visibility of farming in many pollen records that we know as the Late Iron Age Lull. It is perhaps particularly pertinent that the Late Iron Age Lull is time-transgressive and in some places begins within the Developed Iron Age, negating the likelihood of any single environmental trigger, and instead increasing the prospect that this was a more gradual, socially-determined process[163] involving both economic and political re-organisation. Although none of the palaeoecological proxy records from Ireland can match the dendrochronological record or tree-ring-derived climate reconstructions for their chronological resolution, we observe no firm indications of long-term repercussions on the subsistence economy of the environmental events in 207 BC or 44–42 BC. Broadly speaking, the decline of large-scale communal endeavours and farming in the Developed Iron Age took place during the Roman Warm Period, when drier conditions appear usually to have

---

[163] Coyle McClung, 'A palynological investigation of land-use patterns in first millennium AD Ireland; Coyle McClung, 'The Late Iron Age Lull'.

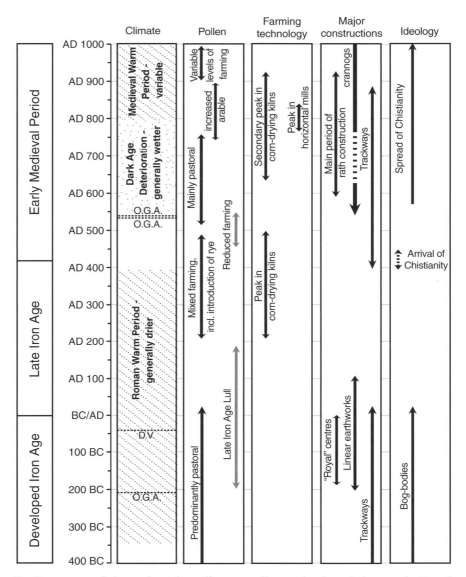

Fig. 7—Summary of the main palaeoclimate, pollen and cultural changes in Developed to Late Iron Age and early medieval period. DV – dust veil event; OGA – oak growth anomaly.

prevailed in Ireland, and although wetter periods did occur, it is difficult to see climate change as a driver in the seeming breakdown of large-scale socio-political power structures over this extended period. In many places, the resumption of farming on a scale perceptible in pollen records, marking the *end* of the Late Iron Age Lull, broadly coincides with a growing body of archaeological evidence (i.e. corn-drying kilns) for an increase in cereal production from at least the third century AD. In view of the seemingly strong spatial relationship between the earliest corn-drying kilns and Roman material, a social stimulus—be that from migration, trade and/or other forms of contact—seems a more plausible explanation for the transition to enclosed settlements and increased cereal production that takes place at this time.

The next major cultural change—the dawn of the early medieval period—is traditionally dated to the fifth century AD, but the most conspicuous aspects of the archaeological record appear a century or more later. We find that the start of this period shows continuity from the final Late Iron Age, at least in terms of land-use and subsistence economy as reflected in the pollen record. In parts of Ulster and Leinster, however, the nature and intensity of farming falter during the middle of the first millennium AD, broadly coinciding with the Dark Age Climatic Deterioration in the mid-sixth century.[164] Further research that combines palaeoclimate and palynological reconstructions is needed to establish the relationship, if any, between these changes. Certainly, it would seem that the characteristic features of early medieval Ireland, such as raths and ecclesiastical settlements, expanded after this time.[165] The pollen record reveals open, pastoral habitats, and it may be at this time that the cow-based wealth system indicated by the later law tracts came to the fore. McCormick has argued that the ringfort emerged as a defence against increased cattle-raiding, precisely because of the value of cows.[166]

The full extent of land under cultivation is difficult to gauge from pollen records, but arable indicators become a more consistent and noticeable feature from the mid-first millennium AD. Cereal production increases in importance by the mid-eighth to ninth centuries, evidenced by a proliferation of horizontal mills and perhaps more efficient corn-drying kilns, as well as the pollen record, and the archaeological record points to an industrious, resourceful society. Kerr and colleagues[167] hypothesised that the shift to increased cultivation may have been an adaptation to a worsening climate and its effect on the cattle economy, a theory that awaits further, in-depth analysis through the palaeoenvironmental record. Climate may not have been the only, or even the principal, catalyst for this shift, however. McCormick has highlighted that the availability of suitable grazing serves as a limiting factor in the accumulation of wealth; eventually, elites needed to find an alternative currency and a move towards greater cereal production and the agricultural surplus it could facilitate may have enabled them to partake in exchanges along wider, regional networks.[168]

---

[164] Coyle McClung, 'A palynological investigation of land-use patterns in first millennium AD Ireland'.

[165] Warner, 'Tree-rings, catastrophes and culture in Early Ireland', 19.

[166] Finbar McCormick, 'Cows, ringforts and the origins of Early Christian Ireland', *Emania* 13 (1995), 33–7.

[167] Kerr, Swindles and Plunkett, 'Making hay while the sun shines?'.

[168] Finbar McCormick, 'The decline of the cow: Agricultural and settlement change in early medieval Ireland', *Peritia* 20 (2008), 210–25; McCormick, 'Agriculture, settlement and society in early medieval Ireland'.

Further incentive for a move away from a cattle-dominated economy may have been the emergence of silver as a currency.[169]

A construction gap during the tenth century seems puzzling and prompted Brown and Baillie to consider if a lack of building was linked to a possible environmental downturn.[170] They point to a series of growth anomalies in North American and Mongolian pines in the 930s that indicate severe growing conditions and which have been variously attributed to the eruption of Eldgjá, now dated by ice core chronology to AD 939.[171] Whether or not extreme weather was manifest in Ireland at these times or impacted on human activity in the short-term, certain pollen records demonstrate that intensive land-use and human activity continued, despite the absence of oak-built constructions, during this period. The hiatuses in construction could alternatively be explained by an over-exploitation of the woodlands following decades of intensive building in the previous century.

Conclusions

All too often, cultural changes, particularly those involving a shift to a more obscure archaeological record in which evidence for structures and other categories of material culture is less visible, are readily interpreted in terms of system collapse. Increasingly, yet harking back to modes of thinking in the earlier twentieth century, theories of environmentally-driven cultural changes are propounded, perhaps themselves stimulated by on-going concerns about current climate change and its potential future social impacts.[172] In this paper, we have critiqued the relationship between past climate change and perceived cultural change during the final prehistoric and early medieval periods. Ireland is endowed with extensive peatlands and lakes that have yielded invaluable records of past climate and vegetation change. Using these records, it is possible to reconstruct general climate trends over extended periods, and to evaluate the impact of climate conditions on the subsistence economy, thus constructing an important bridge with the archaeological record.

Although we cannot in these records identify sub-decadal environmental events, such as those suggested by the tree-ring record, we can investigate if such events had longer-term repercussions on subsistence strategies. We find that the pollen record concords well with the archaeological record in terms of reflecting the fluctuating importance of cereal cultivation and pasture, and that for the most part these fluctuations appear to be socially-driven. Some potential climate impact may have been experienced in the mid-first millennium, giving rise to a shift in emphasis towards pastoral farming. The outcome, however, is not one of social collapse, but rather a new socio-political structure built upon cattle

---

[169] McCormick, 'Agriculture, settlement and society in early medieval Ireland', 28.
[170] Brown and Baillie, 'Confirming the existence of gaps and depletions'.
[171] Sigl *et al.*, 'Timing and climate forcing of volcanic eruptions'
[172] Butzer, 'Collapse, environment, and society'.

ownership. Further climate changes in the late eighth century may have fostered an economic adaptation that undermined the existing cow-orientated wealth system. On balance, however, it was probably internal and external politics that sowed the seed for a new socio-economic power base that stimulated changes in settlement types and the farming economy, with a greater emphasis on arable in many areas of Ireland. In short, though extreme weather anomalies will almost certainly have adversely impacted the populations who experienced them, the available evidence suggests that in the longer-term, climate trends played no major, or certainly not a detrimental, role in determining cultural evolution during the final prehistoric and early historical periods.

Acknowledgments

The authors wish to thank Brian Sloan for making available the photograph of the Tullahoge corn-drying kiln, and David Brown for supplying the image of the oak growth anomaly as well as his comments on the dendrochronological record. We are grateful also to the Editor, Tomás Ó Carragáin, and to two anonymous referees for their comments and suggestions that have helped improve this paper.

Climate, disease and society in late-medieval Ireland[1]

BRUCE M.S. CAMPBELL
School of the Natural and Built Environment,
Queen's University Belfast

FRANCIS LUDLOW*
Trinity Centre for Environmental Humanities, and Department of History,
Trinity College Dublin, Ireland

[Accepted 4 November 2020. Published 14 January 2021.]

Abstract

Palaeoclimatic data are used to track the significant changes in atmospheric circulation patterns and weather conditions that affected Ireland between 1000 and 1500 CE. How these climatic developments and associated shifts in the epidemiological environment were mapped onto Irish society is explored using a tree-ring chronology reflecting the retreat and advance of oak woodland. Years characterised by significant weather-related food scarcities are identified from the Gaelic and Anglo-Irish Annals in combination with the independent record

---

*Author's email: ludlowf@tcd.ie
ORCID iD: https://orcid.org/0000-0003-0008-0314
doi: https://doi.org/10.3318/PRIAC.2020.120.13

[1] This paper is dedicated with affection and respect to Professor Mike Baillie without whose pioneering research and the stimulus of many conversations it could not have been written. Particular thanks are due to David Brown of the Queen's University Dendrochronology Laboratory, who assembled and made available the oak sample data upon which the paper's outline chronology is based. The superposed epoch analysis results presented in the paper were developed with the assistance of Al Matthews, and Old World Drought Atlas data were processed with the help of John Nicholls. An anonymous reader gave encouragement and made helpful comments on the penultimate draft. For the commission to write this paper and for their forbearance and support (along with that of the publications committee of the Royal Irish Academy) when it became more substantial than originally envisaged, the authors are indebted to the editors, James Kelly and Tomás Ó Carragáin. For Francis Ludlow, this publication represents a contribution to the Irish Research Council project, 'Irish droughts: environmental and cultural memories' (COALESCE/2019/43), which has assisted with the cost of this paper's publication. The paper also builds upon the Marie Skłodowska-Curie fellowship project (grant agreement No 709185), 'Historical dynamics of violence, conflict and extreme weather in medieval Ireland' (CLIMCONFLICT). Further support has been provided by the 'Volcanic impacts on climate and society' (VICS) Working Group of PAGES, which is funded by the Swiss Academy of Sciences and the Chinese Academy of Sciences. The paper also draws upon the results of the Economic and Social Research Council project (RES-000-23-0645) 'Crops yields, environmental conditions, and historical change, 1270—1430'. The term 'late-medieval' is used throughout to refer to the half millennium from 1000 to 1500 CE, and 'English' used in place of multiple other possible terms such as 'Anglo-Norman'.

of English chronicles, grain yields and prices. Between the thirteenth and the fifteenth centuries the experience of the two countries is shown to have diverged. It is suggested that in late-medieval Ireland scarcity heightened the resort to violence and from 1348 was often a proximate cause of plague outbreaks. In combination, scarcity, violence and plague helped entrap fifteenth-century society in a low-level equilibrium of sparse population, economic underdevelopment, scarcely disguised poverty and low resilience to natural hazards.

Introduction—climate change as a major but neglected grand theme of late-medieval Irish history

Ireland 'more than any other [country] suffers from storms of wind and rain': thus wrote Gerald of Wales in his *History and topography of Ireland*, based upon first-hand observations from his two extended Irish visits in 1183 and 1185.[2] It constitutes what is probably the first reasonably detailed extant account of Ireland's climate. As a Welshman he does not appear to have been unduly perturbed by these now well-known characteristics of the Irish weather, rather, he comments favourably on the generally temperate nature of the climate and absence of extremes of either summer heat or winter cold. He was struck by the fact that the grass remained green throughout the winter, so that haymaking and the winter housing of livestock were not practised, and noted that snow was seldom seen and rarely lasted long. In his experience, thunder and lightning were equally rare, partly because 'you will scarcely see even in summer three consecutive days of really fine weather'. Hence his stress upon the windiness of the Irish weather ('a north-west wind, along with the west wind to its south, prevails here, and is more frequent and violent than any other') combined with its cloudiness and 'plentiful supply of rain'. These natural attributes meant that the island was 'richer in pastures than in crops, and in grass than in grain', with obvious influences on the agrarian economy and the composition of diets. He also considered the air 'so healthy' that 'you will not find many sick men, except those that are actually at the point of death'. On his testimony, fevers, apart from the ague, were comparative strangers to Ireland, whose insularity partially shielded it from the germs which circulated more readily on the continent.[3]

These observations about the Irish weather at the end of the twelfth century accord with what palaeoclimatic reconstructions are revealing about the distinctive climatic conditions prevailing at that time when the atmospheric circulation patterns characteristic of the Medieval Climate Anomaly (formerly the Medieval Warm Period) were firmly in the ascendant. For Ireland that meant a dominant Atlantic airstream, especially in the winter when a characteristically steep pressure gradient between the Azores and Iceland ensured that the North Atlantic Oscillation (NAO) was typically strongly positive. When the NAO was in positive mode Irish winters were usually mild, windy and wet, while incursions of cold, dry Arctic or continental air masses were kept at bay. One recent

---

[2] Gerald of Wales, *The history and topography of Ireland*, trans. and intro. John O'Meara (Dundalk, 1951), 34–5, 53–4.

[3] J.M. Diamond, *Guns, germs and steel: a short history of everybody for the last 13,000 years* (London, 1997), 202-05, 357-8.

reconstruction suggests that these conditions prevailed in four out of five years during the second half of the twelfth century and were the established norm from 1183 to 1200, at the time when Gerald of Wales was in Ireland.[4] The comparative stability of the NAO at this time is consistent with the unusually settled state of the weather during this benign climatic interlude (as expressed in the low year-on-year variance of a range of climate proxies—Appendix 5) and which not even a notable northern hemisphere volcanic eruption in *c.*1182 was able to disturb.[5] At this time Atlantic storms were to be expected but not, as Gerald says, extremes of cold, heat or drought. In these respects, the findings of climate science broadly corroborate his qualitative account.[6]

Yet the climate would not remain so temperate, nor had it always been so, as Gerald, a learned man, could have discovered for himself by consulting the Gaelic Irish Annals (hereafter Annals) which, by the late-twelfth century, already spanned more than 600 years. Within living memory, in 1156, these recorded that Ireland had endured 'great snow and intense frost…so that the lakes and rivers of Ireland were frozen over' and 'most of the birds of Ireland perished' (*Annals of the Four Masters*).[7] Lightning strikes (either because they damaged ecclesiastical buildings or were interpreted as acts of God) were regularly reported in the Annals, as in 1135 when the *Chronicon Scotorum* reported: 'Lighting took the roof from the tower of Clonmacnoise and made a hole in the tower of Roscrea'.[8] A few years earlier, in 1129, the *Annals of Inisfallen* noted a hot summer and

---

[4] Appendix 3; Pablo Ortega *et al.*, 'A model-tested North Atlantic Oscillation reconstruction for the past millennium', *Nature* 523:7558 (2015), 71–4. Data: www.ncdc.noaa.gov/paleo/study/18935.

[5] Appendix 5.

[6] Gerald's retrospective account of the stormy winter of 1171–2 is also consistent with NAO reconstructions for those years: 'The storms raged so unceasingly and with such persistence that throughout that whole winter scarcely a single ship had succeeded in making the crossing to the island, and no one could get any news whatsoever from other lands': A.B. Scott and F.X. Martin (eds) *Expugnatio Hibernica: the conquest of Ireland by Giraldus Cambrensis* (Dublin, 1978), 103 (who, in corroboration of Gerald's account, cite the tempestuous seas preventing re-supply of Henry II's forces in Ireland. See p. 316 of Thomas Jones (ed.) *Brut y Tywysogyon, or the chronicle of the princes: red book of Hergest version* (Cardiff, 1955), and William Stubbs (ed.) *Radulfi de Diceto decani Lundoniensis opera historica: the historical works of Master Ralph de Diceto, dean of London* (London, 1876). The *Annals of Inisfallen* offer a less specific description of 'Very bad weather this year, which killed the better part of the cattle of Ireland' in 1172: Francis Ludlow, 'The utility of the Irish Annals as a source for the reconstruction of climate' (unpublished PhD thesis, Trinity College Dublin, 2010), vol. 2, 193. Hereafter all Gaelic annalistic texts are referred to by their common titles and their bibliographical details may be found under these at the Corpus of Electronic Texts (CELT) website, www.ucc.ie/celt; unless otherwise stated, references are to the original citations as given in Ludlow, 'Utility of the Irish Annals', vol. 2 (hereafter Ludlow, 'Utility 2').

[7] Ludlow, 'Utility 2', 190–1.

[8] Ludlow, 'Utility 2', 181.

drought so severe that 'the waters of Ireland dried up, and there was a great mortality of beasts and cattle'.[9] And the previous century, in 1095, 'a great sickness' was widely reported 'that killed many people, [lasting] from the first of August until the following May Day—i.e. the year of the mortality' (*Annals of Ulster*).[10] Evidently, Ireland was less immune to epidemics than Gerald supposed and once the Black Death arrived in 1348 plague mortality would weigh heavily upon Ireland's then-shrinking population.

In fact, as the Annals make clear, natural hazards—both physical and biological—posed a recurrent threat to Irish society throughout the late-medieval centuries, as the Irish climate was itself subject to change. Thus, in 1050, at the climax of the Oort Solar Minimum when very different patterns of atmospheric circulation prevailed, 'Much inclement weather happened in the land of Ireland, which carried away corn, milk, fruit, and fish, from the people, so that there grew up dishonesty among all, that no protection was extended to church or fortress, gossipred or mutual oath, until the clergy and laity of Munster assembled, with their chieftains, under Donnchadh, son of Brian, i.e. the son of the King of Ireland, at Cill-Dalua [Killaloe], where they enacted a law and a restraint upon every injustice, from small to great' (*Annals of the Four Masters*).[11] While this account has a clear subtext in the fraught politics of the high kingship of the period,[12] it also bears out the self-evident point that this economically under-developed society was heavily dependent for its subsistence upon the annual harvests of grain, grass, fruit and nuts, milk, meat, wool and hides. When production fell short poverty almost invariably increased and famine not unusually resulted. Scarcity, in turn, might prompt the needy to resort to crime

---

[9] Ludlow, 'Utility 2', 176.

[10] Ludlow, 'Utility 2', 161. For earlier lethal disease outbreaks reported in the Annals: W.P. MacArthur, 'Identification of some pestilences in the Irish Annals', *Irish Historical Studies* 6 (1949-50), 169–88; Ann Dooley, 'The plague and its consequences in Ireland', in L.K. Little (ed.), *Plague and the end of Antiquity: the pandemic of 541–750* (Cambridge, 2006), 215–30; Ciara Crawford, 'Disease and illness in medieval Ireland' (unpublished PhD thesis, National University of Ireland Maynooth, 2011); T.P. Newfield, 'Mysterious and mortiferous clouds: the climate cooling and disease burden of Late Antiquity', *Late Antique Archaeology* 12:1 (2016), 89–115; P.A. Grace, 'From *blefed* to *scamach*: pestilence in early medieval Ireland', *Proceedings of the Royal Irish Academy* 118C (2018), 67–93.

[11] Ludlow, 'Utility 2', 154. Tree-ring evidence suggests that the unspecific 'inclement weather' described in 1050 CE involved severe drought across much of north-west Europe, illustrating the benefits of combining documentary and natural proxy evidence: F. Ludlow and C. Travis, 'STEAM approaches to climate change, extreme weather and social-political conflict', in A. de la Garza and C. Travis (eds), *The STEAM revolution: transdisciplinary approaches to science, technology, engineering, arts, humanities and mathematics* (New York, 2019), 33–65.

[12] Lauren Baker *et al.*, 'Mainstreaming morality: an examination of moral ecologies as a form of resistance', *Journal for the Study of Religion, Nature, and Culture* 11:1 (2017), 23–55.

and the powerful to violence.[13] Such circumstances were the breeding ground of disease, as in 1189 when the *Annals of Inisfallen* noted 'Great warfare and sickness and much bad weather this year'.[14] The weather was not, of course, the sole cause of violence and plague, rather it was the catalyst that often triggered and magnified them and to a degree shaped their courses.[15] As yet there has been little systematic investigation of these interactions,[16] which often weighed more heavily upon the poor than the privileged, partly because they have been eclipsed by the traditionally dominant historiographic grand themes of Church reform, the emergence of a high kingship, English invasion, conquest and colonisation, and the Gaelic revival.[17] Relevant palaeoclimatic information has also been wanting.[18] That has now changed and it is at last possible to place Gerald of Wales's description and the many environmental observations of the annalists in a proper scientific context.

Recent advances in palaeoclimatology have equipped historians with an array of high-resolution datasets constructed from a variety of natural and historical archives and now frequently spanning the entirety of the medieval

---

[13] B.M.S. Campbell, 'Nature as historical protagonist: environment and society in pre-industrial England' (the 2008 Tawney Memorial Lecture), *Economic History Review* 63:2 (2010), 281–314: 291–6.

[14] Ludlow, 'Utility 2', 198.

[15] As in 1447 (*Annals of Ireland 1443 to 1468*): 'Great famine in the spring of this year throughout all Ireland, so that men were then wont to eat all manner of herbs for the most part. Great plague in summer, harvest, and winter, by which died the Prior of Ballyboggan and the Prior of Connell [Co. Kildare], and the Baron of Calatrym [Galtrim], and Gerott the sons [*sic*] of Walront, and the Listel, and many more in Meath, in Munster, in Leinster died of that plague, and it is difficult to get an account of the innumerable multitudes that died in Dublin by that plague': Ludlow, 'Utility 2', 275. For the association between plague outbreaks and spells of extreme weather in the bacterium's reservoir regions in inner Eurasia: B.M.S. Campbell, *The Great Transition: climate, disease and society in the late-medieval world* (Cambridge, 2016), 227–30, 246–52, 349–51; B.V. Schmid et al., 'Climate-driven introduction of the Black Death and successive plague reintroductions into Europe', *Proceedings of the National Academy of Sciences* 112:10 (2015), 3020–5.

[16] A rare exception (but for the early-medieval period) is Donnchadh Ó Corráin, 'Ireland c.800: aspects of society', in D. Ó Cróinín (ed.), *A new history of Ireland, vol. 1, prehistoric and early Ireland* (Cambridge, 2005), 549–608.

[17] These themes are given pride of place in Art Cosgrove (ed.), *A new history of Ireland, vol. 2, medieval Ireland 1169–1534* (Oxford, 1987), and Brendan Smith (ed.), *The Cambridge history of Ireland, vol. 1, 600–1550* (Cambridge, 2018). Neither volume makes more than fleeting mention of the weather or pays serious attention to the frequency and severity of famine.

[18] Commenting in 1987, R.E. Glasscock ('Land and people, c.1300' in Cosgrove, *New history of Ireland, vol. 2*, 205–39: 206) observed that 'until there is more scientific study of this country's medieval climate we shall have to continue to pin our faith on Giraldus's random observations.' As noted above, however, the scientific evidence itself suggests Gerald's few remarks on the Irish climate might not be so random.

period.[19] These datasets have continued to clarify the geographical and temporal character of the often profound changes in climate that occurred over the course of the late-medieval centuries as temperatures and atmospheric circulation patterns transitioned from the relative warmth and stability of the Medieval Climate Anomaly to the cooler and more unsettled conditions of the Little Ice Age, with the critical tipping point from one global climate regime to the other occurring during the first half of the fourteenth century.[20] At the same time, a conjuncture of demographic, economic, commercial, political, military, religious and epidemiological developments was variously placing societies from Iceland to China under increasing stress.[21] Climate change thus emerges as an additional grand theme of late-medieval history and one of overarching global significance.[22] What ecological, epidemiological and societal relevance it may have had for late-medieval Ireland remains to be established.

Climate and society in late-medieval Ireland—the evidence

The evidence currently and potentially available to study climate change and extreme weather events across the first five centuries of the second millennium CE is better than that available to investigate interactions between climate and society.

From ice cores and tree rings, increasingly sophisticated reconstructions are available of two of the key drivers of global climate change, notably the varying output of solar irradiance and the scale, incidence and generalised location of sulphur-rich mega eruptions (Fig. 1). Successively, the years from

---

[19] Relevant datasets are hosted on the National Oceanic and Atmospheric Administration's (NOAA) Paleoclimate Data website: www.ncdc.noaa.gov/data-access/paleoclimatology-data. Recently a curated compilation of datasets has also been released by the PAGES2k Consortium, 'A global multiproxy database for temperature reconstructions of the Common Era', *Nature Scientific Data* 4(170088) (2017), doi:10.1038/sdata.2017.88.

[20] J.L. Brooke, *Climate change and the course of global history: a rough journey* (Cambridge, 2014), 350–444; Campbell, *Great Transition*, 1–19, 277–86.

[21] A.J. Dugmore, Christian Keller and T.H. McGovern, 'Norse Greenland settlement: reflections on climate change, trade, and the contrasting fates of human settlements in the North Atlantic islands', *Arctic Anthropology* 44:1 (2007), 12–36; R.D. Oram, and W. Paul Adderley, 'Lordship and environmental change in central highland Scotland, c.1300–c.1400', *Journal of the North Atlantic* 1 (2008), 74–84; Timothy Brook, *The troubled empire: China in the Yuan and Ming Dynasties* (Cambridge, MA, 2010), 50–78; Victor Lieberman, *Strange parallels: Southeast Asia in global context, c.800–1830, vol. 2, mainland mirrors: Europe, Japan, China, South Asia, and the Islands* (Cambridge, 2009), 1–112, 182–205; Tana Li, 'The Mongol Yuan Dynasty and the climate, 1260–1360', in Martin Bauch and Gerrit Jasper Schenk (eds), *The crisis of the 14th century: teleconnections between environmental and societal change?*, Das Mittelalter: Perspektiven mediävistischer Forschung, Beihefte 13 (Berlin and Boston, 2020), 153–68.

[22] Brooke, *Climate change and the course of global history*; Campbell, *Great Transition*; Lieberman, *Strange parallels*.

Climate, disease and society in late-medieval Ireland

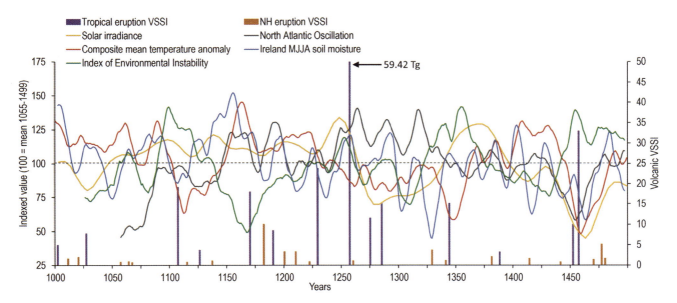

FIG. 1—Indexed solar irradiance, northern hemisphere and European temperatures, Irish spring–summer soil moisture (i.e., MJJA precipitation), the NAO and an Index of Environmental Instability, plus estimated volcanic stratospheric sulphate injections (VSSI; in mass units of teragrams, i.e., Tg) for major tropical and northern-hemisphere extratropical eruptions, 1000–1500 CE. Note the VSSI value of 59.42 for the 1257 Samalas eruption has been truncated at 50 Tg for visual clarity.

Note: temperatures, precipitation, environmental instability and the NAO are centred eleven-year moving averages.

Sources: Solar Irradiance: Friedhelm Steinhilber, Jürg Beer and Claus Fröhlich, 'Total solar irradiance during the Holocene', *Geophysical Research Letters* 36 (2009), L19704. Data: Steinhilber *et al.*, 'Holocene total solar irradiance reconstruction', IGBP PAGES/World Data Center for Paleoclimatology, Data Contribution Series # 2009-133, NOAA/NCDC Paleoclimatology Program, Boulder CO, USA. www.ncdc.noaa.gov/paleo/study/8744. Accessed 25 August 2016.

Composite mean temperature anomaly: Appendix 1.

Ireland MJJA soil moisture: Appendix 2. Data downloaded from Edward R. Cook *et al.*, 'Old World megadroughts and pluvials during the Common Era', *Science Advances* 1:10 (2015), e1500561. doi: 10.1126/sciadv.1500561

North Atlantic Oscillation: Appendix 3.

Index of Environmental Instability: Appendix 5.

Volcanic stratospheric sulphur injections: Matthew Toohey and Michael Sigl, 'Volcanic stratospheric sulfur injections and aerosol optical depth from 500 BCE to 1900 CE', *Earth System Science Data* 9:2 (2017), 809–31: 822.

1000 to 1500 CE spanned the Oort Solar Minimum (*c.*1010–50), Medieval Solar Maximum (*c.*1050–1265), Wolf Minimum (*c.*1282–1342), Chaucerian Maximum (*c.*1350–95) and Spörer Minimum (*c.*1416–1534), with each upturn or downturn in irradiance having potentially far-reaching consequences for global temperatures, sea-surface temperatures, ocean currents, pressure gradients and patterns of atmospheric circulation.[23] Across these centuries, major volcanic forcing events such as those dated approximately to 1108, 1170, 1182, 1229, 1257, 1275, 1285, 1344, 1452 and 1457 triggered a series of short-term but severe climate anomalies of (sometimes) up to three years' duration that were geographically selective in their weather effects and on occasion, via sea-ice formation, may have initiated positive feedback effects of far greater duration.[24] An array of chronologies, from tree rings, speleothems, ice cores, lake sediments and other 'natural archives' (i.e., biological and physical 'proxies'), shed light on the extent to which these climate-forcing events then affected weather conditions over Ireland, Britain and adjacent parts of mainland Europe.

Thanks to research stemming from current concerns about global warming and whether or not the peak temperatures of the Medieval Climate Anomaly have now been exceeded, there are many good temperature reconstructions extending back over the whole or most of the last millennium for the northern hemisphere, the North Atlantic and continental Europe (Appendix 1). Increasingly ingenious methods have been devised for estimating both temperatures and precipitation from tree rings, but with the limitation that the results relate almost exclusively to conditions during the growing season from (broadly) March to August. Tree-ring-derived precipitation series are available for southern England and the Old World Drought Atlas has reconstructed annual patterns of spring–summer soil-moisture content across Europe from a pan-continental network of tree rings from oak and other species, from which a subsidiary chronology for Ireland can be disaggregated (Fig. 1 and Appendix 2).[25] Precipitation series have also been derived from speleothems. That inferred from a speleothem from

---

[23] The dates are given by Minze Stuiver and Paul D. Quay, 'Changes in atmospheric Carbon-14 attributed to a variable sun', *Science* 207:4426 (1980), 11–19; also N.R. Rogozo *et al.*, 'Reconstruction of Wolf sunspot numbers on the basis of spectral characteristics and estimates of associated radio flux and solar wind parameters for the last millennium', *Solar Physics* 203 (2001), 179–91. The reconstruction of solar irradiance by Gilles Delaygue and Edouard Bard, 'An Antarctic view of Beryllium-10 and solar activity for the past millennium', *Climate Dynamics* 36:11–12 (2011), 2201–18, supersedes that of Edouard Bard *et al.*, 'Solar irradiance during the last 1200 years based on cosmogenic nuclides', *Tellus* 52B (2000), 985–92: the correlation between the two series for the years 868–1936 is +0.897.

[24] Markus Stoffel *et al.*, 'Estimates of volcanic-induced cooling in the northern hemisphere over the past 1,500 years', *Nature Geoscience* 8:10 (2015), 784–8. For the hypothesis that the sequence of large explosive eruptions in the later thirteenth century may have initiated the Little Ice Age with reinforcement from positive Arctic sea-ice-formation feedbacks: Gifford H. Miller *et al.*, 'Abrupt onset of the Little Ice Age triggered by volcanism and sustained by sea-ice/ocean feedbacks', *Geophysical Research Letters* 39:2 (2012), L02708, and Joanna Slawinska and Alan Robock, 'Impact of volcanic eruptions on decadal to centennial fluctuations of Arctic sea ice extent during the last millennium and on initiation of the Little Ice Age', *Journal of Climate* 31 (2018), 2145–67.

[25] More formally, the Old World Drought Atlas (OWDA) offers a reconstruction of the self-calibrating Palmer Drought Severity Index (scPDSI), reflecting spring–summer

the Cnoc nan Uamh cave system in the extreme north-west of Scotland is regarded as especially diagnostic of the strength and direction of the rain-bearing winter westerlies.[26] In conjunction with evidence from more southerly latitudes, it has been used to reconstruct annual variations in the NAO (Appendix 3),[27] a dominant determinant of winter weather conditions over Ireland and the British Isles generally. More basically, the Irish oak chronology of annual ring widths spans eight millennia and provides a crude but effective barometer of annual variations in growing conditions, with oaks typically thriving under the cool and moist spring and summer conditions that were least favourable to grain production (Appendix 4). Years with wide or narrow rings may thus prove diagnostic of periods when weather conditions proved either challenging or beneficial to agricultural producers.[28]

It is likely that environmental variability, particularly when rapid and pronounced, may have as great an impact upon society as the absolute magnitude of singular weather extremes experienced historically.[29] An Index of Environmental Instability (Appendix 5), which measures how stable or otherwise prevailing climatic conditions were over time, has therefore been derived from these annual series of temperatures, growing-season soil-moisture availability and tree-ring widths. This is particularly useful for identifying the episodes of intensified environmental stress to which ecosystems and human societies were periodically exposed, as in the 1090s, 1350s and 1450s (Fig. 1).

Taken together, this array of climate variables reveals a complex picture of ongoing episodic change (Fig. 1), in which no combination of climatic circumstances ever persisted for long or recurred in quite the same configuration. The trends summarised in Fig. 1 are generalised by smoothing and hence omit the sometimes

---

soil-moisture availability: E.R. Cook *et al.*, 'Old world megadroughts and pluvials during the common era', *Science Advances* 1:10 (2015), e1500561.

[26] C.J. Proctor, A. Baker, and W.L. Barnes, 'A three thousand year record of North Atlantic climate', *Climate Dynamics* 19:5–6 (2002), 449–54.

[27] V. Trouet *et al.*, 'Persistent positive North Atlantic Oscillation mode dominated the Medieval Climate Anomaly', *Science* 324 (2009), 78–80; Ortega, 'Model-tested North Atlantic Oscillation reconstruction'.

[28] Thus, years with moderately below average oak growth may be indicative of dry spring and early summer conditions more conducive to grain growth, but years with particularly extreme oak growth, whether negative or positive, may be considered potentially stressful for society. For example, very deep growth minima, as seen in Irish oaks in 737 and 738 CE, indicate severe drought likely to be of net harm to grain crops (Ludlow and Travis, 'STEAM approaches to climate change', 54). The detrimental character of this drought is confirmed by a continuator of Bede's *Ecclesiastical History*, who for 737 CE reports 'A great drought rendered the land infertile' (B. Colgrave and R.A.B. Mynors (eds) *Bede's ecclesiastical history of the English people* (Oxford, 1969), 573).

[29] For the impact of rapid environmental variability: A.J. Dugmore *et al.*, 'The role of climate in settlement and landscape change in the North Atlantic islands: an assessment of cumulative deviations in high-resolution proxy climate records', *Human Ecology* 35:2 (2007), 169–78.

extreme annual and seasonal variations that occasionally caused so much grief to society and moved annalists to comment. Fleeting but dramatic events, such as the steeple-toppling St Maur's Day wind of 15 January 1362, 'which wrecked churches and houses and sank many ships and boats', are simply not captured at this scale of analysis, although the generally disturbed climatic context from which this particularly destructive cyclone emerged does show up quite clearly.[30]

Close scrutiny of the variations plotted in Fig. 1 reveals some striking temporal contrasts. Note, for instance, the exceptional weakness of the NAO, driver of the mild and rain-bearing winter westerlies, in the mid-eleventh century following the Oort Solar Minimum. A century later, the Medieval Solar Maximum had become firmly established, the NAO was back up to strength, temperatures and rainfall were both well above average and, with few major volcanic eruptions to perturb global circulation patterns, Ireland's weather appears relatively settled. Never again would the Index of Environmental Instability remain so low on average for so long. These stable weather patterns were eventually unsettled in the 1250s when one of the greatest of all tropical eruptions came hard on the heels of exceptionally strong solar forcing at a time when the NAO was approaching its maximum strength.[31]

Nevertheless, across these five centuries the period of most critical instability was during the middle decades of the fourteenth century, when solar irradiance swung from the low of the Wolf Minimum to the high of the Chaucerian Maximum and renewed volcanic forcing reinforced a notable climate anomaly in the 1340s.[32] The NAO decisively weakened (Appendix 3) and, as North Atlantic sea-surface temperatures alternated with ever increasing amplitude between warm and cold, temperature and precipitation patterns fluctuated between extremes and became conspicuously asynchronous (Fig. 7 and Appendices 1 and 5). The last quarter of the fourteenth century brought a return to more settled conditions, which lasted until well into the opening decades of the fifteenth century.

From the 1430s, with gathering momentum, climatic conditions changed yet again (Fig. 1). The onset of the Spörer Solar Minimum, reinforced during the

---

[30] The *Annals of Ulster, of Connacht, of Loch Cé* and *of the Four Masters* all report the *gaeth mór*: Ludlow, 'Utility 2', 261. It is, however, English chronicles that supply its precise within-year date: C.E. Britton, 'A meteorological chronology to A.D. 1450', *Meteorological Office Geophysical Memoirs 70* (London, 1937), 144–5; Britton reports that according to John of Reading 'the strength of this wind did not abate for seven days and nights following' and that it came from the south and west.

[31] Clive Oppenheimer, *Eruptions that shook the world* (Cambridge, 2011), 261–7; B.M.S. Campbell, 'Global climates, the 1257 mega-eruption of Samalas Volcano, Indonesia, and the English food crisis of 1258', *Transactions of the Royal Historical Society* 27 (2017), 87–121.

[32] Campbell, *Great Transition*, 277–86. Fredrik C. Ljungqvist *et al.*, 'Linking European building activity with plague history', *Journal of Archaeological Science* 98 (2018), 81–92: 86, note significantly reduced levels of felling in 1340 and 1344. For the c.1344 volcanic event: Michael Sigl *et al.*, 'Timing and climate forcing of volcanic eruptions for the past 2,500 years', *Nature* 523 (2015), 543–9: 'Extended data', Tables 4–6.

1450s by a succession of mega eruptions, initiated the first genuinely severe and sustained cold phase of the Little Ice Age. Simultaneously, the NAO weakened decisively, temperatures and precipitation fell and instability rose. Although Irish annalists commented with awe on the 'great frosts' of 1434 and 1435 it was in the 1450s and 1460s that the circulation patterns associated with this distinctive climatic episode were at their most pronounced.[33] At the same time, plague became a recurrent scourge. These environmental circumstances were more or less the opposite of those that had prevailed in the mid-thirteenth century when the circulation patterns of the Medieval Climate Anomaly had been securely in place, delivering on average a mild and moist maritime airstream to Ireland. The evidence as presently assembled thus suggests that the fourteenth century marks the point of transition between these two very different climate regimes.

Investigating how Irish society was affected by these climatic trends and variations is contingent in large part upon the availability of written records, which are limited in survival, uneven in their chronological, geographical and thematic coverage and, for a variety of reasons, may be problematic to date. The Gaelic Annals, compiled up to (and into) the thirteenth century primarily by monastic chroniclers and thereafter by hereditary historians in the employ of the Gaelic nobility, together with the few surviving Latin chronicles of the English Lordship (collectively termed the Anglo-Irish Annals), are the one genre of record with continuous annual coverage of the entire five centuries under consideration (Fig. 2).[34] Unusual weather events are frequently recorded in the Annals, along with their biospheric and human impacts, albeit with an inevitably greater focus on the fates of high-status individuals than those of the humble majority.

Extreme weather was deemed record-worthy by Irish annalists for many reasons, but particularly for its deleterious material impacts and perceived religious significance (e.g., as divine portent or vehicle of divine retribution).[35] The uneven occurrence of extreme weather phenomena will have acted as one fundamental control on the frequency with which they were reported; their perceived relevance to unfolding human events was another.[36] There is therefore an

---

[33] For descriptions in the Annals of cold conditions in 1435 and 1435: Ludlow, 'Utility 2', 271–74. Chantal Camenisch *et al*., 'The 1430s: a cold period of extraordinary internal climate variability during the early Spörer Minimum with social and economic impacts in north-western and central Europe', *Climate of the Past* 12:11 (2016), 2107–26. For conditions in the 1450s: Campbell, *Great Transition*, 371–3, and below, pp. 225–6.

[34] Daniel McCarthy, *The Irish Annals: their genesis, evolution, and history* (Dublin, 2008). For the varying temporal coverage of sixteen Irish annalistic texts: Francis Ludlow, 'Assessing non-climatic influences on the record of extreme weather events in the Irish Annals', in P.J. Duffy and W. Nolan (eds), *At the anvil: essays in honour of William J. Smyth* (Dublin, 2012), 93–133: 113.

[35] Ludlow, 'Utility of the Irish Annals', vol. 1, 149–201. See also the compilation of weather events from the Annals in Ludlow, 'Utility 2'.

[36] Ludlow, 'Assessing non-climatic influences'. The frequency of weather events (and related societal stresses such as famine and plague) represent only a small subset of

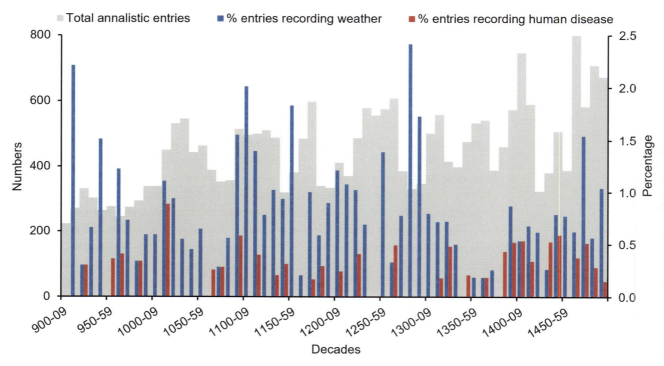

Fig. 2—Decadal totals of all Gaelic annalistic entries and the percentages of those entries recording extreme weather and human disease, 900–1500 CE.

Source: Francis Ludlow, 'The utility of the Irish Annals as a source for the reconstruction of climate', unpublished PhD thesis, Trinity College Dublin, 2010, vol. 2.

important distinction to be drawn between the frequency with which weather phenomena are reported and the frequency of their actual occurrence. Further, although events of national significance are recorded in all Annals, annalists were typically provincial in their interests with the result that there are some conspicuous regional imbalances in their collective coverage. Frustratingly, and in contrast to the situation before the English invasion, it is the more densely

---

the total number of reported events, yet periods with a greater surviving record density still tend to report more weather events, making climatic inferences from raw counts of weather events hazardous (e.g., see the approach and resultant interpretation of weather event frequencies offered by T.R. Kerr, G.T. Swindles and Gill Plunkett, 'Making hay while the Sun shines? Socio-economic change, cereal production and climatic deterioration in early medieval Ireland', *Journal of Archaeological Science* 36 (2009), 2868–74). One method of controlling for changes in record density is to express events as a percentage of total record availability, as per Fig. 2. In this paper it is also assumed that the more extreme the event the greater the probability that it will have been recorded and thereafter survived the process of copying through time (hence the reported frequency of the more extreme events may be less affected by record density), but the issue of recording bias merits further investigation.

populated and commercialised territories of the south and east of the country that are the least well represented (Fig. 3).

Of changes in annalistic recording tradition through time, perhaps the most important is the move from the late-thirteenth-century away from monastic recording to secular recording by hereditary Gaelic scholars. This was accompanied by a heavy (if not complete) shift in the centres of recording to the west of the Shannon and north of the island, where exposure to Atlantic and Arctic weather systems was greatest and grass-based pastoral agriculture predominated. Nonetheless, the full spectrum of extremes of temperature, wind and precipitation nominally continued to receive attention. Geographically, the resultant change in coverage is particularly evident in the case of the *Annals of Ulster* which, after *c*.1300, has significantly less to say about events within the province of Leinster and especially little within the counties of Dublin, Wicklow, Carlow and Wexford (Fig. 3). The best national coverage is therefore obtained by pooling the information contained in all the surviving Annals. Whether any of them individually were qualified to speak of conditions across Ireland as a whole, as in 1461 when the *Annals of Connacht* claimed a 'great dearth throughout Ireland', is nevertheless an open question.[37]

Few of the surviving Annals provide an entirely independent record, since much that they contain was copied from other earlier Annals and therefore reported at second and third hand, although sometimes this has the merit of providing different versions of the same event.[38] For example, the *Annals of Ulster*, *of Loch Cé*, *of Connacht* and *of Clonmacnoise* (or *Mageoghagan's Book*) all effectively repeat the same underlying original report of the frost and heavy snow that prevailed from late December 1281 to the start of February 1282. By contrast, the *Annals of Inisfallen* offer a more independent Munster perspective and add that 'there was very bad weather generally from then on, which prevented any useful work being done', not least through the 'many a violent wind-storm' that

---

[37] Ludlow, 'Utility 2', 276. The annalists sometimes reveal networks of information that would have provided at least a wider regional perspective. Thus for 1471 the *Annals of Connacht* report that 'Showers of hail fell each side of Beltaine [1 May], with lightning and thunders, destroying much blossom and beans and fruits in all parts of Ireland where they fell. One of these showers, in the east, had stones two or three inches long, which made large wounds on the people they struck and destroyed...and a dog in Mag Trega [Moytra, a plain in Co. Longford] and about Cluain Lis Beci [near Rathowen, Co. Westmeath] and in every place it visited. There was another, in the north, which did much damage in Moylurg [in Co. Roscommon] and at the monastery of Boyle [also Co. Roscommon]; and a boat could have floated over the floor of the great church of the monks, as we have heard from the folk of that place.' This report is also found much-abbreviated in the *Four Masters*: Ludlow, 'Utility 2', 279–80.

[38] These are often simple duplicates of lost original observations, but certain texts (or combinations of texts) may provide a fuller or more faithful account of these lost originals: McCarthy, *Irish Annals*. The complexity of this situation makes the collation of all available records a necessity, as per Ludlow, 'Utility 2'.

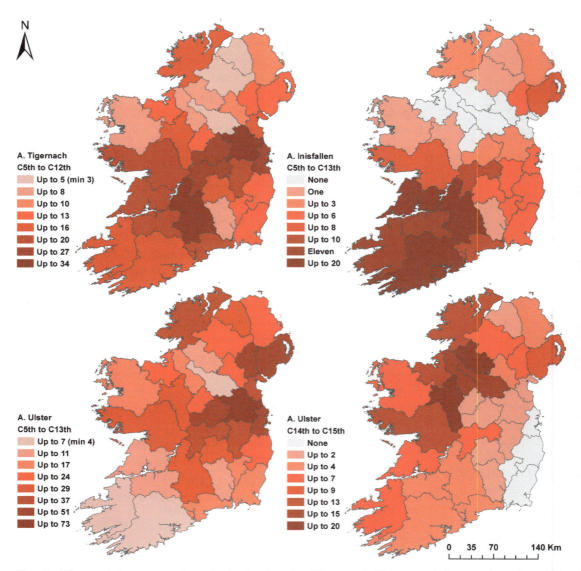

Fig. 3—The spatial coverage of entries in the *Annals of Tigernach*, fifth to twelfth centuries, *of Inisfallen* and *of Ulster*, fifth to thirteenth centuries, and again *of Ulster*, fourteenth to fifteenth centuries CE.

Note: Entries are mapped by sampling the first year of each decade, excepting in the fifth and sixth centuries, where every fifth year is mapped to compensate for lower average entry numbers in this early period. Divisions in the scale (i.e., entry numbers up to 15, 20, etc.) are generated by Jenks Natural Breaks. For expediency, modern county boundaries are used even though they are anachronistic for much of the period being mapped. Although uncertainties remain respecting the identification of many place names, and territories reported in connection with events are often poorly constrained and vary through time, most can be attributed with some confidence to a particular county or group of counties. These are still sufficiently numerous and granular to offer a broad impression of the changing spatial focus of annalistic recording.

Note also that the *Annals of Tigernach* end in 1178 and although the *Annals of Inisfallen* end in 1450, the bulk of their coverage ends in the early fourteenth century. The *Annals of Ulster*, which end in 1538, thus better reveal the shift in spatial focus to the west and north, post *c.*1300.

Source: Counts made by Francis Ludlow and Brianán Nolan for this paper.

wrought considerable damage to agriculture and infrastructure.[39] Additionally, because annalists differed in the dating conventions they followed and those conventions evolved considerably through time, there are often significant discrepancies between Annals in the precise dating of events. Transcription, translation and linguistic change can also distort the intended meaning of entries originally recorded in Old and Middle Irish or Latin.[40] Application of the chronological corrections pioneered by Daniel McCarthy and verified by reference to independently known events has, however, gone far in resolving the multiple divergent dates for the same events often seen between texts.[41] Establishing whether the multiple translations offered by the modern editors of these texts are largely in agreement can similarly resolve uncertainties of meaning and translation.[42] Calibrating weather events recorded in the Annals against relevant independent palaeoclimate proxies can further help verify their general reliability and highlight potentially significant omissions and thematic biases.

From the thirteenth century, comparing Ireland's annalistic record against the robustly documented and quantitative English record of grain prices, daily real wage rates, harvests and crop yields (for none of which are there Irish counterparts, bar scattered references in manorial extents and other records of the English colony in Ireland) can potentially serve the same validating purpose, with the advantage of revealing similarities and discrepancies between the nature and experience of climate change on opposite sides

---

[39] Ludlow, 'Utility 2', 237–8.

[40] An example, from duplicate entries in the *Annals of Connacht* and *of Loch Cé* for 1308, is the Irish word '*donenn*' with its adjectival variant '*doinend*'. A.M. Freeman (editor of the *Annals of Connacht* in 1944) is alone in translating this as 'storm' or 'stormy' weather, rather than a more general inclemency or badness of weather, as rendered by W.M. Hennessy for the *Annals of Loch Cé* (1871) and by multiple modern editors. P.S. Dinneen (*Foclóir Gaedilge agus Béarla: an Irish-English dictionary, being a thesaurus of the words, phrases and idioms of the modern Irish language* (Dublin, 1927, new edition), 355) translates '*doineann*' variously as 'bad weather, storm, tempest' and, in adjectival form, '*doineannac*' as 'stormy, wintry, tempestuous'. The correct choice is thus unclear, but has a bearing upon climatic reconstructions, e.g., storm chronologies, attempted using the Annals: Ludlow, 'Utility of the Irish Annals', vol. 1, 139–41.

[41] Daniel McCarthy, *Irish chronicles and their chronology* (Dublin, 2005, 4th edition), available at www.cs.tcd.ie/Dan.McCarthy/chronology/synchronisms/annals-chron.htm (last updated: 21/03/05; accessed: 06/01/18). These corrections are applied to all reports taken from the Annals, and extended to the small number of texts not fully covered by McCarthy (e.g., the *Annals of Inisfallen, of the Four Masters,* and *of Clonmacnoise*): Ludlow, 'Utility 2'. For further insights into the dating of the Annals: Daniel McCarthy, 'Analysing and restoring the chronology of the Irish Annals', in Ralph Kenna, Máirín MacCarron and Pádraig MacCarron (eds), *Maths meets myths: quantitative approaches to ancient narratives* (Switzerland, 2017), 177–94; Daniel McCarthy, 'The genesis and evolution of the Irish Annals to AD 1000', *Frühmittelalterliche Studien* 52 (2018), 119–55.

[42] For weather references in the Gaelic Annals, this exercise has been undertaken in Ludlow, 'Utility 2'.

Bruce M.S. Campbell and Francis Ludlow

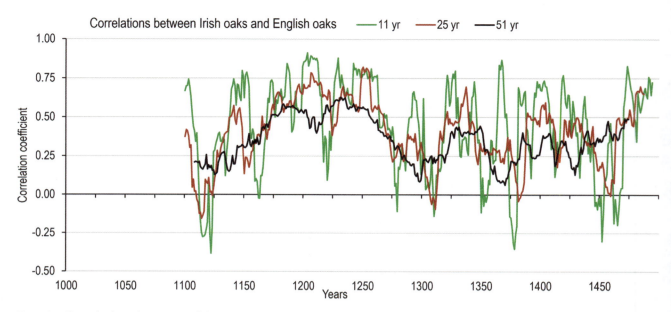

Fig. 4—Correlations between Irish and English oak ring widths, 1100–1499 CE, at different levels of smoothing.
Sources: Oak ring width data (Appendix 4) supplied by M.G.L. Baillie from the Queen's University dendrochronology database.

of the Irish Sea. This is important because it cannot be assumed that climatic trends and variability always occurred consistently across this wider region.[43] Of course, the case in principle for making such a comparison, despite some meaningful differences between the regional extremities of the north and west of Ireland versus the south and east of England, is that Ireland and England are located within a common north-west European temperate maritime climate zone. They were therefore exposed to most of the same macro-scale changes and fluctuations in climate. In different ways, they are also likely to have suffered from many of the same specific synoptic-scale extreme weather events such as the windstorms and heavy precipitation swept east by Atlantic cyclones, and particularly conditions of drought or frost from even larger-spatial-scale anti-cyclonic weather systems.

Fig. 4 demonstrates that from 1100–1499 CE, with only sporadic and brief exceptions, the ring widths of climate-sensitive Irish and southern-English oaks (i.e., those likely to exhibit least agreement) are positively correlated. Values range from a minimum of +0.23 across the fourteenth century to a maximum of +0.45 across the thirteenth century, with an overall correlation of +0.27 between 1100 and 1499. Correlations across shorter time spans

---

[43] Gerard Kiely *et al.*, *Extreme weather, climate and natural disasters in Ireland. Synthesis report. Climate change research programme (CCRP) 2007–2013*, Environmental Protection Agency, Report Series 5 (Wexford, 2010).

are often much higher and, irrespective of the levels of smoothing, range between +0.5 and +0.8 for much of the period 1250–75 when, significantly, the NAO was mostly strongly positive. Instances when the observed correlation between Irish and southern English oaks is weak or even inverted are both fewer and briefer and show up most clearly when correlations are calculated across short time frames of 25 years or less. Thus, the most conspicuous deviations between oak growth on opposite sides of the Irish Sea occurred in the 1110s, early 1310s, late 1370s and around 1450, with other lesser and briefer divergences focused on 1162–3, 1220, 1279, 1350 and 1465. To Mike Baillie, each inversion 'suggests that some environmental boundary has shifted ... as if someone has drawn a line down the middle of the Irish Sea on a weather map' and each may therefore be diagnostic of some fundamental anomaly in North Atlantic climates.[44] The rarity of these exceptions nonetheless proves the rule that under 'normal' conditions Ireland and England exist in the same climatic region, at least as far as oak trees are concerned. Herein lies the case for matching the Irish annalistic record of bad weather, poor harvests, famines and mortality crises against the corresponding English record of harvests, wages, harvests and crop yields, provided that the comparison is not pushed too hard. Contextualising the Annals in these ways brings the information they contain (and do not contain) into sharper focus and, as the rest of this paper demonstrates, lends new significance to some of the human and environmental events that are recorded.

Climate and society 1000–1500 CE—an outline chronology

Land clearance, construction, economic expansion and population growth tended to march together, as did societal contraction, land abandonment and the re-expansion of woodland, but they rarely did so in perfect step.[45] For example, in an Irish context, counting backwards to obtain the age of oaks sampled from historical, archaeological and natural contexts suggests that much of the woodland extant in the sixteenth century had regenerated in the aftermath of the devastating plague outbreaks of the fourteenth century, as was the case in many

---

[44] Mike Baillie, *New light on the Black Death: the cosmic connection* (Stroud, 2006), 105 and 105–13 for a fuller discussion of the potential significance of this phenomenon.

[45] Baillie, *New light*, 21–3; Rowan McLaughlin, Emma Hannah, and Lisa Coyle-McClung, 'Frequency analyses of historical and archaeological datasets reveal the same pattern of declining sociocultural activity in 9th to 10th century CE Ireland', *Cliodynamics: The Journal of Theoretical and Mathematical History* 9:1 (2018), 1–24; F.C. Ljungqvist *et al.*, 'Linking European building activity with plague history', *Journal of Archaeological Science* 98 (2018), 81–92; Eltjo Buringh *et al.*, 'Church building and the economy during Europe's "Age of the Cathedrals", 700–1500 CE', *Explorations in Economic History* 76 (2020), e101316.

other parts of Europe.[46] Kenneth Nicholls subscribes to 'a considerable regrowth of woodland' following a 'collapse of the intensive colonial economy of the thirteenth century and of the population of Ireland as a whole', while suggestive palynological evidence of the landscape abandonment that may have facilitated Irish oak regeneration in the fourteenth century is also noted by Valerie Hall, albeit with some notable exceptions.[47] Dendrochronological evidence of the contraction or expansion of tree cover can therefore offer an instructive guide to the direction and timing of prevailing societal trends when, as in the case of late-medieval Ireland, independent historical evidence of the latter is fragmentary. It is thus, in an exploratory way, that it is employed here and in the certain knowledge that relationships between the dendrological and human populations were non-stationary through time and space. Its value lies in the unique chronological framework that it provides for contextualising the evidence of environmental and societal conditions contained in the Annals (compare Figs 2 and 5).

The chronological distribution of Irish oak samples dated at the dendrochronological laboratory at the Queen's University of Belfast constitutes the essential quantifiable data necessary to this task.[48] For any given year, the

---

[46] David Brown and M.G.L. Baillie, 'How old is that oak?', in Ben Simon (ed.), *A treasured landscape: the heritage of Belvoir Park* (Belfast, 2005), 85–97; Baillie, *New light*, 21–3; Per Lagerås, *The ecology of expansion and abandonment: medieval and post-medieval land-use and settlement dynamics in a landscape perspective* (Stockholm, 2006), 77–92; Dan Yeloff and Bas van Geel, 'Abandonment of farmland and vegetation succession following the Eurasian plague pandemic of AD 1347–52', *Journal of Biogeography* 34:4 (2007), 575–82; Ulf Büntgen et al., 'Filling the Eastern European gap in millennium-long temperature reconstructions', *Proceedings of the National Academy of Sciences* 110:5 (2013), 1773–8: 1776.

[47] Kenneth Nicholls, 'Woodland cover in pre-modern Ireland', in P.J. Duffy, David Edwards and Elizabeth FitzPatrick (eds), *Gaelic Ireland c.1250—c.1650: land, lordship and settlement* (Dublin, 2001), 181–206: 202; V.A. Hall, 'The vegetation history of monastic and secular sites in the midlands of Ireland over the last two millennia', *Vegetation History and Archaeobotany* 15:1 (2006), 1–12; V.A. Hall, *The making of Ireland's landscape since the Ice Age* (Cork, 2011), 126–7.

[48] This work began in the late 1960s and by 1984 had contributed to an unbroken 7,272-year oak chronology: J.R. Pilcher et al., 'A 7,272-year tree-ring chronology for Western Europe', *Nature* 312:5990 (1984), 150–2. Because no other native British and Irish trees with a clearly defined annual ring pattern are as well represented by living trees, preserved timbers, and excavated and fossil timbers, oaks are almost exclusively the main species for which dendrochronologies have been developed in Britain and Ireland. A recent exception is a native pine chronology for the northern Cairngorms of Scotland: Miloš Rydval et al., 'Reconstructing 800 years of summer temperatures in Scotland from tree rings', *Climate Dynamics* 49:9–10 (2017), 2951–74. For a pilot study of the use of multiple species in Ireland (e.g., beech and ash) to derive a clearer climate signal than that embedded in oak chronologies alone: A.M. García-Suárez, C.J. Butler and M.G.L. Baillie, 'Climate signal in tree-ring chronologies in a temperate climate: a multi-species approach', *Dendrochronologia* 27 (2009), 183–98.

Climate, disease and society in late-medieval Ireland

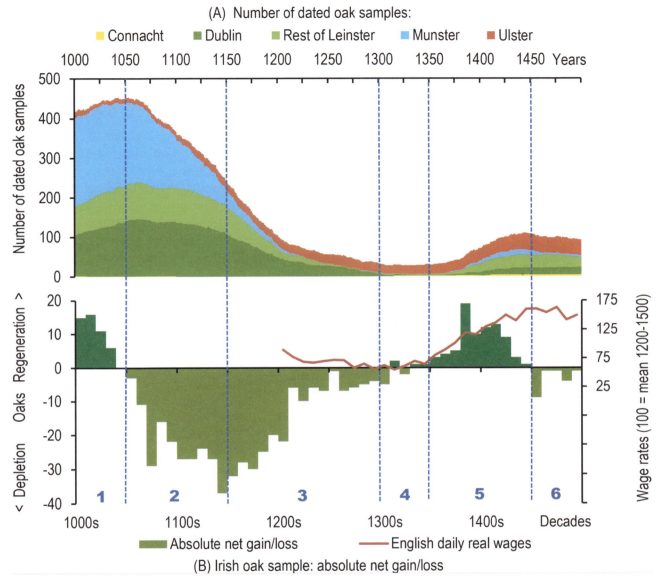

Fig. 5—(A) Numbers of dated annual Irish oak samples by province. (B) The decadal net balance between the start and end dates of sampled timbers, 1000–1500 CE with the daily real wage rates of English adult male labourers, 1200–1500 CE.

Key: 1 = regeneration; 2 = depletion phase 1; 3 = depletion phase 2; 4 = stasis; 5 = regeneration; 6 = stasis.

Note: Connacht is scarcely visible in Panel B due to the small number of samples.

Sources: Oak sample data supplied by David Brown of the Queen's University dendrochronology laboratory.

English adult male daily real wage rates calculated from: Gregory Clark, 'English prices and wages 1209–1914', Global Price and Income History Group (Davis, 2009), www.iisg.nl/hpw/data.php#united; J.H. Munro, 'The Phelps Brown and Hopkins "basket of consumables" commodity price series and craftsmen's wage series, 1264–1700: revised by J.H. Munro' (Toronto, no date), www.economics.utoronto.ca/munro5/ResearchData.html.

number of dated oak samples retrieved from archaeological excavations and historical structures provides a crude index of the number of oak trees then growing which, evidence suggests, tended to expand when human population levels were low and construction activity was slack, and contract when settlement was expanding and levels of economic activity were rising (Fig. 5A).[49] Since all dated timbers have a start and an end date (although the latter is rarely the exact felling date), for each year the net balance struck between the numbers of trees starting or ending their lives indicates whether oak numbers were increasing or decreasing (Fig. 5B).[50] Thus, when felling exceeded regeneration, the implication is that woodland depletion was ongoing, as trees were cleared for construction, fuel, agriculture and the lumber trade, whereas the opposite conditions prevailed when regeneration was in excess and populations and economic activity were in retreat (note the similar course charted by English daily real wage rates—Fig. 5B—which likewise were driven by changing land to labour ratios).

Together these measures have the merit of chronological accuracy but are qualified by the fact that the sampled oaks reflect patterns of archaeological survival and the excavation opportunities and priorities of archaeologists. It is therefore no surprise that 54 per cent of the dated samples derive from sites and excavations in Leinster, with more than half of these from Dublin alone, followed by 31 per cent from Munster, where samples from the urban sites at Cork and Waterford bulk large, 14 per cent from Ulster (notwithstanding the location of the dendrochronology laboratory within that province) and less than 1 per cent from Connacht.[51] These biases mean that the absolute magnitude of trends should not be interpreted too literally, although it is notable, and indeed reassuring, that all the regions display effectively the same chronological pattern (Fig. 5A). The geographical composition of the sample also changes over time and is least representative of Ireland as a whole, or at least of its most closely settled parts, during the critical first half of the fourteenth century (Fig. 5A). Most likely this was because the most heavily settled regions were the most denuded of oaks by this time. By its nature, therefore, this evidence must be considered a better guide to relative trends in, rather than absolute levels of, human population and/or associated construction activity. As will be noted, however, a clear six-part chronology emerges from the results set out in Figs 5A and 5B.

---

[49] Baillie, *New light*, 21–3; Ljungqvist, 'Linking European building activity with plague history'; Lagerås, *Ecology of expansion and abandonment*, 77–92.

[50] Most of these end dates will not strictly represent the final year of growth because only a minority of the oak samples contain the last ring out to the bark: Ljungqvist, 'Linking European building activity with plague history', 82–3. Limiting analysis to these samples would improve the chronological precision of the results but at the expense, in the Irish case, of sample size and spatial and chronological coverage, i.e., it would refine without fundamentally changing the basic trends.

[51] The Ulster location of the Queen's dendrochronological laboratory is evident in a larger number of samples taken from natural contexts such as lake and bog margins in and near the province, but primarily pertaining to periods before 1000 CE.

Pre 1050— relative resource abundance

When the first millennium dawned, the number of then-living oaks represented in the Irish oak dendrochronology dataset was close to its late-medieval maximum. As Fig. 5A shows, many oaks felled in later centuries were actively growing at that time.[52] Because regeneration exceeded depletion (Fig. 5B), the number of precisely dated ring-width observations continued to rise to a temporal peak in the 1040s and 1050s. No subsequent period in the second millennium is better documented, with one plausible inference being that oak woodland was abundant because population was comparatively scarce and building in oak consequently slack.[53] One of the more remarkable statements in the Annals for explicitly documenting a mass internal migration is given by the *Annals of Inisfallen* for 1004 (a year of conspicuously limited Irish oak growth in Ireland).[54] It reports that 'The Ulaid [a people in eastern Ulster] abandoned their land on account of scarcity and scattered throughout Ireland', conveying an impression of a sparse and (when needed) highly mobile population responding to environmental stress. Available palynological evidence from the north of Ireland is consistent with such a reading, which also accords with the telling absence from the dendrochronological record from the 930s to the 1020s of almost any building using newly felled oaks.[55]

Also plausibly linked to this regeneration phase is the potential cumulative impact of an increase in violence and conflict reported in the Annals. Initially this is associated with Viking-related violence from approximately 910 to 950 CE, with peaks in the 920s–930s and 940s.[56] Thereafter, an escalation can be seen in vio-

---

[52] The situation in Scotland was much the same: Anne Crone and Fiona Watson, 'Sufficiency to scarcity: medieval Scotland, 500–1600', in C.T. Smout (ed.), *People and woods in Scotland: a history* (Edinburgh, 2003), 60–81: 80; C.M. Mills and Anne Crone, 'Dendrochronological evidence for Scotland's native timber resources over the last 1000 years', *Scottish Forestry* 66:1 (2012), 18–33: 22, 30.

[53] Note that England in 1086 supported a historically small population of under two million, which, by extrapolation, implies that Ireland's population was less than 0.75 million and quite possibly less than 0.5 million: Stephen Broadberry *et al.*, *British economic growth 1270–1870* (Cambridge, 2015), 6–8; B.M.S. Campbell, 'Benchmarking medieval economic development: England, Wales, Scotland, and Ireland *circa* 1290', *Economic History Review* 61:4 (2008), 896–945: 930–2.

[54] The year 1004 exhibits the fourth narrowest oak growth-ring in the eleventh century, in a detrended oak growth chronology (by application of a 30-year cubic spline); data supplied by Mike Baillie, in personal communication with F. Ludlow, 22 December 2003.

[55] V.A. Hall, J.R. Pilcher and F.G. McCormac, 'Tephra-dated lowland landscape history of the north of Ireland, AD 750–1150', *New Phytologist* 125:1 (1993), 193–202; J.P. Mallory and M.G.L. Baillie, '*Tech nDaruch*: the fall of the House of Oak', *Emania: Bulletin of the Navan Research Group* 5 (1988), 27–33; M.G.L. Baillie and D.M. Brown, 'Dendrochronology and Deer Park Farms' in C.J. Lynn and J.A. McDowell (eds), *Deer Park Farms: the excavation of a raised rath in the Glenarm Valley, County Antrim (Northern Ireland)*, Northern Ireland Archaeological Monographs (Belfast, 2011), 558–67: 560; D.M. Brown and M.G.L. Baillie, 'Confirming the existence of gaps and depletions in the Irish oak tree-ring record', *Dendrochronologia* 30 (2012), 85–91: 88.

[56] Violence in the *Annals of Ulster* is charted by Matthew Stout, *Early medieval Ireland 431–1169* (Dublin, 2017), 139, 173.

lence from c.950–c.1050 CE, including the murder of members of the elite, mass killings and large-scale devastations of territories, which is frequently associated with dynastic rivalry for the high-kingship of Ireland.[57] Persistent slave raiding to supply the Dublin export trade must also have stoked a sense of insecurity and sapped populations of their demographic vitality.[58] McLaughlin, Hannah and Coyle-McClung have proposed that the shrinking volume of material evidence over this period,[59] along with a thinning of entries in the Annals (Fig. 2), implies a persistent downward trend in socio-cultural activity.[60] For reasons that will require much further multidisciplinary effort to resolve, society in this period appears caught in a low-equilibrium trap characterised by endemic violence, low and possibly declining population densities and an inability to capitalise upon what seem to have been increasingly favourable land to labour ratios.[61] It was from this low base and relative abundance of natural resources that, from the mid-eleventh century, renewed expansion was launched, as signalled, on the one hand, by an archaeologically well-documented upsurge in new construction activity, especially in the Hiberno-Norse towns of Dublin, Waterford and Cork, and, on the other, the diminution of violence recorded by the Annals.

---

[57] This is observed in the counting of such events for the analysis presented in Appendix 6. For a classic account of the contestation for the high kingship: F.J. Byrne, *Irish kings and high-kings* (Dublin, 2001, revised edition).

[58] Poul Holm, 'The slave trade of Dublin, ninth to twelfth centuries', *Peritia* 5 (1986), 317–45; Poul Holm, 'Slaves', in Seán Duffy (ed.), *Medieval Ireland: an encyclopedia* (New York and London, 2005), 430–1.

[59] For a specific example of material-archaeological evidence in the form of grain-drying kilns, excavated and radiocarbon-dated in large numbers during the Celtic Tiger construction boom: Scott Timpany, Orla Power and Mick Monk, 'Agricultural boom and bust in medieval Ireland: plant macrofossil evidence from kiln sites along the N9/N10 in County Kildare' in Sheelagh Conran, Ed Danaher and Michael Stanley (eds), *Past time, changing fortunes: proceedings of a public seminar on archaeological discoveries on national road schemes, August 2010* (Dublin, 2011), 73–83; Mick Monk and Orla Power, 'More than a grain of truth emerges from a rash of corn-drying kilns?', *Archaeology Ireland* 26:2 (2012), 38–41. The date distribution of kilns shows an early-medieval peak followed by a (regionally variable) decline that may reflect some of the same processes driving the observed oak regeneration phase and tenth- to early-eleventh-century hiatus in oak building.

[60] McLaughlin, Hannah, and Coyle-McClung, 'Frequency analyses of historical and archaeological datasets', 11–12, 17. The authors study the *Annals of Ulster* and observe a declining number of entries centred in the tenth century. Given the differing spatial foci of the extant Annals (e.g., Fig. 3), and given that other compilations such as the *Annals of the Four Masters* include lost sources not incorporated into the *Annals of Ulster* during its own compilation from 1498 onward, there is a need to examine the changing density and geography of recording in as many texts as possible. Here, word counts may prove a useful alternative metric to event counts: E. Purcell, 'Ninth-century Viking entries in the Irish annals: "no 'forty years' rest"' in John Sheehan and Donnchadh Ó Corráin (eds), *The Viking age: Ireland and the west* (Dublin, 2010), 322–37: 323–4).

[61] It has been suggested that Ireland had a population of 0.5 million c.1000: Margaret Murphy, 'The economy', in Smith (ed.), *Cambridge history of Ireland, vol. 1*, 385–414: 387.

Why an increasingly favourable land to labour ratio should for so long have failed to elicit a positive demographic response is an enigma. Political instability and the violence it engendered must have been a factor. Recurrent raiding to supply the export trade in slaves will certainly have been corrosive.[62] There are also sporadic reports in the Annals of heavy disease-related mortality in the tenth and eleventh centuries that may further have destabilised society, notwithstanding that this was an era free from bubonic plague.[63] Whether these events precipitated or otherwise contributed to any substantial depopulation on the basis of the available descriptions invites closer examination.

The weather, by contrast, seems not to have been as deserving of comment by the annalists. Although solar irradiance, likely a prime driver of global climates, was subsiding from the 960s there was a lag of some decades before a corresponding decline in northern hemisphere, North Atlantic

---

[62] Holm, 'Slave trade of Dublin'; Holm, 'Slaves'; Benjamin T. Hudson, 'The changing economy of the Irish Sea province', in Brendan Smith (ed.), *Britain and Ireland 900–1300: insular responses to medieval European change* (Cambridge, 1999), 39–66: 49–50.

[63] Examples (non-exhaustive, and focusing on apparent epidemics rather than reports of important individuals dying of disease) include: 987 (*Annals of the Four Masters*, also *of Tigernach* and *Chronicon Scotorum*): 'Preternatural (i.e. magical) sickness [was brought on] by demons in the east of Ireland, which caused mortality of men plainly before men's eyes'. 993 (*Annals of Ulster*, also *of Clonmacnoise* and *Chronicon Scotorum*): 'A great mortality of people, cattle, and bees throughout Ireland this year'. 1012 (*Annals of the Four Masters*, also *of Ulster* and *Chronicon Scotorum*): 'A great malady, namely, lumps and griping, at Armagh, from Allhallowtide [31 October] till May, so that a great number of the seniors and students died, together with Ceannfaeladh of Sabhall, bishop, anchorite, and pilgrim; Maelbrighde Mac-an-Ghobhann, lector of Armagh; and Scolaighe, son of Clercen, a noble priest of Armagh. These and many others along with them died of this sickness'. 1019 (*Annals of Inisfallen*): 'A great pestilence, i.e. a colic, in Ára [Aran Islands, Galway] in the above year, and many people died there'. 1061 (*Annals of Tigernach*, also *of the Four Masters* and *Chronicon Scotorum*): 'A great pestilence in Leinster, to wit, the smallpox and colic, so that there was a destruction of people throughout Leinster.' 1084 (*Annals of Tigernach*): 'A great pestilence in this year, which killed a fourth of the men of Ireland. It began in the south, and spread throughout the four quarters of Ireland. This is the *causa causans* of that pestilence, to wit, demons that came out of the northern isles of the world…'. This entry continues at length with mythological and fantastical elements that suggest its veracity should be carefully considered. 1095 (*Annals of Ulster*, also *of Loch Cé*, *of the Four Masters*, *of Clonmacnoise* (a.k.a. *Mageoghagan's Book*), *of Inisfallen* and *Chronicon Scotorum*): 'A great sickness in Ireland that killed many people, [lasting] from the first of August until the following May Day—i.e. the year of the mortality'. Ludlow, 'Utility 2', 143–4, 146, 156–9, 161–4. The events of 1012 are misattributed to 1013 in Ludlow's compilation. The quoted entry in the *Four Masters* for 1012 (an apparent conflation of the earlier and perhaps part-independent entries from the *Annals of Ulster* and *Chronicon Scotorum*) is also omitted. So too is the 1019 event from the *Annals of Inisfallen*. Note that Ludlow's compilation explicitly focuses on extreme weather and conditions of famine and scarcity (which often, but not always, overlap in years of epidemic disease). A full compilation of disease reports from the Annals is thus long overdue.

sea-surface and European summer temperatures set in (Appendix 1). In fact, temperatures rose to a peak of warmth in the 980s and only then slowly began to cool, with the result that they were all still above average when the new millennium opened. Cooling then set in and in Europe the summers of 1014, 1017, 1029, 1032 and 1046 were notably chilly and also, in the main, dry over the British Isles.[64] This probably coincided with a significant weakening of the NAO, facilitating ingress of the cold winter weather reported in the Annals in 1008, 1026, 1031 and 1047.[65] Despite these changes in circulation patterns, growing-season precipitation appears to have held up well in many years, to the extent that in 1012 the *Annals of Inisfallen* complained of a great downpour, and in 1037 the *Annals of Clonmacnoise* observed that 'It rained much this summer'.[66]

The Annals suggest that perhaps the most testing years concerning food security were 1016 and 1047. The former may have been the part result of climate forcing from a possible cometary impact in 1014 and was a year notable for spring–summer drought, when the *Annals of Clonmacnoise* reported 'a great scarcity of corn and victuals this year in Ireland'.[67] A generation later, the latter year witnessed the return of 'great famine' to Ulster, associated at least partly with heavy snowfall and cattle mortality between December 1046 and March 1047, when, according to both the *Chronicon Scotorum* and *Annals of Tigernach*, 'Ulster was almost wholly devastated, and its people went into Leinster'.[68] By the yardstick of other extreme years, however, neither year stands out in the palaeoclimatic record as experiencing a major climate forcing event. Rather, on the testimony of the Annals, it is the responses to these climatic conditions that were dramatic. Society was certainly fortunate in not having to contend with the serious short-term effects of a major tropical or northern hemisphere explosive eruption. The last such volcanic events on any serious scale had been the major Icelandic eruption of Eldgjá in *c*.939 CE and the Volcanic Explosivity Index 7 (VEI7) eruption of Changbaishan on the Chinese/North Korean border seven

---

[64] J. Luterbacher *et al.*, 'European summer temperatures since Roman times', *Environmental Research Letters* 11:2 (2016), L024001 (data: www.ncdc.noaa.gov/paleo/study/19600; accessed 19/08/2016). The OWDA suggests conditions of widespread soil-moisture deficit for much of north-west Europe in 1014, 1017 and 1046. 1032 is similarly dry over north-west Europe, though parts of Ulster and the Irish midlands seem to have escaped. 1029 stands out as the exception, with average- to above-average soil-moisture across Ireland, though parts of Britain and northern Europe experienced drought (Cook, 'Old World megadroughts').

[65] Ludlow, 'Utility 2', 145, 149–50, 152–4.

[66] Ludlow, 'Utility 2', 146, 151. The wet spring–summer conditions of 1012 and 1037 are also amply documented in the OWDA (Cook, 'Old World megadroughts'.)

[67] For the 1014 extra-terrestrial event: Baillie, *New light*, 118–25; Baillie and Brown, 'Dendrochronology and Deer Park Farms', 565–7. Ludlow, 'Utility 2', 147.

[68] Ludlow, 'Utility 2', 152–3.

years later in *c*.946 CE.[69] Any persistent climatic constraints upon Irish society at this time are, therefore, elusive of identification and it is the recurrent and self-perpetuating dynastic warfare, slave raiding and other predatory human actions that may be posited as more likely thwarting renewed expansion and growth, with the role of epidemic disease remaining an open question.

Paradoxically, expansion eventually began during the final years of the Oort Minimum of *c*.1010–1050 (although moderate relative to later minima (Fig. 1)) and when the NAO—source of winter mildness—was exceptionally weak (Fig. 1). What role these environmental developments played in helping to kick-start growth awaits closer investigation. Perhaps these were largely coincidental as Ireland was belatedly drawn into European-wide currents of expansion, as existing constraints upon growth were relaxed, and societies across the continent were reinvigorated?[70]

1050–1150—expansion, phase one

In Ireland, as in much of Europe, the mid-eleventh century brought an unmistakable change in trends, when, on the evidence of the Irish dendrochronological record, a sustained expansion of construction activity began which was to last until the end of the thirteenth century.[71] This is marked by an implied switch from net regeneration to net depletion, as sustained felling made inroads into Ireland's oak woodlands (Fig. 5). This interpretation is reinforced by the European-wide building boom known at this time, which in Italy, France, Germany and the Southern Low Countries shows up most conspicuously in the widespread building and rebuilding of churches. Church building in all these regions increased both absolutely and relatively per head of population.[72] References to church buildings in the Annals (all physically far smaller than their European counterparts) can also be seen to increase steadily from *c*.1010.[73] This reinforces the interpretation that the dramatic increase in excavated Irish oak timbers represents the indelible signature of a corresponding increase in building activity, both in the Hiberno-Norse

---

[69] Chunqing Sun *et al.*, 'Ash from Changbaishan millennium eruption recorded in Greenland ice: implications for determining the eruption's timing and impact', *Geophysical Research Letters* 41:2 (2014), 694–701; Matthew Toohey and Michael Sigl, 'Volcanic stratospheric sulfur injections and aerosol optical depth from 500 BCE to 1900 CE', *Earth System Science Data* 9:2 (2017), 809–31: 814.

[70] For the upward trajectory of European population trends from the eleventh century: Campbell, *Great Transition*, 58–60; B.M.S. Campbell, 'From boom to bust: the Lordship of Ireland and the European "commercial revolution"', in Peter Crooks and Seán Duffy (eds), *Invasion 1169* (Dublin, forthcoming).

[71] Baillie and Brown, 'Dendrochronology and Deer Park Farms', 559–60; Brown and Baillie, 'Confirming the existence of gaps and depletions', 88.

[72] Buringh *et al.*, 'Church building and the economy'.

[73] Tomás Ó Carragáin, *Churches in early medieval Ireland: architecture, ritual and memory* (New Haven, CT, 2010), 111.

trading towns of Dublin, Waterford, Cork and Limerick and more generally.[74] The upshot was a steep increase in oak depletion rates to a maximum in the 1140s and a concomitant decline in the annual number of dated oak samples contained in the dendrochronology dataset. The implication is that sustained felling was eroding the number of standing trees, which would help explain the switch from church-building in wood to building in stone evident from 1050–69, as documented in the Annals, with references to wooden churches almost disappearing from the record after 1110.[75]

Elsewhere in Europe, these years from the 1050s to the 1140s mark the initial and most pronounced phase in the great high-medieval cycle of demographic and commercial growth, when populations and settlement evidently expanded almost everywhere and woodland, felled for timber and firewood and cleared for farmland, retreated.[76] On the available archaeological evidence, Ireland appears to have been no exception. The Viking menace had receded, slave raiding had abated, the Hiberno-Norse trading towns were thriving, and important political developments were also afoot with the emergence of an increasingly viable, if still contested, high kingship.[77]

Climatically, these years coincide with the opening phase of the Medieval Solar Maximum, when sustained high levels of solar irradiance powered the patterns of atmospheric circulation—a mostly positive El Niño Southern Oscillation, a strong South Asian monsoon, an arid Central Asia and a mostly-positive NAO—which gave the Medieval Climate Anomaly its distinctive character.[78] For Ireland this implies that from the late-eleventh century winters became on average milder and moister, as the winter westerlies strengthened, so that Ireland became significantly wetter than England. North-west Scotland experienced a similar increase in precipitation at this time but correlations between the ring widths of Irish and English oaks weakened (Fig. 4). Under these circumstances it is hardly surprising that references to drought are largely absent from the Annals. The sole exception is the hot and dry summer of 1129 already referred to, conditions which at Athlone may have been seized upon to facilitate construction of a new bridge across the River Shannon.[79] Temperatures were less buoyant and trended down, with significant drops in

---

[74] For a comparable situation in Scotland: Crone and Watson, 'Sufficiency to scarcity', 80.

[75] Ó Carragáin, *Churches in early medieval Ireland,* 110–11.

[76] Campbell, *Great Transition*, 30–133; H.C. Darby, 'The clearing of the English woodlands', *Geography* 36:2 (1951), 71–83.

[77] H.B. Clarke, 'Gaelic, Viking and Hiberno-Norse Dublin', in Art Cosgrove (ed.), *Dublin through the Ages* (Dublin, 1988), 4–24; Holm, 'Slave trade of Dublin'; Duffy, 'Ireland, c.1000–c.1100'; Byrne, *Irish kings and high-kings*; Stout, *Early medieval Ireland*, 215–40.

[78] Campbell, *Great Transition*, 36–58.

[79] Above, pp. 161–2. 1129 (*Annals of the Four Masters*, also *of Inisfallen, of Boyle* and the *Chronicon Scotorum*): 'The castle of Athlone and the bridge were erected by Toirdhealbhach Ua Conchobhair in the summer of this year, i.e. the summer of the drought': Ludlow, 'Utility 2', 176.

North Atlantic sea-surface temperatures and European growing-season temperatures in the 1070s and again during the opening quarter of the twelfth century (Appendix 1): 1107 was cold and 1109 and 1127, following major (probably tropical) eruptions in 1108 and 1126, especially so (Fig. 1).[80]

The period was not, therefore, without setbacks. The worst, as based upon the descriptions provided in the Annals, were in 1050 (inclement weather leading to dearth and triggering societal instability),[81] 1099 (famine widespread across Ireland),[82] 1107 (mass cattle and human mortality from wind and cold, and scarcity of grain from wet weather),[83] 1115–16 (a cold winter with mass mortality of wild and domestic animals, and humans, followed by famine and pestilence and claims of cannibalism),[84] 1133 (mass cattle mortality),[85] and 1137

---

[80] Sébastien Guillet et al., 'Climatic and societal impacts of a "forgotten" cluster of volcanic eruptions in 1108–1110 CE', *Scientific Reports* 10:6715 (2020), doi:10.1038/s41598-020-63339-3 (which discusses the complexity of the ice-core volcanic signals starting in 1108); Stoffel, 'Estimates of volcanic-induced cooling', Table S4; Sigl, 'Timing and climate forcing of volcanic eruptions', 'Extended data', Tables 4–6; Toohey and Sigl, 'Volcanic stratospheric sulfur injections', 822. Francis Ludlow thanks Matthew Toohey for making a copy of the original dataset available to him. Note that Toohey and Sigl place some probable tropical eruptions a year earlier than dated by Sigl, the better to account for potential transport times of sulphate from tropical locations to the polar ice sheets.

[81] 1050 (*Annals of the Four Masters*), quoted in full above, p. 162: Ludlow, 'Utility 2', 154. This example and the linkage between weather and violence is noted by Elizabeth Fitz-Patrick, 'Raiding and warring in monastic Ireland', *History Ireland* 1:3 (1993), 13–18: 17.

[82] 1099 (*Annals of Loch Cé*, also *of Ulster*): 'Great famine throughout all Erinn in this year': Ludlow, 'Utility 2', 166.

[83] 1107 (*Annals of Ulster*, also *of Loch Cé*): 'Much wet and bad weather in this year, and it ruined the corn'; 1107 (*Chronicon Scotorum*, also *Annals of Tigernach*, and *of the Four Masters*): 'Great wind and lightning in Ireland this year, and it killed many people and cattle'; 1107 (*Annals of Ulster*, also *of Loch Cé*): 'Snow fell for a day and a night on the Wednesday before the feast of St. Patrick [17 March], and inflicted slaughter on beasts in Ireland': Ludlow, 'Utility 2', 167–8.

[84] 1115 (*Annals of Ulster*, also *of Loch Cé*, *of the Four Masters*, *Chronicon Scotorum* and *of Boyle*): 'Extremely bad weather in the form of frost and snow from the fifth of the Kalends of January [i.e., 28 December] to the fifteenth of the Kalends of March [i.e., 15 March], or a little longer, and it inflicted slaughter on birds and beasts and men, and from this great want arose throughout all Ireland, and particularly in Laigin [Leinster]'. 1116 (*Annals of Ulster*, also *Chronicon Scotorum*, *Annals of Tigernach*, *of the Four Masters* and *Mac Carthaigh's Book*): 'a great pestilence; hunger was so widespread in Leth Moga [the southern half of Ireland], both among Laigin [Leinster] and Munstermen, that it emptied church and forts and states, and spread throughout Ireland and over sea, and inflicted destruction of staggering extent': Ludlow, 'Utility 2', 173–4.

[85] 1133–4 (*Annals of Loch Cé*, also *of the Four Masters* and *Chronicon Scotorum*) 'A great cow mortality occurred throughout all Erinn, for which no likeness was found since the great cow mortality came before that in the time of Flaithbertach, son of Loingsech; and 432 years [elapsed] between them': Ludlow, 'Utility 2', 179–80. For the cited precursors of this cattle mortality, first reported in England in 699 CE and reappearing down to 708 CE in Ireland: Ludlow, 'Utility 2', 60–73; also Chaochao Gao et al., 'Reconciling

(disease, scarcity, attacks by wolves and human and animal mortality from severe wind).[86] Note, however, that on the evidence of the Annals, in the space of 100 years there were only half-a-dozen years of environmentally related difficulty that are explicitly documented as more than local or regional in their impact. Alone, 1115–16 unequivocally stands out as a back-to-back crisis, with the worst of its effects apparently confined to Munster and south Leinster.[87] The *Annals of Clonmacnoise*, *of Tigernach*, *of Ulster* and *of the Four Masters* all reported that Laigin [Leinster] was almost emptied of people as its population took flight and migrated to wherever they could find succour and refuge in Ireland and overseas.[88] Good years generally attracted less comment in the Annals. For instance, following the scarcity of 1107, relief is apparent in the report of the *Annals of Loch Cé* that 1108 was 'A sappy year, with good weather, and with much corn and produce', and in 1130, after a year of drought, the same text noted 'A great crop of every kind of produce generally in Erinn this year'.[89] Whereas years of benign weather afforded opportunities for recovery, none of the bad years can be seen to have inflicted a reversal so general and severe that the prevailing momentum of expansion was more than briefly interrupted.

Two of the worst setbacks—those of 1115–16 and 1137—were possibly triggered or compounded by short-term volcanic forcing from northern hemisphere eruptions dating to the same years.[90] This was a recurrent pattern.[91] On both occasions it elicited in response an increased resort to, and perhaps

---

multiple ice-core volcanic histories: the potential of tree-ring and documentary evidence, 670–730 CE', *Quaternary International* 394 (2016), 180–93.

[86] 1137 (*Annals of Loch Cé*): 'A great colic disease in Erinn generally, which killed many'; 'A great scarcity in the province of Connacht, *et multi mortui sunt ab ea*'; 1137 (*Annals of Tigernach*): 'The Blind One of…that is, Gilla Maire, was killed by wolves'; 1137 (*Annals of the Four Masters*, also *of Loch Cé* and *of Clonmacnoise* (a.k.a. *Mageoghagan's Book*)): 'A great wind-storm throughout Ireland, which prostrated many trees, houses, churches, and buildings, and swept men and cattle into the sea, in Magh-Conaille [centred in County Louth]': Ludlow, 'Utility 2', 180–1. Other, perhaps more regionally specific stresses (e.g., cattle mortality) and weather events (e.g., lightning strikes) without documented widespread impacts are also noted across these years, with their abundance at least partly the result of the fuller recording provided by the Annals in this period (Fig. 2).

[87] It is unclear whether the conditions reported in 1115 started in late-December 1114 or late-December 1115. Determining which annual winter season is described is a recurring challenge in medieval annals: Michael McCormick, P.E. Dutton and Paul Mayewski, 'Volcanoes and the climate forcing of Carolingian Europe, A.D. 750–950', *Speculum* 82 (2007), 865–95: 876.

[88] Ludlow, 'Utility 2', 173–4. The *Annals of Tigernach* provide a unique observation of 'A murrain great and sudden, and most tormenting diseases in this year': Ludlow, 'Utility 2', 172.

[89] Ludlow, 'Utility 2', 169, 177–9.

[90] Sigl, 'Timing and climate forcing of volcanic eruptions'.

[91] For the repeated link between volcanic forcing and adverse weather reported in the Annals: F. Ludlow *et al.*, 'Medieval Irish chronicles reveal persistent volcanic forcing of severe winter cold events, 431–1649 CE', *Environmental Research Letters* 8:2

opportunistic use of, violence, which greatly exacerbated the effects of the bad weather. Thus, in 1116, as reported in the *Annals of Inisfallen*, 'Muirchertach Ua Briain invaded Laigin [Leinster]' and 'countless injuries were committed on that expedition: raids and conflicts, war and famine during that time'.[92] The combination of adverse weather, scarcity and warfare recurred in 1137 when, according to the *Annals of Tigernach*, 'Connacht, then, was laid waste from Assaroe to the Shannon and to Echtach [Slieve Aughty] of Munster, and the people themselves were driven into the west of Connacht'.[93] Hunger was, of course, a frequent consequence of military violence, since putting people to flight, driving off their cattle and torching the crops of the enemy were standard military ploys. In 1139, for example, the *Annals of the Four Masters* reported that the men of Meath destroyed the corn crops of the Ui-Briuin 'so that an insufferable famine prevailed amongst them [the men of Fermanagh] the year following'.[94]

Among scholars, the extent to which severe weather conditions have, in turn, historically promoted violence, and of what kind, in what contexts, and whether only rarely or more persistently, remains highly debated. Beyond the more obvious potential for conflict arising from scarcity induced resource competition, linkages may have been subtle and indirect. For instance, advantage may have been taken of crises to launch opportunistic attacks on weakened rivals or to question and challenge the fitness of dynasties to rule.[95] For medieval Ireland, the Annals do offer occasional explicit confirmation and explanation of such occurrences, not least the inclement weather, subsistence crisis and ensuing breakdown of order in 1050.[96] But in many instances they hold to the traditional annalistic style of presenting apparently disconnected events with little explanation of any causal connections.[97] Quantitative approaches that also make use of the independent evidence of palaeoclimatic proxies can here complement traditional readings of the annalistic evidence. An initial study (employing superposed epoch analyses) of the frequency and timing of a range of violent

---

(2013), L024035; Gao, 'Reconciling multiple ice-core volcanic histories'; McCormick, 'Volcanoes and the climate forcing of Carolingian Europe'.

[92] Ludlow, 'Utility 2', 174.

[93] Ludlow, 'Utility 2', 181.

[94] Ludlow, 'Utility 2', 182–3.

[95] A perceived link between the fertility of the land and quality of its ruler certainly existed in early medieval Ireland, persisting (if more ambiguously) into later centuries: Maxim Fomin, 'The early medieval Irish and Indic polities and the concepts of righteous ruler', *Cosmos* 15 (1999), 163–97; Lauren Baker, 'Mainstreaming morality'; Ludlow, 'Utility of the Irish Annals', vol. 1, 172, 190, 198–200, 217.

[96] The links between adverse weather and socio-political conflict in medieval Ireland are further explored in: Ludlow and Travis, 'STEAM approaches to climate change'.

[97] This tendency diminishes from the late-thirteenth century once hereditary professional historians in the employ of the Gaelic nobility took over recording of the Annals (McCarthy, *Irish Annals*, 245) and began to place the exploits of that nobility in a more narrative (but still annually arranged) structure.

events reported in the *Annals of Ulster* relative to the ice-core-based dates of 32 major volcanic eruptions is thus presented in Appendix 6. While there is much more to learn by examining the influence of a fuller spectrum of extreme events (e.g., droughts, wet weather), for different seasons and of different apparent severities, it is clear that violence is reported with increased frequency (sufficient to appear statistically non-random) in the aftermath of these eruptions.[98] It follows that other adverse weather events may have triggered similarly destructive behaviours, as evidenced in the years 1115–16 and 1137.

1150–1300—expansion, phase two

When Gerald of Wales visited Ireland in the 1180s he was impressed by the 'many woods' that yet remained, notwithstanding the rising rates of felling that had prevailed for the previous 30 to 40 years.[99] By the time of his visit, however, such high rates of felling were evidently becoming unsustainable and as the stock of oaks (represented in Fig. 5 by the annual number of dated oak samples) dwindled so felling and depletion rates began to subside. In parallel, references to church buildings in the Annals increase consistently into the twelfth century, but with a notable shift after *c.*1110 from construction mainly in oak (*dairthech*) to stone (*damliac / teampal*).[100] Although there are complexities to the interpretation of this information from the Annals, it is broadly consistent both with an expansion of building and, progressing from this, a depletion of oak. English demand for Irish oak was also a factor.[101] From an annual average of 226 oak samples in the 1150s, sample numbers decline to 93 in the 1200s, 55 in the 1250s and 29 in the 1300s. Although construction activity had to cope with a dwindling supply of oaks it was sustained until well into the thirteenth century by the first wave of new continental religious foundations and the great building boom—of fortifications, religious houses, churches, towns and settlements—that followed the English invasion of 1169–71 and the substantial influx of colonists to which

---

[98] Appendix 6 presents a series of superposed epoch analyses of the temporal relationship between 32 major explosive eruptions with an estimated volcanic stratospheric sulfur injection (VSSI) of at least 1.0 Tg (a measure reflecting climate forcing potential, and thus excluding nineteen eruptions discernable in the ice cores but of minimal climatic forcing potential and likely to introduce noise into the analyses) and levels of violence recorded in the *Annals of Ulster*. The effects were typically lagged, perhaps with production adversely affected the year following an eruption and recorded violence thus surging thereafter, though with some variability as to exact timing.

[99] Gerald of Wales, *History and topography of Ireland*, 34.

[100] Ó Carragáin, *Churches in early medieval Ireland*, 110–11.

[101] Tim Tatton-Brown, 'The roofs of Salisbury Cathedral', *Spire: Annual Report of the Friends of Salisbury Cathedral* 71 (2001), 18–23; Nicholas Vincent, 'Angevin Ireland', in Smith (ed.), *Cambridge history of Ireland, vol. 1*, 185–221: 203–4; Margaret Murphy and Michael Potterton, *The Dublin region in the middle ages: settlement, land-use and economy* (Dublin, 2010), 375–6.

it gave rise.[102] That, no doubt, is why net depletion rates remained at a relatively high level until the 1200s. Only thereafter did the number of annually-dated samples shrink to single figures.

The evidence suggests that oaks had become so scarce by the mid-thirteenth century throughout the most closely settled parts of Munster and Leinster that datable oak samples from Leinster outside Dublin drop to single figures from 1239 and from 1250 to 1278 there are none at all from Munster. What appears to have been almost 200 years of more-or-less continuous felling had taken its toll. From this point, and as the country's population rose to what is likely to have been its medieval maximum of 1.25 to 1.5 million, Ireland's surviving timber resources appear to have been under considerable pressure.[103] Hereafter the Irish oak chronology becomes increasingly attenuated and, as samples from Munster and Leinster (outside Dublin) peter out, those from Ulster come increasingly to the fore. The smaller oak sample depth that this entails means that by the end of the century the oak-ring-width evidence and climate reconstructions derived from it are less robust, representative and stable than before. Fortunately, it is when the Irish oak record is thinnest that the English evidence of prices, wages, harvests and crop yields comes strongly on stream (Fig. 6).

For all that the English invasion of 1169–71 represents one of the deepest and most profound of all historical divides, environmentally the period that it punctuated is remarkable for its continuity. The defining feature of this era, from the 1050s until the early 1260s (when the Wolf Solar Minimum set in), was a consistently high level of solar irradiance (Fig. 1). Irradiance levels were especially elevated from the 1190s to the 1210s and again, and more impressively, from the 1230s to the 1250s, with an absolute peak between 1244 and 1253. It may be coincidence, but at this apogee of solar output in 1252 the *Annals of Loch Cé* (as also *of Connacht* and *of the Four Masters*) reported 'Great heat and drought in the summer of this year, so that people used to cross the Sinuinn

---

[102] Lydon, *The Lordship of Ireland in the middle ages*, 61, 91–3; Aubrey Gwynn and R. Neville Hadcock, *Medieval religious houses: Ireland* (London, 1970); Roger Stalley, 'Irish gothic and English fashion', in James Lydon (ed.), *The English in medieval Ireland: proceedings of the first joint meeting of the Royal Irish Academy and the British Academy, Dublin, 1882* (Dublin, 1984), 65–86: 68–77; Rachel Moss, 'Material culture' in Smith (ed.), *Cambridge history of Ireland, vol. 1*, 469–97: 471–2.

[103] Campbell, 'Benchmarking medieval economic development', 927; Máire Ní Mhaonaigh, 'Perception and reality: Ireland c.980–1229', in Smith (ed.), *Cambridge history of Ireland, vol. 1*, 131–56: 153. For the scarcity of woodland in the Dublin region by the thirteenth century and near exhaustion of local supplies of oak timbers: Murphy and Potterton, *Dublin region in the middle ages*, 357–76, 380–2. By the early fourteenth century the immediate environs of Drogheda seem to have been similarly denuded of woodland: J.A. Galloway, 'The economic hinterland of Drogheda in the later middle ages', in Vicky McAlister and Terry Barry (eds), *Space and settlement in medieval Ireland* (Dublin, 2015), 167–85: 179–80.

Bruce M.S. Campbell and Francis Ludlow

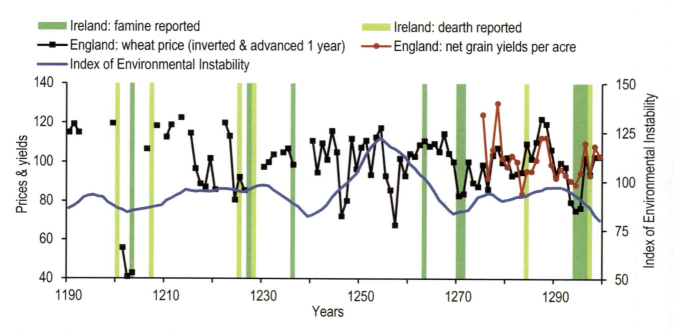

Fig. 6—Reports in the Gaelic and Anglo-Irish Annals of dearth and famine in Ireland, English wheat prices and net grain yields, and an Index of Environmental Instability, 1190–1300 CE.

Sources: *Dearth and famine in Ireland*: authors' own survey of Gaelic and Anglo-Irish Annals.

Wheat prices (percentage of 25-year moving average centred, inverted and advanced one year): Gregory Clark, 'English prices and wages 1209–1914', Global Price and Income History Group (Davis, 2009), www.iisg.nl/hpw/data.php#united. Accessed 15 Aug. 2015; extended and interpolated from 1166–1265 with prices from D.L. Farmer, 'Prices and wages', in H.E. Hallam (ed.), *The agrarian history of England and Wales, vol. 2: 1042–1350* (Cambridge, 1988), 716–817: 787–9, and additional prices for 1237–62 from the manorial accounts of Froyle, Hampshire: British Library, Add. Charters 17, 459–78, 13,338–9; Hampshire Record Office, Winchester, 123M88W/1.

Net grain yields per acre (deviations from trend in net wheat-barley-oats [W-B-O] yields, averaged using the weighted ratio 2:1:1): B.M.S. Campbell and Cormac Ó Gráda, 'Harvest shortfalls, grain prices, and famines in pre-industrial England', *Journal of Economic History* 71:4 (2011), 859–86: 866; B.M.S. Campbell, *Three centuries of English crop yields, 1211–1491* (Belfast, 2007), www.cropyields.ac.uk.

Index of Environmental Instability: Appendix 5.

[Shannon] without wetting their feet; and the wheat was reaped twenty nights before Lammas [1 August], and all the corn was reaped at that time; and the trees were burning from the sun'.[104] The following year the same Annals celebrated 'the

---

[104] Ludlow, 'Utility 2', 225–6. The *Annals of Ulster*, followed closely by the *Annals of Inisfallen*, simply note 'A hot summer in this year'. The Welsh *Brut y Tywysogyon* (pp. 243–5) is less laconic: 'the heat of the sun was so great that the whole earth dried therewith, so that hardly any crops grew on the trees or in the fields and neither sea nor river fish were found. And that summer was called the Hot Summer. And at the close of that autumn the rains were so great that the floods covered the face of the earth, so that the extreme dryness of the earth could not absorb the waters, and the rivers flooded so that

best year that had ever come for nuts, and the produce of the earth, and of cattle, and of trees and herbs'.[105] Then, the very next year, the *Annals of Boyle* recorded another possible dividend of the fine weather: 'peace in Ireland'.[106] Abundance, it would seem, suppressed the propensity to violence. Unfortunately, such nominal tranquility was not to last.

Incoming solar irradiance was, of course, the energy source that powered the world's ocean currents, determined pressure gradients and shaped and directed patterns of atmospheric circulation. In the case of Ireland and Britain that meant the prevalence of a strongly positive NAO. In a recent reconstruction, the NAO was positive for two out of three years from 1150 to 1300, was never weaker than -1.0 but on 22 occasions was stronger than +1.0 and in 1252 reached an absolute extreme of +2.5 (Appendix 3).[107] While this climate regime prevailed, a westerly Atlantic airstream powerfully influenced meteorological conditions in Ireland and precipitation, especially in winter, was rarely deficient, credibly prompting Gerald of Wales's comments about the windiness and wetness of the Irish weather.[108]

Warm and dry summers were not unknown but only in 1252 and 1263 did Ireland's annalists explicitly note drought and heat as problems.[109] The aridity of 1252, when 'people crossed the principal rivers of Ireland with dry feet', was therefore remarkable.[110] The opposite was more commonly the case and, on the evidence of the climate reconstructions, the wettest growing seasons were

---

the bridges and the mills and the houses close to the rivers were shattered, and the trees and the orchards were swept away, and many other losses were caused'. For England, chronicles such as that of Bury St. Edmund's furnish report of '…an exceptionally hot summer [that] killed many people, and alarming thunder was heard on the day after the Assumption of the Blessed Virgin [16 August]' (Antonia Gransden (ed.), *The chronicle of Bury St Edmunds, 1212–1301* (London, 1964): 17–18); also Kathleen Pribyl and R.C. Cornes, 'Droughts in medieval and early modern England, part 1: the evidence', *Weather* 75:6 (2020), 168–72: 168. On the Scottish border, the Lanercost Chronicle makes similar reference to the exceptional heat: Richard Oram, '"The worst disaster suffered by the people of Scotland in recorded history": climate change, dearth and pathogens in the long 14th century', *Proceedings of the Society of Antiquaries of Scotland* 144 (2014), 223–44: 226. The OWDA clearly registers severe drought of unusual extent across much of northern, southern, western and eastern Europe for 1252, with only parts of central Scotland and north-west Ulster (alone in Britain and Ireland) apparently spared the worst: Cook, 'Old World megadroughts'. For the direct and indirect socioeconomic and health impacts of the 1252 drought and others: Kathleen Pribyl, 'A survey of the impact of summer droughts in southern and eastern England, 1200–1700', *Climate of the Past* 16 (2020), 1027–41.

[105] Ludlow, 'Utility 2', 226.
[106] Ludlow, 'Utility 2', 227.
[107] Ortega, 'Model-tested North Atlantic Oscillation reconstruction'.
[108] Above, p. 160; Gerald of Wales, *History and topography of Ireland*, 34–5.
[109] 1263 (*Annals of Clonmacnoise* (a.k.a. *Mageoghagan's Book*), also *of Ulster*, *of Loch Cé* and *of Connacht*): 'There was a great drought this year in the earth and a very hot summer': Ludlow, 'Utility 2', 235.
[110] Ludlow, 'Utility 2', 225–6.

in 1153, 1156, 1159, 1229 (the year of a notable tropical eruption),[111] 1255 and 1292–3 (Appendix 2). In 1158, the *Annals of the Four Masters* reported 'great rain in the summer' and, more seriously, in 1236 the same Annals, along with those *of Loch Cé* and *of Connacht*, complained of 'heavy rains, harsh weather, and much war'.[112] The occasional cold and snowy winters, when Arctic high pressure presumably kept the normally mild westerly Atlantic airstream at bay, also attracted comment, especially when, as in 1156, 1178, 1234 and 1251, lakes and rivers froze over and were passable on foot.[113] These extreme once-in-a-generation events were no doubt recorded, remembered and talked about precisely because they were so rare.[114] They were particularly hazardous to Gaelic

---

[111] Sigl, 'Timing and climate forcing of volcanic eruptions' place this event in 1230, while Toohey and Sigl, 'Volcanic stratospheric sulfur injections' place it in 1229, adjusting for estimated sulphate travel time to the polar ice-sheets.

[112] Ludlow, 'Utility 2', 191, 217–18.

[113] 1156 (*Annals of the Four Masters*, also *of Tigernach*): 'There was great snow and intense frost in the winter of this year, so that the lakes and rivers of Ireland were frozen over. Such was the greatness of the frost, that Ruaidhri Ua Concobhair drew his ships and boats on the ice from Blean-Gaille [Galey, an island on Lough Ree] to Rinn-duin [Rindoon or Rindown, Co. Roscommon]. Most of the birds of Ireland perished on account of the greatness of the snow and the frost'. 1178 (*Annals of Tigernach*): 'A great frost, so that for the space of a month one went on foot on the lakes of Ireland'. 1234 (*Annals of Connacht*, also *of Ulster*, *of Loch Cé* and *of Boyle*): 'Heavy snow fell between the two Christmases, followed by such a frost that men and laden horses walked on the great lakes and rivers of Ireland'. 1251 (*Annals of Loch Cé*, also *of Connacht*): 'Great frost in the early winter, so that the lakes, and the bogs, and the waters were all frozen'. Ludlow, 'Utility 2', 190–1, 195–6, 215–16, 224–5.

[114] In 1165 the *Annals of Tigernach* reported 'A great snow in this year, so that it was a labour for men and for cattle to go about in it' (Ludlow, 'Utility 2', 191), but make no mention of frozen or load-bearing ice, animal mortality, or the localities affected. More intriguing is the report in 1179 (*Annals of Ulster*, also *of Inisfallen*, *of Boyle* and *Mac Carthaigh's Book*) that 'The snow of the destruction [fell] this year': Ludlow, 'Utility 2', 196. This curious entry and its companions in the other Annals—variously translated as noxious, venomous or poisonous from effectively the same Irish phrase, '*sneachta na n-emhi*', reproducing here the text of the *Annals of Inisfallen*, from which only the *Annals of Ulster* depart with *sneachta na mure*—may reflect snowfall laced with poisonous volcanic acids or indeed volcanic ash. A comparable entry is also found in the *Annals of Connacht* (also *of Loch Cé*) in 1245: 'Virulent snow fell on the eve of St Nicholas [6 December], and folk who walked in it lost their heels and toes. The snow lay until Great Christmas [25 December]': Ludlow, 'Utility 2', 223. On both occasions fallout from eruptions in c.1179 and 1245 by the major Icelandic volcano of Katla may have been responsible: Thorvaldur Thordarson and Guðrún Larsen, 'Volcanism in Iceland in historical time: volcano types, eruption styles and eruptive history', *Journal of Geodynamics*, 43 (2007), 118–52: 134. For the potential impact of volcanic tephra on Irish vegetation in the early medieval period: V.A. Hall, 'Assessing the impact of Icelandic volcanism on vegetation systems in the North of Ireland in the fifth and sixth millennia BC', *The Holocene* 13 (2003), 131–8. For a suggestion that an eruption of Hekla, Iceland, may lie behind a further event in the Annals in 1224 (quoted in Ludlow, 'Utility 2', 208–11) in which apparently toxic materials were deposited: M.G.L. Baillie, *A slice through time: dendrochronology and precision dating* (London, 1995), 102.

pastoralists who relied upon grass rather than stored fodder to see their livestock through the winter.[115]

Plainly, even though geographical and temporal coverage by the Annals is exceptionally good at this time (Figs 2 and 3), the weather events reported by them must be considered an incomplete record of those extremes that occurred in this period.[116] Further, the stochastic nature of the occurrence of those events means that, even with a complete record of, say, all extremes passing a minimum threshold of severity or spatial extent, trends in their occurrence need not perfectly follow trends in background average climatic conditions.[117] Yet some degree of correspondence between trends in averages and extremes can still plausibly be expected, and the annalistic evidence is broadly consistent with one of the most striking features of this climatic era, namely, the relatively muted scale of annual weather variations identifiable from available palaeoclimatic proxies. Across these years the Index of Environmental Instability based on the variance of six independent environmental variables is persistently subdued and in the 1160s sank to a historical low (Fig. 1). The one episode of notably heightened instability was in the 1250s and 1260s, when powerful volcanic forcing came hard on the heels of conspicuously strong solar forcing and the NAO was close to maximum strength (Appendix 3).[118]

---

[115] Ó Corráin, 'Ireland c.800: aspects of society', 571–2; A. Keleman et al., 'Indigenous agriculture and the politics of knowledge', in Paul Sillitoe (ed.), *Indigenous knowledge: enhancing its contribution to natural resources management* (Cambridge, 2017), 203–17: 206–8.

[116] Ludlow, 'Assessing non-climatic influences'; Ludlow, 'Utility of the Irish Annals', vol. 1, 231–82.

[117] If average temperatures fall in a given period it is more likely, but not guaranteed, that the incidence of extremes of cold will also increase. The probability of this depends upon how the shape of the distribution of temperatures (or precipitation, windiness, etc.) has changed (e.g., even if the average shifts lower, the incidence of extreme cold—defined as temperatures falling below some threshold—may not increase if temperatures also range more narrowly about that average).

[118] The explosive eruption of the Samalas volcano, Indonesia, in spring/summer 1257 was the main forcing event (VSSI of 59.42 Tg: Toohey and Sigl, 'Volcanic stratospheric sulfur injections'), but in its wake a minor extratropical northern-hemisphere eruption in 1260 (VSSI of 1.05 Tg: Toohey and Sigl, 'Volcanic stratospheric sulfur injections') may have helped produce the reduced temperatures and depressed southern English grain harvests that followed in 1261–2: F. Lavigne et al., 'Source of the great AD 1257 mystery eruption unveiled, Samalas volcano, Rinjani volcanic complex, Indonesia', *Proceedings of the National Academy of Sciences* 110:42 (2013), 16742–7; Campbell, 'Global climates'; Sigl, 'Timing and climate forcing of volcanic eruptions'; S. Guillet et al., 'Climate response to the Samalas volcanic eruption in 1257 revealed by proxy records', *Nature Geoscience* 10 (2017), 123–8; F. Ludlow, 'Volcanology: chronicling a medieval eruption', *Nature Geoscience* 10 (2017), 77–8. Note that a small northern hemispheric eruption placed in 1262 by Sigl and others, is now considered southern hemispheric by Toohey and Sigl. On issues of dating concerning this complex conjuncture of events: Martin Bauch, 'Chronology and impact of a global moment in the thirteenth century: the Samalas eruption revisited', in Andrea Kiss and Kathleen Pribyl (eds), *The dance of*

While Scotland experienced significant weather-related problems at this time and these years brought some serious harvest problems to England, and in 1258 a much commented upon flood of famine refugees to London,[119] the Irish annalists are silent on any extreme weather experienced at this time in Ireland and rather ambiguous as to any potentially related societal stress.[120]

High levels of volcanic activity, with half-a-dozen major tropical eruptions between 1170 and 1300—including the largest of them all in 1257—and almost as many mid- to high-latitude northern hemisphere eruptions (Fig. 1), ensured that the otherwise fairly stable climatic conditions were interrupted by multiple short-term climate anomalies. This conjunction of bouts of strong volcanic forcing with strong background solar forcing likely overrode more localised and regionally specific expressions of climate variance and helps to explain why correlations between the ring widths of Irish and English oaks are mainly strongly positive from the 1170s until the 1260s (Fig. 4). As shown in Fig. 6, reports in the Annals of poor harvests, dearth and, worst of all, famine, commonly coincided with the high-price years that followed poor harvests in England. There were, of course, exceptions, as most conspicuously in 1246–7 and (as discussed) 1257 when there appears to have been no clear counterpart in Ireland to the stressful conditions experienced in England, but this may reflect the selective nature of what the Irish annalists recorded (or later copied from older texts), especially when significant religious, political and military events claimed their attention.

It should not be forgotten that the Annals were primarily concerned with the Gaelic Irish regions of the midlands, north and west (Fig. 3), whose stronger focus upon pastoral agriculture proved less vulnerable to the types of weather extremes that impacted most negatively upon the more arable-focused economies of both the English Lordship of Ireland and England.[121] Frustratingly, the more populous grain-growing lands of the English Lordship, where weather-induced harvest failures may have had some of their greatest impacts, are more poorly served by surviving chronicles. Thus, without the lone testimonies of the Anglo-Irish *Annals of Ireland, A.D. 1162–1370* and Grace's *Annales Hiberniae*

---

death in late medieval and Renaissance Europe: environmental stress, mortality and social response (London, 2019), 214–32.

[119] In the Scottish Cairngorms the summers of 1256 and 1261 were significantly cold and colder than that of 1258: Rydval, '800 years' (the authors are grateful to Rob Wilson for making the detailed temperature chronology available); Oram, 'Worst disaster', 225, 227; Campbell, 'Global climates'.

[120] Of possible Irish impacts, the *Annals of Inisfallen* report for 1259: 'A common cough this year affecting human beings and horses, which was called *galar na placodi*': Ludlow, 'Utility 2', 234–5; Martin Bauch, 'Chronology and impact of a global moment in the thirteenth century'. For 1260, the *Annals of Inisfallen* also report: 'Much sickness this year and death of noble folk', and for 1263 (perhaps too distant in time from Samalas in 1257) other Annals variously note drought, plague and famine: Ludlow, 'Utility 2', 234–5.

[121] Keleman, 'Indigenous agriculture', 206–8.

there would be little explicit to indicate that eastern Ireland, like much of neighbouring England, experienced 'great dearth and pestilence' for three consecutive years from 1294 to 1296.[122]

If the testimony of the Annals is taken at face value, crisis years tended to come in clusters with often quite long intervals in between. The opening years of the thirteenth century are a case in point. Problems began in 1200 (the year of a notable extratropical northern hemispheric volcanic eruption),[123] described in the *Annals of Loch Cé* as a 'cold, foodless year, the equal of which no man witnessed in that age'.[124] The *Annals of Inisfallen* followed this for 1201, noting that 'The greater part of the corn crop of Desmumu [Desmond territory, southern Munster] was laid waste…', and by 1203 difficulties had escalated to the point where the *Annals of Loch Cé* recorded 'great famine [*Gorta mhór*] in all Erinn generally in this year'.[125] More explicitly, the *Annals of Clonmacnoise* stated 'there was great scarcity of victuals throughout the whole kingdom of Ireland this year, [such] that infinite numbers of *the meaner sort* [emphasis added] perished for want…'.[126] Excess mortality, especially among the poorer classes, is a hallmark of genuine famine.[127] England, too, was in trouble. Following storms

---

[122] 'Annals of Ireland, A.D. 1162–1370 [MS Laud, No. 526—Bodleian Library Oxford]', in J.T. Gilbert (ed.), *Chartularies of St Mary's Abbey, Dublin* (2 vols, London, 1884–6, reprinted Cambridge, 2012), vol. 2, 303–98: 323; Richard Butler (ed.), *Jacobi Grace, Kilkenniensis, Annales Hiberniae* (Dublin, 1842), cited in M.C. Lyons, 'Weather, famine, pestilence and plague in Ireland, 900–1500' in E.M. Crawford (ed.), *Famine: the Irish experience 900–1900* (Edinburgh, 1989), 31–74: 61; E.M. Crawford (ed.), 'William Wilde's table of Irish famines 900–1850', in Crawford, *Famine: the Irish experience*, 1–30: 5. The closest the Irish Annals come here is a 1296 report of snow and bad weather (but without any associated societal stresses), and a report for 1297 of inclement weather, cattle murrain and heightened human mortality: Ludlow, 'Utility 2', 239–40.

[123] Sigl, 'Timing and climate forcing of volcanic eruptions'; Toohey and Sigl, 'Volcanic stratospheric sulfur injections' (3.29 Tg VSSI).

[124] Ludlow, 'Utility 2', 201–3. Intense conflict and a near scorched earth policy undoubtedly contributed to the severity of this year, such that 'never before was there inflicted on the Connachtmen any punishment of famine, nakedness, and plundering like this punishment' (*Annals of Loch Cé*, also *of Boyle*). This would not be the last time such devastation arose from the interplay between Gaelic and English lords, climate and landscape in thirteenth-century Connacht: Thomas Finan, *Landscape and history on the medieval Irish frontier: the king's cantreds in the thirteenth century* (Turnhout, 2016).

[125] Ludlow, 'Utility 2', 205.

[126] The *Annals of Loch Cé* note in full that 'Great famine [prevailed] in all Erinn generally in this year, so that the clergy used to eat meat in Lent', invoking an image for contemporaries of a situation so dire that religious observances were abandoned and valuable cattle were slaughtered. *Mac Carthaigh's Book* also opines that 1203 experienced 'A windy, wet summer, with famine and wars': Ludlow, 'Utility 2', 205. The summer of the previous year, 1202, had been conspicuously cold in the northern Cairngorms of Scotland: Rydval, '800 years'.

[127] Symptoms of famine include 'rising prices, food riots, an increase in crimes against property, *a significant number of actual or imminent deaths from starvation* [emphasis

and unseasonable weather in 1201 and 1202, grain and livestock prices soared in 1203 and remained very high the following year (Fig. 6), when many in Ireland were succumbing to 'severe pestilence'.[128] A hard winter followed in 1205 and then serious problems returned in 1206, when the *Annals of Ulster* reported a 'great destruction on people and cattle in this year'.[129] On and off, this was a crisis of seven years duration and it undoubtedly left Irish society diminished in size and vigour.

The next clutch of difficult years began in 1219, which the *Annals of Clonmacnoise* reported to have been 'wet, windy, and boisterous, with great destruction of corn'.[130] Persistently disturbed weather conditions then followed from 1222–5, perhaps as a part consequence of the extratropical northern-hemisphere eruption of Hekla in Iceland in *c.*1222.[131] For 1222 the Annals report a great storm that caused widespread damage to buildings, forests and ships, followed in 1223 by a 'great wind on the day after the festival of Matthew [21 September], which injured all the oats of Erinn that it found standing', while in 1224 'the corn remained unreaped, until the festival of St. Brigid [1 February], when the ploughing was going on, in consequence of the war and inclement weather'.[132] English chroniclers reported stormy weather and a bad harvest in 1225 and the same year the harvest in Ireland was late and the *Annals of Loch Cé* and

---

added], a rise in temporary migration, and frequently the fear and emergence of famine-induced infectious disease': Cormac Ó Gráda, *Famine: a short history* (Princeton, 2009), 7.

[128] Britton, 'Meteorological chronology', 73–9; C.R. Cheney, 'Levies on the English clergy for the poor and for the king, 1203', *English Historical Review* 96 (1981), 577–82: 580–1; D.L. Farmer, 'Some price fluctuations in Angevin England', *Economic History Review* 9 (1956), 34–43. 1204 (*Annals of Inisfallen*): 'A very severe pestilence in the above year, and houses were emptied in Mide, Laigin, Áth Cliath, Cell Dara, Ferna Maedóc, Cell Chainnig, and in Maethal Brócáin in the Déisi, and it reached Ailén Maíl Anfaid and killed a large number of the seniors of the community, including the abbot Ua Lígda': https://celt.ucc.ie//published/T100004/index.html (AI1204.2).

[129] For the 1205 hard winter, the *Annals of Loch Cé* uniquely report: 'Great frost and snow from the kalends of January [1 January] to the festival of Patrick [17 March] in this year'. The report cited in the main text for 1206 is given effectively verbatim in the *Annals of Ulster* and *of Loch Cé*: Ludlow, 'Utility 2', 206. Note that the Icelandic volcano Hekla erupted in 1206, leaving no clear sulphate signature in the Greenland ice but with this volcano's joint-second greatest tephra release by volume in the second millennium CE: Thordarson and Larsen, 'Volcanism in Iceland in historical time', 141.

[130] For 1219 the *Annals of Loch Cé* also stated that '…Droichet-atha [Drogheda, Co. Louth] was carried away by the flood': Ludlow, 'Utility 2', 206–7.

[131] Thordarson and Larsen, 'Volcanism in Iceland in historical time', 141. Given its proximity to Greenland, Hekla may be responsible for the small sulphate signal in Greenland in 1222 (VSSI of 0.87 Tg: Toohey and Sigl, 'Volcanic stratospheric sulfur injections').

[132] Ludlow, 'Utility 2', 207–9. The storm of 1222 is documented in the *Annals of Ulster, of Loch Cé*, and *Mac Carthaigh's Book*, while that of 1223 is found in the *Annals of Loch Cé* and the adverse conditions of 1224 are reported in the *Annals of the Four Masters*.

of Ulster reported a 'great destruction of people'.¹³³ Two years later, in 1227, the situation had deteriorated further: the *Annals of Connacht*, *of Boyle* and *of Loch Cé* all reported upon the 'Great famine [*Gorta mór*] throughout Ireland this year, and much sickness and death among men from various causes: cold, famine and every kind of disease'.¹³⁴ The next year, 1228, brought little respite: European summer temperatures dropped sharply and in Connacht war again compounded the adverse effects of the weather.¹³⁵ Ongoing warfare prolonged this miserable state of affairs into the following years as the bad weather continued and in one way or another affected the whole of Britain and Ireland. Thus, in 1232, following renewed volcanic forcing in c.1229/30 (this time from a substantial tropical eruption), the Scottish Cairngorms experienced the coldest summer of the thirteenth century and English chroniclers reported, first, a summer with too little rain and, then, a summer with too much.¹³⁶ Finally, in 1236, the *Four Masters*

---

¹³³ 1225 (*Annals of Loch Cé*, also *of Ulster*, *of Connacht*, *of the Four Masters*, *of Boyle* and *Mac Carthaigh's Book*): 'The corn was reaped immediately after the festival of [St] Brigid [1 February]; and the ploughing was going on at the same time': Ludlow, 'Utility 2', 211–12. The *Annals of Connacht* and *of the Four Masters* are explicit in their accounts of the intersection of conflict, climate, disease and hunger in Connacht at this time: 'After the plunderings and slaughter of men and beasts and the exposure of the inhabitants to cold and hunger, a severe attack of sickness came upon the countryside, a kind of fever, which emptied towns of every living soul; and though some who took this sickness did recover, they were but a few' (*Annals of Connacht*, with a shortened notice of disease in the *Annals of Boyle*); 'Woeful was the misfortune, which God permitted to fall upon the best province in Ireland at that time! For the young warriors did not spare each other, but preyed and plundered each other to the utmost of their power. Women and children, the feeble, and the lowly poor, perished by cold and famine in this war!' (*Annals of the Four Masters*): Ludlow, 'Utility 2', 211–12.

¹³⁴ Ludlow, 'Utility 2', 212–13. The summer of 1227 was exceptionally cold in the Scottish Cairngorms: Rydval, '800 years'.

¹³⁵ 1228 (*Annals of the Four Masters*, also *of Ulster*, *of Loch Cé* and *of Connacht*): 'An intolerable dearth prevailed in Connaught, in consequence of the war of the sons of Roderic. They plundered churches and territories; they banished its clergy and ollaves into foreign and remote countries, and others of them perished of cold and famine': Ludlow, 'Utility 2', 213.

¹³⁶ This (VSSI of 23.78 Tg) tropical eruption is dated 1229 by Toohey and Sigl, 'Volcanic stratospheric sulfur injections', and 1230 by Sigl, 'Timing and climate forcing of volcanic eruptions'. 1230 (*Annals of Loch Cé*, also *of Connacht*): '…the Foreigners sent out great predatory bands as far as Sliabh-an-iarainn [Sliabh Anierin, Co. Leitrim], and subjected multitudes to cold and hunger on this occasion. And women and children were killed; and all that were not killed were stripped; and they carried off great, fruitful preys to the camp of the Foreigners'. 1234 (*Annals of Ulster*, also *of Loch Cé*, *of Connacht* and *of Boyle*): 'Great snow between the two Nativities in that year [25 December to 6 January]. Great frost thereafter, so that persons and horses went under burdens upon the rivers and lakes of Ireland'. 1235 (*Annals of Loch Cé*): 'The Foreigners afterwards left Connacht without food, clothes, or cattle; and they did not carry off with them either pledges or hostages on this journey; and they left neither peace, nor quietness, nor tranquillity, nor happiness in the country; but the Gaeidhel themselves were robbing and killing one

annalist recorded 'Heavy rains, harsh weather, and much war prevailed in this year'.[137] This is the last such report in the Annals for over 25 years.

Ireland was, however, revisited by serious harvest-related crises on three further occasions before the thirteenth century ended. The first was in 1263, when, following a summer of heat and drought, the *Annals of Ulster* reported 'great destruction on [*sic*] people this year by plague and by famine'.[138] Then, in 1270, 'great, unbearable famine in all Ireland', 'great famine and scarcity in all Erinn' and 'hunger and great destitution throughout Ireland' were reported, respectively, by the *Annals of Ulster*, *of Loch Cé* and *of Connacht*.[139] According to the *Annals of Inisfallen* the year had begun with heavy snow, while a severe winter followed by a wet spring is reported by English chroniclers.[140] This was the first year of a back-to-back crisis. It was followed in 1271 by 'very bad weather in that year, and general warfare between the foreigners [English] and Gaedil of Ireland; and there was a great famine in the same year so that *multitudes of poor people died of cold and hunger and the rich suffered hardship* [emphasis added]' (*Annals of Inisfallen*).[141] Note that in this second year of the crisis both rich and poor were adversely affected, and that among the poorer classes many were now reportedly paying the ultimate penalty of death. In Scotland, too (but dated 1272 by the fifteenth-century chronicler Walter Bower), 'many people fell ill and many animals died', while in England the continuing wet weather depressed grain yields and drove up prices (Fig. 6).[142] In Ireland, where the language of the

---

another regarding the residue which the Foreigners left in it on this occasion': Ludlow, 'Utility 2', 213–14. Rydval, '800 years'; Britton, 'Meteorological chronology', 88–90.

[137] Ludlow, 'Utility 2', 217–18. The *Annals of Connacht* (with a close duplicate in the *Annals of Loch Cé*) also summarises the civil-war-like conditions prevailing during the preceding years: 'This was a year of wet and storm and war, of hunger and scarcity of food and clothing; armed bands and evil-doers without reverence for church or privilege, being excommunicated by the hands of bishops; the reverend clerics of the Catholic Church in fear and dread every day and night; frequent routs and escapings from Gael and Gall to the churches and churches used as dormitories, this year and for the space of 12 years ever since O Neill's war; Galls and Gaels plundering by turns; no lordship or government, but Connacht lying open for the Galls to ruin whenever they came into it, and its King and eligible princes plundering and violating church and countryside in their wake'.

[138] Ludlow, 'Utility 2', 235.

[139] Ludlow, 'Utility 2', 236. The underlying Irish and Latin identifies these three entries as duplicates of a lost original.

[140] 1270: 'A heavy fall of snow about the Epiphany [6 January]': Ludlow, 'Utility 2', 236. Britton, 'Meteorological chronology', 114–15. There had been a VSSI 3.13 (Tg) southern-hemisphere eruption in 1269, but further work is required to assess the impacts of such events on northern-hemisphere climates: Toohey and Sigl, 'Volcanic stratospheric sulfur injections'.

[141] Ludlow, 'Utility 2', 236. For the spur the famine gave the Wicklow Irish to raiding of the archbishop of Dublin's neighbouring lowland manors: James Lydon, 'A land of war' in Cosgrove (ed.), *New history of Ireland*, vol. 2, 240–74: 256–7; Katherine Simms, 'The political recovery of Gaelic Ireland', in Smith, (ed.), *Cambridge history of Ireland*, vol. 1, 272–99: 275.

[142] Oram, 'Worst disaster', 225.

annalists implies that the situation had become particularly grave, the weather-induced food scarcity was greatly compounded by the outbreak of 'general warfare between the foreigners and Gaedil of Ireland' (*Annals of Inisfallen*).[143] This was an increasingly familiar pattern.

Nevertheless, it was the last harvest crisis of the thirteenth century that was probably the most punitive, at least within the territories of the English Lordship. Here the Anglo-Irish Annals attest that for three consecutive years from 1294 to 1296 the weather ruined crops 'resulting in great dearth' and 'many deaths from hunger'.[144] Wheat prices in the Dublin region in 1294–5 and 1295–6 rose to 80 per cent above the recorded average for 1280–1300 and the records of Christ Church Cathedral claimed that 'people ate the corpses of those who had been hanged at the crossroads'.[145] Friar John Clyn of Kilkenny refers to 'the greatest scarcity' and many dying of hunger during these years and, according to the *Annals of Ireland, A.D. 1162–1370*, 'pestilence' contributed to the death toll.[146] James Lydon believes that the dearth drove the Gaelic Irish of the Leinster mountains into rebellion.[147] Further problems were created by the bitter feud that broke out between the earls of Kildare and Ulster.[148] These were also crisis years in England, when, on both sides of the Irish Sea, depressed temperatures and elevated rainfall resulted in a succession of inferior harvests.[149] Thus, the six consecutive years 1290–95 stand out as persistently wet in the OWDA spring–summer soil-moisture reconstruction for Ireland (Appendix 2), more so than in dearth-bound England, with 1292 the wettest in more than a hundred years. These were cold years as well, with a significant drop in summer temperatures in the northern Cairngorms of Scotland in 1294–6 and the European summer of 1294 the coldest since 1127.[150] The Munster-focused *Annals of Inisfallen*, as previously noted, reported that the winter of 1296 brought 'heavy snow and bad weather', followed in 1297 by 'very stormy weather…with wind, snow, and lightning, and a great murrain of cattle and loss of life also'.[151] Evidently the cooling effects

---

[143] Ludlow, 'Utility 2', 236. For 1271, Grace's *Annales Hiberniae* recount 'Pestilence, famine, and the sword in Ireland, and chiefly in Meath': Richard Butler (ed.), *Jacobi Grace, Kilkenniensis, Annales Hiberniae* (Dublin, 1842), 37.

[144] 'Annals of Ireland', 323; 'William Wilde's table of Irish famines', 5; Lyons, 'Weather, famine, pestilence and plague', 61.

[145] Murphy and Potterton, *Dublin region in the middle ages*, 478–9; cannibalism is cited in Maria Kelly, *The great dying: the Black Death in Dublin* (Stroud, 2003), 41.

[146] Bernadette Williams (ed. and trans.) *The Annals of Ireland by Friar John Clyn* (Dublin, 2007), 154–5; 'Annals of Ireland', 323.

[147] Lydon, 'A land of war', 260–1.

[148] Seán Duffy, *Ireland in the middle ages* (Basingstoke, 1997), 127–8.

[149] Britton, 'Meteorological chronology', 127–9; Campbell, *Great Transition*, 201–2; P.R. Schofield, 'Dearth, debt and the local land market in a late thirteenth-century village community', *Agricultural History Review* 45:1 (1997), 1–17.

[150] Rydval, '800 years'; Luterbacher, 'European summer temperatures since Roman times', (data: www.ncdc.noaa.gov/paleo/study/19600; accessed 19/08/2016).

[151] Ludlow, 'Utility 2', 240.

of the Wolf Solar Minimum were beginning to bite, reinforced at their nadir by the climate-forcing from major tropical eruptions (VSSI of 11.53 and 15.06 Tg, respectively) in 1275 and 1285 (Fig. 1).[152] Such powerful environmental forces challenged agrarian societies almost everywhere: Britain and Ireland were far from unique in the difficulties experienced at this time.[153]

By the 1290s the relatively stable and benign weather that had prevailed for so much of the previous 150 years had passed. The Medieval Solar Maximum that had helped to sustain it had ended. Under the influence of the Wolf Solar Minimum and reinforced by powerful volcanic forcing and consequential Arctic sea-ice formation,[154] global temperatures were cooling and long-established tendencies of atmospheric circulation were beginning to unravel.[155] The climate system was losing its resilience, as was Irish society, most particularly in areas of the English Lordship in Ireland. Whereas the periodic crises of the first half of the thirteenth century had been characteristically followed by a return to the *status quo ante*, that was no longer the case. One symptom of the change is the progressive weakening of the correlation between the ring widths of Irish and English oaks over the course of the second half of the thirteenth century (Fig. 4). Another is the clear testimony of the chroniclers that these later subsistence crises and famines, in 1270–1 and 1294–6, resulted in significant fatalities. War and disease and the heavy fiscal and military demands of an increasingly belligerent crown upon its Irish Lordship were also sapping society of its ability to recover,[156] and doing so as Europe's once vibrant commercial economy entered a prolonged and deepening recession.[157] The institutions

---

[152] Sigl, 'Timing and climate forcing of volcanic eruptions'; Toohey and Sigl, 'Volcanic stratospheric sulfur injections' (whose dating, in both cases one year earlier than that of Sigl, is followed here); Ludlow, 'Medieval Irish chronicles'. The Annals record a sequence of inclement and often cold conditions with major societal stresses during the confluence of these forcings from 1279 through the 1280s, including heavy snow and mass mortality of domestic animals in 1279 and 1280, mass human mortality and implied scarcity in 1281, snow, frost, windstorms and agricultural difficulties in 1282, conflict-driven migration and famine in Munster in 1283, unspecific but severe weather in 1284, violent wind in 1285 and scarcity of corn with high prices also in 1285, alongside mass cattle mortality from disease: Ludlow, 'Utility 2', 237–9.

[153] Campbell, *Great Transition*, 250–4.

[154] Miller, 'Abrupt onset of the Little Ice Age'.

[155] Campbell, *Great Transition*, 198–208.

[156] Mark Hennessy, 'Making Ireland English in the thirteenth century: the evidence of the Irish lay subsidy of 1292', in P.J. Duffy and W. Nolan (eds), *At the anvil: essays in honour of William J. Smyth* (Dublin, 2012), 81–91; Campbell, 'Boom to bust'.

[157] Campbell, *Great Transition*, 267–77; Ljungqvist, 'Linking European building activity with plague history', 85–6; Buringh, 'Church building and the economy'. Irish government and customs revenues shrank continuously from their peak in the early 1280s, with a particularly marked fall following the Scottish invasion of 1315–18: Campbell, 'Benchmarking medieval economic development', 896–7; Lydon, *Lordship of Ireland*, 131–8; Duffy, *Ireland in the middle ages*, 128–33.

and resources required to counter scarcity and the lawlessness that it could nurture were being weakened and depleted at the very time the need for them was growing. The weather was on the change and so, too, was society.

1300–1340s: resource scarcity

Frustratingly, the Irish oak chronology becomes perilously thin during the first half of the fourteenth century (Fig. 5A), rendering it less robust and less representative of growing conditions across Ireland than at any other time during the late-medieval centuries. These limitations may partly explain why correlations between the English and Irish oak chronologies become significantly weaker at this time (Fig. 4), although this may also reflect divergences in weather conditions at a time when atmospheric circulation patterns were in a state of flux. The scarcity of datable oak timbers is, of course, a consequence of the excess of felling over regeneration during the previous two centuries (Fig. 5B). But owing to the deteriorating security and economic situations, construction activity was also at a low ebb, with dwindling additions to the established stock of buildings.[158] Construction activity was also on the wane across the German- and French-speaking parts of the former Holy Roman Empire of the German Nation and in most parts of Europe investment in the building of new and enlargement of existing churches was being scaled down.[159] Everywhere, including Ireland, the high-medieval building boom was effectively over, partly because the great demographic and economic efflorescence that had long sustained it had run its course.[160] Nevertheless, society was not yet in full-scale retreat, witness the fact that as late as the 1320s in Ireland, marginally more oaks continued to be felled than were regenerating (Fig. 5B).[161]

Once the serious subsistence crisis of 1292–7 had passed, weather patterns across Ireland and Britain settled into a deceptively stable state, when all the available environmental indices—reconstructed Irish spring–summer soil moisture, European summer temperatures, Irish oak ring widths and English grain yields—display low year-on-year variability (Appendix 5). In fact, during the opening years of the fourteenth century the Index of Environmental

---

[158] For the problems besetting the English Lordship from the 1280s: Duffy, *Ireland in the middle ages*, 128–33; Cormac Ó Cléirigh, 'The problems of defence: a regional case-study', in James Lydon (ed.), *Law and disorder in thirteenth-century Ireland: the Dublin parliament of 1297* (Dublin, 1997), 25–56; Campbell, 'Boom to bust'.
[159] Ljungqvist, 'Linking European building activity with plague history', 85–6; Buringh, 'Church building and the economy'.
[160] Campbell, *Great Transition*, 3–10, 267–77.
[161] Murphy, 'The economy', 410, finds 'some surprising evidence of economic resilience in the period between 1320 and 1340'. In contrast, Raymond Ruhaak, 'Towards an alternative Black Death narrative for Ireland: ecological and socio-economic divides on the medieval European frontier', *Journal of the North Atlantic* 39 (2019), 1–16: 9–12, infers significant woodland regeneration in north-east Ulster from the early fourteenth century based upon unspecified pollen evidence.

Instability subsided to a level not experienced since the late twelfth century (Fig. 1). This was just as well, for the outbreak of the Anglo-Scottish war in 1296, on top of the Anglo-French war of 1294, brought financial, political and military turbulence and uncertainty to the English Lordship of Ireland and the Lordship's internal borders came under increasing attack from the Gaelic Irish.[162] The only recorded instances of dearth were in the early summer of 1305, following a poor harvest in the previous year when in England, unusually, all grains had yielded poorly, and in 1310, following a 'hard spring' which hit English wheat yields hard, when the Anglo-Irish *Annals of Ireland, A.D. 1162–1370* also report a scarcity of grain and high prices.[163] Earlier, for 1308, the *Annals of Loch Cé* report '…there was destruction of people and cattle in it, and also great inclemency of weather in it' and thereby leave open whether these societal hardships were caused by the inclement weather or were merely coincidental.[164] Certainly in no case do the annalists explicitly describe conditions at this time as so bad as to amount to famine. For almost 20 years, then, following the extended crisis of 1292–7, no weather-related famine appears to have materialised. The draining of revenues, provisions and able-bodied men out of Ireland in support of the defence of Gascony and of Edward I's ambitious Scottish enterprise, disastrously continued by Edward II, ostensibly posed a far greater threat to the political, economic and demographic *status quo* than the weather.[165]

The comparatively moderate and settled weather of 1298 to 1314, which included a run of above-average summer temperatures in the Scottish Cairngorms, was, however, quite literally the lull before the storm.[166] Already, out in the North Atlantic, sea-surface temperatures were beginning to seesaw

---

[162] James Lydon, 'The years of crisis, 1254–1315', in Cosgrove (ed.), *New history of Ireland, vol. 2*, 179–204: 196–204; Ó Cléirigh, 'The problems of defence'.

[163] For 1305, the *Annals of Inisfallen* uniquely report 'Great hardship at the beginning of the summer of this year': Ludlow, 'Utility 2', 241. 'Annals of Ireland', 339; Lyons, 'Weather, famine, pestilence and plague', 62. For 1310, the *Annals of Loch Cé* and *of Connacht* duplicate the reported 'hard spring', but without further detail regarding weather or impacts. The *Annals of Inisfallen* do report 'A very violent wind destroyed trees, houses and churches in the above year, and there was also a great crop of masts, nuts, and apples in the same year': Ludlow, 'Utility 2', 242–3. For yields in England: B.M.S. Campbell, *Three centuries of English crop yields, 1211–1491* (Belfast, 2007), www.cropyields.ac.uk. For a European perspective on this episode: Martin Bauch *et al.*, 'A prequel to the Dantean Anomaly: the water seesaw and droughts of 1302–1307 in Europe', *Climate of the Past Discussions* (2020): 1–25.

[164] Ludlow, 'Utility 2', 241: The *Annals of Loch Cé* and *of Connacht* again duplicate this entry for 1308, with very similar phraseology and orthography in the underlying Irish: above note 40.

[165] Lydon, *Lordship of Ireland*, 131–4; Beth Hartland, 'The height of English power: 1250–1320', in Smith (ed.), *Cambridge history of Ireland, vol. 1*, 222–43: 242–3; Campbell, 'Boom to bust'.

[166] Rydval, '800 years'.

Climate, disease and society in late-medieval Ireland

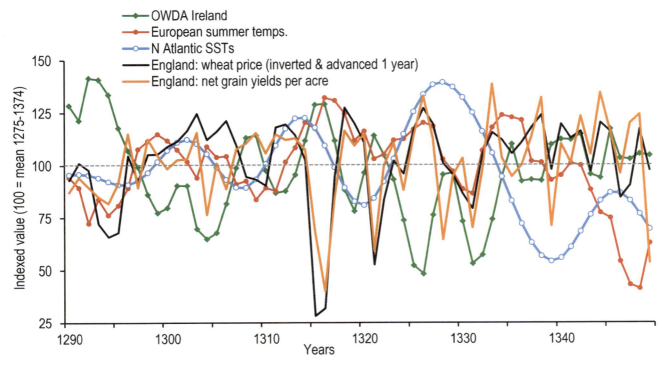

Fig. 7—Proxy measures of weather conditions affecting Ireland, 1290–1350 CE.

Note: all variables are indexed on their respective means for 1275–1374 and their variances standardised.

Sources: *North Atlantic sea-surface temperatures and European summer temperatures*: Appendix 1.

Irish OWDA (spring–summer soil moisture): Appendix 2.

English wheat prices (inverted and advanced one year) and net grain yields per acre as deviations from trend: sources to Fig. 5.

between warm and cold, with each swing more pronounced than the one before (Fig. 7). The warm episodes delivered a mild and humid airstream to Ireland and Britain, elevating precipitation, while the cold episodes had the opposite effect. The variance of annual North Atlantic sea-surface temperatures was rising from c.1300, became conspicuously inflated from 1313, and was exceptionally high from 1327–41, when the single greatest swing from warm to cold conditions occurred. Nevertheless, it was the warm episode of 1311–16 that had the more devastating consequences for food producers when '"overheating" of Atlantic surface ocean waters ... provided a source of moisture for prolonged summer rains as well as winter storms'.[167] Recent work on the marine equivalent of dendrochronology, namely examining temperature-sensitive annual shell-growth bands from the long-lived bivalve *Arctica islandica* in the North Sea, has also revealed marked variability

---

[167] A.G. Dawson *et al.*, 'Greenland (GISP2) ice core and historical indicators of complex North Atlantic climate changes during the fourteenth century', *The Holocene* 17:4 (2007), 427–34: 433; Campbell, 'Nature as historical protagonist', 293–4.

of sea surface temperatures in the 1290s, followed by a dramatic increase in mean temperatures through the first two decades of the 1300s, on a scale not seen in the remainder of this millennium-long reconstruction.[168] This short-term climate event (which has entered the historical lexicon as the 'Dantean Anomaly') came with heavy, persistent and untimely rain that ruined harvests across Ireland, Britain and much of Europe north of the Alps in 1315 and 1316 and triggered the Great Northern European Famine of those years.[169]

In England this is one of the greatest back-to-back yield failures on record and the consequent grain-price inflation was equally extreme (Fig. 7).[170] The ensuing full-scale agrarian crisis that ensued is well documented, as is the resulting excess mortality.[171] In Ireland, where the impact of the bad weather was massively compounded by a Scottish invasion, the crisis is likely to have been even more acute.[172] Although there are no Irish statistical series of yields and prices, palaeoclimatic reconstructions leave little doubt that Ireland experienced weather of comparable severity to England.[173] The *Annals of Loch Cé* testify that 1315 brought 'intolerable, destructive bad weather', while the *Annals of Clonmacnoise* elaborate slightly on what was a common earlier account from a shared exemplar, describing 'ugly and foul weather' in the summer.[174] Almost all annalists also

---

[168] H.A. Holland *et al.*, 'Decadal climate variability of the North Sea during the last millennium reconstructed from bivalve shells (*Arctica islandica*)', *The Holocene* 24:7 (2014), 771–86.

[169] The term was coined by Neville Brown, *History and climate change: a Eurocentric perspective* (London and New York, 2001), 251–4. It has since been employed by Campbell, 'Nature as historical protagonist', 287–301; Martin Bauch, 'The Dantean Anomaly (1309–1321): rapid climate change in late medieval Europe with a global perspective', *Mittelalter. Interdisziplinäre Forschung und Rezeptionsgeschichte* 1 (2018), 92–103; M. Bauch and G.J. Schenk (eds), *The crisis of the 14th century: teleconnections between environmental and societal change?* (Berlin, 2019).

[170] B.M.S. Campbell and Cormac Ó Gráda, 'Harvest shortfalls, grain prices, and famines in pre-industrial England', *Journal of Economic History* 71:4 (2011), 859–86: 869–71.

[171] Ian Kershaw, 'The Great Famine and agrarian crisis in England 1315–22', in R.H. Hilton (ed.), *Peasants, knights and heretics* (Cambridge, 1976), 85–132 (reprinted from *Past and Present* 59 (1973), 3–50); William Chester Jordan, *The Great Famine: Northern Europe in the early fourteenth century* (Princeton, 1996); Campbell, 'Nature as historical protagonist', 287–301; Jordan, *Great Famine*; Philip Slavin, *Experiencing famine in fourteenth-century Britain* (Turnhout, 2019).

[172] J. Lydon, 'The impact of the Bruce invasion', in Cosgrove (ed.), *New history of Ireland, vol. 2*, 275–302; Colm McNamee, *The wars of the Bruces: Scotland, England and Ireland, 1306–1328* (East Linton, 1997), 169–86; Brendan Smith, *Colonisation and conquest in medieval Ireland: the English in Louth, 1170–1330* (Cambridge, 1999), 105–12; Seán Duffy (ed.), *Robert the Bruce's Irish wars: the invasions of Ireland 1306–1329* (Stroud, 2002).

[173] Grace's *Annales Hiberniae* quotes a price of 24 shillings for a crannock of wheat in 1317 and 20 shillings in 1330: Ludlow, 'Utility 2', 252, 255. This compares with a price of at least 8 shillings a crannock in the crisis years of 1294–6 but only 2 shillings following the bumper harvest of 1286–7: Murphy and Potterton, *Dublin region in the middle ages*, 479.

[174] Ludlow, 'Utility 2', 244–51. The *Annals of Connacht* (also *Annals of Loch Cé* and *of Clonmacnoise* (a.k.a. *Mageoghagan's Book*)) summarise 1315 thus: 'Many afflictions in

describe how the opposing armies of Edward Bruce and Richard Earl of Ulster were kept apart at Coleraine by the swollen waters of the swift-flowing River Bann.[175] The following year brought no let-up in the weather, when, as reported in the *Annals of St Mary's Abbey, Dublin*, 'tempests of wind and rain did great damage on land and sea'.[176] The resulting back-to-back harvest failure proved catastrophic so that by 1317, according to the *Annals of Connacht* (similarly reported in the *Annals of Ulster* and *of Clonmacnoise*), 'throughout Ireland' a 'great famine' prevailed, and 'many poor people perished of hunger and disease' (*Annals of Ireland, A.D. 1162–1370*).[177] These crisis conditions and the accompanying 'innumerable deaths' continued into 1318 when a winter of unusually heavy snow added to society's woes.[178] Not until late June did the prospect of a good harvest bring some easing of the situation, which was reinforced by the defeat and death of Edward Bruce at the Battle of Faughart on 14 October.[179]

None of Ireland's annalists leave any doubt that the depredations of Edward Bruce's for-long invincible Scottish army greatly magnified the misery inflicted by the weather during these three-and-a-half grim years.[180] The Scots, in requisitioning and destroying food stocks, caused many to abandon their homes and lands and flee as refugees, and so paralysed Church, state and civic society that they were rendered incapable of relieving the desperate situation and providing succour to the needy.[181] Campaigning amidst a famine-stricken landscape also contributed to the eventual failure of Edward Bruce's attempted conquest. Several annalists employed the classic famine trope of people resorting to cannibalism—last used in 1116 CE—to illustrate the breakdown of the moral order.[182] Such language conveys the impression that this famine was more

---

all parts of Ireland: very many deaths, famine and many strange diseases, murders, and intolerable storms as well'.

[175] Ludlow, 'Utility 2', 244–51.

[176] Gilbert, *Chartularies of St. Mary's Abbey*, vol. 2, 298.

[177] Ludlow, 'Utility 2', 251–2; 'Annals of Ireland', 354.

[178] 'William Wilde's table of Irish famines', 5–6; Lyons, 'Weather, famine, pestilence and plague', 61–3. Ludlow, 'Utility 2', 252–3.

[179] G.O. Sayles, 'The Battle of Faughart', in G.A. Hayes-McCoy (ed.), *The Irish at war* (Cork, 1964), 23–34; 'Annals of Ireland', 359; Lyons, 'Weather, famine, pestilence and plague', 63.

[180] Owing to the adverse weather conditions, Hartland ('Height of English power', 226) considers it 'difficult to estimate the specific impact of the Bruce Invasion on the situation in Ireland'.

[181] Lydon, 'Impact of the Bruce invasion'; McNamee, *Wars of the Bruces*; Smith, *Colonisation and conquest*; Duffy, *Robert the Bruce's Irish wars*.

[182] For example, the *Annals of Clonmacnoise* (also *of Connacht*) reported (1318): '…for there reigned scarcity of victuals, breach of promises, ill performance of covenants, and loss of men and women throughout the whole realm for the space of three years and a half that he [Edward Bruce] bore sway. In so much that men did commonly eat one another for want of sustenance during this time': Ludlow, 'Utility 2', 251–2; Kelly, *Great dying*, 41; Cormac Ó Gráda, *Eating people is wrong, and other essays on famine, its past, and its future* (Princeton, 2015), 14–5, 25–6.

terrible than almost any that had gone before. Occurring after two centuries of population growth and reinforced by a deliberately destructive Scottish invasion, it was likely the greatest famine that late-medieval Ireland endured and in the suffering and excess mortality that it inflicted was maybe more terrible than the more graphically recorded contemporary catastrophe in England.

The damage inflicted upon capital stock by the Scots undoubtedly rendered post-famine recovery and reconstruction the more difficult and left the population more vulnerable to further weather extremes.[183] The return of wet and cold weather in 1321 therefore brought renewed hardship,[184] rendered all the more traumatic by the introduction to Ireland of the rinderpest panzootic—the *Mael Domnaig*—which had already devastated herds in England (Fig. 8). This was a virus that thrived when, as in 1321, temperatures were low and humidity high. The disease appears to have originated in Bohemia in 1316, when weather-induced ecological stresses were at their greatest, and thence spread ineluctably westwards at alarming speed to reach the Channel coast by 1318 and eastern England by Easter 1319.[185]

The Anglo-Irish *Annals of Ireland, A.D. 1162–1370*, and the Gaelic *Annals of Inisfallen, of Loch Cé, of Connacht, of Clonmacnoise* and *of Ulster* all make some cryptic note of the 'great cow-destruction throughout all Erinn, the like of which was not known before'.[186] Collectively, however, they are frustratingly silent on the contagiousness of its spread, the scale of the resultant mortality, the reduced milk yields and fertility of those animals that recovered, the effects upon arable production of the sudden death of many of the essential plough oxen, the time it took to make good the losses, and the repercussions of this epizoological disaster for the pastorally based economic and social order of much of the north and west of Ireland.[187] Certainly, the shock can hardly

---

[183] James Lydon, 'Ireland: politics, government and law', in S.H. Rigby (ed.), *A companion to Britain in the later middle ages* (Oxford, 2003), 335–56: 345–6.

[184] *Annals of Inisfallen* (1321): '…there was a great famine [*illegible*] in the same year': Ludlow, 'Utility 2', 253. These conditions appear replicated in Scotland: Oram, 'Worst disaster', 228.

[185] T.P. Newfield, 'A cattle panzootic in early fourteenth-century Europe', *Agricultural History Review* 57:2 (2009), 155–90; Campbell, *Great Transition*, 209–27.

[186] Ludlow, 'Utility 2', 253–4. The main text quote comes from the *Annals of Loch Cé*, an entry duplicated in the *Annals of Connacht, of Ulster* and *of Clonmacnoise* (a.k.a. *Mageoghagan's Book*). The report in the *Annals of Inisfallen* may be considered independent: 'A great murrain of the cows of Ireland in the above year, and there was a great famine [*illegible*] in the same year'.

[187] For the potential impact of cattle plague upon the Gaelic socio-political order of highland Scotland: R.D. Oram and W.P. Adderley, 'Lordship, land and environmental change in west Highland and Hebridean Scotland, *c.*1300 to *c.*1450', in Simonetta Cavaciocchi (ed.), *Le interazioni fra economia e ambiente biologico nell'Europe preindustriale, secc. XIII–XVIII* (Prato, 2010), 257–67: 262; R.D. Oram, 'Climate, weather and the rise of the Lordship of the Isles', in R.D. Oram (ed.), *The lordship of the isles* (Leiden, 2014), 40–61: 57–8.

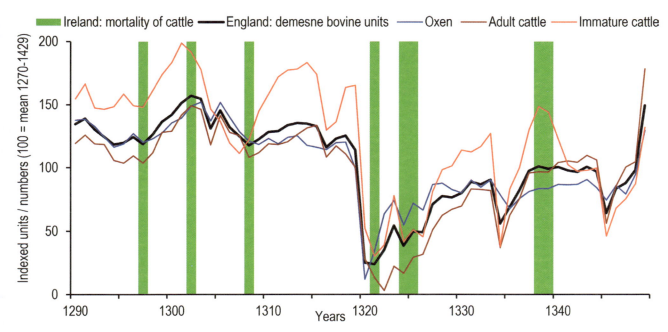

Fig. 8—Reports of mass cattle mortalities and murrains in the Gaelic and Anglo-Irish Annals and indexed numbers of cattle units on English demesnes, 1290–1350 CE.

Sources: *Reports of cattle mortalities and murrains in Ireland*: authors' own survey of Gaelic and Anglo-Irish Annals.

Cattle units on English demesnes (*oxen and cows* × *1.2* + *immature cattle* × *0.8*): B.M.S. Campbell, *The Great Transition: climate, disease and society in the late-medieval world* (Cambridge, 2016), 214, 223; Manorial Accounts Database.

have been smaller in pastoral Ireland than in mixed-farming England, where the overall bovine mortality rate has been estimated at 62 per cent and the national demesne herd sustained an immediate reduction of approximately 60 per cent (Fig. 8).[188] In Ireland, as in England, recovery was handicapped by repeat outbreaks of the disease, as explicitly reported by both the Gaelic Irish and Anglo-Irish Annals in 1324–5 and subsequently,[189] and these setbacks were

---

[188] Philip Slavin, 'The great bovine pestilence and its economic and environmental consequences in England and Wales, 1318–50', *Economic History Review* 65:4 (2012), 1239–66.

[189] Grace's *Annales Hiberniae* thus report for 1324, 'A murrain amongst oxen and the cows': *Jacobi Grace, Kilkenniensis*, 101. The (Gaelic) Annals confirm this report for 1324, with the *Annals of Loch Cé* noting 'The same cow-destruction in all Erinn in *hoc anno*; and it was it that was usually called the *Maeldomhnaigh*' (also in the *Annals of Ulster* and *of Connacht*). For 1325, the *Annals of Loch Cé* (also *of Connacht, of Ulster* and *of Clonmacnoise*) note 'The cow-destruction still throughout Erinn'. To compound these difficulties, the Annals see out the decade by reporting a visitation of epidemic disease in 1327, described in the *Annals of Loch Cé* (also *of Connacht, of Ulster*, and *of the Four Masters*) as 'A great epidemic of the *galar-brec* [literally, specked disease, taken as small pox by most editors of

compounded by harsh winter weather in 1338–9.[190] Since this was an enduring biological shock, as the example of England implies, full recovery to pre-1321 levels of stocking may have taken decades to achieve (Fig. 8). In effect, the cattle plague was the sting in the tail of a seven-year agrarian and military crisis that had begun in 1315 with the coincidental arrival of terrible weather and the Scots.[191] Nor did Ireland's sheep flocks, source of the wool that was the country's single most valuable export, escape unscathed, for in 1338 the *Annals of Loch Cé* and *of Connacht* report that 'the sheep of Erinn died in this year, excepting a few'.[192] No cause is given but sheep scab (which had devastated English flocks in 1279–80) and liverfluke (to which cattle are also susceptible) are prime suspects; the latter is caused by the flatworm *Fasciola Hepatica* which, along with the freshwater snails that are its intermediate host, thrives in rain-sodden pastures.

Meanwhile, as the twin dramas of the cattle plague and sheep murrain unfolded, weather conditions across Ireland remained decidedly unsettled. Following the Dantean Anomaly, the NAO weakened decisively (Appendix 3) with the result that in the mid 1320s and early 1330s Ireland experienced several consecutive years of unusually cold and dry weather, marked in the Irish oak chronology by the narrow ring years of 1325–6, 1334 and 1336 (Appendix 4).[193]

---

the Annals] throughout all Erinn widely, which brought destruction on people small and great, in this year'. 1328 saw continued epidemic disease (now named the '*slaedan*' and apparently not small pox), extreme weather with thunder and lightning that damaged fruit and arable crops, a wind storm during summer and dearth of food and clothing, reported in the *Annals of Ulster, of Connacht, of Loch Cé, of Clonmacnoise* and *of the Four Masters*. See Ludlow, 'Utility 2', 109–11. Ludlow's compilation omits the cattle mortality reported in 1324, and smallpox in 1327 due to the lack of overt linkage to weather conditions. See https://celt.ucc.ie/publishd.html for the relevant texts in 1324 and 1327.

[190] 1338–9 (*Annals of Ulster*, also *of Connacht* and *of Clonmacnoise*): 'A great plague of snows and of frost prevailed that year from the beginning of a fortnight of winter [i.e., 15 November, if using the Celtic seasonal calendar] until a part of spring came, so that much of the cattle of Ireland suffered death and the green crops of Ireland went to nought the same year'. Likewise, for 1338, Grace's *Annales Hiberniae* reports 'Intense frost with very deep snow from the 2nd of December to the 10th of February': *Jacobi Grace, Kilkenniensis*, 131. See also 'Annals of Ireland', 362. The *Annals of Connacht* (also *of Clonmacnoise*) further report 'Great war all over Meath between Galls and Gaels. The corn crops of Ireland were destroyed and there was famine in the land'. See Ludlow, 'Utility 2', 257–8, for the Gaelic annalistic entries cited here.

[191] For the combined impacts of war, weather and disease in this period: B.M.S. Campbell, 'Ecology versus economics in late thirteenth- and early fourteenth-century English agriculture', in Del Sweeney (ed.), *Agriculture in the Middle Ages: technology, practice, and representation*, Philadelphia, 1995), 76–108; Campbell, 'Nature as historical protagonist'; Philip Slavin, 'Warfare and ecological destruction in early fourteenth-century British Isles', *Environmental History* 19 (2014), 528–50.

[192] 1338: see https://celt.ucc.ie/publishd.html for the relevant texts.

[193] Baillie, *New light*, 41–50, 107–11. For the situation in England: David Stone, 'The impact of drought in early fourteenth-century England', *Economic History Review* 67:2 (2014), 435–62; Pribyl and Cornes, 'Droughts in medieval and early modern England', 168–9.

Of these unusual conditions, however, the Gaelic Annals make no mention and, in fact, after 1338–9's report of cold conditions there is a significant decline in references to the weather for most of the remainder of the century (Fig. 2). What makes this development both surprising and frustrating is that the weather was taking an unusual turn, and the nominal level of recording of other events remained quite high (Figs 1 and 2).[194] The Anglo-Irish chronicles are marginally more informative and report the heavy and continuous rain, flooding and violent winds in 1330–31 that were responsible for the late and poor harvest of 1331 and the high Dublin grain prices that followed.[195] This was a bad harvest year in England, too, where low yields were followed by high prices (Fig. 7). This, however, was a crisis of one year's duration as, in its aftermath, the wet weather was replaced by dry. This culminated in the 'dry and fruitful summer' and early and abundant harvest of 1333 reported by the Anglo-Irish *Annals of Ireland, A.D. 1162–1370*,[196] while across the Irish Sea southern English demesnes enjoyed similar bumper yields (Fig. 6). It was a harvest that would not be bettered for over a hundred years.[197]

These comparatively benign weather conditions did not last for long. From the mid-1330s, sea-surface temperatures in the North Atlantic were cooling fast (Fig. 7). In 1335, great damage to wildlife was wrought by heavy snow in spring and then, in 1338–9, the long hard winter proved seriously harmful to livestock and crops alike (Fig. 8).[198] In both Dublin and Kilkenny winter began wet then in December turned so cold that the River Liffey froze for weeks.[199] The prolonged frost was followed by heavy snow, halting grass growth and blanketing the pastures upon which oxen, cows and sheep, more typically in Gaelic-dominated areas kept out of doors during the winter, depended for their

---

[194] Baillie, *New light*, 30–9, 107–13; Ludlow, 'Assessing non-climatic influences'.

[195] *Annals of Ireland by Friar John Clyn,* 200–1; 'Annals of Ireland', 372, 373; 'William Wilde's table of Irish famines', 6; Lyons, 'Weather, famine, pestilence and plague', 65. Grace's *Annales Hiberniae* describes conditions for 1330: 'Most violent storms, by which a house was blown down which killed the wife of Milo Verdon and his daughter. There was also a great flood, especially of the Boyne, by which all the bridges on that river, except Babe's, were carried away, and other mischief done at Trim and Drogheda. A crannock of wheat is sold for 20s., [and] of oats for 8s., this scarcity was occasioned by the rainy season, on which account the greatest part of the wheat could not be reaped before Michaelmas': *Jacobi Grace, Kilkenniensis*, 117–9.

[196] 'Annals of Ireland', 380.

[197] Campbell, *Three centuries*.

[198] 1335 (*Annals of Clonmacnoise* (a.k.a. *Mageoghagan's Book*), also *of Connacht*): 'There was such great snow in the spring of this year that the most part of the small fowl of Ireland died'. 1338–9 (*Annals of Connacht*, also *of Ulster*): 'The cattle and winter grass of Ireland suffered much from frost and snow, which lasted from the end of the first fortnight in winter into spring' [note: the translation of '*gortaib gemair*' as 'winter grass' by A.M. Freeman (*Annals of Connacht*) is rendered 'green crops' by B. MacCarthy and W.M. Hennessy (*Annals of Ulster*)]: Ludlow, 'Utility 2', 257–8.

[199] *Annals of Ireland by Friar John Clyn*, 224–5; 'Annals of Ireland', 381.

frugal sustenance.[200] In the more mixed-farming countryside around Kilkenny, as Friar John Clyn reported, as well as heavy livestock losses, the autumn-sown grain crops were adversely affected.[201] The upshot, according to the *Annals of Connacht*, was that 'the corn crops of Ireland were destroyed and there was famine in the land'.[202] Similar difficulties beset English grain producers and problems returned on both sides of the Irish Sea in 1346, which was evidently as 'barren and costly' (*Annals of Friar John Clyn*) in Ireland as in England (Fig. 7).[203] The following year prices in England were high (Figs 6 and 8) and attempts to export grain provoked the first recorded English grain riots.[204] Edward III had already launched his ambitious and expensive invasion of France in the opening phase of the Hundred Years War, so the fiscal and economic situation was once again volatile and the capacity of both English and Irish society to cope with bad harvests correspondingly reduced.[205]

The timing of this new military initiative, and the strain it placed upon the financial resources of the English crown, could hardly have been worse since from the early 1340s another short-term global climate anomaly had begun.[206] Across Europe its onset was characterised by significant cooling of temperatures (Appendix 1), further weakening of the NAO (Appendix 3) and some violent oscillations in precipitation (Appendix 2). These sudden changes elevated the Index of Environmental Instability to a level not experienced since the late-eleventh century (Figs 1 and 7). Across the world from 1342 the cooler temperatures depressed tree growth.[207] The downturn, possibly initiated by the cumulative cooling effects of the Wolf Solar Minimum, was reinforced from 1341 by a notable

---

[200] Ludlow, 'Utility 2', 257–8.

[201] *Annals of Ireland by Friar John Clyn*, 224–5.

[202] Ludlow, 'Utility 2', 257–8.

[203] *Annals of Ireland by Friar John Clyn*, 238–9. In England, autumn 1345 through to April 1346 were exceptionally wet, to the great harm of the autumn-sown crops: Britton, 'Meteorological chronology', 141.

[204] Buchanan Sharp, *Famine and scarcity in Late Medieval and Early Modern England* (Cambridge, 2016), 56–87; Buchanan Sharp, 'The food riots of 1347 and the medieval moral economy', in A. Randall and A. Charlesworth (eds), *Moral economy and popular protest: crowds, conflict and authority* (London, 2000), 35–54.

[205] H.G. Richardson and G.O. Sayles, 'Irish revenue, 1278–1384', *Proceedings of the Royal Irish Academy* 52C (1962), 87–100; W.M. Ormrod, 'The crown and the English economy, 1290–1348', in B.M.S. Campbell (ed.), *Before the Black Death: studies in the 'crisis' of the early fourteenth century* (Manchester, 1991), 149–83; W.M. Ormrod, 'The relative income from direct and indirect taxation in England, 1295–1454', in *European State Finances Database*: (2010), www.esfdb.org/table.aspx?resourceid=11762; Campbell, *Great Transition*, 267–71, 277–86.

[206] Campbell, *Great Transition*, 267–86.

[207] B.M.S. Campbell, 'Grain yields on English demesnes after the Black Death', in Mark Bailey and S.H. Rigby (eds), *Town and countryside in the age of the Black Death: essays in honour of John Hatcher* (Turnhout, 2012), 121–74: 122–47; Campbell, *Great Transition*, 277–9.

extratropical explosive eruption in the northern hemisphere, and then, particularly from 1344, by a much more substantial injection of sulphate into the high atmosphere by an unknown tropical eruption.[208] Cooling was at its most pronounced by 1348–9 (Fig. 1, Appendix 1).

Whether these climate forcings played any role in the first appearance of the bubonic plague in late-medieval Europe is not known, but this merits further scrutiny.[209] Regardless, from an origin in central Asia, the disease that has become known as the Black Death surfaced in the Crimea in 1345–46, whence it spread across the Black Sea and into the busy coastal ports of the Mediterranean in 1347. By 1348 it had crossed Europe to reach the south-coast English ports and east-coast Irish ports.[210] Its outbreak in England coincided with renewed bad weather and in 1349–51 a rare double back-to-back harvest failure, no doubt made much worse by dramatic plague-induced depletion of the agricultural labour force.[211]

Whether Irish harvests similarly plummeted in 1349–51 is unknown, for none of the Annals gives any hint of weather conditions, other than the (suggestive) report by Friar John Clyn that in 1349 there was a great scarcity of both corn and spices.[212] Irish (mostly Ulster) and English oak ring widths moved more-or-less in tandem during the 1340s but then deviated from 1354 (Appendix 4).[213] Narrow Irish oak rings in 1344 were followed by wide rings until 1349, consistent with the prevalence of cool wet weather during the growing seasons. Growth was then reduced from 1350 to 1352, with the latter being another narrow-ring year. In north-west Scotland, band widths from the Cnoc nam Uamh Cave speleothem suggest that 1341 and 1342 were exceptionally dry, 1348 and 1349 unusually wet and 1352 and 1353 moderately dry again, as the NAO swung between negative and positive modes (Appendix 3). In the northern Cairngorms, summer temperatures sank into a conspicuous trough from

---

[208] Toohey and Sigl, 'Volcanic stratospheric sulfur injections', estimate the VSSI of the 1341 extratropical northern hemispheric event at 1.17 Tg, and the 1344 tropical event at 15.11 Tg; Sigl, 'Timing and climate forcing of volcanic eruptions' date the tropical event to 1345.

[209] Jürg Luterbacher et al., 'Past pandemics and climate variability across the Mediterranean', *Euro-Mediterranean Journal for Environmental Integration* 5:46 (2020), https://doi.org/10.1007/s41207-020-00197-5.

[210] Campbell, *Great Transition*, 300–5. For a detailed reconstruction of the spread of the Black Death across Europe: Ole J. Benedictow, *The Black Death 1346–1353: a complete history* (Woodbridge, 2004). The fullest contemporary account of the Black Death's arrival and spread in Ireland is given in *Annals of Friar John Clyn*, 246–53. Prevailing weather conditions in Ireland are discussed in Maria Kelly, *A history of the Black Death in Ireland* (Stroud, 2001), 32–3.

[211] Campbell and Ó Gráda, 'Harvest shortfalls, grain prices, and famines', 865–72; Campbell, 'Grain yields on English demesnes', 144–7.

[212] *Annals of Ireland by Friar John Clyn*, 252–3.

[213] Baillie, *New light*, 109.

1346–51, with 1348 the second coldest summer of the fourteenth century.[214] There is also the circumstantial evidence that, almost without exception from 1270 until 1346, poor harvest years in England were problem years in Ireland too. There is no reason to suppose that this correlation did not also hold to some extent in 1349–51 when the palaeoclimatic evidence implies that Irish grain producers faced the combined challenge of low temperatures and high rainfall. What is beyond doubt, however, is that Ireland did not escape the plague, whose fearful appearance aroused panic in the populace and prompted morbid comment in the Annals.[215]

As in the case of the earlier rinderpest panzootic, the reactivation of plague occurred in inner Eurasia under climatically-induced conditions of ecological stress.[216] Originally a zoonotic disease of wild ground-burrowing rodents, by degrees it was transformed into a fast-spreading pandemic whose invasion of north-western Europe coincided with the advent of unusual weather conditions arising from a pronounced global climate anomaly. Everywhere the impact of such a deadly disease upon biologically virgin human populations proved devastating and both in Ireland and England the resultant mortality greatly amplified the concurrent effects of the bad weather. Disease achieved what the weather alone did not and helped launch Irish society on a new trajectory. Ireland, in effect, was ensnared in global processes of climate reorganisation with which ecologically driven changes in the epidemiological environment were acting in concert, and all at a time when the country's economic, political and military situation was fast disimproving.[217] It was this conjuncture of circumstances that differentiated this climatic tipping point from all others and rendered its consequences so irreversible.[218]

1350–1450—contraction

By the early fourteenth century, European woodlands had been massively depleted by the cumulative impact of over two centuries of arable expansion, iron smelting and timber construction.[219] Jed Kaplan, Kristen Krumhardt and

---

[214] Rydval, '800 years'.
[215] Benedictow, *Black Death*, 143–5; Kelly, *History of the Black Death in Ireland*, 23, 34–8; Grace's *Annales Hiberniae* thus notes for 1348: 'Very great pestilence in Ireland, which had before gone through other countries': *Jacobi Grace, Kilkenniensis*, 143. Of Gaelic Annals, the *Annals of Ulster* (also *of Loch Cé, of Connacht, of the Four Masters* and *of Clonmacnoise* (a.k.a. *Mageoghagan's Book*)) note for 1349 that: 'The great plague of the general disease that was throughout Ireland [prevailed] in Moylurg [Co. Roscommon] this year, so that great destruction of people was inflicted therein. Matthew, son of Cathal Ua Ruairc, died thereof': Ludlow, 'Utility 2', 259 (Ludlow reports only the entry from the *Annals of Ulster*; see https://celt.ucc.ie/publishd.html for the relevant additional texts).
[216] Campbell, *Great Transition*, 241–52.
[217] Campbell, *Great Transition*, 328–9; Duffy, *Ireland in the middle ages*, 148–51.
[218] Campbell, *Great Transition*, 10–15, 20–4, 332–5, 395–401.
[219] J.O. Kaplan, K.M. Krumhardt, and Niklaus Zimmermann, 'The prehistoric and pre-industrial deforestation of Europe', *Quaternary Science Reviews* 28:27 (2009), 3016–34;

Niklaus Zimmermann reckon that between 1000 CE and the Black Death the share of usable agricultural land occupied by forest in central, alpine, northern and western Europe had reduced on average by 54–63 per cent.[220] They estimate the equivalent reduction in Ireland at 66 per cent. Certainly, the Irish oak chronology (Fig. 5) suggests that by 1340 CE the country's oak woodlands had been substantially reduced and building in oak had virtually ceased. Nevertheless, the 1320s was the last decade in which the number of oak-sample end dates exceeded the number of start dates. Thereafter, for the first time in almost 300 years, the balance tipped in favour of regeneration, almost imperceptibly at first but then with gathering momentum. There was a noticeable upturn in the pace of regeneration from the 1380s and with it, after a century almost devoid of samples (Fig. 5A), an increase in the number of oak samples from sites in Leinster and Munster. By the end of the fourteenth century, oak woodland was clearly becoming re-established in many parts of Ireland and it was at this time that numbers of the oaks felled in later centuries commenced their growth.[221] The change in the appearance of the Irish landscape, evident also to some extent in the country's pollen record, must have been considerable and exemplified a trend evident across Europe at this time.[222]

The catalyst for this sustained switch from depletion to regeneration was the substantial and abrupt reduction in population caused by the Black Death.[223] Mortality in the first wave of plague that struck England in 1348–9 is thought to have been at least 30 per cent and conclusive evidence remains to be presented that in Ireland, infected at the same time, mortality was substantially any less.[224] In its aftermath there was an immediate slump in construction activity almost

---

Campbell, *Great Transition*, 148–9, 312–13. Stripped of their protective tree cover, Tuscany and parts of central Germany were plagued by floods and serious soil erosion: R.C. Hoffmann, *An environmental history of medieval Europe* (Cambridge, 2014), 325–7; Markus Dotterweich, 'The history of soil erosion and fluvial deposits in small catchments of central Europe: deciphering the long-term interaction between humans and the environment — a review', *Geomorphology* 101 (2008), 192–208. For the sparseness of woodland in much of lowland England by the early fourteenth century: B.M.S. Campbell and Ken Bartley, *England on the eve of the Black Death: an atlas of lay lordship, land, and wealth, 1300–49* (Manchester, 2006), 150–7.

[220] Kaplan, Krumhardt and Zimmermann, 'Prehistoric and preindustrial deforestation', 3023.

[221] In striking contrast, woodland remained scarce in Scotland and from 1450 eastern Scotland became increasingly dependent upon imported timber from Scandinavia and the Baltic: Crone and Watson, 'Sufficiency to scarcity', 80–1; Mills and Crone, 'Dendrochronological evidence', 29–31.

[222] Hall, *Making of Ireland's landscape*, 126–7; Büntgen, 'Filling the Eastern European gap', 1776; Lagerås, *Ecology of expansion and abandonment*, 77–92; Yeloff and Van Geel, 'Abandonment of farmland'.

[223] This was anticipated in the 1310s by the minor switch to regeneration that accompanied the Dantean Anomaly and followed the Bruce Invasion (Fig. 5).

[224] Campbell, *Great Transition*, 306–13; Murphy, 'The economy', 409–10.

everywhere and building workers found that there was a corresponding fall in demand for their labour.[225] With perhaps a third fewer mouths to be fed and a corresponding contraction in the available agricultural labour force, much land was withdrawn from cultivation. Arable land was converted to grass, thereby reinforcing the strong pastoral bias of Irish agriculture, and a great deal of land, especially the more marginal, was allowed to revert to woodland.[226] In Ireland, oaks were among the dendrological beneficiaries of the latter significant and, as it turned out, enduring land-use shift. Their re-advance (Fig. 5) is a clear indication that the era of declining land to labour ratios and mounting resource scarcity was over. A new age had dawned, characterised by reduced and reducing population densities, a profound and lasting transformation of the epidemiological environment, and a progressive weakening of English crown authority.[227] A new socio-ecological equilibrium was in the process of becoming established and the prospects of any return to the *status quo ante* were increasingly remote.

What now preoccupied Ireland's new breed of non-monastic and secular annalists, as is clearly apparent in Fig. 9, was not the triumvirate of bad weather, famine and war, although violence and fighting remained relatively commonplace, but plague and the sudden death of great men because of it (Fig. 2). The fates of women, other than the obits of high-ranking females, and of ordinary people, unless dying *en masse* and within the annalist's geographical sphere of interest, were mostly not deemed of relevance. Thus, only in 1349, a year following the plague's first arrival on the island when it reached into a Gaelic heartland, west of the Shannon, and only when an important member of the Gaelic nobility—Matthew, son of Cathal O'Rourke—had succumbed, do the surviving Gaelic Annals note plague's existence.[228] Explicitly quantitative reports of the scale of plague mortality are also few and far between and mostly concern Dublin.[229] The Anglo-Irish Latin chroniclers of the English Lordship are barely more informative; witness the generalised description respecting the third plague of 1370 in the *Annals of Ireland, A.D. 1162–1370* that 'countless nobles, townsmen and children died'.[230]

Usefully, the Anglo-Irish *Annals of Ross* identify five distinct Irish plague pandemics over the course of the fourteenth century: the first in 1348–9, the second in 1361–2, the third in 1370–1, the fourth in 1382–5 and the fifth in 1391 (Fig. 8).[231] The Gaelic Annals do attest to large outbreaks in most of

---

[225] Campbell, *Great Transition*, 310–12.
[226] Nicholls, 'Woodland cover', 186–9, 202–3.
[227] James Lydon, *Ireland in the later middle ages* (Dublin, 1973), 77–152.
[228] Ludlow, 'Utility 2', 259.
[229] The *Annals of the Four Masters* reported the deaths from plague of 3,000 Dubliners in 1439: https://celt.ucc.ie//published/T100005D/index.html (M1439.16); Kelly, *Great dying*.
[230] 'Annals of Ireland', 397.
[231] 'The Annals of Ross', in Richard Butler (ed.), *The Annals of Ireland by Friar John Clyn, of the convent of Friars Minor, Kilkenny; and Thady Dowling, Chancellor of Leighlin; together with the Annals of Ross* (Dublin, 1849), 38.

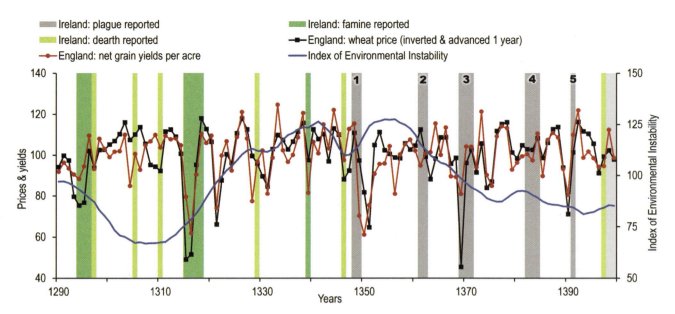

Fig. 9—Reports in the Gaelic and Anglo-Irish Annals of dearth, famine and plague in Ireland, alongside English wheat prices and net grain yields and an Index of Environmental Instability, 1290–1400 CE.

Sources: *Dearth, famine and plague in Ireland*: authors' own survey of Gaelic and Anglo-Irish Annals.

Wheat prices (percentage of 25-year moving average centred, inverted and advanced one year); net grain yields per acre (deviations from trend in net wheat-barley-oats [W-B-O] yields, averaged using the weighted ratio 2:1:1); Index of Environmental Instability: see sources to Fig. 5.

these cases, but note individual instances of the death of notable persons from the third plague in 1369 rather than 1370 and add a sixth widespread event—'A great plague this year' (*Annals of Connacht*)—in 1398.[232] These synchronise well

---

[232] For the fourteenth century, the Gaelic Annals report widespread plague in 1349 (*Annals of Loch Cé*, *of Connacht*, *of Ulster*, *of the Four Masters*, and *of Clonmacnoise* (a.k.a. *Mageoghagan's Book*)), 1361 (*Annals of Loch Cé*, *of Connacht*, *of Ulster*, *of the Four Masters*, with further reports of notable individuals dying of the disease in 1362, but no explicit statement of a continuance of a widespread outbreak), 1383 (*Annals of the Four Masters*, *Annals of Clonmacnoise* (a.k.a. *Mageoghagan's Book*), and with reports of notables dying from plague in 1384 but again without explicit attestation of more general severity or geographical scope), 1392–3 (*Miscellaneous Irish Annals – Fragment 3 – Annals of Oileán na Naomh*; but without explicit use of the word 'plague') and 1398 (*Annals of Loch Cé*, *of Connacht*, *of the Four Masters* and *of Clonmacnoise* (a.k.a. *Mageoghagan's Book*)), with notables again dying in 1399 and 1400 from plague, but no confirmation of broader severity or scope). No explicit Gaelic attestation of a widespread outbreak is given for 1370–1 (as per the *Annals of Ross*), but the *Annals of Ulster* attest to several notables dying of plague in 1369. Lastly, the *Annals of Ulster* for 1376 note the death of just one individual from plague—this is the only instance during these years in which an explicit plague attestation is unrelated (falling either in the same or an adjacent year) to a wider outbreak noted either within the Gaelic Annals or Anglo-Irish Annals. See https://celt.ucc.ie//published for the relevant texts.

with more comprehensively documented English plague outbreaks in 1348–9, 1361–2, 1368–9, 1382 and 1391, of which the first two were the most devastating and the cumulative effect of all five was to reduce that country's population by at least half.[233] In Ireland the combined demographic impact of these same five plague outbreaks may credibly have been similar, but this awaits confirmation.

Especially intriguing, given the ecologically sensitive character of this host- and vector-dependent disease, is the close association between the poor harvests of 1349, 1361, 1369 and 1390 and plague outbreaks in the same or sequel years.[234] In fact, an initial statistical analysis of English harvest yields and Jean-Noël Biraben's counts of reported plague outbreaks in Europe (between 1346 and 1476) reveals a statistically significant negative correlation, with plague counts rising in bad harvest years and falling in abundant harvest years.[235] Harvests are, of course, also influenced by human factors, not least the incidence of plague itself, which may reduce the availability of labour to sow and especially harvest crops and disrupt the continuity of management. This may explain why harvests following within one or two years of a plague outbreak also tended to be reduced.[236] This observation highlights the complexity of the interactions between the human and natural systems under examination, in which depressed harvests might be caused by bad weather and plague outbreaks acting both independently or together. In this materially poor society, harvest shortfalls, in turn, will have adversely affected nutrition and thereby morbidity and mortality and, through scarcity-induced migration, may have further encouraged the

---

[233] S.K. Cohn Jr, *The Black Death transformed: disease and culture in early renaissance Europe* (London, 2002), 184–5, 197; Broadberry, *British economic growth*, 12–15; Campbell, *Great Transition*, 311, 313–19.

[234] Campbell, *Three centuries*; 'Annals of Ross', 38.

[235] The Pearson correlation value for English grain yields versus plague incidence between 1346 and 1476 amounts to $r = -0.214$, a moderate negative correlation, but statistically highly significant with $p = 0.014$ (i.e., there is only a 1.4 per cent chance that the observed correlation could have arisen purely by chance). The sources upon which this analysis are based are Campbell, *Three centuries,* and Jean-Noël Biraben, *Les hommes et la peste en France et dans les pays européens et méditerranéens, vol. 1: la peste dans l'histoire* (Paris and The Hague, 1975), 363–74; U. Büntgen *et al.*, 'Digitizing historical plague', *Clinical Infectious Diseases* 55:11 (2012), 1586–8. There are well-known drawbacks to the Biraben dataset: Joris Roosen and D.R. Curtis, 'Dangers of noncritical use of historical plague data', *Emerging Infectious Diseases* 24:1 (2018), 103–10 (but these are rebutted by Ole Jørgen Benedictow, 'Biraben's lists of the plague epidemics of the second plague pandemic, 1346–*c*.1690: problems, basis, uses', *Annales de Démographie Historique* 138:2 (2019), 213–23).

[236] Pearson cross-correlation values show that for any given year's harvest, plague incidence in the second year preceding correlated negatively at $r = -0.233$ and $p = 0.008$ (i.e., there is a 0.8 per cent chance that the observed correlation has arisen by chance). Plague incidence for the first year preceding is also negatively correlated at $r = -0.326$ and $p = 0.0002$ (i.e., there is just a 0.02 per cent chance that the observed correlation has arisen by chance).

spread of disease or relocated rural populations to urban locations with higher infection rates.

Weather conditions, especially temperature and humidity levels, also powerfully influenced the ecological interlinkages between the plague bacterium (*Yersinia pestis*), its wild and domestic mammalian hosts, the insect vectors—mostly fleas but also, possibly, lice—by which it was spread, and its human victims.[237] This is evident in the statistically significant negative correlation to be observed between recorded plague outbreaks and reconstructed European summer temperatures across the years 1346 to 1499, with cooler summers associated with increased counts of plague outbreaks in the same year and vice versa.[238] Cross-correlation reveals a lagged and/or multi-year response, in which lower summer temperatures in each of the three years preceding a given year also tend to be associated with a higher incidence of reported plague outbreaks in that given year.[239] For medieval Ireland, the available data are not particularly suited to correlation analysis, but an assessment of the association between plague incidence in Ireland and weather conditions can be undertaken by conducting a further set of superposed epoch analyses in which the timing and frequency of epidemics reported in the Annals is examined relative to the date of major explosive volcanic eruptions (Appendix 7). This reveals a statistically significant increase (at p = 0.06 for the post-1348 era) in the reporting of epidemics in the year of volcanic eruptions, attesting to an association between volcanically induced climatic stress and disease outbreaks in Ireland. These implied climate–plague interactions may have operated through the reactivation of local European reservoirs of infection or by intensifying the severity of plague outbreaks already

---

[237] Campbell, *Great Transition*, 228–9, 286–9, 295–9.

[238] The strength of this association is moderate, at r = -0.297 (Pearson correlation coefficient), leaving room for many other influences (including other weather variables such as precipitation) on plague frequencies beyond summer temperatures. It is, however, statistically highly significant, with just a 0.02 per cent probability of having occurred purely by chance (i.e., p = 0.0002). The sources upon which this analysis are based are Biraben, *Les hommes et la peste*, vol. 1, 363–74; Büntgen et al., 'Digitizing historical plague'; PAGES2k Consortium, 'Continental-scale temperature variability during the past two millennia,' *Nature Geoscience* 6 (2013), 339–46.

[239] For the third, second and first years preceding, statistically significant negative Pearson correlation coefficients (at the 5 per cent or p = 0.05 level) are observed between summer temperatures and plague incidence of, respectively, r = -0.161 (p = 0.048), r = -0.247 (p = 0.002), and r = -0.217 (p = 0.007). European summer temperatures are themselves correlated positively with English harvest yields, but only statistically significantly for the second and third years preceding, respectively r = 0.158 (p = 0.073), and r = 0.208 (p = 0.017). These correlations, although not strong, suggest that temperatures may have acted upon plague incidence via their effects on harvest yields. Paradoxically, temperatures do not exhibit any clear correlation with harvests in the same years (i.e., this year's summer temperatures are not strongly correlated with this year's harvests), but do influence plague incidence in the same years, implying other temperature-related influences on plague incidence are also at play.

occurring. On a larger geographical scale and longer time-frames, climatic factors are likely to have triggered (with a 10–12-year lag) the periodic reintroduction of plague to Europe from its heartlands in Asia's continental interior.[240] These mechanisms are certainly not mutually exclusive.

These observations suggest that in this new epidemiological environment the more critical association for society at large had become that between the weather and plague rather than the weather and food scarcity. Indeed, with more land to go around and fewer people to be fed, the risk of dearth escalating into full-scale famine was significantly diminished. Across Europe, in fact, during the land-abundant century-and-a-half that followed the Black Death, there is a conspicuous reduction in the number of recorded subsistence crises and famines.[241] Irrespective of climatic trends and weather conditions, acute scarcity was for the moment something that fewer people had to fear.

The unstable and inclement weather with which arrival of the Black Death coincided persisted for some years afterwards and was much commented upon by English chroniclers.[242] These years witnessed some of the most repeatedly below-average English harvests on record.[243] Yet in Ireland whatever the weather was doing attracted significantly diminished comment by the country's annalists (Fig. 2). Only the most unusual meteorological occurrences, or those damaging to physical infrastructure, were recorded. These include, in 1358, a hail storm with stones the size of crab apples at Carbury, Co. Sligo,[244] the devastating

---

[240] K.L. Kausrud *et al.*, 'Modeling the epidemiological history of plague in Central Asia: palaeoclimatic forcing on a disease system over the past millennium', *BMC Biology* 8:112 (2010), 14; Schmid, 'Climate-driven introduction of the Black Death'. The lagged introduction of plague to Europe is consistent with statistically significant negative correlations between European summer temperatures and Biraben's plague incidence with lags of 12–13 years (having examined the preceding 30 years in the present study) with r = -0.365 (p < 0.001) and r = -0.332 (p < 0.001), respectively.

[241] Guido Alfani and Cormac Ó Gráda, 'Famines in Europe: an overview', in Guido Alfani and Cormac Ó Gráda (eds), *Famine in European history* (Cambridge, 2017), 1–24: 8–9.

[242] There is, for example, no counterpart in the Irish sources to Henry Knighton's account of the wintry weather that persisted from 6 Dec. 1353 until 12 Mar. 1354: 'there was a long, hard and cold winter. It began at the feast of St Nicholas and lasted continuously until the feast of St Gregory: and there followed a great and severe storm of wind destroying the roofs of churches, mills and great trees, and doing much damage: such a tempest had not been seen in our day': Britton, 'Meteorological chronology', 142, also 141–6.

[243] Campbell, 'Grain yields on English demesnes', 147–9.

[244] Reported in the *Annals of Ulster* (also *of Connacht*, *of the Four Masters*, and *of Clonmacnoise* (a.k.a. *Mageoghagan's Book*)): 'A great [hail] shower came in that summer in Carbury [Co. Sligo] and not less than a very ripe [full-grown] apple was every stone of them': Ludlow, 'Utility 2', 260–1.

St Maur's Day wind on 15 January 1362,[245] and in the *Annals of Connacht* (also *of Ulster*) for 1373 another 'very great wind…which wrecked many churches'.[246] Of bad weather, poor harvests and scarcity there is no mention until 1397, when reference is made in the *Miscellaneous Irish Annals* to 'insufficiency of food in the summer, and the autumn wet, windy, destructive and cold'.[247] For once, in contrast to earlier weather-related crises, C.E. Britton reports no corresponding complaint made by English chroniclers about the weather that same year.[248]

Until this point, the indifference of both Gaelic and Anglo-Irish annalists to the weather is striking. Good and (presumably) bad harvests alike passed without mention. Thus, the better weather that prevailed during the Chaucerian Solar Maximum is ignored, notwithstanding that England enjoyed harvests so bountiful in the 1370s and 1380s that they initiated a prolonged grain-price deflation which on many estates brought the era of direct demesne management to an end.[249] It is as though, in an age overwhelmed by repeated tsunamis of plague (Fig. 9), the weather scarcely merited a mention when it came to chronicling important events. Possibly, too, with a reduced, more resilient and more pastoral population, harsh weather was less likely to translate into serious subsistence crises. What is plain is that in Ireland as well as England the return to more settled and clement weather during the final decades of the fourteenth century and opening decades of the fifteenth century (Fig. 1), in combination with re-establishment of favourable land to labour ratios and, in the case of England, materially improved living standards, were still insufficient to halt the demographic rot and set their depleted populations back on the road to recovery.[250] For almost another hundred years, and possibly considerably longer in Ireland, the countervailing effect of high disease mortality hindered positive rates of natural increase from becoming established. Security problems arising from the waning authority and shrinking territorial control of the English administration in Ireland and

---

[245] Carefully calibrated English sources date this gale reliably to 15 January 1362. Grace's *Annales Hiberniae* reports this event under 1361 as 'A great storm on the feast of St. Maur': *Jacobi Grace, Kilkenniensis*, 153. The dating system employed by the *Annales Hiberniae* correctly puts the storm in 1362. The *Annals of Connacht* (also *of Ulster*, *of Loch Cé*, and *of the Four Masters*) also report a 'Great wind … which wrecked churches and houses and sank many ships and boats', but for 1363: Ludlow, 'Utility 2', 261. While the first two St Maur's Day events are undoubtedly the same it is conceivable that the last is distinct.

[246] Ludlow, 'Utility 2', 263. Was this the same gale that in Scotland damaged property and flattened woodland but is retrospectively dated by fifteenth-century Walter Bower to December 1372? (Oram, 'Worst disaster', 228).

[247] Ludlow, 'Utility 2', 264; Lyons, 'Weather, famine, pestilence and plague', 67.

[248] Britton, 'Meteorological chronology', 152.

[249] Campbell, 'Grain yields on English demesnes', 141, 149–51.

[250] Broadberry, *British economic growth*, 13–22, 203–8, 229–34; Jane Humphries and Jacob Weisdorf, 'Unreal wages? Real income and economic growth in England, 1260–1850', *Economic Journal* 129 (2019), 2867–87.

resurgent rivalries and conflicts between Anglo-Irish and Gaelic lords, may have been a further factor keeping replacement rates in check.

Owing to their preoccupation with the deaths of prominent individuals, Ireland's annalists never abandoned their interest in plague and they continued to note related fatalities even after the great initial pandemic outbreaks of the fourteenth century had ended (Fig. 9). Both larger outbreaks and the plague deaths of notable persons are frequently recorded throughout the fifteenth century and imply that the disease was repeatedly re-introduced to Ireland, as in 1478 when 'A great plague came in a ship to the harbour of Assaroe [Co. Donegal] and that plague spread throughout Tirconnell [Co. Donegal], and in Fermanagh and in the Province [of Ulster] in general'.[251] Dublin is, however, likely to have been its most common port of entry. In 1439, '… three thousand persons, both male and female, large and small, died of it [in Dublin], from the beginning of spring to the end of the month of May…' (*Annals of the Four Masters*).[252] Eight years later, in 1447, 'it is difficult to get an account of the innumerable multitudes that died in Dublin by that plague'.[253] On this occasion Meath, Munster and Leinster also became infected, as plague presumably circulated from Dublin to other towns and settlements within the English Lordship, with the *Annals of the Four Masters* adding that 'some say that seven hundred priests died of this plague'.[254] Nor, given the numbers of plague deaths recorded in the Gaelic Annals, in addition to reports such as the above-cited plague-bearing ship arriving in County Donegal in 1478, should it be supposed that the more thinly peopled and pastoral regions of the north and west were little visited by the disease.[255] The initial sparseness of plague citations in the Gaelic Annals from 1349 might suggest that to begin with these regions got off more lightly than the more closely settled mixed-farming regions

---

[251] Reported in the *Annals of Ulster* (also *of the Four Masters* and *of Loch Cé*—though the latter dates the event to 1477). See https://celt.ucc.ie//published/ for the relevant texts.

[252] https://celt.ucc.ie//published/T100005D/index.html (M1439.16).

[253] John O'Donovan (ed.), 'The Annals of Ireland, from the year 1443 to 1468, translated from the Irish by Dudley Firbisse…', *The Miscellany of the Irish Archaeological Society* 1 (1845), 198–301: 218.

[254] https://celt.ucc.ie//published/T100005D/index.html (M1447.2). Beyond the *Annals of the Four Masters* here, and 'Annals of Ireland, from the year 1443 to 1468' above, widespread plague conditions are also reported this year in the *Annals of Ulster* (https://celt.ucc.ie//published/T100001C/index.html (U1447.8)).

[255] For a recent reiteration of, and ecological justification for, the oft-cited view (which has similarly been advanced for Scotland) that the Gaelic regions of the north and west were less impacted by plague: Ruhaak, 'Alternative Black Death narrative', 1–16. This might be tested by mapping all plague deaths in the Gaelic and Anglo-Irish Annals against high-resolution regional pollen profiles. For Scotland, however, Oram ('Worst disaster', 231) has emphasised that 'there is no evidence to support views that plague was ever purely or even largely an urban problem in later medieval Scotland, or that rural populations were any less severely affected by plague epidemics'.

of the south and east, as remarked by some contemporaries.[256] Nevertheless, at least from the 1380s, as oak regeneration became established across the island (Fig. 5), references to plague deaths in the Annals increase (Fig. 2), with the implication that a process of epidemiological levelling-up was taking place. Certainly, the frequency with which the fifteenth-century Annals report notable individuals, both Gaelic and English, succumbing to sickness and disease implies that plague and the other diseases circulating at this time were widespread in their impacts.[257] Ultimately, therefore, morbidity and mortality rates in both communities may have become relatively high.[258]

References to weather also re-appear in the fifteenth-century Annals (Fig. 2) and are a reminder of its continuing capacity to cause hardship and havoc even in an era of relative land abundance. Between 1406 and 1409 a run of poor harvests in England (Fig.10) were closely matched by a sequence of weather-related problems in Ireland. These began in the winter of 1405 with 'very tempestuous weather and very heavy rainfall ... causing much destruction' (*Miscellaneous Irish Annals*), continued in 1407 with 'foul and bad weather and a great murrain of cattle' (*Annals of Clonmacnoise*; also *of Connacht* and *Miscellaneous Irish Annals*), and then, possibly with a greater implicit focus on the lands of the English Lordship, culminated in 1410 with 'great famine in Ireland' (*Annals of Thady Dowling*).[259] At much the same time outbreaks of plague were reported on both islands: in England in 1405, 1406 and 1407 (triggering a spate of will-making in London) and then, with a characteristic lag of a year, in Ireland in 1406 and 1408.[260]

Directly and indirectly, the bad weather very likely facilitated the re-emergence, intensification and diffusion of plague in these years. This, in turn,

---

[256] Maria Kelly, '"Unheard-of mortality": the Black Death in Ireland', *History Ireland* 9:4 (2001), 12–7.

[257] The Annals frequently eschew detailed descriptions and diagnoses of the cause of death. Typical are the unspecific accounts of '*dith mor*' ('great destruction', as per 1406) or the somewhat more specific '*pestilencia magna*' ('great pestilence', as per 1408). Often, explicit mention is made of 'plague', as in 1406 (*Annals of Connacht*, also *of Loch Cé*)) when various named notables '... *mortui sunt don plaig in hoc anno*' ('...died of the plague in this year'): https://celt.ucc.ie/published/G100011/text174.html (1406.2). Such a description is still somewhat ambiguous as to the underlying pathogen, but a broad view is taken in identifying possible bubonic plague incidence (Fig. 10). This is an area of annalistic reporting that merits further study.

[258] For the situation in fifteenth-century England, where disease mortality remained high and the downward demographic trend was not arrested until the middle years of the century: Campbell, *Great Transition*, 349–55.

[259] Ludlow, 'Utility 2', 265–6; Richard Butler (ed.) 'The Annals of Thady Dowling, Chancellor of Leighlin', in *Annals of Ireland by Friar John Clyn*, 27; 'William Wilde's table of Irish famines', 6; Lyons, 'Weather, famine, pestilence and plague', 68.

[260] Biraben, *Les hommes et la peste, vol. 1*, 363–74; Cohn, *Black Death transformed*, 197; *Annals of Loch Cé, of Connacht, of Clonmacnoise*, and *Miscellaneous Irish Annals – Fragment 3 – Annals of Oileán na Naomh*: Ludlow, 'Utility 2', 266; Lyons, 'Weather, famine, pestilence and plague', 68. The close chronological juxtaposition of these English and Irish plague outbreaks helps clinch their identification.

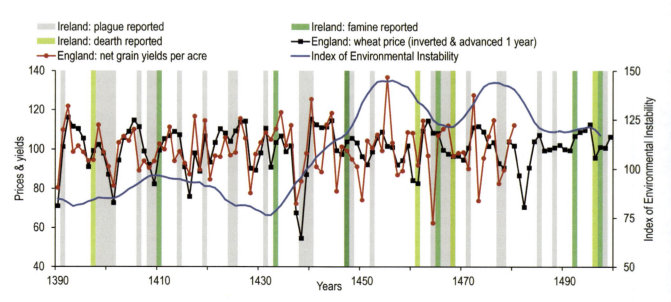

Fig. 10—Reports in the Gaelic and Anglo-Irish Annals of dearth, famine and plague in Ireland, alongside English wheat prices and net grain yields and an Index of Environmental Instability, 1390–1500 CE.

Sources: Dearth, famine and plague in Ireland: authors' own survey of Gaelic and Anglo-Irish Annals.

Wheat prices (percentage of 25-year moving average centred, inverted and advanced one year); net grain yields per acre (deviations from trend in net wheat-barley-oats [W-B-O] yields, averaged using the weighted ratio 2:1:1); Index of Environmental Instability: see sources to Fig. 5.

compounded the social impacts of poor harvests and cattle murrains and made these years deadly on both sides of the Irish Sea. Plague broke out again in Meath and Leinster in 1414, despite the intervention in 1411 of 'The Holy Cross at Raphoe [which] shed blood from the wounds this year and performed many miracles, checking sicknesses and many ills'.[261] Five years later in 1419 the *Annals of Connacht* reported 'much plague in England and in Ireland', although in Ireland this was apparently better remembered as 'the year of the hot summer', when 'burning heat' and drought extended from summer into autumn (*Annals of Connacht*).[262] As in England, this resulted not in scarcity but in 'a great yield of

---

[261] *Annals of Connacht* (also *of Loch Cé*, *of the Four Masters* and *of Ulster*): https://celt.ucc.ie/published/T100011/text179.html (1411.24). Such reports offer a window into how the annalists (representative of the educated Gaelic elite) contextualised the new disease environment of the fourteenth and fifteenth centuries.

[262] Also reported in the *Annals of Ulster*: Ludlow, 'Utility 2', 269–70; Lyons, 'Weather, famine, pestilence and plague', 68. This drought is confirmed by the OWDA, registering as severe throughout Britain and Ireland and across north, north-west, central and eastern Europe: Cook, 'Old World megadroughts'. The summer heat did not apparently extend to include the Scottish Cairngorms, where 1419 marks the start of a 20-year decline in summer temperatures: Rydvale, '800 years'.

every fruit and crop'.[263] Thereafter, northern hemisphere temperatures cooled, atmospheric circulation patterns decisively shifted, the NAO switched from predominantly positive to negative modes (it was negative for three out of five years during the fifteenth century and seven out of ten years between 1425 and 1474: Appendix 3), and environmental instability rose once again (Fig. 1 and Appendix 5). The upshot was that the synchronicity of weather patterns and impacts which had hitherto prevailed between Ireland and England appears to have weakened and on occasion lapsed altogether.

Correlations between the ring widths of Irish and English oaks, which had been so strongly positive when the circulation patterns of the Medieval Climate Anomaly had been firmly in the ascendant from the 1170s to 1260s, were significantly weaker during the opening phase of the Little Ice Age in the fifteenth century (Fig. 4). In fact, during the middle years of that century there were periods when growing conditions in Ireland diverged so widely from those in England that there was effectively no correlation at all, and for short periods, notably 1452–3 and 1462–6, correlations actually turned negative. This may explain why there was no equivalent in England to the 'great inclemency' of (presumably) November 1424 to May 1425 reported by the *Annals of Ulster*, which 'brought great destruction on cattle and loss of tillage and loss of people on the whole of Ireland'.[264] Although this Irish episode does coincide with worsening summer temperatures in the Scottish Cairngorms, a stark distinction between Irish and English weather conditions (in terms of wetness) is well captured by the Old World Drought Atlas.[265] Conversely, on the silence of the Annals, Ireland seems to have escaped the worst of the wet weather that in 1428 ruined the English wheat harvest (Fig.10).[266] Spring-sown oats, in contrast, yielded at well above average, which may explain why there is no mention of subsistence difficulties in the oats-growing north and west of Ireland.[267] Certainly, the Old World Drought Atlas indicates that in 1428 wet weather conditions prevailed right across Britain and Ireland, including the western and northern domains of most Gaelic annalists. Consequently, this may be a case of divergent impacts, in which the oats- and grass-growing Gaelic and 'Gaelicising' areas were less sensitive to the wet conditions that were so damaging to the English wheat and barley crops. Regardless, five years later, it was England's turn to escape apparently unscathed when serious dearth struck

---

[263] Campbell, *Three centuries*; Ludlow, 'Utility 2', 270.
[264] Ludlow, 'Utility 2', 270; Britton, 'Meteorological chronology', 157–8.
[265] Rydvale, '800 years'. The OWDA reveals wet spring–summer conditions across much of Ireland for 1425 (following a notably wet 1424) and neutral to quite dry conditions across much of Britain (following only a moderately wet 1424): Cook, 'Old World megadroughts'.
[266] Britton, 'Meteorological chronology', 158–9; Campbell, *Three centuries*.
[267] Campbell, *Three centuries*.

Ireland in the summer of 1433, although both countries experienced the long and hard winter that followed.[268]

By the second quarter of the fifteenth century the interval of relatively stable and benign weather conditions that followed the Wolf Solar Minimum and coincided with the Chaucerian Solar Maximum was effectively over. Thereafter, onset of the Spörer Solar Minimum initiated the first decisively cold phase of the so-called Little Ice Age (Fig. 1), characterised by cooler global and northern hemisphere temperatures. In the Scottish Cairngorms, summer temperatures were cooling from 1419 to 1441 (the coldest summer in over 200 years) and remained depressed until at least 1450.[269] Meanwhile, Ireland, along with much of northern Europe, experienced some notoriously cold winters.[270] In the aforementioned 1433–4, the rare phenomenon of frozen-over rivers and lakes, last explicitly reported in 1251, is again described in the Annals. So intense was the freezing that 'numerous herds of cattle and horses and people and pack-horses used to go upon the chief lakes of Ireland' (*Annals of Ulster*).[271] Wildfowl, however, suffered grievously and, although it is not mentioned, casualties among livestock customarily over-wintered out of doors may also have been heavy.[272] The following winter seems to have been as bad.[273] Even so, the annalists convey a stronger impression of the remarkable nature of these freezing winter conditions, which had much of Europe in their grip, than of the hardship they presumably inflicted upon society, other than that, for the duration of the frost, the ground was frozen too hard to be worked.[274] Nor is there any hint that serious subsistence problems resulted or mention of plague or other disease-related deaths.

At a European scale 'there seems to have been only one major famine in the fifteenth century (that of 1437–8, affecting central European countries as well

---

[268] 1433 (*Annals of the Four Masters*, also *of Ulster* and *of Loch Cé*): 'There was a famine in the summer of this year, called, for a very long time afterwards, *samhra na mear-githne* [Summer of the Aberration], because no one used to recognise friend or relative, in consequence of the greatness of the famine': Ludlow, 'Utility 2', 271. 1433–4 (*Annals of Ulster*, also *of Loch Cé* and *of Connacht*): 'Great frost began at the end of this year (the year of the great frost); namely [it began] five weeks before Christmas and lasted to the end of seven weeks after. And numerous herds of cattle and horses and people and [pack-]horses used to go upon the chief lakes of Ireland. And great destruction was inflicted upon the fowl of Ireland during that frost and so on': Ludlow, 'Utility 2', 271–2. Britton, 'Meteorological chronology', 161. There is some doubt over the exact winter season in question in the Annals: 1433–4 or 1434–5 are both plausible, though consideration of the English evidence suggests 1433–4.

[269] Rydvale, '800 years'.

[270] Camenisch, 'The 1430s'.

[271] Ludlow, 'Utility 2', 271–2.

[272] Ludlow, 'Utility 2', 271–2.

[273] 1435 (*Annals of the Four Masters*): 'An unusual frost and ice occurred in this year, so that people used to traverse the lakes and rivers of Ireland on the solid ice': Ludlow, 'Utility 2', 272–4. The *Annals of Ulster* and a second entry in the *Four Masters* provide incidental corroboration of the severe conditions in 1434 when describing the evacuation for safekeeping of livestock and belongings over a frozen Lough Erne [County Fermanagh].

[274] *Annals of Connacht*: Ludlow, 'Utility 2', 271–2; Camenisch, 'The 1430s'.

as Britain)'.[275] Its trigger was a classic back-to-back harvest failure that stands out clearly in the English record of grain yields and prices (Fig. 10).[276] As was often the case, persistent and unseasonable cool and wet weather were to blame. Across Europe, this climate-related crisis was followed immediately by one of the most widely recorded of all fifteenth-century plague outbreaks, which strikingly illustrates the potential causal relationship between the two.[277] Intriguingly, if the testimony of Ireland's annalists is to be believed, Ireland, unlike neighbouring Scotland, was spared the famine but not the plague.[278] Thus, the Annals have nothing to say about either the weather or the harvests of 1437–8 but then, in the spring of 1439, the *Annals of the Four Masters* report 3,000 plague deaths in Dublin and the next year plague counted many notables in Connacht among its victims.[279]

In contrast to England, in Ireland the weather in the 1440s appears to have been worse and to have had more serious consequences than that in the 1430s. The decade was also conspicuously cold in the Scottish Cairngorms.[280] Respecting Ireland, the set of Gaelic Annals written by Gaelic scholar Dubhaltach Mac Fhirbhisigh in 1666 and spanning 1443 to 1468 is particularly informative.[281] They note the wetness of the summers of 1443 and 1444 and that the former proved good for fish but bad for bees and sheep and the latter 'made all corn maltish [i.e., fermented] for the most part'.[282] The next year witnessed heavy cattle mortality and the dearth of victuals and corn.[283] This was followed in 1446 by another 'hard year'.[284] The upshot of these four consecutive years of miserable weather was that by the spring of 1447 'all Ireland' was reduced to a state of hunger, whereby 'men were then wont to eat all manner of herbs for the most part'.[285] To make matters worse, plague broke out in both England and Ireland and raged throughout summer and autumn. In Ireland, the many who succumbed to the disease included, by repute, 700 priests (*Annals of the Four Masters*), who, as frontline workers, presumably often contracted plague when

---

[275] Alfani and Ó Gráda, 'Famines in Europe', 8–9.
[276] Campbell, 'Grain yields on English demesnes', 152–5.
[277] Biraben, *Les hommes et la peste, vol. 1*, 363–74; Campbell, *Great Transition*, 314.
[278] Oram, 'Worst disaster', 231; Rydvale, '800 years'; https://celt.ucc.ie//published/T100005D/index.html (M1439.16).
[279] https://celt.ucc.ie/published/T100005D/index.html (M1440.1).
[280] Rydvale, '800 years'.
[281] 'The Annals of Ireland, from the Year 1443 to 1468'. The sheer density of entries in the 26 years covered by these Annals attests to the scope of recording undertaken by the Gaelic learned families, much of which is now lost. For the author (a.k.a. Duald MacFirbis or Dudley Firbisse), who also compiled the *Chronicon Scotorum*: Nollaig Ó Muraíle, *The celebrated antiquary Dubhaltach Mac Fhirbhisigh (c.1600–1671): his lineage, life and learning* (Maynooth, 2002, 2nd edition).
[282] 'The Annals of Ireland, from the Year 1443 to 1468', 207; Ludlow, 'Utility 2', 274–5.
[283] Ludlow, 'Utility 2', 275.
[284] Ludlow, 'Utility 2', 275.
[285] Ludlow, 'Utility 2', 275.

ministering to the sick and dying.[286] In a now established pattern, plague once again followed on the heels of bad weather and scarcity.

From this point, that plague continued to be widespread is attested by outbreaks in Meath and Armagh in 1448,[287] while further outbreaks and suggestive notices of possible plague deaths reappear variously in 1452, 1464–5, 1466 (wider outbreak), 1467, 1468 (wider outbreak), 1470 (wider outbreak) and 1471 (Fig. 2).[288] Other deadly diseases were also likely abroad.[289] From their descriptions, however, none appears to have been as devastating as the 1447 plague outbreak. Meanwhile, serious losses of cattle were noted in 1450 and 1473 and dearth recurred in 1450, 1461, 1462, 1465 and 1468.[290] Environmental instability was at a high level (Appendix 5) and weather extremes were common. The annalists, unaware that they were living at a time of depressed global temperatures and altered atmospheric circulation patterns, described 1450 as a 'hard warlike year... with many storms, and great loss of cattle'.[291] The spring and summer of 1462 were 'very hard', following a winter (presumably of 1461–2) characterised by a

---

[286] Biraben, *Les hommes et la peste, vol. 1*, 363–74; Lyons, 'Weather, famine, pestilence and plague', 69–70; Ludlow, 'Utility 2', 275; https://celt.ucc.ie//published/T100005D/index.html (M1447.2).

[287] 'A great plague raged in Meath, of which Conor, son of Hugh O'Farrell, Dermot Mac Conmaighe, and Henry Duv Mac Techedain, three friars of Longphort-Ui-Feargail, died' (*Annals of the Four Masters*): https://celt.ucc.ie//published/T100005D/index.html (M1448.1). In Armagh, plague led Archbishop Fey to conduct court proceedings outside the city: Anthony Lynch, 'Documents of Franciscan interest from the Episcopal Archives of Armagh 1265–1508', *Collectanea Hibernica* 31/32 (1989/1990), 9–102: 12.

[288] *Annals of the Four Masters*: https://celt.ucc.ie//published/T100005D/index.html (M1452.21; M1464.4-5, 7; M1467.15; M1468.9; M1471.3). *Annals of Connacht*: https://celt.ucc.ie/published/T100011.html (1464.2-4; 1464.11; 1464.13-14; 1464.53; 1465.13; 1466.28 (reportedly widespread: 'A great plague in Dublin, in Meath and in Leinster'); 1467.15; 1468.15; 1468.37 (reportedly widespread: 'There was great scarcity throughout Ireland this year, the result of plague, treachery(?), murder and general war'); 1471.28-29). *Annals of Ulster*: https://celt.ucc.ie//published/T100001C/text093.html (U1470.3 ('Great plague, namely, Airaing, in Fermanagh this year and Ua Flannagain (that is, Cormac, son of Gilla-Isu) of Tuath-Ratha and many others that are not reckoned died thereof')).

[289] While both the *Annals of the Four Masters* and *of Connacht* often cite '*plaig*' for large outbreaks, readily translated as 'plague', many of the above-cited reports (see previous footnote) of individual deaths cite '*tregait*' as the underlying disease. O'Donovan renders these instances as 'plague' (perhaps on contextual grounds) in translating the *Four Masters*, while Freeman renders this 'colic' in translating *Connacht*. Crawford's coverage of this term ('Disease and illness', 208–11) considers examples reported in the Annals between the tenth and eleventh centuries, and hence, if the same as these fifteenth century instances, not bubonic plague. There is no definitive diagnosis, but, as Crawford notes, the term is often also associated with 'lumps' and 'gripping', in addition to 'colic'. Also note that the epidemic reported uniquely by the *Annals of Ulster* in 1470 cites 'airaing', left untranslated by Hennessy and MacCarthy.

[290] Ludlow, 'Utility 2', 276–9, 281.

[291] Ludlow, 'Utility 2', 276.

'great frost…that slaughtered many flocks of birds'.[292] Spring in 1465 was delayed by 'great frost and snow and stormy weather', and 1471 witnessed localised but destructive hail storms followed by a hot summer and very dry autumn.[293] They had only to read Gerald of Wales's *Topographia Hibernica* to discover how much more mild and temperate meteorological conditions had been in the 1180s.[294] Some of these problem years matched years of poor weather and deficient harvests in England, notably 1461, 1462 and 1465, but not all, for although the unsettled character of weather conditions at this time was general, the actual weather experienced in Ireland and England appeared often quite different. This is suggested in the significantly narrower rings displayed by English oaks between 1461 and 1468 compared with their Irish counterparts (Appendix 4) and the absence of much correlation between the two oak-ring series throughout the 1440s, 1450s and 1460s (Fig. 4).[295]

Ireland's agrarian economy, particularly in the Gaelic-dominated regions of the north and west most familiar to the annalists, was also less tillage based and more grass dependent than England's, which is no doubt why cattle mortalities were evidently of such concern.[296] Murrains, hard winters and deficiencies of winter pasture were more to be dreaded than cool and damp summers in places where dairy produce featured prominently in diets, and where wealth and status were measured in cattle. Given that cattle were typically over-wintered on standing herbage rather than fed on hay and that most were not housed, as Kenneth Nicholls notes, 'a severe winter and delayed spring could lead to a heavy mortality of cattle, with consequent famine'.[297] Back in the twelfth century Gerald of Wales had described how in Ireland 'The grass is green in the fields in winter, just the same as in summer', thereby highlighting the climatic characteristics that justified these methods of stock management.[298] Their economic rationale

---

[292] 'Annals of Ireland 1443 to 1468': Ludlow, 'Utility 2', 277.

[293] 1465 (*Annals of Connacht*, also 'of Ireland 1443 to 1468'): 'Exceeding great frost and snow and stormy weather this year, so that no herb grew in the ground and no leaf budded on a tree until the feast of St. Brendan [16 May], but a man, if he were the stronger, would forcibly carry away the food from the priest in church, even though he had the Sacred Body in his hands and stood clothed in Mass-vestments'. 1471 (*Annals of Connacht*, also *of the Four Masters*): 'Showers of hail fell each side of Beltaine [1 May], with lightning and thunders, destroying much blossom and beans and fruits in all parts of Ireland where they fell…'; (*Annals of Ulster*) 'A hot summer this year'; (*Annals of Connacht*) 'An abundant nut-crop this year; the summer and autumn very dry and all the crops very early'. Ludlow, 'Utility 2', 278–80.

[294] Gerald of Wales, *History and topography of Ireland*, 34–5, 53–4.

[295] The correlation coefficient of the ring widths of Irish oaks to southern English oaks from 1440 to 1470 is +0.007 (between 1240 and 1270 it is +0.616).

[296] Katharine Simms, 'Gaelic culture and society', in Smith (ed.), *Cambridge history of Ireland, vol. 1*, 415–40: 417–18.

[297] Kenneth W. Nicholls, *Gaelic and Gaelicized Ireland in the middle ages* (Dublin, 2003, 2nd edition), 137.

[298] Gerald of Wales, *History and topography of Ireland*, 53.

lay in the calculation that the costs of the losses inflicted by occasional extreme winters were less than those of investing scarce capital in housing animals and scarce labour in making hay (itself problematic in a rainy climate), especially if byres, barns and ricks were liable to become the targets of violent and destructive attacks.

In the thinly peopled countryside of the north and west, where cattle raiding and rustling were endemic, there were sound socio-economic as well as environmental reasons for practising a form of transhumance and removing cattle to higher or less fertile grounds in the summer months of strongest grass growth and then returning them for the winter to more sheltered or fertile pastures to graze upon the accumulated summer grass as foggage.[299] Elsewhere, from the mid-fourteenth and into the fifteenth century, the shrinking labour force in combination with the expansion of the area under pasture encouraged wider adoption of these practices. Combined with the greater general resilience of pastoral agriculture to cool and wet conditions, the 'Gaelicisation' of agriculture in much of the previous English Lordship, alongside the evolution of hybrid farming systems that employed haymaking and winter housing to provide greater security against winter cold, can be seen as rational adaptations to the evolving climatic, economic and cultural contexts.[300]

Adopting these extensive methods of agriculture made sense in a situation where land was increasingly abundant and labour scarce, as, by the mid-fifteenth century, had been the case for more than a hundred years. Their corollary was that, until at least the 1440s, as the Belfast dendrochronological database indicates (Fig. 5), oak woodland was actively regenerating as demographic pressure upon woodland resources remained weak. By implication, Ireland's population was now reduced to a very low ebb, with average densities probably less than half those of its pre-1315 peak. It was as well that per capita landed resources were now available in relative abundance, because, as documented by the Annals and discussed above, society was exposed to significant climatological and epidemiological stress during these middle years of the fifteenth century. In Fig. 1 the decades of the 1440s to the 1460s stand out as one of the most distinctive episodes on palaeoclimatic record, when a duo of major tropical eruptions (in 1452 and 1457) coincided with weak solar forcing at the nadir of the Spörer Solar Minimum.[301] Further volcanic forcing

---

[299] On foggage: Ó Corráin, 'Ireland c.800: aspects of society', 571–2. On a modified transhumance as a cultural adaption: Keleman, 'Indigenous agriculture', 206–8. For the continuation of such arrangements deep into the Little Ice Age in the seventeenth century: Gerard Boate, *Ireland's natural history. Being a true and ample description of its situation, greatness, shape, and nature...* (London, 1652), 174.

[300] Nicholls, *Gaelic and Gaelicized*, 137; Seán Duffy, 'The problem of degeneracy', in James Lydon (ed.), *Law and disorder in thirteenth-century Ireland: the Dublin parliament of 1297* (Dublin, 1997), 87–106: 103–4.

[301] 1452 (VSSI of 9.97 Tg) and 1457 (VSSI of 32.98 Tg): Toohey and Sigl, 'Volcanic stratospheric sulfur injections'.

then followed from a closely timed trio of northern hemisphere extratropical eruptions in 1470, 1477 and 1480.[302] Collectively, these forcings can be credited with initiating and reinforcing a general lowering of global and hemispherical mean temperatures and an associated reconfiguration of atmospheric circulation patterns.[303] Hence the persistent weakness of the NAO, the occasional Arctic winters and cool summers, and elevated level of environmental instability experienced by Ireland at this time, following more than a hundred years of fairly relentless demographic and economic contraction, political readjustment, and concomitant social and cultural change. These fifteenth-century weather conditions stand in stark contrast to those that had prevailed almost 300 years earlier, when the Medieval Solar Maximum was at full strength, the NAO was predominantly positive, environmental instability was more muted, the high-medieval demographic and economic boom was in full swing, and woodland almost everywhere was in retreat.

Post 1450—low-level equilibrium

By the second half of the fifteenth century Irish society was almost back at the stage it had been in the mid-eleventh century: people were scarce, in per capita terms land was relatively abundant, and, after a century of regeneration, oak woodland was becoming plentiful (Fig. 5).[304] Eventually, however, building in oak resumed on a modest scale. From the 1420s tower houses were erected in growing numbers, almost fifty new friaries were founded (numbers of them in the south and west of Ireland), many of the older monasteries were remodeled, often on a reduced scale, and, in the more important towns, existing churches were added to and embellished.[305] This building revival, however, was altogether less dramatic than the construction boom which had taken off with such dynamism 400 years earlier and then been lent added momentum by the English invasion and settlement. Its mainsprings were the ending of population decline and settlement retreat, some abatement of endemic levels of violence, and the establishment of a degree of political and social stability adapted to the altered economic and environmental circumstances then prevailing.

---

[302] Individually small to moderate, this trio is notable for its clustering within a decade, with VSSI of 1.39 Tg for 1470, VSSI of 5.12 Tg for 1477 and VSSI of 1.66 Tg for 1480: Toohey and Sigl, 'Volcanic stratospheric sulfur injections'.
[303] Campbell, *Great Transition*, 335–49.
[304] Kaplan, Krumhardt and Zimmermann reckon that woodland's share of agriculturally usable land increased by over two-thirds during the half-century or so that followed the Black Death: Kaplan, Krumhardt and Zimmermann, 'Prehistoric and preindustrial deforestation', 3023.
[305] H.G. Leask, *Irish castles and castellated houses* (Dundalk, 1977), 75–124; H.G. Leask, *Irish churches and monastic buildings, vol. 3, medieval gothic the last phases* (Dundalk, 1978); S.G. Ellis, *Tudor Ireland: crown, community and the conflict of cultures 1470–1603* (London and New York, 1985), 39–40; Moss, 'Material culture', 485–90.

Although there are signs that in England demographic replacement rates were fitfully edging upwards during the final decades of the fifteenth century,[306] in Ireland disease appears to have remained a significant burden. The great plague (*pladh mor*) of 1470 is reported as an outbreak of '*airaing*' by the *Annals of Ulster*, a case of what may have been smallpox ('*galar breac*') is noted by the *Annals of Loch Cé* (also *of Connacht, of Ulster* and *of the Four Masters*) in 1488, and four years later the *Annals of Ulster* record the notable death of James Fleming, Baron of Slane, from the 'English sweat'.[307] Plague itself had returned with outbreaks in 1478 and in 1488, continuing into 1489, for which year the *Annals of the Four Masters* reported great numbers dying of a 'great plague' (*pláigh mhór*) 'so devastating that people did not bury the dead throughout Ireland'.[308] Not unusually, reports of plague in the Annals follow reported plague outbreaks in England with a one- or two-year lag, which implies that the disease was often sustained by repeated ship-borne reintroduction from either England or Europe.[309] The introduction of plague to north-west Ulster in 1478 via the minor west-coast port of Assaroe demonstrates that a single infected ship was all that was required to ignite an outbreak.[310] For that reason the country's port towns and their hinterlands were especially susceptible, with Dublin, on the evidence of the Annals, not unusually the epicentre of Irish plague outbreaks. Reports of plague outbreaks in the Annals only finally slacken over the course of the sixteenth century.

More positively, there appears to have been some easing of overall levels of violence, for violent actions and events loom (proportionately) less prominently in the Annals, and D.B. Quinn considers that 'under screens of defence of one kind or another, most parts of late-fifteenth century Ireland, both Gaelic

---

[306] Broadberry, *British economic growth*, 15–20; Campbell, *Great Transition*, 351–5.

[307] Ludlow, 'Utility 2', 279, 282–3, 285–7. As bemoaned by J.F.D. Shrewsbury (*A history of the bubonic plague in the British Isles* (Cambridge, 1970), 154), '*airaing*' in 1470 is left untranslated by Hennessy and MacCarthy. Guy Thwaites, Mark Taviner, and Vanya Gant, 'The English sweating sickness, 1485 to 1551', *New England Journal of Medicine* 336 (1997), 580-2.

[308] 1478: below, note 312. 1488 and 1489 (when the *Annals of Ulster* and *of the Four Masters* additionally report many individual plague deaths): Ludlow, 'Utility 2', 282–3, 285–7.

[309] Biraben, *Les hommes et la peste, vol. 1*, 363–74; Lyons, 'Weather, famine, pestilence and plague', 71–2.

[310] *Annals of Ulster*, 1478: https://celt.ucc.ie//published/T100001C/index.html (U1478.6). Also in the *Annals of the Four Masters*: https://celt.ucc.ie//published/T100005D/index.html (M1478.11) and (under 1477) in the *Annals of Loch Cé*: https://celt.ucc.ie//published/T100010B/index.html (LC1477.4). The provenance of the ship is not stated, although by the late-fifteenth century Ireland's west-coast ports were visited by merchant vessels from both Bristol and Spain: Wendy Childs and Timothy O'Neill, 'Overseas trade', in Cosgrove (ed.), *New history of Ireland, vol. 2*, 492–524: 504–5; Michael Bennett, 'Late medieval Ireland in a wider world', in Smith (ed.), *Cambridge history of Ireland, vol. 1*, 329–52: 348–9.

and Anglo-Irish, were prospering'.[311] That prosperity, however, was shallow and unevenly spread and the bulk of the country's small population lived in material poverty. Bioarchaeological evidence from the graveyard at Ballyhanna, near Ballyshannon, Co. Donegal, reveals a late-medieval predominantly Gaelic population characterised by poor life expectancy, nutrition and health.[312] In a country where power was so fragmented and personalised, peace and improved security were essential preconditions for demographic and economic recovery: when that began it must have done so as a piecemeal process dependent upon favourable local political circumstances. Meanwhile, developments in maritime technology were creating the potential for a sea-borne commercial revival, in which Ireland was geographically well placed to participate. Nevertheless, while European bullion supplies remained scarce and access to the Orient was obstructed by the emergent power of the Ottomans, there was little prospect of Ireland becoming swept up in the momentum of another continent-wide commercial revolution.[313] That would be delayed until the second half of the sixteenth century or, indeed, later.[314]

As the English author of the *Libelle of Englyshe polycye* acknowledged, mid-fifteenth century Ireland was endowed with an array of natural resources in relative abundance.[315] What was deficient, while international commerce remained slack, domestic demand limited and labour scarce, were the incentives to exploit them more intensively. By 1500, Dublin, still probably the largest Irish town, had a population of less than *c*.8,000, down from *c*.11,000 in 1290, and the share of the population living in towns of all sizes had also probably shrunk.[316]

---

[311] D.B. Quinn, 'Aristocratic autonomy, 1460–94', in Cosgrove (ed.), *New history of Ireland, vol. 2*, 591–618: 597; Ellis, *Tudor Ireland*, 39–40.

[312] Catriona McKenzie and Eileen Murphy, 'Health in medieval Ireland: the evidence from Ballyhanna, Co. Donegal', in Sheelagh Conran, Ed Danaher and Michael Stanley (eds), *Past times, changing fortunes* (Dublin, 2011), 131–43. The bulk of the skeletons date from 1200 to 1650 CE: C.J. McKenzie and E.M. Murphy, *Life and death in medieval Gaelic Ireland: the skeletons from Ballyhanna, Co. Donegal* (Dublin, 2018), 9–12.

[313] Campbell, *Great Transition*, 332–5, 364–73, 388–92.

[314] W.J. Smyth, *Map-making, landscapes and memory: a geography of colonial and early modern Ireland c.1530–1750* (Cork, 2006), 345–450; Raymond Gillespie, 'Economic life, 1550–1730' in Jane Ohlmeyer (ed.), *The Cambridge history of Ireland, vol. 2, 1550–1730* (Cambridge, 2018), 531–54; Francis Ludlow and Arlene Crampsie, 'Environmental history of Ireland, 1550–1730', in Ohlmeyer (ed.), *Cambridge history of Ireland, vol. 2*, 608–37: 611–13.

[315] The list of commodities comprises woollen and linen cloth and frieze; fells and fleeces of sheep, lambs and kids, cattle hides, harts' hides and 'other hides of venery', marten furs and the pelts and skins of rabbits, hares, foxes, squirrels and otters, and fish (salmon, hake and herring); all except cloth were the products of grazing, hunting, trapping and fishing: G. Warner (ed.), *The libelle of Englyshe polycye: a poem on the use of sea-power 1436* (Oxford, 1926), 34–6.

[316] H.B. Clarke, *Dublin, part I, to 1610*, Irish Historic Towns Atlas 11 (Dublin, 2002), 12. Available population estimates for Dublin are discussed in Murphy and Potterton, *Dublin region in the Middle Ages*, 30–1. For the numbers and sizes of Irish towns in 1290: Campbell, 'Benchmarking medieval economic development', 931.

Away from the handful of modestly prosperous walled coastal ports, urban demand was therefore of little consequence in shaping land-use and promoting agricultural specialisation. At a national scale, the country's low urbanisation ratio is symptomatic of economic underdevelopment and, by contemporary standards, of relatively low gross domestic product (GDP) per head.[317] Society therefore remained materially poor and overwhelmingly rural and agrarian; hence the paradox that, amidst seeming plenty, Ireland's population remained susceptible to weather-induced output failures. Fortunately, during the final decades of the fifteenth century few of these risks appear to have materialised.

In the absence of further significant volcanic forcing and as the Spörer Solar Minimum ended and the output of solar irradiance rose, environmental instability slowly subsided from its peak in the 1450s (Fig. 1 and Appendix 5). From the 1470s the NAO was back to close to normal strength and precipitation and temperatures had both recovered to near their long-term averages (Appendices 1–3). Once the difficult 1460s had passed, the worst years according to the Annals were 1478 and 1487. The first, a plague year, followed a VSSI of 5.12 Tg from a northern-hemisphere extratropical eruption the previous year and began with 'a mighty wind' on the the eve of the Epiphany [6 January] which 'laid low' 'men, cattle, trees, lake and land buildings...throughout Ireland'.[318] The rest of the year provided almost ideal growing conditions for Irish oaks, whereas according to the *Annals of Connacht, of Ulster, of Loch* Cé and *of the Four Masters* it was 'a hard, niggardly year' for crops.[319] As already noted, it was also a plague year.[320] Conditions were similar in 1487, with a 'great wind' on 24 February 'whereby many houses and churches were unroofed' and trees broken and then 'great inclemency of rain in the summer of this year, like a winter of inclemency, so that much of the crops of Ireland was destroyed thereby'.[321] More happily, 1471 (also following a northern hemisphere eruption—VSSI of 1.39 Tg—the previous year) was remembered for its hot summer, dry autumn

---

[317] On the positive association between urbanisation ratios and estimates of GDP per head in late-medieval Europe: B.M.S. Campbell, 'National incomes and economic growth in pre-industrial Europe: insights from recent research', *Quaestiones Medii Aevi Novae* 18 (2013), 167–96: 170–2.

[318] Lyons, 'Weather, famine, pestilence and plague', 71–2; Toohey and Sigl, 'Volcanic stratospheric sulfur injections'; (*Annals of Connacht*, also *of Ulster, of Loch* Cé, and *of the Four Masters*) Ludlow, 'Utility 2', 282–3. The summer of 1477 stands out as especially cold in the Scottish Cairngorms (Rydvale, '800 years') and both 1477 and 1478 are quite dry in the OWDA (Cook, 'Old World megadroughts').

[319] Lyons, 'Weather, famine, pestilence and plague', 71–2; Ludlow, 'Utility 2', 284.

[320] Above, p. 230.

[321] Lyons, 'Weather, famine, pestilence and plague', 71–2; 1487 (*Annals of Ulster*): Ludlow, 'Utility 2', 284. 1488 appears exceptionally wet across Ireland in the OWDA (Cook, 'Old World megadroughts').

and early harvest.[322] There would not be a summer as good from the perspective of the annalists for another 21 years.[323]

It was the 1490s that brought the most testing weather. Conditions were particularly bad in 1491, 'called by the natives the Dismal Year, by reason of the continual fall of rain all the summer and autumn'.[324] The year began with a blast of Arctic cold admitted by a weak NAO; in Burgundy a cool summer delayed the Pinot Noir grape harvest, and in Ireland persistent wet weather ruined that year's harvest.[325] This ensured that a great famine (*Ascalt mor a n-Erinn*) followed in 1492, which was also, as noted by the *Annals of Ulster*, memorable for its hot summer.[326] The first of three consecutive years of drought, it was a conspicuously narrow-ring year for oaks in Ireland as across Europe.[327] By 1494 or early 1495, wheat and beef were sold at elevated prices in Drogheda.[328] Worse was to follow: in 1496 (a wide-ring year for oaks, implying abundant spring–summer precipitation) a 'great inclemency' of weather prevailed.[329] This brought

---

[322] Toohey and Sigl, 'Volcanic stratospheric sulfur injections'. 1471 (*Annals of Ulster*): Ludlow, 'Utility 2', 279. The *Annals of Connacht* usefully add 'An abundant nut-crop this year; the summer and autumn very dry and all the crops very early'. The OWDA confirms moderate spring–summer dryness this year (Cook, 'Old World megadroughts').

[323] 1492 re. 1471 (*Annals of Ulster*): 'A hot summer this year; to wit, a year and twenty since the hot summer before': Ludlow, 'Utility 2', 285.

[324] 'William Wilde's table of Irish famines', 7.

[325] Ortega, 'Model-tested North Atlantic Oscillation reconstruction'. Isabelle Chuine *et al.*, 'Burgundy grape harvest dates and spring–summer temperature reconstruction' (2005), IGBP PAGES/World Data Center for Paleoclimatology Data Contribution Series, NOAA/NCDC Paleoclimatology Program, Boulder CO, USA # 2005-007, http://www.ncdc.noaa.gov/paleo/paleo.html. Ludlow, 'Utility 2', 285: 1491 (*Annals of Ulster*, also *of the Four Masters*): 'Great inclemency of wetness during the greater part of the summer of this year and the self-same in harvest of the same year, so that likeness to the extent of the inclemency was not found since the Deluge poured upon the world, so that the corn of all Ireland, save a little, failed and particularly in Fermanagh' [this year the OWDA appears in rare contradiction to the Annals, with spring–summer 1491 registering notably dry (Cook, 'Old World megadroughts')]. The *Annals of Ulster* also report a major windstorm, though without explicitly associated impacts. Summer 1491 was cold in Scotland: Rydvale, '800 years'.

[326] 'William Wilde's table of Irish famines', 7; Lyons, 'Weather, famine, pestilence and plague', 72; 1492 (*Annals of Ulster*): 'Great famine in Ireland this year': Ludlow, 'Utility 2', 285.

[327] Cook, 'Old World megadroughts'.

[328] Reported under 1494, but using Annunciation ('Old Style') dating, meaning that these conditions may also pertain to the first months of 1495 (up to 24 March): Diarmuid Mac Iomhair, 'Two old Drogheda chronicles', *Journal of the County Louth Archaeological Society* 15:1 (1961), 88–95: 92.

[329] Confirmed by the OWDA, with a notably wet spring–summer in 1496: Cook, 'Old World megadroughts'. In Dublin the River Poddle caused serious flooding: J.H. Bernard, 'Calendar of documents contained in the chartulary commonly called "*Dignitas decani*" of St Patrick's Cathedral', *Proceedings of the Royal Irish Academy* 25C (1904–5), 481–507: 491; Peter Crooks (ed.), *A calendar of Irish chancery letters, c. 1244–1509*, Patent Roll 11 Henry VII, §30: https://chancery.tcd.ie/document/patent/11-henry-vii/30.

'enormous destruction on beeves and on other cattle also' and inflicted 'great dearth [on] the greater part of Ireland ... and great hindrance on the husbandry of the year ... whereby everyone in general was ruined in his crops'.[330] This led in 1497 to a 'very great, grievous famine throughout all Ireland ... to which the folk of this time saw not the equal, nor like; for there was scarce an angle or recess in all Ireland wherein died not many persons of that hunger'.[331] Faced with starvation, according to the *Annals of the Four Masters*, 'people ate of food unbecoming to mention, and never before heard of as having been introduced on human dishes', with these desperate conditions persisting into 1498.[332] The language of the Annals leaves little doubt of the magnitude and severity of this event which unfolded over a Biblical seven years.

The run of adverse meteorological conditions that triggered the 1497–8 food crisis had more to do with bad luck than any specific forcing event or climate anomaly. No volcanic eruption was culpable and all fell within the statistical norms of Ireland's variable maritime climate. Nor was this in any sense a 'Malthusian crisis', for the population had shrunk to no more than 0.75 million and resources per head were abundant.[333] That, on the testimony of the Annals, so many should have been affected so grievously therefore bears witness to Irish society's lack of resilience to weather-induced output shortfalls at this time: storage was limited, wealth polarised, charity localised and unequal to the scale of the challenge, organised relief effectively absent and faith in divine intervention too blind.[334] On this occasion, agricultural production systems well adapted to the climatic norm fell disastrously short when confronted by a close succession of far-from-unprecedented meteorological extremes. The conditions of 1497–8 can thus be posited as a famine borne not from overpopulation but from underdevelopment. In this sense, the famine of 1497–8 and many others beforehand can also be more clearly seen as a failure of production than of distribution.[335]

Only by evolving more effective institutions of government and administration, developing more efficient markets and networks of distribution,

---

[330] 'William Wilde's table of Irish famines', 7; 1496 (*Annals of Ulster*): Ludlow, 'Utility 2', 287.

[331] 'William Wilde's table of Irish famines', 7; Lyons, 'Weather, famine, pestilence and plague', 72–3. 1497 (*Annals of Ulster*, also *of Loch Cé, of Connacht*, and *of the Four Masters*): Ludlow, 'Utility 2', 288.

[332] Ludlow, 'Utility 2', 288.

[333] Raymond Gillespie, *The transformation of the Irish economy, 1550–1700* (Dundalk, 1991), 12–3.

[334] For comment on how adaptation to extremes may be hampered by a belief in divine intervention: J. Haldon *et al.*, 'Demystifying collapse: climate, environment, and social agency in pre-modern societies', *Millennium* 17:1 (2020), doi: 10.1515/mill-2020-0002. Also, Ludlow and Travis, 'STEAM approaches to climate change', 56–8.

[335] Guido Alfani and Cormac Ó Gráda, 'The timing and causes of famines in Europe', *Nature Sustainability* 1 (2018), 283–8.

investing in the infrastructures of transport and storage, diversifying economic output, raising levels of agricultural productivity and putting in place practical welfare measures—achievements that did follow in later centuries—would society slowly escape the tyranny of the weather. In these respects, at this midway point in the second millennium, Irish society was little more advanced than it had been at the beginning of that millennium when it had been hit so hard by the scarcities of 1004 and 1047. At no point during the intervening centuries had it enjoyed sufficient food security to withstand the potentially harmful effects of sustained runs of adverse meteorological conditions or individual extremes of great (but not necessarily exceptional) magnitude. Late-medieval Ireland was a country inescapably in thrall to episodic subsistence crises, the worst of which escalated into famines displaying many or all of the attributes itemised by Cormac Ó Gráda as characteristic of such catastrophes.[336]

Conclusion—extreme weather, famine, violence and plague in late-medieval Ireland

Gerald of Wales's characterisation of Ireland's temperate and healthy, wet and windy, climate as essentially extreme free is belied by the testimony of the Annals.[337] Over the 500 years surveyed in this paper, they record rivers and lakes frozen so hard that flocks and herds could pass over them, summers so hot and droughts so severe that the River Shannon could be forded on foot, harvest seasons that were a washout, floods that swept away bridges, mills and houses, lightning strikes that ignited and destroyed buildings, hail storms with stones the size of crab apples, and great winds that toppled steeples and sank ships.[338] None of this should be a surprise, for Ireland's climate is also marginal in terms of its exposure to fluctuations in the rival strengths of maritime and continental, Atlantic and Arctic, pressure systems as mediated by solar and volcanic forcing and the internal dynamic of the multidecadal Atlantic climate variability.[339] Also, all climates are capable of throwing up random extremes and Ireland's is no exception. Its annalists plainly took grim and sometimes even moralising delight in recording those freak meteorological events responsible for bizarre deaths, as in 1134 when the *Annals of Tigernach* recorded that 'the Kindred of Eoghan of Tulach Óc conspired against Mael Maedhóig and a flash of lightning consumed twelve men of them on the spot where they conspired against him'.[340] Or in 1177 when the same Annals described 'a mighty outbreak of water, for greatness resembling a mountain, [that] went through the midst of Glendalough [Co. Wicklow], carried away the bridge and mill of the town and left some of its fish amid the town. Then it entered Inbhear Mór [Arklow, Co. Wicklow], drowned

---

[336] Ó Gráda, *Famine*, 7; above, note 127.
[337] Gerald of Wales, *History and topography of Ireland*, 34–5, 53–4.
[338] As exemplified above and abundantly detailed in Ludlow, 'Utility 2'.
[339] Jianglin Wang *et al.*, 'Internal and external forcing of multidecadal Atlantic climate variability over the past 1,200 years', *Nature Geoscience* 10:7 (2017), 512–17.
[340] Ludlow, 'Utility 2', 179–80.

the fisherman, and swept his net into the sea'.[341] In both cases the victims were unlucky enough to be in the wrong place at the wrong time.

Nevertheless, intervention by the weather to overtly facilitate or shape the course and outcome of major historical events was altogether more exceptional.[342] That was the case in a small way during the bitter winter of 1433–4 when the inhabitants of Fermanagh were able to escape from an army led by the O'Neill by fleeing westwards with their cattle and moveables across an ice-bound Lough Erne.[343] More crucially, it is interesting to speculate what the counterfactual of the ill-timed Scottish invasion of 1315–18 might have been, and what direction Irish history might consequently have taken, had the attempted conquest not coincided so exactly with the worst years of the Dantean Anomaly.[344] As it was, the devastating combination of war, bad weather and back-to-back harvest failure, followed within three years by the rinderpest panzootic, ensured that the famine of 1315–18 was one of the greatest, if not the greatest, to have afflicted late-medieval Irish society.[345] Moreover, largely because of the reinforcing effect of the Bruce invasion, it stands out as perhaps the only late-medieval famine to have had an unambiguously enduring historical impact.

Famines—*gorta, gorta mór*—punctuate the record of the Annals and are the most explicit demonstration of the negative impact that extreme weather could have upon Irish society. What exactly Ireland's annalists meant by the term *gorta* they do not define but from the contexts in which it appears it was clearly intended to convey the extreme hardship that arose from acute hunger and starvation, with all the desperate nutritional, economic and criminal measures to which its victims might resort. Thus, the *Chronicon Scotorum* provides an unusually graphic description of one such famine in 1116: 'Great famine [*Gorta mor*] in the spring so that a man would sell his son and his daughter for food and men would even eat one another, and dogs'.[346] Modern definitions of famine are tighter. Specifically, Ó Gráda has defined famine as 'A shortage of food or purchasing power that leads directly to excess mortality from starvation or

---

[341] Ludlow, 'Utility 2', 194.
[342] For later examples of such interventions: Ludlow and Crampsie, 'Environmental history of Ireland, 1550–1730', 627–36; and Francis Ludlow and Arlene Crampsie, 'Climate, debt and conflict: environmental history as a new direction in understanding early modern Ireland', in Sarah Covington, Vincent Carey and Valerie McGowan-Doyle (eds), *Early modern Ireland: new sources, methods, and directions* (London, 2019), 269–300: 278–90.
[343] Ludlow, 'Utility 2', 272–4.
[344] McNamee, *Wars of the Bruces*, 166–205.
[345] The costs in the Dublin region of wet weather and flooding, opportunistic Gaelic raiding, and the burden of sustaining the king's forces in transit to fight the Scots are reflected in detail in Crooks, *Calendar of Irish chancery letters*, Close Role 9 Edward II, §1 (16 December 1315): https://chancery.tcd.ie/document/close/9-edward-ii/1. For the impacts of harvest failure, devastating Scottish raids and rinderpest upon northern England: Ian Kershaw, *Bolton Priory: the economy of a northern monastery 1286–1325* (Oxford, 1973); McNamee, *Wars of the Bruces*, 72–122.
[346] Ludlow, 'Utility 2', 173–4.

hunger-induced diseases'.[347] Of the many famines reported in the Annals only a minority unequivocally meet the criterion of excess mortality on the basis of the descriptions given.[348] One such is that reported in the *Annals of Loch Cé* for 1227: 'a great famine in this year; and people died of it'.[349] The number that died, however, is never indicated. In a rare entry for 1271, the *Annals of Inisfallen* state that 'multitudes of poor people died of cold and hunger'.[350] Another for 1497 in the *Annals of Ulster* says 'there was scarce an angle or recess in all Ireland wherein died not many persons of that hunger'.[351] In two cases alone between 1000 and 1500 CE, specifically the famines of 1116 and 1315–18, the annalists state that the starving populations made resort to cannibalism, which, irrespective of whether it was true, reveals that in the minds of the annalists these were particularly terrible events when normal taboos and moral scruples were abandoned.[352]

Famine is often regarded as a symptom of Malthusian demographic pressure upon scarce resources, but it is difficult to interpret any of late-medieval Ireland's subsistence crises and famines in such narrowly economic terms. In fact, when famine struck Ulster in 1004 and 1047 and Ireland in 1497, the fundamental problem may have been more a deficit than a surfeit of people.[353] The crises of 1270–1, 1294–6 and 1315–18 alone coincide with the period when Ireland's population may have risen to a historically modest total of around 1.25 to 1.5 million and when, on the evidence of the oak dendrochronology dataset (Fig. 5), available landed resources were coming under pressure.[354] But the deteriorating political, fiscal and military situation in the English Lordship was also a significant contributing factor. Rather, insofar as famine in late-medieval Ireland had a common denominator, it was the negative impact of extreme weather (particularly in back-to-back years) upon agricultural production, often to the detriment of arable output, sometimes to that of pastoral output (especially when hard winters depressed grass growth or access to foggage and sent livestock mortality soaring), and occasionally to both. Thus, in 1115–16 and again in 1294–6

---

[347] Ó Gráda, *Famine*, 4; also, Alfani and Ó Gráda, *Famine in European history*, 2.

[348] Cormac Ó Gráda, 'Ireland', in Alfani and Ó Gráda, *Famine in European history*, 166–84, omits systematic discussion and evaluation of the annalistic record of Irish famines.

[349] Ludlow, 'Utility 2', 212–3.

[350] Ludlow, 'Utility 2', 236.

[351] Ludlow, 'Utility 2', 288.

[352] Ludlow, 'Utility 2', 173–4, 244–53; Ó Gráda, *Eating people is wrong*, 14–16, 26. The same trope was used in four separate chronicles for 700 CE, as in the case of the *Annals of Clonmacnoise* (a.k.a. *Mageoghagan's Book*): 'There was such famine and scarcity in Ireland for three years together, that men and women did eat one another for want': Ludlow, 'Utility 2', 60–2.

[353] Above, pp. 179, 182, and 233–4.

[354] Alfani and Ó Gráda ('Timing and causes', 283) make the general point that in Europe 'up to 1710, the main clusters of famines occurred in periods of historically high population density'.

it was grain-growing Leinster that appears worst affected, whereas in 1203 and 1227 famine was widely reported by annals with a focus on Clonmacnoise and Connacht, which implies that the grazing districts of the Shannon valley and east Connacht were experiencing difficulties. Similarly, in 1433 the *Annals of Loch Cé*, *of the Four Masters* and *of Ulster* all carried reports of the summer of scarcity in regions that were predominantly pastoral.

The recorded experience of food scarcity is, of course, chronologically uneven, not least because some periods were climatically more unsettled than others and the patterns of atmospheric circulation that determined Ireland's weather changed over time (Fig. 1). The available annalistic coverage is also intrinsically uneven, in terms of survival and the attention paid to extreme weather events and their repercussions for humans by individual annalists (Fig.2). Consequently, absence of any mention of food crises, as most conspicuously for the 60 years from 1339 until 1397, does not necessarily mean that none occurred, unless in this case the better wages and improved living standards that followed the Black Death provided some respite.[355] Certainly, at no point does late-medieval Ireland appear to have escaped more than temporarily from a state of chronic food insecurity, as evidenced by the recurrence of famine in 1203, 1227, 1236, 1263 and 1270–1 during a period that was otherwise favourable to demographic and commercial expansion (Fig. 6). War was certainly an important contributory factor, especially given that from the outset the English Lordship had a contested military border, aggressively expanding until the late-thirteenth century and contracting thereafter.[356] The nutritional deficiencies sustained by those repeatedly exposed to such food crises is writ large in the stunted and malnourished skeletons excavated from the late-medieval graveyards at Ballyhanna, Co. Donegal, and Ardreigh, Co. Kildare.[357] Dearth was the periodic lot of all those who made up the humble majority and when conditions were at their worst and dearth escalated into famine, mortality evidently soared. As recorded by the Annals, those faced with starvation typically resorted to desperate measures: flight (that could itself engender conflict and the spread of infection), the selling off of assets (including children into slavery), trading down to substitute and sub-standard foodstuffs and, for those with the weapons and audacity, theft, rustling, plunder and pillage.

It did not help that from the late-twelfth to the early-fourteenth centuries the weather in Ireland and England was so closely synchronised that years

---

[355] An order dated 26 August 1349 to the mayor and bailiffs of Dublin is certainly concerned that 'working men and servants' might, as in England, seek to work only 'for excessive wages' following the first onset of the Black Death, and should be penalised in such cases: Crooks, *Calendar of Irish chancery letters*, Close Role 23 Edward III, §17: https://chancery.tcd.ie/document/close/23-edward-iii/17.

[356] For example, the 1227 famine as it pertained to Connacht: Finan, *Landscape and history*.

[357] McKenzie and Murphy, 'Health in medieval Ireland'; McKenzie and Murphy, *Life and death in medieval Gaelic Ireland*, 394–401.

of scarcity in Ireland typically coincided with problem years in England. Since England was Ireland's nearest source of relief grain supplies, this meant that it was least able to supply them when Ireland's need was greatest. Worse, in common crisis years the greater pulling power of the more commercialised and monetised English market, coupled, during England's Welsh, Scottish and French wars, with heavy demands from the royal purveyors for victuals to provision the king's armies overseas, may have caused the normal net exodus of grain, meat and butter from Ireland to persist and what little came in the opposite direction is likely to have remained within the confines of Ireland's port towns, thereby providing scant relief to those in the country's rural interior.[358] At such times the prospects of Ireland receiving substitute food supplies from elsewhere were negligible and society had to get by on whatever, domestically, was available.

De facto, the food crises and famines that punctuate Ireland's late-medieval history underline the want of resilience that might have prevailed had there been greater solidarity between Gaels and Galls, more effective central government, heavier investment in storage facilities and transport infrastructures, more extensive market arbitrage and integration, fuller involvement and greater security in international trade and diplomacy, more generous endowment of charitable institutions, mature land and credit markets, and greater diversification of economic output.[359] Remedies to shortage were not absent but they were imperfectly and unevenly developed and too easily undone by political breakdown. Whatever resilience society may have possessed was also likely to be wholly undermined by the calamity of war, with its demands for manpower and pre-emptive claims on scarce revenues and provisions, threat to law and order, and destruction of capital goods, productive capacity and dis-inducement to investment.[360]

Personal violence, raiding, rustling and pillaging, war and invasion all loom large in the history of late-medieval Ireland and were fostered from 1169 by the intrinsic divisions between Gaels and Galls, the fragmented and personalised

---

[358] Between 1280 and 1300 the limited available price evidence indicates that 'wheat prices in Dublin moved in a similar way to those in England' but with a premium in most years in favour of England: Murphy and Potterton, *Dublin region in the middle ages*, 478.

[359] In England, government efforts to alleviate food crises began in response to the Great Northern European Famine, 1315–7, in the reign of Edward II: Buchanan Sharp, 'Royal paternalism and the moral economy in the reign of Edward II: the response to the Great Famine', *Economic History Review* 66:2 (2013), 628–47. For the political obstacles to such initiatives in Ireland: Art Cosgrove, 'Ireland', in Christopher Allmand (ed.), *The new Cambridge medieval history: vol. VII, c.1415–c.1500* (Cambridge, 1998), 496–513: 510.

[360] On, e.g., the punitive effects of the system of 'coign and livery': Art Cosgrove, 'The Gaelic resurgence and the Geraldine supremacy: c. 1400–1534', in T.W. Moody and F.X. Martin (eds), *The course of Irish History* (Cork, 2011, new edition), 136–150: 137–8. Conducting overseas trade and diplomacy also faced considerable challenges: Brendan Smith, *Crisis and survival in late medieval Ireland: the English of Louth and their neighbours, 1330–1450* (Cambridge, 2013), 169.

nature of authority, and the fluctuating commitment of the English crown to its Irish Lordship. What is less widely recognised by historians is that Irish society's inclination towards violence in multiple forms and at a variety of scales was stoked, not just incidentally but repeatedly (Appendix 6), by hardship and scarcity. James Lydon plainly understood the connection. He considered the 1270–1 harvest crisis to be the catalyst that prompted the Irish of the Wicklow Mountains to raid the vacant archdiocese of Dublin's neighbouring lowland manors and thought it 'no coincidence that when [in 1294] Gaelic Leinster once more rose in rebellion, it was in the year of another great famine'.[361] Even in relatively law-abiding societies supply-side output failures of food and essential raw materials might prompt resort to crime (usually against property), protest, riot and violence.[362] When public authority failed and the moral economies of charitable giving and mutual social support broke down there was an even greater danger that those possessing the necessary armed might would take advantage of the situation and seek plunder, booty and ransom.

If dated volcanic eruptions are taken as a proxy for depressed growing conditions arising from sudden severe short-term climate forcing, the statistical analyses presented in Appendix 6 suggests that violence and war tended to follow in the train of bad weather and poor harvests and thereby greatly magnified the latters' social and economic consequences.[363] This locked society into a self-perpetuating cycle whereby weather-induced output shortfalls promoted lawlessness and lawlessness, in turn, eroded society's resilience to output shortfalls and thereby further endorsed the resort to violence at times of need. Eventually, by the fifteenth century, rustling and raiding had become almost a way of life in the thinly peopled livestock-farming regions of the Gaelic north and west.[364] By then patterns of atmospheric circulation had shifted with the result that years that were bad for England were no longer necessarily bad for Ireland and vice versa. This climatic divergence is manifest in the reduced and at times negligible or even negative correlation between the ring widths of Irish and southern-English oaks (Fig. 4). It was also the case that as the Irish agrarian economy became more pastoral, the hard winter weather that proved most challenging for Irish pastoral producers carried little penalty for English grain producers, who had most to fear from the wet spring and summer weather that was so favourable to grass growth.

---

[361] Lydon, 'Land of war', 256–7, 260. Also, Simms, 'Political recovery of Gaelic Ireland', 275.

[362] Campbell, 'Nature as historical protagonist', 291–2, 296; Guido Alfani, Luca Mocarelli and Donatella Strangio, 'Italy', in Alfani and Ó Gráda, *Famine in European history*, 25–47: 42–3; for scarcity driven violence and rioting in fourteenth century Dublin: Finbarr Dwyer, *Witches, spies and Stockholm syndrome: life in medieval Ireland* (Dublin, 2013).

[363] Ludlow and Travis, 'STEAM approaches to climate change'.

[364] K.W. Nicholls, 'Gaelic society and economy in the high middle ages', in Cosgrove (ed.), *New history of Ireland, vol. 2*, 397–438: 413–15.

Climate, disease and society in late-medieval Ireland

Nevertheless, the vital game-changing development, which in the mid-fourteenth century had sent Ireland's population plunging, with far-reaching consequences for the country's social, economic and political structures, was neither climate nor war *per se* but disease. It was the transformation of the epidemiological environment by the arrival of bubonic plague (*Yersinia pestis*) that gainsaid Gerald of Wales's earlier portrayal of Ireland as a healthy country and initiated a new demographic era dominated by high morbidity, high mortality and negative replacement rates.[365] The deaths of eminent individuals had always preoccupied Ireland's annalists and plague's deadly onset and frequent reappearances ensured that they had plenty to record, as the great and the good succumbed in sometimes dramatic numbers.[366] To add grist to their mill, social opportunism thrived on the sudden death from plague or other diseases of those holding important or administrative office and allowed 'new' families to rise to prominence, sometimes irrespective of their cultural origins.[367] In effect, such mortality crises might engender a 'state of exception', in which normal conventions and cultural norms were temporarily suspended, allowing room for potentially rapid social and political change.[368]

Plague's devastating impact upon population levels in Ireland, both immediately and in the long term, is also writ large in the changes to land use which then ensued. After 250–300 years when woodland had been in more-or-less

---

[365] Between 1150 and 1249 annalistic references to extreme weather outnumber those to epidemic disease by approximately 7.5 to 1.0; by the less-healthy fifteenth century that ratio narrows to 2 to 1 (Fig. 2).

[366] For examnple, in 1489 the *Annals of the Four Masters* (also *of Ulster*) (https://celt.ucc.ie//published/T100005D/index.html (M1489.3-5)) reported: 'A great plague [raged] this year, of which great numbers died. It was so devastating that people did not bury the dead throughout Ireland. Redmond, the son of Owny, son of Farrell, son of Thomas, son of Mahon, son of Gilla-Isa Roe O'Reilly, died of it. Felim Oge, the son of Felim, son of Farrell, son of Thomas, son of Mahon, son of Gilla-Isa Roe O'Reilly; Donnell, the son of Torna O'Mulconry, intended Ollav of Sil-Murray; Donnell Cananach i.e the Canon, the son of Teige O'Birn; Cormac O'Conolly, head of the gallowglasses of O'Conor's rear guard; Ineen-duv, the daughter of O'Conor, i.e. Donough the black-eyed; Hugh Boy and Donnell Caech, two sons of O'Hanly; Rury Glas, the son of Rory, son of Mac Hugh; Mac Donough Reagh, i.e. Hugh; and Finola, the daughter of Mac Dermot Roe, all died of the plague'.

[367] A.S.K. Abraham, 'Upward mobility and seigneurial residences in late medieval Meath' in Arlene Crampsie and Francis Ludlow (eds), *Meath history and society: interdisciplinary essays on the history of an Irish county* (Dublin, 2015), 149–76. For upward mobility by families with Gaelic ancestry within the English Lordship: Sparky Booker, *Cultural exchange and identity in late medieval Ireland: the English and Irish of the four obedient shires* (Cambridge, 2018), 52–96.

[368] On the 'state of exception': Michael R. Dove, *Anthropology of climate change: an historical reader* (Chichester, 2014), 18. A concrete example is given by Jacqueline S. Solway, 'Drought as a revelatory crisis: an exploration of shifting entitlements and hierarchies in the Kalahari, Botswana', *Development and Change* 25 (1994), 471–95.

continuous retreat, the dendrochronological record implies that in the immediate aftermath of the Black Death oaks began to regenerate in increasing numbers, with regeneration accelerating following the fourth major plague outbreak in 1382–5 (Fig. 5). The upshot was that by the mid-fifteenth century Ireland was once again, albeit unevenly, a well-wooded country, with a rich store of timber upon which later builders would be able to draw (Fig. 5).[369] Without the negative and recurrent biological shock inflicted by plague, such a far-reaching landscape transformation (matched, moreover, by a corresponding re-advance of woodland across Europe) would be inexplicable.[370]

Plague, nevertheless, did not act independently of climate and herein, arguably, lies the most profound, if indirect, influence of the weather upon late-medieval Irish society. Plague's ancient reservoir regions in the semi-arid Asian interior were as much exposed to the changes in atmospheric circulation patterns set in motion from the late-thirteenth century as Ireland. The heightened ecological stress generated by abrupt swings from droughts to pluvials and then, suddenly, back to drought reactivated plague from its long dormant enzootic mode and propelled it on its westward migratory course.[371] By 1346, at the climax of a global climate anomaly, the disease had reached the Crimea and crossed over to become a deadly and fast-spreading human pandemic, reaching southern England and eastern Ireland almost simultaneously in 1348. Thereafter, with a ten to twelve-year lag, climatic conditions in newly-established plague reservoirs in inner Eurasia, especially the Caspian Basin, triggered successive reintroductions of the disease to Europe and eventually Ireland.[372]

At the same time, by means not yet fully understood, plague succeeded in maintaining itself within Europe, where it circulated between cities and especially ports and assumed the character of a recurrent background disease with frequent localised outbreaks of the sort reported in the Annals. Contemporaries had good reason to fear cool European summers and poor grain harvests as liable to provoke outbreaks of plague, whereas warm summers and abundant harvests diminished that risk (Appendix 7).[373] Often Ireland was on the receiving end of plague outbreaks that had originated elsewhere, triggered by weather effects and harvest shortfalls that had occurred beyond its shores. The deadly plague outbreak that ravaged Dublin and its hinterland in 1439 is a case in point. In England and Europe this

---

[369] Baillie, *New light*, 15–25; Nicholls, 'Woodland cover', 202–3.
[370] Campbell, *Great Transition*, 312–13; Kaplan, Krumhardt and Zimmermann, 'Prehistoric and preindustrial deforestation', 3023; Ljungqvist, 'Linking European building activity with plague history'.
[371] Campbell, *Great Transition*, 227–30; Kausrud, 'Modeling the epidemiological history of plague in Central Asia'.
[372] Schmid, 'Climate-driven introduction of the Black Death'.
[373] Above, notes 235, 238–9.

erupted in the immediate aftermath of the dreadful weather and back-to-back harvest shortfall of 1437–8.[374] Yet whereas Ireland appears to have been spared that harvest catastrophe it did not escape the continent-wide plague epidemic that followed in its wake and which likely levied a heavy toll on the country's already much diminished population.[375]

Plague in late-medieval Ireland, like famine, is more easily described than quantified. More can certainly be learnt about both from a closer critical engagement with the Annals and other sources, especially those emanating from the English administration in Ireland. Placing that record in the context of the more detailed and quantifiable evidence for England and other adjacent parts of Europe is also revealing. Bioarchaeology, as the excavated graveyards of Ballyhanna and Ardreigh have demonstrated, can also shed unique light on the health, nourishment and life expectancy of the majority of ordinary Irish people in whose fortunes and fates the annalists took such little individual interest.[376] Dendrochronology, too, can provide a chronological framework for contextualising these categories of information. Ireland's oak chronology spans a temporal range at a resolution and standard of chronological accuracy unmatched by any extant historical sources, even the island's remarkable Annals. Pollen preserved in peat bogs, sediments deposited in freshwater lakes, and speleothems formed in the country's many limestone caves are further natural archives from which palaeoclimatic information can potentially be extracted. It is therefore to be anticipated that future research will greatly add to the range of evidence currently available.

This essay therefore offers no more than a first pass at what combining this wealth of evidence from historical and natural archives can eventually reveal about the interactions between climate, disease and society throughout half a millennium when the global patterns of atmospheric circulation that determined Ireland's climate changed profoundly. It reveals an economically under-developed and mostly materially poor society, deficient in food security and, in its Gaelic regions, employing farming methods that exposed it cruelly to weather extremes. Scarcity and famine consequently remained periodically inescapable facts of life, to which violence of one form or another was a normative response. Across these five centuries, breaking this socially corrosive and economically destructive pattern of cause and effect was never long achieved. Nevertheless, it was plague, like violence often an indirect outcome of the weather, which from 1348 had the more decisive and enduring impact.

---

[374] Campbell, 'Grain yields on English demesnes', 153–4; Campbell and Ó Gráda, 'Harvest shortfalls', 870–3; Alfani and Ó Gráda, 'Famines in Europe', 8–9. As well as Ireland, plague was reported in Italy, Iberia, France, the Low Countries, Germany and Austria and Scandinavia: Biraben, *Les hommes et la peste*, vol. 1, 363–74.
[375] *Annals of the Four Masters,* 1439 (https://celt.ucc.ie//published/T100005D/index.html (M1439.16).
[376] McKenzie and Murphy, *Life and death in medieval Gaelic Ireland*, 388.

For all these reasons it is time that historians of late-medieval Ireland begin to take the weather seriously. The climate may scarcely have impinged overtly upon affairs of state and only exceptionally, as in the case of Edward Bruce, unambiguously compromised the grand schemes of ambitious men, but its effects upon the lives and livelihoods of ordinary people and the types and levels of adversity with which they had to contend were profound.

Appendices

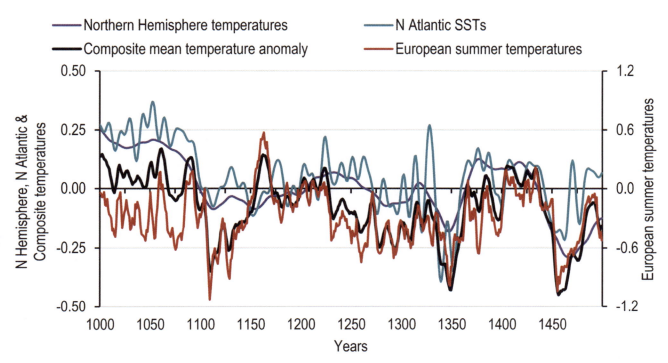

APPENDIX 1—Northern hemisphere temperatures, North Atlantic sea-surface temperatures, European summer temperatures (5 year moving average) and a composite mean temperature series (11 year moving average).

Sources: M.E. Mann *et al.*, 'Proxy-based reconstructions of hemispheric and global surface temperature variations over the past two millennia', *Proceedings of the National Academy of Sciences* 105:36 (2008), 13252–57. Data: www.ncdc.noaa.gov/paleo/metadata/noaa-recon-6252.html.

J. Luterbacher *et al.*, 'European summer temperatures since Roman times', *Environmental Research Letters* 11:2 (2016), L024001. Data: www.ncdc.noaa.gov/paleo/study/19600. Accessed 19/08/2016.

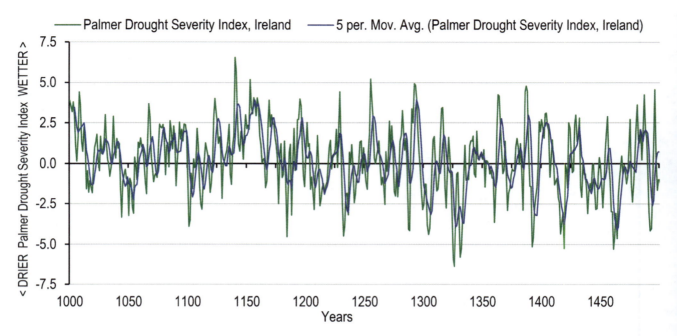

APPENDIX 2—Growing-season (i.e., spring–summer) soil moisture in Ireland according to the Old World Drought Atlas (OWDA).

Source: Data from E.R. Cook *et al.*, 'Old World megadroughts and pluvials during the Common Era', *Science Advances* 1:10 (2015), e1500561. doi: 10.1126/sciadv.1500561.

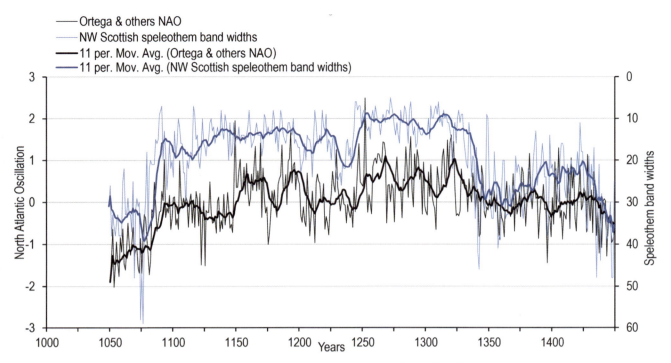

APPENDIX 3—Scottish speleothem band widths and the North Atlantic Oscillation (NAO).

Sources: Pablo Ortega *et al.*, 'A model-tested North Atlantic Oscillation reconstruction for the past millennium', *Nature* 523:7558 (2015), 71–4. Data: www.ncdc.noaa.gov/paleo/study/18935.

C.J. Proctor, A. Baker and W.L. Barnes, 'A three thousand year record of North Atlantic climate', *Climate Dynamics* 19:5–6 (2002), 449–54. Data: www.ncdc.noaa.gov/paleo/study/5418.

Bruce M.S. Campbell and Francis Ludlow

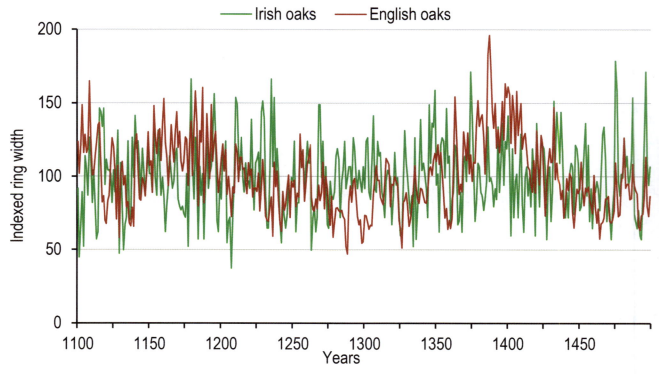

APPENDIX 4—Ring widths of Irish oaks and southern English oaks.
Source: Data supplied by M.G.L. Baillie and David Brown.

Climate, disease and society in late-medieval Ireland

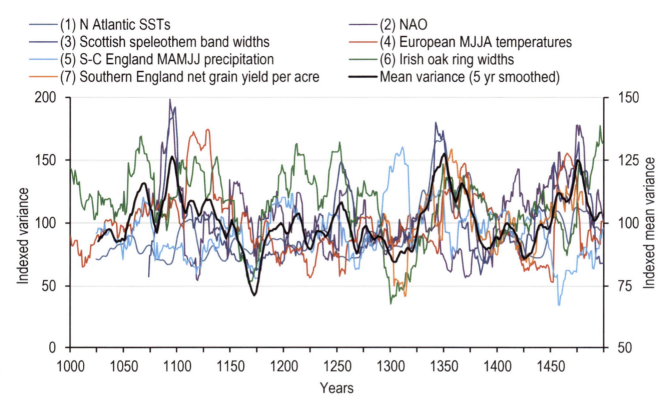

Appendix 5—Index of Environmental Instability.

Note: the variance of each dataset has been standardised.

Sources:

(1) M.E. Mann *et al.*, 'Proxy-based reconstructions of hemispheric and global surface temperature variations over the past two millennia', *Proceedings of the National Academy of Sciences* 105:36 (2008), 13252–57. Data: www.ncdc.noaa.gov/paleo/metadata/noaa-recon-6252.html.

(2) Pablo Ortega *et al.*, 'A model-tested North Atlantic Oscillation reconstruction for the past millennium', *Nature* 523:7558 (2015), 71–4. Data: www.ncdc.noaa.gov/paleo/study/18935.

(3) C.J. Proctor, A. Baker and W.L. Barnes, 'A three thousand year record of North Atlantic Climate', *Climate Dynamics* 19:5–6 (2002), 449–54. Data: www.ncdc.noaa.gov/paleo/study/5418.

(4) J. Luterbacher *et al.*, 'European summer temperatures since Roman times', *Environmental Research Letters*, 11:2 (2016), L024001. Data: www.ncdc.noaa.gov/paleo/study/19600. Accessed 19/08/2016.

(5) R. Wilson *et al.*, 'A millennial long March–July precipitation reconstruction for southern-central England'. *Climate Dynamics*, 40:3–4 (2012), 997–1017. www.ncdc.noaa.gov/paleo/study/12907. Accessed 19/08/2016.

(6) Irish mean master oak-ring chronology supplied by M.G.L. Baillie (2003).

(7) B.M.S. Campbell and Cormac Ó Gráda, 'Harvest shortfalls, grain prices, and famines in pre-industrial England', *Journal of Economic History* 71:4 (2011), 859–86.

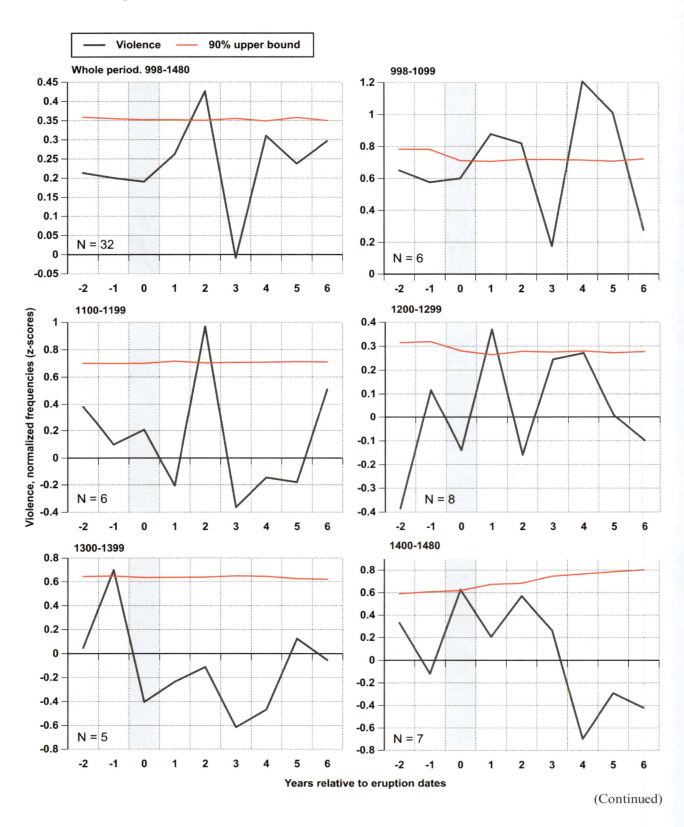

APPENDIX 6—Superposed epoch analyses (SEA) of a broad spectrum of violence reported in the *Annals of Ulster*, 998–1499 CE, relative to a polar ice-core-based reconstruction of volcanic climate forcing.

Notes and sources: Violence included in the analyses range from individual murders and homicides to mass killings and large-scale armed attacks on properties and territories reported in the *Annals of Ulster*. Each year's value is normalised according to the mean and standard deviation of itself and the previous 49 years, in order to ensure statistical comparability in the response to volcanic eruptions throughout the period under consideration.

The analysis focuses upon 32 major explosive eruptions with a VSSI of at least 1.0 Tg (an estimate of volcanic sulphate injected into the stratosphere, reflecting climate-forcing potential, and thus excluding 19 eruptions discernable in the ice-cores but of minimal climatic-forcing potential and consequently likely to introduce noise into the SEA analyses). Most eruption dates are estimated based upon counts of ice core layers, calibrated against tree rings and other independently dated records. They are therefore liable to a small chronological error of at most +/-2 years: Matthew Toohey and Michael Sigl, 'Volcanic stratospheric sulfur injections and aerosol optical depth from 500 BCE to 1900 CE', *Earth System Science Data* 9:2 (2017), 809–31: 812, 822 (original dataset made personally available to Francis Ludlow).

A whole-period analysis is presented first (top-left panel), compositing violence (black line) relative to all 32 volcanic events using a ten-year window, running two years before the estimated eruption dates (Years -2 to -1 on the horizontal axis), the estimated dates of the eruptions (Year 0) and the first six years following (Years 1 to 6). The red line depicts the 90 per cent upper bound of a randomly generated reference distribution (based upon 10,000 sets of random, Monte Carlo-style, draws from the whole-period violence dataset). Thus, any observed value that reaches or exceeds this bound (i.e., in which the black line meets or rises above the red line) can be deemed to have a 10 per cent or less chance of occurring purely by chance, if there were no underlying association between volcanism and violence. This exercise reveals a notable peak in average violence in Year 2. The specific probability of observing such a high value in Year 2 by chance alone is just 5.0 per cent (i.e., $p = 0.05$).

The next five panels examine the response in successive centuries, starting with the eleventh century. This confirms that in most centuries elevated levels of violence occurred in the first and/or second year following eruptions. This exercise complements the testimony of the texts themselves, which are only occasionally explicit respecting possible links between climatic stress and violence, but also cautions against assuming a simple mechanistic relationship between eruptions, weather effects and societal responses, in which violence can be expected to spike systematically in a particular post-eruption year. The uniqueness of each eruption event in location, magnitude, character, seasonality and background climatic context, as well as some small dating uncertainty, is likely the origin of much variation in the observed response, as indeed is the changing societal context in which each eruption occurred (with potentially varying levels of societal resilience and stability in the different periods).

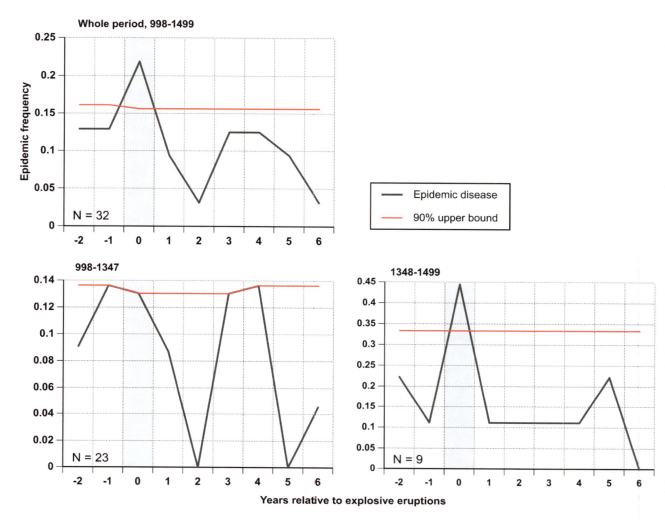

Appendix 7—Superposed epoch analyses (SEA) of outbreaks of epidemic disease reported in the *Annals of Ulster*, 998–1499 CE, relative to a polar ice-core-based reconstruction of volcanic climate forcing.

Notes and sources: Epidemic disease as reported in the *Annals of Ulster*. In order to ensure comparability in the response to volcanic eruptions throughout the period under consideration, each year's epidemic disease count (in binary presence-absence (0,1) format) is normalised according to the mean and standard deviation of itself and the previous 49 years. The analysis is based on the same 32 major explosive eruptions with an estimated VSSI of at least 1.0 Tg as described in Appendix 6.

The results of this analysis suggest a genuine (if obviously indirect) association between explosive volcanism and epidemic disease outbreaks, which is conspicuously stronger for the bubonic plague era 1348–1499 than the pre-plague era 998–1347. Thus, in the plague era, 44.4 per cent of volcanic events (N = 9) coincide with reported epidemic outbreaks in the same year. The probability of such a high value occurring randomly in this year is just 6 per cent (see the note to Appendix 6 for details on the specific statistical testing underlying this probability estimate). Unsurprisingly, the result for the pre-1347 period is less clear, but still suggestive of an association between volcanically induced climatic disturbances and reported epidemics.

Climate, weather and social change in seventeenth-century Ireland

RAYMOND GILLESPIE*
Department of History, Maynooth University

[Accepted 7 August 2020. Published 25 September 2020.]

Abstract

In attempting to construct a model of social and political change in early modern Europe some historians have turned to climate change as a way of integrating other developments. Climatic deterioration placed pressure on resources that had impacts on population and food supply that generated political crises across the globe. This article points not to the similarities in the changes across Europe but rather on the divergences from the general pattern, especially at the margins such as Ireland where the general model does not seem to apply. By focusing on the everyday experience of climate, weather, this essay argues that the important variable in such change is not climate per se but how local societies reacted to the changing weather patterns and adapted to them. Using the harvest crisis of 1673 as a case study it charts the response in the regions of Ireland to a deterioration of weather and stresses the need for local study of reaction to climatic change rather than global approaches.

Introduction

Most historians attempting to weld an incoherent mass of evidence into some semblance of an argument, or even a story, have been attracted by two strategies. The first is to survey the problematic landscape from above in the hope of detecting a regular pattern of events and exceptions that might well provide the basis for a synthesis. The second is to isolate the local and the specific in the hope that a detailed and local microhistory will provide clues to the more perplexing general topography of the past. Historians of the seventeenth century are no exception to this generalisation. Since 1959 a magisterial overview of seventeenth-century Europe has been available, complete with an organising principle for understanding that world, in the form of Hugh Trevor-Roper's 'The general crisis of the seventeenth century'.[1] Trevor-Roper's case for a general crisis has been elaborated and refined by a succession of scholars but most successfully by Geoffrey Parker. In a number of works Parker has not only developed Trevor-Roper's argument but also substantially improved on it, not least by arguing for an underlying agent that drew together the variables making

---

*Author's email: raymond.gillespie@mu.ie
doi: https://doi.org/10.3318/PRIAC.2020.120.07
[1] H.R. Trevor-Roper, 'The general crisis of the 17th century', *Past and Present* 16 (1959), 31–64.

for a crisis which by themselves had more limited explanatory potential (such as economics or politics). The agent he identified was the 'little ice age', a collective name for the shifts that took place in the world's climate from the late fifteenth century, and in particular the Maunder Minimum from roughly the 1640s to the 1720s which saw lower average summer temperatures than previously in the northern hemisphere. This, Parker persuasively argued, intensified the pressure on resources that a growing population in the late sixteenth and early seventeenth centuries had created. As climate deteriorated, marginal land became less productive (sometimes being abandoned) and so food supplies for a growing population became problematic: 'climate-induced dearth'. The crisis was concentrated in three zones: marginal farming lands, cities and 'macro regions' (regional economies). Each of these zones displayed their own vulnerabilities but they were all characterised by hardship produced by disruption. Reductions in food supply meant that a weakened population became more vulnerable to disease and other forms of demographic crisis. Not all suffered equally with women and the 'have nots' being the most vulnerable, though life on the battlefield was still more dangerous. Migration (both voluntary and involuntary) rose as did suicide, epidemic diseases such as smallpox or plague gained ground, and the live birth rate fell through a rise in the marriage age or by infanticide. In this already weakened state the population was subjected to growing fiscal demands from an increasingly militarised and centralised state as warfare became more and more expensive and local rights came under threat from emerging centralised states. The result was war, population dislocation, plague and famine followed by a dramatic contraction in world population. Climate itself was not the sole cause of this, it 'required the misguided policies pursued by religious and political leaders to turn the crisis caused by sudden climate change into catastrophe'.[2] Thus local and minor problems were exacerbated into major crises that fed off each other and ensured that war was the characteristic feature of the seventeenth-century world. Indeed it is Parker's contention that 'the 1640s saw more rebellions and revolutions than any comparable period in world history'.[3] It was climate that provided the unifying and organising principle of the crisis and ensured that it would be global, from China and Japan in the east to France and England in the west.

Models and problems

Viewed from the perspective of a gently descending historian equipped with a parachute this is a persuasive argument that has the potential to account for a wide range of phenomena in early modern Europe. Those, for instance, who see witchcraft as the product of social tensions can be provided with a convenient

---

[2] The most recent formulation of the argument is in Geoffrey Parker, *Global crisis: war, climate change and catastrophe in the seventeenth century* (Yale, 2013), especially 1–110. The quotation is on page 25.
[3] Parker, *Global crisis*, 112.

explanation for its demise in the release of those tensions as population fell in the late seventeenth and early eighteenth centuries. However, from the perspective of the shape of regional and local change in specific, and often unusual, contexts the argument works less well. On the margins of Europe the patterns posited by Parker's argument seem in need of dramatic modification. The Dutch golden age, for example, stands in sharp contrast to the story of decline but others have found that the model fits, albeit with some chronological adjustment.[4] In seventeenth-century Ireland, for instance, population size may not have posed the problem that it did in other parts of Europe. Ireland's population problem in the early seventeenth century was not a surplus of people, as in many parts of seventeenth-century Europe, but a shortage of them. Moreover, it was a population that was expanding rather than contracting. Between 1600 and 1641 it probably grew from about 1.4 million to about 2.1 million. The effects of war and disease meant that it stood at about 1.9 million in the 1680s.[5] The reasons for this are fairly clear: immigration coupled with a low death rate ensured that population rose rapidly, though briefly checked by war in the 1640s and an isolated outbreak of plague in 1650. Plague was noticeably absent in Ireland throughout the century as a whole. Between the middle of the sixteenth century and the middle of the seventeenth century there were no significant outbreaks of plague in Ireland despite a number of outbreaks in England.[6] It was only with the outbreak of plague in Ireland in 1650 that this changed, but after this brief appearance it did not recur for the rest of the century. This does not mean that the inhabitants of Ireland did not fear plague and outbreaks in London in the 1620s occasioned proclamations for quarantine and sermons of warning in Ireland.[7] Contemporaries certainly noted the low incidence of other diseases in the country. Gerard Boate, for instance, commented in 1657 that 'though Ireland is obnoxious to excessive wetness, nevertheless it is very wholesome for the habitation of men as clearly doth appear by that there are as few sickly persons…as in any of the neighbouring countries'. Ireland was free of scurvy, plague and ague (all present in England) and only troubled by malignant fevers ('Irish agues'), rickets, leprosy (presumably a skin disease), and 'the bloody flux'. This Boate attributed to the environment, from 'some hidden property of the land itself', as there certainly

---

[4] For example, Thorkild Kjærgaard, *The Danish revolution, 1500–1800: an ecohistorical interpretation* (Cambridge, 1994).
[5] Raymond Gillespie, 'Economic life, 1550–1730', in Jane Ohlmeyer (ed.), *The Cambridge history of Ireland, 1550–1730* (4 vols, Cambridge, 2018), vol. 2, 539, 549.
[6] Chronologies of plague can be followed in J.F.D. Shrewsbury, *The history of bubonic plague in the British Isles* (Cambridge, 1971), chapters 6–8.
[7] R.R. Steele, *A bibliography of royal proclamations of the Tudor and Stuart sovereigns, 1485–1714* (2 vols, Oxford, 1910), vol. 2, pt 1, no. 262; Henry Leslie, *A warning for Israel* (Dublin, 1625); J.T. and Lady Gilbert (eds), *Calendar of the ancient records of Dublin* (19 vols, Dublin, 1889–1944), vol. 3, 536–7, vol. 4, 345–7.

does seem to be a clear link between climatic conditions and plague outbreaks.[8] Why this might be is still unclear. Ireland's very low levels of urbanisation (with no 'palace cities') may be one factor avoiding Parker's 'urban graveyard' in all but Dublin and possibly Cork.[9] This had an impact on the death rate and late seventeenth-century Irish Quakers, for instance, lived longer than their English counterparts, married younger and had more children.[10] It also contributed to a rapid growth in the Irish population over the century, but even by the 1700s it was not yet straining the resources of Ireland to accommodate it. This is a demographic regime very different to that described for other parts of the world, whose population, Parker estimates, may have fallen by one third as Ireland's population increased by almost 50 per cent.

The problem of European regional variation in the relationship of population to resources is not simply a matter of demographics. Cultural differences across Europe could generate significant differences in local responses to climatic change. Perhaps the most significant variable here was diet. Deterioration in climatic conditions is most easily measurable in the grain supply through the impact of weather on the harvest. The importance of the grain harvest varied according to the composition of diet. In Ireland, for instance, the diet in the sixteenth and early seventeenth centuries was much more heavily based on meat, offal and dairy products than in most other parts of Europe. This meant that the sort of conditions that impacted badly on harvests in other places had a more limited effect in Ireland but conversely outbreaks of cattle disease would have had a disproportionate impact. Over the seventeenth and eighteenth centuries the Irish diet modernised under pressure from urbanisation and commercialisation, incorporating both more grains and the potato. This created a cultural situation that seems to have protected Ireland, in part, from the climatic problems of the 1690s and early eighteenth century resulting in what historians have termed 'a gap in famines'.[11] This is not to argue that grain was completely absent from the Irish diet in the early seventeenth century but rather that its production and consumption was localised. This localism in grain consumption was accentuated by the very low levels of commercialisation of the Irish economy at this point. The poorly developed marketing system created problems in moving food within Ireland in times of difficulty and thus ensured that most food was locally

---

[8] Gerard Boate, *Ireland's natural history* (Dublin, 1725), 89–92, 97–102. The text was first published in London in 1657.

[9] Parker, *Global crisis*, 58–66.

[10] D.C. Eversley, 'The demography of the Irish Quakers, 1650–1850' in J.M. Goldstrom and L.A. Clarkson (eds), *Irish population, economy and society: essays in honour of the late K.H. Connell* (Oxford, 1981), 57–88.

[11] On diet see L.A Clarkson and E.M. Crawford, *Feast and famine: a history of food and nutrition in Ireland, 1500–1920* (Oxford, 2001), 9–29; L.M. Cullen, *The emergence of modern Ireland, 1600–1900* (London, 1981), 140–171. For the gap in famines see David Dickson, 'The gap in famines: a useful myth?' in E.M. Crawford (ed.), *Famine: the Irish experience, 900–1900* (Edinburgh, 1989), 96–111.

produced, accentuating and reinforcing the highly regional character of the Irish diet.

Weather and climate

Variations in social, economic and cultural structures on the margins of Europe are not the only problems in attempting to apply a model of climatic deterioration forcing resource depletion in the early seventeenth century. Climate change was not a phenomenon that most contemporaries would have recognised or recorded: weather was immediate and measurable, climate was not. Most did not understand the idea of climate as a pattern of weather events. For instance those who migrated to the new world in the sixteenth and seventeenth centuries assumed that they would encounter a weather regime similar to that which they had left behind, with disastrous consequences.[12] Indeed there is some evidence to suggest that the idea of climate, as opposed to that of weather, was only being shaped in the late seventeenth century as contemporaries compared the climatic regimes of Ireland and America.[13]

Understanding weather shaped how many contemporaries viewed their world. As a product of the natural world, it was not regarded as a result of a series of impersonal natural processes to be described by scientific laws but rather as God's providence, manifesting itself in a particular social context. In articulating a view of the world one did not ask what controlled the weather but who controlled it. Thus if one wished to predict weather the evidence of experience or advice from almanacs could be relied on, but better was consulting the bible. One late seventeenth-century Dublin man did exactly that, drawing up a list of weather prognostications using biblical types as his model and scribbling these in a pamphlet that he owned.[14] Weather was not random but seen as part of the matrix of reward and punishment allocated by God as a result of moral behaviour. In 1628 William Bedell, the newly appointed provost of Trinity College, Dublin, observed the reactions in Dublin to the disastrous harvest of the previous year and the widespread cattle disease of that year. The response was a series of 'fast days' in which, he noted, 'our preachers lay the higher cause on the tolerating and countenancing idolatry, church robbery, swearing and blasphemy, blood, drunkenness, pride and other open and insolent sins'.[15] While this sort of providential immediacy may have lessened somewhat in the late seventeenth century it certainly did not disappear. During the bad harvest years between 1688 and 1693 Bishop Anthony Dopping of Meath turned to the same sermon on four occasions. It spoke of the plague of 'immoderate rain and water and by an unusual clap of thunder…He [God] hath in effect told us that he hath

---

[12] Sam White, *A cold welcome: the little ice age and Europe's encounter with north America* (London, 2018).
[13] Brant Vogel, 'The letter from Dublin; climate change, colonialism and the Royal Society in the seventeenth century', *Osiris* 26:1 (2011), 111–28.
[14] Dublin City Library, Pearse Street, volume of bound pamphlets, 1813/1/7F.
[15] Charles McNeill (ed.), *The Tanner letters* (Dublin, 1943), 84–5.

greater degrees of anger in reserve to deal with whoring, failure to pay debts and drinking'.[16] It was not a view confined to Protestant churchmen for when the harvest crisis of 1673–4 was at its height in the spring of 1674 the Catholic archbishop of Armagh, Oliver Plunkett, wrote 'because of our sins these hardships have afflicted us'.[17] The response to such dramatic crises was as much moral and theological as practical. In the main that response was conditioned by the state which sanctioned days of fasting and repentance for exactly such situations, but local weather crises could also provoke local responses. In 1624 when heavy rain threatened to destroy the harvest around Bangor, Co. Down, the whole parish fasted and prayed all day for a change in weather. After the weather duly changed everyone worked for two days without a break while the local ministers continued fasting and praying.[18] Again, the 1673 crisis produced a highly traditional response from the Kerry parishioners of the Church of Ireland minister Devereux Spratt who crowded into their parish church to repent their sins.[19] Weather and its meanings were not morally neutral subjects nor was it seen as an exogenous shock over which contemporaries had no control.

The centrality of weather and its supernatural origins, rather than the more amorphous idea of climate, makes it easier to construct the pattern of weather activity in the seventeenth century. While tree ring data may be good proxies for years with abnormal growth patterns, they are rather less useful when it comes to measuring the impact of weather on other resources, in particular the harvest. Urban growth and changing dietary patterns in late seventeenth-century Ireland made a stable grain harvest increasingly important to maintain food supply. The dramatic growth of Dublin, for instance, meant that grain was sourced from as far away as Wexford and Lecale, Co. Down, as well as the adjacent county of Kildare. Dublin was not the only expanding urban centre demanding grain; Galway, Belfast, Cork and Derry relied on increasing volumes of grain from their hinterlands.[20] Government was therefore sensitive to the supply of grain not just because of its moral message but because a poor harvest might presage food shortages and ultimately unrest. As a result, authorities monitored the grain supply regularly and thus identifying years of difficulty with the grain supply is a relatively simple matter despite the absence of a grain price series. Proclamations for prohibitions of grain exports from Ireland can act as markers of years in which the harvest was felt to be in danger and food supplies needed to be conserved. Such proclamations were issued in 1622, 1631, 1633, 1662, 1674,

---

[16] Trinity College, Dublin (TCD), MS 1688/1, 288, 306; MS 866, ff 234^v–5.
[17] John Hanly (ed.), *The letters of Saint Oliver Plunkett* (Dublin, 1979), 416.
[18] Thomas McCrie (ed.), *The life of Mr Robert Blair* (Edinburgh, 1848), 62–3.
[19] St John D. Seymour (ed.), *The adventures and experiences of a seventeenth-century clergyman* (Dublin, 1909), 23.
[20] Raymond Gillespie, 'The changing structure of Irish agriculture in the seventeenth century', in Margaret Murphy and Matthew Stout (eds), *Agriculture and settlement in Ireland* (Dublin, 2015), 127–31.

1681, 1687, 1697, 1698 and 1699.[21] Using only one indicator of adverse weather, such as the prohibition of grain exports, is a relatively crude measure of the impact of bad harvests. Moreover, events such as war in the 1640s and 1688–91 interfered with the workings of government resulting in the failure to issue proclamations. Again wartime conditions rather than harvest situations may have resulted in the regulation of the price of grain.[22] Prohibitions on exports are, however, an effective way of measuring problems with the harvest. When compared with a more detailed range of sources for a restricted time period (the early seventeenth century alone) the evidence of the prohibition of grain exports is a good measure of the wider realities of the state of the grain harvest.[23]

Using centralised measures of harvest conditions also ignores the problems of regional variation. Weather conditions may have varied a good deal over Ireland and its neighbouring areas. Thus the 1690s in south-west Scotland witnessed disastrous harvests and a severe demographic crisis, while in adjacent east Ulster conditions were relatively benign although a number of years in the 1690s do have spikes in burials in some parish records.[24] The 1690s were thus characterised by migration from south-west Scotland to adjacent Ulster pushed by conditions in Scotland and the possibility of cheap land in post-war Ireland. The migrants brought with them their assets resulting in a significant capital inflow that permitted post-war reconstruction in Ulster at a time of crisis in Scotland.[25]

Anatomy of a crisis

If we can understand both the chronology of harvest crises and the ways in which contemporaries regarded such crises then it may be possible to begin to understand something of the wider question of climate change. For most of the seventeenth century the inhabitants of Ireland thought in terms of the immediacy of weather and did not consider longer term and more subtle shifts of climate. In this world climate was experienced through weather, particularly erratic or extreme weather events. Climate change, in short, influences people through

---

[21] Steele, *Tudor and Stuart proclamations*, vol. 2, pt 1, nos 243, 289, 299; James Kelly with Marian Lyons, *The proclamations of Ireland, 1660–1820* (5 vols, Dublin, 2014), vol. 1, nos 61, 232, 233, 235, 293; vol. 2, nos 29, 149, 150, 193, 196, 216. I have not included the prohibition of May 1684 since this was revoked a month later (Kelly with Lyons (eds), *Proclamations*, vol. 1, nos 303, 306) and seems to have been a panic proclamation rather than a substantive fear of grain shortage.

[22] For example, Kelly with Lyons (eds), *Proclamations*, vol. 1, nos 148, 152, 154.

[23] Raymond Gillespie, 'Harvest crises in early seventeenth-century Ireland', *Irish Economic and Social History* 11 (1984), 5–18.

[24] For instance, Valerie Morgan, 'A case study of population change over two centuries: Blaris, Lisburn, 1661–1848', *Irish Economic and Social History* 2 (1976), Fig. 1. On the Scottish crisis see Karen J. Cullen, *Famine in Scotland: the 'ill years' of the 1690s* (Edinburgh, 2010).

[25] K.J. Cullen, 'Scottish migration to Ulster during the "seven ill years" of the 1690s' in Anders Ahlqvist and Pamela O'Neill (eds), *Celts and their cultures at home and abroad* (Sydney, 2013), 35–54.

weather and weather creates particular relationships between local environments and human activities. That is not to say that weather or other natural processes determine outcomes, rather weather events provide possibilities for those who lived in the seventeenth-century world to exploit or to be dominated by those phenomena. How contemporaries responded to those challenges shaped their world and provides a way of understanding the link between climate change and society.[26] There are relatively few examples of studies of individual climate events in Ireland, though such studies are crucial to understanding how contemporaries responded to climate change.[27] For contemporaries, weather and climate was situated in local contexts and is best understood in those contexts. This essay adds one further study: a consideration of the weather and social context of the harvest crisis of 1672–4, identified above as one of the few harvest crises of the late seventeenth century in Ireland despite the apparent degeneration of the weather during the climatic shift of the Maunder Minimum.

The harvest crisis of 1672–4 was mainly the result of a variety of weather types, though the outbreak of the Dutch war exacerbated the problems. The summer of 1672 was hot; John Brennan, Catholic bishop of Waterford, described it as being the 'hottest season within human memory' and George Rawdon at Lisburn commented to Lord Conway on the 'want of rain and burning weather beyond example here'.[28] In June, Rawdon further reported that the excessive drought was affecting grass growth and the cattle. There was a want of flour since there was no water to drive the mills. This was somewhat alleviated by some rain in June and the heat does not seem to have done lasting damage to the harvest or to have had a long-term effect on the mainstay of the Lagan valley economy, the butter trade.[29] Some of the earliest evidence of the crisis of 1673–4 is provided by the observation in June 1673 of Nicholas Jones, the agent for Captain George Legg's lands in Connacht, that he was having difficulty in collecting his rents because of the 'hardship their [the tenants'] cattle has been put to this last winter by extremity of the weather and the scarcity of fodder…for it is hardly to be believed the poverty the country is reduced to, unless you were here to see it'.[30] The winter of 1672–3 had been difficult, and by the spring of 1673 this was having an impact on fodder supplies. It is clear that the weather was the immediate cause for the poor harvest of the autumn of 1673. Oliver Plunkett, the Catholic archbishop of Armagh, reported in May 1674 that the previous

---

[26] I have been influenced by the approach here of Dagomar Degroot, *The frigid golden age: climate change, the little ice age and the Dutch Republic, 1560–1720* (Cambridge, 2018).
[27] Raymond Gillespie, 'Meal and money: the harvest crisis of 1621–4 and the Irish economy' in Crawford (ed.), *Famine*, 75–95.
[28] Patrick Power (ed.), *A bishop of the penal times* (Cork, 1932), 22; *Calendar of State Papers, domestic series, 1672* (London, 1856) (henceforth *Cal. S.P. Dom., 1672*), 90.
[29] *Cal. S.P. Dom., 1672*, 159, 184.
[30] Historical Manuscripts Commission (HMC), *The manuscripts of the earl of Dartmouth* (3 vols, 1886–96), vol. 3, 117.

autumn had been so wet that the grain could not be harvested, a fact confirmed by the County Down landowner William Waring. However, caution should be exercised about claims of overly wet summers since soil moisture evidence extracted from Irish oak tree ring growth suggests that the early 1670s were drier than the years before 1640 and after 1700 (which may help explain why there were more difficult years before 1650 than after).[31] That situation worsened over the winter of 1673/4. In January of 1674 Plunkett in Armagh described heavy snow and hailstones with cold winds.[32] Into the spring little had improved with Lord Conway's agent at Lisburn commenting that the weather had continued so extreme that there had been no market at all.[33] The heavy snow and ice of the winter meant that the spring sowing was late because the ground could not be ploughed.[34] Some, however, were optimistic. In March and April 1674 George Rawdon reported 'we have very good weather here' but warned that the impact of the previous winter would be severe.[35] More pessimistically, Nicholas Jones reported from Connacht in May 1674 'there is a greater danger of famine than hopes of raising rents' and, by July, he was of the view that 'the extremity of weather that is now' would quash the hope of the harvest.[36] The spring proved to be cold which restricted growth, and in particular grass growth, which left farmers reliant on scant supplies of hay.[37] Certainly by June 1674 things were getting worse with Oliver Plunkett observing 'corn cannot be had for love or money and the wars on the continent prevent importation'.[38] If anything, the summer of 1674 was not wet but very hot. While this may have improved the situation for livestock it was less successful in enhancing the grain harvest right across the country. In Connacht the antiquarian Roderic O'Flaherty noted that 1674 was 'a year memorable for the dearth of corn through all Ireland'.[39] The harvest of autumn 1674, though much reduced on normal yields, was better than that of the previous year. Into the autumn the County Down landowner William Waring was still describing the tenants as 'impoverished' and he continued to lament local conditions in the spring of 1675, claiming that 'this country is so

---

[31] Francis Ludlow and Arlene Crampsie, 'Environmental history of Ireland, 1550–1730' in Jane Ohlmeyer (ed.), *The Cambridge history of Ireland, 1550–1730* (4 vols, Cambridge, 2018), vol. 2, 619 (Fig. 3).
[32] Hanly (ed.), *Letters,* 398, 407. 'Great snow' was also reported in Scotland this winter: *Register of the privy council of Scotland, 1673–4*, 416–7.
[33] *Cal. S.P. Dom., 1673–5,* 193–4.
[34] Hanly (ed.), *Letters*, 407.
[35] *Cal. S.P. Dom., 1673–5,* 212, 217.
[36] HMC, *Dartmouth,* vol. 3, 118, 119.
[37] *Cal. S.P. Dom., 1673–5,* 225.
[38] Hanly (ed.), *Letters*, 410.
[39] Roderic O'Flaherty, *A chorographical description of west of h-Iar Connaught* (written 1684, published Dublin, 1846), 63. It has been suggested that one poem by Dáibhí Ó Bruadair may be dated to this summer, see J.C. Mac Erlean (ed.), *Duanaire Dháibhidh Uí Bhruadair* (3 vols, London 1910–17), vol. 2, 34–7.

impoverished that unless God mend the time as I hope he will some of the tenants will not be able to pay any rent'.[40] Yet this was special pleading since even at the worst of the crisis in the spring of 1674 Waring was acquiring land and undertaking to drain and build on it at a point when the collection of rents seemed uncertain. Some accused him of using this as a bargaining point to better the terms on which he got the property.[41] By the summer of 1675 Oliver Plunkett could look back and talk about the famine of the previous two years as a historic event and in November 1675 the future again looked promising and the summer of 1676 would, if anything, be on the dry side but the butter trade was 'very great' that year in the Lagan valley. By the summer of 1677 corn was reported to be 'very cheap' and having learnt the lessons of 1673–4 the accountant on the Conway estate was proposing that it was 'a good way to buy a good stock this year, for fear that another may not be so good, we having so good room for keeping them sweet and good'.[42] The speed with which Ulster recovered from the harvest crisis of 1673–4 was as much due to the commercial structures, especially mercantile credit, that had developed there after the 1660s and the ending of the Dutch war in February 1674 that opened up the expanding markets for butter and beef in Low Countries, as it was to the amelioration of the weather. Increased commercialisation after 1660 in the form of the growth of fairs and the advertising of these in almanacs, spread information and lowered transaction costs; it certainly meant that restocking cattle was easier after the crisis than it otherwise might have been as breeding replacements was a protracted process.

What is clear is that the impact of the weather conditions of 1673–4, unlike the drought of 1672, was not national but strongly regionalised. In July 1674 Nicholas Jones commented on 'the dearth and famine that is generally in the north and west of Ireland' and when George Rawdon described the crisis in the spring of 1674 it was only from Ulster and Connacht that he reported 'sad stories of the like kind' about cattle deaths and grain shortages.[43] This regional bias is supported by other evidence. In October 1674 when the export of grain was prohibited by proclamation the prohibition was restricted to Ulster.[44] There were reports of difficulty from other parts of the country but hardly distress. Parker has suggested that cities might pose particular problems for those who fled to them in their bid to survive, creating an 'urban graveyard effect'.[45] Certainly in the short term this did not happen in Ireland in 1673–4 though it did happen during other crises. The Dublin parish registers for the 1670s are fragmentary and not amenable to detailed statistical analysis but, apart from that of St Peter's and St Kevin's parishes, they do not show marked spikes in burials in 1673 and

---

[40] Public Record Office of Northern Ireland (PRONI), Waring papers, D695/7, 18.
[41] PRONI, Waring papers, D695/9, 13A, 13B.
[42] Hanly (ed.), *Letters*, 455; *Cal. S.P. Dom., 1675,* 397; *Cal. S.P. Dom., 1676–7,* 333, 533, 548.
[43] HMC, *Dartmouth,* vol. 3, 119; *Cal. S.P. Dom., 1673–5,* 225.
[44] Kelly with Lyons (eds), *Proclamations,* vol. 1, no. 233.
[45] Parker, *Global crisis,* 58–66.

1674 but that does not rule out the possibility of distress. The vestry records of the Dublin parish of St Bride's demonstrate that the amount expended on poor relief between 1670 and 1675 only increased marginally, which does not suggest that the parish resources were strained by growing numbers of poor due to problems with weather and food supply.[46] Similarly, in Youghal in July 1674 the town council concluded that there was no need to increase the poor cess over the level of the previous year, suggesting no significant growth in the levels of distress that might have been expected to follow from a severe harvest failure. There are some indications, though not many, from other parts of the country that there may have been difficulties. Although grain riots were rare in seventeenth-century Ireland, in County Tipperary the Clonmel assize book for October 1674 records what may be a grain riot in the townland of Kilkoky on the Purcell of Loughmoe estate where some twenty-nine individuals were indicted for stealing 10,000 sheaves of corn and for assaulting one Mathew Shanaghane, and imprisoning him for two days. On another part of the estate corn worth 10*s.* was taken by three men.[47] However there is nothing to connect these raids on grain with the sort of food shortages that can clearly be identified in Ulster and Connacht. Evidence of difficulty outside Ulster and Connacht is not easy to find. On the Boyle estates in Cork and Waterford, for instance, the arrears listed in the rentals for 1675 are not significantly higher than the arrears listed for March 1672 to March 1673 which clearly contrasts with the significant arrears that landlords reported in Ulster and Connacht.[48]

Those with an eye for the main chance saw the possibilities of profit in the fact that parts of Ireland were little affected by the crisis. As Viscount Conway, the landlord of the Lisburn area in Ulster, who was in Dublin in July 1673, commented to his agent George Rawdon, 'I wonder to hear that wheat is sold at 5*s.* the barrel, considering this bad season likely to destroy both hay and corn. I believe it will raise the price in England sufficiently and if it be so cheap amongst us, we may make good merchandise there'.[49] Conway was not the only person with an eye toward this profit for in May 1674 and again in December there were proclamations against engrossers and forestallers on the grain market and prohibitions on the export of grain until Michaelmas and Easter respectively.[50]

It seems clear that the main impact of the 1673/4 harvest crisis was in Ulster and Connacht. Yet within these regions there were significant differences in how the crisis impacted the population. Connacht and west Ulster, for instance, were much less commercialised regions than the eastern half of Ulster and therefore could avoid something of the commercial disruption that often

---

[46] W.J.R. Wallace (ed.), *The vestry records of the parishes of St Bride, St Michael Le Pole and St Stephen, Dublin, 1662–1742* (Dublin, 2011), 47–8, 53–55, 58, 62,70.
[47] National Library of Ireland (NLI), Clonmel assize book, MS 4908, ff 82ᵛ, 85.
[48] NLI, Lismore papers, MSS 6272, 6275, 6277, 6279.
[49] HMC, *Report on the manuscripts of Reginald Rawdon Hastings* (4 vols, London 1928–47), vol. 2, 381.
[50] Kelly with Lyons (eds), *Proclamations*, vol. 1, nos 232, 235.

accompanied weather-induced disruptions to the market. East Ulster, however, was more sensitive to commercial trends.[51] Moreover, parts of Ulster previously lightly settled had seen significant population growth in the seventeenth century within a tenurial framework that limited expansion without subdivision. While this rigid system of ownership was one of the reasons for the economic progress of this region it worried some who feared a rise in poverty as a result of pressure on resources. Thus the parish of Shankill (Lurgan) in the highly commercialised Lagan valley seems to have been the first place in Ireland outside Dublin to badge its beggars in 1669 and in the 1670s it began to maintain a regular poor list.[52] In this area, too, landlords attempted to encourage the commercial linen trade as a way of diversifying their local economy and making it less dependent on agriculture.[53]

The most immediate impact of the crisis was a fall in agricultural output. A cold winter followed by a wet spring both retarded growth and promoted plant diseases such as moulds, rusts and mildews. As John Tattnall, one of the agents on the Conway estate, described the situation:

> …corn is so scarce that many of your tenants have not as much as will sow their land nor bread to eat, and as far as I can apprehend there is like to be a great scarcity amongst the tenants both for want of money and bread, for there has not been so scarce a time of victuals since the wars [of the 1640s], for not one family in 20 has bread to serve them till harvest and many have not to sow half their land for want of seed.[54]

Grain output was most immediately affected since that was both an important food source and the main source of seed for the following year. Shortage of grain from one harvest had an impact on the availability of grain for a subsequent one, making the impact of harvest crises cumulative. As Oliver Plunkett fretted about the harvest of 1674 he noted: 'we had such a frost during the winter and the continual snow killed the wheat and the barley after it had been sown in the fields and as a result we have a very thin crop. As soon as it ripens it will be devoured and we are afraid that the shortage will continue during the coming year.'[55] The impact seems to have been across the range of cereal crops for

---

[51] For an overview of developments see Raymond Gillespie, 'The early modern economy, 1600–1789' in Liam Kennedy and Philip Ollerenshaw (eds), *Ulster since 1600* (Oxford, 2013), 19–22.
[52] T.G.F. Patterson, 'A Co. Armagh mendicant badge, inscribed Shankill Poor, 1669', *Ulster Journal of Archaeology* 10 (1947), 113.
[53] For this argument see Raymond Gillespie, *Seventeenth-century Ireland* (Dublin, 2006), 245–58.
[54] *Cal. S.P. Dom., 1673–5*, 226.
[55] Hanly (ed.), *Letters*, 416.

Plunkett commented in May 1674 that bread was unavailable, even oaten bread which suggests that the usually robust oat crop had been affected.[56]

If the failure of the grain harvest attracted attention because of its importance as a dietary crop, possibly more significant was the extensive mortality of livestock for as Oliver Plunkett commented of Armagh, livestock 'were the wealth of the poor Irish people'.[57] As early as April 1673 Nicholas Jones observed to George Legg that in Connacht the country was reduced to poverty by dearth of 'all sorts of cattle' and rents would not be paid until the cattle were in a better condition to sell.[58] The following spring it was reported from the Conway estate that a great many cattle in the country were dead and more were continuing to die every day. From this situation little could be salvaged except 'mort hides', which were the 'chief market commodities here weekly' and beef was in short supply to sell to merchants.[59] For such cattle as did survive the shortage of fodder reduced dead weights and therefore the profit that could be made from them on slaughter. Presumably, the reduction in milk yields from surviving cattle also impacted diets as Oliver Plunkett reported in the spring of 1674 that the poor were eating horseflesh in Armagh.[60] Perhaps more important was the long term effect on the butter trade that was a vital part of the Lagan valley economy. The reduction in milk yields reduced butter supplies for sale, most of the Lagan valley output being bought by the Belfast merchants for export to European markets. A practice developed in the late seventeenth century of Belfast merchants providing credit to farmers along the Lagan valley over the winter by pre-paying for butter that would be delivered the following summer. It is clear that some survived the winter on this credit but, in 1674, credit had been advanced based on the previous year's lower prices. While the farmers had been advanced 12*s.* or 14*s.* a cwt the actual price was likely to be 30*s.* As a result, John Tattnall on the Conway estate observed in April 1674, 'although corn and butter are likely to give a good rate this year, but few have any to sell for most of their cows is dead'.[61] The Belfast merchant George McCartney, who acted as a factor for others in Belfast and therefore was not directly affected by price movements, agreed to pay market prices thus providing a cushion for at least some who survived the crisis of the winter.[62] Such credit could not be expected to last more than one season.

The cause of the significant livestock mortality is elusive. Fodder shortages were clearly a problem. By the spring of 1673 fodder was already in short supply partly because of the 'extremity of weather'.[63] Wet weather, for instance,

---

[56] Hanly (ed.), *Letters,* 404.
[57] Hanly (ed.), *Letters,* 407, 410.
[58] HMC, *Dartmouth,* vol. 3, 116; *Cal. S.P. Dom., 1673–5,* 194, 212.
[59] *Cal. S.P. Dom., 1673–5,* 194, 212.
[60] Hanly (ed.), *Letters,* 414, 420.
[61] *Cal. S.P. Dom., 1673–5,* 226.
[62] *Cal. S.P. Dom., 1673–5,* 213.
[63] HMC, *Dartmouth,* vol. 3, 117.

made it impossible to cut hay and drying it in the fields was even more difficult. Fodder shortages were quickly compounded by the spread of disease among cattle. What this disease was is unclear. It is unlikely to have been rinderpest, which was a viral disease of ruminants, since it also affected deer, sheep and horses; further, its regional nature is atypical of rinderpest which spread rapidly and virulently.[64] The wet summer conditions would certainly have encouraged liver fluke in sheep, especially in the badly drained parts of Connacht. It may well have been a combination of a number of diseases coupled with a shortage of fodder and the cold weather of the winter and spring weakening the animals. It may be no accident also that in the middle of the crisis a Dublin publisher produced a handbook for the management of cattle disease authored by the Cheshire Quaker and astrologer Michael Haward who had moved to Ireland. While this was written a year earlier, the notes for the diagnoses and treatment of cattle fever and murrain in both cattle and sheep had immediate applicability in the summer of 1673.[65] The impact of all this was potentially serious: loss of dung for fertiliser but, more importantly, as George Rawdon explained, there was 'very little ploughing for want of horses and seed' in the spring of 1674.[66] Clearly the crisis had the potential to get a great deal worse.

One of the by-products of the crisis may have been a rise in petty theft. No assize or quarter sessions records survive that would allow this to be quantified but over the winter of 1673–4 there were certainly more complaints about petty theft and burglary. Writing of the situation around Monaghan, one man informed Lord Conway in February 1673 of 'frequent stealths and petty and some greater robberies of late', and observed, 'their numbers are likely to increase, unless some speedy course be taken to reclaim them or render them amenable to the law', and that one of the more prominent victims was Lord Massareene.[67] By the end of the year George Rawdon commented that around Lisburn 'none dare keep money in their houses' and that he had increased the watch in local parishes where cattle and horses were being stolen.[68] It would be unwise, however, to read too much into such comments. Local tensions were high, exacerbated by factors such as the anti-Catholic proclamations issued earlier in the year and the resurgence of Tory activity in south Ulster. This situation may have made the complainants more aware of disorder rather than reflecting the state of the harvest.

If the damage to the agricultural economy was severe the potential demographic impact of this harvest crisis was even worse. The comments of Oliver Plunkett in Armagh would indicate widespread hunger at least and in some cases

---

[64] *Cal. S.P. Dom., 1673–5*, 194, 212, 226; Hanly (ed.), *Letters*, 407.
[65] Michael Haward, *The herds-man's mate or a guide for herdsmen teaching how to cure all diseases in bulls, oxen, cows and calves gathered from sundry good authors and well approved by the author in his thirty year practice* (Dublin, 1673). The preface is dated 6 June 1682. On Haward, see TCD, MS 883/1, 147.
[66] *Cal. S.P. Dom., 1673–5*, 225.
[67] *Cal. S.P. Dom., 1672–3*, 616; *Cal. S.P. Dom., 1673*, 182–3.
[68] *Cal. S.P. Dom., 1673–5*, 62.

death from starvation. In May of 1674 he wrote 'famine is so widespread that the people are beginning to die from hunger'.[69] The following month he added 'at present you can see hundreds and hundreds of starved skeletons rather than men walking the roads' and people were eating horse flesh.[70] George Rawdon agreed. Writing from Lisburn in April 1674, he observed that there were 'many families starving for want of bread, wheat scarce and dear, 20s. a barrel in the market'.[71] In Connacht Nicholas Jones recorded in April 1674 'since my coming here I have been eye witness of the death of many, and [the] continued outcry of the people, by the scarcity of corn and horn.'[72]

Such comments by Plunkett, Rawdon and Jones were the result as much of fear as detailed observation and are not borne out by the contemporary evidence of the parish registers. Two sets of parish registers survive for Ulster in the 1670s that allow the measurement of vital events over the years of the harvest crisis. The register for Blaris covers the town of Lisburn and part of the surrounding area owned in the late seventeenth century by Lord Conway. The parish was in the centre of the dramatic commercial expansion of the Lagan valley region in which butter and beef came to dominate the trade with Belfast merchants in the late seventeenth century. It was also an important grain growing area for supplying Belfast. A description of the barony of Oneiland in Armagh in 1683 noted that it had 'a vast quantity of wheat that is yearly carried hence into the county of Antrim beside the maintenance of above two thousand families with bread … [that] do plainly demonstrate it to be the granary of Ulster'.[73] For 1673 and 1674 the burials recorded at Blaris did not spike significantly although in 1675 baptisms fell, reflecting a reduction in conceptions the previous year.[74] Overall baptisms remained well in excess of burials indicating that the population continued to grow. This suggests that the demographic impact of the crisis of 1673–4 in Blaris was restricted. It did not generate significant excess mortality but rather reduced confidence in the future and the result was delayed childbearing. The admissions to freedom from Belfast, the main port for the Lagan valley region, in the 1670s provide a similar picture. The seventeen individuals admitted to freedom in 1673 was a long way short of the average of sixty-eight in each of the preceding three years. Equally the recovery in 1674, with fifty-two admissions, was rapid since this was roughly the average for the next three years.[75] The evidence would suggest that rather than abandon Belfast

---

[69] Hanly (ed.), *Letters*, 404.
[70] Hanly (ed.), *Letters*, 414, 416.
[71] *Cal. S.P. Dom., 1673–5*, 225.
[72] HMC, *Dartmouth*, vol. 3, 118.
[73] TCD, MS 883/1, 223. For the wider context see Raymond Gillespie, S*ettlement and survival on an Ulster estate: the Brownlow leasebook, 1667–1711* (Belfast, 1988), xxv–xxviii.
[74] Morgan, 'A case study of population change', Fig. 1.
[75] R.M. Young (ed.), *Town book of the corporation of Belfast* (Belfast, 1892), 270–83. The year is taken as beginning on 1 Jan.

individuals simply postponed their admission to freedom until the future appeared more propitious, and this accounted for the rapid recovery.

The demographic response to the crisis revealed by the second Ulster parish register, that of Derry, is rather more complex. Derry was similar to Belfast in that it acted as the port for a major marketing area defined by the Foyle valley though it was less reliant on the butter and meat trades than Belfast. By the 1670s it was dwarfed by its east coast rival. In 1671–2 registered burials averaged 126 a year but in 1673 they rose to 169 and to 177 in 1674 before falling back to eighty-five for the next two years. The increase in burials for the crisis years is almost entirely accounted for by the increases in the months of November 1673 and August and September 1674, the months immediately after the harvest of 1673 and the months immediately before the harvest of 1674. Such a pattern of very short term autumnal rises in mortality would not suggest an outbreak of epidemic disease but is almost certainly related to food supply with diseases already present in the population having greater effect on a weakened population.[76] Disease was a factor in the drought of the summer of 1672 when there was an outbreak of smallpox in Ulster but this does not appear as a major event in any of the parish registers, which suggests that it did not sweep the countryside in epidemic form but was probably endemic at local level with periodic outbreaks.[77]

The evidence also suggests that the demographic impact of the crisis was not spread evenly. In Connacht Nicholas Jones was clear that it was the under-tenants who would suffer as a result of the crisis since landlords would continue to extract their rent.[78] Those with even less financial security were more severely affected. Archbishop Oliver Plunkett continually complained to Rome in 1674 of the problems of the Catholic clergy during the crisis. Their income had shrunk to almost nothing because parishioners had little to spare.[79] Clergy in turn had nothing to spare for their archbishop and the harvest crisis may well have sharpened the dispute over questing rights between the Franciscans and Dominicans in Ulster that had already rumbled on for a number of years.

If the demographic impact of the crisis was less than might be expected the commercial impact was more severe. As early as September 1673 there were complaints of cash shortages in Ulster but one cannot ascribe this entirely to the weather or agricultural situation.[80] War in early 1672 had taken its toll with a collapse in trade.[81] As George Rawdon wrote to Lord Conway in May 1672: 'you will find strange alteration here of scarcity of money, all Spanish and other

---

[76] Richard Hayes (ed.), *The register of Derry cathedral* (Dublin 1910). The year is taken as beginning on 1 Jan.
[77] *Cal. S.P. Dom., 1672,* 310, 370.
[78] HMC, *Dartmouth,* vol. 3, 116.
[79] Hanly (ed.), *Letters,* 407, 410, 453.
[80] PRONI, D 693/12.
[81] Osmond Airy (ed.), *Essex papers, 1672–79* (London, 1890), vol. 1, 78.

carried away daily, no trading of merchants abroad or buying anything'.[82] Shortage of cash meant that rents remained unpaid and the prospect of collecting rents seemed slim. As John Tattnall commented of the Conway estate in the spring of 1674: 'I fear it will [be] the worst year for getting rents that was this many years'.[83] Nicholas Jones commented in June 1673 that he had not received any of the spring rents and that 'I am sure that I must use all severity possible before I get in anything considerable, for it is hardly to be believed the poverty of the country is reduced to unless you were here to see them'. By April 1674 he was forced to abate the rents.[84] On the Conway estate George Rawdon reported to the landowner, Lord Conway, that he had only managed to collect between 10 and 20 per cent of the November rents due which, he commented, was 'not worse hereabouts than in other parts'.[85] Moreover the property market dried up; Nicholas Jones noted that he could not get tenants for his own Connacht property.[86]

Some were of the view that the crisis would cause widespread dislocation of population, and especially of tenants. John Tattnall on the Conway estate, for instance, feared that tenants would flee leaving land to waste.[87] Oliver Plunkett thought he observed exactly this phenomenon since 'now you can see hundreds of Catholic families which last year were comfortable now reduced to hunting and begging from door to door, from town to town' and 'thousands upon thousands of Catholic families in my province have left their homes and have taken to hunting'.[88] While this may have been true of the poorest, the fears were unfounded, at least for the more substantial leaseholders. On the Brownlow estate at Lurgan, in the middle of the Lagan valley, there are no new leases for 1674 and only one for 1673 recorded in his leasebook despite regular entries for new leases being entered before and after that.[89] It is also significant, however, that the immediate years after the crisis did not see new leases being made of properties leased before the crisis. In short, the crisis appears not to have broken leaseholders on this estate.

The problem of collecting rents was only part of a wider problem with the circulation of money in a world that relied on a trade surplus for enough specie to allow the local economy to work. The problem long pre-dated the 1670s, but it was made worse by the outbreak of the Dutch war in 1672 that slowed markets and reduced the flow of specie. The collapse in confidence as a result of a drought and the Dutch war in the summer of 1672 further worsened the situation with George Rawdon observing that 'those who have money will not

---

[82] *Cal. S.P. Dom., 1672*, 90.
[83] *Cal. S.P. Dom., 1673–5*, 226.
[84] HMC, *Dartmouth*, vol. 3, 117, 118.
[85] *Cal. S.P. Dom., 1673–5*, 62, 225.
[86] HMC, *Dartmouth*, vol. 3, 118–9.
[87] *Cal. S.P. Dom., 1673–5*, 226.
[88] Hanly (ed.), *Letters*, 407, 410.
[89] Gillespie, *Settlement and survival*, passim.

be willing to part with it yet a while'.[90] That was compounded by the harvest crisis of 1673–4. The cattle murrain and grain shortages meant that there was little to sell. In March 1674 Richard Mildmay, the agent on the Conway estate in Co. Antrim, complained that he could not get money, because there 'has been no market at all the two market days past'.[91] Oliver Plunkett readily admitted in May 1674 there was a shortage of money but also noted that 'indeed whoever has money cannot find corn to buy'.[92]

Conclusions

The detailed consideration of the harvest crisis of 1673–4 in Ulster and Connacht has attempted to understand how one weather event impacted on the workings of a society. It has tried to do so not by seeing weather as a primary cause of events or as a variable that pre-determined events. Weather was nor an exogenous shock that caused inevitable catastrophe. Weather events were compounded or mitigated by the social and economic systems in which they occurred. The fact that contemporaries saw weather and climate not as something outside their world over which they had no control but rather internalised it by ascribing a religious significance to it as the outworkings of providence, meant that it was not a determinant of their actions but rather one variable whose impact was shaped within a social and political order.

Climate change, as Parker uses it, may well prove to be the unifying factor in a global history but, as understood by contemporaries as weather events, it was capable of producing not unity but widely differing experiences with significant spatial and chronological variations. Thus apparently persuasive general models must be tested against local evidence. Different parts of Ireland responded to the 1673–4 crisis differently. For some the crisis was mild and they were relatively unaffected. For others it was clearly much more severe with other types of problems being created. One instance may be the varying levels of commercialisation across the island. The commercial impact of the crisis varied a good deal with less commercialised Connacht being less affected than the east of the country, which relied more heavily on markets. Slowdowns in trade reduced circulation of coin and made markets difficult with complaints about the shortage of specie. One response to this was the striking of large numbers of tokens by merchants and shopkeepers in the Lagan valley area from the 1660s that helped to improve the circulation of small coin. In October 1673 their striking was prohibited by proclamation and few such tokens survive from 1674 and 1675 but enough were already in circulation to make life easier for the poor who relied on the small-scale commercial world for their subsistence.[93] It did not solve

---

[90] *Cal. S.P. Dom., 1672*, 159.
[91] *Cal. S.P. Dom., 1673–5*, 193–4.
[92] Hanly (ed.), *Letters*, 404.
[93] Kelly with Lyons (eds), *Proclamations*, vol. 1, no. 224; W.A. Seaby, *Coins and tokens of Ireland* (London, 1970), 108.

all problems for as George Rawdon noted in January 1674: 'I hear poverty is increasing everywhere and scarcity of money'.[94] In the west of the country there were almost no token issues suggesting that the circulation of goods was not a difficulty there since reliance on coin was less and it may be, paradoxically that the marginal lands of Ireland were best placed to survive harvest crises and the associated commercial disruption.

Responses to adverse weather certainly varied over space but contemporaries also observed similarities in reactions to bad weather over time. When considering the events of 1673–4 some contemporaries were struck by the similarities between the politics of those years and the events of 1641. Oliver Plunkett drew explicit parallels between the events of 1640 and 1641 and those of 1673 and George Rawdon at Lisburn did likewise.[95] In late 1673 or early 1674 when Lord Herbert of Castleisland in Kerry described the 1640s he was clear that 'a bloody enemy [Irish Catholics] (as they are expected to be in another rebellion) and 'tis possible they look upon themselves as now provoked'.[96] While contemporaries certainly saw these parallels, temptation to see underlying common causes should be resisted. The weather conditions of the early years of the 1640s and those of 1673–4 were remarkably similar with cold winters and wet springs and summers.[97] Political conditions too seemed similar. Rather, it is what contemporaries made of these circumstances, including the weather events, that gives them their significance. As with 1640–41, 1673–4 was a period of economic and social crisis occasioned by the Dutch war, harvest failure and livestock disease that quickly evolved into a commercial crisis with market failures in some of the more commercialised parts of Ulster. Yet the results of these apparently similar sets of variables was radically different. There was no rebellion in Ireland in 1674 and the tensions that the crisis created were rapidly defused. The responses to the conjunction of harvest crisis, commercial crisis and political crisis were different in 1673–4 to those of the autumn of 1641. That this was so is the result of what contemporaries chose to do with such variables rather than being shaped by them. Understanding past climates as contemporaries understood them is as much about recovering past mentalities as it is about discovering the mechanics of weather. The effects of climate, understood by contemporaries as patterns of weather, were real but they were mediated though complexities of human and biological agencies.

---

[94] *Cal. S.P. Dom., 1673–5*, 94.
[95] Hanly (ed.), *Letters*, 386; *Cal. S.P. Dom., 1673–5*, 225.
[96] W.J. Smith (ed.), *Herbert correspondence* (Cardiff, 1968), 214.
[97] Ludlow and Crampsie, 'Environmental history', 633–6.

Climate, weather and society in Ireland in the long eighteenth century: the experience of the later phases of the Little Ice Age

JAMES KELLY*

School of History and Geography, Dublin City University

[Accepted 7 August 2020. Published 28 September 2020.]

Abstract

This paper aspires to map the climate and weather experience of the population of Ireland during the later phases of the Little Ice Age (LIA). Comprising four sections, it begins with an examination of the impact of the Late Maunder Minimum spanning the challenging 1690s—the coldest decade of the LIA—and the amelioration in temperature that was a feature of the early decades of the eighteenth century. Though Ireland was not as severely impacted as other parts of western Europe at this time, the population experienced its share of weather-induced crises—severe cold, serious flooding, high winds and, on occasion, drought—accounts of which can be found in contemporary weather diaries and newspapers. Weather-induced harvest crises posed a still more formidable challenge, and part two of the paper seeks, by correlating these events with volcanic forcing, both to identify those episodes that can be ascribed to specific volcanic events, and to make a case for the inclusion of larger environmental forces in the historic reconstruction of the island's climate. Volcanic forcing is most readily illustrated in the case of the major Lakagígar eruption (1783–4), but the temporal correlations that can be drawn with famines and subsistence crises in 1740–41, 1755–6, 1766 and 1815 suggests that it was a more persistent factor. The population was insufficiently informed to make such connections, of course, and parts three and four of the paper focus on the impact of extreme weather events on people and on identifying how economic growth and the improvement to the kingdom's infrastructure enhanced their capacity to negotiate climatic and weather induced crisis into the early nineteenth century when, following a phase of reduced temperature—the so-called Dalton Minimum *c.* 1795–1825—the LIA can be said to have concluded.

Introduction

On 21 July 1787, readers of *Saunders' News Letter* were informed that 'farms' on the 'banks' of 'all the country rivers' had suffered 'great damage' due to flooding caused by 'the late rains'.[1] It was one of a sequence of reports

---

*Author's email: james.kelly@dcu.ie
ORCID iD: https://orcid.org/0000-0003-1423-9226
doi: https://doi.org/10.3318/PRIAC.2020.120.08

[1] *Saunders' News Letter*, 21 July 1787.

recounting the effects of the heavy 'rains' experienced in the summer of 1787.[2] What distinguished this report from others was not the specificity of its focus but the fact that it was accompanied by a positive reflection on the island's climate:

> Ireland, happily…does not experience those hurricanes, tornadoes and earthquakes, which terrify the minds of the inhabitants in other countries. Dangerous lightning is seldom seen among us, though the neighbouring countries, and even the nearest, Great Britain, furnishes frequent instances of the mischiefs done by that elementary fire. France, one of the finest and most fruitful kingdoms, has been visited by such storms of hail, thunder and lightning, as have blasted the hopes of the year, while happier Ireland has escaped like calamities.[3]

The ability to make such comparisons and to acknowledge that 'great and manifest alterations have taken place in the climate of most countries' over time was one of the outcomes of the increased interest in weather reporting that was a feature of the eighteenth century.[4] It was integral to the data collection pursued by John Rutty, the physician, whose 'chronological history of the weather' is the fullest Irish statement of the proposition that 'the weather has a powerful immediate influence…in the propagation, increase and abatement of diseases'. Indeed, Rutty's contention that the population of Ireland was less susceptible to plague because 'the air…[was] peculiarly wholesome and healthful' and less prone to fever because of 'the coolness and temperateness of our summers' provided the foundation for his conclusion that 'the healthiness of our climate in general appears from the rarity of any notable depopulating epidemics'.[5] Other observers were more cautious but increased meteorological curiosity, the most material evidential legacy of which is the weather diary, attests to the appreciating interest in identifying weather patterns. The number of individuals who maintained weather diaries, whether for the purposes of facilitating inquiry or, as has also been suggested, as an exercise in 'self-discipline', was modest. But

---

[2] *Dublin Evening Post*, 30 June, 5, 10, 26 July, 18, 21, 23 Aug., 25 Sept. 1787; *Saunders' News Letter*, 24 July, 2 Aug. 1787.
[3] *Saunders' News Letter*, 21 July 1787.
[4] *Saunders' News Letter*, 6 Mar. 1786.
[5] John Rutty, *A chronological history of the weather and seasons, and of the prevailing diseases in Dublin, with their various periods, successions, and revolutions during the space of forty years, with a comparative view of the differences of the Irish climate and diseases and those of England and other countries* (Dublin, 1770), xxvi, xxix, xxxv–vi; 'A preface shewing the importance and usefulness of histories of the weather' in John Rutty, *An essay towards a natural history of the county of Dublin* (2 vols, Dublin, 1772), vol. 2, 271–9.

their existence is testament to the increased recognition of the impact of climate and weather on life and the desire to penetrate its secrets.[6]

Because 'agrarian systems are directly dependent on climate', it is appropriate at the outset to observe that the system of food production in Ireland and France in the seventeenth and eighteenth centuries 'was not resistant to climatic shocks'. As Axel Michaelova and Louis Cullen have pointed out, since both 'short term climate shocks and long-term climate change' have 'a higher probability of extreme events', 'most periods of serious crisis were accompanied by harvest problems'.[7] This was an inevitable consequence of the fact that, by comparison with England where 'agriculture was quite diversified', the 'structure' of food production in Ireland and France was not. As a result, the impact of 'climate extremes', especially when they occurred in 'clusters' was more consequential than 'an isolated climate extreme', which might not cause 'long-term economic damage'.[8] A negative outcome was certainly a possibility during the Little Ice Age (LIA), assuming one accepts (and not all do) that the 1–2°C decrease that defines this climatic era merit this appellation.[9] What is not in dispute is that the temperature oscillated between the onset of the LIA in the fourteenth century and its conclusion in the mid nineteenth, and that the eighteenth century, which is the focus of this paper, spans a number of its later phases. These are, first, the later years of the Late Maunder Minimum ('the coldest phase of the "Little Ice Age"')[10] spanning the final quarter of the seventeenth century and the early decades of the eighteenth (*c*.1675–*c*.1720). Second, a warmer phase, peaking in the 1730s but which also includes a cooler, less stable period spanning

---

[6] Rutty, *Chronological history of the weather*, xxix; Jan Golinski, '"Exquisite atmography": theories of the world and experiences of weather in a diary of 1703', *British Journal for the History of Science* 34 (2001), 149–71; Jan Golinski, *British weather and the climate of Enlightenment* (Chicago, IL, 2007), 80–91.

[7] Axel Michaelova, 'The impact of short-term climate change on British and French agriculture and population in the first half of the eighteenth century' in P.D. Jones *et al.* (eds), *History and climate: memories of the future?* (New York, 2001), 205; L.M. Cullen, 'The study of economic fluctuations 1660–1800: problems and sources', *Irish Economic and Social History* 41 (2014), 4–5; also Guido Alfani and Cormac Ó Gráda, 'Famines in Europe: an overview' in Alfani and Ó Gráda (eds), *Famine in European history* (Cambridge, 2017), 16–17.

[8] Michaelova, 'The impact of short-term climate change', 206–7.

[9] Mike Lockwood *et al.*, 'Frost fairs, sunspots and the Little Ice Age', *Astronomy and Geophysics* 58:2 (2017), 2.17–2.23; K.R. Briffa and J.A. Matthews, 'The Little Ice Age: reevaluation of an evolving concept', *Geografiska Annaler* 87A (2005), 17–36; Morgan Kelly and Cormac Ó Gráda, 'The waning of the Little Ice Age', *Journal of Interdisciplinary History* 44 (2013), 301–25; Morgan Kelly and Cormac Ó Gráda, 'Change points and temporal dependence in reconstructions of annual temperature: did Europe experience a Little Ice Age?', *Annals of Applied Statistics* 8:3 (2014), 1372–94.

[10] J. Luterbacher *et al.*, 'The Late Maunder Minimum (1675–1715) – a key period for studying decadal scale climatic change in Europe', *Climatic Change* 49 (2001), 441.

most of the rest of the century; and, third, the ensuing cold phase—the Dalton Minimum—spanning the final years of the eighteenth century and most of the first three decades of the nineteenth century. Though crucial features of each of these phases remain opaque, they provide a framework for this attempt to map the climatic experience of the population of Ireland between *c.* 1690 and 1830. Moreover, when set beside the calendar of crisis events—famines and subsistence crises particularly—they support the findings of historical climatologists that volcanic forcing exerted such influence on weather patterns during this period that it deserves a prominent place in the history of Irish climate.

Climate and society in early eighteenth-century Ireland—the final phase of the late Maunder Minimum

Jürg Luterbacher's arresting claim that 'the climax of the Little Ice Age [in Europe] was reached in the 1690s' is supported by the evidence of temperature records (most pertinently from an Irish perspective the long running Central England Temperature series (CET)) and by the pattern of extreme events. Among these, the demographically costly famines of 1693–4 in France, 1693–5 in Italy, and the 'ill years' that ravaged Scotland in the second half of the decade stand out.[11] The absence of a comparable crisis in Ireland[12] is intriguing therefore, as it suggests that the island negotiated the worst years of the Late Maunder Minimum without an equivalent increase in mortality or climate-induced distress. Ireland did not escape these ill effects, though the efforts of the Irish Privy Council to obviate the prospect of 'a great scarcity and dearth of corn' by embargoing its export from Ulster in January 1697 is consistent with the conclusion that the

---

[11] Jürg Luterbacher, 'The late Maunder Minimum (1675–1715): climax of the 'little ice age' in Europe', in P.D. Jones *et al.* (eds), *History and climate: memories of the future?* (New York, 2001), 30; Gordon Manley, 'Central England temperatures: monthly means 1659–1973', *Quarterly Journal of the Royal Meteorological Society* 100 (1974), 389–405; Alfani and Ó Gráda, 'Famines in Europe: an overview', 10, 14, 15; K.J. Cullen, *Famine in Scotland: the ill years of the 1690s* (Edinburgh, 2010); Rosanne D'Arrigo *et al.*, 'Complexity in crisis: the volcanic cold pulse of the 1690s and the consequences of Scotland's failure to cope', *Journal of Volcanology and Geothermal Research* 389 (2020), 106746; Richard Hoyle, 'Britain' in Alfani and Ó Gráda (eds), *Famine in European history* (Cambridge, 2017), 161–3.

[12] This is not to imply that events in Scotland did not impact Ireland; the late 1690s witnessed a reversal of the pattern of migration from Ireland to Scotland in the early 1690s to migration from Scotland to Ireland: K.J. Cullen, 'Scottish migration to Ulster during the "seven ill years" of the 1690s', in Anders Ahlqvist and Pamela O'Neill (eds), *Celts and their cultures at home and abroad* (Sydney, 2013), 35–54. There is no reason, however, to challenge the view of Alfani and Ó Gráda ('Famine in Europe: an overview', 15) that, apart from the Netherlands (D'Arrigo *et al.*, 'Complexity in crisis', 3), Ireland and England were the 'only regions' in Europe that 'seem to have been spared'. It is noteworthy also that the Church of Ireland burial register for Youghal indicates no increase in mortality in the late 1690s: Clodagh Tait, 'Causes of death and cultures of care in county Cork 1660–1720: the evidence of Youghal parish registers' in John Cunningham (ed.), *Early modern Ireland and the world of medicine* (Manchester, 2019), 134–6.

country was not then hurting severely.[13] If so, this did not remain the case, and the subsequent extension of the embargo to embrace Leinster and, when a 'great scarcity and dearness of all manner of corn and grain' was experienced across the island in the summer of 1697, to 'all…ports', indicates that the country was then in the throes of a serious subsistence crisis. Moreover, matters continued to disimprove as 'unseasonable weather during the harvest' generated concerns 'that multitudes of the poor…may be in danger of perishing' if food exports were not interdicted.[14] The absence of reference to excess mortality suggests that the extension of the embargo in October 1698 in order 'that the stock of corn within this kingdom may be preserved for the use of the inhabitants thereof during this time of general scarcity…in most of Europe' achieved its purpose. If so, it did not insulate the 'poorer sort' against distress. Indeed, though the harvest was adequate in 1699, prices remained 'so high and dear' that the embargo was renewed once again to ease the threat to the well-being of the 'poorer sort', who were then 'in greater danger of being starved than formerly'. It remained in force until April 1700 when normal trading in foodstuffs finally resumed.[15]

Though the order and frequency of the Privy Council's interventions suggest that the margin between famine and survival in the 1690s was not large, the fact that Ireland did not experience difficulties equivalent to those that afflicted Scotland and much of continental Europe is not easily explained climatically. It may be that the island's 'proximity to the…North Atlantic Drift' assisted it to escape the worst effects of four unusually cold winters in the 1690s (1692, 1694, 1695 and 1698), and the longer spate of reduced temperatures that defines the decade 1696–1705 as one of the coldest in the northern hemisphere during the second millennium.[16] But it is difficult to conceive how variation in ocean circulation (the North Atlantic Drift) or in atmospheric circulation as the North Atlantic Oscillation moved into a negative phase, which may have reduced winter temperatures in the northern hemisphere by between 1–2°C and summer temperatures by 0.3–.6°C, would not have had a comparable impact on Scotland and Ireland.[17] At any event, it is not incompatible with the 'substantial temporal and spatial variability' (observed by Luterbacher) in cold conditions during the

---

[13] Proclamation, 12 Jan. 1697 in James Kelly and M.A. Lyons (eds), *The proclamations of Ireland 1660–1820* (5 vols, Dublin, 2014), vol. 2, 370–71.
[14] Proclamation, 29 Mar., 22 June 1697, 8 Oct. 1698 in Kelly and Lyons (eds), *The proclamations of Ireland*, vol. 2, 371–2, 373, 424–5.
[15] Proclamation, 18 Nov. 1698, 7 Feb., 20 Oct. 1699, 26 Apr. 1700 in Kelly and Lyons (eds), *The proclamations of Ireland*, vol. 2, 428–9, 435–7, 466–9, 486–7.
[16] Engler *et al.*, 'The Irish famine of 1740–41: famine vulnerability and "climate migration"', *Climate of the Past* 9 (2013), 1169; D'Arrigo *et al.*, 'Complexity in crisis', 1–9.
[17] Luterbacher, 'The late Maunder Minimum', 30; Luterbacher *et al.*, 'The Late Maunder Minimum (1675–1715) – a key period', 441–2; M.F. Glueck and C.W. Stockton, 'Reconstruction of the North Atlantic Oscillation', *International Journal of Climatology* 21 (2001), 1453–65; see the correlation of sunspot number and northern hemisphere temperatures in Lockwood *et al.*, 'Frost fairs, sunspots and the Little Ice Age', 2.18–19.

Little Ice Age; or with temperature reconstructions (such as those analysed by the Pages 2K Consortium), which indicate that 'the specific timing of peak warm and cold intervals varies regionally'.[18] It is the case, of course, that the multi-decadal trends upon which this conclusion is grounded are less compelling in accounting for Ireland's ostensibly anomalous experience during the 1690s and first decade of the eighteenth century, but it is at the least tenable to ascribe it to variation within the broader hemispheric pattern of low temperatures.[19]

Moreover, it is clear from the documentary record that the weather in Ireland in the 1690s was extremely challenging. One may instance the 'great frost' that gripped the country between the 19 January and mid-February 1692 and the 'very hard frost' experienced in 1693. The former echoes the 0°C temperature return for February 1692 recorded in the CET series, and the impression it provides is consistent with the CET record, which indicates that air temperatures fell below the decadal norm during five of the ten years 1691–1700. Saliently, this decadal average was 8.4 per cent below that experienced in the 1680s (8.79°C) and 13.5 per cent in arrear of that recorded for the first decade of the eighteenth century (9.21°C) (see Table 1).[20] Furthermore, it was conducive to the spread of 'rheums of all kind', such as that which 'seized great numbers of all sorts of people in Dublin' before it took hold in 'the country as well as the city' in the winter of 1693–4.[21] It is not clear from Thomas Molyneux's account of this 'distemper' if it resulted in increased mortality; it is not unlikely, but the absence of reference then and later to significant excess mortality supports the conclusion that Ireland was less seriously troubled by the difficult climate conditions of the 1690s than most of Europe.

This remained the case, moreover, as the increase in average annual air temperature attributable to warmer winters in 1698–9 and 1699–1700 paved the way for an aggregate improvement in the decadal average in the 1700s and 1710s (Table 1).[22] It was not that the population did not experience severe weather related challenges.[23] According to reports from Limerick, seventeen people were

---

[18] Jürg Luterbacher, 'European summer temperatures since Roman times', *Environmental Research Letters* 11 (2016), 5–6; Pages 2KConsortium, 'Continental-scale temperature variability during the past two millennia', *Nature Geoscience* 6 (2013), 341–2.

[19] It also gives additional weight to Karen Cullen's argument that, as well as the weather, the decision to introduce a bounty to incentivise grain exports in 1695 was an important causative factor: Cullen, *Famine in Scotland*, chapter 3.

[20] Manley, 'Temperatures in England', 393–4; F.H. Tuckey, *The county and city of Cork Remembrancer* (Cork, 1837), 120; John Burns, *An historical and chronological remembrancer of all the remarkable occurrences from the creation to…1775* (Dublin, 1775), 217.

[21] Benjamin Franklin, 'On colds', 30 Nov. 1732 in L.W. Labaree (ed.), *The papers of Benjamin Franklin, volume 1* (New Haven, CT, 1959), 252–4. Franklin's paper draws on an original account of the episode by Thomas Molyneux (1661–73), which was published in the *Philosophical Transactions* 18 (1694), 105–11.

[22] Manley, 'Temperatures in England', 393–4.

[23] D.W. Hayton and Michael Page (eds), *Anglo-Irish politics, 1680–1720: the correspondence of the Brodrick family of Surry and county Cork – volume 1, 1680–1714*

TABLE 1—Decennial temperature (degrees centigrade): yearly average by decade, 1661–1810 (CET series)

Decade	Degrees Celsius
1661–70	9.14
1671–80	8.6
1681–90	8.79
1691–1700	8.11
1701–10	9.21
1711–20	9.14
1721–30	9.43
1731–40	9.57
1741–50	9.17
1751–60	9.09
1761–70	8.65
1771–80	9.32
1781–90	8.92
1791–1800	9.11
1801–10	9.13
1811–20	8.77

Source: Calculated from data in Gordon Manley, 'Central England temperatures: monthly means 1659–1973', *Quarterly Journal of the Royal Meteorological Society*, 100 (1974), pp 389–405.

drowned in December 1705 in 'a most violent storm' that flooded 'most of the cellars in town' and obliged 'the inhabitants of the suburbs of the English town… to crawl naked from the inside to the tops of their cabbins'.[24] However, this was on a modest scale by comparison with the explosive storm that devastated England's southern coast in November 1703.[25] Similarly, though it was so cold in Dublin during the 'great winter' of 1708/09 that Alan Brodrick was 'hardly able to keep my house warm with all the fires I can make and the shutters I can use', the 1.5°C below zero average January temperature in the British Isles indicates that conditions in Dublin were markedly less severe than they were in Paris, which registered a minus 20°C night time temperature.[26] Moreover, this pattern persisted through the final years of the Late Maunder Minimum as the weather diarist Isaac Butler recounts. Butler's approach to record keeping was impressionistic rather than precise, but he was alert to the wider environment, which makes his diary particularly useful. And it provides the context for his observation that the impact of the 'ragged weather' experienced in Dublin during the hard winter

---

(*Parliamentary History*: texts and studies 15: Chichester, 2019), 221, 244.
[24] *Boston News Letter*, 25 Mar., 10 June 1706.
[25] Golinski, 'Exquisite atmography', 161–4; Golinski, *British weather*, 42–53.
[26] Manley, 'Temperatures in England', 394; Hayton and Page (eds), *Anglo-Irish politics, 1680–1720: the correspondence of the Brodrick family*, 231.

of 1715–6, when there was a record number of frosty days and Lough Neagh famously froze over, was exceeded by the 'unspeakable misery' that precipitated 'vast numbers' to premature death in Paris, Germany and Poland.[27] The winter of 1717–8 was not equally grim, but even then reports from Europe offered some vicarious comfort as the snow, frost and 'violent stormy winds' experienced in Ireland in December 1717 were less demographically costly than flooding in north Holland and Germany, which may have resulted in 2,500 deaths in the Groningen area alone.[28]

One must not conclude from this that the country exited the Maunder Minimum in the early eighteenth century without loss of life or serious travail. It is notable, for example, that the violent storms that cost seventeen people their life in Limerick in 1705 was accompanied by a significant loss of 'cattle and corn in the low lands near the Shannon…as well as the corn and rape in stack as that in the ground' that might, at another time, have prompted justifiable fears for the well-being of the populace.[29] The situation was more serious in early 1709 because the intense cold came in the wake of a poor harvest, but the authorities contrived—by introducing an embargo on 'the exportation of all manner of corn, grain and meal'—to calm prices by pre-empting merchants who had already embarked on 'buying great quantities…to export…to parts beyond the seas'.[30] These efforts did not dispel public disquiet, as the occurrence of food protest in Cork demonstrates, but the absence of similar protests in 1710 suggests that the population's concerns soon eased.[31] This is notable as

---

[27] Isaac Butler, 'The diary of the wind and weather, 1716–1734' (Dublin Public Library (DPL), Gilbert Collection), 1, 2–4; F.E. Dixon, 'An Irish weather diary of 1711–1725', *Quarterly Journal of Royal Meteorological Society* 85 (1959), 380; Rutty, 'A monthly registry of the weather and seasons in Dublin', in *Natural history of Dublin*, vol. 2, 350–51, 352. There was frost on a total of 10 days in December 1715, 18 days in January and 15 days in February 1716. This was true also of the 'perfect tornado tempest with violent rains' that caused significant death on the English south coast in September 1716; it did 'great damage' to Sir John Rogerson's Quay but there were no reports of casualties: Butler, *The diary of the wind and weather, 1716–1734*, 15; Rutty, *Natural history of Dublin*, vol. 2, 350.

[28] Butler, 'The diary of the wind and weather, 1716–1734', 46–7; Rutty, 'Registry of the weather', 285. The Irish reading public was provided with further grounds for comparison by newspaper reports, such as that carried in *Pue's Occurrences*, 5 Sept. 1719, that the 'excessive heats' experienced in France and England in the summer of 1719, which resulted in serious water shortages, contributed to an 'epidemical distemper' in humans and to unseasonal cattle mortality.

[29] *Boston News Letter*, 25 Mar., 10 June 1706.

[30] Michaelova, 'The impact of short-term climate change on British and French agriculture', 207; Kelly and Lyons (eds), *The proclamations of Ireland 1660–1820*, vol. 2, 616–17. The prohibition was reiterated on 19 December and rescinded on 26 Apr. 1710: Kelly and Lyons (eds), *The proclamations of Ireland 1660–1820*, vol. 2, 623–4, 629–30; *Dublin Intelligence*, 14 Jan. 1710.

[31] James Kelly, *Food rioting in Ireland in the eighteenth and nineteenth centuries* (Dublin, 2017), 31–2.

the weather conditions were often difficult. An incomplete listing of the most challenging moments experienced in the 1710s include above average rainfall in 1712, 1715 and 1720; 'a great snow', which was responsible for the loss of 'an abundance of sheep', in January 1716; 'exceeding stormy bad weather' that battered the Irish and English coastlines in September 1716 and the spring of 1717; damage to 'fields and gardens' caused by thunderstorms in July 1717; and serious flooding in Dublin attributed to 'the greatest thunder and lightning…ever…seen' in July 1719.[32]

While it is unclear how much distress these events caused, weather extremes lay at the root of the most serious environmental challenges the population encountered in the early eighteenth century. By comparison with England, Ireland's agricultural system was insufficiently 'diversified' to evade famine when extreme weather endangered the food supply.[33] This is what occurred in 1720–21 and 1725–9. Though neither episode has been reconstructed in sufficient detail to provide a precise picture of the centrality of the weather in their gestation, course and impact, Isaac Butler's observation that 'much damage was done to the corn and hay by the…violent storms of wind and rain that fell' in the months of July and August 1720 indicates that it was a factor.[34] Moreover, the difficulties this caused were compounded by a wet and cold autumn and early winter, though the worst of the weather was not experienced until February and March 1721 when eleven days with snow and 35 'days with frost' took a heavy toll on cattle across the island. Sections of the population were reduced to extremis as a result, and obliged to look for relief from wherever it could be acquired.[35] Incidents, such as that described by Bishop Nicolson of Derry in June 1721, when scores of 'starving' cottagers descended on and butchered the carcass of a coach

---

[32] A.F. Jenkinson *et al.*, 'Monthly and annual rainfall for Ireland, 1711–1977' (Met 0 13 Branch Memorandum, no. 77, Apr. 1979, Meteorological Service Library, Dublin); Butler, 'The diary of the wind and weather, 1716–1734', 1, 29, 36, 84, 85; Rutty, 'Registry of the weather', 282–3, 290; *Newcastle Courant*, 4 Feb. 1716; *Pue's Occurrences*, 5 Sept. 1719; Conolly to Bonnell, 21 July 1719 in M.L. Jennings and G.A. Ashford (eds), *The letters of Katherine Conolly* (Dublin, 2018), 15; Graeme Kirkham, 'Ulster emigration to North America, 1680–1720' in H.T. Blethen and C.W. Wood (eds), *Ulster and North America: transatlantic perspectives on the Scotch Irish* (Tuscaloosa, 1997), 80–91.

[33] Michaelova, 'The impact of short-term climate change', 205–7; Hoyle, 'Britain', 141–2, 148–9, 156–9.

[34] Butler, 'The diary of the wind and weather, 1716–1734', 109; Rutty, 'Registry of the weather', 291.

[35] James Kelly, 'Harvests and hardship: famine and scarcity in Ireland in the late 1720s', *Studia Hibernica* 26 (1991–2), 66–7; Butler, 'The diary of the wind and weather, 1716–1734', 113, 115; Rutty, 'Registry of the weather', 292–3; Jenkinson *et al.*, 'Monthly and annual rainfall for Ireland, 1711–1977'; DPL, Wake papers, Gilbert MS 27 ff 286–7, Nicolson to Wake, 2 June 1721; Dixon, 'An Irish weather diary of 1711–1725', 380; M.G. Sanderson, 'Daily weather in Dublin 1716–1734: the diary of Isaac Butler', *Weather* 73:6 (2018), 181; 'Petition from Limerick', 1721 (National Archives of Ireland (NAI), Isabel Grubb's notes from petitions in the Public Record Office, 1915).

horse that had died in an accident provide a window onto their desperation. Their plight was certainly not eased by further heavy rain in the late summer and early winter of 1721, which inundated 'lowlands' and 'a vast quantity of hay [was] for ever lost by the floods'.[36]

The population was hardly better equipped to deal with unusual warmth, for though the improvement of the weather that occurred in 1722 and 1723 was welcome the 'exceeding hot weather' that threatened drought in the summer of 1723 was equally discomfiting. In point of fact, the concerns this aroused were unjustified for though the effects of this anomalous warmth were exacerbated by 'a month of extraordinary thunder' in July, it impacted Ireland less severely than elsewhere in Europe, and it brought some an unexpected bounty in the form of 'a second crop of the fruit of the earth'.[37] This was a welcome bonus for a population that had endured a sequence of difficult seasons, though it hardly compensated all for the 'incredible mischief' the 'excessive heat did...the grass and other vegetables' in May 1723.[38] Moreover, the respite it gave was short-lived as, beginning in 1725, the country endured a sequence of poor weather years that underlined their continuing vulnerability to extreme weather.

The sequence of events that reduced parts of the island to famine in 1727 and 1729 commenced, not with severe storms and the inundation of large areas alongside the river Liffey in the winter of 1724–5, but with an unusually 'wet and cold' summer in 1725, the most material ill-effect of which was a 'spoiled' harvest.[39] This outcome, inevitably, presented the public and the political elite with a serious challenge, and while the difficulties they encountered were exacerbated by below average temperatures and precipitation in January 1726 ('a month of the hardest weather'), they were dealt a more serious blow when a further wet summer contributed to a second less than full harvest necessitating a significant increase in grain imports.[40] Had the weather facilitated planting the population might quickly have put the challenges posed by inflated food prices behind it.

---

[36] DPL, Wake papers, Gilbert MS 27 ff 286–7, Nicolson to Wake, 2 June 1721; National Library of Ireland (NLI), Smythe of Barbavilla papers, MS 41589/3, Fitzsimons to Smyth, 16 Sept. 1721; Butler, 'The diary of the wind and weather, 1716–1734', 117.

[37] Butler, *The diary of the wind and weather, 1716–1734*, 135, 137, 139, 149, 151, 155, 157, 161; Dixon, 'An Irish weather diary of 1711–1725', 380. According to Jenkinson *et al.*, 'Monthly and annual rainfall for Ireland, 1711–1977', 1723 was the sixth driest year in the eighteenth century.

[38] Rutty, 'Registry of the weather', 297.

[39] Kelly, 'Harvests and hardship', 72–3; Butler, 'The diary of the wind and weather, 1716–1734', 189, 200, 203; Rutty, 'Registry of the weather', 302, 303–4, 307; DPL, Wake papers, Gilbert MS 27 f. 360, Nicolson to Wake, 13 July 1725. According to Jonathan Swift on 14 Aug. 'in four months we have had two odd fair days, and 13 more, and all the rest foul from the 20th of April': Harold Williams (ed.), *The correspondence of Jonathan Swift* (5 vols, Oxford, 1963-5), vol. 3, 87.

[40] Butler, 'The diary of the wind and weather, 1716–1734', 217; Rutty, 'Registry of the weather', 306; Manley, 'Central England temperatures', 394; Kelly, 'Harvests and hardship', 77–8.

Primate Hugh Boulter, at the head of the Irish executive, favoured introducing a tillage quota in order to augment the food supply, but it was already too late to avert the impact of shortages and high prices and continuing difficulties caused by 'exceeding bad weather'. Mortality increased as a result in 1727, and, for the second time in less than a decade, the country tasted the bitter fruits of famine.[41] The most accessible index of its impact is provided by the bill of mortality for Dublin, which rose by 8 per cent between 1726–7 and 1727–8 (Table 2). It would probably have been worse had the 'very terrible rainy weather' of March and April 1728 and the 'very cold and unseasonable weather' experienced in June (which brought ice briefly to the river Liffey) persisted. As it was, rain in July and 'terrible storms' in August 1728 had such a negative impact on the harvest that when, in December 1728, the country experienced what Katherine Conolly described as 'the greatest snow and hardest frost I ever remember' the condition of the country deteriorated appreciably.[42] The population's predicament was not eased when, in January 1729, the air temperature approached the low level it had last registered in January 1726, and the country endured 'a long tedious winter', and 'a cold backward spring', with average air temperatures in February and March 1729 colder than they had been at any time since the exceptional winter of 1709.[43] This resulted, inevitably, in further excess mortality, evidenced by the annual bill of mortality in Dublin, which peaked in 1729–30 at 18 per cent above its previous level (Table 2). The impact across the island is less identifiable, but 'the province of Ulster suffered greatly'. Further, calculations based on the hearth money returns, which suggest that the country's population may have fallen (because of emigration as well as famine mortality), by 0.2 per cent per annum between 1725 and 1732 provide an indication of the order of its demographic impact.[44] It was a matter of great significance therefore that improved

---

[41] Kelly, 'Harvests and hardship', 82–3, 95; Boulter to Cartaret, 20 July 1727 in Kenneth Milne and Paddy McNally, *The Boulter letters* (Dublin, 2016), 214; Butler, 'The diary of the wind and weather, 1716–1734', 245, 249, 268–9, 271, 275; Rutty, 'Registry of the weather', 309–10; *Stamford Mercury*, 18 Apr. 1728; *Ipswich Journal*, 20 Apr. 1728.

[42] Butler, 'The diary of the wind and weather, 1716–1734', 276, 277, 278, 279, 286; Rutty, 'Registry of the weather', 311–3; *Stamford Mercury*, 18 Apr. 1728; Conolly to Delafaye, 23 Dec. 1728 in Jennings and Ashford (eds), *The letters of Katherine Conolly*, 49; Kieran Hickey, 'The historic record of cold spells in Ireland', *Irish Geography* 44:2–3 (2011), 306.

[43] Manley, 'Central England temperatures', 394; Kelly, 'Harvests and hardship', 84–6; Butler, 'The diary of the wind and weather, 1716–1734', 288, 294.

[44] According to Butler the mortality in Dublin was 'greater than ever was known': Butler, 'The diary of the wind and weather, 1716–1734', 210; for Ulster, see Rutty, 'Registry of the weather', 313; David Dickson, Stuart Daultrey and Cormac Ó Gráda, 'Hearth-tax, household size and population change, 1672–1821', *RIA Proceedings* 82C (1982), 155, 156, 164; Patrick Walsh, 'Free movement of people? Responses to emigration from Ireland, 1718–30', *Journal of Irish and Scottish Studies*, 3:1 (2009), 221–36; Benjamin Franklin, 'Affairs in Ireland, 20 Nov. 1729' in Labaree, *The papers of Benjamin Franklin, volume 1*, 162.

weather conditions in the summer and autumn of 1729 resulted in a good harvest as it meant the country had eased out of crisis in advance of the commencement of the high temperature that distinguished the 1730s.[45]

Ireland experienced fewer climate induced crises during the final decades of the Late Maunder Minimum than many other parts of Europe. This is consistent with Luterbacher's conclusion that Europe's exit from this cold phase, which can be said to have commenced in the British Isles in the winter of 1699, took a number of decades.[46] The most significant difficulties were encountered during the late 1690s, late 1700s, and in 1720–21 and 1725–9 when the country either experienced famine or was obliged to take emergency action to prevent this happening. In addition, one must not overlook the more numerous episodes of bad weather in which lives were lost and property was destroyed on land and on sea, or the discomfort, cost and inconvenience caused by the storms, flooding, lightning and other meteorological phenomena that feature disproportionately in weather diaries, correspondence and news reports. While these documents are of interest for what they reveal of the embryonic attempts of contemporaries to identify patterns in the ostensibly random events they chronicled, meteorological analysis of their data confirms that the population lived through an era during which severe frosts, prolonged snows, persistent heavy rain and severe storms were regular occurrences.[47] The climate in the early decades of the eighteenth century was not as forbidding as it was when the Maunder Minimum was at its most acute in the 1690s.[48] But the famines of 1720–21 and 1725–9 demonstrated that the population was ill circumstanced to deal with the challenges the weather presented. This was as true of warm weather as it was of extreme cold.

The impact of volcanic forcing on climate in Ireland in the eighteenth century

The increased air temperature identifiable in north-west Europe in the 1730s represented a significant shift away from the cold extremes that were a feature of the Late Maunder Minimum.[49] One of its initial registers was the near complete absence of frost during the high winter of 1729–30, but it also had a broader register evident in the reduced number of extreme weather events recorded in the weather diary of Isaac Butler in 1730, 1731 and early 1732.[50]

---

[45] Manley, 'Central England temperatures', 394; Michaeolova, 'The impact of short-term climate change', 205.
[46] Luterbacher, *et al.*, 'The Late Maunder Minimum (1675–1715) – a key period', 442.
[47] Dixon, 'An Irish weather diary of 1711–1725', 376–80.
[48] Above pp 4–6.
[49] P.D. Jones and K.R. Briffa, 'Unusual climate in north west Europe during the period 1730 to 1745 based on instrumental and documentary data', *Climate Change*, 79 (2006), 361–79.
[50] Rutty, *Chronological history of the weather*, 18; Rutty, 'Registry of the weather', 314–5; *Hibernian Chronicle* (Cork), 4 Feb. 1773; Butler, *The diary of the wind and weather, 1716–1734*, 313–60, 363; Sanderson, 'Daily weather in Dublin 1716–1734: the diary of Isaac Butler', 181

TABLE 2—Bill of Mortality: Dublin, 1717-65 (year ending 25 March and total)

1683-4	1717-8	1718-9	1719-20	1720-21	1721-2	1722-3	1723-4	1724-5	1725-6
2173	3021	–	–	–	–	3023	2963	2915/2941	–
1726-7	*1727-8*	*1728-9*	*1729-30*	*1730-31*	*1731-2*	*1732-3*	*1733-4*	*1734-5*	*1735-6*
2723	2946	2700	3206	2184	2184	2534	2608	2466	2196
1736-7	*1737-8*	*1738-9*	*1739-40*	*1740-41*	*1741-2*	*1742-3*	*1743-4*	*1744-5*	*1745-6*
2101	2217	2506	2201	3304	2792	2320	2193	1705	2265
1746-7	*1747-8*	*1748-49*	*1749-50*	*1750-51*	*1751-2*	*1752-3*	*1753-4*	*1754-5*	*1755-6*
1957	1827	1530	1817	2088	2030	1844	1825	1732 (or 1897)	1896 (or 2002)
1756-7	*1757-8*	*1758-9*	*1759-60*	*1760-61*	*1761-2*	*1762-3*	*1763-4*	*1764-5*	*1765-6*
1550	1825 (or 1639)	1558	1752	1993	2292	2490	2605	2307	2275

Source: John Rutty, *A chronological history of the weather and seasons and of the prevailing diseases in Dublin ... with a comparative view of the differences of the Irish climate and diseases and those of England and other countries* (London, 1770); *Dublin Gazette*, March 1724-32; *Belfast News Letter*, 5 Jan. 1762.

Moreover, this pattern persisted through the decade, for as well as the 'mild' winter of 1730–31, an 'unseasonably warm' winter in 1732–3 and 'warm' and 'mild winters' in 1733–4, 1734–5, 1735–6 and 1737–8, the country experienced a 'hot summer' in 1733, 1736 and 1737. As a result, and consistent with the trend in western Europe, the average decadal temperature achieved its eighteenth-century peak in the 1730s (Table 1).[51] This was not without negative implication, if John Rutty's conclusion that warm weather facilitated the spread of epidemical diseases such as the 'catarrhal fever' (which inflated the Dublin bill of mortality in 1732, 1733 and 1737) is correct (Table 2).[52] Moreover, the increased temperature was accompanied by increased precipitation. The 1730s were distinguished, as a longitudinal study of rainfall in Ireland has revealed, by 'persistently wet conditions'.[53] Four years (1730, 1733, 1735 and 1738) stand out, but 1735, which was the second wettest year in the whole of the eighteenth century, was the most challenging as 'the cold winds attended with rain' experienced in the summer drove up bread prices. And, Lord Fitzwilliam's Dublin agent, Richard Mathew reported, 'but for the wheat imported from France, we should have suffered by famine'. Mathew may have exaggerated the order of the threat, but the high food prices he reported were very real and the condition of the population was not eased when August and September were also 'very bad'.[54] Then there was the obvious downside when warmer temperatures were accompanied by drought as was the case in 1737, as another of Earl Fitzwilliam's correspondents explained; writing from Kilkenny at the height of summer heat, he noted worriedly that 'the cattle [are] in a poor way' because 'the herbage by the extraordinary drought is all burnt up'.[55]

It might have been worse, of course. The early and mid-1730s was more benign climatically than the crisis years of the late 1720s and, still more starkly, the famine of 1740–41. The latter event stands apart as the most demographically

---

[51] Rutty, *Chronological history of the weather*, 28, 36–7, 49, 54, 60, 68, 69–70; Rutty, 'Registry of the weather', 317–30, 334, 337; Manley, 'Central England temperatures', 394; Butler, 'The diary of the wind and weather, 1716–1734', 393–4, 414; 'Conolly to Bonnell, 6 July 1737' in Jennings and Ashford (eds), *The letters of Katherine Conolly*, 153–4; NAI, Pembroke estate papers, 97/46/1/2/3/3, Mathew to Fitzwilliam, 14 Feb. 1738.

[52] Rutty, *Chronological history of the weather*, 30–31, 100.

[53] Conor Murphy *et al.*, 'A 305-year continuous monthly rainfall series for the island of Ireland (1711–2016), *Climate of the Past* 14 (2018), 435–6; Jenkinson *et al.*, 'Monthly and annual rainfall for Ireland, 1711–1977'. According to John Rutty, a 'long wet season', which began on 12 June 1734, 'continued generally until 2 February 1736, which amounted to a year and eight months': Rutty, *Chronological history of the weather*, 43; Murphy *et al.*, 'A 305-year continuous monthly rainfall series', 430.

[54] Butler, 'The diary of the wind and weather, 1716–1734', 414, 416, 423, 425; Rutty, 'Registry of the weather', 331, 342, 344; NAI, Pembroke estate papers, 97/46/1/2/4, Mathew to Fitzwilliam, 24 July 1735.

[55] NAI, Pembroke estate papers, 97/46/1/2/2/3, Martin to Fitzwilliam, 20 Aug. 1737.

costly crisis of the eighteenth century.[56] It is of interest also because it is the first attributed to the impact of volcanic forcing.[57] This is not a claim that can be made unequivocally, for the simple reason that volcanic activity is not always securely connectable to those moments when the disruption to the normative weather pattern was the primary cause of famine or, when the alimental and demographic impact was less acute, to a subsistence crisis. But the recognition by historic climatologists that 'volcanic eruptions are primary drivers of natural climate variability—their sulphate aerosol injections into the stratosphere shield the earth's surface from incoming solar radiation, leading to short-term cooling at regional to global scales' means that that it must be given serious consideration.[58] To date, 'volcanic aerosol loading and forcing' have been identified 'from 283 individual eruptive events' over two and a half millennia. The implication that the earlier inquiry pursued by the Smithsonian Global Volcanism Programme, which 'identified 37 annually dated explosive eruptions in the northern hemisphere and tropics…that likely injected sulfate aerosols into the stratosphere', understated the significance of this phenomenon is reinforced by claims that the Little Ice Age may have been precipitated by the massive Samalas eruption of 1257.[59] The fact that there are a number of securely identifiable eruptive events dating from the long eighteenth century among the 'large volcanic eruptions' tabulated by Sigl *et al.* underlines the importance of exploring their significance for the climate history of Ireland if we are better to understand the pattern of

---

[56] David Dickson, *Arctic Ireland: the extraordinary story of the great frost and forgotten famine of 1740–41* (Belfast, 2007); James Kelly, 'Coping with crisis: the response to the famine of 1740–41', *Eighteenth-Century Ireland* 27 (2012), 99–122; Ó Gráda, 'Ireland', 168–73.

[57] Ó Gráda, 'Ireland', 168; Kelly, 'Coping with crisis', 102–03; Hickey, 'The historic record of cold spells in Ireland', 303–04. Jones and Briffa, by contrast, have suggested 'that there does not appear to have been any simple cause for the event, such as a single or a series of large volcanic eruptions': Jones and Briffa, 'Unusual climate in northwest Europe', 362.

[58] G.M. Miles *et al.*, 'Volcanic aerosols: the significance of volcanic eruption strength and frequency for climate', *Quarterly Journal of the Royal Meteorological Society* 128 (2003), 1–16; Michael Sigl *et al.*, 'Timing and climate forcing of volcanic eruptions for the past 2500 years', *Nature* 523 (July 2015), 543; Michael Sigl *et al.*, 'A new bipolar ice core record of volcanism', *Journal of Geophysical research: atmospheres* 118 (2013), 1151–2; Alan Robock, 'Volcanic eruptions and climate', *Review of Geophysics* 38:2 (2000), 191–219; Eythor Halldorsson, 'The dry fog of 1783: environmental impact and human reaction to the Lakagígar eruption' (University of Vienna, MA thesis, 2013), 17–18; Dagomar Degroot, *The frigid golden age: climate change, the Little Ice Age and the Dutch Republic 1560–1720* (Cambridge, 2018), 22–3. Samalas/Rinjani has a VEI of 7.

[59] Sigl *et al.*, 'Timing and climate forcing of volcanic eruptions', 543; Jan Esper *et al.*, 'European summer temperature response to annually dated volcanic eruptions over the past nine centuries', *Bulletin of Volcanology* 75 (2013), 2–3; G.H. Miller, *et al.*, 'Abrupt onset of the Little Ice Age triggered by volcanism and sustained by sea-ice/ocean feedbacks', *Geophysical Research Letters* 39 (2012) Bibcode:2012GeoRL..39.2708M.

climate driven crises that shaped people's lives. It is given added impetus by the identification, in a related inquiry into 'volcanic stratospheric sulfur injection', of seven 'matches of [Greenland] ice core sulfate signals to volcanic eruptions' since these provide tangible evidence that the climatic and environmental effects of volcanic activity is not confined to the immediate locality in which volcanic explosions occur.[60] The relationship of volcanic activity, even that bearing a high Volcanic Explosivity Index (VEI), and identifiable climatically induced food crises is not always readily demonstrable, however. 'Volcanic eruptions that inject large quantities of sulphur-rich gases into the stratosphere have the capability of cooling global climate by 0.2–0.3°C for several years', but this is neither invariable nor equal because the effects do 'not scale proportionately with the size of the eruption'.[61] Various studies 'suggest a significant role of [sic] [for] volcanism in decadal-scale climate fluctuations, with eruptions between 1400 and 1850 explaining 18%–25% of the decadal variance in Northern Hemisphere mean temperature', but volcanic activity was, as these percentages attest, not the only force at play.[62] Furthermore, its impact might be indirect and short term; it was, according to Esper, typically 'stronger during the summer', more marked 'in high European latitudes compared with lower latitudes' and generally of no 'longer than two years' duration.[63]

Demonstrating the impact of volcanism in historical time is inherently problematical given the difficulty in measuring the amount of sulphate aerosol

---

[60] The 'large volcanic eruptions', their dates and ranking are: Tambora (Indonesia), 1815, rank 6; Laki (Iceland), 1783, rank 8; unidentified, 1809, rank 12; and unidentified, 1695, rank 19: Extended data, table 4 in Sigl *et al.*, 'Timing and climate forcing of volcanic eruptions; the seven 'proposed matches' of volcanic eruptions (all of whom have a VEI of 4 or above (see table 3) and ice core sulphate signals are, in chronological order, Fujissan (Japan), 1707; Katla (Iceland), 1721; Shikotsu/Tarumai (Japan), 1739; Katla (Iceland), 1756; Hekla (Iceland), 1766; Laki/Grímsvötn, 1783 and Tambora (Indonesia), 1815: Matthew Toohey and Michael Sigl, 'Volcanic stratospheric sulphur injections and aerosol optical depth from 500 BCE to 1900 CE', *Earth Systems Science Data* 9 (2017), 814.

[61] Luterbacher, 'The late Maunder Minimum', 48. Degroot, *The frigid golden age*, 23. Moreover, this figure may understate its temperature impact as others suggest a figure of .2–.5 degrees centigrade and still others up to 1 degree: S.D. Galvin, Kieran Hickey and A.P. Potito, 'Identifying volcanic signals in Irish temperature observations since AD 1800', *Irish Geography* 44:1 (2011), 7; Halldorsson, 'The dry fog of 1783', 18.

[62] The main 'external forcing' agents were: variation in solar activity, volcanic eruptions and changes in atmospheric circulation in the Atlantic (the North Atlantic Oscillation): for a case study involving their application, see Luterbacher, 'The late Maunder Minimum', 37–50.

[63] Degroot, *The frigid golden age*, 24; Luterbacher, 'The late Maunder Minimum', 47–48, citing Alan Robock; Luterbacher *et al.*, 'European summer temperatures', 8–9; Esper *et al.*, 'European summer temperature response to annually dates volcanic eruptions over the past nine centuries', 1–3; Sigl, 'A new bipolar ice core record of volcanism', 1151–2.

precipitated into the atmosphere, its dispersal and impact at a given moment. The challenge is particularly acute when the focus is an island with a predisposition to climate variability, and when the pertinent characteristics of some of the most likely volcanic eruptions remain opaque. But if volcanic forcing impacts the North Atlantic Oscillation, which when it was in its positive, or high phase, may have led to milder winters and cooler summers and when it was in its negative, or low phase, to severe winters, it is incumbent to try. This is supported by the fact that while a majority of the 39 years between 1690–1810 when the NAO was positive are concentrated in the first half of the eighteenth century, the larger number of years (81) when the NAO was negative embrace years (1708–12, 1715–20, 1724–33, 1762–80, 1782–92, 1804–10) when the kingdom experienced significant weather fuelled difficulties.[64] One cannot assert, however, that volcanic activity affected the weather in a manner that led invariably to a food crisis, because this does not take account of variations in the order and impact of volcanic forcing, still less other relevant and not all equally well-tested variables.[65] Yet the temporal correlation that can be drawn between volcanic incidents with a significant VEI (3 or above) and food crisis in Ireland suggests that it is more than coincidence (Table 3). Moreover, it is consistent with the conclusion of Frank Ludlow, who has identified a strong statistical correlation between 38 volcanic events and cold weather in Ireland over a period of 1,200 years between the fifth and the seventeenth century.[66] It is implicit also in the finding of the investigation (overseen by Graeme T. Swindles) into the occurrence of volcanic ash clouds in northern Europe over 7000 years, which has highlighted the importance of Iceland as their place of origin. This project has identified 33 layers of tephra in Ireland and concluded, based on their frequency (there and elsewhere), not only that 'Icelandic volcanic ash has demonstrably reached Europe between one and five times per century' but also that the number of instances in which such layers have been located in Ireland may have increased during the past 1500 years. The most recent of these events discussed by Swindles is not dated any more precisely than AD1600–1700, but the identification at Brackloon, Co. Mayo of a further tephra deposit, which has been linked to the major Lakagígar eruption of 1783–4, is evidence of the impact of an eighteenth century event. It is also consistent with the conclusion that since Ireland was 'more likely than other parts of Europe to be in the

---

[64] Pablo Ortega *et al.*, 'A model tested North Atlantic Oscillation reconstruction for the past millennium' *Nature*, 523 (no 7556), (2015), 71–4; Glueck and Stockton, 'Reconstruction of the North Atlantic Oscillation', 1453–65. It was at its most negative in 1728 and 1762, and most positive in 1745.
[65] See Sigl, 'Timing and climate forcing' for the argument that volcanic forcing exerted a significant but not always consistent effect.
[66] Francis Ludlow *et al.*, 'Medieval Irish chronicles reveal persistent forcing of severe winter cold events 431–1649', *Environment Research Letters* 8 (2013), 24035–10.

path of anticyclonic airflows bringing ash southwards from Iceland', Icelandic eruptions deserve particular attention.[67]

Because the Lakagígar eruption excepted, the register of most eighteenth-century volcanoes remains opaque, any attempt to establish their climatic impact on Ireland individually or severally, is necessarily tentative. One can be confident, however, based on the work that has been undertaken to calculate the magnitude (VEI) of every episode, to fix its geographical and hemispherical location and, in a minority of instances, to calculate the volume of sulphate issued, that the main eruptions have been identified. Problems persist, of course, notably the identification of major eruptions in 1694, 1762–3 and 1809–12.[68] But the list of volcanoes on the Smithsonian Institution's database is a helpful point of departure.[69] And, as Table 3 suggests, the temporal proximity of global volcanic activity and harvest crisis supports the conclusion that volcanic forcing contributed to the climatic conditions that precipitated the crises—famines and scarcities—that constitute the most consequential manifestations of the impact of climate and weather on the Irish population during the long eighteenth century. It is not possible (as already indicated) to claim an invariable link, given the limits of our knowledge of both the weather in Ireland and volcanic activity. Yet, a case can be made that the impact of volcanic forcing on the weather and food crises in Ireland ranges from strong, as in 1783–4 and 1815–7, to weak (1727–9). This leaves a significant number of instances where, even when a putative link can be claimed, the conclusions must be regarded as provisional.

It is especially difficult to demonstrate that 'the explosive events' that fuelled the Late Maunder Minimum had a formative influence on the weather in Ireland in the late 1690s. But if, as has been suggested, 'the cool summers of 1695 and 1698…have volcanic causes', and that this was the case in Scotland, it is improbable that the Irish Privy Council's decision to embargo food exports for some three years as an insurance against domestic shortage can be divorced from the often forbidding weather of these years.[70] If so, this is true

---

[67] G.T. Swindles et al., 'A 7000 year perspective on volcanic ash clouds affecting northern Europe', *Geology* 39 (2011), 887–90; G.T. Swindles et al., 'Volcanic ash clouds affecting northern Europe: the long view' *Geology Today*, 29:6 (2013), 214–17; Valerie Hall and J.R. Pilcher, 'Late quaternary Iceland tephras in Ireland and Great Britain: detection, characterization and usefulness', *The Holocene* 12:2 (2002), 225, 226–30; Eileen Reilly and F.G.J. Mitchell, 'Establishing chronologies for woodland small hollow and mor humus deposits using tephrachronology and radiocarbon dating', *The Holocene* 25:2 (2015), 248.

[68] See Sigl et al., 'A new bipolar ice core record of volcanism', 1158 for an indicative list.

[69] Global Volcanism Program, 2013. Volcanoes of the World, v.4.7.7. E. Venzke (ed.) Smithsonian Institution (accessed May 2019): https://doi.org/10.5479/siGVP.VOTW4-2013.

[70] D'Arrigo, 'Complexity in crisis', 2–9; Luterbacher, 'The late Maunder Minimum', 48; Table 3.

TABLE 3—Putative correlation of major episodes of volcanic activity and food crisis in Ireland, 1690-1815

	Volcanic activity			Putative register (Ireland)	
Date	Name	Volcanicity Explosivity Index (VEI)	Dust Veil Index	Type of crisis	Date
13 Feb.-14 Sept. 1693	Hekla (Iceland)	4	300	Severe cold and subsistence crisis	Mid and late 1690s
4 June-July 1693; 1694	Serua (Indonesia)	4; 3			
Dec. 1693-Nov. 1694	Etna (Italy)	3			
4-6 July 1694	Hokkaido-Komagatake (Japan)	4			
1694-97	Unknown tropical eruption	N/A			
31 July 1696; Sept. 1697-July 1698	Vesuvius (Italy)	3; 2			
1697-8	Klyuchevstoy (Russia)	3			
16 Dec. 1707-24 Feb. 1708	Fujissan (Japan)	5	500	Subsistence crisis	1709-10
Aug. 1708-23	Vesuvius	3			
23 May 1707-14 11	Santorini (Greece)	3	500		
4 Aug. 1717; 1720	Barbardunga (Iceland)	3:2		Minor famine	1720-21
11 May-15 Oct. 1721	Katla (Iceland)	5	750		
Aug. 1727- May 1728	Oraefajökull (Iceland)	4	70	Subsistence crisis and famine	1725-9
Aug. 1727, 18 Apr., 18 Dec 1728, 30 June 1729 (4 episodes)	Krafla (Iceland)	2/2/2/2	350		
1 Sept. 1730- 16 Apr. 1736	Lanzarote (Canary Islands)	3	400	Increased temperatures and drought/flooding	
Aug. 1737	Avachinsky	3		Famine	1740-41
1739	Sheveluch (Kamchatka)	3			
Feb. 1739 – Dec. 1740	Tolbachik (Kamchatka)	2			
19 Aug.1739-June 1740	Shikotsu (Tarumai) (Japan)	5			
Aug.-Sept. 1749	Taal (Phillipines)	4		—	—
1750(?)	Ksudach (Kamchatka)	4		—	—
15 May-4 Dec. 1754	Taal (Phillipines)	4			
9-15 Mar. 1755	Etna (Italy)	3		Subsistence crisis	1756-7

TABLE 3—(Continued)

Date	Volcanic activity Name	Volcanicity Explosivity Index (VEI)	Dust Veil Index	Putative register (Ireland) Type of crisis	Date
17 Oct.1755-13 Feb.1756	Katla (Iceland)	5	1200		
Aug. 1763-69	Mikakejima (Japan)	4	650	Subsistence crisis	1766
1764	Vesuvius (Italy)	3			
Apr 1766-May 1768	Hekla/Bjallagigar (Iceland)	4			
8 Nov. 1779-May 1781; Jan. 1782	Aira (Japan)	4;2		Subsistence crisis	1782-4
1 May-15 Aug. 1783	Reykjanes	3	} 2,300		
8 June 1783-Feb. 1784	Lakagigar (Shafkar)/Grímsvötn (Iceland)	4			
4 June-11 Aug. 1787	Etna (Italy)	4		Periodic climate difficulties	Late 1780s/ early 1790s
9 June 1790-93	Alaid (Kurile Islands, Russia)	4			
9 June 1798	Tenerife (Canaries)	3		Subsistence crisis	1799-1801
15 Jan.-Apr. 1800	Mount St Helens (USA)	5			
1800?	Witori (Papua)	4			
April 1809-Jan. 1812	Unidentified tropical location	6		Economic difficulties	1810-12
Apr-July 1815	Mount Tambora (Indonesia)	7	3,000	Subsistence crisis	1816-17

Source: 'Global Volcanism Program, 2013, Volcanoes of the World, v.4.7.7. Venzke, E. (ed.), Smithsonian Institution: https://doi.org/10.5479/51 (accessed 2019); M. Sigl et al., 'A new bipolar core record of volcanism from WAIS divide and NEEM and implications for climate forcing of the last 2000 years', *Journal of Geophysical Research: Atmospheres*, 118 (2013), pp 1151–69; M. Toohey and M. Sigl, 'Volcanic stratospheric sulphur injections and aerosol optical depth from 500BCE to 1900 CE', *Earth System Science Data*, 9 (2017), p. 814; R.S. Bradley and P.D. Jones, 'Records if explosive volcanic eruptions over the last 500 years', in idem eds, Climate since AD 1500 (revised edition, London, 1995), table 31.1; H.H. Lamb, 'Volcanic dust in the atmosphere: with a chronology and assessment of its meteorological significance', *Philosophical Transactions of the Royal Society*, 226A (1970), pp 425–533; Michael Sigl et al., 'A new bipolar ice core record of volcanism', *Journal of Geophysical research: atmospheres*, 118 (2013), pp 1151–2.

TABLE 3.1.1— Dust Veil Index

H.H. Lamb's Dust Veil Index (major eruptions with an individual and collective impact of above 500)

1693-98	1707	1721	1724-9	1755	1763-70	1765	1775-6	1783-4	1793-6	1798-1803	1805-09	1812-15
Hekla and others	Fujissan (Japan)	Katla (Iceland)	Hekla, Krafla etc.	Katla	Etna, Hekla, Vesuvius	Hekla	Etna, Vesuvius	Laki etc	Mexico, Alutians	Central America	Central America; Azores	Tambora etc.
3000-3,500	500	750	420	1200	3400	650	1000	2300	1000	1100	1500	4400

TABLE 3.1.2—Dust Veil Index

Northern Hemisphere: Years with a Dust Veil Index in excess of 200, 1690-1820

1694	1707	1708	1752	1755	1783	1784	1785	1815	1816	1817
285	300	200	200	255	400	300	200	695	490	375

Source: H.H. Lamb, 'Volcanic dust in the atmosphere: with a chronology and assessment of its meteorological significance', *Philosophical Transactions of the Royal Society*, 226A (1970), pp 425–533.

also of their interventions in March and December 1709 as the consequences of a poor harvest in 1708 and the 'Great Winter' that gripped Europe during the first three months of 1709, which has been linked to the Fujissan (Japan) and, less commonly, the Santorini eruption in Greece, hit hard.[71] Though the imposition of an embargo is generally a reliable pointer to the fact that the kingdom was experiencing serious food supply issues, the fact that these were subsistence crises rather than famines is consistent with the conclusion that the impact of volcanic forcing on the climate in Ireland at this time was less severe than it was elsewhere. If so, the margin between crisis and survival could be thin. For if the improvement in conditions, whose most obvious index was the improvement in air temperature (Table 1), facilitated the country to negotiate these potentially difficult years in the early eighteenth century, the disimprovement in economic conditions culminating in the crisis of 1720–21 meant the country was still vulnerable when climate conditions were difficult.[72] This is not to imply that the volcanic eruptions of Bárbardunga in August 1717 and Katla between May and October 1721 played no part. The obscuring of the sun in parts of France, Germany and northern Italy in June 1721 indicates that the Katla volcano had an impact on the weather across Europe. But the link between events in Iceland and Ireland is not strong, even if the sizeable dust veil Katla spawned (Table 3.1.1) may have contributed to the difficult weather experienced in Ireland during the second half of 1721, and, perhaps, the warmth experienced in 1722.[73] If so, though there were a series of Icelandic volcanoes (Krafla most notably) in the late 1720s, the fact that their cumulative Dust Veil Index was less than that of Katla in 1721 is consistent with Engler and Werner's conclusion that these had 'no influence on Irish weather'.[74] Indeed, though 'unusual temperature and precipitations conditions' played a

---

[71] Kelly and Lyons (eds), *Proclamations*, vol. 2, 616–8, 623–4. The proclamation was rescinded on 26 Apr. 1710.

[72] The picture is very unclear for the 1710s, but the 'upsurge' experienced in the middle years of the decade ceded to 'depression in 1718 into 1720': Cullen, 'A study of economic fluctuations', 18.

[73] Above pp 9–10; T. Thordarson and G. Larsen, 'Volcanism in Iceland in historical time: volcano types, eruption styles and eruptive history', *Journal of Geodynamics* 43 (2007), 134, 142, 143; G.R. Demarée and Øyvind Nordli, 'The Lisbon earthquake of 1755 vs volcanic eruptions and dry fogs: are its 'meteoric' descriptions related to the Katla eruptions of mid October 1755?' in A.C. Arújo *et al.* (eds), *O terramoto de 1755: impactos históricos* (Lisbon, 2007), 120; G.R. Demarée and A.E.J. Ogilvie, '*Bon baisers d'Islande*: climatic, environmental and human dimensions impacts of the Lakagigar eruption (1783–1784) in Iceland' in P.D. Jones *et al.* (eds), *History and climate: memories of the future?* (New York, 2001), 240. It may also be significant that the weather diarist Thomas Neve recorded above average solar activity in 1721 and 1722: Dixon, 'An Irish weather diary of 1711–25', 383–4.

[74] Steven Engler and J.P. Werner, 'Processes prior and during the early eighteenth century Irish famines – weather extremes and migration', *Climate* 3:4 (2015), 1040; Thordarson and Larsen, 'Volcanism in Iceland, 145.

crucial part in the descent of the country into famine in 1727 and 1729, the 'adverse weather' was not inconsistent with the weather norms of the Little Ice Age.[75] This is a more difficult argument to sustain when we come to the extreme weather conditions experienced between 1738 and 1741. For though the late 1730s produced a sequence of volcanic eruptions in eastern Russia and Japan (Table 3), which have been tentatively linked to the remarkable weather conditions that made the 1740–41 famine the most costly environmental crisis the Irish population endured in the eighteenth century, there is no direct evidence. Indeed, until a plausible explanation of the exceptional weather conditions experienced across Europe in these years is arrived at, the crisis is better accounted for as an extreme illustration of the demographic toll a weather-induced crisis could take on a vulnerable population.[76]

Whatever its source, the deterioration in weather conditions that anticipated the end of the 1730s warm spell may be said to have commenced in the spring of 1738. Air temperatures were in keeping with the decadal norm, but heavy snow in February and 'a runn of extraordinary raine' in the summer combined to make for a wet year.[77] Since this did not greatly damage the hay harvest, it was not a cause of serious disquiet.[78] It was just a foretaste of what was to come, however, as the country was precipitated into its most testing climatic experience of the eighteenth century.[79] The first hint of the severity of what was to come was provided in the spring of 1739 when 'the most unaccountable weather…frost, haile and snow', followed by unusually heavy rain, 'deprived' gardeners and their families 'of their early crops'.[80] This was less ominous, however, than what ensued when a rainy July was followed by an exceptionally wet September (the high point of which was 40 hours of 'the most violent and continued rain' on the sixth and seventh). The rain inevitably damaged grain crops, much of which rotted in the ground or was too damaged

---

[75] Engler and Werner, 'Processes', 1038.
[76] See Engler *et al.*, 'The Irish famine of 1740–41: famine vulnerability and "climate migration"', 1161–79, for the most sustained statement of this case.
[77] NAI, Pembroke estate papers, 97/46/1/2/3/3, 7, Mathew to Fitzwilliam, 14 Feb., 17 June 1738; Rutty, 'Registry of the weather', 339, 344; Manley, 'Central England temperatures', 394; Jenkinson *et al.*, 'Monthly and annual rainfall', 1739; *Newcastle Courant*, 18 Nov. 1738.
[78] NAI, Pembroke estate papers, 97/46/1/2/3/7, 10, Mathew to Fitzwilliam, 17 June, 14 Sept. 1738.
[79] The finest account of this episode is Dickson, *Arctic Ireland*, passim, which informs what follows; see also Engler *et al.*, 'The Irish famine of 1740–41', 1163–74; J.D. Post, 'Climate variability and the European mortality wave of the early 1740s', *Journal of Interdisciplinary History* 15:1 (1984), 1–30.
[80] NAI, Pembroke estate papers, 97/46/1/2/4/1, 3, Mathew to Fitzwilliam, 14 Feb., 22 Mar. 1739; Rutty, 'Registry of the weather', 344–5; Conolly to Bonnell, 22 Mar., 14 Apr., 16 May 1739 in Jennings and Ashford (eds), *The letters of Katherine Conolly*, 181, 182.

to harvest, and the 'quantity and quality of hay, [which] was much lessened'.[81] Since the more robust potato crop was largely unaffected, hopes persisted that the implications of the bad weather for food prices, which were already rising, could be kept under control, but, they were exploded when, beginning on 24 December, the country experienced the most acute and enduring frost 'in the memory of man'.[82] Actually, the CET suggests that January 1684 may have been marginally cooler than January 1740, but February 1740 was colder than the same month in 1684.[83] Moreover, it was of little consolation to the Dublin 'poor', which was reduced to 'going about the streets half naked and half-starv'd for want of food'.[84] Their main source of difficulty, besides the numbing cold, which was responsible for many fatalities among the young, 'the old, infirm and asthmatic', was inflated food prices as it became clear that the frost had destroyed much of the potato crop.[85] Death attributable to hypothermia constitutes one index of the challenge posed by sub-zero temperatures, but still more harm was caused by the shortage of flour as the freezing of waterways meant that mills could not function.[86] To make matters worse, farm labourers were deprived of the opportunity to earn as they were unable to work for the duration of the frost, and for some time afterwards, because the thaw that commenced in mid-February was slow to penetrate the surface. As a result 'a great deal of corn perished in the ground'.[87] Nor did livestock escape; cattle

---

[81] Jenkinson, 'Monthly and annual rainfall', 1739; Rutty, *A chronological history of the weather*, 76, 78; NAI, Pembroke estate papers, 97/46/1/2/4/10, Mathew to Fitzwilliam, 12 Sept. 1739; *Pue's Occurrences*, 15 Sept. 1739; National Library of Wales (NLW), Puleston papers, MS 3584D, Kingsbury to Price, 16 Sept. 1739; British Library (BL), Egmont papers, Add. MS 46991 ff 11–12, Powell to Egmont, 22 Feb. 1740; Michael Drake, 'The Irish demographic crisis of 1740–41', in T.W. Moody (ed.), *Historical Studies VI* (London, 1968), 106–07.

[82] J.D. Post, *Food shortage, climatic variability and epidemic disease in preindustrial Europe: the mortality peak in the early 1740s* (Ithaca, NY, 1985), 58; *Freeman's Journal*, 20 Jan. 1776; Rutty, 'Registry of the weather', 346, 347–8.

[83] Manley, 'Central England temperatures', 393–4; Samuel McSkimin, *The history and antiquities of the county of the town of Carrickfergus*, ed. E.J. McCrum (Belfast, 1909), 79.

[84] *Dublin Daily Post*, 3 Jan. 1740.

[85] Rutty, *A chronological history of the weather*, 79; *Dublin Daily Post*, 2 Jan. 1740; *Dublin Newsletter*, 11 Jan. 1740.

[86] *Dublin Daily Post*, 2 Jan. 1740; *Dublin Gazette*, 5 Jan. 1740; *Faulkner's Dublin Journal*, 12 Jan. 1740; *Dublin Newsletter*, 11 Jan. 1740; BL, Egmont papers, Add. MS 46991 ff 4, 5, Taylor to Egmont, 26 Jan., Purcell to Egmont, 29 Jan. 1740; *Newcastle Courant*, 2 Feb. 1740; Rutty, 'Registry of the weather', 349.

[87] NLI, Lucas farm journal, MS 14101, Entries 27 Jan.–19 Feb. 1740; *Dublin Newsletter*, 11 Jan. 1740; *Faulkner's Dublin Journal*, 15 Jan. 1740; NAI, Pembroke estate papers, 97/46/1/2/4/10, Mathew to Fitzwilliam, 13 Jan. 1740; BL, Egmont papers, Add. MS 46991 f. 13, Purcell to Egmont, 25 Feb. 1740; *Freeman's Journal*, 20 Jan. 1776.

and sheep 'died' in large numbers 'for want of fodder, occasioned by the long continuance of the frost and snow on the ground'.[88]

It was clear by then that the hopeful anticipation that the country might be quickly released from its weather-born travails was not destined to be realised. If, as the CET indicates, the air temperature for the first six months of 1740 was lower than it had been since 1709, the negative implication of this was intensified by drought. April was, John Rutty recorded, 'preternaturally cold and dry'. Planting was disrupted as a result, cattle mortality increased and as food prices sustained a relentless upwards trajectory, there was an inevitable increase in the number of 'the poorer sort of people [who] die with hunger'.[89] Hopes were raised by the welcome arrival of rain during the same month that 'the dreadfull apprehensions of a famine' might be dispelled by 'a good harvest' but northern winds (there was even 'some frost and ice') in July and 'a most violent storm' in August, which did further damage, ensured the harvest 'sadly fail'd'.[90] By then the country was firmly in the grip of famine as 'the common people', subsisting in the countryside on a diet of 'sour milk, nettles and charnock' and in cities on alms, found it increasingly difficult to secure nourishment. It was necessary, as a result, to bury the increasing number of dead in mass graves in the most severely impacted areas; in Cork 'several hundred indigent persons were buried, for want of money to purchase graves for themselves' in 'a large pit at the back of the green in Shandon church yard'.[91]

Without the easement in their circumstances that would have resulted from an improved food supply, whether that was a result of imports or a good harvest (the harvest of 1740 was 'thin'), the fate of the population depended more than ever on the amelioration of the weather. They experienced the opposite. Fuelled by temperatures lower than those they had endured in 1739–40, the population was buffeted during the winter of 1740–41 by heavy falls of snow and sleet and frost beginning in late October, storms and flooding that were particular acute in late November–early December and 'a great frost' that was at its most severe in the second half of December. These were trying conditions in

---

[88] *Dublin Daily Post*, 27 Feb., 16 Apr. 1740; Public Record Office of Northern Ireland (PRONI), Wilmot papers, T3019/223, Potter to Legge, 30 Jan. 1740; BL, Egmont papers, Add. MS 46991 ff 11–12, 20, Purcell to Egmont, 22 Feb., Taylor to Egmont, 3 May 1740.

[89] BL, Egmont papers, Add. MS 46991 f. 20, Taylor to Egmont, 3 May 1740; Rutty, *A chronological history of the weather*, 80; Post, *The 1740s*, 119; *Caledonian Mercury*, 17 Apr. 1740; Rutty, 'Registry of the weather', 353–4.

[90] BL, Egmont papers, Add. MS 46991 f. 27, Taylor to Egmont, 10 June 1740; Rutty, *A chronological history of the weather*, 81, 84; Rutty, 'Registry of the weather', 354–5, 356; NAI, Pembroke estate papers, 97/46/1/2/4/18, Mathew to Fitzwilliam, 8 Aug. 1740; *Newcastle Courant*, 23 Aug. 1740; *Derby Mercury*, 5 Mar. 1741.

[91] BL, Egmont papers, Add. MS 46991 f. 29, Purcell to Egmont, 13 June 1740; *Caledonian Mercury*, 7 Aug. 1740; Tuckey's *Cork Remembrancer*, 130. Charnock was 'a yellow flavoured weed', of the brassica genus, which grew alongside corn.

any context, but they bore heavily on a population whose reserves were depleted.[92] The most visible manifestation of this was the increase in the number of 'starving' poor on the streets of Dublin and Cork, and the fact that the ranks of those who were reduced to 'begging to survive' included 'some who, two years ago were in a very good way'.[93] Their predicament was exacerbated by 'fevers and fluxes', which caused an 'uncommon mortality among the poor'. But a still more vivid insight into the 'misery' that gripped the country at this moment is presented by the observer, who invoked the 'moans and groans' of the 'many miserable objects' he observed 'dying by the ditch side…for want of bread' in rural county Cork in January 1741.[94] It provided contemporaries with a graphic (possibly indelible) image not only of what conditions were like in those parts of the country (Munster most notably) where the crisis was felt most acutely in 1740–41 but also of just how easily 'the poor' could be reduced to 'a most miserable condition' in one of Europe's 'least developed…societies'.[95]

This remained the case, moreover, for six further months, for though the 'fine warm, mild we[a]ther' of February was a welcome relief to rich and poor alike, the 'great drought' that followed meant that food prices during the spring and summer of 1741 remained at the 'excessive rate' they had previously scaled in the summer of 1740.[96] One consequence of this was the decision of 'many familys in the country [to] abandon their dwellings and crowd [into] the city'.[97] Moreover, since the fever, first identified in 1740, 'raged through the summer' of 1741, there was no visible decrease in the death rate until August, by which time the combination of food imports, charitable endeavour, improved weather and the prospect of a good harvest assisted the country to emerge out of crisis.[98] It left deep scars. The most consequential obviously was the great loss of life. John

---

[92] *Dublin Gazette*, 28 Oct., 25, 29 Nov. 1740; *Dublin Newsletter*, 1, 4, 22 Nov., 9, 13, 16, 23 Dec. 1740; *Derby Mercury*, 11, 25 Dec. 1741; Rutty, 'Registry of the weather', 354–5; NLI, Domville papers, MS 11793/11, Madden to Lord Santry, 19 Dec. 1740; NLW, Puleston papers, Add. MS 3584D, Pearde to Price, 14 Dec. 1740; Conolly to Bonnell, 19 Dec. 1740 in Jennings and Ashford (eds), *The letters of Katherine Conolly*, 201.

[93] NLI, Domville papers, MS 11793/11, Madden to Lord Santry, 19 Dec. 1740; NLW, Puleston papers, Add. MS 3584D, Pearde to Price, 14 Dec. 1740.

[94] Post, 'Climate and mortality', 20–25; *Derby Mercury*, 25 Dec. 1740, 5 Mar. 1741; *Ipswich Journal*, 7 Mar. 1741.

[95] Conolly to Bonnell, 19 Dec. 1740 in Jennings and Ashford (eds), *The letters of Katherine Conolly*, 201; Post, 'Climate and mortality', 17–18. Post places Ireland in this category with Finland and Norway.

[96] Conolly to Bonnell, 2 Feb. 1741 in Jennings and Ashford (eds), *The letters of Katherine Conolly*, 203; Rutty, *A chronological history of the weather*, 84; Post, *The 1740s*, 119; Rutty, 'Registry of the weather', 356–7.

[97] NAI, Pembroke estate papers, 97/46/1/2/4/21, Mathew to Fitzwilliam, 20 Apr. 1741.

[98] Rutty, *A chronological history of the weather*, 86; Rutty, 'Registry of the weather', 283; Kelly, 'Coping with crisis', 105–19; PRONI, Wilmot papers, T3019/295, Potter to Wilmot, 30 May 1741; *Dublin Gazette*, 11 July 1741; NAI, Pembroke estate papers, 97/46/1/2/4/23, Mathew to Fitzwilliam, 11 July 1741.

Climate, weather and society in Ireland in the long eighteenth century

Rutty's claim that 'eighty thousand died…of…fever, dysentery and famine' in the years 1740 [and] 1741' does not sit easily with the number implied by the Dublin bill of mortality (Table 2), or with recent calculations which suggest that the percentage of the population that died was of the order of 13 to 20 per cent. Though this is, in the estimation of some, unduly high,[99] it underlines how friable were the population's defences in the face of extreme weather.[100]

This was in evidence once more four years later, when, following a late and 'damaged' harvest due to prolonged 'wet and stormy' conditions, the anticipated 'scarcity' forecast in November 1744 came to pass.[101] As in 1739–41, crisis was precipitated by a sustained spell of low temperatures. For though the first three months of 1745 were not especially harsh, 'great falls of snow', sharp frosts and 'violent heavy rains' caused severe flooding in Dublin and its hinterland and the death in Connaught and Ulster of 'vast numbers of cattle and sheep'.[102] Distress was experienced throughout the country, but it was particularly acute in Ulster. Reports of 'a great famine' were unwarranted, but the combined impact of the 'want [of] firing' (due to the failure in 1744 'to get in there [sic] turfe'), and cattle mortality was exacerbated by high food prices. Some resorted to scavenging the 'wasted carcases' that were to be encountered in 'fields and ditches' such was their despair; others took to the roads and headed for Dublin bringing contagion in their wake. The demographic consequences of this for Dublin are not immediately identifiable, but it took the combined impact of a synchronous increase in July in the supply of (imported) corn and an improvement in the weather to ensure there was no repeat in 1745 of what transpired in 1740–41.[103]

If the crises of 1740–41 and 1744–5 can reasonably be portrayed as extreme examples of a pattern of weather that was characterised, as J.G. Tyrell has pointed out, by longer and 'more intense' winters than was the case in the twentieth century, this does not mean that there is no place for volcanic forcing in the

---

[99] To give some context: the percentage of the population lost in Scotland in the 1690s is put at 10–15 per cent: D'Arrigo, 'Complexity in crisis', 2.
[100] Rutty, *A chronological history of the weather*, 86–7, 91; Dickson, *Arctic Ireland*, 62–69, 72; Brian Gurrin, 'Population and emigration, 1730–1845' in James Kelly (ed.), *The Cambridge history of Ireland, vol 3, 1730–1880* (Cambridge, 2017), 210–12.
[101] NLW, Puleston papers, MS 3580 ff 23, 26, 27, Spencer to Price, 29 June, 29 Sept., 5 Nov. 1744; NAI, Pembroke Estate papers, 97/46/1/2/5/18, Mathew to Fitzwilliam, 7 Nov. 1744; Rutty, 'Registry of the weather', 364–6, 368–9.
[102] *Newcastle Courant*, 9 Feb. 1745; Conolly to Conolly, 9 Feb. 1745 in Jennings and Ashford (eds), *The letters of Katherine Conolly*, 265–6; 'Galway scrapbook', *The Galway Reader*, 2 (1950), 152; NAI, Pembroke Estate papers, 97/46/1/2/5/22, Mathew to Fitzwilliam, 8 Mar. 1745.
[103] Conolly to Bonnell, 26 Feb. 1745 in Jennings and Ashford (eds), *The letters of Katherine Conolly*, 267; NLW, Puleston papers, MS 3580 ff 29, 32,33, 36, Spencer to Price, 4 Mar., 1, 26 July, 10 Oct. 1745; *Derby Mercury*, 12, 26 Apr. 1745; Burns, *An historical and chronological remembrancer*, 219; Rutty, *A chronological history of the weather*, 127; Rutty, 'Registry of the weather', 372–3; NAI, Pembroke Estate papers, 97/46/1/2/5/23, 25, Mathew to Fitzwilliam, 5 July, 20 Aug. 1745.

narrative of these events.[104] Our knowledge of the history of volcanism in the early eighteenth century is very incomplete, and it may be that further research will affirm the tentative links drawn here between volcanic dust veils and Icelandic volcanoes and food crises in the late 1690s and 1720–21, and Asian eruptions in the 1730s and the 1740–41 famine. It is also pertinent that a more definite link can be drawn between seismic activity (in Iceland specifically) and food crises in Ireland in the second half of the century. It is notable that this took place at a time when greater notice was taken of unusual atmospheric and meteorological phenomena.[105] It may be that this was an offshoot of the identifiable increase in weather reporting, one manifestation of which was the increased number of reports of extreme weather conditions in Europe in the Irish press.[106] It certainly acquired a higher profile when in early 1750, at the same time that reports that London was subject to two small earthquakes circulated in the Irish press, an 'aurora borealis' appeared in the evening sky over Cork.[107]

Since the population at the time had neither a meteorological, a geological or a seismological framework in which to locate these events, they did not elicit any more notice than reports of lightning strikes, or the increasingly common (and costly) sea storms.[108] This was true also in 1755 when in the wake of the earthquake, which reduced Lisbon to rubble, it emerged that the tsunami that struck Kinsale in the course of the afternoon of 1 November and destroyed a sloop and fishing boats in the harbour was part of the same phenomenon.[109] In point of fact, it was not the only unusual event to strike the island at that time. 'A very sensible shock of an earthquake', which was felt in Cork city on the morning of the same day, also made the news, but other than the obvious speculation that both originated 'at the bottom of the sea', no tenable natural explanations were forthcoming.[110] There were a few other pointers, which had they been picked up, might have suggested that something else was afoot. The

---

[104] J.G. Tyrrell, 'Paraclimatic statistics and the study of climate change: the case of the Cork region in the 1750s', *Climate Change* 29 (1995), 238, 243.

[105] For example, Tuckey's *Cork Remembrancer*, 131; *Derby Mercury*, 12 Apr. 1745; *Belfast News Letter*, 6 Feb. 1750; Rutty, 'Registry of the weather', 290, 328, 367, 378, 402–3, 425–6, and below p. 29.

[106] As instanced by the number of reports of the wet summer experienced in 1749: *Pue's Occurrences*, 4, 15, 25 July, 2 Sept., 3 Oct. 1749.

[107] *Belfast News Letter*, 27 Feb., 20, 23 Mar. 1750.

[108] Tuckey's *Cork Remembrancer*, 131; *Belfast News Letter*, 3, 11, 20 Aug., 21 Dec., 1750, 27 Feb., 14 Aug. 1753, 17 Dec. 1754.

[109] *The Scots Magazine* 16 (1755), 552–3, 595; It is notable also that this link was made in the discussion of the matter on 5 May 1756 at the Dublin Medico-Philosophical Society (Royal College of Physicians if Ireland, Dublin Medico-Philosophical Society papers, vol. 1, 5 May 1756).

[110] *The Scots Magazine* 16 (1755), 553; Tuckey's *Cork Remembrancer*, 137; *Newcastle Courant*, 22 Nov. 1755; see also David McCallam, *Volcanoes in eighteenth-century Europe: an essay in environmental humanities* (Liverpool, 2019) for a discussion of the interpretative frameworks then applied.

appearance in the evening sky near Tuam, Co. Galway, in the afternoon of 2 January of 'an unusual light, far above that of the brightest day', followed three hours later (7 pm) by 'a sea of streamers,...which undulated like a winnowing sheet' was one indication. But the fact that the display was succeeded by an 'uncommon shock' that threw those who experienced it to the ground, and that one or two locations, measuring two or seven acres, in the vicinity were discovered the next morning 'covered with water' was still more suggestive.[111] Nobody, however, had any awareness of the fact that several hundred miles north of where they were located, Ketla volcano was nearing the conclusion of an extended high mass eruption (it lasted 120 days) that produced atmospheric effects across Europe comparable to (but on a grander scale than) those witnessed in County Galway. They were still less aware that it had cast a volume of tephra capable of sustaining a dust veil (Table 3.1) greater than anything experienced in Europe since the seventeenth century and was responsible for 'lowering the mean annual temperature in northern mid-latitudes by approximately 0.7°C'.[112]

It is not possible to demonstrate with evidential exactitude a direct link between volcanic events in Iceland in 1755–6 and the 1756–7 subsistence crisis in Ireland, but the winter of 1755–6 is the first occasion when one can make a connection (via the Lisbon earthquake) between an identified eruption (Katla) and meteorological events in Ireland. What is also demonstrable is that the weather in 1756–7 contributed to the difficulties the population experienced and moulded their response. The most striking illustration of this is the spike in food rioting that took place in 1756 and 1757, but since this is more useful as an index of popular apprehension than a measure of actual experience, the weather itself offers a better guide.[113] What this reveals is that eleven of the twelve months of 1756 were more than usually 'wet' and 'winter-like',[114] and that this exacerbated ongoing financial problems attributable to the collapse of five merchant banks in 1754–5 and 'the catastrophe of Lisbon'.[115] The situation was particularly concerning in

---

[111] *Caledonian Mercury*, 27 Jan. 1756; *Derby Mercury*, 30 Jan. 1756.

[112] Tyrrell, 'Paraclimatic statistics', 243; Gudrun Larson, 'Holocene eruptions in the Katla volcanic system, south Iceland: characteristics and volcanic impact', *Jokull* 49 (2000), 1–28; Demarée and Nordli, 'The Lisbon earthquake of 1755 vs volcanic eruptions and dry fogs', 118–20; J. Schmith, 'Large explosive basaltic eruptions at Katla volcano, Iceland', *Journal of Volcanology and Geothermal Research*, 354 (2018), 140–52; Thordarson and Larsen, 'Volcanism in Iceland', 134, 142.

[113] Kelly, *Food rioting in Ireland*, 35; Eoin Magennis, 'In search of the "moral economy": food scarcity in 1756–57 and the crowd' in Peter Jupp and Eoin Magennis (eds), *Crowds in Ireland c. 1720–1920* (Basingstoke, 2000), 189–211.

[114] November was the exception: see Rutty, 'Registry of the weather', 407; and for corroborating evidence: *Pue's Occurrences*, 14 Feb., 18 Sept. 1756; *Derby Mercury*, 5 Mar. 1756; *Universal Advertiser*, 19 July 1757.

[115] L.M. Cullen, *Anglo-Irish trade 1660–1800* (Manchester, 1968), 197; L.M. Cullen, *An economic history of Ireland since 1660* (London, 1972), 73; NAI, Pembroke estate papers, 97/46/1/2/7/71, Fitzwilliam to Fitzwilliam, 29 Jan. 1756: according to Fitzwilliam 'the towns of Corke and Bandon are by it sufferers to the tune of £37,000.'

Connaught where, Charles O'Conor of Belanagare (Co. Roscommon) noted in May, 'two thirds of the inhabitants are perishing for want of bread'. And it got worse when, as apprehended, the harvest was both 'late and very bad', and regional concerns appreciated—in Ulster particularly.[116] The impact of the severe frost in January was especially troubling in this context. But while the citizenry of Dublin breathed a sigh of relief that the 'gentle thaw' that followed in February did not bring the flooding that must inevitably have occurred 'had the thaw been attended with rain', the situation remained bleak elsewhere. It was particularly so in Ulster, as the cumulative impact of six weeks of frost and snow pushed the province to the verge of famine.[117] Though the clergyman writing to the Earl of Abercorn exaggerated when he compared the environment in County Tyrone then to that of 'Lapland', he captured the public's perception for while conditions inevitably eased, 1757 was, as anticipated, 'a very hard summer with the poor people'.[118]

It would have been still worse had the Irish administration not made a sustained attempt to secure the food supply by, among other actions, imposing an embargo on food exports and encouraging imports.[119] Their efforts were not without impact, even if they were insufficient to prevent people dying of 'want'.[120] Moreover, they remained in arrear of what was required to neutralise the effects of weather as problems persisted even after the worst phase of this subsistence crisis had passed, with the result that there was no respite from weather-induced difficulties. They did not experience another subsistence crisis until 1766, however, and the fact that this also coincides with a further Icelandic eruption—the Hekla volcano, which embarked on its two-year eruptive course

---

[116] O'Conor to Curry, 21 May 1756 in R.E. Ward *et al.* (eds), *Letters of Charles O'Conor of Belanagare* (Washington, 1988), 13; NAI, Pembroke estate papers, 97/46/1/2/7/90, Fitzwilliam to Fitzwilliam, 30 Nov. 1756; Magennis, 'In search of the "moral economy"', 199–200.

[117] Rutty, *A chronological history of the weather*, 197; Rutty, 'Registry of the weather', 409–10; NAI, Pembroke estate papers, 97/46/1/2/8/11, Fagan to Fitzwilliam, 3 Feb. 1757; *Universal Advertiser*, 5 Feb. 1757; Rigby to Bedford, 3 Feb. 1757 in Lord John Russell (ed.), *The correspondence of John, fourth duke of Bedford* (3 vols, London, 1842–6), vol. 2, 232; J.H. Gebbie (ed.), *An introduction to the Abercorn letters* (Omagh, 1972), 51.

[118] Magennis, 'In search of the "moral economy"', 201; Charles O'Conor, *The Protestant interest re-considered, relative to the operation of the Popery acts in Ireland* (Dublin, 1757), 30; PRONI, Villiers Stuart papers, T3131/C/10/16, Grandison to [Kennedy], 6 May 1757.

[119] Bedford to Lords Justices, 3 July 1757 in A.P.W. Malcomson (ed.), *Eighteenth-century Irish official papers in Great Britain* (2 vols, Belfast, 1973–92), vol. 2, 166; Kelly and Lyons (eds), *Proclamations*, vol. 3, 462, 465–6, 473.

[120] *Pue's Occurrences*, 2 Nov. 1756; P. Ó Maidin (ed.), 'Pococke's tour of south and south west Ireland in 1758', *Journal of the Cork Historical and Archaeological Society* 65 (1960), 136.

in April 1766—raises the question once more as to the role volcanic forcing may have played in creating the conditions that brought it about.

The dust veil weighting attributed to the Hekla eruption of 1766–8 is comparatively modest (Table 3.1), but it may be that this is not the most reliable guide to its climatic significance for northern and western Europe, as it was responsible for the largest lava flow and the third largest volume of tephra of any Icelandic volcano in historical times.[121] Assessing its impact is complicated further by its duration, but it is tempting to speculate that it may have contributed to the recurring drought (attributable to dry winters) experienced in the second half of the 1760s.[122] Since this was at its most acute in 1765, it may be that it has an independent genesis. If so, one is on securer ground in concluding that the impact of the poor harvest (potatoes, grain and hay) that resulted was intensified, first by the harsh frost and snow that fuelled the cold temperatures experienced in January and February 1766, and, second, by the 'wet and cold' summer that followed.[123] Despite this, hopes were high in July that the kingdom would soon shake of the legacy of the preceding bad harvest, but this expectation was exploded late in August 'when a sudden change of weather from heat to violent wind and rain' contributed to ensure, when the wheat harvest 'failed' once more, that action was required.[124] The expeditious introduction on 7 October of an embargo 'on all manner of corn, grain and meal' attests to the responsiveness of the authorities, but while this alleviated the severity of the threat to the population, its inadequacy was exposed when a 'very bad frost' in January 1767 injured the potato crop, which had been harvested successfully. Though claims that the frost was 'as severe as that' experienced in 1740 were inaccurate, there was no doubting the acuity of conditions as, in a repeat of that terrible year, manufacturers and tradesmen were unable to work, roads were impassable, the Liffey and other rivers were frozen solid, and deaths due to hypothermia and exposure were reported.[125] These conditions are of a kind identifiable with the weather extremes

---

[121] Thordarson and Larsen, 'Volcanism in Iceland', 134, 141; Sigundur Thorarinsson, *Hekla: a notorious volcano* (Reykjavik, 1970).

[122] Conor Murphy *et al.*, 'The forgotten drought of 1765–68: reconstructing and re-evaluating historic droughts in the British and Irish Isles', *International Journal of Climatology* 40 (2020), 1–23. For corroborating contemporary references to the 'hot weather' and the damage it inflicted on 'the fruits of the earth' see Rutty, 'Registry of the weather', 450; NAI, Pembroke estate papers, 97/46/1/2/8/65, Cantwell to Fitzwilliam, 8 Aug. 1765; *Freeman's Journal*, 1 July 1766; Ryder to Ryder, 27 Jan. 1766 in Malcomson (ed.), *Eighteenth-century Irish official papers in Great Britain*, vol. 2, 6.

[123] NAI, Irish correspondence, i, MS 2446, Hertford to [Conway], 30 Nov. 1765; Rutty, 'Registry of the weather', 451–2; *Freeman's Journal*, 15 Feb., 1 July 1766; *Dublin Courier*, 14, 17, 19, 21, 24, 28 Feb. 1766.

[124] *Dublin Mercury*, 10 July, 2 Aug., 14 Oct. 1766; *Dublin Courier*, 18 July, 29 Aug. 1766; *Public Gazetteer*, 11 Oct. 1766; Richard Caulfield, *The Council book of the corporation of the city of Cork* (Guilford, 1876), 811.

[125] Kelly and Lyons, *Proclamations*, vol. 4, 93–4; *Belfast News Letter*, 16 Dec. 1766; NAI, Alcock papers, BR Wat/10/1/23; Tuckey's *Cork Remembrancer*, 147; *Dublin Mercury*, 17,

attributed to the impact of volcanic forcing. But though it is tempting to link the challenging environmental conditions of the late 1760s—the difficult winters of 1767–8 and 1768–9 notably—to the enduring impact of the extended Hekla eruption, this requires more investigation.[126]

Yet the possibility is intriguing and it is given impetus by the fact that the Lakagígar fissure eruption of 1783–4 had 'a momentous impact on the environment' and that this served in Ireland to transform the difficulties posed by the poor harvest of 1782 into a major subsistence crisis.[127] As the cumulative dust veil of Lakagígar and Reykjanes (which preceded it) attests (Table 3.1) this was an eruption on an exceptional scale. It has been calculated that it may have released in the order of 122 megatons of sulphur dioxide (SO_2) into the atmosphere and maintained a sulphuric aerosol veil in the northern hemisphere for some five months.[128] The first manifestation of this was the slow spread of what contemporaries denominated a 'dry fog' (or sulphuric haze) across the northern hemisphere in July and August 1783. The failure to locate any reference to a fog or haze comparable to those identifiable across Europe suggests that Ireland did not experience the first effects of the volcano as severely as other parts of the continent, but the identification of Laki tephra in County Mayo indicates that the island did not escape untouched.[129] Moreover, as understanding of the climatic effects of the eruption has increased, and these have expanded to embrace the 'the abnormally hot summer' of 1783 as well as the 'cold winter' of 1783–4, it is apparent that the eruption affected Ireland severely. It may be that the country did not experience an increase in mortality in the summer of 1783 equivalent

---

20, 27, 30 Jan. 1767; *Finn's Leinster Journal,* 21 Feb. 1767.

[126] *Finn's Leinster Journal,* 9 Dec. 1767, 6, 16, 20 Jan. 1768, 25 Jan., 14 June 1769; Tuckey's *Cork Remembrancer*, 150. Sigl *et al.* calculate its sulphate deposition, based on the examination of a Greenland ice core, at *c.* 13.8kg per square km: Sigl *et al.*, 'A new bipolar ice core record', 1158.

[127] Thorvaldur Thordarson and Stephen Self, 'Atmospheric and environmental effects of the 1783–84 Laki eruption: a review and reassessment', *Journal of Geophysical Research* 108 (2003), AAC7, 2; James Kelly, 'Scarcity and poor relief in eighteenth century Ireland: the subsistence crisis of 1782–84', *Irish Historical Studies* 28 (1992), 38–62.

[128] Thordarson and Self, 'Atmospheric and environmental effects of the 1783–84 Laki eruption', 1. Other calculations put the combined sulphuric acid aerosol at 200 megatons, when the sulphur dioxide combined with water: Halldorsson, 'The dry fog of 1783', 35.

[129] Thordarson and Self, 'Atmospheric and environmental effects of the 1783–84 Laki eruption', 2, 7, 15, 18, 20, appendix A; John Grattan, 'Pollution and paradigms: lessons from Icelandic volcanism…', *Lithos* 79 (2005), 344; Reilly and Mitchell, 'Establishing chronologies for woodland small hollow and mor humus', 248; Demaree and Ogilvie, '*Bon baisers d'Islande*: climatic, environmental and human dimensions impacts of the Lakagígar eruption', 219–46. It is noteworthy that the presence of the 'fog' in Europe was reported in Irish newspapers: *Saunders' News Letter*, 22 July, 1, 14,16, 26 Aug., 9, 20 Sept 1783; *Finn's Leinster Journal*, 30 Aug. 1783; *Freeman's Journal*, 23 Sept. 1783.

to that identified in England.[130] But the 'very hot weather' experienced in June and July and the 'balls of fire' that accompanied the 'violent thunder storms' that were particularly severely felt in County Cork demonstrate that the country did not evade its climatic effects.[131] More significantly as far as the population was concerned, they anticipated a spell of 'melancholy weather' characterised by 'high wind' and 'heavy rain' that destroyed the hopes they had placed in a good harvest relieving them of the problems caused by the rain damaged grain crop harvested in 1782.[132] The acknowledgement in September that 'rains and storms had blasted the hopes of the husbandman, and furnished the most gloomy apprehensions of another year of scarcity' aptly summarised the order of the transformation that had taken place.[133]

If this meant inevitably that conditions in Ireland in the autumn of 1783 were more testing than the population had anticipated, they were less forbidding than what was to come, as the winter of 1783–4 was one of the coldest on record. Temperatures did not quite plumb the depths they had reached in 1740 but the sub-zero averages recorded in January and February attest to the severity of the winter.[134] For two months from Christmas day 1783, the country was gripped by frosts that were so severe 'water-pipes…[were] frozen so hard as to be unserviceable', rivers and lakes froze over, and, in a repeat of what had happened 43 years previously, the potato crop froze and was rendered inedible in places. With the frost came heavy snow, which piled in drifts, sometimes 15–20ft high, which made roads impassable, labouring impossible and fatalities inevitable as people 'perished through the inclemency of the weather'.[135] Since conditions were equally harsh elsewhere across the northern hemisphere, there is a near consensus among historical climatologists that this was a consequence of the disruptive impact of volcanic forcing, but this was of no consolation to a population which was ill-prepared to negotiate continuous frost of more than seven weeks.[136] The acute cold was especially challenging for the poor, who were further discomfited

---

[130] Neil Ogle et al., 'Palaeovolcanic forcing of short-term dendroisotopic depletion: the effect of decreased solar intensity on Irish oak', *Geophysical Research Letters*, 32 (2005), 1–4; C.S. Witham and Clive Oppenheimer, 'Mortality in England during the 1783–84 Laki craters', *Bulletin of Volcanology*, 67 (2005), 16–26.

[131] *Dublin Evening Post*, 26 June 1783; Tuckey's *Cork Remembrancer*, 186-7; *Cork Hibernian Chronicle*, 17 July 1783; *Saunders' News Letter*, 22 July 1783.

[132] *Dublin Evening Post*, 8 July 1783; *Saunders' News Letter*, 9 July, 1, 6, 19,20 Sept. 1783; *Freeman's Journal*, 19 June, 12, 16 Sept. 1783; *Finn's Leinster Journal*, 10, 13,17, 20 Sept. 1783.

[133] *Freeman's Journal*, 12 Sept. 1783.

[134] Manley, 'Central England temperatures', 395.

[135] *Saunders' News Letter*, 1, 2, 6, 15, 24, 26, 27, 31 Jan., 3, 4, 5, 6 Feb. 1784; Notebook Jan. Feb. 1784 (Historical Society of Pennsylvania, Pemberton papers, Miscellaneous Box 1); *Hibernian Journal*, 30 Jan., 9 Feb. 1784; *Freeman's Journal*, 31 Jan. 1784; *Volunteer Evening Post*, 5, 12 Feb. 1784.

[136] John Warburton, Robert Walsh and John Whitelaw, *History of the city of Dublin* (2 vols, London, 1818), vol. 1, 231; *Saunders' News Letter*, 5, 11, 12 Feb. 1784.

by flooding when the daytime thaw combined with heavy rain to cause rivers to overflow, but this was less serious for their general well-being than the high price of staple foodstuffs. Indeed, but for the 'timely aid distributed [in Dublin] by the House of Industry, hundreds must have perished for absolute want'.[137] The House of Industry did not act alone. Parish relief committees, voluntary organisations and individual donors contrived, when conditions were at their worst in the capital to provide basic relief—a pound of bread a boiled herring and a pint of small beer—to as many as 20,000 people, and thereby to stave off a major loss of life.[138] Such efforts were not sufficient to prevent some excess mortality in the city. The situation was worse in those parts of the countryside—in Leinster especially—where relief was not available. But there was no repeat there or elsewhere of the famine conditions of 1740–41, and the 1784 harvest was sufficiently hearty to remove the threat.[139]

The 1782–4 subsistence crisis is the most clear-cut illustration of the disruptive climatic impact of volcanic forcing on the population of Ireland in the eighteenth century.[140] Furthermore, though the harvest in 1784 was 'plenteous', with the result that food prices moderated and the population at large was relieved of the threat of hunger in the autumn of 1784, the winter of 1784–5 was challenging.[141] Matters were at their worst in December 1784 and February 1785 when the sharp decline in temperature elicited the by now familiar comparison with 1740.[142] This was unwarranted but the 'visible increase of severity in our winters' that was a feature of the mid-1780s suggests that, based on the Irish experience, the Lakagígar eruption may have had a more enduring effect on weather patterns than is generally assumed.[143]

The link established between Lakagígar and the challenging weather experienced in Europe, and beyond, in 1783–4 is consistent with the conclusion that volcanic forcing had a direct and identifiable short-term influence on weather patterns in Ireland. While geographical proximity can be cited as to why Icelandic eruptive activity is an obvious place to look for evidence of this in Ireland,

---

[137] *Saunders' News Letter*, 5 Jan., 4, 5, 10, 12 Feb. 1784; *Dublin Evening Post*, 24 Feb. 1784.

[138] *Saunders' News Letter*, 4 Feb. 1784; Kelly, 'The subsistence crisis of 1782–84', 56–9; James Kelly, 'Charitable societies: their genesis and development' in James Kelly and Martyn Powell (eds), *Clubs and societies in eighteenth-century Ireland* (Dublin, 2010), 99–100.

[139] David Dickson, 'The gap in famines: a useful myth' in E.M. Crawford, *Famine: the Irish experience 900–1900* (Edinburgh, 1989), 101–3.

[140] Witham and Oppenheimer, 'Mortality in England', 19–24.

[141] Kelly, 'The subsistence crisis of 1782–4', 41, 61; *Saunders' News Letter*, 22 May, 10 June, 18 Dec. 1784; *Hibernian Journal*, 30 Aug., 17 Sept., 6, 20 Dec. 1784.

[142] Manley, 'Central England temperatures', 395; *Saunders' News Letter*, 28 Oct., 14, 16, 18 Dec., 1784, 15 Feb., 9 Apr., 5 May 1785; *Hibernian Journal*, 27 Oct., 15, 17, 20 Dec. 1784.

[143] *Saunders' News Letter*, 10 Nov. 1786; below p. 44.

TABLE 4—Volcanic Sulphate deposition for NEEM S1 Ice Core, Greenland

Volcano, location	Ice core date	Deposition SO_4^{2-} [kg km^{-2}] ± 1σ
Unidentified	1695-Mar. 1696	20.0 ± 2.3
Fujissan, Japan	Aug. 1707-Apr. 1709	5.8 ± 1.4
?Lanzarote, Canary Islands	Feb. 1729-May 1732	27.0 ± 3.7
Tarumai, Japan	1739-June 1740	24.6 ± 3.0
Katla, Iceland	Mar. 1755-June 1756	7.9 ± 2.6
Unidentified	Aug. 1761-Mar. 1763	12.7 ± 3.2
Hekla, Iceland	Apr. 1766-May 1765	13.8 ± 2.5
Lakagígar, Iceland	Aug. 1782-May 1784	178.6 ± 4.3
Unidentified	July 1809-Feb. 1811	30.6 ± 2.0
Tambora, Indonesia	June 1815-June 1817	39.0 ± 2.4

Source: Michael Sigl *et al.*, 'A new bipolar ice core record of volcanism from WAIS Divide and NEEM and implications for climate forcing of the last 2000 years', *Journal of Geophysical Research: Atmospheres*, 118 (2013), pp 1151–69 (doi:10.1029/2012JD018603).

the connection that has been established between the Tambora eruption in Indonesia (1815) and the subsistence crisis of 1815–17 cautions against applying a hemispherically exclusive focus.[144] This draws additional impetus from a possible link between a still unidentified tropical eruption in the early nineteenth century (1809–12) and the economic travails that prompted a spike in food protest in Ireland in 1812 though the fact that even the location of this eruption is unknown underlines just how provisional our conclusions can be.[145] This is true also for the eighteenth century generally, for while a tabulation of major volcanic activity and food crisis (Table 3) provides a *prima facie* case that the climatic disruption attributable to volcanic forcing played a part in the generation of the environmental conditions that were a precondition for a sequence of food crises, this was not inevitable. There are many reasons. The first and most important is that volcanoes took different forms. They all possessed transformative capacity but, as the variation in the order of the dust veil they created shows, they did not affect the weather equally, and some had little or no impact. Indeed, based on current knowledge, it is reasonable to conclude that a minority of volcanoes (Lakagígar, most notably) had a transformative impact on the weather in Ireland; that others, such as Heckla, exerted a lesser but still identifiable impact; while others, such

---

[144] See J.D. Post, *The last great subsistence crisis in the western world* (Baltimore, 1977); Clive Oppenheimer, 'Climatic, environmental and human consequences of the largest known historic eruption: Tambora volcano (Indonesia) 1815', *Progress in Physical Geography* 27:2 (2003), 230–59; Clive Oppenheimer, *Eruptions that shook the world* (Cambridge, 2011), 295–319; Gillen D'Arcy Wood, *Tambora: the eruption that changed the world* (Princeton, 2014), chapter 8.
[145] Kelly, *Food protest*, 35, 48–9.

as those that occurred in the 1720s, may have had little or no effect. Identifying which belongs in which category and connecting them to the weather in Ireland is fraught with difficulty, but the order of the volcanic sulphate deposition identified in the Greenland ice core is useful in this respect. Sigl *et al.* have identified ten examples spanning the time period 1690–1815 (see Table 4). Of these, Lakagígar was by far the largest, but the presence of Tambora (1812–5), Hekla (1766–7), Katla (1755–6), Tarumai (1739–40), Fujissan (1707–09) and three unknown signatures dating from 1695–6, 1761–63 and 1809–11 is so alike the known pattern of harvest crisis in Ireland during this time (Table 3) as to suggest that there may be a deeper underlying influence. The presence of a sulphate deposition tentatively identified with the island of Lanzarote and dated 1729–32, which does not coincide with a harvest crisis, is thus puzzling. But it may be that its disruptive weather impact is to be found in the usual warming experienced in the 1730s, and that the source of the unknown deposition dateable from the early 1760s also had a different register, but this too requires investigation. It certainly cautions against exaggerated or simplistic conclusions, and highlights the desirability of an interpretative structure that, as well as volcanic forcing, takes other factors (solar irradiance, the North Atlantic Oscillation, pressure gradients, for example)[146] on board to assist with the task of constructing a picture of how the large environmental forces that influenced climate shaped the weather in Ireland. It also echoes the argument of Philip Slavin that 'climate and short term weather anomalies do not create famines', and the recent account of Scotland's 'ill years', which emphasise the 'importance of considering multiple climate variables as well as regional and local circumstances if we are to understand the complexity and impacts of… volcanic climate forcing'.[147]

The weather and the population in the middle decades of the eighteenth century

While the addition of volcanic forcing brings a new dimension to our efforts to understand how climatic and weather patterns shaped the lives of the population in eighteenth-century Ireland, the recognition that this was typically short term underlines the importance of constructing a picture of the weather more generally. Important work on precipitation, storm frequency, lightning and other 'climatic hazards' is helpful in this undertaking.[148] These climate events occurred against the backdrop of the higher air temperature that defined the era after the conclusion of the Maunder Minimum. As the CET series bears out, the high

---

[146] D. Justin Schove, 'The reduction of annual winds in north western Europe, A.D. 1635–1960', *Geografiska Annaler* 14:3/4 (1962), 317.
[147] Philip Slavin, 'Climate and famines: a historical reassessment', *WIREs Climate Change* 7 (2016), 441; D'Arrigo, 'Complexity in crisis', 9.
[148] Murphy *et al.*, 'A 305-year continuous monthly rainfall series'; Conor Murphy *et al.*, 'Irish droughts in newspaper archives: rediscovering forgotten hazards', *Weather* 72:6 (2017), 151–5; K.R. Hickey, 'The historical record of lightning in Ireland' (unpublished, 2014); J.K. Mitchell, 'Looking backward to see forward: historical changes of public knowledge about climatic hazards in Ireland', *Irish Geography* 44:1 (2011), 7–26.

temperature levels of the 1730s were not sustained for though the record low temperatures that distinguish 1740 did not establish a new norm, there was no return to the highs reached in 1733 and 1736. Indeed, the decadal average for the 1740s was closer to that of the 1710s than the 1720s. More significantly, perhaps, the average for the four decades 1740–80, while higher than that of the Maunder Minimum, was below that of the first three decades of the eighteenth century. This remained the case, moreover, as the decadal average fell to a century low in the difficult 1760s. The 1770s witnessed an improvement, back towards the level registered in the 1720s, and there were already signs that this would be repeated in the 1780s (1782 was a cold year) before the effects of the Lakagígar eruption were felt and temperatures reverted to their mid-century norm for the remainder of the century (Table 1).[149]

The complexity of the temperature picture this suggests is compounded by the fact that the number of instances in which the annual average temperature fell below 9°C increased from five in the 1740s to eight (or just one below the number registered in the 1690s) in the 1760s. The 1770s was warmer (only one year averaged less than 9°C), but (paradoxically) it was the decade with the coldest January average in the 40 years 1741–80.[150] The 1770s was anomalous in several respects therefore, as the decadal average in the 1780s echoed their mid-century average.

The precipitation record oscillated in broad parallel with that of temperature, as in a break with the rain experienced in the 1730s (and indeed the 1710 and 1720s), the 1740s was the driest decade of the century, with three of the driest years (1740, 1741 and 1745). In obvious contrast, the 1750s was wettest, with two of the wettest years (1755 and 1756), though the wettest year of all took place a decade later; in 1768 there was almost 30 per cent more rain than the yearly average for 1741–80 (Table 5). 1768 excepted, the 1760s were not especially wet. Indeed the decade set a trend that was sustained for the remainder of the century, though the decennial averages that informs this observation need to be read in conjunction with the fact that the volume of rain was above average in nineteen of these 40 years and that 1773 and 1775 were two of the six wettest.[151]

Consistent with these temperature and precipitation trends and the characterisation of the weather advanced by John Tyrell and Kieran Hickey, the population of Ireland in the mid-eighteenth century experienced a seasonal weather pattern that produced sustained periods of frost and heavy falls of snow.[152] The negative impact of this on society is most clearly illustrated by the frequency with which exceptionally cold winters, particularly those that followed a poor or

---

[149] Manley, 'Central England temperatures', 395.
[150] Manley, 'Central England temperatures', 395.
[151] Jenkinson et al., 'Monthly and annual rainfall for Ireland 1711–1977', table; Murphy et al., 'A 305-year continuous monthly rainfall series', 428–30.
[152] Tyrrell, 'Paraclimatic statistics', 235–8; Hickey, 'The historic record of cold spells in Ireland', 308–09.

TABLE 5—Rainfall: Decennial totals and year average, 1711-1820

Decade	Decennial Rainfall (in millimetres)	Yearly average (millimetres)
1711-20	1088.8	108.88
1721-30	1047.9	104.79
1731-40	1022.7	102.27
1741-50	937	93.7
1751-60	1112.9	11.29
1761-70	997.1	99.7
1771-80	988.6	98.86
1781-90	941.6	94.6
1791-1800	992.4	99.24
1801-10	1071	107.1
1811-20	1013.7	101.37

Source: A.F. Jenkinson *et al.*, 'Monthly and annual rainfall for Ireland, 1711–1977' (Met 0 13 Branch Memorandum No. 77, Apr. 1979, Meteorological Service Library, Dublin).

deficient harvest, plunged the population into crisis.[153] But it was not confined to these occasions, and it did not always weigh so heavily on the population as the winter of 1775–6 attests. Having enjoyed several bumper harvests in the early 1770s that were in welcome contrast to their experience in the late 1760s, the population was better positioned to cope with the more challenging conditions they encountered in the winter of 1775–6.[154] These can be said to have commenced with 'tempestuous weather' and 'violent gales' in October 1775 that resulted in damaged property and lost shipping that, among its other effects, disrupted the supply of coal to Dublin.[155] Yet worse was to come as a sharp fall in temperature in November produced the first reported casualty—a man who died of cold in a doorway in Thomas Street, Dublin.[156] Flooding later in the month compounded the challenge of living in the capital.[157] But it was not until January 1776 when temperatures exceeded the low level experienced in 1709, and fell within a degree of the record low of 1740, that the worst effects of the severe cold were felt. Rivers and lakes froze, roads were rendered impassable by heavy snow and ships were bound in ice in Dublin Bay. As the cold hit home, the number of beggars plying the streets in the hope of assistance rose; so too did the number that fell victim to the cold. This was ominous, but the country was saved from a significant increase in mortality by the onset of thaw, which eased

---

[153] Above, p. 3.
[154] As well as the evidence of reports to the contrary, there are reports of 'greatest plenty' in 1774: *Hibernian Journal*, 30 Sept. 1774; *Finn's Leinster Journal*, 29 Oct. 1774.
[155] *Hibernian Journal*, 23 Oct., 1, 3, 8 Nov 1775; *Finn's Leinster Journal*, 28 Oct., 1 Nov. 1775.
[156] *Hibernian Journal*, 15 Nov. 1775.
[157] *Hibernian Journal*, 24, 27 Nov. 1775.

conditions, by the fact that food prices did not surge and by the improved availability of poor relief.[158] It was a telling illustration, however, of how rapidly the country's fortunes could switch from contentment to crisis, and of the enduring precarity of life for a sector of society.

This was not a lesson that the population needed to learn. They had come through a number of comparable (if not so severe) cold spells in the 1760s (in 1763, and in 1766, 1767, 1768 when they effectively prolonged the subsistence crisis that had made the mid-1760s especially challenging). They also experienced other, shorter, cold spells during the longer, colder winters that are emblematical of climate during the mid-eighteenth century, and that can be identified in 1754, 1763–4, 1768, 1772, 1777, 1779, and January and November 1780.[159] They were the most discommoding weather events that the population had to negotiate, though they were exceeded statistically by the number of storms (sea and land), instances of thunder and lightning and flooding incidents that account for a majority of 'the natural hazards' that were reported in the press.[160]

Even more so than snow and frost, storms had the capacity to transform quickly the immediate environment in which people lived. They were not equally disruptive, still less equally destructive, though it was the latter quality, next to their frequency, that attracted contemporary attention.[161] This was especially true of sea storms, which could be depended on, during the winter months, to provide a quotient of harrowing stories involving the loss of life and property.[162] This outcome was the most serious consequence of the vulnerability of wooden sailing vessels to the destructive power of the sea, and it took a regular toll on

---

[158] *Hibernian Journal*, 17, 26, 29, 31 Jan., 7, 9, 16 Feb. 1776; *Saunders' News Letter*, 15, 19 Jan., 2, 7, 16 Feb. 1776; *Finn's Leinster Journal*, 20, 27, 31 Jan., 3, 7, 10 Feb. 1776: *Freeman's Journal*, 23 Jan. 1776; Gebbie (ed.), *Abercorn letters*, 322; Kelly, 'Charitable societies', 96–100.

[159] Tyrrell, 'Paraclimatic statistics', 235–8; PRONI, Villiers-Stuart papers, T3131/C/14/2, Musgrave to Grandison, 23 Dec. 1763; *Finn's Leinster Journal*, 6 Jan. 1768; Tuckey's *Cork Remembrancer*, 150, 161, 179; *Hoey's Publick Journal*, 3 Feb. 1772; *Hibernian Journal*, 10 Feb., 1772, 22 Nov. 1780; BL, Hardwicke papers, Add. MS 35610 f. 174, Bishop of Clogher to Hardwicke, 17 Mar. 1772; *Saunders' News Letter*, 24 Feb. 1777.

[160] This conclusion is supported by Mitchell's categorisation of 130 reports in the *Belfast News Letter*, 1738–92: Mitchell, 'Looking backward to see forward', 16.

[161] It is noteworthy that it did not elicit any comparative reflection, which would echo the modern suggestion that there were possibly fewer gales then than was the case during the Maunder Minimum: see V. Trouet et al., 'North Atlantic storminess and Atlantic meridional overturning circulation…', *Global and Planetary Change* 84–5 (2012), 51–2. For the 'principal storms from 1715–58' see Rutty, 'Registry of the weather', 471–8, tables II, III and IV.

[162] Many examples might be given: the destructive impact of the sea was well revealed in January 1757 when two Whitehaven vessels both foundered in rough seas 'in sight of… shore' near Dublin, and in October 1775 when the Irish casualties who died en route to Holyhead included Alderman Forbes and a Mrs Farrell, her son and three daughters: *Finn's Leinster Journal*, 28 Oct. 1775.

sailors, fishermen and passengers whether they plied the coast, crossed the Irish sea, or ventured further afield. The loss of cargo and the disruption of the mails that complicated the management of the Anglo-Irish nexus, which was regularly commented on by those at the political helm, were less consequential by comparison. But they were as revealing, in their own way, as the inability of the wealthiest to stay warm during extreme cold spells, of the population's limited capacity to insulate itself against the power of the elements.[163]

Lightning excited comparable interest for the same reason. It is unsurprising therefore that, in a continuation of the pattern identifiable with respect to incidents recorded in the 1690s and early eighteenth century, a high proportion of the lightning episodes reported in the mid eighteenth century featured the loss of life (human and animal) and the destruction of property.[164] This was true also of thunderstorms, which were normally reported as being accompanied by lightning and therefore as inherently destructive, for even when this was not the case it was their destructive capacities that took precedence.[165] By comparison, most of the more numerous instances of flooding seemed more matter of fact though they usually left a larger trail of destruction. A survey of reported instances suggests that hardly a year passed when there was no significant incident of this kind, and there were identifiable occasions—January 1754, October 1763 and January 1786—when significant numbers of 'people were drowned, bridges swept away, crops and roads inundated, peat supplies lost, ships driven aground and cargoes damaged or destroyed'.[166] Most were localised and intermittent, but there were a variety of lowland areas—river floodplains and estuaries particularly—that were prone to repeated serious flooding. Though this can be attributed, in part at least, to incautious, or ill-considered urban development and land use, it also attested, more broadly, to the inadequacy of municipal and national infrastructure.[167] It may be that the problems to which this gave rise

---

[163] James Kelly, *Poynings' Law and the making of law in Ireland 1660–1800* (Dublin, 2007), 175–6, 264–5; Conolly to Bonnell, 6 Feb. 1742, 10 Jan, 1 Feb. 1743 in Jennings and Ashford (eds), *The letters of Katherine Conolly*, 216, 230, 231.

[164] Hickey, 'The historical record of lightning', passim; *Pue's Occurrences*, 28 Jan, 4, Feb., 27 May, 29 Aug. 1749, 8, 29 Nov., 9 Dec. 1757; *Belfast News Letter*, 3 Aug. 1750; *Aberdeen Press*, 12 Aug. 1750; Tuckey's *Cork Remembrancer*, 134; *Dublin Courier*, 13 June 1760, 29 June 1761, 7 July 1762, 10 June, 1 Aug., 19 Sept. 1763, 29 June, 2, 6 July, 24 Aug 1764; *Hibernian Journal*, 3 Mar. 1773, 26 June 1775, 24 June 1776; *Saunders' News Letter*, 5 Feb., 3 Aug. 1778, 1 May, 21 July 1779, 18 Aug. 1780; *Dublin Evening Journal*, 5 Feb. 1778; *Dublin Evening Post*, 8 Aug., 1 Sept. 1778, 2, 4 Sept. 1779.

[165] *Pue's Occurrences*, 14 Feb. 1756, 8 Nov. 1757; *Belfast News Letter*, 14 Aug. 1753; *Aberdeen Press*, 12 Aug. 1750; Tuckey's *Cork Remembrancer*, 131–2,134, 155, 149, 165; *Dublin Courier*, 13 June 1760, 29 June 1761, 7 July 1762, 10 June 1763, 24 Nov. 1766; *Public Gazetteer*, 13 Feb. 1768; *Saunders' News Letter*, 5 Feb. 1778; *Dublin Evening Post*, 2 Sept. 1779.

[166] Mitchell, 'Looking backward to see forward', 17.

[167] See David Dickson, 'Large scale developers and the growth of eighteenth-century Irish cities' in Paul Butel and L.M. Cullen (eds), *Cities and merchants: French and Irish*

were felt most acutely in the largest urban centres—Dublin, Cork, Kilkenny, Limerick and Belfast—since this is where a majority of reported cases occurred, but allowance should also be made for the fact that, since these were also centres of newspaper publication, they may be over-represented in the record.

Be that as it may, it is still apparent based on the number of occasions when flooding was reported on Main Street, Dunscombe's Marsh, Hammond's Marsh, Tuckey's and other quayside locations that Cork was especially vulnerable to tidal flooding.[168] This was a less common problem elsewhere, but notable incidents at Carrickfergus (in 1750), Waterford (in 1766), Youghal (in 1771) and Dublin (see below) demonstrate that while it may have been most commonplace on the south coast it was not confined to there.[169] It was less common, moreover, than heavy rain causing rivers to surge and overflow, which was the occasion of disruptive flooding in Enniscorthy (1765), Galway (1773) and Tralee (1778). An earlier incident of this kind on the river Blackwater in 1769, which resulted in 'great loss' to farmers in the vicinities of Tallow, Lismore and Cappoquin, Co. Waterford, indicates that flooding could result in significant damage to hay and corn crops. This is also what ensued in County Down in 1751, when the rivers Mourne and Finn overflowed, but bleach greens were also vulnerable, as was the case in County Antrim in 1761 when the Bann overflowed.[170]

As the island's fastest growing urban centre, it was inevitable that Dublin encountered problems not only with the river Liffey, but also with its tributaries, the Dodder and Poddle. Dublin certainly experienced its share of floodwater with notable incidents in 1745, 1749, 1750, 1754, 1760, 1761, 1762, 1764, 1774, 1776 and 1784. As was the case in Cork, 'the overflowing of the quays' was an ongoing concern when the Liffey ran high, whether the source was a high tide, rainfall or an unexpected surge in the volume of water due to a rapid thaw.[171] This was the source of the problems experienced in 1745 when 'a sudden thaw came on, attended by heavy violent rains, which…penetrated most of the houses in the city, doing great damages to roofs, rooms and cellars'. If, one well informed contemporary maintained, as few as one house in 40 avoided water penetration on this occasion it was a once in a lifetime event.[172] But the fact that 'the great rains' that

---

perspectives on urban development, 1500–1900 (Dublin, 1986), 109–23 for some perspective on this.

[168] *Belfast News Letter*, 6 Feb.1750; *Derby Mercury*, 16 Feb. 1750; Tuckey's *Cork Remembrancer*, 131, 132, 153, 160, 166; *Public Gazetteer*, 21 Jan. 1764; *Finn's Leinster Journal*, 19 Aug. 1769.

[169] *Derby Mercury*, 16 Feb. 1750; *Belfast News Letter*, 16 Dec. 1766; Tuckey's *Cork Remembrancer*, 160.

[170] *Dublin Courier*, 4 Nov. 1761; *Belfast News Letter*, 25 Jan. 1765; *Saunders' News Letter*, 8 Sept. 1773, 13 Nov. 1778; *Finn's Leinster Journal*, 16 Aug. 1769; Mitchell, 'Looking backward to see forward', 15–16.

[171] *Dublin Weekly Journal*, 1 June 1751.

[172] Burns, *An historical remembrancer*, 248; Rutty, 'Registry of the weather', 368–9; Delany to Dewes, 10 Jan 1745 in Lady Llanover (ed.), *The autobiography and correspondence …*

fell in February and March 1749 'caused such great floods that several parts of this city is under water' indicates that the city and its environs were ill-prepared to cope with major inundations.[173] This was confirmed in 1762 when 'heavy rains' resulted once more in 'most parts of the city being overflowed' because the city's 'sewers' were 'too small to carry off the quantity of water'.[174] A more persistent problem was highlighted in January 1764, when, as well as the cellars on the Liffey quays, 'houses in Patrick Street, Little Ship Street, the Lower Castle yard, Castle Lane and Dame Street' were submerged under 'several feet under water'.[175] Next to the quays, Patrick Street was particularly susceptible to flooding because of the inability to control the flow of the Poddle, and further incidents in that location in 1774 and during the cold winter of 1775–6, in particular, underlined the Poddle river's enduring disruptive capacity.[176]

One of the implications of river flooding that elicited particular notice was its impact on the country's communications infrastructure, bridges specifically. Thus in the report of the damage caused to Tralee by floodwater in 1778 it was claimed that 'most of the bridges in the county are destroyed'.[177] This is hardly more tenable than the near contemporary report that 'fourteen bridges' were swept away by the impetuosity of the torrents' that followed when County Donegal was inundated 'by sudden and excessive rains' in the same year'.[178] But the loss of bridges was a useful proxy both of the seriousness of a particular flood and of how much it would cost to set matters right. With this in mind, the 'dreadful flood' that inundated the eastern half of the country in October 1763 set a high benchmark. Prompted by a combination of storms and exceptional rain, the effects of which were registered as far north as Belfast and as far south as Cork, it hit the eastern counties of Leinster hardest.[179] As the loss of a number of 'small craft' on the Liffey, the destruction of the bridge linking Dirty Lane on the south side with Queen Street on the north, the toppling of two houses in Ringsend and 'damage to gardens' attests, Dublin received more than a glancing blow, but the impact was worse elsewhere.[180] In Wexford, for example, where

Mrs Delany (3 vols, London, 1861), vol. 2, 334; *Newcastle Courant*, 9 Feb. 1745; Jennings and Ashford (eds), *The letters of Katherine Conolly*, 205.

[173] NAI, Pembroke estate papers, 97/467/1/2/5/58, 59, 60, Mathew to Fitzwilliam, 24 Jan., 7 Feb., 14 Mar. 1749; *Pue's Occurrences*, 28 Feb. 1749.

[174] *Dublin Courier*, 22 Oct. 1762; Rutty, 'Registry of the weather', 440.

[175] *Dublin Courier*, 13 Jan. 1764; *Public Gazetteer*, 17 Jan. 1764.

[176] *Saunders' News Letter*, 9 Dec. 1774; *Hibernian Journal*, 24, 27 Nov. 1775; *Finn's Leinster Journal*, 7 Feb. 1776.

[177] *Saunders' News Letter*, 13 Nov. 1778.

[178] *Dublin Evening Post*, 17 Sept. 1778. As well as those mentioned there are other reports of bridges being lost in Wicklow in 1761 (*Dublin Courier*, 30 Nov. 1761); Enniscorthy in 1765 (*Belfast News Letter*, 25 Jan. 1765); Co. Antrim (*Dublin Courier*, 27 Dec. 1766); and on the Bandon river in 1749 (*Pue's Occurrences*, 16 Dec. 1749).

[179] *Dublin Courier*, 10, 12 Oct. 1763; Rutty, 'Registry of the weather', 445; Mitchell, 'Looking backward to see forward', 17.

[180] *Dublin Courier*, 5, 10 Oct. 1763.

'the lowest part of the town' was submerged under 4ft of water, the damage was computed 'to amount to more than £1000'. The loss inflicted on property and livestock in the neighbourhood of Celbridge, Co. Kildare, which was also inundated, was comparable, while the reported loss of seventeen bridges in County Wicklow suggests that the damage inflicted in that county was on a still larger scale.[181] And yet it was modest compared to the experience of County Kilkenny, where the combination of heavy rain and a strong northern wind 'raised such a flood in the river Nore' and its tributaries as 'to totally destroy all before it'. As an inventory of the damage was not prepared, it is not possible to determine its full extent. But the fact that as well as the 'many people' (perhaps as many as two hundred) that gave their lives, eight bridges were 'swept away' and the village of Thomastown was 'almost entirely destroyed' provides some justification for the claim that the 'county is ruined'.[182] It was not, of course. Kilkenny soon put the experience behind it. But the loss of life and the destruction wreaked in 1763 is a further striking illustration of the heavy toll the elements could and did take in lives and infrastructure during one of the more benign phases of the Little Ice Age.

Experiencing the Dalton Minimum: the weather in the late eighteenth and early-nineteenth centuries

The early eighteenth-century improvement in temperatures that signalled the end of the Maunder Minimum was brought to a close by the commencement of another cooling phase towards the end of the eighteenth century. Prompted by the decline in solar irradiance identified by the meteorologist John Dalton, and dated to the period 1790–1830, Wagner and Zorita have suggested more recently that the 'reduction of the near-surface global temperature' that defines the Dalton Minimum was a consequence, primarily, of volcanic forcing because the cooling effect is not demonstrable prior to the unidentified tropical eruption dated to 1809–11.[183] This conclusion is not incompatible with the decennial average temperatures of the CET series (Table 1), but it is not in keeping with the 'annual mean temperature series' for Ireland recorded at Armagh Observatory beginning in 1796. Both the annual mean spot temperatures and the 'equivalent mean' of the maximum and minimum temperatures recorded at this location are not directly comparable to those of the CET series, but they support the conclusion that, beginning in the second half of the 1790s, the weather in Ireland embarked on a phase, extending over three and a half

---

[181] *Dublin Courier*, 5, 10 Oct. 1763; *Oxford Journal*, 22 Oct. 1763.
[182] *Dublin Courier*, 5, 10 Oct. 1763; *Freeman's Journal*, 8, 11 Oct. 1763; NAI, Prim Collection, BR no 87/84, Prim to Jones, 5 Oct. 1763; Canon Carrigan, *The history and antiquities of the diocese of Ossory* (4 vols, Dublin, 1905), vol. 3, 46.
[183] Sebastian Wagner and Eduardo Zorita, 'The influence of volcanic, solar and CO_2 forcing on the temperature in the Dalton Minimum (1790–1830): a model study', *Climate Dynamics* 25 (2005), 205–18.

TABLE 6—Annual Mean Temperatures, 1796–1870 at Armagh Observatory

Years	Annual Mean Spot temperatures (°C)	Equivalent mean of Maximum/ Minimum temperature (°C)
1796–1800	7.72	8.14
1801–10	8.07	8.47
1811–20	7.82	8.21
1821–24	8.075	8.475
1834–40	8.67	8.66
1841–50	8.92	8.91
1851–60	8.80	8.80
1861–70	8.94	8.94

Source: C.J. Butler *et al.*, 'A provisional long mean air temperature series for Armagh Observatory', *Journal of Atmospheric and Terrestrial Physics*, 58 (1996), table 3.

decades, of reduced temperatures (Table 6). It is not that these decades are without other distinguishing features, moreover.

The 1780s and 1790s were among the driest decades in the eighteenth century. Furthermore, it is improbable that the subsistence crisis experienced in 1799–1801 is unconnected to the reduced temperatures experienced in the late 1790s, which reached their nadir in 1799, for (though there were a number of notable volcanic episodes in the late 1790s (Table 3)) no evidence has been aduced to suggest that volcanic forcing was a significant factor in this instance. The early years of the nineteenth century were somewhat more benign, but consistent with the findings of Wagner and Zorita, temperatures fell back in the 1810s to the levels experienced in the late 1790s, and, according to the CET series, close to the level previously encountered in the 1760s (Tables 1 and 6). This cold spell was not sustained into the early 1820s but as the average annual mean temperature during this decade did not exceed that experienced between 1801 and 1810, they are no less securely identified as a continuing part of the Dalton Minimum.[184] As this suggests, and as the pattern of cold winters, and episodes of serious flooding identifiable in the 1780s and 1790s illustrate, the weather continued to test the population as much during the final phase of the Little Ice Age as it did in the mid-1780s as it came to terms with the enduring effects of Lakagígar.[185]

Though the good harvest of 1784 came as a relief to a population that had endured the long and severe winter in 1783–4, there was no early relief from

---

[184] C.J. Butler *et al.*, 'A provisional long mean air temperature series for Armagh Observatory', *Journal of Atmospheric and Terrestial Physics,* 58 (1996), table 3; C.J. Butler *et al.*, 'Air temperatures from Armagh Observatory, Northern Ireland, from 1796 to 2002', *International Journal of Climatology*, 25 (2005), table 4.

[185] Murphy *et al.*, 'Irish droughts in newspaper archives', *Weather* 72:6 (2017), 151–2.

severe winter weather as 1784–5 and 1785–6 were also difficult.[186] Unlike its predecessor, the winter of 1784–5 started early. It was subsequently claimed that it began with 'a shower of snow' on 25 September, but a sudden change in the weather—'from…benign to…severe'—in late October sits more readily with the temperature record, as the lower than average temperatures experienced in October and November were a prelude to the exceptional cold experienced in December. Featuring hail, snow and 'very strong frost', it obliged farmers 'to fodder' cattle early, while reports of death by exposure and hypothermia among the human population underlined the continuing vulnerability of the poor when this happened.[187] Conditions improved temporarily alongside a 'gentle thaw' in January 1785, but the respite was brief as the return at the end of the month of low temperatures and the associated frost and snow and heavy rain prolonged the winter cold. Conditions were not made any easier by the 37 days of drought that followed for though there was sufficient moisture in the ground to ensure that growth was not long interrupted, it is clear from the warmth of the commentary that greeted the fine autumnal weather and 'plentiful harvest' in 1785 that the population was relieved.[188] If so it was relief, tinged with anxiety that was in evidence once more during the winter of 1785–6, as, in a repeat of 1784–5, winter began early once again. It did not quite follow the same pattern for though there was 'heavy snow' and 'sharp frosts' in early January and again in February–March 1786 that exacerbated the plight of the 'poor and miserable' and caused further deaths due to exposure and hypothermia, the 'incessant rains' that accelerated the initial thaw were more disruptive. They caused major flooding in the heart of Leinster as 'hundreds of acres' were inundated, bridges were swept away, mills and houses were damaged or ruined and numerous towns and villages were submerged.[189] It would have been worse, of course, if the heavy April rains had persisted, whereas they were succeeded by a further spring drought that proved no less difficult for 'the poor' who continued to bear the brunt of the extreme conditions.[190] It so happened that the wet summer and autumn that followed posed a more serious threat to the quality of the harvest, but it was safely saved, and since the winter of 1786–7 was 'uncommonly mild' it was the first

---

[186] *Saunders' News Letter*, 28 Oct. 1785.
[187] *Saunders' News Letter*, 14, 15, 16, 18 Dec. 1784, 28 Oct. 1785; *Hibernian Journal*, 27 Oct., 15, 17, 20 Dec 1784.
[188] *Saunders' News Letter*, 15 Feb., 9 Apr., 5, 20, 27 May, 21 June, 1 Dec. 1785; *Exshaw's Gentleman's and London Magazine*, 55 (Feb. 1785), 112; *Dublin Evening Post,* 21 May, 4, 9 June, 12 July, 6 Aug., 6 Sept. 1785.
[189] *Dublin Evening Post,* 27 Oct., 22 Nov., 29 Dec. 1785; *Saunders' News Letter*, 31 Dec. 1785, 4, 5, 9, 10, 12 Jan., 7, 9 Mar. 1786.
[190] *Saunders' News Letter*, 22, 24 Apr. 1786; *Tuckey's Cork Remembrancer*, 193; *Hibernian Chronicle (Cork)*, 29 May 1786.

winter in several years in which rain induced flooding posed a greater challenge than cold or drought.[191]

The milder winters of 1786–7 and 1787–8 were a relief to a population that had negotiated a sequence of testing winters since 1782–3. It was not that the weather was invariably benign. Heavy rains in 1787 resulted in serious flooding across the island in November, and 1788 was unusually dry.[192] These conditions were far from ideal, but they were less forbidding for the population than acute cold, as the winter of 1788–9 demonstrated once more. As was the usual pattern, the onset of cold weather was signalled by 'a great fall of snow' and a 'severe frost' in mid-December 1788, that, mirroring the severity of the season across Europe, elicited comparisons with the exceptional winters of 1708–9, 1740–41 and 1783–4.[193] Conditions were not sufficiently severe in Ireland to justify such claims. Indeed, some took advantage of the opportunity to ice skate and others to throw snowballs. But the indulgence of these recreational impulses was put in proper perspective by the experiences of those for whom the interruption of economic activity, which was one of the primary indices of the 'severity of the weather', increased the likelihood of death by exposure and hypothermia.[194] Drifting snows, which reached an exceptional 15–20ft in Crumlin, Co. Dublin, in January 1789, were certainly disruptive, rendering roads impassable and interrupting the movement of foodstuffs. But it was 'the extreme cold' that had the greatest effect, as those engaged in trades as varied as building, clothmaking, milling and agriculture were reduced to nearly the same condition as the 'poor wretches immersed in the depths of woe'.[195] Had this happened earlier in the century, it is likely that many would have fallen victim to 'corrosive famine and consuming disease', but the fact that Dublin was well supplied with coal and that the dispensers of charitable relief were better equipped than ever to respond to those in need kept casualty rates low.[196] The population was assisted by the fact that the thaw that separated the early January snows from those in the second half of the month permitted the resumption of economic activity, for though the thaw combined with 'a heavy fall of rain' to submerge a large part of Cork city on 17 January, it was of short duration.[197] This was true also of the Liberties of

---

[191] *Saunders' News Letter*, 13 June, 18, 28, 29 Aug., 1, 8, 11, 13, 15 Sept., 2 Oct., 24, 27 Nov., 4, 6, 13, 16 Dec. 1786, 28 Feb. 1787; *Freeman's Journal*, 10 Mar. 1787.
[192] *Dublin Evening Post,* 24 May, 30 June, 5, 9, 21, 24, 26 July, 21, 23 Aug., 1, 4, 25 Sept., 22, 24 Nov. 1787; *Saunders' News Letter*, 25 July, 2, 13, 25 Aug., 19, 27 Sept., 5, 24 Oct., 13, 16, 19, 20, 22, 28 Nov., 8 Dec. 1787; *Ramsey's Waterford Chronicle*, 20, 27 Nov. 1787.
[193] For reference to the conditions in Europe, see *Saunders' News Letter*, 3, 10, 13, 15, 23, 28 Jan., 3,11, 12, 18 Feb. 1789; *Dublin Evening Post*, 6 Jan. 1789.
[194] Tuckey's *Cork Remembrancer*, 200; *Saunders' News Letter*, 15, 16, 17 Jan. 1789.
[195] *Dublin Evening Post,* 6 Jan. 1789; *Saunders' News Letter*, 14,15, 23 Jan. 1789; *Freeman's Journal*, 15 Jan. 1789.
[196] *Dublin Evening Post,* 6 Jan. 1789; *Dublin Chronicle*, 13, 15 Jan. 1789.
[197] Tuckey's *Cork Remembrancer*, 200–01; *Saunders' News Letter*, 14, 15,19, 20, 24, 27 Jan., 4 Feb. 1789.

Dublin, which was inundated when the Poddle overflowed, but other locations were less fortunate. The destruction of three bridges in the vicinity of Macroom, Co. Cork, was one of the most notable infrastructural losses of a season that concluded, almost as rapidly as it had begun, with 'the extraordinary change in the weather from intense cold to warmth' at the beginning of February.[198]

The winter of 1788–9 demonstrates that Irish society had developed to a point where it possessed the capacity to cope with the problems posed by extreme weather. This was due to a combination of factors. The increased effectiveness of the network of relief services that had evolved over several decades against a background of strong economic growth was crucial. But mention should also be made of infrastructural improvements, such as those in Dublin aimed at taming the unruly Dodder and at corralling the flood waters that had for decades 'occasioned...considerable damage in many parts of the city and along the line of the Liffey'.[199] Such improvements were not of sufficient scale to neutralise the environmental effects of seriously bad weather, but when it was within expected parameters, and the harvest was adequate, the population could usually get by. Thus, though localised flooding in the summer of 1789, caused by 'seven weeks incessant rain', and the anticipated 'retarded harvest' were sufficient to arouse genuine concerns, the imposition of an embargo on exports (in December) combined with a reasonable harvest to ensure there was no repeat of the difficulties experienced in 1788–9.[200] The country certainly did not experience conditions as challenging as England, or those parts of France and Austria which endured 'all the miseries of famine' in 1789.[201] Indeed, because the 1789 harvest was better than anticipated, and the winter of 1789–90 mild, the country embarked on the 1790s better circumstanced to negotiate weather extremes than it had been at any prior point in the eighteenth century. It so happened that the country then experienced a sequence of good years spanning the early 1790s that were essentially free of climate-induced stress.[202] It was not that what one perceptive contemporary denominated 'the terrors of a ruined harvest, and consequent scarcity' did not persist in the public mind.[203] Concerns were expressed in the summer and autumn in virtually every one of these years at the implications of persistent

---

[198] *Saunders' News Letter*, 19 Jan., 3, 4 Feb. 1789.

[199] Above, 41–2; Kelly, 'Charitable societies' 98–101; *Saunders' News Letter*, 20 Jan. 1789; Michael Branagan, *Dublin moving east: how the city took over the sea* (Dublin, 2020), passim.

[200] *Saunders' News Letter*, 27 May, 3, 18, 20, 25 June, 7, 14,15, 22, 25 July, 3,12 Sept. 1789; *Dublin Chronicle*, 18 July 1789; *Dublin Evening Post*, 25 July 1789; Newenham to Washington, 14–26 Aug. 1789 in *The papers of George Washington, presidential series*, vol 3, accessed at http://founders. archives.gov/documents/ Washington/05-03-02-0263.

[201] *Saunders' News Letter*, 1 June, 8, 9, 10, 11, 15, 17, 21, 24 July, 6, 7, 25 Aug., 9 Sept. 1789; *Hibernian Journal*, 26 Aug. 1789.

[202] *Hibernian Journal*, 28 Sept. 1789; *Freeman's Journal*, 12 Jan. 1790; *Saunders' News Letter*, 25 Sept. 1789.

[203] *Dublin Evening Post*, 15 July 1790.

rain, but the harvest was sufficiently 'abundant' every time to allay unease, even when winters were not 'uncommonly fine', which was the case in 1793–4.[204]

By contrast, the winter of 1795, which was one of the most testing for some time, set the tone for what was to follow over a sustained period. As was now commonplace, comparisons were drawn with the winter of 1740, but whereas the grounds for doing so previously were generally unwarranted, this was not so on this occasion; the low January average temperature in the CET series was more severe than that registered in January 1740.[205] Moreover, this was not the extent of the challenge posed by the elements as problems for the population had commenced in November 1794 with 'a very severe storm...accompanied by heavy rain'. Dublin was particularly badly affected then, as the flood waters not only 'totally inundated' Patrick Street and environs and rendered Dame Street 'impassable' to those on foot, but also posed a threat to life as the four individuals who were 'swept' to their death in flood waters off George's Quay learned to their cost. In addition, it did 'irreparable damage to many poor and industrious families' in suburban New Street and Blackpitts, and caused the partial destruction of the 'new bridge' (Annesley Bridge) linking the North Strand to Clontarf.[206] The next phase was longer and still more testing. Beginning with frost on 21 December, the country was plunged anew into another 'severe winter' of 'constant frost and snow' that continued, 'with only six days intermission', 'until the nineteenth of January', following which it resumed and persisted 'with more or less rigour' through the remainder of January and February.[207] It also had a familiar register, since, as well as reports from Dublin of 'poor creatures' (male and female) 'perishing from want and the inclemency of the weather', the disruption of incoming traffic, as roads within a 25 or 30 mile radius of the city were rendered impassable, took a heavy toll on the 'multitudes' that were 'reduced...to the very extremity of existence' by 'the want of food and fuel'.[208] Indeed, but for the efforts of the Church of Ireland parish relief

---

[204] *Freeman's Journal*, 15 July 1790, 15, 22 Sept. 1791; *Dublin Evening Post*, 24 Aug. 1790, 30 Aug. 1792; *Dublin Morning Post*, 23 Sept. 1790, 6, 24 Sept., 2 Oct. 1792, 14 Oct. 1794; *Hibernian Journal*, 2 Sept. 1791, 25 Apr., 6 June, 23, 28 Nov 1792; *Dublin Weekly Journal*, 3 Sept. 1791; *Finn's Leinster Journal*, 28 Sept. 1791; *Ennis Chronicle*, 12 Nov. 1792; *Saunders' News Letter*, 6 Apr., 16 July, 17 Aug., 26 Sept., 12 Nov. 1793, 12 June, 21 July 1794; Newenham to Washington, 11 Feb. 1794 in C.S. Patrick (ed.), *The papers of George Washington*, presidential series, vol. 15 (Charlottesville, VA, 2009), 218–22; Newenham to Washington, Nov. 1794 in D.R. Hoth and C.S. Ebel (eds), *The papers of George Washington*, presidential series, vol. 17 (Charlottesville, VA, 2015), 136–40; Tuckey's *Cork Remembrancer*, 205.

[205] Manley, 'Central England temperatures', 395; for analogies with 1740 see *Scot's Magazine*, 57 (Jan. 1795), 67; *Oxford Journal*, 10 Jan. 1795; *Stanford Mercury*, 16 Jan. 1795.

[206] *Dublin Evening Post*, 22 Nov. 1794; *Dublin Morning Post*. 22 Nov., 13 Dec. 1794; *Ennis Chronicle*, 27 Nov. 1794.

[207] Newenham to Washington, 9 Mar. 1795 in Hoth and Ebel (eds), *The papers of George Washington*, vol. 17, 637–41; *Belfast News Letter*, 23 Mar. 1795.

[208] *Dublin Evening Post*, 27 Dec. 1794; *Saunders' News Letter*, 23, 26, 29 Jan. 1795.

committees, which distributed aid in the form of 'bread and broth', fuel and 'fresh straw' to 'a great number of unfortunate persons' in the metropolis, still more must have died. Meanwhile, in the countryside landowners like the Duke of Leinster sought to aid the distressed on their estates, who were prevented 'from working and earning bread' for six weeks until the second week of February when the commencement of a thaw released the populace from the worst of this weather fuelled crisis.[209] As usual, it did not relieve them of anxiety (as the by now familiar vernal drought kept prices high) until 'the completion of the harvest' brought about a normalisation in the environment.[210] The ensuing years (1797 and 1798) were without equivalent weather-induced challenges, moreover, as temperatures improved. Heavy rains were a source of intermittent anxiety; so too was snow, but so long as the harvest was good (as it was in 1796 and 1797), the population was not tested severely.[211]

These generally benign conditions did not inhibit weather speculation, however. The observation carried in a May 1796 issue of the *Dublin Evening Post* that 'old people generally agree that our climate has changed for the worse even within the experience of their own time' was a comprehensible response to a May day featuring 'sharp frost', 'deluges of rain', impetuous gusts of wind and 'thunder and lightning'.[212] Moreover, the speculation echoed the increased efforts that were being made across society to make sense of the weather.[213] The publication in the second half of the 1790s of data from two weather diaries—one for Belfast in 1794 the other for Limerick in 1798—which suggested that each city experienced 200 rainy days offered one solid pointer to the nature of Irish weather. The greater variation in the number of frost days (eight in Belfast in 1794 and 48 in Limerick in 1798) provided an equally useful perspective on just how different conditions could be from year to year, and how material this was when it came to establishing the impact of the weather at any given time.[214] This was underlined once more in 1799–1801 when the country experienced another subsistence crisis. Precipitated in the first instance by exceptionally cold conditions in the winter and spring of 1798–9, which delayed planting, a dry summer that inhibited growth, and a rain-weakened harvest, the difficulties this created were compounded in 1800 when a still more severe summer drought encouraged

---

[209] *Saunders' News Letter*, 27, 29 Jan., 9, 11 Feb., 18 Mar. 1795; *Freeman's Journal*, 5, 7 Feb. 1795.
[210] *Freeman's Journal*, 5 June 1795; *Saunders' News Letter*, 22 July, 5, 7, 13, 19, 31 Aug., 8, 19, 21 Sept. 1795.
[211] *Saunders' News Letter*, 5, 7, 22 Oct., 3, 25 Nov. 1795, 4 Aug., 4, 5, 12, 19 Sept., 5 Dec. 1797; *Dublin Evening Post*, 1 Dec. 1796, 7, 24 Jan., 10 Oct. 1797; Washington papers, Newenham to Washington, 15 Feb., 30 Oct. 1797, accessed at http://founders.archives.gov/documents/ Washington/05-03-02-0263; W.W. Abbot (ed.), *The papers of George Washington, retirement series* (Charlottesville, VA, 1998), vol. 1, 441–4.
[212] *Dublin Evening Post*, 14 May 1796.
[213] See, for example, *Saunders' News Letter*, 20 Dec. 1797.
[214] *Belfast News Letter*, 16 Jan. 1795; *Saunders' News Letter*, 9 Jan. 1799.

disease (curl) and resulted in a poor potato harvest. The impact of the weather varied across the country in both years, but the net effect was a depleted harvest, and serious distress that, the efforts that were made to mitigate its impact notwithstanding, resulted in extensive distress and (possibly) greater excess mortality than the country had experienced in a number of decades.[215] Moreover, it was a pattern that was not just sustained during the first decades of the nineteenth century, it was exacerbated when in the 1810s volcanic forcing pushed temperatures downwards.[216] The most notable manifestation of this globally occurred in 1816 when in the wake of Tambora, the world experienced a 'year without a summer'. Saliently, conditions were more difficult in Ireland in 1817 than they were in 1816, but this was less consequential in explaining the sharp rise in excess mortality that was to define Irish food crises in the nineteenth century than the country's record population. At *circa* seven million in 1821, it was more vulnerable than it had been at any time since the second quarter of the eighteenth century when climate driven crises had precipitated two significant famine episodes in 1727–9 and 1740–41. Since history does not repeat itself, there was no obvious reason why the population should apprehend further disasters on this scale. But the fact that weather driven crises were a defining feature of life in eighteenth-century Ireland and that 'multiple eruptions closely spaced in time', such as occurred in the 1810s, 'are more likely to have a major impact' meant that further crises were virtually inevitable given the ongoing deterioration in the economic environment.[217] On the positive side, the palpable improvement in air temperatures recorded at Armagh Observatory from the late 1820s (Table 6) served to diminish the threat presented by extreme cold. It did not remove the threat, of course, but the decline in the number and frequency of temperature extremes thereafter was a pointer towards 'the mid-19th century warm period',

---

[215] Roger Wells, 'The Irish famine of 1799–1801: market culture, moral economies and social protect' in Andrew Charlesworth and Adrian Randall (eds), *Markets, market culture and popular protest in eighteenth-century Britain and Ireland* (Liverpool, 1996), 164; Butler *et al.*, 'A provisional long mean air temperature series for Armagh Observatory', table 3; Liam Kennedy and Peter Solar, 'The famine that wasn't: 1799–1801 in Ireland' (unpublished paper, 2019); *Saunders' News Letter*, 22 Feb., 8 Apr., 22 June, 2, 17, 19 July, 5, 23 Aug., 27 Nov. 1799.

[216] Wagner and Zorita, 'The influence of volcanic, solar and CO_2 forcing on the temperature in the Dalton Minimum (1790–1830)', 206–8, 210; *Saunders' News Letter*, 12 Jan. 1802; Angela Byrne (ed.), *A scientific, antiquarian and picturesque tour: John (Fiott) Lee in Ireland 1806–07* (London, 2018), 24–5; Manuscript diary of John Loftie, Tandragee, Co. Armagh, De Burca Books Catalogue (2020).

[217] G.A. Zielinski, 'Stratospheric loading and optical depth estimates of explosive volcanism over the last 2100 years derived from the Greenland Ice Sheet Project 2 ice core', *Journal of Geophysical Research: Atmospheres* 100 D10 (1995), abstract; Slavin, 'Climate and famines', 440–41; Jonas Gudnason *et al.*, 'The 1845 Hekla eruption: grain-size characteristics of a tephra layer', *Journal of Volcanology and Geothermal Research*, 350 (2018), 33–46; Cormac Ó Gráda, *Ireland: a new economic history* (Oxford, 1993), part 2.

which 'started in the late 1820s and continued till *c.* 1870', that signalled the end of the Dalton Minimum and, with it, the Little Ice Age.[218]

Conclusion

When in 1809 Thomas Newenham engaged with the subject in his seminal *View of Ireland*, he observed that the country was possessed of 'a climate highly favourable to health and longevity, to the labour of man, and to the production of such articles of food as deserve a place among the real necessaries of life'.[219] It was a more than slightly rose-tinted perspective on Irish climate, for while he was secure in the conviction that Ireland possessed ample resources to flourish, he did not take sufficient cognizance of the repeatedly depressive difficulties caused by the weather. The most striking manifestation of this is the link that can be drawn between extreme weather and harvest crises, for while it is evident that each crisis impacted the population differently, it is also the case that each possessed an identifiable climatic dimension. It may be that the role climate played differed in every case. Yet, the recognition that volcanic forcing played an important part in creating the conditions is not just consistent with Campbell's characterisation of nature as a 'historical protagonist' it brings an important additional dimension to bear.[220] It certainly provides a compelling reason to embrace climate in any account of why and when they took place. This may seem to state the obvious, as various engagements with individual harvest crises in Ireland have highlighted the importance of the weather to their origin and course, but an acknowledgement that climate was neither static nor an inexplicable supra-ordinate force facilitates the location of Ireland in its hemispheric and climatic historical context. It also provides an opportunity to combine the different methodologies—the scientific and quantitative favoured by historical climatologists with the qualitative empiricism favoured by historians—in a manner that will enhance the perspective both can bring to bear, because there is, as this attempt to identify the phenomenon in Ireland in the long eighteenth century attests, much that is unclear. The most obvious, given the attention it has been accorded in this paper, may be the gaps in our understanding of the timing, order and impact of volcanism. But the limitations in our appreciation of the importance of solar irradiance, the movements of large bodies of air and (sea) water, the amount of carbon dioxide in the atmosphere and so on is even more striking. And then there is

---

[218] Butler *et al.*, 'Air temperatures from Armagh Observatory, Northern Ireland, from 1796 to 2002', 1068–9, 1072–5, 1078.

[219] Thomas Newenham, *A view of the natural, political and commercial circumstances of Ireland* (London, 1809), 40.

[220] B.M.S. Campbell, 'Nature as historical protagonist: environment and society in pre-industrial England', *Economic History Review* 62 (2009), 282–314.

the matter of establishing how people understood, related to and engaged with the weather and climate.

The increased frequency with which the weather was referred to in the public sphere, and the expanded attempts that were made to trace and explain events scientifically are a manifestation of this that might usefully be explored. But there are other responses that do not fit easily into a scientific paradigm. One may instance the prayers for 'fair weather' that were offered up in 'several' Church of Ireland churches in Dublin on Sunday 7 May 1749 and Cork in 1763 and 1768, or the prayers for 'rain' that were offered up in 'all the churches' in Cork in the 'remarkably dry summer' of 1762, and again in 1776.[221] It is not apparent what, if any, psychological assistance these services provided their congregations, but their occurrence is as indicative in its own way as the inability to keep warm, or ink freezing in inkwells, which were inconveniences complained of by the rich, of the fact that the climate impacted lives in a myriad of ways.[222] The enduring fascination with lightning is another manifestation of this.[223] The upshot is that, no less than the manner in which people worshipped or rioted, recreated or expressed their political sentiments, their interaction with the weather was crucial to how they lived, and it deserves a commensurate place in the narrative and analysis of their lives.

---

[221] *Pue's Occurrences*, 9 May 1749; Tuckey's *Cork Remembrancer*, 139, 140, 153, 171.

[222] Brodrick to Brodrick, 9 Feb. 1709 in Hayton and Page (eds), *The correspondence of the Brodrick family*, 231; Conolly to Bonnell, 18, 29 Jan., 19 Dec. 1740, Conolly to Conolly, 9 Feb. 1745 in Jennings and Ashford (eds), *The letters of Katherine Conolly*, 190, 191, 201, 266; NAI, Pembroke Estate papers, 97/46/1/2/4/12, Mathew to Fitzwilliam, 13 Jan. 1740.

[223] Above 9, 28, 39–40; *Saunders' News Letter*, 19 Feb., 12 June 1781, 22 June 1782, 22 July 1783, 10 June 1784, 24 June, 2 Aug. 1785, 28 June, 7, 10 July, 21 Dec. 1786, 17, 21, 23 July 1789, 15 Aug. 1795; *Hibernian Journal*, 20 Jan. 1783; *Dublin Evening Post*, 25 June 1785.

'Nature herself seems in the vapours now': poetry and climate change in Ireland 1600–1820

Lucy Collins*
School of English, Drama and Film, University College Dublin

[Accepted 7 August 2020. Published 30 September 2020.]

Abstract

Long before climate change became a recognised phenomenon, unusual weather patterns were affecting our lives and being recorded in our literature. Referred to as the 'Little Ice Age', the period between 1450 and 1850 saw severe weather conditions in Europe and North America, and during this time both private and published writings show a particular sensitivity to meteorological description. Turbulent weather, both at sea and on land, was a feature of much seventeenth- and eighteenth-century poetry, combining experience and observation in powerful ways. The Romantic era brought further change to the literary representation of weather, when heightened attention to subjective states was matched by an increased awareness of the relationship between natural forces and political upheaval. In this essay I will explore the changing representation of weather in poetry written in Ireland between 1600 and 1820 and examine the relationship between literary convention and political and intellectual transformation in these texts.

Introduction

'Civilization inevitably runs to its end with a blindfold over its eyes' wrote Eugène Huzar in 1855, before going on the predict that in 'one or two hundred years' the emissions from the world's railways and steamships, factories and workshops would 'disturb the harmony of the world'.[1] This prescient awareness of the influence of human action on the wellbeing of the world is testament to the significant evolution of responses to the human relationship with atmospheric events over the preceding centuries. The need to recognise climate change as not only a scientific, but also a cultural, phenomenon means there is much to be discovered from the representation of weather before the systematic development of scientific learning.[2] The changing representation of weather in English-language verse of the seventeenth and eighteenth centuries attests to the impact of the growth

---

*Author's email: lucy.collins@ucd.ie
ORCID iD: https://orcid.org/0000-0003-4118-3520
doi: https://doi.org/10.3318/PRIAC.2020.120.10

[1] Eugène Huzar, '1855: Paris', *Lapham's Quarterly* 12:4 (Special Issue: Climate, 2019), 155.
[2] 'Climate – as it is imagined, studied and acted upon – needs to be understood, first and foremost, culturally. Since climate is a complex and abstract idea, it cannot be understood independently of the cultures within which the idea takes place': Mike Hulme, *Weathered: cultures of climate* (London, 2017), xii.

in natural philosophy and the early development of science, while the evolving use of natural imagery enriches the way poets investigate and express political dynamics. For poets, Ireland has for centuries constituted a space of detailed observation as well as for elaborate metaphorical meaning. This essay explores what these texts reveal about the evolving relationship between humans and their environment, and how the language of poetry shapes this understanding.

From its inception in the 1990s ecocriticism as a discipline has been concerned with the capacity of literary texts to foster environmental awareness. Foundational texts in British ecocriticism focused on Romantic poetry as a means to explore human consciousness of the natural world and acknowledge the shared vulnerability of all living things.[3] The social and political implications of this analysis were soon evident and shaped the first ecocritical engagements with early modern texts, which challenged previous assumptions of their anthropocentric character. While one would be mistaken, as Todd Borlik has argued, to expect these writings to represent 'fully formulated theories of biotic egalitarianism', they nonetheless exhibit a complex awareness of the relationship between human and non-human life.[4] Early work in the discipline returned to canonical texts, reading Shakespeare and Milton through an ecocritical lens and paying particular attention to the political and theological implications of climate imagery.[5] Recent ecological readings of the early modern period have opened the work of less well-known writers to scrutiny, revealing how overlooked texts shed light on everyday experiences of natural phenomena, and inform the relationship between literature and other modes of writing. In this way environmental debates have paved the way for a more inclusive literary canon and a greater depth of political engagement by critics.

In Ireland between the Tudor conquests and the Romantic period, representations of the natural world were shaped, firstly, by the dynamics of the Gaelic Irish, Old English and New English communities, and, secondly, when this triangular nexus was reduced in the seventeenth century to a more straightforward binary rivalry, to that of the Protestant and Catholic interests. The variable relationships this fostered between different linguistic, religious and intellectual traditions is evident in the evolving understanding of climate events and their

---

[3] The first major work of British ecocriticism is Jonathan Bate's *Romantic ecology: Wordsworth and the environmental tradition* (London, 1991). For an extended description of the field see Kevin Hutchings, 'Ecocriticism in British Romantic studies', *Literature Compass* 4:1 (2007), 172–202.

[4] Todd A. Borlik, *Ecocriticism and early modern English literature: green pastures* (London, 2011). Borlik notes the pioneering work by Keith Thomas in *Man and the natural world: changing attitudes in England 1500–1800* (London, 1983).

[5] See, for example, early modern ecocritical work by Paul Alpers (1996), Ken Hiltner (2003, 2008, 2011), Rebecca Bushnell (2003), Gabriel Egan (2006, 2015), Simon C. Estok (2011) and Dan Brayton (2013, 2018).

impact on individual human experience.[6] Nature could no longer be construed as stable and comforting, as 'a consoling cycle of growth, decay and renewal'.[7] Increased understanding of the links between meteorology and physiology in the early modern period has underlined human embeddedness in the material world and this, in turn, has indicated the challenges to direct representation of extreme weather events.[8] These challenges sometimes resulted in stylistic experimentation, but in other cases yielded a reluctance to engage directly with the extremity of experience. Poetry from mid-seventeenth-century Ireland not only drew on English literary conventions when depicting the natural world but also reflected the particular anxieties provoked by war and its attendant social and political upheaval. A century later, extreme weather was not always described as frightening; storms or floods could serve to intensify the sense that Ireland was a wild and untamed place, and to provide for the reader a frisson of excitement. During the Romantic period, roughly from the 1790s to the 1850s, poetry combined close connection to the landscape with forms of ethical or emotional reflection. It increasingly engaged with the world of empire, and explored relations between Ireland and Britain directly, as well as meditating on larger questions concerning human hierarchy and social order.[9]

Understanding climate

Ireland's position as an island in the north Atlantic Ocean at the edge of Europe has ensured that it has experienced variable and comparatively clement weather conditions. From the onset of the Little Ice Age *c.*1400, however, Europe underwent an extended period of volatile weather; periods of excessive rainfall were interspersed with years of extreme heat, leading to drought and bad harvests,

---

[6] For an exploration of land in Irish poetry of the eighteenth century see Andrew Carpenter, 'Land and landscape in Irish poetry in English, 1700–1780', in Moyra Haslett (ed.), *Irish literature in transition 1700–1780* (Cambridge, 2020), 151–70.

[7] Timothy Clark, citing Timothy Morton, *The value of ecocriticism* (Cambridge, 2019), 35. In Morton's view, however, this fundamental understanding of nature as a reliable backdrop to human experience persists and is responsible for our continuing exploitation of natural resources.

[8] Rebecca Totaro argues that we have underestimated the importance of meteorology to early modern writers by assuming that their references were always figurative. Rebecca Totaro, *Meteorology and physiology in early modern culture: earthquakes, human identity, and textual representation* (New York and London, 2018)

[9] Ecocritical perspectives on texts from early modern Ireland have been limited to date. While digital projects such as *Deep maps: West Cork coastal cultures* (www.deepmapscork.ie) draw on material— including poems—from 1700 onward, there are no book-length studies of environmental issues in pre- Romantic writing from Ireland. Critics of Spenser and Swift have engaged with the role of the environment in their work, for example J.D. Bernard, *Ceremonies of innocence: pastoralism in the poetry of Edmund Spenser* (Cambridge, 1989) and Carole Fabricant, *Swift's landscape* (Notre Dame IN, 1982). A few monographs and essay collections on Irish ecocriticism have included reference to the seventeenth and eighteenth centuries—see Wenzell (2009), Faragó and Kirkpatrick (2016).

and sustained periods of lower than average temperatures. The climate of the British Isles as a whole, being temperate in character, was less susceptible to extreme weather events than elsewhere, as John Campbell observed in 1774: 'if therefore our Weather be...less steady and serene than in some other Countries of Europe, it is not so sultry in one Season, or so rigorous in another'.[10] Periods of good weather facilitated farming development and, as Geoffrey Parker argues, encouraged agricultural expansion on lands 'already close to the limits of viable cultivation'.[11] This increased the likelihood of severe human hardship when, as happened in the 1640s and 1650s, a combination of war and failed harvests reduced many to destitution. The scale of the hardship then was remarkable: in the words of preacher Jeremiah Whitaker, God planned 'to shake all nations collectively, jointly, and universally'.[12]

Early representation of climatic conditions attributed them to divine power. This was especially true of extreme weather events, as John Calvin, writing in 1536, set out in characteristically explicit terms:

> In the Law and the Prophets, [God] repeatedly declares that as often as he waters the earth with dew and rain, he manifests his favour, that by his command heaven becomes hard as iron, the crops are destroyed by mildew and other evils, that storms and hail, in devastating the fields are signs of sure and special vengeance. This being admitted, it is certain that not a drop of rain falls without the express command of God.[13]

The seventeenth century was a period of rapid developments in scientific instrumentation,[14] yet this had little identifiable impact on the power of religious and folk belief. Key figures in early meteorology, such as Robert Boyle (1627–91), acknowledged the difference between scientific and popular thinking. Some argued that all atmospheric events were natural and 'that God's providence took the form of upholding the regular laws of nature, laws that might ultimately become known by systematic study'.[15] As late as 1772, however, the Quaker John Rutty saw the weather as an expression of divine wisdom.[16] Popular accounts dwelt on

---

[10] John Campbell, *A political survey of Britain* (1774), quoted in Jan Golinski, *British weather and the climate of Enlightenment* (Chicago and London, 2007), 59.

[11] Geoffrey Parker, *Global crisis: war, climate change and catastrophe in the seventeenth century* (New Haven and London, 2013), 57.

[12] Quoted in Parker, *Global crisis*, xxiv.

[13] John Calvin, *Institutes of the Christian religion*, Henry Beveridge (trans.) (Peabody, MA, 2008), 118.

[14] Brendan McWilliams, 'The kingdom of the air: the progress of meteorology', in John Wilson Foster (ed.) *Nature in Ireland: a scientific and cultural history* (Dublin, 1997), 115–32: 123.

[15] Golinski, *British weather and the climate of Enlightenment*, 41.

[16] John Rutty, *An essay towards a natural history of the county of Dublin* (2 vols, Dublin, 1772), vol. 2, 280–81. Dr Johnson mocked Rutty's 'Spiritual Diary' but his scientific work was of lasting value: see F.E. Dixon, 'Weather in Old Dublin', *Dublin Historical Record* 13; 3–4 (1953), 94–107: 95.

the religious connotations of extreme weather: for example, the authors of pamphlets and sermons addressing the Great Storm of 1703 understood the event as a punishment for the sins of humanity.[17] Daniel Defoe asserted that 'Nature plainly refers us beyond her Self, to the Mighty Hand of Infinite Power, the Author of Nature, and Original of all Causes'.[18] Yet he also recognised the value of testimony, as demonstrated by his call for personal accounts of the storm, which he edited and published the following year.[19] Defoe's *The Storm*, judged the first significant work of modern journalism, explicitly recognised the validity of personal experience in assembling accurate records: 'No pen could describe it, nor tongue express it, nor thought conceive it unless by one in the extremity of it'.[20]

The observation of weather can be found in a variety of discourses in the early modern period. Diaries and letters from people in varied walks of life—gentlemen, clergymen, physicians, sea-captains and travellers—are important sources of information on weather events. The development of natural philosophy throughout Europe, in Ireland through the Dublin Philosophical Society (1684–1709) and the Medico-Philosophical Society (1756–84), encouraged sustained observation of weather patterns. This did not always dispel long-held folk beliefs about the weather, many of which were disseminated through almanacs, published for all areas of the British Isles, including Dublin and Cork. But almanac-writers were increasingly disparaged, as an anonymous Irish poet who experienced the rigours of the 'Great Frost' of 1739–40 suggested in a wry verse, with its final distorted rhyme: '…it does appear/By all our Almanacks this year,/That ne'er an author of them all,/Foreknew that such a storm would fall;/So far from that, the ninnies rather/Tell us of rain, and pleasant weather.'[21]

The process of record-keeping shaped how the weather was perceived in a number of ways. As well as emphasising cyclical patterns, it stressed the importance of instruments for reading the weather accurately, and of long-term strategies for recording and framing these findings. Instead of being an unpredictable phenomenon, the weather exhibited continuities that were there to be identified.[22] Local observation formed an important dimension of this analysis, affinities with place lending authority to the accumulated detail, as Gilbert

---

[17] Golinski, *British weather and the climate of Enlightenment*, 41.

[18] Daniel Defoe, *The Storm: or a collection of the most remarkable casualties and disasters which happen'd in the late dreadful tempest both by sea and land* (London, 1704), 2.

[19] See Robert Markley, '"Casualties and disasters": Defoe and the interpretation of climatic instability', *Journal for Early Modern Cultural Studies* 8:2 (2008), 102–24.

[20] Defoe, *The Storm*, 68.

[21] Anonymous, 'On our modern astrologers. Written in the time of the Great Frost, 1740', *The Ulster Miscellany* (1953), 310–11. Borlic notes, however, that in some quarters interest in almanacs increased after the Reformation, when there was a greater need 'to appease uncertainty through prophecy and meteorological forecasts', *Ecocriticism and early modern English literature*, 116.

[22] Arden Reed, *Romantic weather: the climates of Coleridge and Baudelaire* (Hanover and London, 1983), 8.

White observed: 'Men that undertake only one district are much more likely to advance natural knowledge than those that grasp at more than they can possibly be acquainted with'.[23] This material formed the basis of larger-scale comparisons throughout Europe. In Ireland, the members of the Dublin Philosophical Society studied the weather in various locations around the country and tried to assemble topographical details of the counties of Ireland for Moses Pitt's planned atlas of England and Ireland.[24] Yet weather accounts combined anecdotal and scientific processes, showing the role that collective memory continued to play:

> On Monday, June 18th, 1748, about four of the clock in the afternoon, happened the most violent storm of hail that was known in the memory of man, attended with lightning and thunder, which held above a quarter of an hour; several hail-stones measured five inches square, and others had five or six forks from the main body, of an inch long each, which broke several windows, and did other considerable damages in and about Cork.[25]

Many records confined themselves to unusual or extreme events; imaginative literature, in its turn, drew on the experience and representation of weather to add drama and intensity to observed scenes but also to explore the changing fates of humanity, and to express singular and collective moods. Jonathan Bate has argued that the evidential importance of weather observation remains despite its increasing metaphorical use,[26] meaning that the poem is an important response to natural phenomena as well as a space of imaginative engagement.

Writing the seasons

The representation of the weather in Irish literature prior to the Romantic period reflects many of the complex dynamics of wider attitudes towards natural phenomena. Though rarely explicit in poetry, the relationship between personal observation of nature and a sense of its symbolic potential can be traced in the evolving voice of the poet during this period, which at times conjures allegorical representations, and at times records experiential detail directly. The process of learning about distant weather events, as well as experiencing those close at hand, offers a means of linking specific experiences to larger patterns of human life. Yet how weather is understood and how it is felt may be quite different:

---

[23] Gilbert White, quoted in W.J. Keith, *The rural tradition: A study of the non-fiction prose writers of the English countryside* (Toronto and Buffalo, 1988), 42. The value of consistent observation meant that those who never left home made a particularly valuable contribution to these records; see Adeline Johns-Putra (ed.), *Climate and Literature* (Cambridge, 2019), 119.

[24] See for example Samuel Molyneux to Charles Norman, 29 Jan. 1708, in K.T. Hoppen (ed.), *Papers of the Dublin Philosophical Society 1683–1709* (2 vols, Dublin, 2008), vol. 2, 813.

[25] Charles Smith, *The ancient and present state of the county and city of Cork* (2 vols, Dublin, 1774), vol. 2, 403.

[26] Jonathan Bate, 'Living with the Weather', *Studies in Romanticism* 35 (1996), 431–47.

increased knowledge of meteorological systems may mitigate risks, but it does not alter a person's fear of immediate destruction and loss of life.

Reflections on the seasons drew on traditional modes but could be inflected by personal, religious or political readings, since they were a means to confront change within the stable framework of recurring patterns of experience.[27] Nahum Tate's 'On Snow fall'n in Autumn, and dissolv'd by the Sun' typifies the personification of nature in the period by a writer born and educated in seventeenth-century Ireland:

> Nature now stript of all her Summer Dress,
>   And modestly supposing 't were unfit
> For each rude Eye to view her Nakedness,
>   Around her bare Limbs wraps this snowy Sheet.[28]

Tate pursued this image further in his description of the earth as 'made big with the fair Spring to come',[29] the generative power of seasonal change realised in human terms. Yet even in such a poem, the expectations of cyclical change are addressed, and the close relationship between human mood and conduct and the rhythms of nature is asserted. A century later, William Tighe of Ashford, Co. Wicklow, in his 'Elegy to the Gales of Spring', addressed the resonance of these seasonal transitions in more declarative terms: 'Ye animating gales, your powers restore/The lingering pulse of Nature, and unclasp/The glowing buds of Spring, whom Frost no more/Benumbs, and prisons in his icy grasp!'[30] In the meantime the power of the seasons as a way of shaping human action and thought was ambitiously demonstrated by Scottish poet James Thomson in his influential work *The Seasons*, which was particularly praised by the Cork poet James De-La-Cour.[31] The first part of Thomson's popular poem, *Winter*, appeared in 1726; the complete text was published four years later. It demonstrated the role that weather could play in unifying a diverse range of themes and enquiries.

Later in the eighteenth century, the representation of weather plays an important role in the development of sensibility, being a vehicle for the transmission of sentiment within poems that continued to gesture towards traditional genres and modes. Volatile weather conditions feature frequently in topographical poetry, as both observed and felt elements, and with the rise of labouring class writers, the immediate impact of the weather became more pronounced, as demonstrated by the declamatory effect of Henry Jones's 'On a fine Crop of Peas being spoil'd by a storm': 'Shall one tempestuous Hour thus spoil/The Labours

---

[27] Hulme, *Weathered*, xv.
[28] Nahum Tate, 'On Snow fall'n in Autumn, and dissolv'd by the Sun', *Poems* (London, 1684), 80.
[29] Tate, 'On Snow fall'n in Autumn, 80.
[30] William Tighe, 'Elegy to the Gales of Spring', *The plants: a poem, cantos the first and second, with notes; and occasional poems* (London, 1808), 147.
[31] See James De-La-Cour, *A prospect of poetry: address'd to the right honourable John, Earl of Orrery. To which is added a poem to Mr Thomson on his Seasons* (Dublin, 1734).

of a Year!'.[32] The importance of agricultural production in Ireland meant that the close connections between weather events and social and economic stability were never far from the surface of literary representation.

Storms at sea in the seventeenth century

Relations between Ireland and England shaped all Irish climate poems in the seventeenth and eighteenth centuries. The proximity of the two islands meant that they often experienced similar weather conditions but travel between them was sufficiently dangerous to offer opportunities for reflection on both personal and political realities. Though the rhetoric of Ireland's sixteenth-century colonists presented the landscape as one of plenty and opportunity, the dangers inherent in travelling from England or Wales was often dramatised in poetry. The trope of the sea storm, which was prevalent during the sixteenth and seventeenth centuries especially, reflected the real dangers of such journeys, as well as affording an opportunity to affirm weather as a manifestation of divine power. In Richard Stanihurst's reworking of a famous passage by St Thomas More, which he entitled 'Of a tempest Quayling', the immediacy of present action and the sensory character of the language draws the reader into the scene of disaster: 'Theare rose in sayling a rough tempestuous owtrage,/With watrye plash bouncing, thee ribs of giddye ship hitting./Thee mariners fearing, al hoap eeke of salftye reiecting'.[33]

Other poems placed personal experience, rather than textual borrowing, at the centre of their work. Frances Cooke's mid-seventeenth century account of surviving a storm off the coast of Cork records her distress and disorientation and thanks God for her deliverance: 'Landing in *Kinsale*, I said, am I alive or dead? Doth not the ground move under mee? I have been dying all this storme, and I cannot tell whether I am yet alive'.[34] The verse with which the pamphlet concludes affirms the intervention of a benevolent God: 'For with his Word the Lord did make/the sturdy storms to cease:/So that the great waves from their rage,/be brought to rest and peace'.[35] The Catholic lawyer, Richard Bellings, brings greater suspense to his recounting of a trip from Wales to Ireland. He recalls when the seamen—frustrated at their becalmed ship and the 'pale,

---

[32] Henry Jones, 'On a fine crop of Peas being spoil'd by a storm', in Andrew Carpenter and Lucy Collins (eds), *The Irish poet and the natural world: an anthology of verse in English from the Tudors to the Romantics* (Cork, 2014), 228.

[33] Richard Stanihurst, 'Of a tempest quayling', in Edward Arber (ed.), *Translation of the first four books of the Æneid of P. Virgilius Maro* (Westminster, 1895), 144.

[34] Frances Cooke, *Mrs. Cooke's meditations, being an humble thanksgiving to her heavenly Father, for granting her a new life, having conclnded [sic] her selfe dead, and her grave made in the bottome of the sea, in that great storme. Jan. the 5th 1649. Composed by her selfe at her unexpected safe arrival at Corcke* (Cork, 1650), 2.

[35] Cooke, *Meditations*, 15.

breathlesse, prostrate' sea—whistle up a storm.[36] Likening the ensuing scene to a stage set, Bellings emphasises the dramatic action by drawing classical parallels: King Eolus is summoned and offers a portent of disaster to come. This framing yields to writing of intense descriptive force, recording the rhythm of the moving ship:

> But when the winds these waves doe beare away,
> She hangs in ayre, and makes a little stay:
> But downe againe from such presumptious height
> Shee's headlong borne by her attractive weight
> Into the hollow of a gaping grave.[37]

The detailed attention to the experience of the storm gives ways to despair. Bellings is resigned to death and, being saved, thanks God that he has given him 'time to live and to repent'.

    The sea voyage offered both time and occasion to reflect on the power of divinity, and a demonstration of the vulnerability of humans in the natural world. Some twenty years after Bellings' text, Payne Fisher's description of a storm in Lough Neagh also dwells on the drama of the event, and remarks too on the failure of the travellers to understand the weather—the 'Heat/Which we presum'd a Fortune, proved our Fate.'[38] The crew are unable to deal with such severe weather, bringing the 'larboard' or port side of the vessel broadside to the gale. With the mainsail lost and the rudder broken, the sailors lose control of the ship and are rendered inert—they stand 'like senseless stones, or statues made of wood', at the mercy of these elemental forces.[39] In the face of such extremity, all lose the use of their senses—they cannot see clearly, and the sound of the wind drowns out their voices. The deities they invoke cannot come to their aid, and the divergence between the force of nature and the presumption of higher power is made horrifyingly clear. The terrors of the storm function as a purgative, first emotional, then physical. The weeping and despair of those on the boat is a human response to the extreme weather they experience, and in marked contrast to the Romantic tendency to impute human emotions on inanimate forms.[40] When dawn comes on Lough Neagh and the wind abates a little, the men can begin to move once more, revealing the traumatic effects of the events on their bodies. They are sick and battered—abject figures no longer recognisable

---

[36] Richard Bellings, 'The description of a Tempest', in Carpenter and Collins (eds), *The Irish poet and the natural world,* 81–3: 81.
[37] Bellings, 'Description of a Tempest', 82.
[38] Payne Fisher, 'On a Dangerous Voyage', in Carpenter and Collins (eds), *The Irish poet and the natural world,* 98.
[39] Fisher, 'On a Dangerous Voyage', 98.
[40] The term normally used for this practice, 'pathetic fallacy', was first used by John Ruskin in *Modern Painters* (1856), to criticise this aspect of work from the Romantic period.

as the men they once were and evidence of the vulnerability of human lives in the larger scheme of divine power.

As well as reflecting the realities of perilous sea voyages, these intense experiences also found their way into texts concerned with imaginative journeys and intended to entertain. Richard Head, whose hybrid and transgressive work often crossed the boundaries of expected tastes, uses the trope of the sea storm to heighten tensions in his poem, published in 1674, about the discovery of O Brazeel, an enchanted island off the coast of Ireland.[41] Head mocks the conventions of the shipwreck poem, interjecting whimsical comments on the sea's elemental strength and complaining about the incomprehensible language of sailors: 'I know not which was loudest, their rude Tongues/Or the big Winds with their whole Cards of Lungs'.[42] Here the fruitless actions of those aboard ship are the source of both fear and amusement:

> We pumpt the Ship, but to as little end,
> As to repent, yet never to amend:
> For all the Water we pumpt out with pain,
> The Sea with scorn returns, and more again.[43]

This sideswipe at the practice of repenting *in extremis* yet never changing one's ways acknowledges the religious rituals often described in the narratives of extreme weather experience during the period.

All of these poems use the prolonged drama of a storm at sea to lend narrative tension to the text, but others suggest a more peremptory fate. Nahum Tate's 'The Hurricane', published in 1676, picks up the energy of the seafaring life in the declamatory tone of the speaker on board ship. Even more than those on land, the sailor must read the signs to prepare for difficult conditions, and the space of the poem expresses the speed with which the weather can change— 'That Northern Mist fore-bodes a Hurricane/See how th'expecting Ocean raves/ The Billows roar before the Fray'.[44] The prediction is correct and soon the text itself begins to fragment under pressure from the elements: long dashes signify the lurching of the ship and panic of the sailors: 'Port, hard, a'port ------ The Tackle fails./Sound ho! ------ Five Fathom and the most./A dangerous Shelf! sh'as struck, and we are lost'.[45] Unlike many other seafaring poems, this does not end in rescue and redemption, but stoical death. The sailors form a ring and perish in this collective embrace: 'Now to new Worlds we steer, and quickly shall arrive/Our Spirits shall mount, as fast as our dull Corpses dive'.[46] Their journey

---

[41] Richard Head, 'A Great Sea-Storm describ'd' in Carpenter and Collins (eds), *The Irish poet and the natural world*, 115–18. O Brazeel, or Hy-Brazil, is said to become visible just one day every seven years.
[42] Head, 'Great Sea-Storm', 116.
[43] Head, 'Great Sea-Storm', 117.
[44] Nahum Tate, 'The Hurricane', *Poems written on several occasions* (London, 1684), 119.
[45] Tate, 'The Hurricane', 119.
[46] Tate, 'The Hurricane', 120.

to heaven is far less arduous than their earthly struggle, and affirms Tate's use of the sea voyage as a metaphor for the toil of fallen man.

The Great Frost 1739–41

Human mortality remained a preoccupation in the representation of extreme weather events throughout the eighteenth century. As engagement with natural philosophy grew, the metaphorical intensity and divine preoccupation of seventeenth-century poems gave way to more realistic and socially descriptive texts, attuned not only to the world of sensory experience but also to the stratification of human society. The cooling temperatures of the Little Ice Age altered the mobility of people and goods, changing patterns of trade as well as resource consumption. Poets engaged both with the immediate ways in which human activity altered, as well as more fundamental ethical and political issues. Though extreme conditions meant that fleets were stilled, other energies informed the frozen world, as Nahum Tate's 1684 poem 'Sliding on Skates in a Hard Frost' suggests.[47] This world is conversely one of stability and freedom—'Tho' Hurricanes shou'd rage…' they can't 'curl the water's brow'.[48] The poem presents a unified scene, where the earth and sky act as mirrors; nature, man and the material enact an imaginative exchange, and skaters become as ships as 'on keels of polish steel [they] secretly sail…' freer than fish or birds.[49]

The previous year, John Evelyn sketched a less tranquil scene in his diary, that of the Thames Frost Fair—a 'bacchanalian triumph, or carnival on the water' as 'sleds, sliding with skates, a bullbaiting, horse and coach races, puppet plays and interludes', not to mention less savoury pursuits, took place on the frozen river.[50] More serious in a severe frost was the destruction of human and animal life, with 'men and cattle' dying and 'fowls, fish and birds and all our exotic plants and greens universally perishing'. This world was memorably represented in Virginia Woolf's *Orlando*: 'Birds froze in mid-air and fell like stones to the ground. In Norwich a young country woman started to cross the road in her usual robust health and was seen by the onlookers to turn visibly to powder and be blown in a puff of dust over the roofs'.[51] Both in personal records and imaginative texts, we see the extreme effects of climate change, and its impact on every dimension of human life.

The magnitude of the Great Famine of 1845 has tended to obscure the relative frequency of food crises in Ireland between 1290 and 1890.[52] James Kelly

---

[47] Nahum Tate, 'Sliding on Skates in a Hard Frost', *Poems written on several occasions* (London, 1684), 69.
[48] Tate, 'Sliding on Skates', 69.
[49] Tate, 'Sliding on Skates', 69.
[50] Austin Dobson (ed.), *The diary of John Evelyn* (3 vols, Cambridge, 2015), vol. 3, 121.
[51] Virginia Woolf, *Orlando: a biography* (1928) (Oxford, 1992), 32.
[52] But see, E. Margaret Crawford (ed.), *Famine: the Irish experience 900–1900* (Edinburgh, 1989); James Kelly, *Food rioting in Ireland in the eighteenth and nineteenth centuries* (Dublin, 2017).

has identified the early eighteenth century as a period of frequent harvest crises and the role of bad weather in precipitating these disasters: 'The weather was the link in the chain that bound the annual harvest and the wellbeing of the population'.[53] It was during the years 1739–41 that Ireland experienced some of the most severe weather conditions ever recorded in the country. Over two harsh winters lakes and rivers froze, crops were destroyed, and animals and humans died from hypothermia and starvation. This gave rise to considerable social unrest, partly owing to the systemic inequalities that prevailed in rural areas.[54] The freezing weather pervaded the imagination, even for those poets who were not immediately inspired to engage with it. An anonymous poem hymning the virtues of the Earl of Roscommon uses the extreme cold to argue for the warmth of the poet's feelings, and his pure—and divinely sanctioned—love 'of Virtue, Honour, and a Friend'.[55] It is through metaphors of weather, and topographical imagery, that this love is both understood, and directly communicated to its object—'Fly ye North-winds, and let Rosscommon know/That neither Flakes of Ice nor Hills of Snow,/Can set my anxious mind at ease or rest'.[56]

Other poets meditated directly, and at length, on the impact of the Great Frost on those that lived through it, and many also reflected on the aesthetic challenges presented by this beautiful yet destructive scene. William Dunkin's 'The Frosty Winters of Ireland' (1742) represents extreme weather first in supernatural terms: in place of a 'Heaven' of fair weather and 'fields/A-float with golden grain', there comes from Hell the vengeful cold, severe enough to destroy all forms of life.[57] It is a dynamic that also informs the poems of Peter Brett, the parish clerk of Clondalkin, in his 'Verses on the Hard Frost' (1757): 'The Black north East from rough tartarian Shores,/O're Europe's realms its freezing rigour pours/Stagnates the flowing Blood in human Veins,/And binds the Silver streams in icy chains.[58] For both poets, one a schoolmaster in Co. Fermanagh, the other a schoolmaster in Co. Dublin, these events are beyond human imagination; the combination of wonder and rigorous attention expresses the contest between religious and scientific

---

[53] James Kelly, 'Harvests and hardship: famine and scarcity in Ireland in the late 1720s', *Studia Hibernica* 26 (1992), 65–105: 66; Kelly, 'Climate, weather and society in Ireland in the long eighteenth century', (this volume).

[54] David Dickson, *Arctic Ireland: the extraordinary story of the Great Frost and forgotten famine of 1740–41* (Belfast, 1997), 300.

[55] Anonymous, 'To the Earl of Rosscommon, at the time of the Great Frost in 1739, by a noble peer', *Poems written occasionally by John Winstanley, interspers'd with many others, by several ingenious hands* (Dublin, 1751), 45.

[56] Anonymous, 'To the Earl of Rosscommon', 44.

[57] William Dunkin, 'The Frosty Winters of Ireland', in Carpenter and Collins (eds), *The Irish poet and the natural world,* 208–12.

[58] Peter Brett, 'Verses on the hard Frost, that began December, 22nd. 1739, and held till February 1st. 1739–40; and then began to thaw and continued as fine a thaw as ever was known', *The fourth volume of Brett's miscellany: containing above one hundred useful and entertaining particulars…* (Dublin, 1757), 129.

'Nature herself seems in the vapours now': poetry and climate change in Ireland 1600–1820

thinking that many poems of this time enact. Dunkin's text is dense with metaphor, as the poet attempts to make sense of the phenomenon by comparing it to disease and warfare. The calamity is linked to the earth as a whole, perhaps because this weather phenomenon was known to be extensive. Some of the most memorable description in this poem is of a purely sensory kind, as the poet bears witness to the stilling of natural energy, the power sufficient to arrest rivers mid-flow:

> The vagrant rivers, in their prone career
> Congeal'd, arrested, at the voice divine
> Horrific stood, and through the liquid lakes
> And arms of ocean, watry fields admire
> Unwonted burthens. Fiery foaming steeds
> Bound o'er the polished plain, and human crowds
> Securely glide, and glowing chariots fly
> With rapid wheels. Beneath the glassy gulph
> Fishes benumb'd, and lazy sea-calves freeze
> In crystal coalition with the deep.[59]

The formal control that Dunkin exerts through alliteration and syllabic variation allows him to present the interconnected character of all life. The fecund earth is rendered barren and all life decays, from cattle to the blades of grass on which they feed. Neither do gardens afford shelter and that sturdiest of trees, the regal oak, 'imbibes the horror keen, the polar bane';[60] birds and insects, deprived of a sustaining habitat, perish. Even the salt water of the advancing tide 'stiffen[s] at the breath/Of Boreas', effectively stopping time and depicting this freezing state as never-ending.[61] The earth is powerless to generate new life and so the poem comes full circle; the swain who appeared at its opening dies, as his wife and child sit in freezing silence: 'the faultring accents, on her tongue/Stiff, into silence everlasting freeze'.[62] This final tableau evokes the powerlessness of man against these elements, and the silencing of human reason and explanation in the face of such terrible suffering.

Such scenes remain powerfully in the reader's mind. Other poets too attempted to capture them in verse; Samuel Shepherd's topographical poem *Leixlip* was written during the 'Great Frost', a fact which he stresses in the prefatory note to its first printing in 1747: 'It may be proper to take Notice that the following Poem was written during the Great Frost in the Year 1739. The Reader will easily judge why some particular Incidents are more largely insisted on than the Subject might seem naturally to require'.[63] Though the poem is principally concerned with the beauty and harmony of the landscape in and around Leixlip created by Shepherd's patron William Conolly, the text stresses the extraordinary impact of extreme weather on that landscape, particularly on the waterfalls of

---

[59] Dunkin, 'Frosty Winters', 209.
[60] Dunkin, 'Frosty Winters', 210.
[61] Dunkin, 'Frosty Winters', 211.
[62] Dunkin, 'Frosty Winters', 212.
[63] Samuel Shepherd, *Leixlip: a poem* (Dublin, 1747), n. p.

the river Liffey: 'the Waves above/Freeze, as they flow; and stiffen, as they move:/Pendent in Air the new-born Chrystals spread;/And Rocks of Ice enclose the dumb Cascade'.[64] Embedded within a poem that seeks to offer a many-faceted response to place, these scenes emphasise the onward rush of time, and show the poet's concern to place this tragic phase of history within a wider context.

Assertions of poetic control are evident also in 'To Francis Bindon Esq', a poem inspired by the public response to the sufferings brought about by the Great Frost. The author was Thomas Hallie Delamayne (1718–73), a poet active throughout the middle years of the eighteenth century. Delamayne draws attention to the power and responsibility of visual as well as verbal representation, and claims the space of the poem as one in which political and social events can find expression. The poem addresses a portrait of Archbishop Hugh Boulter dispensing charity to the needy, and is fundamentally concerned with the recognition and alleviation of suffering caused by extreme natural events. Both William Dunkin and Delamayne personify famine and disease in their poems on the frost, aiming to dramatise the shocking effects of both on the people of Ireland; the culminating image in Delamayne's poem—reflected also in Dunkin's—is of a starving infant for whom the milk of the sick mother becomes a kind of poison.[65] The greater social implications of the epidemic caused by the severe weather begin to be felt in the poem when those who have died must remain unburied, the ground frozen too hard to admit their coffins.

So, while the immediate effects of extreme weather may be those of wonder or fear of divine displeasure,[66] there are also severe social and economic consequences that are most strongly felt in societies where significant hardship already exists. Laurence Whyte (c.1683–c.1753), a prolific Irish poet of the early eighteenth century, was aware that the suffering caused by these climate events had an enduring impact for ordinary people. Two of his poems —'Famine' and 'Plenty'—made an important intervention in the debates during the early 1740s about the effects of Ireland's Great Frost. The poem 'Famine' begins by noting the silence of poets on the conditions of want: 'How comes it now that in this Year of Want,/When Famine reigns and Bread so very scant,/That Wit and Humour rather sink than rise,/And seem to tally with the Baker's size'.[67] Though Whyte's concern was with the suffering of the urban poor—primarily because of the shortage of wheat—it was the loss of the potato crop that was the primary indicator of a forthcoming crisis in food supply,

---

[64] Shepherd, *Leixlip*, 13.
[65] Thomas Hallie Delamayne 'To Francis Bindon Esq' in Carpenter and Collins (eds), *The Irish poet and the natural world,* 213–17; William Dunkin, *Select poetical works* (2 vols, Dublin, 1769–70), vol. 1, 443.
[66] *The judgments of God upon Ireland, or sickness and famine, God's visitation for the sins of the nation*, was published in Dublin. Two editions appeared in 1741.
[67] Laurence Whyte, 'Famine' in Michael Griffin (ed.), *Collected poems* (Lewisburg, PA, 2016), 291. The size of a loaf of bread was determined by statute, though when wheat was in short supply bakers reduced the size: see Carpenter and Collins (eds), *The Irish poet and the natural world*, 218.

'Nature herself seems in the vapours now': poetry and climate change in Ireland 1600–1820

which peaked in the summer of 1740 after a long period of drought.[68] The continued exporting of grain from Ireland, in the face of extreme food shortages, sparked riots in the spring of 1740, and the return of harsh weather conditions in October of that year indicated that the crisis would be prolonged, and that it would no longer be felt by the poor alone.[69] Whyte links these events explicitly to climate crisis:

> When Heav'n was pleas'd to visit us with Woe,
> With Cold intense, uncommon Frost and Snow:
> Each rapid River then was at a Stand,
> And greatest Lakes as passable as Land…
> The Earth lock'd up her Treasures under Ground,
> And Dearth began to spread itself around.[70]

Both the scale and the severity of the crisis were extraordinary, and just as they confounded attempts to bring both social and medical problems under control, so they created representational challenges for those who wished to address these experiences in verse. The most significant texts to engage with the events explicitly invoke aesthetic dilemmas, as well as revealing the artistic reach needed to confront such a complex set of circumstances.

Revolutionary weather

Whyte's engagement with the economic implications of Ireland's 'Great Frost' is a striking example of the political reading of weather events that would become increasingly important as the century progressed. These observations are the precursors of our contemporary understanding of the role of natural resources in the negotiation of human power. Extreme weather events were sometimes linked in the public mind to politics:[71] the 1703 storm was figured in this way, and the Great Frost of 1739 also functioned as a metaphor for national resilience. The parish clerk Peter Brett, for whom patriotism means loyalty to Protestant Britain, picks up on this tendency in the simple message of his eight-line poem 'On the War with Spain, 1739–40, Hard Frost': 'Let all the proud of every Nation know,/*Britain's* true sons, tho' cas'd with Ice and Snow,/Their native warmth and vigour still retain,/Fix'd on revenge against insulting *Spain*'.[72] Reference to Spain or France in

---

[68] David Dickson, '1740–41 Famine', in John Crowley, M.J. Smyth and Mike Murphy (eds), *The atlas of the Great Irish Famine* (Cork, 2012), 24.
[69] Dickson, '1740–41 Famine', 27.
[70] Whyte, 'Famine', 292.
[71] For further discussion see G.H. Endfield and Lucy Veale (eds), *Cultural histories, memories and extreme weather: a historical geography perspective* (London, 2018), 78.
[72] Peter Brett, 'On the War with Spain, 1739–40, Hard Frost', *The second volume of Brett's miscellany: being, a collection of divine, moral, historical and entertaining sayings and observations…* (Dublin, 1752*)*, 131.

eighteenth-century Ireland invoked militant Catholicism and the threat of invasion by the forces of arbitrary rule— another form of the 'extreme'.

Though he wrote for a local readership in Castleknock and Dublin, Brett's weather poems engaged with a wide geographical context, suggesting that he gleaned news of events abroad from newspapers and used these as inspiration. His poem on the tremors preceding the London earthquake of 1751, an event that had little direct impact on Ireland, acknowledges the global context for extreme weather, and the larger lessons that could be derived from these accounts. Natural traumas reinforced human vulnerability, and the inescapability of these weather events made their impact on humanity of universal importance:

> When dread convulsions shake this Ball of Earth
> Adore the Power who gave Creation Birth:
> With deep Contrition think on Failings past
> And live, as tho' this Sun might shine your Last.[73]

Brett urged on his readers a traditionally Christian response to natural disasters, but the panic that the earthquakes inspired certainly affected human and animal lives, as an eyewitness account of the London shock testified: 'It awoke people from their sleep and frightened them out of their houses…dogs howled in uncommon tones; and fish jumped half a yard above the water.'[74]

These extreme weather events, known about though not directly experienced by Irish people, all contributed to the sense of existential and political uncertainty that shaped the latter part of the eighteenth century. Weather observations became linked more strongly to emotional responses, even in personal accounts. Bishop Synge, writing to his daughter in July 1751, makes this understanding explicit:

> …doleful tidings of much rain in the night, and a sky that threaten'd more…Corn bent, and bending, Mowers struck off. Cut grass poss'd in wet, the ground all sloppy, and Men, Horses, and Mules, where they could at all work, labouring and suffering by return of violent rain… But why all this to you? I hope you see already…. What happens in the Farm and Harvest, happens in all other affairs, in all Circumstances, every Condition of life. Nothing is certain, but uncertainty.[75]

Synge's letters are full of references to the weather, in particular of accounts of storms and heavy rains, and their impact on agriculture. For those directly involved in farming this concern was still more acute. Olivia Elder

---

[73] Peter Brett, 'Several persons leaving London in 1749 being frightened at the Earthquakes, occasioned the following lines', *The fourth volume of Brett's miscellany,* 108.

[74] The eyewitness account of William Hone: see BBC Radio 4, *Making History,* 19 Apr. 2005 (www.bbc.co.uk/radio4/history/making_history/making_history_20050524.shtml)

[75] On 19 Aug. 1747 Synge wrote: 'On Saturday night we had here a terrible storm. But it has done no damage, or next to none. The rain of the day secur'd the corn. All my wheat was in stack'; and on 18 July 1749: 'We had your storm, and broken Weather ever since… It is unpleasant, and will be mischievous': Marie-Louise Legg (ed.) *The Synge letters:*

(1735–80), the daughter of a prominent New Light Presbyterian minister at Aghadowey near Coleraine, helped her father on the small farm that supplemented his limited income in the 1760s and 70s. Though she read widely, Elder's poetry often drew directly on her everyday experiences and emphasised not only the drama of extreme climate events, but also the constant challenges of inclement weather. Departing from literary convention, she depicted nature's capacity to dispirit, rather than to foster creativity. In a verse letter to Anna Laetitia Barbauld, she described the conditions of her life in Ulster:

> Around me, too, external things conspire
> To damp the genius rather than inspire.
> Far north in bleak Hibernias stormy Isle
> Where softest seasons scarcely know to smile;
> Where fruitless labour toils the painfull year,
> Scarce ploughs in hope, and often reaps despair.[76]

She continued the poem by suggesting that the Irish weather was linked to the depressing political events of the day and, specifically, that the miserable life endured by Presbyterians under the Penal Laws was reflected in the unremitting gloom of the weather. When she referred to an extreme event—such as a storm so violent that it uprooted trees—Elder seems to have seen it as a metaphor for the violent changes that convulsed her part of rural Ulster in the 1770s.[77]

Elder's work was closely associated with her regional identity, both in its rendering of community and in its use of dialect.[78] As the eighteenth century drew to a close, greater attention was paid to the specific character of Ireland's landscape and weather. A curious example of the intensification of interest in extreme weather can be seen in the two versions of Joseph Atkinson's *Killarney*. Atkinson, who was an army officer, first published the poem in 1769, producing an extended version of it in 1798.[79] Having had opportunities to revisit 'this terrestrial Paradise' in the intervening years, Atkinson 'endeavoured to correct,

---

Bishop Edward Synge to his daughter Alicia, Roscommon to Dublin 1746–1752 (Dublin, 1996), 76–7, 139; see also 324.

[76] Olivia Elder, 'To Miss Aikin, now Mrs Barbauld' (1774), in Andrew Carpenter (ed.), *The poems of Olivia Elder* (Dublin, 2017), 103. Elder frequently linked environment and emotion in her work: 'Where e'er I turn me round methinks I see/Each object kindly sympathize with me'. 'A Pastoral, written on the departure of Miss J.P. from A-------y, which happen'd when there were great floods after a lot of fine weather', in Carpenter (ed.) *Poems of Olivia Elder*, 18–21: 19.

[77] Olivia Elder, 'Some lines written extempore…the morning after a violent storm', in Carpenter (ed.), *Poems of Olivia Elder*, 27.

[78] See Andrew Carpenter, 'Working-class writing in Ireland before 1800: 'Some must be poor – we cannot all be great'' in Michael Pierce (ed.), *A history of Irish working-class writing* (Cambridge, 2018), 72–88.

[79] *Killarny: a poem* (Dublin, 1769), was eighteen pages in length. The later printing — *Killarney* (1798) —was expanded to twenty-eight pages and included an engraved view of the lakes of Killarney and a fulsome dedication to the Earl of Moira.

enlarge and embellish' the original text, increasing the romantic perception of Killarney as a kind of Eden.[80] The picture of the landscape is peaceful and idyllic in both versions of the poem, but among the additions to the later version of the text is a passage on Ireland's temperate climate:

> But since, nor earthquakes nor volcanos dire
> Convulse our shores, nor burst with liquid fire,
> Nor furious hurricanes, which storm the deep,
> And o'er the land with desolation sweep....
> But we, to chartered, lawful Freedom born,
> May brave all despots, and their minions scorn.
> Then freed from ills, which richer climes annoy,
> Our native pleasures let our sons enjoy.[81]

Just as Spenser characterised Ireland as a 'bewtifull and sweete Countrie',[82] praising its plentiful natural resources and a temperate climate, so Atkinson drew a direct link between the benign character of Ireland's weather and the peace and stability of her political circumstances though, by the time of this rewriting, the country was in the grip of a bitter and violent insurgency.

Ironically, though, climate played an important role in preserving Ireland from revolution. The French landing at Bantry Bay in 1796 was thwarted by storms and, in addition, bad weather played a significant role in several of the skirmishes of the 1798 rising.[83] The American Revolution of 1775 had ushered in an extended period of political uncertainty throughout Europe as a whole and in Ireland in particular. Yet few Irish poets writing at the time explicitly linked political insecurity to unstable climate conditions. In fact, though he was writing after the Act of Union, William Drennan suggested the opposite: that if Nature had been less kind to Ireland, her men would have been more vigorous and her path less peaceful.

> Had Nature been her enemy,
> IERNE might be fierce and free.
> To the stout heart, and iron hand,
> Temp'rate each sky, and tame each land;
> A climate and a soil less kind,
> Had form'd a map of richer mind.[84]

---

[80] Joseph Atkinson, *Killarney* (Dublin, 1798), iv.
[81] Atkinson, *Killarney*, 9. A comparison of the two texts can be found in Carpenter and Collins (eds), *The Irish poet and the natural world*, 393–405. For an interesting analysis of the significance of Killarney in eighteenth-century writing, see Luke Gibbons, 'Topographies of terror: Killarney and the politics of the sublime', *South Atlantic Quarterly*, 95 (1996), 23–44.
[82] Edmund Spenser, *A view of the present state of Ireland*, W.L. Renwick (ed.) (London, 1934), 25.
[83] See John Tyrell, *Weather and warfare: a climatic history of the 1798 Rebellion* (Cork, 2001).
[84] William Drennan, 'To Ireland', in Carpenter and Collins (eds), *The Irish poet and the natural world*, 342.

'Nature herself seems in the vapours now': poetry and climate change in Ireland 1600–1820

For others, however, there was a clear imaginative link between weather conditions and revolutionary violence and some poets writing at the turn of the nineteenth century clung to the notion that both climatic and political violence, such as that which had toppled regimes in America and France, would remain at a distance from Ireland. In 1805, Matthew Weld Hartstonge, a Dublin-born lawyer, wrote a poem describing Kilcarrick, Co. Carlow, as a place 'shelter'd from the boisterous gale' and home to insects and birds, to the goat, hare and fox. The tranquillity of the scene the poet paints is also due to its distance from 'trump or drum' and it becomes clear that Hartstonge values it specifically as a refuge from revolutionary strife: 'While nations rage for sov'reign sway,/Contented here I lonely stray'.[85] By combining weather imagery with military reference, he demonstrates how closely these elements could become entwined at times of political upheaval. His characterisation of the landscape emphasises the possibility of peaceful containment while such places can be preserved:

Then hail, ye pleasing rural charms,
Unstain'd with blood, or faction's arms;
And ever peaceful may remain,
The rocks that bound Kilcarrick's plain;
Tranquil, green Erin's sea-girt shore,
Though loud the storm at distance roar![86]

As at any time of political upheaval, the poets of late eighteenth-century Britain and Ireland were inclined to place their personal meditations within a wider scope, often using topographical modes to do this. If, in the words of John Barrell, 'landscape becomes a theatre where the poet's own moral reflections are acted out', then the weather plays an important part in that dramatic representation.[87] So, climate poems in this phase of Irish literary history sometimes use the weather for rhetorical effect suggesting some kind of stability in an unstable world. It is worth noting that Thomas Moore, a student at Trinity College Dublin during the tumultuous years following the outbreak of the French Revolution, while the United Irishmen—including his friend Robert Emmet—were actively thinking of revolution in Ireland, chose to write of love; Moore only mentions extreme weather in one of his early lyrics, 'Love in a Storm'. The lady concerned 'felt not a fear' as 'the tempest did frown'. On the contrary, she 'nestled' to the poet's bosom: 'Dread was the lightning, and horrid its glare,/But it showed me my Julia in languid delight'.[88]

The rise of Romanticism articulated modes of feeling that, for many poets, drew together representations of landscape and the ancient past and

---

[85] Matthew Weld Hartstonge, 'Lines written at the rocks of Kilcarrick', in Carpenter and Collins (eds), *The Irish poet and the natural world,* 354.
[86] Hartstonge, 'Kilcarrick', 355.
[87] John Barrell, *The idea of landscape and the sense of place 1730–1840* (Cambridge, 1972), 35.
[88] [Thomas Moore,] *The poetical works of the late Thomas Little* (London, 1810), 62.

acknowledged—though did not necessarily centre on—ideas of nationality. While the political tensions underpinning Celtic modes were undeniable, Irish writers of the period absorbed influences from England and Europe, even as they mourned a lost national tradition. Matthew Campbell has noted the archipelagic character of early nineteenth century poetry in English, and has linked MacPherson's pseudo-Celtic *Ossian*, Thomas Chatterton's invented medievalism and the reclaimed songs of Robert Burns to the *Lyrical Ballads* of William Wordsworth and Samuel Taylor Coleridge.[89] The intensification of a poetics of sensibility linked feeling and environment in important ways and increased the affective power of the verse published at the turn of the nineteenth century. Though most Irish poets were more drawn to the 'beautiful' than to the 'sublime'—to use Burke's terms—there are ways in which Irish Romanticism combined engagement with the Enlightenment ethos with an awareness of political events.

One example is that of William Hamilton Drummond's *The Giant's Causeway* (1811). This extraordinary poem of nearly 2,000 lines comprehends history, mythology and folklore, as well as providing a striking physical description of this natural feature. It is most remarkable for its representation of geology, demonstrating at once the importance of regional topographies and the larger forces that bring them into being. Here is evidence of what Noah Heringman has called 'geology's becoming naturalized in poetry',[90] and of the form of a poem extending to accommodate the breadth and ambition of its subject matter. As well as highlighting the important intersection between poetry and science for this generation of writers and causing controversy in its handling of much-debated theories, the poem places human history within a vast temporal frame.

Drummond chooses Norse mythology to represent the power of storms, emphasising the extreme force of the weather and its power to shape the earth:

> Swift down the bow of many a fulgent dye,
> Bridge of the Gods, th'immortal footsteps hie;
> Hail, sleet and darkness o'er his bosom spread,
> The rush of waters roared around his head,
> While wrapt in light'ning and devouring storm,
> He swept the winds, a dim terrific form.[91]

Here the many facets of extreme weather are linked in one mythic figure orchestrating hurricane and flood and, in the actions of his own body, encompassing elemental forces. Though representing the human form, the scope and grandeur of Odin diminishes mortal man, just as our greatest buildings are dwarfed by natural wonders. Here climate is linked to the extraordinary

---

[89] Matthew Campbell, *Irish poetry under the Union, 1801–1924* (Cambridge, 2014), 7.
[90] Noah Heringman, *Romantic rocks, aesthetic geology* (Ithaca and London, 2004), 157.
[91] William Hamilton Drummond, *The Giant's Causeway: a poem* (Belfast, 1811), 14.

formation of the earth itself, a phenomenon only beginning to be understood in early nineteenth-century Ireland.

Drummond's ambitious scientific enquiries had found a more human scale a generation earlier in poems about storms—not only that by Olivia Elder but also that by the eccentric Tipperary recluse, Dorothea Herbert. Her poem 'The Storm' dwells on the impact of extreme weather on every aspect of middle-class life in rural Ireland in the late eighteenth century. Herbert figures the storm not as an exceptional event, but as an inevitable feature of winter, both a fated part of the cycle of human experience and a purging of the earth before new beginnings. Winter spreads desolation 'o'er half the World', yet its power seems greater still: 'The bow'ry Grove the beauteous Meadows green/Are all laid waste and under Heaven's high Dome/All Natures wrapt in universal Gloom'.[92] As in Drummond's poem, the elemental force is remarkable but for Herbert its power to strike terror in the human heart is indicative of an enduring fear of latent violence and its indiscriminate effects:

> The Elements in mad Combustion toss'd
> All Vegetation's now destroy'd and lost
> Nor can the rugged Elm or Sturdy Oak
> Withstand stern Winter's fell relentless Stroke
> The tottering Tower whose thick Ivy'd Walls
> For ages stood with dreadfull Crash now falls.[93]

This fundamental disturbance has political connotations too. Even the most established trees —elm and oak, with their various connotations of revolution and authority—are felled. A lengthy passage in the poem dwells on the destruction of the house, whose 'stubborn, shatter'd Roof' gives way at length, leaving those trapped within to try in vain to escape their fate.[94] Herbert emphasises the indiscriminate nature of the storm; neither the 'Lowly peasant's mud built Cot' nor the 'Abode of power' can 'Escape the ruin of the Dreadfull hour'.[95] Culture and nature are destroyed together—the 'glittering Spire' alongside the forest —and Herbert takes a certain aesthetic pleasure in the intensity of the destruction she conveys.[96] All is restored by the 'unbounded Spring' of death.[97]

The height of climate upheaval in the Romantic period is the three-year period between 1816 and 1818, when the eruption of Mount Tambora on the island of Sumbawa near Java caused widespread environmental effects throughout the world. The sole eyewitness account described 'three distinct columns of flame' bursting forth near the top of the mountain, which

---

[92] Dorothea Herbert, 'The Storm', in Frances Finnegan (ed.), *Introspections: the poetry and private world of Dorothea Herbert* (Kilkenny, 2011), 313.
[93] Herbert, 'The Storm', 313.
[94] Herbert, 'The Storm', 314.
[95] Herbert, 'The Storm', 313.
[96] Herbert, 'The Storm', 315.
[97] Herbert, 'The Storm', 315.

'appeared like a body of liquid fire extending itself in every direction'.[98] Though the relationship between this event and the weather conditions of the 1810s was not discovered until the twentieth century, unseasonable weather was remarked by contemporary commentators and writers, most famously in the letters of Mary Shelley, written from Sécheron, just outside Geneva, in June 1816: 'An almost perpetual rain confines us principally to the house; but when the sun bursts forth it is of a splendour and heat unknown in England. The thunder storms that visit us are grander and more terrific than I have ever seen before'.[99] The summer of 1816 was up to six degrees cooler than normal, yielding radical change in agricultural production around the world, and leading to famine, disease and social unrest. Even two years later, in August 1818, abnormal weather persisted. The *Freeman's Journal* noted that 'the present summer, so remarkable for the extreme heat of the weather, has also been, in different parts of the world, attended with severe storms of hail, thunder and lightning'.[100] Though no Irish poets wrote directly of these conditions, they must have influenced the increasingly dramatic way the weather was represented in texts from these years. Anna Liddiard's 1819 poem *Mount Leinster* represents weather as the subject of fear and awe[101]—here the natural environment was closely connected to recent political events in Ireland. Growing up in Corballis, Co. Meath, Liddiard likely experienced revolutionary disturbance first-hand.[102] Her poetry reflects the contemporary interest in antiquarian materials but her commitment to Irish interests was more cultural than political. Julia Wright identifies *Mount Leinster* as the most nationalist of her Irish interest poems.[103] It is a poem in the topographical tradition, celebrating the beauty of Ireland and strongly criticising Britain's treatment of her, especially under the Penal Laws.

---

[98] [Charles Assey], 'Narrative of the effects of the eruption from the Tomboro Mountain, in the island of Sumbawa, on the 11th and 12th of April 1815', quoted in David Higgins, *British Romanticism, climate change and the Anthropocene: writing Tambora* (London, 2017), 2.

[99] [Mary Shelley and Percy Bysshe Shelley], *History of a six weeks tour* (London, 1817), 96–7.

[100] *Freeman's Journal*, 21 Aug. 1818.

[101] There is a question concerning the authorship of this poem, which some believe to be written by Anna's husband, William Liddiard. The two were known to have co-authored poems and this text is both more scholarly and more anti-British than other texts attributed to Anna Liddiard. For further discussion of her work see Julia Wright, 'Introduction: Anna Liddiard', in Stephen Behrendt (ed.), *Irish women poets of the romantic period* (Alexandria, VA, 2008) [online database].

[102] Wright, 'Anna Liddiard'. Julia Wright's introduction to Anna Liddiard notes that the house was 'forced in the night' in 1795.

[103] Wright, 'Anna Liddiard'.

> Red lightnings glare, the thunders awful sound;
> Peal rolls on peal, and shakes the solid ground:
> The winds let loose roar dreadful from afar,
> And, rushing onward, mix in mighty war:
> On ocean's bed they fix with eddying sweep,
> Roused are the waves and boiling foams the deep.[104]

Here, probably more vividly than in any other Irish poem, we see extreme weather and extreme political violence yoked together, metaphorical storms and real storms linked within the framework of verse.

Conclusion

The representation of weather in Irish poetry between 1650 and 1820 reveals the varied and complex relationship between the natural world and human social and political formations during these years. Extreme climate events inspired extended reflection and influenced the creative decisions of writers both at the time and later; even those who did not address these phenomena directly often registered their influence in passing textual references. Poets engaged with the weather both experientially and metaphorically, and their approaches were shaped by the expectations of their time, but also by their larger thematic interests and personal preoccupations. From poems of religious contemplation to those with an implicit political message, these texts demonstrate not only the evolving relationship between humans and their environment but also the co-existence of apparently divergent attitudes towards the natural world. The space of the poem offers an opportunity to combine intellectual enquiry with flights of imagination, and reveals the many ways in which these generations sought to understand climate events and to represent them for their readers.

---

[104] J.S. Anna Liddiard, *Mount Leinster; or, the prospect: a poem descriptive of Irish scenery etc* (London and Dublin, 1819), 3.

Seeing the natural world: *Comhbhá an Dúlra*

Máire Ní Annracháin*

School of Irish, Celtic Studies and Folklore, University College Dublin and Sabhal Mòr Ostaig

[Accepted 7 August 2020. Published 29 September 2020.]

ABSTRACT

Comhbhá an dúlra is the name given to the idea that Nature acts in sympathy with rightful rulers. It is one of the most enduring tropes of Gaelic literature from earliest times. If the correct ruler was in place and acted justly, Nature was deemed to flourish and the weather would conspire to support him. If he died, suffered mishap or misbehaved, Nature would be held to wither and even the weather would deteriorate. Modern poets, whose work is examined in this paper, have taken up the trope of *comhbhá an dúlra* in intriguing and fruitful ways. Their work often display a high degree of irony as they reflect on non-traditional forms of relationship between humans and the natural world. In doing so they demonstrate the malleability and acuity of the modern Gaelic poetic tradition, which now challenges the supremacy of humans, sometimes in an ecocritical spirit, while reconfiguring some of the most deeply rooted Gaelic images.

Anthropocentric concepts of Nature

Irish literature has from earliest times been imbued with three core concepts that relate to the relationship between humans and the land. Collectively they served to affirm the sovereignty of political or other leaders. They were, first, the understanding that Ireland, or individual parts of it, could be personified as a woman, whether goddess, human, or of intermediate status; second, that Nature was a site of almost paradisiacal abundance; and third, that Nature responded to the fortunes of those who inhabit the land and in particular to the fortunes of the rightful leader. The sympathy of nature, *comhbhá an dúlra*, is the focus of this paper. It is somewhat akin to, but not identical with pathetic fallacy. The latter attributes human feelings to Nature or can seem to a human observer to do so, while *comhbhá an dúlra* represents a quasi-magical response by the natural world to important events in a leader's life, for good or ill. Thus, Nature would rejoice and be fruitful if a leader or other important man, or a man whom one wished to construe as important, succeeded in important ways; however if he died or failed in some respect, Nature had many ways to express distress: it might scream

---

*Author's email: maire.niannrachain@ucd.ie
ORCID iD: https://orcid.org/0000-002-2884-7620
doi: https://doi.org/10.3318/PRIAC.2020.120.09

in pain or wither, crops might fail, birds might fall silent. Its sympathy was to an extent conditional, in that it could be withheld in response to culpable failure.

Although a trope of great antiquity, for the sake of brevity I confine myself for background to three still popular examples from the relatively recent eighteenth and nineteenth century. Consider first 'Bímse buan ar buairt gach ló', by Seán Clárach Mac Domhnaill, an eighteenth-century song that laments the absence of the Stuart king, figured here as a lion. The birds, it says, have fallen silent, the sun has failed to rise, the moon is overshadowed and hurricanes roar. All this, improbably, is a result of his departure:

> Ní haoibhinn cuach ba suairc ar neoin…
> Níor éirigh Phoebus féin ar cóir
> Ar chaoinchneas ré tá daolbhrat bróin
> Tá saobhadh ar spéir is spéirling mhór
> Chun sléibhe i gcéin mar d'ealaigh an leon.
> (The cuckoo no longer rejoices at noon / even the sun failed to rise / a dark shadow of sorrow spreads across the moon / the sky is turbulent and the hurricane is mighty / since the lion departed to distant mountains.)[1]

Another near contemporary, but more intimate, example is Eibhlín Dubh Ní Chonaill's lament for her husband, Art Ó Laoghaire, killed in an ambush in May 1773. She exhorts his dead body to mount his horse and take the road to the east where even 'the streams will narrow for you, the bushes will thin out for you' ('mar a maolóidh romhat an sruth, mar a n-ísleoidh romhat na toir').[2] The circumstances of the composition of this lament are unclear in certain respects but a number of the strophes included in Seán Ó Tuama's edition are generally taken as having been composed at the end of the summer of 1773, when Ó Laoghaire's body was exhumed and transferred for burial in a different cemetery. They relate that his crops are growing and his cows are giving milk: 'Tá do stácaí ar a mbonn' and 'Tá do bha buí á gcrú'. These strophes appear at odds with Eibhlín Dubh's earlier confidence in the sympathy of Nature; they are either an instance of literal truth colliding with imaginative fictions, or alternatively, if they belonged after all to the days in May directly after his death, they could be considered a call to Ó Laoghaire to return to life and take charge of the chores that are pressing. Either way, there is a disjuncture between his widow's reiteration that she herself is still locked in her grief, and the continuing abundance of Nature.

A third well-known example is 'Cill Aodáin',[3] a pre-famine poem by Antoine Ó Reachtabhra (now commonly spelt 'Raifteataí') which is a proven favourite of many Irish people. His home district, to which he longs to return, is presented as overflowingly fertile to the point of being paradisiacal, with overtones

---

[1] E. Ó hÓgáin (ed.) *Seán Clárach Mac Dónaill* (Baile Átha Cliath, 2011), 59.
[2] E. Dubh Ní Chonaill, 'Caoineadh Airt Uí Laoghaire' in Seán Ó Tuama (ed.), *Caoineadh Airt Uí Laoghaire* (Baile Atha Cliath, 1961).
[3] A. Ó Reachtabhra, 'Cill Aodáin' in P. Ó Canainn (ed.) *Filíocht na nGael*, (Baile Átha Cliath, 1958), 151–52.

of the Book of Isaiah, a place of harmonious human relations, care for the weak, abundance of flora and fauna, and drink available gratis.[4] The poem starts out moderately, stating that Cill Aodáin is a fertile place: 'Cill Aodáin an baile a bhfásann gach ní ann / Tá sméara, subh chraobh ann is meas ar gach sórt' ('Cill Aodáin is the townland where everything grows / Berries, raspberries, fruit of all kinds'). However two points should be noted. First, the extravagant bounty of nature is secondary to the presence and company of the community. To be among his people would be akin to being in a paradisiacal, timeless world that would restore him to youth: 'Dá mbeinnse im sheasamh i gceartlár mo dhaoine / D'imeodh an aois díom is bheinn arís óg' ('If I stood right among my people / age would leave me and I would be once again young'). Moreover the picture he paints of life in Cill Aodáin is that of the traditional big house, the realm of the rightful lord in traditional terms, with feasting among nobles, leisure games and copious drinking, all generating a clear link between abundance and political sovereignty. Second, as in the pieces by Seán Clárach Mac Domhnaill and Eibhlín Dubh Ní Chonaill, an element of the fantastical interposes itself, suggesting in each case that it is not to be understood entirely literally. Raiftearaí's extravagant litany of abundance and fertility, too long to quote here, verges on the extreme. To give just one example, he names no fewer than fourteen sea creatures that can be found inland in Cill Aodáin, in a list that is nothing short of fanciful: pike, trout, eel, crab, periwinkle, mackerel, seal, salmon, wrasse, basking shark, tortoise, lobster, turbot, gurnet and to cap it all, generalised 'fish'.

The examples quoted underscore the discontinuity between the trope of *comhbhá an dúlra* and actual circumstances, whether by veering into plainly absurd exaggeration or, in Éibhín Dubh's case, by poignant reference to the continued flourishing of Nature. Irish literature is replete with more plausible assertions of Nature's sympathy. Eleanor Knott, however, in her introduction to *The bardic poems of Tadhg Dall Ó hUiginn*, one of the best known and most revered formal bardic poets of the sixteenth century, refers somewhat disparagingly to Tadhg Dall's tendency to use what she terms 'stereotyped phrases':

> The beneficial influence of a rightful ruler is usually pictured in stereotyped phrases with little reference to actualities: the chief pacifies the raging sea; the trees of the forest bend down to him in reverence; the earth yields her fruits in abundance even before their due season; the weather is all that can be wished for…[5]

Leaving aside the fact that not everyone would concur with the implied valorisation of originality in her words, Knott's observation is a reminder that the figurative dimension of *combhá an dúlra*, which was in full flower during the bardic

---

[4] L. Ó Laoire, '"…d'imeodh an aois díom": Tír na nÓg agus Talamh na hÉireann' in W. McLeod and M. Ní Annracháin (eag-í) *Cruth na tíre* (Baile Átha Cliath 2003), 39–68.
[5] E. Knott, *The bardic poems of Tadhg Dall Ó hUiginn (1550–1591)*, (London, 1922), LXII.

period, was established in Ireland well before the eighteenth century, and also that it should not always be interpreted as fully realist.

The concept of the sympathy of Nature, where Nature is conceived as the female spouse of the rightful leader, is connected with the traditional concept of the divine right of kings. It raises obvious issues of gender inequality, which have been analysed in detail by scholars. Of more immediate relevance to this paper, it also raises more general issues of the power relations between humans and the natural world. Not all Irish scholars subscribe to the idea that the relationship was one of unremitting male dominance. Breandán Ó Buachalla for instance, argued for the existence of a partnership, on the grounds that the bestowal of sovereignty on the male leader was depicted as the gift of the goddess of the land, and she moreover was represented as proactive in responding to his life, which included her being willing to express disapproval of his misdemeanours, military defeats or other failures to live up to the obligations of his role.[6] Thus Ó Buachalla argues against the by-now widely held feminist view that the female personification of the land and the concomitant sympathy of Nature serve as a bulwark of male power and prestige, leaving the male leader as protagonist and the female role as one of response.[7]

Whether traditionally an expression of partnership or of a relationship of dominance and subordination, post-Revival poetry throughout the twentieth and into the twenty-first century takes up these and many other traditional tropes, reimagining them creatively and often ironically. Finding or imagining a fissure in the idea of Nature's supposed sympathy with male leaders has led to radical reassessment of gender relations, both public and private. Over and above gender, it is clear that with the shift in perspective brought about by the current era of climate disruptions, new and fruitful ways of relating to Nature are discernible, or can be inferred from the radical engagement with traditional tropes that certain poets have undertaken.

Not all relevant social and political developments are of recent origin. Most obvious from the eighteenth century was the failure of the messianic king-over-the-water to fulfil his promise to Ireland; the success of democracy more widely, which undermined the belief in great leaders automatically possessing the right to rule; Freudian insight into the controlling power of the unconscious over the will; and the belief, since Darwin, that it is humans who adapt to their environment, not Nature that responds to them in a subordinate manner. More recently, the women's movement has been remarkably instrumental in challenging the belief in a strong, dominant individual man with a God-given right to control his own mind and actions, his territory, his people and in some cases large swathes of the planet with its multitude of inhabitants. A word of warning

---

[6] B. Ó Buachalla, *Aisling ghéar: na Stíobhartaigh agus an t-aos léinn, 1603–1788* (Baile Atha Cliath, 1998), 469–82.
[7] See, for instance, M. Nic Eoin, *B'ait leo bean: gnéithe den idé-eolaíocht inscne i dtraidisiún liteartha na Gaeilge* (Baile Átha Cliath, 1998).

against two interpretative extremes is warranted. First, the long tradition of *comhbhá an dúlra* from which contemporary poets emerged did imply a recognition of the interdependence of the land and the people, but, Ó Buachalla's analysis notwithstanding, it is difficult to characterise it as anything other than firmly anthropocentric, to the extent that Nature responded to and reflected human action (or in certain cases reflected the glory of God or other supernatural figures, notably Fionn Mac Cumhaill). Thus it is fair to say that Irish remained largely free of the popular semi-mystical ascription to the Celtic world of an undifferentiated unity between humans and all other life forms, expressed by, for example, Bartosch as an awareness of a 'shared creaturely situation of human and nonhuman animals'.[8]

On the other hand, notwithstanding its anthropocentrism, Irish literature does not give widespread witness to the enthronement of the sovereign human subject within the context of 'burgeoning enlightenment concepts of freedom and human dignity...[as Adorno] stresses how freedom and dignity for the subject are bought at a high price, namely the price of unfreedom for everything non-human, for the other, that is, for nature'.[9] The Irish language world, at least when expressed in literature produced in Ireland, has no real tradition of the extremes of extractivist exploitation that came to characterise the industrial revolution and the conquering of the new world by empire builders. We will see later some examples of struggle between besieged humans and a harsh land, but nothing to compare with, for example, the characterisation by Theodore Roosevelt in his address to the Sorbonne University of the American taming of the new world as out and out subjugation: 'To conquer a continent, to tame the shaggy roughness of wild nature, means grim warfare...To conquer the wilderness means to wrest victory from the same hostile forces with which mankind struggled on the immemorial infancy of our race.'[10]

This then is the current local context for Irish-language literature: neither mistily at one with Nature nor fully dominant over it. Thus current trends in post-human analysis would require a degree of modification for Irish-language literature, which retains a memory of *comhbhá an dúlra*, unbroken, from earliest times. The global context may be a little different. If individual leaders may have lost their sheen, they have been replaced by other forms of human dominance. The current climate emergency reinforces the doubly ironic message

---

[8] R. Bartosch, 'Against exuberant ecocentrism: Kafka, Coetzee and transformative mimesis' in S.L. Muller and T.-K. Pusse (eds), *From ego to eco: mapping shifts from anthropocentrism to ecocentrism* (Leiden and Boston, MA, 2018), 218.

[9] C. Schmitt-Kilb, '"Poetry's a line of defence": ecopoetry and politics in the 21st century' in Muller and Pusse (eds), *From ego to eco*, 140.

[10] T. Roosevelt, (1910) 'Citizenship in a Republic', delivered at the Sorbonne, in Paris, France on 23 April 1910. http://www.worldfuturefund.org/Documents/maninarena.htm accessed 3 July 2020.

that Nature resists human control and, simultaneously, that the crisis is indeed a response by Nature to human actions.

Ironic modern re-imaginings

The remainder of this paper will consider a small cross-section of recent and contemporary efforts to re-imagine the relationship between nature and humans on the part of poets who are themselves immersed in a tradition that foregrounded *comhbhá an dúlra*, the sympathy of nature.

Seán Ó Ríordáin: personal memory, cultural depression

Few readers of modern Irish-language literature would dispute the canonical status of Seán Ó Ríordáin's poem 'Adhlacadh mo mháthar' ('My mother's burial').[11] Ostensibly, it is a reflection on an incident in a blossom-filled orchard in June as the poet-speaker reads an old tattered letter from his deceased mother and is transported back in memory to the day of her burial: 'Thit an Meitheamh siar isteach sa ngeimhreadh / Den úllghort deineadh reilig bhán cois abhann...' ('June fell back into winter / the orchard became a white cemetery by the river...'). The high status this poem enjoys derives not only from the personal grief of the speaker but from its resonance as a dark, ironic evocation of the main traditional tropes that pertain to the land of Ireland. The identity between the woman, in this case the speaker's mother, and the land is no longer one of supernatural personification but of cold materiality as she literally becomes part of the soil she in which she is buried; the woman is no radiant otherworldly young woman or *spéirbhean* but a dead elderly woman for whom the process of transformation back from aged hag or *cailleach* to young fertile woman has stalled, and the land, initially a fertile orchard and a site of abundance, has become, in the poet's imagination, a cemetery. Through this funereal vision the poem can readily be considered to reflect an attitude of cultural depression of a type not uncommon in the literature of recently liberated nations, when self-determination fails to produce the hoped-for transformations, and the life-cycle from youth to old age and back to youth is interrupted at the point of death.

In describing the effect on Nature of the death of the speaker's mother the poem breaks new ground, combining personal memory and the sympathy of Nature with the speaker's plight. The sudden regression of June into winter ('Thit an Meitheamh siar isteach sa gheimhreadh') is consistent with the magical response by Nature to human calamity, while simultaneously making it clear that that response is also an obvious metaphor for the speaker suddenly remembering the day of his mother's burial. In traditional Irish poetry Nature often falls silent when mourning a death, or alternatively screams in pain, particularly in the poetry of the eighteenth-century Munster poet Aogán O Rathaille, whose

---

[11] S. Ó Ríordáin, *Eireaball spideoige* (Baile Átha Cliath, 1952), 56–8.

influence can be discerned throughout Ó Ríordáin's work. Following Ó Rathaille, Ó Ríordáin then presents the black hole of his mother's grave in the whiteness of the snow covered cemetery, as a mouth screaming: 'Do liúigh sa sneachta an dúpholl' ('The dark hole screamed out from the snow'). To refer to June as falling back into winter is a metaphor for losing oneself in memory; yet by retaining the memory of the older trope, a sense is retained of Nature empathising with the grieving man. There is a further complexity in that the speaker's trauma—the death of the woman-mother-goddess and the transformation of the fertile orchard in his mind into a cemetery—is both the immediate cause of his grief and a traditional response to a calamitous event in a hero's life. This poem has gripped the imagination of Irish language speakers for reasons that are not entirely clear, but that may well derive at least in part from the recognition of the deep roots of its basic premises regarding the land of Ireland. Those roots appear here in a form that accords with a prevailing mood of cultural depression in the mid-twentieth century.

Máirtín Ó Direáin: heroic struggle, nostalgic memory

Máirtín Ó Direáin, a mid-twentieth century contemporary of Seán Ó Ríordáin's, is the poet who more than any other found himself at odds with the pre-Famine idea, *à la* Raiftearaí, that Nature was a source of rich bounty and support for humans. Men could survive and proved themselves by their struggle with Nature, in particular the harsh terrain of his native Aran. He largely abandons the traditional heroic understanding that men were to act and Nature's role was one of response; rather a man becomes heroic now through engaging with Nature as adversary. The mark of a man was his own resilience, strength and determination and the support of his family and community as in 'Gleic mo dhaoine'[12] ('My people's struggle')

> Cur in aghaidh na hanacra
> Ab éigean do mo dhaoine a dhéanamh
> An chloch a chloí, is an chré
> Chrosanta a thabhairt chun míne
> Is rinne mo dhaoine cruachan,
> Is rinne clann chun cúnaimh.
> Dúshlán na ndúl a spreag a ndúshlán…
> (Fighting against adversity / Was what my people had to do; / Subduing stone and levelling out / The stubborn clay, they toughened up / And raised a family to help. / Nature's defiance made them defiant…)

Men must take on the might of Nature, not that of other men. Nature's power and agency appear implacable in Ó Direáin's work, even casting men in its

---

[12] M. Ó Direáin, *Selected poems /Rogha dánta*, ed. and trans. F. Sewell (An Spidéal, 2018), 96, 97.

own image, and usurping the role of artist and creator, as in 'Cuimhne an Domhnaigh'[13] ('A Sunday Memory'):

> Chím mar a chaith an chloch gach fear
> Mar lioc ina cló féin é
> (I see how the stone has sculpted each man / Worn him down to its own shape)

Although the iconic anti-urban poem 'Stoite'[14] ('Uprooted') admits that the forebears who lived on Aran recognised 'féile chaoin na húire' ('the soil's beneficence'), and even admits the possibility that a sense of exultation might accompany the struggle, this acknowledgment is slight compared to the account given of the struggle. It recalls that 'our fathers / and forefathers / Grappled with life / Wrestling the bare rock…As they withstood / The power of the elements'. ('Ár n-aithreacha bhíodh / Is a n-aithreacha siúd, / In achrann leis an saol / Ag coraíocht leis an gcarraig loim…Ag baint ceart / De neart na ndúl.')

  Even a heroic struggle with Nature, the same poem says, is not enough; Nature must be transformed by cultural activity, such as house building, if the traditonal requirement of heroic poetry is to be met, namely that one ensure that one's memory be preserved: 'Thóg an fear seo teach / Is an fear úd / Claí nó fál / A mhair ina dhiaidh / Is a choinnigh an chuimhne buan'. ('One man builds a house, / Another a boundary / Or dry stone wall / That outlived him / And preserved his memory.') To build a house or a wall may be a feasible alternative to a life in the civil service which was a target of Ó Direáin's particular opprobrium. Less realistic is his Canute-like apostrophic address to the drifting sand that threatens to engulf St Enda's church on Aran. 'Teaghlach Éinne'[15] ('Eanna's Household') is a strenuous exhortation, emphasising how cultural heritage is at risk from the power of Nature. Its final stanza makes this clear:

> Fóill, a ghaineamh, fóill!
> Stad is lig don bhall,
> Fág binn, stua, is doras;
> Ní cuibhe ar shaothar Mhic Chonaill
> Brat an dearmaid ar deireadh.
> (Hold back, sand, hold back! / Halt, and let the wall be. / Leave gable, arch and doorway. / Mac Conaill's work does not deserve / To end in a shroud of oblivion.')

Ó Direáin's adversarial attitude to Nature does not always entail a desire to abandon it. In one of his best known poems, 'Ár ré dhearóil'[16] ('Our wretched era'), he compares a life separated from Nature to a prison, leaving him surrounded by prisoners 'Since we said goodbye / To the land and shore, / And necessity crashed /

---

[13] Ó Direáin, *Selected poems /Rogha dánta*, 102, 103.
[14] Ó Direáin, *Selected poems /Rogha dánta*, 68, 69.
[15] Ó Direáin, *Selected poems /Rogha dánta*, 112, 113.
[16] Ó Direáin, *Selected poems /Rogha dánta*, 140–53.

Seeing the natural world: Comhbhá an Dúlra

Down upon us' ('Ó d'fhágamar slán / Ag talamh, ag trá / Gur thit orainn / Crann an éigin'). Strikingly, the deprivation suffered by the urban migrant is expressed in language of a type commonly used to express traditional *comhbhá an dúlra*. No birdsong or murmuring streams for such workers: 'Níl éan ag ceol / Ar chraobh dó, / Ná sruthán ag crónán / Go caoin dó.' Striking, too, in this poem is the characterisation of life in the city and in offices as one of struggle and sterility, while the former relationship with the land is expressed almost neutrally, without criticism or praise and without reference to a struggle: 'Níl a ghiodán ag neach / Le rómhar ó cheart' ('Here no one has / His plot of earth / to dig…')

It is becoming clear that Ó Direáin's position was more nuanced than some of the examples first quoted from his work would suggest. Poems that register childhood memories confirm this nuanced approach. His memory of the natural world of his childhood, admittedly nostalgic, was predominantly of a halcyon world. In 'Maidin Dhomhnaig'[17] ('Sunday Morning') he recalls his grandmother praying with '[A] rainbow-coloured butterfly / Extending its empire / On the wing of a gentle breeze' ('Féileacán ildaite / Is a ghlóir-réim á leathadh / Ar eite na leoite séimhe'. A similarly romantic impulse generates a series of vignettes in the iconic 'An tEarrach Thiar' ('Springtime in the West'), in which he recalls a series of treasured memories.[18] First is the 'sweet sound' ('[b]inn an fhuaim') of a man scraping his spade clean 'In the peace and calm / Of a warm day' ('sa gciúnas séimh i mbrothall lae'). This is followed by the 'shimmering vision' ('Niamhrach an radharc') of a man with a creel with 'the red mayweed / Glistening / In a ray of sunlight' ('an fheamainn dhearg / Ag lonrú / I dtaitneamh gréine'). Next is a 'dreamy sight, / Springtime in the West' ('Támhradharc sítheach / San Earrach thiar') of women gathering shellfish in ebb-tide pools. Finally, the sound of the fishermen's oars sounded across 'a slow, gold sea' ('órmhuir mhall'). These memories have either elided or contradicted the rhetoric of struggle, and add a certain counterpoint to his grimmer pronouncements.

Nature even occasionally appears as a defence for the older way of life on Aran, to which Ó Direáin was greatly attached, in which he found solace, and whose passing he lamented. In 'Ómós do John Millington Synge' ('Homage to J.M. Synge') he laments: 'Tá cleacht mo dhaoine ag meath, / Tá cabhair feasta an tonn mar fhalla' ('My people's ways are in decline, / The wave no longer a protective wall').[19] Synge, a visitor to the Aran islands on five separate occasions at the turn of the nineteenth century, asserted that 'In Inismaan one is forced to believe in a sympathy between man and nature'.[20] Arguing that Synge reveals the sea as both provider and potential, indeed probable, killer, Kennedy-O'Neill suggests

---

[17] Ó Direáin, *Selected poems / Rogha dánta*, 62, 63.
[18] Ó Direáin, *Selected poems / Rogha dánta*, 72–75.
[19] Ó Direáin, *Selected poems / Rogha dánta*, 106, 107.
[20] Quoted in J. Kennedy-Ó'Neill, '"Sympathy between man and nature": landscape and loss in Synge's Riders to the Sea' in C. Cusick (ed.) *Out of the earth: ecocritical readings of Irish texts* (Cork, 2010), 36.

that 'his work is hard to place in a strictly pastoral, Romantic or transcendental pigeonhole' and suggests, as an alternative, a view of Nature as 'Darwinian indifference'.[21] For Ó Direáin, writing within an Irish tradition albeit with a clear familiarity with Synge's work, the relationship with nature is best viewed less as one of indifference but as one in which the traditional belief in the responsiveness of Nature to human action comes under pressure from the specific harshness of the terrain in Aran.

Somhairle MacGill-Eain: Nature flourishing despite human death and loss

It is appropriate to adopt an inclusive Irish–Scottish approach to the analysis of Gaelic literature in view of the deep shared roots and shared literary language until the early modern period of Irish and Scottish Gaelic. In that spirit, and because *comhbhá an dúlra* was a literary cornerstone in Gaelic Scotland, just as in Ireland, the poetry of the Scottish Gaelic poet Somhairle MacGill-Eain demands attention. His poem 'Hallaig'[22] is arguably the most radical mid-twentieth century evocation of the trope of the sympathy of Nature and, incidentally, of *aisling*-type visions, in either Irish or Scottish Gaelic. The poet-speaker relates an otherworldly vision he had with the cleared and subsequently deceased community from his native island, Raasay.

To describe a visionary encounter with the dead in the wild trees that spread freely across the townland of Hallaig after the people were cleared was a remarkable reversal of the core Gaelic trope that traditionally maintained that land prospers when its rightful sovereign is in place and ruling wisely, and withers or suffers when he dies. Here the land blooms and is beloved not only despite the catastrophic loss of the people, but directly as a result of it, as the departure of the people allowed the trees to extend over the area.

> Tha iad fhathast ann an Hallaig
> Clann Ghill-Eain 's clann MhicLeòid,
> Na bh'ann ri linn Mhic Ghille-Chaluim:
> Chunnacas na mairbh beò.
> Na fir 'nan laighe air an lianaig
> aig ceann gach taighe a bh'ann
> na h-igheanan 'nan coille bheithe,
> dìreach an druim, crom an ceann.
> (They are still in Hallaig, / MacLeans and MacLeods, / all who were there in the time of Mac Gille Chaluim: / the dead have been seen alive. The men lying on the green / at the end of every house that was, / the girls a wood of birches, / straight their backs, bent their heads.)

---

[21] Kennedy-Ó'Neill, 'Sympathy between man and nature', 43.

[22] S. MacGill-Eain / S. MacLean, *Caoir gheal leumraich / White leaping flame: Collected poems in Gaelic with English translations*, eds and trans, C. Whyte and E. Dymock, (Edinburgh, 2011), 230–35.

The poem is too long and complex to analyse fully here but it should at least be noted that no real restitution takes place through the vision in 'Hallaig' and none is claimed, apart from a temporary respite from the enduring pain of the Highland Clearances in the nineteenth century, and that only for the duration of the speaker's life. If there is a disjuncture in 'Hallaig' between the glorious vision of the resurrected dead and the admission that Nature appears to be flowering in spite of the suffering of the people, some parallels can be seen with the fact that Eibhlín Dubh Ní Chonaill's assurance of the support of Nature for her dead husband came, in the end, to nought, as Nature continued to bear fruit in his absence. Subtle levels of irony pervade both poems: Nature will continue to flourish notwithstanding the plight of the people.

Pádraig Mac Fhearghusa: frozen Nature withholds support

A generation after Ó Ríordáin, Ó Direáin and MacGill-Eain, Pádraig Mac Fhearghusa has published six volumes of remarkable, if under-acknowledged, poetry. Among his various sources of inspiration is an extended consideration of the grief that endured for many decades following the loss of what is presented as an early love. With the title of his first volume, *Faoi léigear (Under siege)* the sense of life as an assault takes hold and persists throughout much of the subsequent work.[23] Perhaps unsurprisingly in such a context, the heroic relationship with supportive and responsive natural forces is undermined.

If Ó Direáin figured the relationship as one of a struggle for dominance against a harsh land and sea, Mac Fhearghusa, at some distance from the extremes of Aran, is free from the obligation to wrestle physically with the land for survival. He writes as though personally thwarted by the forces of Nature, which treat him as an interloper. I draw attention to two aspects of this hostility on the part of Nature. The first is a marked preference for images of frozen landscapes. In 'Dó seaca faoi chorrán gealaí'[24] ('Frostbite under a crescent moon') he proclaims that his separation from the beloved is a source of pain-as-coldness that remains unabated long after their separation. His frequent returns to where she lived have been of no avail; all he has from her is cold: 'An fuacht, b'shin díot mo chuid'. A focus on her hard, cold breasts sets up a clear echo of another cornerstone trope, namely the female personification of the land, which is closely related to the belief in the sympathy of Nature. His lost love has become the whole cold world: her breasts are described as 'cruinne-chíocha', where 'cruinne' denotes both 'round', and 'the universe'. This poem, in which the woman and the world are cold and the male speaker is frozen by them, sets up a remarkable circular movement whereby Nature on the one hand empathises with him in his loss and sorrow by freezing over, and on the other hand, ironically, it is the coldness of the Nature-woman that causes him to freeze. It is as though a mutual

---

[23] P. Mac Fhearghusa, *Faoi léigear* (Baile Átha Cliath, 1980).
[24] Mac Fhearghusa, *Faoi léigear*, 11.

process of freezing the other were set in motion between Nature and the speaker, in tandem with the freezing he experiences from his beloved. In its examination of the pain of lost love, this poem taps into the complexity of the human–Nature relationship as it has been imagined in Irish literature across the ages, including our own. In the context of *comhbhá an dúlra*, the speaker's sorrow might be considered to have generated the big freeze, placing Nature in the role of sympathetic responder, but its response piles further suffering on the speaker and mirrors closely the actions of the one who initially brought him down.

A second notable elaboration of the relationship between Nature and humans takes place in Mac Fhearghusa's third volume, *Faoi Shliabh Mis agus dánta eile*, a title which translates as both *At the foot of* and/or *Concerning Sliabh Mis and other poems*.[25] Slieve Mis is the mythological site of the fortress of Cú Roí, who abducted a young woman, Bláthnaid, from her father's house. She, in love with the Ulster hero Cú Chulainn, tricked Cú Roí and facilitated Cú Chulainn's entry into the fortress, where he duly killed Cú Roí. An eponymous suite of seventeen poems, 'Fá Shliabh Mis'[26] recounts an ascent of Slieve Mis in Kerry, along the lines of a dark *aisling* or vision poem. Traditional *aisling* visions often take place either in a form of supernatural mist that envelops the fairy woman who comes to visit a poet-speaker, or in sleep. Note that the word 'néall' can denote both 'cloud' and 'sleep'. In Mac Fhearghusa's sequence the mist turns menacing and literal, suggesting that Nature lacks sympathy with the speaker's quest and pointing to his failure as a heroic adventurer along life's journey.

The speaker of the poem sets off one 'long brown' autumn day in the town below the mountain, a dismal place of overflowing rubbish bins. He departs in haste, for fear of the changing weather that threatens to turn the ground to mud and blanket the mountains with snow, a transformation that echoes, but is less dramatic and less magical than the turn from June to winter in the Ó Ríordáin poem discussed earlier. While the journey is an opportunity for reflection, with echoes of pilgrimage, it mainly repeats the ascent into the wilderness that marked the traditional location of many *aisling* poems. After a short respite in a ruined church along the way, as in a pilgrimage, the atmosphere reverts to something seemingly pre-Christian and unremitting as he proceeds through the heather and the 'aiteann Gaelach' ('Gaelic furze' i.e. dwarf whin). There is now no possibility of rest in a place that is described with a hostile martial metaphor:

> Cónaí ná sos ní fhéadaim,
> Saighead gaoithe im dhrom...
> Bíogann íor na farraige aníos
> Bláthaíonn an tsúil ina blár gorm
> (I cannot stop or rest, / An arrow of wind in my back... / The sea on the horizon mounts up / The eye sees a blue battleground)

---

[25] P. Mac Fhearghusa, *Fá Shliabh Mis agus dánta eile* (Baile Átha Cliath, 1993).
[26] Mac Fhearghusa, *Fá Shliabh Mis agus dánta eile*, 38–55.

Combining Christian and heroic pre-Christian language, he admits that 'the sin here is the indifference of cowardice' ('Is é is peaca anseo neamhshuim na meatachta'). It is notable from a Gaelic perspective that the heroic struggle required here is not against an external enemy, in which he might have expected the support of Nature, but with Nature itself, as some of Ó Direáin's poems also contend. The speaker of this poem is a humble searcher after wisdom, who lacks the heroic dimension that Ó Direáin's men displayed in their grappling with the forces of Nature. Nature declines to endorse him but rather ramps up the pressure as he proceeds with his ascent, assailing him with the cold, the approach of darkness and a very literal blanket of fog:

> An fuacht faoi dheoidh a ghoin m'aire,
> An ghrian ag sleabhcadh ar Bhinn os Gaoith,
> …
> An ceo ina míle teanga ar mo shála
> ('It was the cold that took my attention / The sun slipping down on Binn os Gaoith /…The mist a thousand tongues around my feet')

At this point his foot trips on the heather, causing him to fall, terrifyingly, almost losing his life. As in *aisling* poetry, he is now visited by otherworldly beings, three in this case, each of whom exhorts him in a different direction. As he eventually extricates himself from his predicament he is assisted, not by Nature, apart from the light of the moon, but by banal goods manufactured by humans: his protective anorak and coffee from his flask. Such anti-heroic markers indicate that he is no colossus, with no hope of support from Nature.

Dòmhnall MacAmhlaigh: *Contemptuous Nature*

Returning briefly to Scottish Gaelic, the short poem 'Am fiar-Chath' ('Devious fight')[27] by the mid-twentieth century poet Dòmhnall MacAmhlaigh is another clear example of the type of ironic discourse that has in recent times been used to give expression to the awareness that Nature, far from supporting great heroes, defeats them effortlessly.

> An laoch
> a bha gheal an-uiridh
> gabhar am-bliadhna a thuireadh:
> thill e à iomadh cath dìreach
> glan-bhàireach.
> Chaidh e air chall san fhaoilleach
> 's tha a lorg air a bàthadh
> fon t-sìor chathadh air a gilead
> (bha fhuil gun a leigeil

---

[27] Dòmhnall MacAmhlaigh, *Deilbh is faileasan / Images and reflections: Dàin le Dòmhnall MacAmhlaigh / Poems by Donald MacAulay* (Steòrnabhagh, 2008), 48, 49.

> ragadh gu bàs e –
> mullach na tàmailt)
> Choisinn am fiar-chath ùmhlachd.
> 'S e comharra g' eil an t-earrach a' teachd
> gun leagh
> am bodach-sneachd'.
>
> (The warrior / who, last year, shone bright / this year his death-songs are sung: / he returned from many straight fights / leaving a clean trail.
> He got lost in the dead of winter /and his footprint is drowned / by the incessant snow falling on its whiteness / (His blood was not let / his death was by freezing – / a source of the greatest shame) /He succumbed in a devious fight. A sign of spring's approach / is that snowmen / melt.)

No ally of heroes here, Nature is a harsh adversary that refuses to play fair and deprives the warrior of the glory of a bloody and martial death. This inglorious death undermines the heroic code and the traditionally subservient relationship of Nature to humans. The tone, initially respectful of a true hero who had taken part in many glorious battles, slides almost imperceptibly into mock heroic, lightly ironising the tragedy of dying from the cold rather than heroically. To consider such a death tragic is made to seem faintly ridiculous, for who today could seriously hold it against the weather that it fought dirty, or consider it tragic in traditional terms that a hero be forgotten because his footprints in the snow were effaced. Nature has undermined the hero by revealing him as a mere snowman. It is not clear whether the death is caused by a failure of judgment or unavoidable circumstances, but either way, Nature is implacable. But it is also full of life, because it is the advent of spring that heralds the snowman's death.

This poem contrasts with other great struggles between heroic individuals and adverse weather forces, such as Jack London's short story 'To build a fire',[28] in which a foolishly unprepared traveller falls prey to the existential threat of the snow in the Yukon. By underestimating the danger, he is destroyed. In this case he was brought down not only by the power of Nature but also by a combination of his own arrogance and foolishness. MacAmhlaigh makes no such judgment of the hero in his poem but suggests that, since the hero is no more resilient than a snowman in the face of Nature, his demise is simply a part of the natural order, and the natural order is not necessarily at one with or supportive of humans. Intriguingly, this echoes slightly the irony in 'Hallaig'. The two poems offer alternative versions of the strength and independence of Nature. 'Hallaig' investigates its cause; 'Am fiar-Chath' its effect. In 'Hallaig' the forced departure of the people allowed Nature to expand; in MacAmhlaigh's poem it is the gentleness of Nature, not its harshness, that

---

[28] J. London, 'To build a fire' (1908), available at www.owleyes.org/text/build-fire/read/Build-Fire#, accessed 3 July 2020.

brings the hero down, as the snowman melts with the advent of spring. Neither suggests support for humans.

Biddy Jenkinson: towards ecocentrism

An issue that regularly arises for oppressed groups is whether or not they can achieve liberty and equality without seeking to replace their position of subordination with one of dominance. The recognition of Nature as a formidable adversary can seem threatening, or, more hopefully, can seem like a prophetic note of warning about the future relationship of humankind and Nature in a world transformed by climate change. However there are, happily, alternatives to a simple reversal of power relationships. Among contemporary Irish-language poets, the major poetic voice heard expressing a desire to forge a new relationship between humans and Nature is that of Biddy Jenkinson. True, some of her work does appear to engage in a type of polar reversal, which can have radical ethical repercussions, not least because of the degree of precedence afforded the natural world. But other pieces go farther and seek to transcend the binary relationship of dominance and subordination in a more radical way.

At its simplest, Jenkinson allows her speakers to overturn the traditional expectation that Nature would follow the fortunes of people, as in, for example 'Dá mbeadh an lá go breá / Do bhéarfainn gean duit féin…'[29] ('If the day were fine / I would give you love' or 'Tá an fharraige ard, an ghrian go hard is táimse lán de ghrásta'[30] ('The sea is full, the sun is high, and I am full of grace.') In the latter, the benign presence of the sea and the sun appear to take on the mantle of angels, as they bring about the state of grace familiar to Catholics from the prayer known as the 'Hail Mary', which memorialises Mary's visitation by God, through an angel, and her consequent conception of Jesus. Grace in this poem clearly does not require the subjugation of Nature.

Complex statements are found in several poems that probe the implications of a relationship in which Nature is accorded an even greater degree of precedence. The prioritisation of Nature inevitably involves the loss of human privilege. In the poem 'Oileán na Caillí'[31] ('The Hag's Island'), Nature rules in two guises, namely as the sovereignty goddess in her eponymous and familiar hag form, and as the cows that belonged to her and to which she allows free rein, in fact free reign, on her island. These animals, we are informed, have made their own of the land now that humans have left. They

---

[29] B. Jenkinson, *Dán na huidhre* (Baile Átha Cliath, 1991), 13.
[30] B. Jenkinson, *Uiscí beatha* (Baile Átha Cliath, 1988), 16.
[31] Jenkinson, *Uiscí beatha*, 49. (Note that this poem predates recent debates about the climate risks associated with the national herd, which have had the effect of defining cows as part of the problem rather than, as here, a sign of the restitution of the sovereignty of the natural world.)

have assumed sovereignty themselves, somewhat to the dismay of the former owner, the speaker of the poem:

> Tá gréinleach a gcúirt ríoga ar mo léana
> is táimse in amhras i dtaobh uisce an tobair.
> Tá an tseamair dhearg ite síos go fréamh
> is tá steaimpí déanta acu den mhagairlín gaelach…
> Níl claí gan bearna bó.
> (There are tufts of grass covered in dung in their royal courts on my lawn, / and I'm worried about the water in the well. / The clover is eaten to the root, / they have trodden down the wild orchid…/ Not a fence remains without a gap left by a cow.)

The poem's title, 'Oileán na Caillí' ('The Hag's Island') refers to the island as the possession of the hag-goddess of sovereignty and therefore under her sway; it is safe to assume she is satisfied with this new state of affairs. This is corroborated in other poems by conventional examples that indicate the response of Nature to a rightful leader, as in 'Muirfín' ('Merrion'): 'Tá an ghealach ag bláthú; tá searraigh chúir á scaoileadh ag an bhfarraige, éiríonn an spéirlíne ar sciathán éan'[32] ('The moon is waxing; foals of foam are launching onto the ocean, the skyline rises on the wings of birds.') Nature is plainly delighted with the new dispensation; the deposed human owner is left bemused and bereft; and the poem succeeds in aligning itself with the forces of Nature against the human speaker who appears over-controlling and unfree. But the tone is playful, with no sense of violence or domination. If the sovereignty of Ireland was in the gift of the goddess of the land from earliest times, within Biddy Jenkinson's poetry she once more retains it, holding it firm and holding it dear.

    Much more could be added to this paper's investigation of a strand of thought that continues to develop in Irish-language poetry as it seeks new forms of relationship between humans and the natural world. There are poems, not discussed, that revisit the land as human cemetery or as wild paradise; poems that seek to de-commodify the land by exalting the tiniest, shyest and, in instrumental terms, more or less useless, flowers; poems that infuse the naming of the land with love, not ownership; there are many forms of ecopoetry. Like the pieces we have discussed, such poems find multiple ways to ironise traditional tropes. They reside within a tradition of great antiquity, which provides an ethical and emotional ground for reflections on how to live well in the contemporary world. Poets may subvert the tradition, find in it fissures that can act as a foothold for a new vision, or even attempt to displace it, but only rarely, if at all, can they forget it, or pass it on unaltered.

---

[32] Jenkinson, *Dán na huidhre*, 19.

Reconstruction of hydrological drought in Irish catchments (1850–2015)

SIMON NOONE* and CONOR MURPHY

Irish Climate Analysis and Research Units (ICARUS), Department of Geography, Maynooth University, Kildare, Ireland

[Accepted 24 August 2020. Published 15 October 2020.]

Abstract

While long-term records that extend into the nineteenth century exist for various meteorological variables, river flow records of concurrent length do not exist on the island of Ireland. This work attempts to reconstruct monthly river flows for twelve Irish catchments using quality assured long-term precipitation records for the period 1850–2015. A conceptual rainfall-runoff model calibrated and verified on contemporary flow records is used to reconstruct monthly flows for each catchment. Reconstructions are then analysed to identify periods of drought using a threshold-based drought indicator. Results show that the catchments examined experienced protracted drought episodes with seven major drought rich periods identified in 1887–88, 1891–94, 1902–12, 1933–34, 1944, 1953, 1971–76. The timing and severity of hydrological droughts are consistent with previous work that has examined meteorological drought. This work thus provides a first attempt to reconstruct historical river flows to examine hydrological drought in Ireland. We tease out directions for future work and the opportunities presented for using such reconstructions for drought risk management.

Introduction

In recent years significant progress has been made in developing long-term, quality assured records of precipitation for the island of Ireland that stretch back to the eighteenth and nineteenth centuries. These records have been used to extend understanding of past climate variability and change, and to provide further insight into extremes of floods and droughts. For such hydro-climatic extremes it is particularly beneficial to have long river flow records to examine, among other things, how meteorological extremes propagate into hydrological extremes. However, river flow records of concurrent length do not exist on the island. The commencement of river flow monitoring typically coincided with the onset of arterial drainage in the 1940s/1950s and with the occurrence of drought in the

---

*Author's email: simon.noone@mu.ie
ORCID iD: https://orcid.org/0000-0003-1661-1423
doi: https://doi.org/10.3318/PRIAC.2020.120.11

mid-1970s when local authorities became concerned about ensuring adequate supply to meet demand.[1]

In the UK and elsewhere, researchers have used long rainfall records to reconstruct river flows for numerous catchments with the derived series being employed to assess variability and change in flow sequences and to investigate past extremes.[2] Reconstructed flows have also been used to assess the resilience of water company drought plans, noting that severe droughts of the nineteenth century are particularly useful for testing current and future water supply systems and to provide a baseline for climate change adaptation planning.[3] For instance, river flow reconstruction and drought analysis for the Anglian Region, United Kingdom (UK) highlighted periods of prolonged drought in 1854–60 and 1893–1907.[4] While similar work for the Severn Trent water supply region in the UK identified several notable drought periods in the reconstructed flow series in 1887–89, 1892–97, 1921–23, 1933–35, 1975–77 and 1995–98.[5] Each of these studies highlights the utility of long-term reconstructed river flows to water planning and to understanding variability and change in catchment hydrology.

This paper aims, firstly, to use the Island of Ireland Precipitation (IIP) network 1850–2015 to reconstruct monthly river flows for selected catchments and, secondly, to identify hydrological droughts in reconstructed flow records.[6] The paper is organised as follows; first we describe the study catchments and detail the data used in reconstructing river flows. Next, we describe the methods, including the hydrological model employed, its calibration and verification. The drought indicators employed are also described. Following the presentation of

---

[1] Murphy *et al.*, 'Climate-driven trends in mean and high flows from a network of reference stations in Ireland', *Journal of Hydrological Science*, 58:4 (2013), 755–72, doi: 10.1080/02626667.2013.782407

[2] P.D. Jones, 'Riverflow reconstruction from precipitation data', *Journal of Climatology*, 4 (1984), 171–86; P.D. Jones and D.H. Lister, 'Riverflow reconstructions for 15 catchments over England and Wales and an assessment of hydrological drought since 1865', *International Journal of Climatology*, 18 (1998), 999–1013; Spraggs *et al.*, 'Re-construction of historic drought in the Anglian Region (UK) over the period 1798–2010 and the implications for water resources and drought management', *Journal of Hydrology*, 526 (2015), 231–52, doi: 10.1016/j.jhydrol.2015.01.015; Jones *et al.*, 'Extended riverflow reconstructions for England and Wales, 1865–2002', *International Journal of Climatology*, 26 (2006), 219–31.

[3] Watts *et al.*, 'Testing the resilience of water supply systems to long droughts', *Journal of Hydrology*, 414–5 (2012), 255–67, doi: 10.1016/j.jhydrol.2011.10.038.

[4] Spraggs *et al.*, 'Re-construction of historic drought in the Anglian Region', 231–52.

[5] Lennard *et al.*, 'The application of a drought reconstruction in water resource management', *Hydrology Research*, 47:3 (2015), 646–59, doi:10.2166/nh.2015.090.

[6] Noone *et al.*, 'A 250-year drought catalogue for the island of Ireland (1765–2015)', *International Journal of Climatology*, 37 (2017), 239–54, doi:10.1002/joc.4999.

Study catchments and data	In reconstructing river flows, suitable catchments were selected from the Irish Reference Network (IRN), which consists of 35 river flow gauges from the Republic, together with 8 stations from Northern Ireland contained in the UK Benchmark Network.[7] Catchments within the IRN have good quality observed data of at least 25 years duration and are relatively free from confounding factors such as urbanisation and river regulation.[8] Based on proximity to rainfall gauges within the IIP, twelve catchments (see Fig 1) were chosen from the IRN, representing, as far as possible, diversity in catchment characteristics (see Table 1). For each catchment daily mean flow data was obtained from the Office of Public Works (OPW) and the Environmental Protection Agency and converted to mean monthly flows.[9] Fig 1 shows the location of the IIP stations in relation to each catchment. Note that Shannon Airport is matched to two catchments (27002, 23002) and for some catchments the rainfall gauge is located outside of the catchment boundary.

Potential Evapotranspiration (PET) observations are limited across Ireland and rely on approaches to estimate approximate losses. The Penman-Monteith method is recommended by the United Nations Food and Agriculture organisation (FAO). It calculates PET by combining both energy and mass balances to model evapotranspiration. However, the Penman-Monteith method is data intensive to calculate and due to a lack of required long-term data for Ireland it is not possible to derive estimates dating back to 1850 using this approach. While there are other methods for calculating PET, most have significant input data requirements such as temperature, wind speed and radiation. More stringent PET calculation methods that only require mean daily/monthly temperature and the latitude of the site are available.[10] However, given the lack of long-term quality assured temperature records for Ireland this study employs constant monthly PET over the period of reconstruction (1850–2015) as a first pass approach. Long-term average PET (LTA_PET) is calculated from Penman-Monteith

---

[7] Harrigan et al., 'Designation and trend analysis of the updated UK Benchmark Network of river flow stations: the UKBN2 dataset', *Hydrology Research*, 49:2 (2018), 552–67, doi: 10.2166/nh.2017.058; J. Hannaford and G. Buys, 'Trends in seasonal river flow regimes in the UK', *Journal of Hydrology*, 475 (2012), 158–74.

[8] Murphy, et al., 'Climate-driven trends in mean and high flows', 755–72.

[9] Office of Public Works, OPW Hydrodata: http://waterlevel.ie/hydro-data/home.html; Environmental Protection Agency 2016, http://www.epa.ie/water/wm/hydrometrics/network/

[10] C.W. Thornthwaite, 'An approach toward a rational classification of climate', *Geographical Review*, 38:1 (1948), 55–94; H.F. Blaney and W.D. Criddle, 'Determining water needs from climatological data', USDA Soil Conservation Service (1950), SOS–TP, USA, pp 8–9.

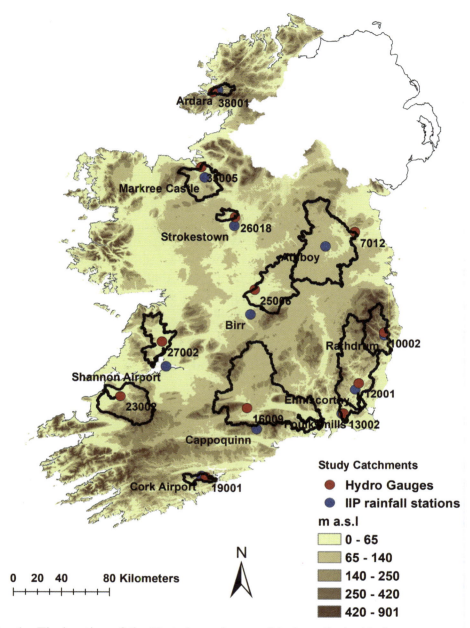

Fig. 1—The location of the 12 study catchments (black outline) with the gauge location (red circle) and gauge number. The blue circles represent each of the Island of Ireland precipitation stations used in reconstructing river flow at each study catchment.

estimates for seven synoptic station records (1955–2015) representing inland and coastal locations (see Fig 2). Firstly, the monthly mean of each station was calculated and then averaged across all stations to obtain the long-term monthly averages employed for reconstruction of flows for each catchment (see Fig 2). The monthly mean PET derived for this study closely corresponds to those

TABLE 1—Details of key catchment characteristics for each of the 12 selected study catchments. The portion of flow (m³/s¹) during low flow periods that derives from stored sources such as groundwater is defined by the Base Flow Index (BFI). Low BFI indicates a river which has lower storage with flow being runoff dominated. In contrast a higher BFI means that flows have a greater groundwater component.

Catchment Gauge ID

Key Catchment Descriptors	7012	10002	12001	13002	16009	19001	23002	25006	26018	27002	35005	38001
Catchment Area (km²)	2460	231	1031	63	1583	106	647	1163	119	564	640	111
Standard-period (1961–1990) average annual potential evapotranspiration (mm)	890	1530	1167	1044	1079	1176	1345	932	1044	1336	1198	1753
Standard-period (1961–1990) average annual rainfall (mm)	504	511	522	537	518	527	514	495	458	533	463	498
BFI soils	0.68	0.54	0.72	0.73	0.63	0.68	0.31	0.71	0.72	0.70	0.61	0.28
Total length of river network above gauge (km)	2146	239	1101	65	1585	108	719	846	99	303	836	264
Main stream length (km)	94	35	89	16	85	24	51	67	25	40	41	26
Slope of main stream (m/km)	0.70	6.90	2.10	4.95	1.00	3.74	4.31	0.75	0.55	1.22	1.15	5.95
Proportion of catchment area mapped as benefitting from arterial drainage schemes	0.21	0.00	0.00	0.00	0.00	0.00	0.00	0.28	0.00	0.00	0.00	0.00
Proportion (as a %) of river network length included in arterial drainage schemes	61	00	00	00	00	0	00	51	00	00	00	00

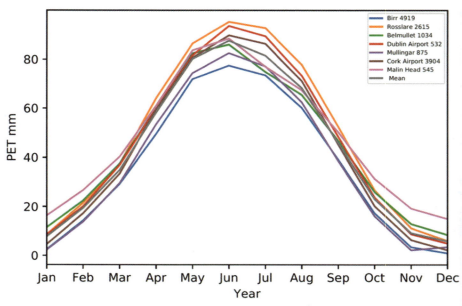

Fig. 2—Long-term monthly mean PET from seven Met Éireann synoptic stations for the period 1955–2015. The black line represents the mean of all seven stations.

values presented in previous work.[11] Other river flow reconstruction work has also used this approach noting that constant evapotranspiration is useful for past reconstructions when only rainfall data are available.[12]

Methods

The hydrological model

The hydrological model HYSIM was chosen to reconstruct monthly river flows for each catchment. HYSIM is a lumped conceptual rainfall runoff model (CRR) that requires monthly/daily precipitation and PET data to simulate river flow.[13] HYSIM has previously been used to model Irish catchments and has also been widely employed in the United Kingdom and elsewhere.[14] HYSIM uses parame-

---

[11] T. Keane, 'Climate, weather and Irish agriculture', Joint Working Group on Applied Meteorology (AGMET) (1986) (Dublin Mount Salus Press, 1986) available at Meterological Service, Dublin 9.

[12] Jones *et al.*, 'Riverflow reconstructions for 15 catchments over England and Wales', 999–1013; Jones *et al.*, 'Extended riverflow reconstructions for England and Wales, 1865–2002', 219–31.

[13] R.E. Manley, 'Calibration of hydrological model using optimization technique', *Journal of the Hydraulics Division* (American Society of Civil Engineers), 104 (1978), 189–202.

[14] Rosemary Charlton and Sonja Moore, 'The impact of climate change on water resources in Ireland' in John Sweeney *et al.*, *Climate Change, scenarios and impacts for Ireland* (EPA Publication, Johnstown Castle, 2003), 81–102; Murphy *et al.*, 'The

ters for hydrology and hydraulics that characterize the catchment rainfall-runoff response. The model represents the catchment as a set of linked storage functions which connect seven hydrological stores (snow storage, interception, upper and lower soil horizon, transitional groundwater, groundwater storage and minor channel storage). HYSIM has two main groups of parameters; physical parameters and process parameters. The physical parameters are measurable properties of the watershed; the process parameters represent the characteristics that are not directly measurable and estimated via calibration against observations. Physically based parameters were set using prior knowledge of soil type, catchment size and observed flow records. Process parameters were calibrated by comparing observed and simulated flows. These include two interflow parameters and two permeability parameters which control movement of water in the soil layers. Fig 3 provides an overview of the model structure.[15]

Before being used for reconstruction, HYSIM was calibrated and validated for each catchment with 75 per cent of available observations used to calibrate the model and the remaining independent data used to verify model performance. For parameters that needed to be estimated by minimising the difference between observed and simulated flows, the Extremes Error of Estimate (EEE) objective function was used to identify optimum parameter values. To assess model performance we employ the Nash Sutcliffe Efficiency (NSE).[16] The NSE is a normalized statistic that determines the relative magnitude of the residual variance compared to the measured data variance. An NSE value of 1 indicates a perfect model fit, whereas a value of 0 indicates that the model performs as well as the mean of the observations. Several other goodness of fit criteria were also calculated across the range of flow conditions, including the Mean Absolute Error (MAE), Percent Bias (PBIAS) and

---

reliability of an "off-the-shelf" conceptual rainfall runoff model for use in climate impact assessment: uncertainty quantification using Latin hypercube sampling', *Area*, 38:1 (2006), 65–78; Murphy *et al.*, 'Climate-driven trends in mean and high flows', 755–72; C.G. Pilling and J.A.A. Jones, 'The impact of future climate change on seasonal discharge, hydrological processes and extreme flows in the Upper Wye experimental catchment, mid-Wales', *Hydrological Processes*, 16:6 (2002), 1201–13; Lennard *et al.*, 'The application of a drought reconstruction in water resource management', 646–59; R. Remesan and I.P. Holman, 'Effect of baseline meteorological data selection on hydrological modelling of climate change scenarios', *Journal of Hydrology*, 528 (2015), 631–42; B.S. Soundharajan, A.J. Adeloye and R. Remesan, 'Evaluating the variability in surface water reservoir planning characteristics during climate change impacts assessment', *Journal of Hydrology*, 538 (2016), 625–39.

[15] Manley, 'Calibration of hydrological model using optimization technique', 189–202; Murphy *et al.*, 'Climate-driven trends in mean and high flows from a network of reference stations in Ireland', 755–72.

[16] J.E. Nash and J.V. Sutcliffe, 'River flow forecasting through conceptual models part I—a discussion of principles', *Journal of Hydrology*, 10:3 (1970), 282–90. doi:10.1016/0022-1694(70)90255-6.

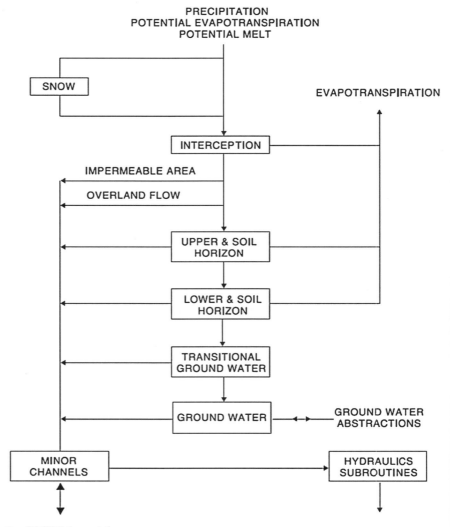

Fig. 3—HYSIM model structure.

coefficient of determination (R^2).[17] Model performance was evaluated for winter (ONDJFM) and summer (AMJJAS) half years.

Drought indicator

There are a wide variety of drought metrics for assessing various types of drought. A commonly used method for drought identification in river flows is

---

[17] Remesan and Holman, 'Effect of baseline meteorological data selection on hydrological modelling of climate change scenarios', 631–42; M.K. Muleta 'Model performance sensitivity to objective function during automated calibrations', *Journal of Hydrologic Engineering*, 17:6 (2011), 756–67.

the threshold level approach where the start and end of a drought is defined by a period when flow is below a certain threshold.[18] The Q95 (the 5th percentile flow) relates to the flow rate equalled or exceeded for 95 percent of the flow record and is an important low flow indicator. Q95 is widely used for monitoring water quality and supply and is thus adopted as a flow threshold here to identify drought events. To implement this procedure, Q95 thresholds were produced by first calculating the 5th percentile for each month (January, February, March etc.) of reconstructed flow from 1850–2015 at each catchment. Next the reconstructed monthly flow was deducted from the 5th percentile value to give the Q95 deficit or surplus for that month at each catchment.[19] The identification of thresholds for each month allows multi-season droughts to be identified. The start of a drought is defined when the reconstructed monthly flow drops below the long term Q95 threshold value for that month, resulting in a Q95 deficit and ends when the reconstructed monthly flow exceeds the Q95 threshold for that month (i.e. returns to surplus relative to Q95 threshold). The drought duration is calculated by summing the number of months from the first month where the simulated flow drops below the Q95 threshold value and ends at the month where the Q95 threshold value is exceeded (note that the first month is inclusive in the drought duration but the end month noted is not inclusive in the drought duration).

Results

Model calibration and validation

The annual model calibration and validation results are presented in Table 2. Overall HYSIM performs well during calibration with NSE values for monthly flows ranging from 0.76 at 12001-Slaney (Co. Wexford) to 0.91 at 38001-Owenea (county Donegal). NSE values for verification range from 0.67 at 12001-Slaney to 0.92 at 26018-Owenure (county Roscommon). The results indicate that the model tends to underestimate flows with PBIAS ranging from -0.6% to -11.2%. The largest underestimation for 23002-Feale (county Kerry) is likely due to the precipitation gauge being located outside the catchment area. For most catchments model performance during verification is in line with calibration results, indicating a robust model. The largest reduction in performance (see Table 2) during verification is for 16009-Suir (county Tipperary) where again the rainfall station may not be adequately representative of the catchment. Fig 4 compares scatter plots of simulated and observed flows for the summer half year during the verification period for each catchment. Despite a slightly weaker performance at

---

[18] Hisdal *et al.*, 'Have streamflow droughts in Europe become more severe or frequent?', *International Journal of Climatology*, 21:3 (2001), 317–33; Fleig *et al.*, 'A global evaluation of streamflow drought characteristics', *Hydrology and Earth System Sciences*, 10:4 (2006), 535–52.

[19] Watts *et al.*, 'Climate change and water in the UK–past changes and future prospects', *Progress in Physical Geography*, 39:1 (2015), 6–28.

TABLE 2—Annual model calibration (Cal) and validation (Val) performance at each catchment.

Catchment	Catchment Area (km²)	Model	Period	NSE	R²	MAE m³/s¹	PBIAS m³/s¹
7012-Boyne at Slane Castle, Co. Meath	2460	Cal	1942–1960	0.88	0.89	6.76	3.1
		Val	1961–1970	0.90	0.93	5.43	0.6
10002-Avonmore at Laragh, Co. Wicklow	231	Cal	1953–1964	0.77	0.93	2.13	-1.3
		Val	1965–1970	0.88	0.86	2.13	-6
12001-Slaney at Scarrawalsh, Co. Wexford	1031	Cal	1990–2010	0.76	0.74	5.61	-2.6
		Val	1970–1980	0.67	0.77	5.12	5.6
13002-Corock at Foulksmill, Co. Wexford	63	Cal	1977–1982	0.88	0.92	0.21	-1.1
		Val	1983–1985	0.83	0.83	0.20	-3.4
16009-Suir at Cahir Park, Co. Tipperary	1583	Cal	1953–1980	0.84	0.84	6.16	-0.6
		Val	1991–2000	0.68	0.77	9.12	-12.1
19001-Owenboy at Ballea, Co. Cork	106	Cal	1974–1990	0.84	0.84	0.64	-1.9
		Val	1991–2010	0.83	0.88	0.57	-1.7
23002-Feale at Listowel, Co. Kerry	647	Cal	1974–1990	0.84	0.87	4.86	-11.2
		Val	1991–2010	0.87	0.88	4.61	-2.41
25006-Brosna at Ferbane, Co. Offaly	1163	Cal	1952–1960	0.89	0.85	3.58	-1.7
		Val	1961–1970	0.77	0.84	4.09	-5.4
26018-Owenure at Bellavahan, Co. Roscommon	119	Cal	1992–2000	0.89	0.87	0.59	1.3
		Val	1976–1980	0.92	0.93	0.39	0.8
27002-Fergus at Ballycorey, Co. Clare	564	Cal	1974–1985	0.88	0.88	2.18	6.4
		Val	1986–1990	0.79	0.81	2.44	-0.8
35005-Ballysadare at Ballysadare, Co. Sligo	640	Cal	1947–1960	0.84	0.84	2.84	-0.7
		Val	2002–2008	0.76	0.82	3.21	-4.6
38001-Owenea at Clonconwall Ford, Co. Donegal	111	Cal	1994–2000	0.91	0.95	0.88	1.7
		Val	2001–2003	0.89	0.91	0.78	-0.7

a couple of catchments (16009, 12001), overall models show an acceptable level of performance during both calibration and verification. The derived models for each catchment were then used to reconstruct monthly river flows at all twelve study catchments for the period 1850–2015. Fig 5 and Fig 6 show the reconstructed flows for the entire reconstructed period for winter and summer half years with observed flows overlaid for each study catchment.

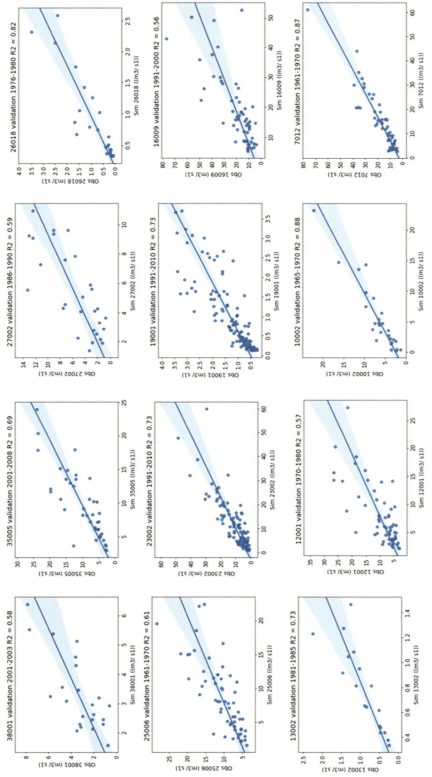

Fig. 4—Scatter plots of simulated and observed summer (April, May, June, July, August and September) half year flows (m^3/s^{-1}) for the verification period indicating the R^2 value at each study catchment between observed (Obs) and simulated (Sim) flows. The solid line indicates the best fit.

Simon Noone and Conor Murphy

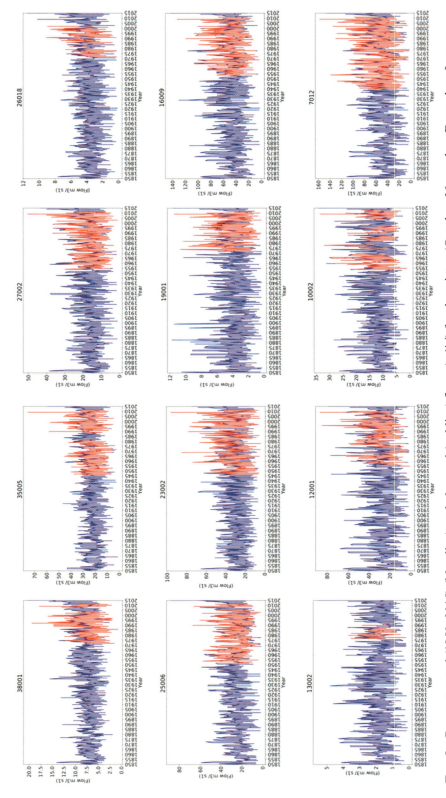

Fig. 5 — Reconstructed (1850–2015) (blue line) and observed (red line) flows (m^3/s^1) for the winter (October, November, December, January, February and March) half year for each of the twelve catchments.

Reconstruction of hydrological drought in irish catchments (1850–2015)

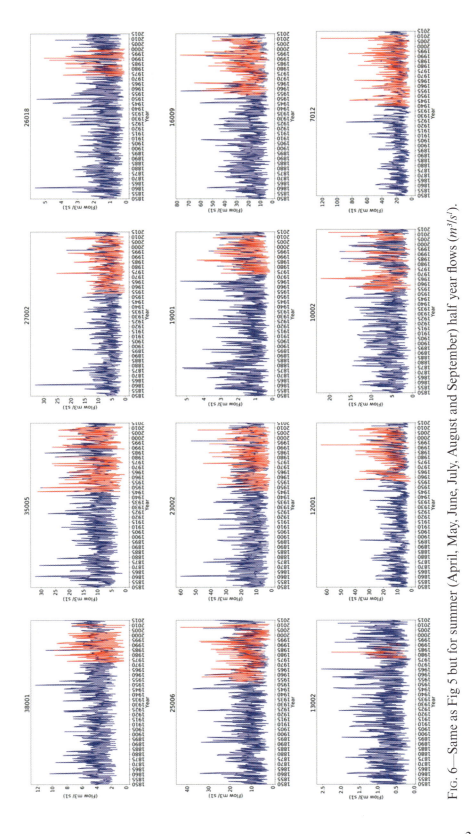

Fig. 6.—Same as Fig 5 but for summer (April, May, June, July, August and September) half year flows (m^3/s).

Q95 Threshold drought results

For the purpose of the drought analysis the following section will focus upon presenting detailed results and analysis for a selection of six study catchments. These have been chosen based on their location to provide good geographical coverage across Ireland and the selection includes catchments of varying size and characteristics. The six selected catchments are as follows: 38001-Owenea at Clonconwall Ford, County Donegal (North-West); 26018-Owenure at Bellavahan, County Roscommon (Mid-West); 7012-Boyne at Slane Castle, County Meath (East); 10002-Avonmore at Laragh, County Wicklow (East); 13002-Corock at Foulksmills, County Wexford (South-East), and 19001-Owenboy at Ballea, County Cork (South) (Fig. 1). We present the top ten ranked Q95 threshold deficit droughts based on drought duration for all twelve catchments in Table 6 of the Appendix of this paper.

Table 3 presents the top ten ranked droughts based on duration for catchments 38001 (North-West) and 26018 (Mid-West). Table 3 also shows the drought period start and end dates, together with the duration in months, the mean flow deficit in m^3/s^1 over the drought duration and the accumulated or total flow deficit in m^3/s^1 over the drought duration.

The results show that catchment 38001-Owenea, County Donegal (North-West) experienced the longest drought from January 1953 to the start of June 1953 with a duration of 5-months below the Q95 threshold. Other noteworthy droughts, each lasting four months, were experienced at 38001-Owenea during 1929, 1933, 1975 and 1984. The largest accumulated deficit at 38001-Owenea (-3.99 m^3/s^1) was experienced from September 1933 to January 1934. The results for 38001-Owenea also show a 3-month drought from March 1875 to the start of June 1875. There were also four two-month droughts with two occurring in 1855 and one each in 1856 and 1873.

The results shown in Table 3 for 26018-Owenure, County Roscommon, demonstrate that the longest drought, which was of seven months duration, occurred between May 1921 and December 1921. The largest accumulated deficit (-1.84 m^3/s^1) was also experienced during the drought of 1953. Droughts lasting six months occurred from April 1893 to the beginning of October 1893 and then again from February 1953 to the start of August 1953. There were three more four-month long droughts during 1891, 1941 and 1944. A further four droughts lasting three-months were identified during 1870, 1879 and 1887.

Table 4 shows the top ten drought events, ranked by duration, for the catchments 7012-Boyne, county Meath and 10002-Avonmore, county Wicklow both in the eastern region of the island. The longest drought at catchment 7012-Boyne occurred from January 1891 to September 1891 with flows persisting below simulated monthly Q95 threshold for eight months. The largest accumulated deficit (-51.82 m^3/s^1) also occurred during this drought period. Several droughts of 7-months duration were experienced in 1893–94, 1934, and again during 1953. In addition, droughts lasting four months were experienced during 1857–58,

TABLE 3—Top ten ranked Q95 drought events based on duration for catchments 38001 and 26018. The drought deficits are negative values derived from the Q95 (5th percentile) threshold across all months. A drought start period is defined when the reconstructed monthly flow value falls below the Q95 threshold and drought ends when the monthly flow value returns above the Q95 threshold. Table shows the drought period start and end dates together with the duration in months, mean low-flow deficit (m^3/s^1) and accumulated deficit (m^3/s^1 over the drought period. Note that the first month is inclusive in the drought duration but the end month noted is not inclusive in the drought duration.

Catchment	Rank	Drought Start	Drought end	Mean Q95 m^3/s^1 deficit	Accumulated Q95 m^3/s^1 Deficit	Drought duration months
38001 Owenea North-west BFI (0.28)	1	1953-01	1953-06	-0.20	-0.99	5
	2	1929-03	1929-07	-0.42	-1.66	4
	3	1933-09	1934-01	-1.00	-3.99	4
	4	1975-06	1975-10	-0.23	-0.94	4
	5	1984-06	1984-10	-0.51	-2.06	4
	6	1875-03	1875-06	-0.15	-0.45	3
	7	1855-01	1855-03	-0.28	-0.56	2
	8	1855-11	1856-01	-0.17	-0.35	2
	9	1856-03	1856-05	-0.06	-0.12	2
	10	1873-12	1874-02	-0.14	-0.28	2
26018 Owenure Mid-west BFI (0.72)	1	1921-05	1921-12	-0.26	-1.84	7
	2	1893-04	1893-10	-0.02	-0.12	6
	3	1953-02	1953-08	-0.22	-1.31	6
	4	1891-02	1891-06	-0.32	-1.27	4
	5	1941-07	1941-11	-0.03	-0.13	4
	6	1944-03	1944-07	-0.14	-0.55	4
	7	1858-01	1858-04	-0.03	-0.08	3
	8	1870-07	1870-10	-0.03	-0.08	3
	9	1879-11	1880-02	-0.33	-0.98	3
	10	1887-06	1887-09	-0.03	-0.08	3

1887, 1892 and 1933–34. Table 4 shows that catchment 10002-Avonmore experienced severe drought commencing at the start of April 1893 and lasting eight months until the beginning of December 1893. The same drought period produced the largest accumulated deficit (-6.18 m^3/s^1). There were three four-month long droughts during the years 1874, 1953 and 1976, several two-month droughts during in 1884, 1906–07, 1938, 1944 and 1978 and a two-month drought in 1854.

Table 5 shows the top ten Q95 drought events, ranked by duration, for catchments 13002-Corock at Foulksmills, county Wexford (South-East) and 19001-Owenboy at Ballea, county Cork (South). Results at catchment

TABLE 4—Same as Table 3 but for catchment 7012 and 10002.

Catchment	Rank	Drought Start	Drought end	Mean Q95 m^3/s^1 deficit	Accumulated Q95 m^3/s^1 Deficit	Drought duration months
7012 Boyne East BFI (0.68)	1	1891-01	1891-09	-6.48	-51.82	8
	2	1893-06	1894-01	-3.31	-23.19	7
	3	1934-02	1934-09	-6.12	-42.82	7
	4	1953-02	1953-09	-2.22	-15.56	7
	5	1857-12	1858-04	-1.69	-6.75	4
	6	1887-07	1887-11	-0.78	-3.12	4
	7	1892-03	1892-07	-0.93	-3.72	4
	8	1933-09	1934-01	-3.36	-13.45	4
	9	1870-07	1870-10	-0.62	-1.87	3
	10	1895-05	1895-08	-1.29	-3.88	3
10002 Avonmore East BFI (0.54)	1	1893-04	1893-12	-0.77	-6.18	8
	2	1874-04	1874-08	-0.41	-1.63	4
	3	1953-01	1953-05	-0.53	-2.13	4
	4	1976-05	1976-09	-0.38	-1.53	4
	5	1884-10	1885-01	-1.11	-3.34	3
	6	1906-12	1907-03	-1.17	-3.51	3
	7	1938-04	1938-07	-0.57	-1.70	3
	8	1944-06	1944-09	-0.06	-0.19	3
	9	1978-09	1978-12	-0.92	-2.77	3
	10	1854-03	1854-05	-0.13	-0.26	2

13002-Corock for December 1975 to the start of October 1976 indicate that the longest drought persisted for 10 months. The largest Q95 accumulated deficit (-1.98 m^3/s^1) also occurred during the drought of 1975–76. The drought from June 1887 to January 1888 was second longest, lasting 7 months. During 1891, 1893 and 1944 catchment 13002-Corock experienced a drought lasting 6 months.

In addition, between May 1905 and December 1906 drought persisted for 5 months and during May to October 1975 drought also lasted 5 months. Drought persisted for 4 months during 1888 and 1953 at catchment 13002-Corock and for 3 months during late 1854–55. For catchment 19001-Owenboy (Table 5) the longest drought started in February 1944 and persisted until September 1944. The second longest drought was experienced during 1887 from May to November and lasted 6 months. There were two 5-month long droughts during 1906–07 and in 1975. The results show that 19001-Owenboy experienced periods of drought with flows consistently below simulated Q95 for 6-months in 1854–55, 1874, 1891, 1921 and 1953, with the largest accumulated deficit (-2.55 m^3/s^1) occurring during the 1854–55 drought.

TABLE 5—Same as Table 4 but for catchment 13002 and 19001

Catchment	Rank	Drought Start	Drought end	Mean Q95 m³/s¹ deficit	Accumulated Q95 m³/s¹ Deficit	Drought duration months
13002 Corock South-east BFI (0.73)	1	1975-12	1976-10	-0.20	-1.98	10
	2	1887-06	1888-01	-0.07	-0.51	7
	3	1891-02	1891-08	-0.12	-0.73	6
	4	1893-06	1893-12	-0.04	-0.27	6
	5	1944-03	1944-09	-0.02	-0.10	6
	6	1906-12	1907-05	-0.22	-1.08	5
	7	1975-05	1975-10	-0.03	-0.14	5
	8	1888-02	1888-06	-0.12	-0.49	4
	9	1953-01	1953-05	-0.05	-0.21	4
	10	1854-12	1855-03	-0.17	-0.52	3
19001 Owenboy South BFI (0.68)	1	1944-02	1944-09	-0.16	-1.13	7
	2	1887-05	1887-11	-0.06	-0.36	6
	3	1906-12	1907-05	-0.51	-2.55	5
	4	1975-04	1975-09	-0.09	-0.45	5
	5	1854-03	1854-07	-0.05	-0.21	4
	6	1854-11	1855-03	-0.85	-3.39	4
	7	1874-06	1874-10	-0.06	-0.25	4
	8	1891-02	1891-06	-0.20	-0.81	4
	9	1921-06	1921-10	-0.05	-0.21	4
	10	1953-01	1953-05	-0.32	-1.29	4

Discussion

Key findings

This paper has reconstructed monthly river flows for twelve Irish catchments for the period 1850–2015. These catchments provide good spatial coverage and incorporate diverse catchment characteristics. Quality assured, long-term monthly precipitation records and long-term average PET data were used to reconstruct historical river flows for each catchment. Using the threshold method to identify droughts as periods during which flows fall below the long-term simulated monthly Q95 threshold, we identify notable drought events in each catchment. The results at six selected catchments are presented and discussed in detail, while the top 10 droughts (by duration) for all catchments are provided in Table 6 in the Appendix.

The results show that the most noteworthy drought years based on the drought indicator used were 1887–88, 1891–94, 1902–12, 1933–34, 1944, 1953, 1971–76. Previous work has compiled a 250-year historical meteorological drought catalogue for Ireland using the Standardised Precipitation Index (SPI) applied to 25 precipitation series contained in the Island of Ireland precipitation network (1850–2015) and a reconstructed precipitation series from 1765 representing the island of Ireland. Although, the previous study used a different drought indicator and concerned only meteorological drought, the periods highlighted as drought rich for the period 1850–2015 are generally consistent across both studies.[20]

Moreover, the identified drought years in this study show good coherence with studies conducted in the United Kingdom, which highlight the large spatial extent of some of the historical droughts. Drought rich periods are noted for many rivers in England and Wales during 1887–89, 1892–97, 1933–34 and 1975–76, which closely correspond to droughts identified in this study.[21] Our results also show that these Irish catchments have experienced a relatively drought sparse period since the 1980s up to 2015.

Limitations of this study and opportunities for future work

This work provides a first pass reconstruction of long-term river flows and as such there is much scope for improving this analysis. Conceptual Rainfall Runoff (CRR) models are a simplified representation of a complex catchment system and the selection of model structure is usually a subjective decision made by the modeller.[22] Some model parameters cannot be measured and need to be estimated; they are also assumed to be constant over time. It is widely acknowledged that most uncertainty in CRR models comes from model structures and parameter selection.[23] Equifinality exists where many model parameter combinations can generate a satisfactory simulation.[24] In addition, only one CRR model was employed in

---

[20] Noone *et al.*, 'A 250-year drought catalogue for the island of Ireland (1765–2015)', 239–54.

[21] Lennard *et al.*, 'The application of a drought reconstruction in water resource management', 646–59; Spraggs, 'Re-construction of historic drought in the Anglian Region (UK) over the period 1798–2010 and the implications for water resources and drought management', 231–52; T. Marsh, G. Cole and R. Wilby, 'Major droughts in England and Wales, 1800–2006', *Weather*, 62 (2007), 87–93; Todd *et al.*, 'Severity, duration and frequency of drought in SE England from 1697 to 2011', *Climate Change*, 121:4 (2013), 673–87. doi:10.1007/s10584-013-0970-6.

[22] Murphy *et al.*, 'The reliability of an "off-the-shelf" conceptual rainfall runoff model for use in climate impact assessment: uncertainty quantification using Latin hypercube sampling', 65–78; Wagener *et al.*, 'Towards reduced uncertainty in conceptual rainfall-runoff modelling: Dynamic identifiability analysis', *Hydrological Processes*, 17:2 (2003), 455–76.

[23] Murphy *et al.*, 'The reliability of an "off-the-shelf" conceptual rainfall runoff model for use in climate impact assessment: uncertainty quantification using Latin hypercube sampling', 65–78.

[24] Wagener *et al.*, 'Towards reduced uncertainty in conceptual rainfall-runoff modelling: Dynamic identifiability analysis', 455–76; R. Wilby, 'Uncertainty in water resource model parameters used for climate change impact assessment', *Hydrological Processes*, 19 (2005), 3201–19.

this study; future work could use other CRR models and modelling techniques to explore additional model structures in reconstructing Irish river flow.

Overall good model performance was maintained even when this study was required to use rainfall stations outside of catchment boundaries. However, increasing the number of long-term rainfall stations available as part of the IIP would also increase confidence in reconstructed flows. Furthermore, gridded reconstructions of precipitation and temperature exist for Europe over the period 1766 to present and their potential for reconstructing river flows should be investigated.[25] A greater spatial distribution of rainfall data would also facilitate an increased sample of catchments for reconstruction so that a more in depth understanding of the role of catchment characteristics in drought propagation could be explored. Here longer droughts seem to be associated with catchments with higher groundwater contribution to river flows; our sample size is too small to draw robust results.

Work is ongoing at the Irish Climate Analysis and Research Units (ICARUS) at Maynooth University in collaboration with Met Éireann to digitise and transcribe daily precipitation records dating back to the nineteenth century in Ireland.[26] These daily precipitation records could be used to expand the IIP monthly network. These daily precipitation records could also be employed to run catchment rainfall runoff models to produce daily reconstructed flow records back to the late nineteenth century to examine variability and change in hydrological extremes more closely.

Another limitation of this study is the lack of long-term temperature records for Ireland. There are monthly temperature records available at Markree (West), Birr (Midlands) and Dublin (East) with records dating back to 1830 but these have not yet been homogenised or quality assured. There are further long-term hard copy daily temperature records in the Met Éireann archives. Researchers at the National University of Galway are in the process of digitising and transcribing these records and they will apply homogenisation methods for data quality assurance.[27] Given that PET is temperature driven, the long-term average PET data used in this study does not take any increase in temperature over the period into account. Future work could address this limitation. Furthermore, the influence of snow during colder periods can cause modelling output errors.[28] In addressing this

---

[25] Pauling *et al.*, 'Five hundred years of gridded high-resolution precipitation reconstructions over Europe and the connection to large-scale circulation', *Climate Dynamics*, 26 (2006), 387–405.

[26] Ryan *et al.*, 'Ireland's pre-1940 rainfall records', *Geoscience Data Journal*, (2020), forthcoming; Ryan *et al.*, 'Integrating data rescue into the classroom', *Bulletin of the American Meteorological Society*, 99:9 (2018), 1757–64.

[27] C. Mateus, A. Potito and M. Curley, 'Reconstruction of a long-term historical daily maximum and minimum air temperature network dataset for Ireland (1831–1968)', *Geoscience Data Journal* (2020), 1–14. https://doi.org/10.1002/gdj3.92.

[28] P.D. Jones, 'Riverflow reconstruction from precipitation data', *Journal of Climatology*, 4 (1984), 171–86.

issue future work could incorporate the long-term temperature records into the CRR models to simulate snow and snow melt. Finally, as with any approach to river flow reconstruction we assume consistent land-use and channel geomorphology over the period of reconstruction. These assumptions are unlikely to hold, but nonetheless assessment of reconstructed flows for catchments in their contemporary state is a useful endeavour for informing variability and change.

Implications

The 1995 drought is often used as the event of record from a water management perspective.[29] Yet the 1995 drought does not feature in the top ten ranked drought events based on duration, as more severe droughts have been identified during the nineteenth century. The past 40 years appear to have been a relatively drought poor period in hydrological terms. However, during 2018 Ireland experienced a very dry summer with the combined three-month rainfall totals (May, June and July) at Phoenix Park, Dublin the lowest on record.[30] The study used the Standardised Precipitation and Evapotranspiration Index (SPEI) to calculate the three-month accumulated deficit (SPEI-3).[31] The value for SPEI-3 for May to July 2018 was -2.70, the most extreme value on record at Phoenix Park. The drought of 2018 caused water supply issues with restrictions in place for most of the summer. As the situation worsened, the utility company Irish Water warned in early August that Dublin would run out of water supply within 70 days if drought conditions continued.[32] During 2020 the east and Dublin region experienced the lowest spring (March, April and May (MAM)) rainfall totals since records began in 1837 at Phoenix Park. In addition, the combined rainfall totals for April to May ranked as the driest consecutive two months ever recorded at Phoenix Park.[33] In the past three years Ireland, and especially the densely populated regions across the east and Dublin, have experienced two extreme three-month drought periods due to rainfall deficits. These recent droughts

---

[29] M. MacCarthaigh, *An assessment of the 1995 drought including a comparison with other known drought years* (Environmental Protection Agency, Wexford, 1996), 70.

[30] S. Noone, C. Murphy and P. Thorne, 'The ongoing flash drought is (probably) the most intense experienced at Phoenix Park since records began', Irish Climate Analysis and Research Units, Maynooth University, Ireland, 2018), http://icarus-maynooth.blogspot.com/2018/08/the-ongoing-flash-drought-is-probably.html (accessed 28/05/2019).

[31] Beguería *et al.*, 'Standardized precipitation evapotranspiration index (SPEI) revisited: parameter fitting, evapotranspiration models, tools, datasets and drought monitoring', *International Journal of Climatology*, 34 (2014), 3001–23. doi:10.1002/joc.3887

[32] *Irish Times*, 7 Aug. 2018: https://www.irishtimes.com/news/ireland/irish-news/dublin-could-run-out-of-water-in-70-days-irish-water-warns-1.3589156 (accessed 28/05/2019).

[33] S. Noone and C. Murphy '2020: the driest spring in Dublin since records began in 1837', Irish Climate Analysis and Research Units, Maynooth University, Ireland, 2020. http://icarus-maynooth.blogspot.com/2020/05/2020-driest-spring-in-dublin-since.html (accessed 29/07/2020).

caused severe water supply issues but are significantly shorter than the historical droughts identified in recent research.[34]

The results of this study indicate that catchments located in the south, midlands, east and south-east have been prone to long duration hydrological droughts in the past. For example, flows persisted below monthly Q95 for a period of ten months at 13002-Corock in the south-east from the start of December 1975 to beginning of October 1976. In addition, drought at 7012-Boyne in the east lasted for eight months during 1891. Therefore, if future droughts like those experienced in the past reoccur, they may have serious implications for water supply and water quality in vulnerable regions.

Conclusion

Reconstructed monthly flows for twelve catchments were derived and analysed to identify historical hydrological droughts. The results identified seven major hydrological drought rich periods which affected most study catchments. While the methods available to reconstruct flows are subject to limitations, the consistency of the timing of these drought periods with those identified in previous work, both in Ireland and the UK, builds confidence in the subsequent results, which provide new insights into historical river flow and droughts in Ireland. This work also provides a basis from which future research can build, to expand the spatial and temporal context of river flow reconstructions and to develop fuller estimates of the uncertainties associated with reconstructions and hydrological droughts.

---

[34] Noone *et al.*, 'A 250-year drought catalogue for the island of Ireland (1765–2015)', 239–54.

Appendix supplementary material

Appendix tables present the top ten ranked Q95 drought events based on duration for all catchments. The drought deficits are negative values derived from the Q95 (5th percentile) threshold across all months. A drought start period is defined when the reconstructed monthly flow value falls below the Q95 threshold and drought ends when the monthly flow value returns above the Q95 threshold. The tables show the drought period start and end dates together with the duration in months, mean low-flow deficit (m^3/s^1) and accumulated deficit (m^3/s^1) over the drought period. Note that the first month is inclusive in the drought duration but the end month noted is not inclusive in the drought duration.

Catchment	Rank	Drought Start	Drought end	Mean Q95 m^3/s^1 deficit	Accumulated Q95 m^3/s^1 Deficit	Drought duration months
38001 Northwest BFI (0.28)	1	1953-01	1953-06	-0.20	-0.99	5
	2	1929-03	1929-07	-0.42	-1.66	4
	3	1933-09	1934-01	-1.00	-3.99	4
	4	1975-06	1975-10	-0.23	-0.94	4
	5	1984-06	1984-10	-0.51	-2.06	4
	6	1875-03	1875-06	-0.15	-0.45	3
	7	1855-01	1855-03	-0.28	-0.56	2
	8	1855-11	1856-01	-0.17	-0.35	2
	9	1856-03	1856-05	-0.06	-0.12	2
	10	1873-12	1874-02	-0.14	-0.28	2

Catchment	Rank	Drought Start	Drought end	Mean Q95 m^3/s^1 deficit	Accumulated Q95 m^3/s^1 Deficit	Drought duration months
35005 West BFI (0.61)	1	1864-02	1864-11	-1.08	-9.70	9
	2	1953-01	1953-08	-1.69	-11.85	7
	3	1956-02	1956-07	-1.17	-5.87	5
	4	1941-07	1941-11	-0.60	-2.41	4
	5	1856-10	1857-01	-1.37	-4.11	3
	6	1890-05	1890-08	-0.07	-0.22	3
	7	1891-02	1891-05	-1.17	-3.51	3
	8	1893-06	1893-09	-0.02	-0.05	3
	9	1929-04	1929-07	-0.73	-2.20	3
	10	1975-07	1975-08	-0.34	-0.69	2

Catchment	Rank	Drought Start	Drought end	Mean Q95 m³/s¹ deficit	Accumulated Q95 m³/s¹ Deficit	Drought duration months
27002 West BFI (0.70)	1	1891-02	1891-08	-0.57	-3.40	6
	2	1893-04	1893-10	-0.24	-1.42	6
	3	1953-02	1953-08	-1.25	-7.51	6
	4	1879-11	1880-03	-1.34	-5.38	4
	5	1887-06	1887-10	-0.17	-0.67	4
	6	1895-06	1895-10	-0.19	-0.78	4
	7	1944-03	1944-07	-0.41	-1.64	4
	8	1902-08	1902-11	-0.38	-1.14	3
	9	1905-07	1905-10	-0.21	-0.62	3
	10	1933-10	1934-01	-3.47	-10.41	3

Catchment	Rank	Drought Start	Drought end	Mean Q95 m³/s¹ deficit	Accumulated Q95 m³/s¹ Deficit	Drought duration months
26018 West BFI (0.72)	1	1921-05	1921-12	-0.26	-1.84	7
	2	1893-04	1893-10	-0.02	-0.12	6
	3	1953-02	1953-08	-0.22	-1.31	6
	4	1891-02	1891-06	-0.32	-1.27	4
	5	1941-07	1941-11	-0.03	-0.13	4
	6	1944-03	1944-07	-0.14	-0.55	4
	7	1858-01	1858-04	-0.03	-0.08	3
	8	1870-07	1870-10	-0.03	-0.08	3
	9	1879-11	1880-02	-0.33	-0.98	3
	10	1887-06	1887-09	-0.03	-0.08	3

Catchment	Rank	Drought Start	Drought end	Mean Q95 m³/s¹ deficit	Accumulated Q95 m³/s¹ Deficit	Drought duration months
25006 Midlands BFI (0.71)	1	1887-07	1888-04	-1.29964	-11.6968	9
	2	1850-01	1850-08	-1.71125	-11.9788	7
	3	1864-04	1864-10	-0.29988	-1.79925	6
	4	1973-03	1973-09	-1.00088	-6.00525	6
	5	1976-04	1976-10	-0.83921	-5.03525	6
	6	1891-02	1891-07	-1.4809	-7.4045	5
	7	1953-03	1953-08	-0.63385	-3.16925	5
	8	2004-05	2004-10	-0.4824	-2.412	5
	9	1911-06	1911-10	-0.10513	-0.4205	4
	10	1956-04	1956-08	-0.25294	-1.01175	4

Catchment	Rank	Drought Start	Drought end	Mean Q95 m³/s¹ deficit	Accumulated Q95 m³/s¹ Deficit	Drought duration months
23002 Southwest BFI (0.31)	1	1893-03	1893-08	-0.61	-3.06	5
	2	1902-07	1902-11	-0.82	-3.27	4
	3	1933-09	1934-01	-2.63	-10.53	4
	4	1953-03	1953-07	-1.95	-7.78	4
	5	1971-05	1971-09	-0.15	-0.60	4
	6	1879-11	1880-02	-2.97	-8.91	3
	7	1887-06	1887-09	-0.33	-0.98	3
	8	1895-05	1895-08	-0.31	-0.92	3
	9	1929-04	1929-07	-0.37	-1.12	3
	10	1852-04	1852-06	-0.15	-0.31	2

Catchment	Rank	Drought Start	Drought end	Mean Q95 m³/s¹ deficit	Accumulated Q95 m³/s¹ Deficit	Drought duration months
19001 South BFI (0.68)	1	1944-02	1944-09	-0.16	-1.13	7
	2	1887-05	1887-11	-0.06	-0.36	6
	3	1906-12	1907-05	-0.51	-2.55	5
	4	1975-04	1975-09	-0.09	-0.45	5
	5	1854-03	1854-07	-0.05	-0.21	4
	6	1854-11	1855-03	-0.85	-3.39	4
	7	1874-06	1874-10	-0.06	-0.25	4
	8	1891-02	1891-06	-0.20	-0.81	4
	9	1921-06	1921-10	-0.05	-0.21	4
	10	1953-01	1953-05	-0.32	-1.29	4

Catchment	Rank	Drought Start	Drought end	Mean Q95 m³/s¹ deficit	Accumulated Q95 m³/s¹ Deficit	Drought duration months
16009 South BFI (0.63)	1	1887-05	1887-11	-1.25	-7.50	6
	2	1921-07	1922-01	-4.12	-24.70	6
	3	1854-11	1855-03	-5.28	-21.10	4
	4	1864-06	1864-10	-0.07	-0.29	4
	5	1893-04	1893-08	-1.62	-6.49	4
	6	1850-01	1850-04	-5.27	-15.80	3
	7	1854-03	1854-06	-3.23	-9.70	3
	8	1874-05	1874-08	-0.31	-0.94	3
	9	1879-11	1880-02	-6.31	-18.94	3
	10	1884-09	1884-12	-3.29	-9.87	3

Catchment	Rank	Drought Start	Drought end	Mean $Q95\ m^3/s^1$ deficit	Accumulated $Q95\ m^3/s^1$ Deficit	Drought duration months
13002 Southeast BFI (0.73)	1	1975-12	1976-10	-0.20	-1.98	10
	2	1887-06	1888-01	-0.07	-0.51	7
	3	1891-02	1891-08	-0.12	-0.73	6
	4	1893-06	1893-12	-0.04	-0.27	6
	5	1944-03	1944-09	-0.02	-0.10	6
	6	1906-12	1907-05	-0.22	-1.08	5
	7	1975-05	1975-10	-0.03	-0.14	5
	8	1888-02	1888-06	-0.12	-0.49	4
	9	1953-01	1953-05	-0.05	-0.21	4
	10	1854-12	1855-03	-0.17	-0.52	3

Catchment	Rank	Drought Start	Drought end	Mean $Q95\ m^3/s^1$ deficit	Accumulated $Q95\ m^3/s^1$ Deficit	Drought duration months
12001 Southeast BFI (0.72)	1	1893-06	1894-01	-1.43	-10.01	7
	2	1944-03	1944-10	-1.05	-7.38	7
	3	2015-01	2015-08	-1.03	-7.19	7
	4	1887-07	1888-01	-0.42	-2.55	6
	5	1953-02	1953-07	-1.15	-5.75	5
	6	1874-06	1874-10	-0.39	-1.58	4
	7	1891-03	1891-07	-1.09	-4.36	4
	8	1907-01	1907-05	-5.19	-20.77	4
	9	1941-07	1941-11	-0.36	-1.42	4
	10	1854-12	1855-03	-3.58	-10.74	3

Catchment	Rank	Drought Start	Drought end	Mean $Q95\ m^3/s^1$ deficit	Accumulated $Q95\ m^3/s^1$ Deficit	Drought duration months
10002 Southeast BFI (0.54)	1	1893-04	1893-12	-0.77	-6.18	8
	2	1874-04	1874-08	-0.41	-1.63	4
	3	1953-01	1953-05	-0.53	-2.13	4
	4	1976-05	1976-09	-0.38	-1.53	4
	5	1884-10	1885-01	-1.11	-3.34	3
	6	1906-12	1907-03	-1.17	-3.51	3
	7	1938-04	1938-07	-0.57	-1.70	3
	8	1944-06	1944-09	-0.06	-0.19	3
	9	1978-09	1978-12	-0.92	-2.77	3
	10	1854-03	1854-05	-0.13	-0.26	2

Catchment	Rank	Drought Start	Drought end	Mean $Q95\ m^3/s^1$ deficit	Accumulated $Q95\ m^3/s^1$ Deficit	Drought duration months
7012 East BFI (0.68)	1	1891-01	1891-09	-6.48	-51.82	8
	2	1893-06	1894-01	-3.31	-23.19	7
	3	1934-02	1934-09	-6.12	-42.82	7
	4	1953-02	1953-09	-2.22	-15.56	7
	5	1857-12	1858-04	-1.69	-6.75	4
	6	1887-07	1887-11	-0.78	-3.12	4
	7	1892-03	1892-07	-0.93	-3.72	4
	8	1933-09	1934-01	-3.36	-13.45	4
	9	1870-07	1870-10	-0.62	-1.87	3
	10	1895-05	1895-08	-1.29	-3.88	3

Climate and society in modern Ireland: past and future vulnerabilities

JOHN SWEENEY*

Maynooth University

[Accepted 2 September 2020. Published 30 October 2020.]

Abstract

Sitting astride the main storm tracks of the North Atlantic, Ireland's location has historically rendered it vulnerable to the vicissitudes of weather and climate. Throughout the nineteenth century and for much of the twentieth century, the imperative of achieving a food, fodder and fuel surplus meant agrarian Irish society was a greater hostage to climate than many other parts of Europe where the Industrial Revolution had enabled the worst effects of the Little Ice Age to be mitigated. Closer examination of society–climate relationships has been facilitated by documentary sources and by direct observations from the nineteenth century onwards, which have provided new insights into Irish climate hazards such as storms, floods and droughts. As Ireland modernised, new concerns such as urban flooding emerged, and new ways of managing climate risks were devised. Ultimately though, as more benign climatic conditions in the mid-nineteenth century gave way to more instability and rapid warming in the twentieth and early twenty first, the need for adaptation and mitigation of climate change became evident. Improvements in global and regional climate modelling and forecasting were instrumental in assisting with this. However, Irish society has been slow to react to climate change concerns and only through a series of catalytic extreme events has public and political attitudes shifted, induced by both 'bottom-up' activism and 'top-down' international agreements. Accordingly, Ireland is now on the threshold of taking the radical steps necessary to shed its 'climate laggard' status and embark on the road to a post-carbon society.

Introduction

Though the conclusion in the nineteenth century of the Little Ice Age (LIA) was accompanied by an improvement in average annual air temperature, Ireland remained highly vulnerable to the vagaries of climate. The omnipresent preoccupation with fodder, fuel and food was magnified during the first half of the century by a rapidly rising population. On top of this, the lingering effects of the Little Ice Age continued to be felt and it would be the middle of the century before consistent mildness was experienced. (Ironically the mildness of 1845/6

---

*Author's email: john.sweeney@mu.ie
doi: https://doi.org/10.3318/PRIAC.2020.120.12

brought its own negative consequences as it facilitated the spread of potato blight, which was the source of the Great Famine—the single greatest environmental catastrophe since the Great Frost Famine of 1740–41.) Moreover, the recovery from the harsh winters of the LIA was punctuated by extreme events which brought further challenges to Irish society.

Climate and weather from the nineteenth century to the present

In 1801, Ireland had a population of 5.2 million. The corresponding population of England was 8.9 million. A century later Ireland had 4.5 million people while England had 32.5 million. The Industrial Revolution fundamentally changed the respective demographic and economic positions of the two countries. The Industrial Revolution also strongly incentivised organised weather observations. In the crowded industrial cities of Europe, public health and sanitation became a matter of great concern once the link was established between disease, sanitation and living conditions. A reliable water supply and sewerage network needed objectively measured data on rainfall and river resources. In an Ireland largely bypassed by the Industrial Revolution, it was 'Big House' astronomical observatories such as Armagh (1790), Birr (1845), Dunsink (1788) and Markree (1824) that formed the early observational nucleus. These were all inland. However, many of the climate gradients in Ireland are coastal-interior orientated. This reflects the importance of oceanic influences on temperature and temperature-related parameters such as frost days and measures of the growing season. The skeletal observational network did not address marine issues from the outset. It took the loss of 459 lives in 1854 when a storm sunk the passenger ship Royal Charter off Anglesey to prompt the establishment, at the instigation of Admiral Robert Fitzroy (1805–65), of 15 coastal weather stations across Britain and Ireland. A key component of this network was Valentia, which provided a telegraphic link to the UK to service the transatlantic cable that was laid in 1856. Since then, Ireland's west coast weather stations have acted as valuable sentinels for Atlantic storm systems, providing early warning to locations further east in Europe.

The fear of storm, which lies deep in the Irish psyche, was intensified as early instrumental records emerged. Perhaps the most potent nineteenth-century reminder to Irish society was provided on the night of the Epiphany, 6 January 1839—Oíche na Gaoithe Móire, the Night of the Big Wind—when the country was impacted by a depression which may have had a central pressure as low as 918hPa.[1] At any event, 250–300 people perished, 42 ships were wrecked, 20–25 per cent of the houses in Dublin city were destroyed or damaged, and several thousand trees were blown down. Vegetation was drenched in brine

---

[1] L. Shields and D. Fitzgerald, 'The "Night of the Big Wind" in Ireland, 6–7 January 1839', *Irish Geography* 22:1 (1989), 31–43.

up to 15km from the coast (with anecdotal accounts of herring and other fish being deposited 6km inland). Stacks of hay and corn were devastated by fire, as were many thatched houses, which were disproportionately the residents of the less well off. Such losses may have diminished their capacity to cope with the Great Famine, which was to descend on the island in 1845. So deeply was the event etched in the folk memory that when old age pensions were introduced in Ireland seventy years later, memory of the event was used by the authorities to establish the entitlement of some septuagenarians who could not furnish a birth certificate.

Most storm events in Ireland tend to be felt on a national scale. It is relatively infrequent for an event to be limited to a locality. Such an event occurred on 18 April 1850 in Dublin when the city was subject to its most destructive hailstorm.[2] This storm was accompanied by walnut-sized hailstones which shattered thousands of window panes and roof slates in addition to causing considerable property damage. In College Park, ten trees fell towards the north west at the beginning of the storm while nine trees fell towards the south east later.[3] As the centre of the storm appears to have been distinguishable as it passed directly through the city, it may well have been a tornado. Certainly the damage costs were estimated at 40% of the 1839 event.

The impacts of weather extremes on Irish society in the pre-instrumental period are well documented in Irish newspapers. Titles, such as the *Belfast Newsletter* (1738-present) and the *Freeman's Journal* (1763–1924), and regional newspapers such as the *Kerry Evening Post* (1813–1917), *Tuam Herald* (1837–1955) and *Nenagh Tribune* (1838-present) are a useful source of information on the effects of the weather from the early nineteenth century, and they are augmented from the mid and later decades by the proliferation in local titles in the second half of the century.[4] Of course it is important to interpret reports carefully—the nature and severity of weather events reported echoes the concerns of the middle and better off classes rather than the poor urban dweller or subsistence farmer. But they assist in the construction of the relationship between weather events and Irish society.[5] They also help contextualise the contemporary events such as Storm Emma in 2018 by illustrating the nature and impact of past bitterly cold winters such as that in 1783/84.[6] Noone *et al.* (2017) have also demonstrated the utility of such sources in reconstructing drought

---

[2] F.E. Dixon, 'Weather in Old Dublin', Dublin Historical Record, 13:3 (1953), 94–107.

[3] F.E. Dixon, 'Weather in Old Dublin Part II', Dublin Historical Record, 15:3 (1959), 65–73.

[4] M.L. Legg, *Newspapers and nationalism: the Irish provincial press 1850–1892* (Dublin, 1999).

[5] John Sweeney, 'A three-century storm climatology for Dublin, 1715-2000', *Irish Geography* 33:1 (2002), 1–14.

[6] Conor Murphy, 'An icy blast from the past', *Weather* 74:2 (2019), 74; James Kelly, 'Weather, climate and society in Ireland in the long eighteenth century: the experience of later phases of the Little Ice Age', *Proceedings of the Royal Irish Academy*, 120C (2020).

events and their societal impacts.[7] This has alerted us to persistent multi-season drought episodes in the nineteenth and twentieth centuries. Ireland, it transpires, is much more drought-prone than commonly perceived, with recent decades being unrepresentative of the longer-term drought climatology. During the years 1850–2015 for example Irish society had to cope with seven major island-wide drought-rich periods: 1854–60, 1884–96, 1904–12, 1921–23, 1932–35, 1952–54 and 1969–77. Such work provides important yardsticks for calibrating the magnitude and frequency changes that can be expected under future changed climate conditions.

The years 1800 to 1809, for example, was one of the most sustained drought events over the past 250 years, resulting in the importation of emergency supplies of grain and maize from the U.S., the failure of the potato crop, and great distress for those dependent on the water-powered woollen and linen industries. Again, in 1887, a persistent blocking anticyclone settled over Ireland. Commencing in early spring and only breaking down in November, the drought caused crop failure and public water supply crises, which were at their most acute in the east of the country. Murphy *et al.* (2017) report public health concerns in Dublin due to stagnant sewers and also a call to pray for rain from the Church of Ireland Bishop of Meath in the *Irish Times* in early July 1887.[8]

The interactions between extreme climate events and society are well demonstrated by drought situations. The Dublin water crisis of 1893 is a case in point. By late summer, a drought commencing in the spring threatened the city's supply from the reservoir at Vartry. Despite major reductions in supply and lengthy periods when water was cut off, by the autumn the city was down to its last 16 days of supply. The crisis prompted an extensive debate on how new supplies might be obtained. Damming Lough Dan in Wicklow, piping water from the River Avoca, tunnelling through the watershed between Lough Tay and Lough Dan, exploding dynamite above the city to make rain, were just some of the ideas discussed. It is striking how radical suggestions emerge during severe events, only to wither on the vine once the memory fades. Floods and droughts tend to diminish quickly in importance in Irish public consciousness as the more short-term priorities of daily life take over.

Increasing urbanisation and increased overseas trade in the twentieth century changed Irish society's priorities regarding climate hazards. Intense rainfall events and urban flooding assumed greater importance in the public consciousness as property values increased and concerns for food security decreased. Forecasting skills improved steadily and the value of observations became apparent. The early warning capability of Irish observations for Britain

---

[7] Noone *et al.*, 'A 250 year drought catalogue for the island of Ireland (1765–2015)', *International Journal of Climatology*, 37:S1 (2017), 239–54.

[8] Murphy *et al.*, 'Irish droughts in newspaper archives: rediscovering forgotten hazards?', *Weather*, 72:6 (2017), 151–55.

and Europe was particularly important, and is well demonstrated by the crucial role observations at Blacksod in Co. Mayo played in the timing of the 1944 D-Day landings. The importance of good quality weather data for the transatlantic flying boats service from Foynes in Co. Limerick was also instrumental in the establishment of the Irish Meteorological Service in 1936.

As better understanding of the internal structure of mid latitude depressions is established, better forecasting of major events was also developed. But still, events could cause surprises. The Mount Merrion storm of 11 June 1963 for example dumped over 184.2mm on the Ballsbridge area of Dublin, with over 75mm of it in a single hour.[9] In many ways this event illustrated the new relationship that was developing between modernising Irish society and climate hazards. Urban flooding was henceforth the number one preoccupation.

Many of Ireland's towns and cities are located close to upland catchments that respond rapidly to high rainfall events. While some large rivers have been partially tamed by dams, vulnerability to smaller rivers, swelled up by high rainfall events in their upper courses, has increased significantly as impermeable urban surfaces spread. Such vulnerability was well demonstrated by 'Hurricane Charley' in August 1986. It is not that unusual for the tail end of a hurricane to reach Ireland in late summer/autumn. Heavily laden with water vapour, any forced ascent can result in large quantities of rain, as was the case with Charley. An estimated 280mm fell on the mountains of Wicklow, sending huge amounts of water along the Dodder, Dargle and other rivers down to lower levels (Fig 1). Even at low levels the rainfall received set a new national record of 200mm at Kilcoole, south of Greystones. The worst flooding for over a century in Dublin ensued with over 400 properties affected, some to depths of 2.5m.

As the twentieth century drew to a close, extreme events were more widely reported. This was due in part to an improved monitoring network, but also to increased public sensitivity and awareness. Greater scrutiny of established methods to protect society from extreme events emerged. For society it is the case that a trade-off will always exist between 100% protection and the high cost of bringing this about. Accordingly, a measure of risk generally deemed to be acceptable has for long been used. A well-established practice of characterising extreme events in terms of their probability of occurrence has been employed, especially for infrastructure such as bridges, dams and flood protection measures. Thus the 1-in-100 year event is calculated from a statistical analysis where a sufficient run of data is available, and structures are designed to withstand what is deemed commensurate with such a risk. Accordingly, for example, a major rainfall event on 27/28 October 1989 at Belmullet was described as having a return period in excess of 100 years, and another event on 11 June 1993 at Casement Aerodrome was described as having a 250-year

---

[9] W.A. Morgan, 'Rainfall in the Dublin area on 11th June, 1963', Irish Meteorological Service Internal Memorandum IM 72/71 (Dublin, 1963), 1–8.

Fig. 1—The River Dodder reaching the parapet at Ballsbridge, Dublin during 'Hurricane Charley', 25–26 August 1986. (Photograph: Courtesy *The Irish Times*)

return period.[10] Underlying all of this was the assumption that the database that was used reflected a stationary time series. In the event of a trend embedded in the data, such calculations become unreliable. It became increasingly clear in the late twentieth century that this assumption of stationarity was not justified. Irish climate itself was changing and society would need to adjust to a whole new relationship.

Notwithstanding the occasional exceptional extreme storm event, it is clear that the middle to the end of the nineteenth century was marked by more quiescent and benign climate conditions. A greater frequency of anticyclonic conditions would seem to have prevailed, with fewer storms and generally milder conditions. Butler *et al.* (2005) noted these milder conditions at Armagh Observatory during the middle part of the century,[11] lasting roughly until 1870. From the 1890s onwards, however, all this was to change. A new period of instability emerged as Ireland began to warm more quickly. By the mid-twentieth century around 0.5°C of warming had occurred and, after a mid-century lull, the late twentieth century was marked by further rapid warming. Irish climate was no longer fluctuating according to natural drivers alone. Now it was

---

[10] Met Eireann, Major Weather Events, 2019. Available from: http://www.met.ie/climate/weather-extreme-records (accessed 15 Feb. 2019).
[11] Butler *et al.*, 'Air temperatures at Armagh Observatory, Northern Ireland, from 1796 to 2002', *International Journal of Climatology*, 25 (2005), 1055–79.

becoming clear that global forcing in response to anthropogenic influences was involved. The Anthropocene had arrived.

New societal awareness of vulnerability in an age of climate change

In 1985 the International Council for Science, together with the World Meteorological Organisation (WMO) and the United Nations Environment Programme (UNEP), staged a major conference in Austria which concluded that greenhouse gases could warm the earth by several degrees. While this was to some extent a re-statement of the validity of the pioneering work of the nineteenth-century Irish scientist John Tyndall and the Swedish scientist Svante Arrhenius, what was different was the acceptance that this was the current trajectory of earth's climate, and that actions were required to address this. As a result, WMO and UNEP established the Intergovernmental Panel on Climate Change (IPCC) in 1988, whose Assessment Reports, published every six or seven years, have laid the foundation for efforts to address global warming. These scientific outputs were used by the United Nations Framework Convention on Climate Change, which was established after the Rio Earth Summit of 1992, in their development of emission mitigation strategies.

Climate change was not deemed a serious issue in Ireland, however, at either the academic or public level for a number of years after the IPCC commenced its activities. Some researchers did suggest that rainfall receipt across Ireland would change should the frequency of particular synoptic circulations alter;[12] but climate modelling was only embarked on its rapid development [13] and it was not possible to downscale even the crude outputs from these with confidence. The first national impact assessment for Ireland merely used hypothetical temperature and rainfall parameters to guide their conclusions.[14] However, rapid advances in computing power modelling after the turn of the century meant it was possible not only to produce scenarios of what future Irish climate might look like, but also to use outputs to drive impacts models in areas of wider interest for society and to pose some major questions.[15] How would water availability

---

[12] John Sweeney, 'The changing synoptic climatology of Irish rainfall', Transactions of the Institute of British Geographers, 10:4 (1985), 467–80; John Sweeney, *Global change and the Irish environment* (Royal Irish Academy, Dublin, 1997).

[13] P. Lynch, 'Climate modelling', in John Feehan (ed.), *Climate variation and climate change in Ireland?* (Environmental Institute, University College Dublin, 1994).

[14] Brendan McWilliams, Climatic change: studies on the implications for Ireland (Department of the Environment, Dublin, 1992).

[15] John Sweeney and R. Fealy, 'Future climate scenarios for Ireland using high resolution statistical downscaling techniques', in F. Convery and J. Feehan (eds) Achievement and challenge, Rio+10 and Ireland (Environmental Institute, University College Dublin, 2002), 172–79; John Sweeney, *Climate change: Scenarios and impacts for Ireland* (Environmental Protection Agency, Johnstown Castle, Wexford, 2003); McGrath *et al.*, *Climate change: regional climate model predictions for Ireland* (Environmental Protection Agency, Wexford, 2003).

change?[16] How would yields of agricultural crops such as potatoes change?[17] How would forests change?[18] For some crops, the direct effect of having higher carbon dioxide concentrations in the atmosphere could be expected to increase yields; but only if other limitations did not exist. So cereal crops in Ireland could be expected to do as well as at present, if not better, under the future projected conditions, with maize being a particular winner. But other crops such as grass and potatoes would not welcome the drier summers projected. Livestock farming would also be impacted by the projected higher winter rainfall and consequent decrease in accessibility in spring to waterlogged soils, especially in the west of Ireland.

As both computing power and model reliability increased, refinement of some of these research questions became possible.[19] Wider concerns for biodiversity also emerged. Species with narrow tolerance ranges, especially montane and boreo-arctic species, and those dependent on peatland or coastal habitats, would face increasing pressures.[20] Society became increasingly aware of the multiplier effect climate change might have in accelerating the extinction of iconic species such as the curlew. At the same time as native species were coming under increasing threat, vacant ecological niches, partly helped by ongoing warming in Ireland, encouraged new invasive species to gain footholds. Mobility of people and goods also facilitated this to a great extent as awareness grew of the threats to native species posed by the zebra mussel, Japanese Knotweed, New Zealand Flatworm, and a host of others. By 2013, 48 non-native species were classified as potentially having a high impact.[21] Pests and diseases of plants have also made the journey north and west. The Horse Chestnut Leaf Miner, first identified in the Republic of North Macedonia in 1984, had by the end of the second decade

---

[16] Gerard Mills, 'Ireland's water budget – Model validation and a greenhouse experiment', Irish Geography 33:2 (2000), 124–34; Charlton *et al.*, 'Assessing the impact of climate change on water supply and flood hazard in Ireland using statistical downscaling and hydrological modelling techniques', Climatic Change 74:4 (2006), 475–91.

[17] Holden *et al.*, 'Possible change in Irish climate and its impact on barley and potato yields', *Agriculture and Forest Meteorology*, 116:3–4 (2003), 181–96.

[18] Purser *et al.*, 'The potential impact of climate change on Irish Forestry', Irish Forestry 61 (2003), 16–34.

[19] John Sweeney, Climate Change in Ireland: Refining the Impacts (Environmental Protection Agency, Johnstown Castle, Wexford, 2008).

[20] Coll *et al.*, *Climate change impacts on biodiversity in Ireland: Projecting changes and informing adaptation measures* (Environmental Protection Agency, Johnstown Castle, Wexford, 2012).

[21] https://www.biodiversityireland.ie/projects/invasive-species/species-lists/ (accessed 19/08/2020).

of the twenty-first century attacked chestnut trees along the east coast of Ireland and was moving relentlessly westwards.

Societal perceptions regarding climate change were further catalysed by an increasing frequency of extreme events. Ireland today is at least 0.5°C warmer than the average conditions of the 1961–90 standard reference period (Table 1). Every month shows a similar trend, meaning that about four weeks extra growing season is available on average. It also means that the air can hold more water vapour and deliver more intense rainfall. On average 6% more rain was recorded during the 1981–2010 period than the 1961–90 period. Society therefore has to come to terms with the realisation that not only will places with a history of past flooding experience more frequent and more severe events, but also that places hitherto not at risk will become vulnerable. The Office of Public Works has identified 300 communities at serious risk and commenced a programme of protective measures which will require an expenditure of €1 billion over the next decade. For some of these communities, mistakes were made in allowing urbanisation to occur in areas of known risk such as floodplains, and the reluctance of insurers to provide flood insurance cover once a property had flooded has emerged as a growing problem. The extent to which Irish individuals perceive themselves as primarily responsible for flood protection for their properties, as opposed to relying on state intervention, was studied in the context of social contract theory with reference to two communities affected by the same flood event in November 2009, one in Galway and the other in Cumbria (UK).[22] Significant differences were found in the expectations of both communities of state protection with Irish respondents more inclined to deem their local authorities to be falling short of the responsibilities expected, producing a greater sense of helplessness than in their Cumbrian counterparts.

Growing social awareness of the flood threat was accompanied by increased sensitivity as to whether extreme events were harbingers of wider climate change phenomena which would arrive down the track. This was catalysed by a series of extreme events, both individual and seasonal in nature. In an analysis of storm activity over the Ireland-UK domain, Matthews *et al.* (2014) concluded that the winter of 2013/14 was the stormiest for at least 143 years.[23] Two years later, the winter of 2015/16 turned out to be the wettest ever recorded at more than half the observing stations. Indeed the decade 2006–15 was the wettest 10-year period in more than 300 years.[24] Perhaps the single

---

[22] Adger *et al.*, 'Changing social contracts in climate-change adaptation', *Nature Climate Change* 3 (2013), 330–33.

[23] Matthews *et al.*, 'Stormiest winter on record for Ireland and UK', *Nature Climate Change* 4 (2014), 738–40.

[24] Murphy *et al.*, 'A 305-year continuous monthly rainfall series for the island of Ireland (1711–2016)', *Climate of the Past*, 14 (2018), 413–40.

TABLE 1—Comparison of 1961–90 and 1981–2010 temperature averages for selected Irish stations

1961–90 and 1981–2010 averages for temperature: Dublin

Casement Aerodrome	Jan	Feb	Mar	Apr	May	Jun	Jul	Aug	Sep	Oct	Nov	Dec	year
Mean temperature 1981–2010	5.1	5.1	6.8	8.2	10.9	13.6	15.7	15.4	13.3	10.3	7.2	5.4	9.7
Mean temperature 1961–1990	4.9	4.6	6.0	7.5	10.1	13.1	15.2	14.8	12.6	10.1	6.7	5.6	9.3

1961–90 and 1981–2010 averages for temperature: Cork

Cork Airport	Jan	Feb	Mar	Apr	May	Jun	Jul	Aug	Sep	Oct	Nov	Dec	year
Mean temperature 1981–2010	5.6	5.7	6.9	8.4	10.9	13.5	15.3	15.2	13.3	10.5	7.8	6.1	9.9
Mean temperature 1961–1990	5.1	5.0	6.2	7.7	10.2	12.9	14.8	14.5	12.7	10.3	7.2	6.1	9.4

1961–90 and 1981–2010 averages for temperature: Donegal

Malin Head	Jan	Feb	Mar	Apr	May	Jun	Jul	Aug	Sep	Oct	Nov	Dec	year
Mean temperature 1981–2010	5.9	5.8	6.9	8.3	10.5	12.7	14.5	14.7	13.3	10.8	8.2	6.4	9.8
Mean temperature 1961–1990	5.4	5.2	6.2	7.6	9.9	12.3	13.8	14.0	12.7	10.7	7.5	6.3	9.3

most significant event which shaped Irish society's perceptions of climate change was the arrival of Storm Ophelia in October 2017. Widely regarded as the worst storm to affect Ireland since Hurricane Debbie in 1961, Ophelia intensified into a Category 4 hurricane for a time south of the Azores before moving north-eastwards towards Ireland, losing its tropical characteristics shortly before making landfall on the south coast. Irish society was well prepared for the event, Met Eireann issuing a rare red warning well in advance of its arrival. Despite the country effectively going into lockdown, damage losses of €70 million were estimated and three people lost their lives. A wind gust of 155.6kph was measured at Roches Point, Co. Cork. Offshore at the Fastnet Rock the corresponding figure was 191kph with a nearby weather buoy recording a wave height of 17.81m.

For many people, any lingering doubts they harboured regarding the link between extreme events and climate change were dissipated by the events of 2018. This started after a fairly average winter which culminated in easterly blizzard-like conditions as Storm Emma moved eastwards through the Celtic Sea. A Siberian airflow is not an uncommon event during Irish winters, bringing bitterly cold clear conditions. This often follows a sudden stratospheric warming event which disrupts the normal westerlies and encourages a blocking anticyclone to develop. When this happens the normal passage of depressions from west to east can be disrupted. So it was with Storm Emma which brought tropical air laden with water vapour northwards at the beginning of March to collide with the continental polar easterly airflow dominating Ireland at the time. Snow drifts of over 2m were measured with several stations reporting days with temperatures not rising above 0°C. This was the first time that such conditions were observed in March in Ireland.

The delayed spring of 2018 was followed by a summer of heatwaves and droughts. The all-time record high temperature for Ireland of 33.3°C, which dates from 1887, was approached by a value of 32°C at Shannon Airport on 28 June 2018. A similar temperature was measured in northern Norway, well north of the Arctic Circle, indicating that much of Europe was enveloped by the heatwave. It was estimated that human-induced global warming more than doubled the probability of this event occurring, and in some parts of the continent made it five times more likely. Such estimates are possible because the growth in computing power has enabled customised multiple model runs to be made with, for example, pre-industrial and current levels of greenhouse gas concentrations. The resultant comparisons have provided climate scientists with a powerful tool to demonstrate the role played by anthropogenic influences in individual extreme events. Thus, for example, it can be suggested that the record breaking French heat wave of June 2019 was 10 times more likely than was the case in the last century and that climate change increased the chances of the prolonged Siberian heat wave of 2020, which produced temperatures of 38°C in the high Arctic, 600 times than would be the case in the absence of greenhouse gas loadings of the atmosphere.[25] Such progress enables new, authoritative, public statements to be made by climate scientists, not least in Ireland, finally dispelling the sceptical view that increased frequency of extreme events does not have anthropogenic climate causes.

The 2018 heat wave in Ireland gave way to a prolonged drought which lasted from early June until late July. Absolute drought conditions prevailed in many parts of eastern Ireland throughout this period, with a June rainfall at the Phoenix Park (on average over 69mm) of only 3.8mm, which was its lowest total since 1941. Grass growth failed forcing farmers to house their cattle indoors during the summer months, putting further strains on dwindling fodder resources. Imports of alfalfa from Mediterranean countries continued throughout the summer until benign conditions resumed in the autumn. If further evidence was needed, a recurrence of drought conditions in spring 2020 produced the driest spring since 1837 in the Dublin region. Lengthy periods of water restrictions to towns and cities further reinforced the perception of many citizens that climate change was something that Ireland had to take more seriously.

Facing up to the future as laggard or leader

Decisions on how to cope with climate change ultimately have to be made at local level, and should be based on knowledge of local climate conditions and a prognosis of how they will change over time. The production of future climate scenarios is crucial for this. Limitations in computing power for long restricted the outputs of Global Climate Models to very coarse grid cells, in the case of Ireland perhaps only two or three covering the entire island. This was unhelpful for communities wondering how their particular location would be affected, how their local river would behave, or how their crop yields might change, for example. Fragmenting coarse grid outputs into smaller units was the only way of addressing this. Downscaling techniques evolved initially based on statistical relationships between large and small scale meteorological variables, frequently based on combinations of multiple linear regression techniques and stochastic weather generators.[26] It was with these early scenarios for Ireland that the case for adaptation became clear.[27] Later, the introduction of Regional Climate Models provided a more dynamically grounded approach and, as computing power increased, enabled multiple models to be combined in a configuration aimed at

---

[25] World Weather Attribution, 'Attribution of the 2018 heat in northern Europe', World Weather Attribution, 2018: https://www.worldweatherattribution.org/attribution-of-the-2018-heat-in-northern-europe/ (accessed 2 Mar. 2019).

[26] R. Wilby and C. Dawson, 'The statistical downscaling model: insights from one decade of application', *International Journal of Climatology* 33:7 (2013), 1707–19.

[27] Sweeney, *Climate change: Scenarios and impacts for Ireland* (2003); Sweeney, *Climate change in Ireland: refining the impacts* (2008).

reducing uncertainty.[28] Continuing computing advances have also provided opportunities for the high resolution outputs needed by environmental managers.[29]

Simulations of temperature change from the downscaled models are generally in agreement, showing a likely rise, compared with the 1981–2010 average, of approximately 1°C over the next 30 year period 2021–50 and 2–3°C for the period 2051–80 based on a business as usual trajectory. For precipitation, much greater uncertainty exists, though the models tend to agree on a trend towards wetter winters and drier summers (Fig. 2). If realised, these rainfall changes will have profound consequences for Irish society—an increased winter flood problem and a decreased summer water supply, especially in those parts of the country where the bulk of the population resides. Major infrastructural investments will be required to adapt to both circumstances. Given the lengthy lead times for these, a 'wait and see' approach is not an option.[30] Adaptation to both circumstances requires immediate detailed local planning to enable local authorities to prioritise their responses based on an informed risk assessment.[31] The first National Adaptation Framework, which was published in 2018, required each local authority to develop a local adaptation strategy and established four Climate Action Regional Offices to support both mitigation and adaptation measures at local authority level.

Adapting to climate change is not in itself sufficient. Clearly, as a member of the international community, Ireland has an obligation to contribute to the global effort to avoid a business as usual trajectory materialising. This entails a commitment to emissions mitigation proportionate to its historic contribution to the climate change problem. The UN Framework Convention on Climate Change, to which Ireland is a signatory, requires countries to act on the basis of 'common but differentiated responsibilities and respective capabilities'. As part of the EU effort to comply with this, in 2008 Ireland entered into a legally binding commitment with its European partners to reduce its greenhouse gas emissions in transport, agriculture, buildings and waste by 20% on their 2005 levels by 2020. This figure was agreed by the Taoiseach as a member of the Council of Ministers, and by the European Parliament and European

---

[28] E. Gleeson, R. McGrath and M. Treanor, 'Ireland's climate: the road ahead' (Met Éireann, Dublin, 2013); R. Fealy, C. Bruyére and C. Duffy, Regional Climate Model Simulations for Ireland for the 21st century (Environmental Protection Agency, Wexford, 2018).

[29] O'Sullivan *et al.*, 'A high-resolution, multi-model analysis of Irish temperatures for the mid-21st century', *International Journal of Climatology*, 36:3 (2015), 1256–67.

[30] Murphy *et al.*, 'Against a 'wait and see' approach in adapting to climate change', *Irish Geography*, 44:1 (2011), 81–95.

[31] Sweeney *et al.*, COCOADAPT: Co-ordination, Communication and Adaptation for Climate Change in Ireland: An Integrated Approach (Climate Change Research Programme (CCRP) Report Series No. 30, Environmental Protection Agency, Wexford, 2013).

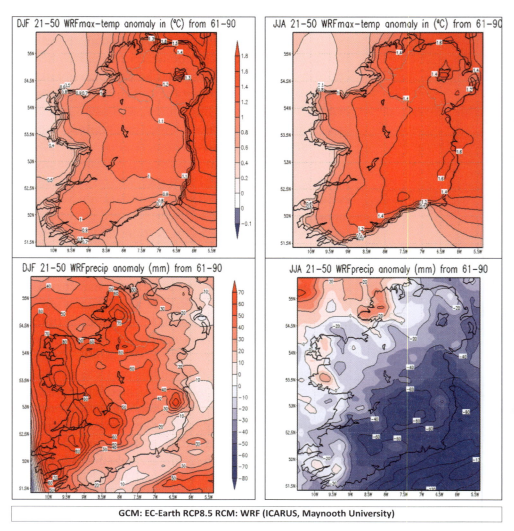

Fig. 2—Downscaled temperature and rainfall projections for Ireland, winter and summer 2021–2050 relative to 1961–1990 (Courtesy R. Teck)

Commission. However, successive National Climate Change policies, and legislation in the form of the Climate Action and Low Carbon Development Act of 2015 have failed to deliver any significant reductions, and breaches of the annual limit values are presently occurring. Indeed, while EU emissions decreased by 25% between 1990 and 2018, Irish greenhouse gas emissions increased by just under 10%. The decoupling of emissions growth from economic growth in Ireland has failed to occur and with the recovery from the recession at the beginning of the first decade of the twenty-first century, emissions began a relentless increase, led by a programme of agricultural intensification and a failure to tackle car dependency in both rural and urban areas. As with the economic crash of 2008–12 and Kyoto Protocol compliance, the Covid-19 pandemic will provide a temporary fig leaf which will partially disguise the policy failures of the past two decades. But Irish society increasingly requires structural change. This is partially in recognition that the costs of inaction are likely to be increasingly felt beyond the climate impacts themselves. Frequently identified as the worst performing country in the EU in annual assessments carried out by international environmental groups,[32] and its 'laggard' status admitted at the highest level of government, Ireland is likely to incur fines and/or emission quota purchasing costs of several hundred million euros for these policy failures. These costs are likely to be levied on society as a whole and not based on the 'polluter pays' principle.

As Irish society has become increasingly sensitised to the gravity of climate change, impatience with the political response has grown. Much of the initial impetus came from young people increasingly aware that climate change posed an issue of intergenerational inequity. The highly successful An Taisce Green Schools programme is currently operational in over 94% of Irish schools and provides a best practice example that has been extensively studied internationally. Although rooted in sustainability in a wider sense, it has become an instrument for climate change awareness that has now been extended to third level colleges, hospitals, parks and volunteer-run community green spaces. Simultaneously, issues of climate justice have achieved prominence due to the work of distinguished individuals such as former President Mary Robinson and charities such as Trocaire which emphasised the message that former UN Secretary General Ban Ki Moon delivered on a visit to Dublin in 2015: 'Today one cannot be a leader on hunger without also being a leader in climate change.'

The reality of an Ireland that emits more greenhouse gases than the 400 million poorest people on Earth has entered the consciousness of key components of Irish society. Citizen litigation has become more common as evidenced by the successful judicial review in 2020 of the National Mitigation Plan, criticised even by the government-appointed Climate Change Advisory Council. Another manifestation of concern has resulted in increasing pressure on individuals, organisations and the State to divert their investments away from fossil fuel interests towards what are considered ethical funds. A movement that started in US universities spread to Europe rapidly to encompass over 1,200 institutions with managed investments worth over €9 trillion. Maynooth University was followed by Trinity College, Dublin, the Church of Ireland, the Catholic dioceses and many other institutions in committing themselves to such a course. With the

---

[32] Burck *et al.*, Climate Change performance Index 2019 (Germanwatch/NewClimate Institute/Climate Action Network International, Bonn, 2018).

passage of the Fossil Fuel Divestment Act 2018, Ireland became the first country in the world to commit to fully divest its sovereign wealth fund out of fossil fuel investments.

Irish society's most innovative and potentially effective engagement on climate change came with the consideration of the topic by the Citizens' Assembly in 2017. This exercise in deliberative democracy comprised 99 citizens chaired by a former Supreme Court judge was given the mandate: *How the State can make Ireland a leader in tackling climate change*. Briefed by expert, impartial and factual advice over two weekends, the Assembly overwhelmingly endorsed thirteen recommendations to be laid before government (Table 2). If implemented these would transform Ireland's position on climate change. The Joint Oireachtas Committee established to consider how best to implement these recommendations, however, provided only a selective response, avoiding recommending the major policy actions which alone will permit the transformation from 'laggard' to 'leader'. At the UN Conference of the Parties to the Paris Agreement in Katowice, Poland in December 2018, Irish negotiators declined to join a group of 26 climate leading countries intent on stepping up their climate ambition in response to the latest scientific findings of the IPCC. This was despite growing awareness that even the most progressive countries, such as Sweden and the United Kingdom, have climate policies which are based on unjustifiably large claims on the dwindling global carbon budget.[33] However, while all this might suggest the disjuncture between Irish society and its decision makers was continuing, the bottom-up and top down pressures are combining to force significant changes in the status quo.

The failure of the adherents to the Paris Agreement to agree a rule book for its implementation over the course of six years, and the realisation that many of the pledges made were subject to unrealistic political and/or economic provisos, as well as the more confident identification of a climate change fingerprint in extreme events, has provided the basis for a groundswell of populist grass-roots activism that could not be ignored by decision makers. Within Irish society, groups, such as 'Fridays for Future', 'Extinction Rebellion', 'Stop Climate Chaos' as well as a wide range of environmental NGOs and faith groups have clustered around the principles of climate justice, mobilised on a national scale via recurring demonstrations and marches. A government Climate Action Plan designed to reduce emissions by 3% per annum to 2030 has been superseded in 2020 by a legislative commitment to achieve a 7% per annum reduction over the same period and to achieve the decarbonisation of the Irish economy by 2050. This highly ambitious target still falls short of the figure estimated by researchers to be appropriate for Ireland's fair share of the remaining carbon

---

[33] K. Anderson, J.F. Broderick and I. Stoddard, 'A factor of two: how the mitigation plans of 'climate progressive' nations fall far short of Paris-compliant pathways', *Climate Policy*, 2020: DOI: 10.1080/14693062.2020.1728209.

TABLE 2—Recommendations of the Citizens' Assembly

i. 97% of the Members recommended that to ensure climate change is at the centre of policy-making in Ireland, as a matter of urgency a new or existing independent body should be resourced appropriately, operate in an open and transparent manner, and be given a broad range of new functions and powers in legislation to urgently address climate change.

ii. 100% of the Members recommended that the State should take a leadership role in addressing climate change through mitigation measures, including, for example, retrofitting public buildings, having low carbon public vehicles, renewable generation on public buildings and through adaptation measures including, for example, increasing the resilience of public land and infrastructure.

iii. 80% of the Members stated that they would be willing to pay higher taxes on carbon intensive activities, subject to the qualifications identified in the question.

iv. 96% of the Members recommended that the State should undertake a comprehensive assessment of the vulnerability of all critical infrastructure (including energy, transport, built environment, water and communications) with a view to building resilience to ongoing climate change and extreme weather events. The outcome of this assessment should be implemented. Recognising the significant costs that the State would bear in the event of failure of critical infrastructure, spending on infrastructure should be prioritised to take account of this.

v. 99% of the Members recommended that the State should enable, through legislation, the selling back into the grid of electricity from micro-generation by private citizens (for example energy from solar panels or wind turbines on people's homes or land) at a price which is at least equivalent to the wholesale price.

vi. 100% of the Members recommended that the State should act to ensure the greatest possible levels of community ownership in all future renewable energy projects by encouraging communities to develop their own projects and by requiring that developer-led projects make share offers to communities to encourage greater local involvement and ownership.

vii. (a) 97% of the Members recommended that the State should end all subsidies for peat extraction and instead spend that money on peat bog restoration and making proper provision for the protection of the rights of the workers impacted; and (b) 61% recommended that the State should end all subsidies on a phased basis over 5 years.c

viii. 93% of the Members recommended that the number of bus lanes, cycling lanes and park and ride facilities should be greatly increased in the next five years, and much greater priority should be given to these modes over private car use.

ix. 96% of the Members recommended that the State should immediately take many steps to support the transition to electric vehicles.

x. 92% of the Members recommended that the State should prioritise the expansion of public transport spending over new road infrastructure spending at a ratio of no less than 2-to-1 to facilitate the broader availability and uptake of public transport options with attention to rural areas.

xi. 89% of the Members recommended that there should be a tax on greenhouse gas emissions from agriculture. There should be rewards for the farmer for land management that sequesters carbon. Any resulting revenue should be reinvested to support climate friendly agricultural practices.

TABLE 2—(*Continued*)

xii. 93% of the Members recommended the State should introduce a standard form of mandatory measurement and reporting of food waste at every level of the food distribution and supply chain, with the objective of reducing food waste in the future.
xiii. 99% of the Members recommended that the State should review and revise supports for land use diversification with attention to supports for planting forests and encouraging organic farming.

budget.[34] It is, however, closely aligned with the ambition of the EU Green Deal, which is aimed at transforming climate and environmental challenges into opportunities, and, as such, may have an expectation over the period 2021–2027 of availing of supports and finance of up to €150 billion designed to facilitate a just transition for people, companies and regions hitherto dependent on carbon-intensive employment sectors, which in Ireland include those engaged in peat related activities.

Conclusion

Consistent with its position as an island on the north western periphery of Europe, climate has always been a major preoccupation in Ireland. It has influenced Irish well-being, shaped its landscapes and imbued its culture with a range of rituals and practices. The intimate interaction between climate and Irish society has posed different challenges as both climate and society have changed over time. Historically, climate determined what crops could be grown in Ireland, when harvests could be made, when venturing on to the open sea was possible, and the extreme events that needed to be coped with. The imprint on Irish society was always therefore, and continues to be, pervasive. This imprint was not mediated through the classical ethnocentric mechanisms espoused by determinists who believed climate was the main driver of global societal differences,[35] instead climate has constituted an omnipresent factor that social organisation has had to come to terms with.

Throughout most of its history, Irish society was a prisoner of climate as mediated through the necessity of a harvest surplus. The wisdom and experience acquired coping with the vagaries of climate had furthermore to be passed on to the next generation. From prehistoric almost to contemporary times this hostage relationship applied. With the coming of objective measurements, the realisation

---

[34] McMullin *et al.*, 'Assessing negative carbon dioxide emissions from the perspective of a national 'fair share' of the remaining global Carbon Budget', *Mitigation and Adaptation Strategies for Global Change* 25, 579–602. https://doi.org/10.1007/s11027-019-09881-6.

[35] E. Churchill Semple, *Influences of geographic environment, on the basis of Ratzel's system of anthropo-geography* (New York, 1911); E. Huntington, *Civilization and climate* (New Haven, 1915).

has dawned that the relationship is now reversed. In a global context, climate is now the prisoner of people. Irish society increasingly recognises that to ensure a sustainable future it must play its part in contributing to mitigating the worst effects of ongoing climate change. No longer is the ninth-century Irish monk's sentiment regarding his fate being determined by uncontrollable atmospheric processes valid:

> Bitter is the wind tonight,
> It tosses the sea's white tresses;
> I do not fear the fierce warriors of Norway,
> Who only travel the quiet seas.[36]

Instead, in the words of a contemporary poet, Seamus Heaney:

> The world where we are to make our tarry ark lies before us.[37]

---

[36] Translation by Kuno Meyer of verse on Cod. Sang. 904: Prisciani grammatica (St. Gallen, Stiftsbibliothek) accessed at http://www.e-codices.unifr.ch/en/list/one/csg/0904.

[37] Seamus Heaney, 'Commencement ceremony at The University of North Carolina at Chapel Hill, 12 May 1996', Internet Poetry Archive: https://www.ibiblio.org/ipa/poems/heaney/unc-commencement.php (accessed 1 August 2020).

PROCEEDINGS OF THE ROYAL IRISH ACADEMY
archaeology • culture • history • literature

The Royal Irish Academy was founded in 1785 to promote the study of science, polite literature and antiquities. It publishes a number of journals in which a large body of research papers appears each year. Its first journal was the *Transactions* of the Academy, which appeared in 1787. This was supplemented in 1836, and eventually replaced by the *Proceedings*.

Proceedings of the Royal Irish Academy is a peer-reviewed journal which publishes original research papers primarily in the fields of archaeology and history, but also welcomes submissions on aspects of culture, including material culture, from the perspectives of other disciplines, as well as submissions in Celtic Studies and literature.

Authors of papers in archaeology are encouraged to relate their findings, where possible and appropriate, to wider themes, in order to connect ideas about Irish local, regional and national material with the outside world. Papers on non-Irish material housed in collections within Ireland, and sites, settlements and cultural landscapes outside of Ireland with significant Irish connections, will also be considered for publication. All submissions are refereed and only papers of a high academic standard are accepted.

ANNUAL SUBSCRIPTION RATES (single annual volume):
Individual (print and online) €35/£30/$45
For institutional rates, please contact JSTOR: support@jstor.org

SUBSCRIPTIONS/ORDERS SHOULD BE SENT TO:
Publications Office
Royal Irish Academy
19 Dawson Street
Dublin 2
Ireland
Tel. +353-1-676 2570

Orders and enquiries may also be emailed to: publications@ria.ie